TH...
ST. MARY'S COLLEGE OF MARYLAND
ST. MARY'S CITY, MARYLAND 20686

ERRATA

Fig. 10: caption should read '*Dutch* **boyer** (left) and armed Dutch merchantman of the mid-sixteenth century, from a painting by Pieter Brueghel the Elder'.

Fig. 16A and Fig. 17: captions should be transposed.

Fig. 19: for 'Engraving' read 'Idealized eighteenth-century reconstuction'.

p. 141, 1.12: for 'spices' read 'no spices'.

p. 288, 1.7: for 'interpreters or' read 'interpreters to'.

The World Encompassed

THE
WORLD ENCOMPASSED

The first

European maritime empires

c. 800–1650

G.V. SCAMMELL

University of California Press

BERKELEY and LOS ANGELES

First published in 1981 by
University of California Press
Berkeley and Los Angeles, California

© 1981 G.V. Scammell

Printed in the United States of America

ISBN 0–520–04422–3
Library of Congress Catalog Card Number 80–6319

All rights reserved. No part of this book may be reprinted
or reproduced or utilized in any form or by any electronic,
mechanical or other means, now known or hereafter invented,
including photocopying and recording, or in any information
storage or retrieval system, without permission in writing
from the publishers.

Library of Congress Cataloging in Publication Data

Scammell, Geoffrey Vaughan.   The world encompassed.

Includes bibliographical references and index.
1. Europe—History—476–1492.   2. Europe—History—1492–1648.
3. Discoveries (in geography)
I. Title.
D104.S35   940.1   81–1076
ISBN 0–520–04422–3   AACR2

Contents

○○

List of maps

○○

vii

List of illustrations

References and abbreviations

∞

It will be noticed that I have used few footnotes, quoting sources only to substantiate some new piece of information, or to support opinions which may seem contentious. A bibliographical note is given at the end of each section of the book. These notes make no claim to be comprehensive, but describe the literature I have found most useful, the place of publication being London unless otherwise stated. The notes vary in scope according to whether a subject has received much attention from scholars (as have the Iberian empires) or not (as is the case with Genoa). The journals mentioned are those which regularly carry materials of relevance. Many others do so occasionally, and of course the periodicals listed in one section are frequently of value for another.

There are a number of books which form admirable introductions to the subject as a whole, or large aspects of it. Amongst them are: Ralph Davis, *The Rise of the Atlantic Economies* (1973); K.G. Davies, *The North Atlantic World in the Seventeenth Century* (Minneapolis, 1974); Charles Wilson, *The Transformation of Europe, 1558–1648* (1976); Jan de Vries, *The Economy of Europe in an Age of Crisis, 1600–1750* (Cambridge, 1976); C.R. Boxer, *The Church Militant in Iberian Expansion, 1440–1770* (Baltimore, 1978). For the torrential flow of new specialist books and articles the reader is referred to the various guides listed in the bibliographical notes already mentioned. There is, however, a useful *Annual Bulletin of Historical Literature*, produced by the Historical Association in Great Britain, and articles in journals are briefly summarized every year in *The English Historical Review*.

The following abbreviations have been used in references.

Annales	*Annales, economies, sociétés, civilisations*, Centre National de la Recherche Scientifique et VIᵉ Section de l'École Pratique des Hautes Études, Paris
APO	*Arquivo Português Oriental, Nova Edição*
BM	British Library, Department of Manuscripts
CIHM	*Travaux des colloques internationaux d'histoire maritime*, Bibliothèque Générale de l'École Pratique des Hautes Études, VIᵉ Section, Paris
CSP	*Calendar of State Papers*, series specified as *D (Domestic) Spanish (Relating to Negotiations between England and Spain)*, etc.
Ec.Hist.Rev.	*The Economic History Review*
HAHR	*The Hispanic American Historical Review*

x

HCA	High Court of Admiralty
Hakluyt	Richard Hakluyt, *Principal Navigations* (MacLehose edn, 12 vols, Glasgow, 1903–5)
HGB	*Hansische Geschichtsblätter*
Hist.	*History*
HJ	*The Historical Journal*
MM	*The Mariner's Mirror*
P&P	*Past and Present*
PRO	The Public Record Office, London
Purchas	*Purchas His Pilgrimes* (MacLehose edn, 20 vols, Glasgow, 1905–7)

Acknowledgements

It is a pleasure to record my gratitude to friends who have answered queries, discussed problems, and provided books and offprints otherwise difficult of access. They are of course in no way responsible for the facts that I have used, or the opinions that are expressed in the book. I particularly wish to thank Dr K.R. Andrews, Professor Sinnappah Arasaratnam, Professor Maria Bogucka, Dr Geneviève Bouchon, Dr Michael Bratchel, Dr Peter Bury, Dr Wendy Childs, Professor J.S. Cummins, Dr Chandra R. de Silva, Professor Klaus Friedland, Professor John Hale, Dr Marie Helmer, Professor Michel Mollat, Comandante Avelino Teixeira da Mota, Professor David Quinn, the late Professor Virginia Rau and Dr Luís Filipe F. Reis Thomaz.

I owe especial thanks to Mel Arnold, at whose urging this book was begun, and to John Naylor whose enthusiasm and patience have ensured its completion. I am particularly grateful for long years of encouragement from Professor John Bromley, and for the friendship, unfailing kindness and never flagging interest of Professor Charles Boxer.

I would also like to record my remembrance of those ships of the Royal Navy in which I served in many of the waters described here during the Second World War, and my affection for those small boats in which, before and since then I have spent so many happy years sailing. But my greatest debt is to my wife, without whose help, encouragement and stimulus the book would have been neither commenced nor finished.

Cambridge
1 October 1979   G.V.S.

Introduction

Between approximately 800 and 1650 the world known to western Europeans was enlarged in a way unparalleled before or since. In the tenth century the Scandinavians reached North America. The high Middle Ages saw Italian traders and missionaries in China, Venetian galleys in ports from Alexandria to Southampton, and German merchants bring the fastnesses of northern Europe into a vital association with the rest of the continent. Then in the fifteenth and sixteenth centuries, in some of the greatest voyages ever made under sail, the Iberians opened the Atlantic and Pacific oceans, subjugating part of the Americas and seizing or obtaining footholds in Africa and Asia. In some cases, as with the Norse in America, settlements soon foundered. In Asia Europeans conquered no more than a few islands, yet established themselves with important economic consequences on the fringes of landmasses whose size and civilizations they only imperfectly understood. But in the Americas whole indigenous societies were destroyed and some parts of the continent brought under European rule in campaigns whose audacity, let alone success, still remains a matter for wonder.

How and why such events came to pass, why the Norse colonies failed whilst those of their successors flourished, why the expansion of the Portuguese should have taken so different a course from that of the Dutch, and why France and England were unable to equal the achievements of the Iberians are some of the questions which this book attempts to discuss. I have compared the ways in which different peoples attempted to handle very similar problems, and I have tried to assess the influence of empire on both colonial and metropolitan societies. The word empire has been used advisedly, notwithstanding the semantic perils this involves. It is here taken to mean the dominion exercised by one people or state over other peoples, lands or states, whether this arises from armed conquest or from the establishment or imposition of economic domination. Maritime is taken to mean that such authority or influence was primarily, though not necessarily entirely, created and exercised by some form of seapower.

The book begins with the voyages of the Norse, the first Europeans successfully to contend with the rigours of the North Atlantic. Their colonization of Iceland and Greenland marked the commencement of the extension of European power (and eventually civilization) beyond the bounds of the continent itself. Their ability, at so early a date, to cross and recross regularly so formidable an ocean raises the whole question as to the extent to which Europe's eventual expansion into the wider world was dependent on technological advances, whether in the design and construction of ships or in the methods of their navigation. There then follows a discussion of the maritime achievements of the Hanseatic League in the north, and of the Venetian and Genoese republics in the south. Between them they bequeathed to Europe major developments in the building and rig of ships, techniques for the exploitation of subject lands, and – in the case of Venice and Genoa – for their rule. The book ends in the mid-seventeenth century. By this date the oceanic empires created by the Portuguese and Spaniards – often with the aid of Italian skills and capital – were resisting with varying degrees of success the assaults of other European states. After a lengthy prelude of failure the first Protestant colonies had been founded, and much of the maritime economy established by the Iberians had passed, or was passing, into the hands of the north European seapowers Holland and England.

Some points of detail call for explanation. Placenames, in many parts of the world subject to sudden change according to the vicissitudes of politics, are given in the forms which (I hope) are most readily identifiable. Measurements drawn from a wide variety of sources have been converted to metric equivalents. The tonnage of ships is thus, for example, given in tonnes. It should, however, be remembered that such figures are rough approximations, since the carrying capacity of a vessel was something that was settled by observation during the early years of her life.

I

The Norse

∞

1 'The seas their land'

The first maritime empire in the west since Antiquity was that of the Scandinavians. From the second century BC the remote north, that 'womb of nations' we now know as Norway, Denmark and Sweden, had pushed out wave after wave of peoples – Cimbri, Goths, Burgundians, Angles – into Roman dominated Europe, their fearsome behaviour and astonishing customs sharply observed by classical historians. The movement died down in the sixth century AD, only to revive 200 years later against a Europe barely recovered from the collapse of Roman government and civilization. Between roughly 750 and 1050 the Scandinavians penetrated on the one hand to the Christian and Islamic civilizations of the Middle East, and on the other to Britain, France, Iberia, the Mediterranean and ultimately, in a series of breathtaking voyages, to Iceland, Greenland and North America. By the eleventh century Knut the Great (1016–35) – that Canute, the legend of whose failure to rule the waves still persists in English popular mythology – controlled an impressive confederacy embracing at the least Norway, Denmark and England, and by about 1100 the Norse had created what, by its bonds of trade, was the first empire of the North Atlantic.

For a hundred years or so before their oceanic voyages Vikings, in fierce, sudden and unheralded assaults, had been raiding east into the Baltic and south and southwest along the coasts of the British Isles and Europe.[1] In the course of the ninth and tenth centuries Scandinavian kingdoms were established in Ireland, Scotland, the Isle of Man, the Hebrides, and in the northern, midland and eastern districts of England. On the whole it was the Danes, whose attacks were of an organized military nature under kings or princes, who came off best, securing land in eastern England and, in 911, in Normandy. The more individualistic and less-purposeful Norse, after some profitable raids on northeastern England in the late eighth century, were confined for a time to land-hunting in the poor and distant islands of the north and west – the Faroes, Shetlands and Orkneys – where they not so much subdued the native populations as were absorbed by them. From these bases they moved into the Irish Sea, to the conquest of Ireland, and to plundering expeditions to the coasts of France. In the Scottish islands, or more probably in Ireland, they could have learned of Iceland, a sanctuary since the late 700s for the wilderness-seeking anchorites of Irish Christianity, and by about 870 the Norse had made their first settlement in that forbidding land. In Scandinavia political change, always a powerful incentive to speedy departure for

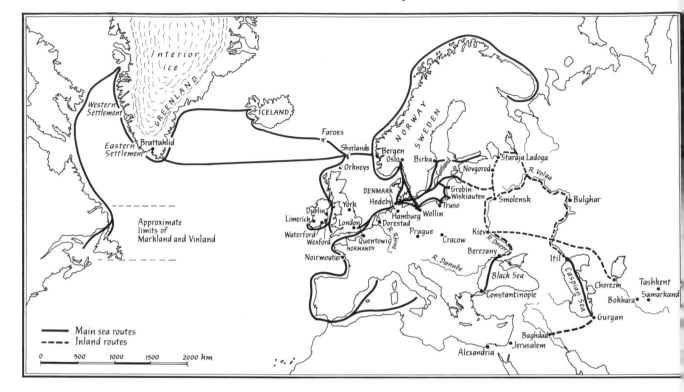

1   The Viking World

distant parts, hastened the flow of migration, whilst a series of defeats at the hands of erstwhile victims who now had the measure of the Vikings – in Lithuania (*c.* 850); France (891); England (892–6); and Ireland (902) – funnelled it into this new direction (see p. 10). Within little more than fifty years the colonization was completed. The Irish hermits, the only people the Vikings found there, were killed, enslaved or driven out, and the little habitable land available was occupied.

Precisely how many Norse migrated to Iceland we shall never know. It has been alleged that between 870 and 930 as many as 25,000 people settled there. That would amount to the equivalent of 8 per cent of Norway's supposed population at the time, and constitute a loss from the mother country on a scale surpassed later only by the Portuguese. Yet admittedly it was the migration of a whole society – of men, women, children, slaves and retainers. As such it bears little resemblance to the male-dominated expansion either of subsequent commercial empires, such as that of the Hanse, or of those of conquest, as that of Spain. The closest parallel is with the exodus of the English Puritans to America in the seventeenth century, where once again, though for very different reasons, whole communities felt impelled to seek new homes. As in other similar movements, power in Iceland passed to those who by birth or achievement commanded resources and respect. *Landnámabók* (*The Book of the Settlements*, see p. 35) records the names of some 400 major settlers and their families. Some were of royal descent, others lesser lords. The majority were from southwest Norway – from that very region in which the king had recently taken vigorous steps to enforce his authority (see p. 10). Some had lived in the Hebrides and Ireland, and several were of mixed Norse and Celtic blood. Like the Spanish conquerors of the American continent or some of the first Portuguese in Brazil and Asia, many settlers moved not directly from the mother country to a new land, but as conditions deteriorated, or as rumours of better things to be had elsewhere spread from colony to colony, giving the growth of empire, then as since, a momentum of its own. Iceland was to see no flowering of some pristine Germanic freedom. Royal authority – that of the king of Norway – was for long ignored and, as was to happen elsewhere, a form of government established reflecting the needs and interests of the dominant minority. Significantly enough, the island was without any central control until 930. Instead it was quickly carved up into a handful of vast and independent estates on which, surrounded by their women, families, slaves and retainers, the chiefs lived in patriarchal style distributing – as every good medieval lord was expected to do – lands to their followers, exacting obedience and dispensing justice. Nor did their authority end here, for in a fierce pagan world the proper worship of the gods demanded costly temples and sacrifices. Such burdens only magnates could bear, and so it was from among the chiefs that there emerged the thirty-six hereditary temple priests who by the tenth century exercised legislative and judicial power in Iceland. Each of these took payments from those who of necessity became their followers, for the right to participate in temple ceremonies, and who were obliged to accompany them to public assemblies. It was these priests who controlled the National Assembly (*Althing*) which appeared in 930 and which, some reforms notwithstanding, continued as a gathering of a few dozen grandees, each adamantly supreme in his own territory. They reached many admirable decisions, but since there was no authority willing or able to enforce them for some three centuries, the republic, with no external threats to inspire any change, went on its turbulent way in that not uncommon state of all law and no government.

There soon emerged in a land without towns, and without even villages, a simple pastoral economy based on scattered single farms – sheep and stock raising, hunting and fishing – enlivened and augmented in the early years by the old basic Viking practices of piracy and raiding. By about 1100 the population of Iceland is thought to have been between 60,000 and 80,000 – though like as not it was considerably less – and the country was no longer, as it had been for the Irish, a remote sanctuary, but an integral part of the flourishing Norse commercial empire which until the mid-twelfth century dominated the North Sea and the Baltic. Icelandic ships appeared in British and European waters, and Iceland was regularly visited by vessels from all parts of the Scandinavian world – Norway, Denmark, Ireland, the Orkneys, Faroes and Shelands.

After the island's conversion to Christianity at the beginning of the eleventh century, Icelanders made pilgrimages to Rome, Jerusalem and Compostella, whilst on a less elevated plane there was a constant coming and going of ecclesiasts, chieftains and merchants between Iceland and Norway.

Cold, wet and barren, much of it – five-sixths perhaps – covered by lava or permanent ice, Iceland produced none of the luxuries of life and few of its necessities. Grass grew plentifully in valleys and on plains and hillsides fronting the sea, and the high moorlands provided good summer grazing. Trout and salmon abounded in lakes and rivers; other fish, together with whales and seals, in the surrounding seas. The coasts and their islets teemed with seabirds, and for a brief time, 'in certain choice places' as tradition has it, wheat was grown. But in an age in which timber was even more vital than steel in the modern world, Iceland had no native oak, beech or conifer; nothing beyond driftwood and scrub for ships and houses.[2] And though a land of 'stones, more stones and all stones' it had virtually none suitable for building, and even gravestones were imported. The country was thus heavily dependent on others, and particularly on Norway, for its survival. It was from Norway that there came timber and meal, and later, as tastes became more sophisticated, a wider range of goods. In payment Iceland exported at first a crude, rough cloth made from the wool of her extensive flocks, to which were subsequently added hides, falcons and fish. The white Icelandic falcon was soon highly esteemed and much sought after in Europe, and in 1262 some were even sent as a present to the Sultan of Tunis. But most important was the fish, the *skreid* or dried cod, which came into prominence in the late Middle Ages. Together with seal oil it was shipped to Norway and thence re-exported, doubtless somewhat past its prime, to feed, amongst others, the peoples of England and Germany.

In the course of the thirteenth century Iceland's dependence on Norway became even closer. Just as in the Americas the heirs of the *conquistadores* were revealed as notoriously unbellicose, so the descendants of the Vikings abandoned the sea. To both peoples the opportunities of the new lands were more attractive than their former ways of life, and in Iceland a falling population and the demands and profits of agriculture removed the previous incentives to seafaring. Icelandic shipping, always difficult to maintain in a country virtually devoid of shipbuilding materials, dwindled into insignificance by 1200, and for contact with the rest of the world the island was at the mercy of the Norwegians. At the same time, in a pattern to become only too familiar in the later Middle Ages, power had become increasingly concentrated in the hands of a small group of magnates, each supported by his retainers, and all warring together with full-blooded Norse vigour. By 1264 the republic, desperately poor even by the unexacting standards of the time, and an anachronism, as a dignitary of the church conveniently and complacently observed, since it was 'against all reason that this country should not serve a king even as all other countries in the world', had collapsed, and Iceland had surrendered her independence to Norway. For a time commercial relations were maintained, but whereas in the 1100s there might have been thirty-five sailings a year from Norway to Iceland, by the 1340s they were down on average to about eleven. And new troubles came fast. The economy of Norway was increasingly dominated by the German Hanse (see p. 67) which had gained its initial foothold as the supplier of grain to the country's growing population in the thirteenth century. At first this gave something of a boost to the Icelandic trade. There was a greater demand for fish; and Norwegian enterprise, blocked by the power of the Hanse in the Baltic and the North Sea, was diverted to the Atlantic. But this was not to last. In the fourteenth century Norway was crippled by the tightening stranglehold of the Hanse. Her ships – small, fast and light – were pushed off the seas by the bulk carriers of the German cities. After the Union of Kalmar (1397), uniting the three Scandinavian kingdoms, the ruling dynasty was Danish or half German. The seat of government was moved from Bergen to Oslo; the centre of gravity shifted away from the west coast as Norwegian products were taken by the Hanse to the Baltic and to Europe; and Norse ambitions and interests in the Atlantic were dead. Iceland, harassed by a worsening climate and a series of fearful volcanic eruptions which established Hekla as one of the gateways to Hell, was abandoned. In 1394 no more than two Norwegian ships reached the island, and its shrinking and impoverished population was only saved when, in the early fifteenth century, the country was drawn back into contact with the world by the arrival on its coasts of English fishermen (see p. 160).

Iceland was the sole survivor, but for a time the Norse empire in the Atlantic had been more extensive. Early in the tenth century one Gunnbjörn, on passage from Norway to Iceland, had been blown past his destination and had sighted new lands to the west. At first nothing came of this, but eventually the lead was followed up by the aptly named Eirik the Red, driven from Iceland (982) by a record of homicide imposing even by Scandinavian standards. He rounded what is now Cape Farewell in southern Greenland, and spent three years exploring the coast between Herjolfsnes (Ikigait) and Eiriksfjord (Tunugdliarfik), noticing the remains of habitations and boats.[3] What he saw he liked, and on the evidence of the pastures at the heads of the fjords of the south-west, optimistically named his discovery *Groenaland*, The Green Land, or *Groenland* – Greenland. He returned in 986 with fourteen ships – survivors of a larger fleet – and a band of settlers, and within a short time his country, in general a gloomy and forbidding land, had attracted a small but vigorous population – probably never more than about 3000. The colonists were chiefly recruited from amongst those who for one reason or another Iceland could no longer contain or support. The migration was once again one of whole communities and families to what, at first sight, was another uninhabited land. As in Iceland there quickly emerged a simple patriarchal society, and Eirik, we hear 'lived in high distinction and all recognized his authority'. Like Iceland, the country was Christian from about 1000 and sustained, in the same way, a pastoral economy of isolated farmsteads. 'The farmers', says the *King's Mirror* of the mid-thirteenth century, 'raise cattle and sheep in large numbers, and make butter and cheese in great quantities. The people subsist chiefly on these foods and on beef; but they also eat the flesh of various kinds of game, such as reindeer (caribou), whales, seals and bears.' And like Iceland, the new colony was heavily dependent on Norway for many of its necessities – timber, grain, iron – and for all its meagre luxuries. In exchange it could offer furs, hides, a cloth of sorts, ropes – reputedly strong enough to take the pull of sixty men – and, more remarkably, polar bears, walrus and narwhal ivory, and those superb white falcons a dozen of which were thought in 1396 to be an adequate ransom for a European prince held by the Sultan of Turkey.

For reasons which are not clear, but which might well be guessed, Greenland, like Iceland, surrendered its independence to Norway in mid-thirteenth century, and like Iceland was doomed as Norway's interest and power in the Atlantic faded. There were originally two major settlements, both on the then more or less ice-free west coast facing North America. One (the western) was in the vicinity of the modern Godthaab, and in its heyday comprised some ninety farms and four churches. The other (the eastern), was much larger with 190 farms, a cathedral, and over a dozen churches and monasteries in its prime, and lay just above Cape Farewell, in what is now the Julianehaab District. Beyond this tiny littoral there was nothing but mountains and ice, though further along the west coast (in roughly latitude 70°N) the two colonies found excellent hunting and fishing grounds, whilst on occasions, as is known from inscriptions, the intrepid pushed up, and even wintered, as far north as latitudes 73°, 76° and 79°. This hard and cruel world, well within the Arctic Circle, called forth staggering feats of enterprise and endurance, none of which, admittedly, have lost anything in the telling. *Flóamanna Saga*[4] describes a shipwreck, with the survivors struggling through the ice in the ship's boat, rowing where they could, and for the rest dragging it and themselves over ice floes and glaciers. *Einars Tháttr* tells of the finding (*c.* 1120), in ominous circumstances, of a beached ship, merchants and crew all dead, and nearby the corpses of two servants, one, it was reckoned, 'who had been chopping wood and had collapsed through hunger', the other 'who had stayed on his feet as long as he could'. The *King's Mirror* is laconic as to those who have been trapped in the ice and how 'they have taken to their boats and have dragged them up on the ice with them, and in this way have sought to reach land; but the ship and everything else had to be abandoned and was lost. Some have had to spend four or five days upon the ice before reaching land, and some even longer.'

Not even the Norse could endure such rigours indefinitely. Survival might have been possible had nothing altered for the worse, but this was not to be the case. From about 1200 the northern climate apparently deteriorated, the sea temperature probably fell, and there was a vast increase in the drift ice which came south with the east Greenland current to Cape Farewell and then swung north-west to enclose first the eastern, and then the western settlement. With the ice came seals, and in pursuit of these the *Skraeling* – the Eskimo – who, having crossed Canada from Alaska, entered northern Greenland about 1200, and commenced to occupy its habitable areas, some moving south down the west coast.[5] By the mid-fourteenth century they had overrun the Norse western settlement. The eastern colony struggled on longer. There were occasional clashes as the Eskimo advanced: the *Icelandic Annals* record that in 1379 'the *Skraelings* attacked the Greenlanders and killed eighteen of them', and among the Eskimo folk tales collected by Henry Rink in the nineteenth century is one, *Ungortok the Chief of Kakortok*, describing a gruesome and bloodthirsty Norse-Eskimo feud. Possibly there was, at least in theory, room enough for the two peoples. The farms of the Greenlanders lay well back up the fjords, where the sea froze late and where the ice was never very safe. This was of little use to the Eskimo whose hunting was concentrated on the headlands, islands and sea ice where seals were most abundant. But neither race was accommodating, and the Norse were radically weakened by the loss of their northern hunting grounds to the Eskimo. And at the same time their contacts with the outside world were fading. What Greenland could offer Europe was no longer particularly attractive. Its cloth could hardly compare with that of Flanders or England; the Hanse could obtain furs more easily and in larger quantities from Russia; and the discriminating found walrus ivory inferior to that of Africa and Asia. Moreover, like Iceland, Greenland had neither the population nor the materials to construct and maintain any sizable ships of its own, and for such relations as it had with the outside world it was entirely dependent on the Norwegians. Just how tenuous these relations were, and how modest the scale of the colony's trade, can be seen from the fact that in the second half of the fourteenth century a single ship did the run from Norway to Greenland fairly regularly – though certainly not annually – until she was lost in about 1370. Thereafter, with Norway's maritime decline, the colony was abandoned, whilst Iceland, desperately fighting for its own life, could do nothing to help. In the last decades of the fourteenth century craft sailing between Norway and Iceland were occasionally blown westwards to Greenland, and English fishermen working in Icelandic waters may, by accident or design, have found their way there from time to time in the early 1400s. By the late fifteenth century the country, though not entirely forgotten – it appears on genuine maps of 1427 and 1485, as well as on the spurious Vinland Map of supposedly *c.* 1440[6] – was so dimly remembered that in the 1470s the king of Denmark is alleged to have sent out expeditions to attempt to find it. The last credible evidence of organized Christian life there dates from about 1410, though roughly eighty years later Pope Alexander VI was expressing a somewhat detached concern at the rumoured spiritual condition of the settlement. Archaeological finds – caps, fragments of dress and the like – suggest Greenland still knew Europe well into the fifteenth century, and it seems very likely that life of some sort dragged on there till about 1500. Most probably the colonists, weakened by generations of inbreeding and by failure – so the remains of fashionable European garments would indicate – to adapt to the rigours of the climate, succumbed in the end to hunger and to Eskimo hostility. The final scene, it has been argued (but not widely accepted) was one of abject misery and degradation, and the contents of a cemetery at Herjolfsnes, in the south of the eastern settlement, have been taken to show that the descendants of the once tall, strong and fertile Norsemen were, by the late 1400s, a handful of feeble and deformed degenerates. The contention is hotly disputed, and the evidence in any case too fragile to support so general a conclusion. But be this as it may, when in 1586 that great English seaman John Davis re-explored the western fjords of Greenland he found no white men, nor any signs of them, 'nor saw anything only gripes, ravens and small birds'.

The ultimate, and the most spectacular achievement of Norse seamen was the discovery of North America. As with Greenland it was found simply by chance. In 986 one Bjarni Herjólfsson, an experienced sailor and trader, or in the more oblique language of the Sagas 'a most promising young man . . . and from his early days a keen traveller abroad', left Norway to winter with his father in Iceland. On arrival, however, he found that his father had sold up and gone to Greenland. Notwithstanding the lateness of the season and his ignorance of the route, Bjarni decided to follow. The result was that three days out 'their favourable wind died down, and north winds and fogs overtook them, so that they had no idea which way they were going'. When eventually they got a bearing and set a course the landfall they made – well-forested and with low hills – was obviously not Greenland. They were, like as not, off southern Labrador, and Bjarni spent a few reluctant days examining the coast – his men would willingly have spent more – before he found his way to Greenland.[7]

Within a few years (perhaps *c.* 1000) the discovery was taken up. The redoubtable Eirik himself was persuaded that his skills and luck were essential to such an undertaking, but fell from his horse on the way to embark. So the leadership passed to his son Leif, a man of equally remarkable parts, reputedly the first seaman to make the round trip from Greenland to Norway and back, and said by some to have improved the hour by converting Greenland (but not his father) to Christianity. Using Bjarni's ship, and possibly some of his crew, he sailed from Greenland to work Bjarni's course in reverse. His first landfall – perhaps the south of the modern Baffin Island – was 'all great glaciers, and right up to the glaciers from the sea as it were a single slab of rock', which, considering useless, he named in good Norse style, *Helluland*, or Flatstone Land. He then moved on south, coming into splendid bays with fine white sands and behind them woodland – apparently the forests of Labrador – which he called *Markland*, Wood or Forest Land. From this he worked further south again to his final point, *Vinland*, probably the northern tip of Newfoundland.[8] Here, where at L'Anse aux Meadows, there are substantial remains of what may have been a subsequent Viking settlement, the expedition wintered and in the spring sailed back to Greenland.

The Norse, and particularly the later Saga writers influenced by classical legends, were vastly impressed by what had been found. It eclipsed Greenland and Iceland; it was a paradise, Wineland the Good, where, as the king of Denmark explained to an inquiring German in about 1075, vines grew of their own accord and there was self-sown wheat in abundance, and where, as the *Greenlanders' Saga* tells 'there was no lack of salmon in river or lake, and salmon bigger than they had ever seen before . . .' whilst 'no frost came during the winter and the grass hardly withered'. Leif himself never returned to America, but an assortment of his relatives made every effort to exploit the promised land, where at last the simple requirements of the Norse were to be satisfied and their years of endurance rewarded. His brother Thorvald spent two summers examining the Markland-Vinland coast until he was killed (*c.* 1005) in a skirmish with (probably) Algonkian Indians somewhere near Lake Melville. Next (*c.* 1009) came Karlsefni, married to another of the Eirikson tribe, bringing with him a body of men – variously put at 160 or 250 – and women, together with the livestock and other essential paraphernalia of settlement. He established himself, as far as can be seen, at the northern end of Belle Isle Strait, on either Belle Isle or on Great Sacred Island. From confused and conflicting accounts it would seem that not all were persuaded that this was the long-awaited paradise, and there was some exploration in search of better things in the Hamilton Inlet – Lake Melville area.[9] Karlsefni himself dug in behind a stockade and traded cloth to the local Eskimo in exchange for furs and pelts, and 'when the cloth began to run short (the Norse) cut it up so that it was no broader than a fingerbreadth, but the *Skraelings* gave just as much for it or more.' Yet notwithstanding this precocious display of imperial enterprise, the Norse were not to succeed. Before long they had clashed with the Eskimo and fallen out amongst themselves over women. After three winters they withdrew, taking with them one Snorri to whom a certain fame is due as the first white man born in America.

Thereafter, to the best of our knowledge, no settlement was attempted or established. There were other voyages to the mainland, such as in 1121 when 'bishop Eirik of Greenland went in search of Vinland'. Unchronicled expeditions may have wandered even further afield, and there was still some contact between Greenland and Markland – probably for timber and furs – as late as the fourteenth century. But the Norse had gone as far as they were going. They lacked if not purpose certainly that overall control and direction essential to the success of any colonizing venture, and their efforts were constantly weakened by feuds and dissensions. They met determined resistance from the local Indians and Eskimo, and they were clearly intimidated by the sheer volume of the native American population. At the same time they themselves were increasingly short of manpower, and as the settlements in Iceland and Greenland decayed they were deprived of the bases, material and incentives for any further endeavour.

II *Land, loot and ships*

The motives underlying the whole great cycle of Scandinavian expansion are as elusive as much of the detail of the achievement itself. Possibly Scandinavia, like Spain, was from its harsh geography and climate, a forcing ground of the heroic, and there was (and is) something in the Scandinavian temperament – a passion for adventure, freedom and action – only to be satisfied in desperate undertakings. Such lofty views echo the highmindedness of Icelandic tradition. In this there is a simple reason why men so readily migrated in the late ninth century: to escape the tyrannous behaviour of King Harald Fairhair of Norway (870–945). It was later reported that

> Once he had established possession of these territories which were newly come into his power he paid close attention to the landed men and the leading farmers, and all those from whom he suspected some rebellion might be looked for. He made everyone do one thing or the other, become his retainers or quit the country, or, for a third choice, suffer harship or forfeit their lives . . . But many a man fled the land from this servitude, and it was now that many desert places were settled far and wide.

This is of course the classic case against any early ruler who exerted himself, and is not to be taken at its face value. Nevertheless there is little doubt that some, though not as many as tradition would have it, were impelled for one reason or another to escape Harald's state-building zeal as he attempted to extend his authority throughout the whole of Norway and to overcome the unruliness – to say the least – of a people accustomed to that freedom of speech and personal liberty deriving from their Germanic ancestry. After a victory at Hafrsfjord (*c.* 885) he got himself as firmly into the saddle as he could. One of the many obstacles to his will were the Vikings of the south-west – the homeland, that is, of the majority of the first settlers in Iceland – long dedicated by tradition, desire and economic necessity to violence, disorder and piracy. It was the king's dealings with these future heroes of Icelandic historiography that largely inspired the passage quoted above. Some fled to the Scottish islands, others to Iceland, and even a number of his erstwhile allies emigrated, we are euphemistically told, with his aid and advice. And much the same had already taken place in Denmark when, in the early ninth century, its ruler had cleared his coasts of Vikings.

Admittedly the wish to escape from some unacceptable regime has at all times been a powerful incentive to migration. But so, too, has been the desire to escape the results of miscalculation, misfortune and misdemeanour, and men have fled to sea and to distant parts to avoid their wives, their creditors and the consequences of their misdeeds. And in a world endowed with an unusually full measure of those wars and disorders endemic in early society, there were always many obliged to go on their travels to escape justice, revenge or some other disaster, without any need of the stimulus of Harald, or those rebuffs we have already remarked, suffered by the Vikings in various parts of Europe in the late ninth century (see p. oo). Gnup, 'a great manslayer and ironsmith' departed to Iceland, *Landnámabók* records, 'because of his own killings and his brother's'; Eirik the Red's magnificent record in discovery was largely inspired by the necessity of avoiding the consequences of an equally outstanding prowess in manslaughter; and the first organized expedition prowess in manslaughter; and the first organized expedition to Iceland, well before Harald's star was so noticeably in the ascendant, was the outcome of an urgent need for land and sanctuary after some disastrous setbacks in feud.

This incessant war and violence doubtless to some degree reflected a struggle to control inadequate resources of land, and therefore of sustenance. Throughout the Viking age there is the constant suggestion of a growing population increasingly pressing on the limited amount of cultivable land available in an area – Norway in particular – scarcely favoured by nature. The northern half of the Swedish-Norwegian peninsula is mountainous, cold and inhospitable. Yet there, as was expected of them, great men sired amazing progenies by their wives, mistresses and concubines. Harald Fairhair had nine sons, one of whom, Eirik Bloodaxe, in turn fathered eight, all needing, and indeed demanding, substantial patrimonies. And no doubt the lesser emulated their superiors, with every Swede who could afford taking, according to one horrified Christian observer, two or three wives. Even without fully accepting evidence so colourful, it would seem that in Scandinavia, as in Europe as a whole, the population was probably rising by the ninth century, and certainly rising in the tenth. So it can be argued that, through the constraints of geography, with nothing to support such numbers, the entire rhythm and pattern of the earliest phases of Scandinavian expansion were dictated by a search for land for settlement by peoples amongst whom there burned an intense love for a holding of one's own, and in whose literature heroes returned from the wars to settle on their farms. The earliest Norse forays to the Shetlands and Orkneys appear to have been less to take plunder than to find land. Then again, after their initial attacks on the rich monasteries of north-eastern England in the late eighth century, and despite the tempting prospects these must have revealed and the absence of any resistance, the Norse failed to turn south to harvest a similar reward but went instead apparently to seek land in the poorer north and west. So also the Danish raids to the west may have begun later than those of the Norse because a growing population could be more easily absorbed in Denmark than in Norway's more extensive, but less tractable lands. And Danish activity was to wane – for a time at least – in the early tenth century when these pressures were relieved by colonization in England and Normandy. The preoccupations were much the same in the migration to Iceland. At its climax (*c.* 900) it perhaps reached something like 2000 people a year, with whole families moving out encumbered in the most unmartial fashion with farm and household gear, livestock, followers and slaves. And when within a short time – by the mid-tenth century – such habitable land as there was had been occupied and famine pressed, there followed a further exodus from Iceland to Greenland.

But the problem was never merely one of subsistence, and it would be a naive simplification to see Norse expansion simply in terms of worthy aristocrats and deserving peasants seeking fair acres to rule, or plots to till. The Danes attacked the Flemish coast in the early 800s as retaliation for the onslaught by the armies of Charlemagne against the neighbouring pagan Saxons. And in a society organized for, and largely devoted to, war, in which strife was a major theme of literature, and where the virtues most highly esteemed were those of the warrior, the chief who would survive had to be able to lead his followers on triumphant and profitable raids. As Tacitus had acutely observed, 'you cannot maintain a large body of companions except by violence and war'. Faithful retainers expected to be rewarded with slaves, fundamental to life in pagan Scandinavia and valuable articles of trade in the Moslem Mediterranean and Near East. They expected, too, cloth, wine, land, and above all that silver so highly regarded as currency, capital and ornament. Once the true wealth of the west was appreciated, and much was discovered to be conveniently housed in churches and monasteries often undefended, and frequently situated on lonely islands or near coasts, it was only a matter of time before Viking attacks increased and spread. They began, as far as can be seen, with Lindisfarne in northeastern England (793); two years later Dublin had been reached, and by the end of the century the coast of Aquitaine. Before long much of the west was subject to what was tantamount to regular taxation, the levying of that Danegeld – the payment by which the raiders were bought off – taken in France from 845 and in England from 865. The amounts raised are unknown, but they were clearly substantial, with seven levies in France alone producing 40,000lb (18,160kg) of silver. Nor was this the Vikings' only source. For much of the ninth and tenth centuries Scandinavians pushing across Russia had acquired, amongst other things, silver from the Moslem world in exchange for furs, slaves and assorted loot (see p. 30). When, however, this flow of bullion towards the north ceased (*c.* 970), those pirates who had flourished by plundering it and the trade it had stimulated in the Baltic, turned with renewed violence to the opportunities of the west. Whole seaborne armies were released against Europe in the late tenth and early eleventh centuries to take the treasure of a continent enriched by the output of the silver mines of the Harz Mountains, and to take in particular that of an ill-defended England, where in 1018 a single Danegeld is said to have yielded £72,000.

In pursuit of such rewards Viking bands moved with speed and secrecy, striking unheralded and enjoying all those tactical advantages of mobility, flexibility and surprise that seapower could then confer. 'It was not thought', wrote a contemporary of the attack on Lindisfarne, in the familiar language of defeat, 'that such an inroad could be made.' Against the Norse ninth-century Europe – the Greeks of Byzantium and the Moslems of south Spain apart – could do little. It had no naval forces of any consequence. Even worse there was no organized, let alone united, power in the British Isles or in Russia, whilst the vast European empire of Charlemagne was disintegrating, with the sons of Louis the Pious engaged in open war against each other after 840. The renewed Scandinavian assault on England from the mid-900s encountered only a realm impotent in the hands of the luckless Ethelred (987–1016). And no more than the Spaniards in America or the Portuguese in Asia in later centuries had the Scandinavians any difficulty in finding allies among their victims. The Irish kings of the ninth century employed Norse mercenaries in their endless internecine disputes; and even the nephew of the English hero Alfred, deserted to the Danes.

Thus we can see for the first time, and however obscurely, something of that pattern of motives and opportunities which was to re-appear in other cycles of maritime expansion. In the aggressor society political discontent; resources in land inadequate to the aspirations, if not necessarily to the needs, of some of its population; a demand for riches; and an admiration for, or devotion to, heroic endeavour. Then, in the neighbouring or distant world, the existence of victims attractive in their wealth, and neither able nor organized to resist. It still, however, remains to explain how and why the Norse should have gone so far afield. Yet of all maritime peoples they were the most maritime. The geography of much of Scandinavia was such that without ships or boats life could hardly have been sustained. Northern Sweden was a land of poor soil and unbroken forest; Finland a mass of lakes and forests; Norway a spine of mountains fringed with an insignificant coastal strip. Everywhere, apart from West Jutland, coasts were so irregular and indented that communication was either only possible by sea, or certainly easier and more rapid, whilst boats were vital for the taking of fish to supplement the meagre diet the land could produce. So from the earliest times the ship was an integral and indeed a fundamental part of Scandinavian life, respected, cherished, and housed for the winter in some specially constructed shelter. It was in ships that the great travelled; from ships that they fought; and, in pagan days, in ships that they were buried. And naturally enough Scandinavian vessels were designed and handled with the skill of a people who, like the equally impressive Polynesians, lived in daily contact with the sea. It was thus clear, from its traditions and from its very geographical location, that if Scandinavia was to expand at all it would be by river and sea. And so until the eighteenth century the Swedes were repeatedly drawn across the Baltic and into Russia. But for Norway the natural outlet was to the west. There are, for instance, some 960km of sailing between Oslo and Bergen; but only 400km between Bergen and the Shetlands and 720km between Bergen and the Faroes. Furthermore the Norse voyages show a steady progression through a belt of latitude whose extremities in Norway are Trondheim in the north and Jaeren or Lindesnes in the south. Roughly within, or adjoining this 576km wide stretch of ocean lie the Faroes, Shetlands, Orkneys and Hebrides; the first settlements in Iceland and Greenland, and the nearest points of the North American continent. Every spring there blow in these waters the east and north-east winds of the Norway Sea, and every summer the south and south-easterlies of the eastern Atlantic, whilst throughout the sailing season (spring to autumn) east and north-easterly winds prevail between Iceland and Greenland. Leaving Norway with a fair wind, as any experienced seaman would do, and as the Norse are known to have done, there was every probability of a landfall in the northern isles, Iceland, Greenland or North America. For the more crucial return journey there were (and are) the westerlies which bring up the rear of every passing depression, and which are particularly frequent, and unruly, in the late summer and early autumn. Geographically, therefore, the Norse were almost as well placed to undertake oceanic voyages as were the Iberians of the sixteenth century. Like them they were in a wind system which carried them out to, and back from, the distant west, and carried them in the same way along routes interspersed with numerous islands from which seamen could check their course and position, and in which they could refit and revictual their ships. But unlike the Iberians, the Scandinavians operated in latitudes of high winds, violent and unpredictable storms and immense seas. Overtaken by such weather it was their practice to run before it. This they were obliged to do by the design of their ships, which sitting low in the water shipped seas if headed into them, or if sailed across strong winds lifted their steering oars, fitted to one side, clear of the water, so leaving the vessel out of control. But the Norse ship could and would run and steer successfully before a following gale. And given the wind systems of the northern latitudes this meant she might well end up off one of the lands of future settlement. Iceland was reached, according to one source, because 'men had a voyage to make from Norway to the Faroes . . . but they were storm-driven into the western ocean and discovered a big country there', or, as another version has it, Gardar had 'made a journey to the Hebrides . . . but as he was sailing through the Pentland Firth a gale drove him off course and he was carried into the western ocean'. Greenland came to light in very similar circumstances when Gunnbjörn, on passage from Norway to Iceland, 'was storm-driven west across the ocean'.

But having reached such regions, willingly or unwillingly, there was much, it was found, to be wished for. True, the islands of the northern seas were conveniently sited as a series of stepping stones or staging posts for further voyages west – the Shetlands and Faroes for Iceland; Iceland for Greenland; Greenland for North America – much as the Atlantic and Caribbean islands later served the Spaniards in relation to the American mainland. But, after the first enthusiasm had moderated, their very insufficiencies were in themselves a powerful incentive to renewed migration, as were, as in all other empires, the dissensions and feuds among the settlers. In Iceland some five-sixths of the country offered no support to human life. Greenland was the same, and in the *King's Mirror* it is significantly recorded that men 'have often tried to go up into the country and climb the highest mountains . . . to look about and learn whether any land could be found that was free from ice'. Even Wineland the Good, apparently so idyllic after the rock, ice and desert of the earlier settlements, was hardly the most attractive part of the American continent, and whatever its undoubted charms they were fatally flawed by the presence of large and hostile native populations. The Norse, in short, under no such purposeful direction as the Danes, and with their migrations so much governed by their own turbulent individualism and determined by where their ships would most easily or safely go, were singularly unlucky in what they found.

But to admit there was clearly a very substantial element of chance about the course of Scandinavian discovery is not to argue that Scandinavian ships were driven aimlessly and helplessly about the Atlantic. Far from it, and an essential factor in the range and success of these voyages was the excellence of the crews and vessels with which they were undertaken. By any reckoning the Scandinavians, and especially the Norse, were among the greatest sailors the world has known. Theirs was the first conquest since Antiquity of an ocean by western man, and that one of the wildest and most dangerous.

In the high latitudes of the North Atlantic there are no reliable trade winds or seasonal monsoons like those which helped later explorers in other seas, but instead sudden shifts of wind, and the skies more often than not blotted out by rain, cloud or fog. Yet from an early date the passage from Norway to Iceland was on occasion made direct, and by the thirteenth and fourteenth centuries this was the usual practice. A successful crossing took something like three weeks – though bad weather and assorted mishaps might prolong it almost indefinitely – and there is no suggestion that the voyage was regarded as a particularly difficult or dangerous undertaking. Even more remarkable is that in the high Middle Ages the Norse were making the far more formidable direct passage from Norway to Greenland (*c.* 2400km) and that for decade after decade these trades were carried on with no more than a reasonable proportion of losses through what are, even in spring and summer, some of the stormiest and most unpredictable seas in the world.

That this was so is testimony to skills developed through centuries of experience in the handling of small craft. Something of these we can gather from the Sagas of the twelfth and thirteenth centuries, when the Norse still remained the only seamen in Europe to sail so far and so frequently out of sight of land. Driven towards destruction among the breakers of a lee shore they might, for instance, save at least crew and cargo by running their ship ashore under full sail – deliberately heading her, that is, towards the land. As any who have beached a boat in even a moderate sea will appreciate this called for consummate skill, perfect control, and confident and accurate steering, since once in the surf the slightest error would cause the vessel to slew round and leave her to be rolled over and destroyed by the sea. And nowhere were the qualities of the Norse more clearly demonstrated than in their techniques of navigation. Like any other competent seamen they could estimate their position out of sight of land by dead-reckoning – calculating from the feel of the wind, and from a knowledge of what speed a particular ship would make under such conditions, their progress in a given direction. With steady following breezes and a passable helmsman it was, and is, no great problem to hold the desired course. But the climate is rarely so accommodating, and with winds fluctuating in force and direction, beam seas and currents of unknown strength, Norse navigators might find themselves lost, or in what the Sagas describe as a state of *hafvilla* – not knowing their course, uncertain as to how far they had travelled, and without any sense of direction. So we hear of those who 'met with bad weather . . . there was much fog, and the winds were light and unfavourable . . . they drifted far and wide on the high sea. Most of those on board completely lost their reckoning', whilst others encountered 'a thick fog which did not lift for many days' after which came bad weather 'and they were in fact hopelessly adrift'. Quite clearly then, mere estimates of course, position and distance run were inadequate and had to be checked by other techniques.

Some of these were of such simple but effective ingenuity that the Norse have at times, and quite wrongly, been credited with some sixth sense, a sort of mystic communion with the sea enabling them to perform the seemingly impossible. Among the stories of the discovery of Iceland is that of Floki who, emulating Noah (and the practice of other early seafarers), sailed on one celebrated occasion with three ravens on board: 'when he set the first free it flew aft over the stern; the second (released later) flew up in the air and back to the ship again; but the third flew forth straight way over the stem' so showing where the promised land lay. And indeed, within limits, it is possible to select or check a course by watching the flight of homing seabirds, observing the changing character of marine life, and noticing the variations in the run and colour of the sea. From all such phenomena a cautious and skilled navigator can deduce a very reasonable notion of his whereabouts, and this ability to read and interpret the waters was common amongst experienced seamen of all nations to within living memory. Thus the *King's Mirror* reveals a remarkable knowledge, based on the closest observation, not only of winds and tides, but of the movements of whales, fish, walrus and seals, and of the character and migration of sea ice. How such information was turned to use is shown in the sailing directions for the direct crossing from Norway to Greenland. The pilot is told to keep so far north of the Shetlands that they were just visible, and then to run south of the Faroes at such a distance that the heights were half hidden by the sea. Next he was to pass to the south of Iceland 'so that the seabirds and whales can be seen' – that vigorous congregation living off the fish and plankton abounding on the edge of the Icelandic continental shelf, so making this otherwise desolate and formidable stretch of ocean particularly conspicuous, and easily identifiable.

But for successful long-distance navigation more was needed than good steering and a keen eye, and it was essential that a pilot should be able to find and hold a course when well clear of the land and such assistance as it offered. It is highly probable that from an early date the Norse, like the Irish before them, could orientate themselves from the noon sun and the Great Bear. Indeed by the 800s they may have been using the Pole Star to get a more precise north than the Bear gave, or so at least it would seem from the *scip steorra* (ship star) and *lád steorra* (lodestar, leading star) of the Anglo-Saxons, whilst an Old English poem of the ninth century tells how mariners relied on the sun 'to guide their craft across the sea and bring them to the land'. And clearly by the age of the great voyages the Norse could, as the seamen of Antiquity had been able to do, work out directions from the major heavenly bodies, and so shape a course across open waters. To landsmen, and particularly to modern landsmen, this sounds a more formidable undertaking than in fact it was. From remotest times men have had some notion of direction from the movement of the sun, infallibly appearing over the horizon in one place and disappearing in another, whilst for the more sophisticated its mid-day position and the shadows it cast, further served to divide east from west, and also to define two more quarters of the sky. But in high latitudes the positions of sunrise and sunset alter rapidly, so that east and west are much less easy to identify than north and south. Furthermore, the coasts of Scandinavia and Denmark run roughly from north to south, making it reasonable to distinguish directions east of the meridian as 'land-north' or 'land-south', whilst the seaward directions are 'out-north' and out-south', i.e.

north-west and south-west. This individual and somewhat cumbersome terminology was modified in the course of time. By the ninth century the Anglo-Saxons had already devised or adopted the system, later to become general, whereby the four basic directions (north, south, east, west) could be combined to define intermediate points (northwest, northeast, southwest, southeast) and to name the winds. Something of this was already known to the Viking Ottar, whose expedition (*c*. 880) from Norway round the North Cape and into the White Sea was recorded by king Alfred. His narrative speaks of a wind 'west and somewhat north', and in the later Sagas the eight divisions of the horizon (north, south, east, west and the four intervening points) and the corresponding wind names are the only ones used.

From occasional hints in the literary sources it would appear that the 'division of the horizon' – the establishing that is of directions – was soon regarded by Norse seamen as an almost routine operation. So in 986 Bjarni Herjólfsson and his companions on passage to Greenland ran into a long spell of fog and northerly winds. Having lost all sense of direction they lowered their sail and drifted until the skies cleared – another invaluable indication of navigational practice. Then, when the sun re-appeared, they were able to get their bearings (*deila aettir* – find the airts or divisions of the horizon), and the voyage was successfully resumed. That this procedure had a long history is suggested by the fact that Ottar, in his voyage at least a century earlier, was apparently able to distinguish the direction of the wind in what were then unknown waters, and at a time of year when the Pole Star was invisible. How such observations were made is unknown. It is possible that the Norse had some kind of bearing dial with which they could find the points of the horizon from the sun and stars, and what is supposed to be such an instrument has been discovered in Greenland. And it has even been claimed that by using Icelandic spar, which polarizes light, they could detect the sun when the heavens were overcast – though had this been so stories of the loss of bearings would surely have been less common. Nor was this all. No more than other early seamen could the Norse determine longitude, but by methods once again unknown they could find their latitude at sea – their 'northing' or 'southing' – a matter of the greatest urgency in voyages along an essentially east-west axis. True, by observing the mid-day sun, even if only by measuring its shadow, or by marking the height of the Pole Star above the horizon, expressed in terms of one's own arm, hand or thumb, some rough indication of latitude could be obtained. But Norse technique may well have been less crude, for there were in existence tables which gave the mid-day latitude of the sun week by week throughout the year, as observed in northern Iceland in the late tenth century. Armed with this, or similar information, recorded on some simple object – a marked stick, for instance – a seaman could tell his latitude in relation to a known place. So the Norse could determine how far north or south they were; could hold a course and could recover it if it should be lost. And so also they could practise, from perhaps the eleventh century, latitude sailing: they would seek, that is, the latitude of their destination, and then with a favouring wind run it down until they arrived where they wished to be.

This rudimentary but nevertheless highly effective celestial navigation lasted unchanged well into the thirteenth century. Its mysteries and merits are expounded by the sage father of the *King's Mirror* to his prentice son, who amongst other things is to master arithmetic, observe the courses of the heavenly bodies, recognize the quarters of the horizon and generally keep his wits about him. Whatever other conclusions we may draw from this evidence it is clear enough that it cannot be assumed that it was the introduction of the magnetic compass which made oceanic navigation possible, no more than it can be held that with the appearance of the compass older methods of navigation were superseded. A primitive compass had been known in European waters since the twelfth century and was probably in general use on the northern sea-routes by about 1300.[10] With a needle to show him where the north lay a pilot could now find the points of the horizon irrespective of whether he could see the sun or stars, and it is highly significant that in the later Sagas we hear no more of *hafvilla* – of loss of bearings. Nevertheless in the Atlantic, as elsewhere, the ancient methods persisted. So the sailing directions for the Greenland voyage (thirteenth and fourteenth centuries) appear to have been based on compass courses, but on astronomical observations. And though the compass was of undoubted assistance in cloudy or foggy weather, the Pole Star – the Guiding Star, the Star of the Sea – its constancy a standing reproach to fickle popes and prelates, retained its age-old importance. Thus, as was to be the case in other maritime societies, existing skills and knowledge were adapted to the needs of seamen. And as in other maritime societies the scope and range of voyages were not determined by the extent of initial navigational techniques, but rather such techniques and skills were improved and extended to meet new demands. So somewhat before the introduction of the compass, the sounding line appears to have come into use to discover the depth and nature of the bottom. To be in soundings – to be able to touch the bed of the sea with a weight on the end of a line – was often the first warning a seaman had that he was coming, willingly or not, to land. Furthermore, since the coverings of the sea-floor (sand, shingle, mud of infinite variety) have a pattern of distribution as characteristic and recognizable as a landscape, the specimens brought up by a tallowed lead enabled an experienced navigator to identify his whereabouts with some confidence. Then as trade developed and voyages ceased to be spasmodic, individual ventures and took on something of the nature of routine commercial operations – of regular runs along established routes – there were produced collections of sailing directions (those for example in the thirteenth-century *Sturlubók* and the fourteenth-century *Hauksbók*), indicating courses, describing landmarks, and generally offering a pilot assorted useful information.

Even more fundamental to Norse success was the quality of their ships, and indeed it has been argued that Scandinavian maritime expansion came when it did, and took the directions it did, since only then were the Norse in possession of craft able to face the rigours of oceanic voyaging. Similar views are often expressed about the later voyages of discovery, but they are, as we shall see, far from satisfactory, and in general overestimate the technological advances needed before man could successfully contend with the ocean. The Irish, after all, reached Iceland in pre-Norse times in boats which, as far as may be seen, had no margin of safety other than that divine intervention so frequently recorded in the lives of the Celtic saints. In Scandinavia there were in existence at a very early date vessels of a highly developed and individual character. Tacitus mentions the double-ended northern ship – pointed at bow and stern in a fashion quite unknown to the Romans – in the first century AD, and a remarkable example of such a craft has survived in the fourth-century boat discovered at Nydam in southern Denmark. In this virtually all the distinguishing features of later Norse vessels are already present in some degree or other. It has a light, flexible and rakish hull, tapering off to a finely pointed and overhanging raised bow and stern – to stem the seas both whilst afloat, and when being launched from, or landed on, a beach. It is long (23.18m), narrow (3.2m), shallow (1.2m) and undecked, built of overlapping planks riveted to each other by iron nails (clinker-built) and then secured to the ribs (the ship's internal frame) by lashings. It has no keel to speak of, no mast or sail, and is simply a large rowing boat controlled by an anticipation, none too crude, of the later and distinctive Scandinavian steering oar. In easy weather it might, though not without danger and discomfort, have crossed the North Sea, and it was perhaps in craft such as this that the Anglo-Saxons had reached England, for many of its features recur in a ship of *c.*625–60, discovered some years ago at Sutton Hoo in Suffolk.

Five centuries after the Nydam boat the vessels of the Scandinavians had reached a perfection which, together with the superb cathedrals of their Norman descendants, constitutes one of the most dazzling achievements of medieval technology. By then the Norse had ships which could cross oceans, land almost anywhere, and from which horses could easily disembark. And they had other craft which could work up rivers into the heart of a continent, and which could, if need be, be carried overland. Some of their vessels were in effect merchantmen (the *hafskip*), others warships (the *langskip*). Of this latter type a magnificent example has survived in the now celebrated vessel excavated at Gokstad, near Oslo, in 1881. She was perhaps built about 850, and though small by modern standards must have been considerably larger than the average Viking ship of her time. Like her Nydam ancestor, she is long (23.33m) and shallow, drawing only 92cm when partly loaded. And, indeed, much in design and construction has remained unchanged over the centuries. Apart from her raised bow and stern the Gokstad ship sits low in the water; she is double-ended; she is built in the same clinker fashion; and the same style lashings are used to secure the planking – though only below the water-line – to the frames. But she is a sailing ship and no longer a rowing boat. She is without rowing benches; is decked; has a recognizable keel; is much broader for the sake of stability (5.25m); and would use her sixteen pairs of oars only as auxiliary power. Every detail of her design shows remarkable ingenuity and sophistication. She set a single large square sail on her one mast. With the aid of special spars the sail could be spread before a light following breeze, or with tackle it could be set to lie at various angles to the

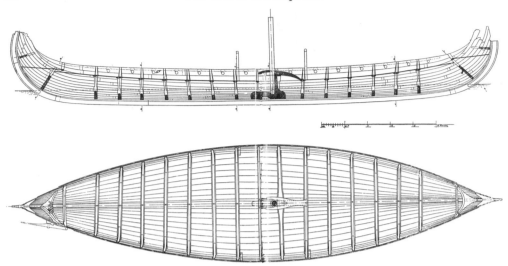

Fig. 1   The Oseberg ship, skeleton drawing by Fr Johannessen.

hull for beating to windward, whilst in strong winds, or for other reasons, its area could be quickly and effectively reduced by a simple reefing system. She was steered not by a stern rudder, but by what was tantamount to a large oar fitted on one quarter. This was fastened to a substantial block of wood attached to the exterior of the hull. Osiers were used for the fastening, knotted on the outside, passing through both rudder and block, and well secured inside the ship. The rudder was thus firmly attached to the hull, whilst at the same time the flexibility of the osiers meant it could be turned in the horizontal plane by a tiller, and another fastening on the hull prevented it from rotating on its axis in the vertical plane. When the ship was beached, or passing through shallows, the rudder could easily be raised by undoing the upper fastening and rotating it on its axis with the help of a rope attached to the lower part of the blade. Whatever the disadvantages of a rudder of this kind, it gave to the helmsman the potential of a powerful transversal thrust, and so to the ship rapid and easy manoeuvrability. In the surf and breakers off a beach, where a stern rudder is either torn from its fittings or useless (being in water moving as fast as the vessel itself), an oar-like projection can be kept off the bottom, and can reach beyond the sea carrying the ship to allow control to be maintained. Then in clear waters the deep rudder (and that of the Gokstad ship is 3.3m in depth) would help to check the tendency of so shallow a hull to fall off to leeward – to drift sideways, that is – when sailing across a wind.[11] True, no more than most other ships was she without her faults. Her performance against a headwind is uncertain. With so little grip on the water, and with a consequent lack of momentum when coming head into sea and wind, and with no sail at either extremity of the hull to pull or push her round, it is very likely that in any sort of a sea she would be prevented by the waves from turning from one tack to another, and would need to be rowed round. Though like as not the Norse could, from an early date, beat to windward they clearly found the process laborious and futile over any length of time, as did many others after them and certainly not the exhilarating experience it is to modern small boat enthusiasts. That numerous promontories on the Norwegian coast have the name *Stad* suggests the frequency with which ships would wait there for fair winds, whilst from the Sagas it is known that on the high seas the Norse meeting with a wind dead against them would lower their sails and drift until it changed. Nevertheless the construction and lines of the Gokstad ship, graceful and almost yacht-like, show a perfect adaptation to the conditions in which she worked – a rising bow and pointed stern to cope with waves and breakers; a broad and flattish hull which would remain upright when beached; a light and flexible build which would let her rise to the seas and ensure lively sailing qualities. Such, indeed, was the excellence of this design that it has survived in some degree even till today amongst many fishing and working boats in the north. That she must have been a fine, fast and seaworthy ship was conclusively shown in 1893 when her replica triumphantly crossed a characteristically stormy Atlantic at an average speed of 3.4 knots but touching eleven at times.[12]

But neither the Gokstad, nor the equally celebrated Oseberg ship was designed for long oceanic voyages, and for such passages the *knarr* was used in the Viking and early medieval centuries. Of this we know very little. It was probably of the same double-ended design, essentially a sailing vessel and rigged in the same way, with a single mast and square sail. It was of perhaps 40 tonnes burden and in general shorter, broader and deeper than the *langskip*, and one discovered at Roskilde is 16.47m long and 4.37m broad, decked fore and aft and with an open hold amidships. It sat higher in the water than a fighting ship, and must have had a distinctively prominent bow, for in the Icelandic Sagas amply bosomed ladies are described as *knarr*-like. Yet in general it is clear that the course of the development of the Viking ship between the fourth and ninth centuries is one of evolution and not revolution, and the significant changes are refinements of a well-established prototype. A rowing boat becomes a sailing ship, and in the process her lines are rounded, filled and smoothed, whilst the whole vessel is made stronger and more seaworthy. But the basic building technique remains constant, though the Gokstad ship, unlike the Nydam boat, has a heavy external keel; has sixteen strakes[13] to a side as against the five of her predecessor; and her hull is braced by transversal strengthening. Why and when such perfection was attained is uncertain, and at what date the sail came into use, the hull was broadened and strengthened, and the ship given a higher freeboard are all disputable. Yet it would seem that in Scandinavia, as later in England and Iberia, ships suitable for oceanic voyages had evolved well before such voyages took place. Tacitus and other classical writers describe sailing craft in the southern North Sea, and a sail of sorts was in use in the Baltic by the seventh century, if not before. A boat found at Kvalsund, probably dating from the 600s, is much more strongly constructed than that from Nydam; has a greater

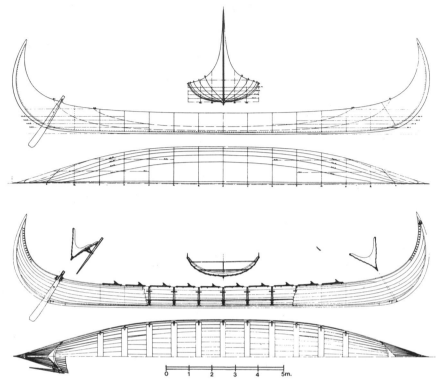

Fig. 2   The Kvalsund boat, seventh century, reconstruction by Fr Johannessen.

beam; an identifiable keel; and conceivably carried a mast and sail. It was probably in some such vessel that the first passages to the Orkneys and Shetlands were accomplished *c*. 700. No more than the crossing of the Anglo-Saxons to England in the equivalent of the Nydam ship were such voyages likely to have been made in safety or comfort. But neither then nor later did safety or comfort count for much. Magellan was to set off round the world with a handful of aged and worn ships; and the bulk of the Viking raiding forces in Europe were probably nothing more than open boats about 9m in length. The reserves of endurance in Scandinavian ships and seamen were forcibly shown when craft designed primarily to operate in the North Sea survived boisterous, involuntary and impromptu passages to Iceland and Greenland. It seems in fact that in general we overestimate the standards which the design and construction of ships would need to have attained before oceanic expansion could begin. The Norse probably had craft suitable for offshore passages by at least the middle of the eighth century, which is to say that had there been sufficient incentive their raids to the west might have started some half century before they did. Once they were in progress, and as their range and scope altered, so, as in other maritime empires, ships were modified and

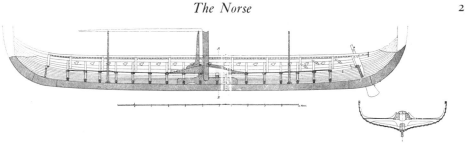

Fig. 3 Reconstruction of the Gokstad ship, built *c.* 850.

improved, with the *knarr* probably appearing in the late eighth century when voyages were regularly being made to the Hebrides, Ireland and the Faroes.

Experiment and change continued after the great age of expansion. As lands were settled and in some degree linked by trade, specialized ships were developed for particular purposes. There was, as we have already seen, a clearly recognized distinction from an early date between the seagoing *hafskip* (such as the *knarr*) and other types – the more sizeable but less seaworthy warship (*langskip*), for example, or the cargo carriers used in the Baltic. By a familiar progression ships became larger, and those of the medieval centuries were frequently bigger, and often considerably so, than those of the heroic age. A late source records the loss of a 54-oared merchantman in Iceland in 1118, whereas the Gokstad ship had only 32 oars. Perhaps this is merely poetic licence, but it is known that warships were increasing in size with Knut the Great owning one with allegedly 120 oars, whilst others with 60 or more are mentioned in the late twelfth century. It may well be that the appearance of vessels of this size was responsible for an important change in building techniques. Twenty metres was probably the largest keel timber available in Scandinavia, so that anything above this size would have to be built up by joining two balks together. But the flexible hull produced by traditional Norse methods imposed enormous stress on the keel as the ship leapt and twisted through the sea, and it seems highly probable that a vessel of such construction with a joined keel would soon have broken her back. It may have been to overcome this difficulty that in the twelfth century traditional techniques were abandoned in large craft.[14] The ribs were moved in closer together and the planking secured to them by rivets or wooden nails. The whole ship was therefore more rigid, but also, as the cost of such progress, much heavier and doubtless a great deal less lively, than her predecessors. At the same time there were attempts to emulate or incorporate innovations developed elsewhere. The stern rudder was introduced (see p. 79), and on the Icelandic run the *knarr* gave way in the late thirteenth century to the *buza*. What lay behind this terminology is by no means clear, but the remains of a vessel, probably dating from the mid-1200s, found at Bergen give a breadth of 9.1m to a length of 25.9m – a ship, that is, both short and fat showing nothing of those lean lines of the early centuries. So also some Scandinavian craft of the 1200s and 1300s appear to have had the form and build of the 'round ship' then common elsewhere in western Europe; a vessel with the improbable appearance of a crescent moon resting on the water. But for the rest, Norse technology, once so fertile and inventive, stagnated. An early thirteenth-century Norwegian representation of a ship recently discovered at Bergen shows, partly because of the artist's incompetence, merely a grotesque parody of the grace and elegance of those from Gokstad and Oseberg, whilst the illuminators of late-medieval Icelandic manuscripts could find nothing better than single-masted vessels of the old style with which to embellish their texts.

But whilst the technology of the Scandinavians languished that of their major rivals, the German cities of the Baltic littoral, showed all the vigour of an economy in full growth (see p. 77). The Germans rose to power by providing grain to help feed the growing population of northern Europe, including that of Scandinavia, in the twelfth and thirteenth centuries, and by marketing textiles produced in the west. From such opportunities the Norse, lacking both resources and suitable shipping, were as effectively excluded as from the frozen seas of Greenland. Meanwhile the Germans, to handle the trades they were developing or extending – all in bulk products – revolutionized northern ship-design by bringing into being a series of capacious carriers, first the cog, then the even larger hulk. The Norse had nothing to compare or to compete with these. Their trade, still vigorous enough in the twelfth century in the Baltic; with the Atlantic settlements; and with England, Ireland, the Low Countries and France, was largely concerned (luxuries apart) with such things as dried fish, hides, butter and relatively small amounts of cloth and timber. There was no bulk traffic to speak of, and it was the bulk trades, as German and Dutch experience was to show, which made ships grow in size and numbers (see p. 426). But Norse craft were designed for a world in which initially the movement of men and loot rather than of primary products or manufactured goods had predominated. In size they were limited by the ancient traditions of building, in which the planking was assembled first and the ribs then inserted, just as in capacity – at best about 40 to 50 tonnes – they were limited by their flat, narrow and shallow hulls. By 1200 the Scandinavians had ceased to be of any importance in the North Sea and the Baltic. In the Atlantic they had longer to go, and then, after something like seven centuries, the great wave of Norse maritime energy and achievement was finally spent.

III *The Norse impact*

The surprising thing is not that the Norse empire collapsed when it did but that the end should have been so long delayed. The pattern of Norse expansion was in part determined by the predilection of the Scandinavians for territory physically resembling their homeland. And it was in larger measure determined by what their ships could most easily do, and so by the wind systems of the waters in which they operated. They were accordingly confined to what lay between roughly latitudes 64° and 58°n – to as inhospitable a collection of shores as could be found anywhere – and to a region in which, as far as can be seen, an already harsh climate was further to deteriorate within a relatively short time. Compared with what the Iberians were to find in America and Asia, or even with what the Germans found in the Baltic, the Norse were singularly unlucky. Their discoveries produced nothing – gold, silver, spices – to satisfy European needs or cupidity, and thus to create a firm bond across the Atlantic. Moreover, in Greenland and Iceland there was, when the Norse arrived, no native population. And the greatest successes in early colonization and empire-building – as with the Spaniards in Mexico and Peru – came where an invader could displace a ruling class in an organized society. In Europe, on the other hand, the Scandinavians met almost everywhere peoples more numerous and – once they had recovered from the initial shock of the assault – better organized and in nearly every way more powerful than themselves. So they succumbed, as did in varying degrees other isolated, or small groups of immigrants, to the cultures amidst which they found themselves. In the east they were Slavicized, Hellenized, and converted to Christianity; in Normandy they became French; whilst in Ireland they were soon sufficiently Celtic to take to the kilt. It was a process by no means peculiar to the Scandinavians, but accelerated by their willingness to serve with absolute loyalty, as their custom dictated, the lord of their choice. Meanwhile, in North America their numbers were insufficient, unlike those of the Germans in the Baltic, to dominate the native populations they encountered. They were hopelessly overshadowed by the Indians and by the vigorously advancing Eskimo who, like other primitive peoples living in difficult terrain, were more than a handful of would-be conquerors or settlers with no marked technological superiority could contain or subdue. And there were other fatal flaws. The initial migrations were in part occasioned by internal political changes within Scandinavia; but resources in men and ships were limited when, in the tenth and eleventh centuries they were frequently diverted into the constant struggles for territory in, and between, the emerging kingdoms of Norway, Denmark and Sweden. Furthermore, Norse expansion was often nothing more than a search for land for settlement rather than the expression of some deliberate plan of conquest, and was not, as was later Spanish enterprise – or that of the Danes under Knut – systematically directed to plunder and subjugation. Instead it was frequently the work of chieftains and their retainers who, as the most ambitious or the most intractable, inevitably recreated in a new setting the anarchy and disorders in part responsible for their departure from the mother country. Such happenings, as the Spaniards were to show in Peru, were far from being a Scandinavian monopoly, nor were they necessarily inimical to imperial success. But whereas Spain quickly established her authority over her possessions, there was no Norwegian monarchy capable of subduing and ruling the communities in Iceland and Greenland, and when they eventually submitted it was an act of desperation, and to a power already doomed.

The comparison with later settlement can be taken further. Nothing characterizes the mother country more clearly than its colonies. Like a catalyst, colonization defines and intensifies, even to the point of parody, the essential, dominant qualities of a society. The fantastic element in Spanish civilization was nowhere better revealed than in Utopian schemes for regenerated mankind in Mexico, or quests for such chimera as the Fountain of Everlasting Youth or the even more promising Land of the Amazons. Nothing defined English Puritanism more closely than the dissenting colonies of New England (see p. 488), just as nothing symbolized better the heroic, anarchical aspirations of Norse aristocratic society than the political structure of Iceland. Nor does the parallel cease here. The Norse, like their European successors in the New World, showed the same – perhaps even greater – unwillingness to adapt to their new environment. In Iceland, in the earliest years, their dwellings were naturally enough the big, rectangular houses they were used to at home, but whose construction and upkeep required more timber and heating than so barren, cold and wet an island could supply. True, this problem was eventually solved, but the Norse never found how to protect themselves against cold and rain; and even when starving never discovered the full range of edible things the country offered.

But this is merely to say that in much, like the rest of mankind, they were naturally conservative. It detracts little from the immensity of their achievement – an achievement all the more remarkable in that their Atlantic voyages were into the unknown. The Iberians of the fifteenth century had at least hopes of the riches of the east, known and rumoured for centuries, to sustain them, and the Portuguese were, in any case, in some measure re-assured by the proximity of the West African coast in the earliest expeditions to the south (see pp. 228–32). But apart from what they had learned about Iceland from the Irish, the Norse knew nothing of what lay over their horizons. To contemporaries, however, Scandinavian expansion was no fine expression of heroic endeavour. Even to a Christian Europe well-acquainted with such misfortunes it was an outburst, mercilessly prolonged, of savagery, destruction and desecration. The damage inflicted on the west by the raiders was graphically, not to say sensationally, recorded by Christian chroniclers, but their statements cannot be accepted at their face value. The losses are not capable of statistical demonstration, but no society, least of all one that was Christian enduring the assaults of pagans, is likely to underestimate the wounds received from an attacker. Yet these could be wounds that quickly healed, for simple economies, provided they are not further disrupted by the introduction of diseases against which they have no natural resistance, are of a remarkable resilience. The ravages of the Vikings were clearly widespread and they were scarcely trivial. Along much of the coasts of western Europe victims were killed, enslaved or exploited. In Iceland a tenuous Celtic Christianity was destroyed, just as monasticism disappeared from the lands eventually to become the Duchy of Normandy. Towns from the Channel to the Mediterranean – like the commercial centre of Dorestad on the Rhine, seven times attacked between 834 and 863 – were plundered; churches, a prime source of wealth to the Vikings, were damaged, destroyed and looted. Combined with the Hungarian raids from the east, the Viking attacks hastened the disintegration of the already decaying Carolingian empire. In its place came a regime of military lordships, since to face these swift and unpredictable onslaughts self help was often the most, if not the only, effective remedy. A local lord who could protect his neighbourhood and its inhabitants had a greater claim to their loyalty – and financial aid – than some remote and ineffective sovereign. But if such opportunities enhanced the authority of a lord it was at the expense of the liberty of those who in time came to be known as his men, and the peasantry, their already precarious livlihood further disrupted, and burdened with the new exactions the crisis either demanded or permitted, moved nearer to serfdom. But this was not simply the bequest of the Vikings who, in many cases, merely accelerated or intensified a process already in progress before their arrival.

Nor was their impact solely destructive. The demands of the Danes for tribute led to the introduction of one of the first general taxes to be levied in Europe, the Danegeld (see p. 12). Moreover, in face of Scandinavian attacks an able ruler might increase his power, whilst resistance to invasion could induce amongst his subjects, actual and potential, a sense of unity and even nationhood. In England the Danish wars of king Alfred (871–99) and his sons added to the power and glory of the crown of Wessex a naval force of sorts equipped with vessels of royal design; a re-organized army capable of reasonably elaborate operations; and a network of fortresses forming part of a comprehensive scheme of national defence. Then Alfred's success in freeing London from the Danes in 886 led to his recognition as overlord of non-Danish England and was a step, however tentative, in the country's advance towards political unification. But the most obvious and direct consequence of the Scandinavian migrations and raids was to scatter across Europe, and momentarily into the New World, a number of remarkably energetic, enterprising and adaptable peoples. Few, or relatively few in number, meeting almost everywhere cultures more powerful than their own, they fused with, or were absorbed into, existing societies in a process the very opposite of that whereby in the sixteenth century the vigorous civilization of Spain was superimposed on those of South America (see p. 353). Even so their impact was far from insignificant. The Swedes may not, as was once thought, have founded the Russian state, but of the importance of their activities in the east there is little doubt (see p. 30). To the Irish the Norse brought (possibly) the battle-axe; swords of a new pattern; and those maritime skills whose adoption or emulation is reflected by the survival in Irish of many nautical terms of Old Norse origin – *scút* (ship, ON *skúta*); *stiúr* (rudder; ON *stýri*). And it was the Norse who founded Cork, Limerick, Wexford and Dublin – soon known as a major port in Arabic, Scandinavian and English sources – to further trade, and to serve as bases for their operations against England and the continent. Meanwhile in the Isle of Man the Scandinavian hegemony was sufficiently complete to make Norse the dominant language from *c.* 900 to *c.* 1300. So also their influence was considerable in England, even though specialist opinion is divided as to its precise nature and extent. The Danes established themselves in the north and east; the Norse and the Irish-Norse in the north-west. Like most conquerors or settlers they were probably few in number to begin with – their 'armies' perhaps 200 or 300 men at the most – followed, as were the *conquistadores* in Mexico and Peru, by traders, colonizers and others as by that common progression plundering raids gave way to settlement. No more than most other builders of empires, formal or otherwise, did they radically and fundamentally change those societies amongst which they took root, and they apparently imported no distinctive legal or administrative methods of their own into England. None the less their impact was powerful. They, or their descendants, were perhaps responsible for bringing into cultivation whole new areas of the country – the Lancashire coastal strip, the marshes of Lincolnshire, the flatlands of the Norfolk Broads. The English language abounds in words of Scandinavian ancestry, from 'awkward' and 'ill' to 'happy' and 'odd', whilst in the Domesday Survey of 1086 40 per cent of the placenames of the East Riding of Yorkshire are of Scandinavian origin, 38 per cent of those of the North Riding. And the very settlement, in more than half of England, of Scandinavian peoples meant that up to, and even beyond the Norman conquest, there was a willingness in regions north of the Humber to welcome kings, or would-be kings, from Scandinavia.

But of far greater consequence was the Danish acquisition, in the early tenth century, of that by no means inviting part of France soon to be known, after its northern conquerors, as Normandy.[15] Here, where hundreds of place-names testify to the density of their colonization, their successors quickly absorbed from the civilization of the Franks the techniques of war and government which were to make them so formidable. Within little more than a hundred years the country, now a French-speaking Duchy, was in every sense of the word too small to hold a people so fecund, energetic and militant, and in the eleventh century the Normans established themselves, to the accompaniment of some spectacular outbursts of violence, in southern Italy, Sicily and England. The vigour and intelligence that in Iceland were devoted to literature, or less happily squandered in feuds, were in these prosperous and sophisticated lands directed to government, and the fusion of Norman energy and adaptability with the civilizations of Sicily and England resulted in the creation of two of the most advanced and effective kingdoms of the early Middle Ages.

Equally far-reaching was the Scandinavian impact on trade. The raids, particularly the earliest, must, in some degree have disrupted the existing patterns and flow of western commerce – that, for example, of the Anglo-Saxons with the continent, or that of the Frisians who, in the eighth century and earlier were in touch with England, what is now France, and the Baltic from their strategically sited city of Dorestad on the old estuary of the Rhine. But clearly the Scandinavians extended, and very considerably, the range of European trade in the way that the Portuguese and Spaniards were later to do. In Ireland the presence of the Norse brought a rapid expansion of the old-established relations with France and Spain, a flourishing commerce in such things as Welsh slaves and horses across the Irish Sea, and the opening up of a trade with the north and east, so that Saga tradition could recall the sale in tenth-century Norway of an Irish princess to an Icelandic farmer by a Russian merchant. The emergence of

Norse colonies in Greenland and Iceland, trading with Norway and, more spasmodically with each other, enlarged, however momentarily and marginally, the nature and scope of northern trade. Again, there had been, since pre-historic times, some commercial contacts between Scandinavia and western Europe. These the Norse and Danish migrations both intensified – as trade developed between settlements – and extended. Ottar's well-known visit to Alfred shows that at even so apparently unpropitious a moment an intelligent Norwegian could hope to sell his ivory, furs and hides in England. Excavations at Kaupang (Vestfold in Norway) suggest ninth-century relations with Britain, the Rhineland and France, whilst a passage in the earliest life of St Oswald records, no doubt with a flourish of local patriotism, that during the writer's time (*c*. 1000) York was filled with the wealth of Danish traders. Thus, and constituting a major step in the expansion of European civilization, Scandinavia was firmly linked to the west. The link was to be reinforced by its conversion to Christianity and by Knut's accumulation of those lands and powers which made him a force to be reckoned with (see p. 1). And it was further reinforced as the fruits of Viking enterprise – whether by piracy or trade – drew to Scandinavia those willing to supply the wants of the newly enriched, just as in later centuries the wealth of Iberia and its colonies was to attract, whatever the hazards, foreign merchants. The Scandinavians demanded pottery, jewels, weapons and in particular those renowned swords of the Franks. Celebrated for their stylish and extravagant sartorial tastes they sought cloths – the silks and satins of the east, and those woollen textiles they acquired in such quantities from England, Ireland, Frisia and France – in sufficient amounts to stimulate the growth of specialized centres of production.

So by the twelfth century the Baltic and the North and Irish Seas were dominated by Scandinavian ships and traders. There was a vigorous Norse association with England, especially with the Scandinavian colonies of the east coast; a number of flourishing commercial centres had been developed in Ireland; and Scandinavian merchants were to be found on the Rhine, in Flanders and in Normandy. To the west they traded to Iceland and Greenland, and to the east, in voyages as remarkable as any even they were to undertake, with Russia, Byzantium and beyond. Thus, not only was Scandinavia, but the Baltic itself, brought permanently within the bounds of western commerce and civilization. Once again the association was not new – already in the ninth century Birka in eastern Sweden was in lively contact with western Europe – but it was strengthened and extended. The wealthy and rewarding littoral of the Baltic was penetrated by Scandinavians who established trading centres at such places as Truso (near the modern Elbing) and Wollin (on the estuary of the Oder). By the eleventh century Gotland was conducting a trade which embraced Russia and Germany alike, and until the great German drive to the east in the 1100s the Scandinavians remained active in Poland and Russia. Nor did their enterprise stop there, and for a brief period, which ended in the tenth century, their expansion brought relations, albeit tenuous, with the civilizations of the east.

In the distant past, before the Slav migrations of the sixth century, the Scandinavian north had been in touch overland with the Byzantine empire centred on Constantinople.[16] This association the Swedes – known first to the Finns and then to other peoples further east as the Rus – before long revived and extended. They were trading and fighting amongst the Letts, Lithuanians and Slavs by the eighth century, and soon after had a base for trade to the south of Lake Ladoga. From here, through a land of rivers, swamps and streams they could reach by boat – carried or dragged overland when necessary – the Dnepr and the Volga, and so the very heart of Russia. They were at Novgorod – which indeed they probably founded – by the ninth century and then at Smolensk and Kiev. In their boats they reached the Black Sea; launched, in the ninth and tenth centuries, a series of maritime assaults against Constantinople, as well as marauding and trading in Greece, the Caucasus and along the southern shores of the Caspian. In Kiev, as in Novgorod, they lived in characteristic style, exacting from the Slavs money, furs and slaves – especially, as an Arabic traveller appreciatively noted, pretty girls. Their settlements were never extensive, and such initially were their relations with the natives that it was alleged that should a man wish to go outside to relieve himself an armed escort was essential. Be this as it may, the Scandinavian colonists were rapidly Slavicized, absorbed by the peoples of the east and powerfully influenced by the Hellenic civilization of Byzantium, so that there was in the end little of Scandinavia about the Russian principality that developed in Kiev. But for a time, and with an energy and daring unmistakably Viking, the Rus and their northern kinsmen carried on, with what they had looted or otherwise acquired from the Slavs, an astonishing trade to the south. In the summer, when the floods had subsided, they descended the Dnepr, leaping naked into its waters to guide their craft by the feel of their feet through the torrents of the rapids at the modern Dnjepropetrovsk. Some traded in Constantinople; others – Swedes from Birka, Rus from Kiev and Novgorod – crossed the Caspian Sea and then travelled by camel train to Baghdad; others met and did business with Moslem merchants from Khazaria and Bulghar on the Volga. Thus they tapped that ancient trade flowing from the Orient, and in exchange for their furs, slaves, weapons, honey and wax, could acquire all those celebrated luxuries and delicacies of the near and distant east – Indian spices, Chinese silk, Persian glass and even more exotic wonders, such as that statuette of Buddha found in Helgö (1955). But above all they could acquire from the Moslem world that silver so highly esteemed in Scandinavia. This rich harvest was carried north to Kiev and Novgorod – themselves linked to towns such as Prague, Cracow and Regensburg – and to the Scandinavian bases on the Baltic. So, for about a century and a half after the early 800s bullion was draining from the Islamic lands in enormous amounts – witness the 120,000 Samanid[17] coins so far found in Russia, and a further 85,000 in Scandinavia. Then, passing through Hedeby (in Jutland) some of this wealth penetrated from the Baltic to the rest of Europe and even to Iceland until (*c*. 970) a silver crisis in Islam diminished the flow, and German and Russian hostility sealed the route.

Whatever losses, therefore, the Vikings may initially have inflicted on it, in the end Europe was to draw considerable material advantages from their enterprise in the often indistinguishable pursuits of piracy, war and trade. With their acquisition in distant lands, and frequently by force, of primary products and of commodities of the highest value, their maritime empire displayed many of the features soon characteristic of more consciously imperial endeavour. So the west received from them on the one hand hides, timber, fish and iron, and on the other silver, ivory and those exquisite furs – fox, sable, bear, ermine – so long the hallmarks of opulence and standing. More than this, their activities gave some stimulus to the whole of Europe's economic life. They opened routes to an unknown west; they opened or re-opened access to the east. Danes, Norwegians and Swedes traded with each other and with peoples as different as the Lapps of the far north, the natives of the Baltic, the Greeks of Byzantium, the Arabs of Spain and the east, the Slavs, Germans, Franks, Frisians, Irish and English, and the inhabitants of the Atlantic islands from the Faroes to Greenland. The new-found riches of the Scandinavians drew to the north trade and merchants, so that at Birka in its heyday (*c.* 800–970) could be found men from Denmark, Frisia, Finland, Germany, England, Sweden, Byzantium and possibly the Arab lands, and goods from the whole known world. The apparent resurgence of the European economy commencing in the tenth century perhaps owed something to that infusion of bullion for which the Scandinavians were responsible, whilst the demands of their trades produced new commercial centres – many destined to survive – from Limerick on the Shannon to Kiev on the Dnepr, in addition to dozens more in Scandinavia itself.

Nor can the balance be struck merely in terms of profit and loss. Admittedly the Norse made no contributions to the techniques of government, commerce or agriculture. Their expansion was the very apotheosis of that of an aristocratic society, or, to be more precise, of a society dominated by an aristocratic ethos: an initial devotion to the exaction of tribute and loot, turning, as was to happen with the Spaniards, Portuguese and English, to commerce, settlement and some form of agrarian endeavour. Like other colonizing peoples, they planted replicas of their own world in distant lands; transmitted their languages far and wide, to survive and flourish in Iceland and to leave vestiges in many other places; and they brought Christianity to Greenland where it was to perish, and to Iceland where it was to endure. Western Europe benefited from an injection of their formidable energy; from their artistic talents; and above all from their superlative skills in all things relating to the sea – a legacy which has left its mark in a leavening of Scandinavian nautical terms in languages ranging from French to Gaelic, and in the unmistakably Norse lines of many small craft still to be seen in northern waters.

The migrations of the fearsome and pagan Norse across the Atlantic and the forays of the equally fearsome and pagan Swedes to the east and to the fringes of Asia made little impact on the literary imagination or geographical understanding of medieval Europe. An English cosmography of the late 1300s records 'Veneland, Gotland, Iceland,

Greenland', and Greenland was, as we have seen, mapped in the early fifteenth century and perhaps visited by a Danish expedition in 1476. The English, who were in Iceland by the early 1400s, may have learned there of lands to the west and so have been inspired to begin their exploration of the Atlantic, and even Columbus himself may have been influenced by knowledge gained in Iceland (see pp. 302 and 460). But be this as it may – and the arguments are far from convincing – Finland was to pass into medieval geography as the march against yet another realm of Amazons, and Scandinavia as yet another island.[18] But though Norse enterprise was to have even less intellectual impact in Christian Europe than the later Iberian discoveries it nevertheless enabled an intelligent man like king Alfred in England to learn something of the geography of Scandinavia from the much-travelled Ottar, just as it permitted the civilized and inquiring chronicler Adam of Bremen to gain, in the eleventh century, some idea of that of the Baltic, the North Sea and the North Atlantic. Indeed it would seem that in early Scandinavia itself there was, for a time, considerable curiosity about what the voyages revealed.[19] There is, for instance, a significant passage in *The Greenlanders' Saga*, telling how Bjarni, the reluctant discoverer of America, visited Norway about 1000 and gave to his audience what was clearly a disappointing account of his adventures, 'and people thought how lacking in enterprise and curiosity he had been in that he had nothing to report to them'. It may well be that this is a later, perhaps thirteenth-century, gloss. Even so it reflects an attitude of mind that assumes that a traveller will take some critical interest in what he encounters. It is an attitude clearly revealed in the *King's Mirror*, with its sharp observation of a mass of natural phenomena (see p. 16), and it is an attitude already implicit in Ottar's refusal, several centuries earlier, to accept the veracity of what he has not seen with his own eyes.

That the Scandinavians, when they first appeared in western Europe, seemed to most civilized men terrible and ferocious we can hardly doubt. They were heavily and effectively armed, violent, rapacious, energetic, self-confident, resourceful and above all pagan. But they had, nevertheless, other talents of which naturally enough, little was said. Their ships, tools, weapons, superb jewelry – their brooches in particular – and their impressive if forbidding carvings are all evidence of craftsmanship and artistic powers of a high order. In stone, but more especially in wood, they worked with amazing technical virtuosity, and with astonishing richness of invention and inspiration. A magnificent example is the carving on the early ninth-century ship and accompanying wagon and sledges excavated (1904) at Oseberg. On the vessel's bow long scrolls of interlaced animal patterns, and on her prow groupings of gripping beasts and lugubriously comic human figures, are all carefully incised within a strictly limited space. One incidental outcome of the Viking migrations was to produce, as was to be the case in other empires, some modest degree of cultural fusion and assimilation. Viking art was influenced, though not profoundly, by the art of other peoples – Irish, English, Franks – whilst Viking influences appear in turn in the art of other societies, as is dramatically instanced by those undated stone crosses of Scandinavian inspiration found in a number of villages in east Yorkshire.

But the Norse voyages and settlements were to have a greater effect than simply to ensure the widespread diffusion of a number of artistic styles. The victories, conquests and discoveries of the Scandinavians may have brought little stimulus to the intellectual life of Europe as a whole, but in Scandinavia their natural outcome was that ebullience and pride in achievement that success brings to all nations, as indeed to all individuals. Ships were named *Strider* and *Flier* and their qualities joyously lauded in verses such as those of the magnificent eleventh-century *Journey to the East*:

> Light my mind was, Lord and
> mirthful, when on firth ways
> with glorious king the stormy
> gales did shake our sailships:
> in glee, swiftly, our sea-steeds
> o'er sounds of Lister bounded
> at will, with the wind bellying
> the wings of heeling keel-birds.

And just as Camões celebrated the triumphs of Portugal, or Ercilla those of Spain, so the *Vikingsavisur* is the heroic recital of the martial achievements, from the Baltic to Iberia, of the Viking chief St Olaf (see p. 280). Yet it was not in Scandinavia that such sentiments achieved their fullest expression, but in Iceland, where there rapidly emerged one of the most original and distinctive civilizations of the Middle Ages, and it is the *Heimskringla*[20] that proudly records the epic career of Harald Hardradi, 'the Thunderbolt of the North', in Russia, the Levant and Byzantium. The achievements crises and disasters of expansion and empire have always left some imprint on the culture of the parent country. But colonial arts and literature have almost invariably been of a modest and derivative quality. In Scandinavian colonization, however, the process was largely reversed, and the literature of the homeland – or at least such as has survived – is insignificant in comparison with that of the colony. Indeed in Iceland a literary culture blossomed with such vigour as to suggest that almost all creative talent had been drained from the parent society. And in a way this was true, and the sudden flowering of Icelandic civilization is to be explained, in part, by the very scale and quality of the migrations which brought to the island not only some of the most obstreperous, but also many of the most enterprising people in Scandinavia. Yet the same might be said of the conquerors of Mexico and Peru in the sixteenth century, whose descendants, nevertheless, produced no Latin-American civilization to eclipse that of Iberia (see p. 332). But in Iceland a peculiar combination of circumstances developed and accentuated all the latent talent of the settlers in a way the Americas never did that of the Spaniards, and – equally important – ensured that its expression should be permanently recorded, whilst in Europe the parent society drifted into political and economic eclipse. The Icelandic colonists came from a strong and individual culture, and many, as we have seen, had lived in Ireland amongst an equally distinctive culture, before their migration. In Scandinavia, or in Ireland, Norse creative impulses had found an outlet in carving, sculpture and metalwork, but in Iceland there was no tractable stone, no metal and virtually no wood. All energies – and with such a people they were clearly considerable – left from feud had thus of necessity to find an outlet in words, and words, which by remarkable good fortune were largely to be preserved. The long dark winters to be filled provided more than adequate opportunity for creative endeavour. Memories of ancient beliefs and practices; of heroic deeds; of battles and of treacheries in strange and distant lands offered magnificent themes. And the need, through the rigours of the climate, to slaughter most of their cattle every year, supplied an abundance of vellum. Then, with the coming of Christianity at the beginning of the eleventh century, the Icelanders acquired a form of writing less cumbersome than their customary runes – an alphabet originally designed for carving on wood or stone. Furthermore, since their conversion was peacefully accomplished it entailed no destruction of the vernacular civilization, but instead added to whatever stimulus the Icelanders had received from the heritage of Celtic Ireland that of the literature and beliefs of the Catholic west. Thus there came about what has been described as transcription on an unprecedented scale. There still survive some 700 complete or fragmentary manuscripts produced in medieval Iceland, and these represent perhaps only one-tenth of what once existed. Given a maximum population of something like 80,000 in 1100, declining thereafter, and that codices were written not only on the estates of wealthy chieftains and bishops, but in the houses of small farmers, production on this scale presupposes one of the most highly literate societies known in the west until modern times.

Much that was transcribed, it is true, was not of remarkable merit – popular histories like the fantasies of Geoffrey of Monmouth; hagiographical tracts; the imported romances that bulk large in any literature. But above these tower the especial fruits of Icelandic inspiration – outpourings of poetry; vernacular epics of Norse history and mythology; and Sagas telling, from an admixture of legend, tradition, history and invention, of the finding of new lands, of feuds, triumphs and disasters. With these there emerges an heroic literature often enough tedious in its genealogical meanderings, and frequently overburdened with violence, lust, marvels and mysteries. Yet at times it is of awesome grandeur in description, and with its theme of man against Fate, of immense emotional power. It is, it has been said, a literature which can stand side by side with those of Greece and Rome and fear nothing from the comparison. Of no other colonial civilization could this ever be thought, and never again were the Scandinavians to make so profound and prolonged an impression on the culture and history of Europe as in these greatest centuries of their seafaring.

Bibliographical note

The sources for Norse history fall into roughly three classes: archaeology; numismatics (the study of coins and coinage); and written records. It is from finds and excavations that so much is known, and in such detail, of the towns, weapons, dress, agriculture and – because of their custom, when pagan, of ship-burial – of the ships of the Vikings. The study of coins and coinage may help, once rulers commenced to mint a currency, to establish otherwise uncertain sequences of kings, and to understand how, in Scandinavia, royal powers and pretensions developed. The discovery of buried collections of coins (hoards) can tell a great deal of the pattern of trade and plunder – a striking instance being the heavy incidence of oriental coins in eastern Sweden and Gotland, indicating the vigour of the association with Russia and the Moslem east. The written records embrace materials differing widely in nature and language. They include runic inscriptions from Scandinavia, written, that is, in an alphabet of angular phonetic symbols, thought to have originated about the beginning of the Christian era, and originally designed to be carved on wood or stone. And they also include descriptions of the Scandinavians as marauders and traders by chroniclers in western Europe, Russia and the Islamic east.

There are no contemporary Scandinavian accounts of the genesis and early centuries of oceanic voyaging. *The Book of the Icelanders (Islendingabók)* is a history of Iceland probably written in the early twelfth century, and though it survives only in seventeenth-century transcripts is the oldest sustained prose narrative in any Scandinavian language, and is accepted as critical, accurate and especially valuable for its chronology. It is available in an English translation by Halldór Hermannsson (New York, 1930) and selections are published in Gwyn Jones, *The Norse Atlantic Saga* (Oxford, 1964).

The Book of the Settlements (Landnámabók) contains a wealth of detail on the colonization of Iceland. It sets out the genealogies and origins of some 400 of the principal settlers, what land they took and where, and what became of them. It exists in five versions dating from the thirteenth to the seventeenth centuries, and perhaps deriving from a lost twelfth- or thirteenth-century original. Two of these versions are of relatively early date, are complete, but are not identical. One is the *Sturlubók* of the mid-thirteenth century, the other the early fourteenth-century *Hauksbók*. There are translated selections in Jones, *The Norse Atlantic Saga.*

The Greenlanders' Saga (Groenlendinga Saga) and *The Saga of Eirik the Red (Eiriks Saga Rauda)* are magnificent examples of that justly celebrated Icelandic literary form, the Saga. This is an epic, written in Icelandic (or Old Norse) prose, and dealing with a biographical, historical or mythical subject. The Sagas were written down by clerks in the late twelfth century, and though not works of history, contain material from earlier ages long kept alive by oral tradition. Later the Saga became an art form and developed as a work of pure imagination. Nevertheless, valuable information is to be had from all the Sagas relating to the time of their composition or transcription. How much reliance is to be placed on what they have to say of earlier events is debatable, though embedded in them are both the traditions and some of the poetry – in the difficult skaldic form – of a previous age.

The Greenlanders' Saga survives as three interpolations in a Saga relating to king Olaf of Norway, itself preserved in a fourteenth-century source. It dates from perhaps *c.* 1200, though its origins are unknown. There is a translation in Jones, op. cit. *The Saga of Eirik the Red* is preserved in two medieval and five later manuscripts. One of these medieval versions is in *Hauksbók* (already mentioned), the other in *Skálholtsbók* of the fifteenth century, considered, however, to contain an earlier and more authentic text. The Saga probably dates from the late thirteenth century. Recent opinion is that *The Greenlanders' Saga* and *The Saga of Eirik the Red*, both containing older and partially oral traditions, were written independently and in ignorance of each other. Texts are published in Halldór Hermannsson, *The Vinland Sagas* (Ithaca, 1944), and Jones, *The Norse Atlantic Saga*.

The Story of Einar Sokkason (*Einars Tháttr Sokkasonar*) describes life in twelfth-century Greenland. It comes from a manuscript of the late 1300s. There is an English version in Jones, *The Norse Atlantic Saga*. Examples of 'legendary' (i.e. purely imaginative) Sagas are translated by Hermann Pálsson and Paul Edwards in *Gautrek's Saga and other Medieval Tales* (1968).

The modern literature dealing with the Vikings, Viking expansion and medieval Scandinavia is of enormous volume, and the following note makes no claim to comprehensiveness. It merely mentions books and articles I have used in those languages more accessible to the non-specialist. Most of the books have full and critical bibliographies, whilst the English-speaking reader may attempt to keep abreast of the flow of scholarship by consulting the *Saga Book of the Viking Society for Northern Research*, and the annual *Bibliography of Old Norse – Icelandic Studies* which has, since 1963, listed all major publications.

There is a useful general introduction to the Vikings by Allen Mawer, 'The Viking Age', in *Travel and Travellers of the Middle Ages*, ed. A.P. Newton (1930). Lucien Musset has a wide-ranging and perceptive study of medieval Scandinavia in his *Les Peuples Scandinaves au Moyen Age* (Paris, 1951). Colourful, slackly written, but still useful and lavishly illustrated is Eric Oxenstierna, *The Norsemen* (1966), an English translation of his *Die Wikinger* (Stuttgart, 1959). Gwyn Jones, *A History of the Vikings* (Oxford, 1968) is a work of outstanding excellence, combining impressive erudition with refreshing common sense and infectious enthusiasm. Equally valuable is P.G. Foote and D.M. Wilson, *The Viking Achievement* (1970), some of whose conclusions are condensed in D.M. Wilson's splendidly illustrated *The Vikings and their Origins* (1970). There are many reflections on Scandinavia as a whole, as well as on the Scandinavians in England in Sir Frank Stenton's *Anglo-Saxon England* (new edn, Oxford, 1971). Some of his opinions are subjected to lively and justifiable criticism by P.H. Sawyer, *The Age of the Vikings* (new edn, 1971). Recent work especially relating to England, is outlined by Gillian Fellows-Jensen, 'The Vikings in England: A Review', in *Anglo-Saxon England*, ed. Peter Clemoes (Cambridge, 1975).

The Norse voyages in the Atlantic are touched on by most of the authors already mentioned. They are examined in convincing detail by Jones, *The Norse Atlantic Saga*, which includes a selection of the literary sources in translation. They are more briefly narrated in W.P. Cumming, R.A. Skelton and D.B. Quinn, *The Discovery of North America* (1971) and, with chracteristic vigour and idiosyncrasy, by S.E. Morison, *The European Discovery of America: The Northern Voyages* (Oxford, 1971). Professor Morison also considers (and rightly dismisses as unsubstantiated) the possibility that the Norse discoveries may have influenced later Atlantic exploration, a subject re-opened with care and imagination in D.B. Quinn, *England and the Discovery of America* (1974).

Jean Young discusses, among other things, Norse commerce in Ireland in 'A Note on the

Norse Occupation of Ireland' in *Hist.*, XXXV (1950). G.J. Marcus outlines the history of the Greenland trade in *Ec. Hist. Rev*, VII (1954), and that of the Norse traffic to Iceland in *Ec. Hist. Rev.*, IX (1957) and *MM*, 46 (1960). The flow of Eastern bullion to Europe in the Viking age is placed in context in an important article by A.M. Watson in *Ec. Hist. Rev.*, XX (1967), 'Back to Gold – and Silver'.

The characteristics, evolution and capabilities of Norse ships have been, and are, the subject of much specialist debate, by no means all particularly rewarding or convincing. There are good and balanced summaries in Jones, *Vikings*, and Sawyer, *The Age of the Vikings*. The classic account is A.W. Brøgger and H. Shetelig, *The Viking Ships, Their Ancestry and Evolution* (Oslo, 1953). Recent advances in knowledge, and current theories of interpretation, are noticed in the contributions of Arne Emil Christensen and Ole Crumlin-Pedersen to the lavishly illustrated *History of Seafaring*, ed. G.F. Bass (1972). Romola and R.C. Anderson, *The Sailing Ship* (1947) is still well worth consulting, as is the controversial paper of P. Heinsius, 'Dimensions et caractéristiques des koggen hanséatiques dans le commerce Baltique', *CIHM*, 3 (1960) for the different techniques of ship-construction in the medieval north. Much research and controversy about seafaring and seafarers is available for this, and all other periods, in English, in *MM*.

E.G.R. Taylor has an excellent outline of Norse navigational methods in her *The Haven-Finding Art* (1956). Of the many contributions of G.J. Marcus I have used those in *MM*, 39 (1953); *Hist.*, XII (1956); *MM*, 44 (1958).

2

The Hanse

1 The German east

The maritime supremacy of the Scandinavians in northern waters was destroyed, replaced and ultimately surpassed by the seapower of a society of a radically different order – urban, bourgeois, commercial, culturally undistinguished and almost uniquely averse to the acquisition of territory. This was the Hanseatic League,[1] an association of north-German towns and cities, and one of the most remarkable manifestations of a more extensive European, and in the end German, push to the East. The Europe of the Romans had, at least in the military sense, ended on the Rhine and the Danube. But under their Germanic, and soon Christian, successors there began a long and arduous eastward expansion. In the early Middle Ages the Saxons of the wooded and swampy lands beyond the Rhine were, with difficulty, subjugated and converted by the great Frankish warrior and ruler Charlemagne (768–814). The following century they in turn assaulted their Slav and pagan neighbours beyond the Elbe with such vigour and brutality as to provoke before long a rising violent enough to throw the linguistic barrier back to where it had been in Carolingian days. Then, in the early 1100s, the whole process re-commenced and within 200 years the Germans had brought under their control eastern lands roughly equal in size to two-thirds of their original territories, the products and needs of whose inhabitants were to form, as with later colonial societies elsewhere, the basis of an impressive maritime economy.

This astonishing achievement was but one aspect of the expansion of Christian Europe in the high Middle Ages, an expansion reflecting in part the growth of the continent's population between *c.* 1100 and 1300. It was marked on the one hand by the reclamation and settlement of unpopulated areas within the existing boundaries, and on the other by the momentary establishment of Christian states in the Moslem Levant, and by the annexation of lands from Moslems in Iberia and from Slavs in eastern Europe. The essence of German expansion in these years was, uniquely, a process of peasant colonization. Yet like the Italian maritime republics in the medieval Mediterranean, and the Portuguese in Asia in the fifteenth and sixteenth centuries (see pp. 90, 233), the Germans were also concerned with the penetration and extension of an already established pattern of commerce. There was, as we have seen, a considerable trade in which the Germans themselves in some degree participated, and which had led to the growth of trading posts and towns so that in the Slav east the Germans were to encounter, as later did the Spaniards in the Americas, societies by no

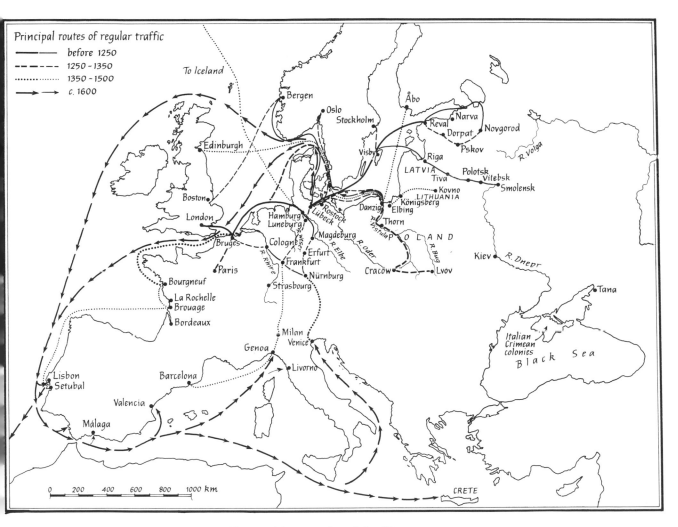

Principal routes of regular traffic
- before 1250
- 1250 – 1350
- 1350 – 1500
- *c.* 1600

2   The maritime empire of the Hanse

means innocent of urban life, even if an urban life at a level more primitive than that of western Europe (see pp. 29–30 and 68–9). And though like the expansion of the Spaniards in the New World in the 1500s, that of the Germans was accompanied by the violent conquest, subjugation and conversion of non-Christian peoples, it was in the same way accompanied by settlement, and by the establishment, on a phenomenal scale, of new towns and cities.

Of these none was more celebrated, or for centuries more influential than Lübeck. Founded in 1143 by that notable colonial entrepreneur, the count of Holstein, it was acquired and re-established fifteen years later by his suzerain, the duke of Saxony who, to protect his precious asset, in 1160 conquered the lands of the (Slav) Abodrites which later became the duchy of Mecklenburg. To foster the trade of his new town, and thereby increase his own revenues, he sent, a contemporary records, 'messengers to all the towns and kingdoms of the north: to Denmark, Sweden, Norway and Russia offering them peace on condition that they traded in Lübeck . . . on which which he conferred the most extensive privileges'. With such purposeful assistance the city flourished to a prosperity which later political hazards, such as the imposition of Danish overlordship early in the following century, left largely untouched. Situated on the Trave, Lübeck was both easily defensible and sufficiently distant from the open sea to escape surprise by pirates. But more than this, established as it was at the eastern foot of the Danish peninsula, within easy reach by land and river of Hamburg, it became, until the opening of a direct maritime route from the Baltic to the North Sea through the Skaggerak, the inescapable point at which goods travelling west were unloaded for carriage across the neck of Jutland, and those moving east reshipped. So for a time it virtually monopolized the trade along this axis, and on the Baltic littoral its power and influence were reflected by a string of daughter-cities.

From Lübeck merchants pushed out in all directions – to Scandinavia; into the North Sea; and in the tracks of the Vikings to tap the trade of the east at Novgorod and in the markets of Polotsk, Smolensk and Kiev (see p. 30). To Novgorod the route by sea and land was relatively straightforward. But to reach the hinterland of the Baltic it was necessary to cross the territories of vigorous pagan peoples, such as the Lithuanians and Livonians, whose determined hostility rendered this pioneering commercial endeavour particularly dangerous. And so it was that in these areas – in the gulfs of Riga and Finland – economic penetration was accompanied, and at times overshadowed, by conquest, conversion and Germanization. Lübeck itself had backed 'with ships laden with arms and foodstuffs' an attempt to convert and settle Livonia before the end of the twelfth century.

Once again, as with the Vikings and the English in North America, we hear of the delights awaiting the intrepid – of fertile fields, abundant pastures, and rivers teeming with fish – and struggling to inherit this paradise the land-hungry of every class from Saxony, Westphalia and Frisia. But despite the potential rewards, and notwithstanding a mighty resolve 'to break the strength of the heathen', little was accomplished. The Gulf of Riga was distant, and worse still, only accessible by sea, so that not surprisingly even the most resolute had doubts. Thus, as in the first attempted Viking and English settlements in the New World, there were never enough colonists to displace or swamp the natives, who in any case, like those of primeval North America, put up a strenuous resistance (see pp. 6, 9 and 482). But unlike the Scandinavians the Germans, with their vast resources in manpower and with a crusading tradition as potent as any, could try other tactics, and at the turn of the century a full-scale crusade was launched against the East. Riga was re-founded and fortified (1201) and a military order, the Brethren of the Sword – significantly open to merchants as well as to men of birth – established, to complete the conquest. Even so it was only with the intervention of another military order, that of the formidable Teutonic Knights (1237), who had in the meanwhile commenced the subjugation of Prussia, that the country was finally brought under control. To the north the advance was pushed as far as Lake Peipus, but to the south the going was much heavier, and until the fourteenth century the Samogites of Lithuania remained an embarrassing barrier between Prussia and Livonia, in contact only by sea. In the meanwhile men of ambition had found their way much further afield. German towns appeared in Estonia at Reval, Dorpat and Narva. By 1212 merchants from Riga had acquired navigational rights on the Dvina and so made their way, Viking style, to Vitebsk and thence to Smolensk, linked by way of the Dnepr with the Black Sea. In Smolensk they were soon established in sufficient strength to negotiate a treaty with the local ruler (1229). But their luck was not to hold. The development and aspirations of the Russian towns restricted the scope of their operations, and in the late 1200s they drew back to Polotsk.

In the meantime the many gaps behind this imposing façade were being stopped. Along the Baltic coast a crop of German maritime towns – Rostock (1218), Wismar (1228), Stralsund (1234), Danzig (1238) – appeared, frequently developed from some existing nucleus by a Slav ruler, colonized from Lübeck, and enjoying as a rule the support and liberties of Lübeck, whose role indeed in the whole process of expansion was comparable to that of Seville and Castile in the establishment of Spanish hegemony in the Americas. Then, in the lands between Germany's fluid eastern frontier and the lower reaches of the Vistula, there was a massive settlement by German peasants, in part encouraged by German princelings, in part by Slav magnates and dynasts. And whilst this movement was at its peak, with the pioneers across the Vistula in the north and the Oder further south, there came a spectacular – and final – extension of German power. At the invitation of a Polish prince the Teutonic Knights undertook the conquest and colonization of the territories of the heathen Prussians, a ferociously independent Lithuanian tribe living on the Baltic littoral, roughly between the basins of the Vistula and the Niemen. The initial strategy of the Knights was to set up a network of strongpoints from which to hold the area down, and thereafter to exploit it with native labour. Starting from a series of bases on approximately the line of the Vistula the attack was pushed forward with fierce determination. With the aid of the ships and resources of Lübeck the coast was taken and secured by the foundation (1237) of Elbing and Königsberg (1255). After the Brethren of the Sword had been absorbed into the Order access to the north was gained by the capture of the Kurische Nehrung and the founding (1252) of Memel, and contact was opened with the southern fringes of the Teutonic empire in Courland, Livonia and Estonia. For a time all things seemed possible, and there were even thoughts of an advance on Novgorod. But such ambitions were curtailed by defeat at the hands of the Russians and by native revolts in Prussia. So the policies of the Knights were changed: the idea of rapprochement with the various indigenous peoples was abandoned; their holy places were desecrated; tribes were deported or reduced to serfdom, and in their place came the ubiquitous German peasant. Indeed the Order long continued to cherish grand designs, but from the mid-thirteenth century much of its energies were diverted to the problems of populating and exploiting some 80,000sq.km (i.e. East Prussia alone) of new German territory.

Yet violent though the Germans undoubtedly were in Prussia, as earlier they had been in Holstein and Mecklenburg, their colonization in the north, as in other Slav regions, was on the whole accomplished not like that of the Spaniards, but by a peaceful penetration comparable to that of North America by the English dissenters in the seventeenth century (see p. 489). The Germans neither transmitted to the east lethal diseases; enslaved nor destroyed the peoples they found there; nor, for the most part, disputed settled lands with their native possessors. Like that of the Iberians in America their colonization was seigneurial in the sense that what was now brought into cultivation belonged to some lord. But it was colonization undertaken by a far wider range of society than in Iberia – by aristocrats, the church, the military orders – just as it brought to the colonial lands a far greater variety of German social classes. True, as in the Spanish Americas, there appeared in the east knights, merchants, the clergy both secular and regular, miners and craftsmen. But there appeared too, and in vast numbers, peasants and their families – the very class, that is, almost totally excluded from overseas colonizing ventures by the refusal of lords to lose labour, and by the costs of shipboard travel. In the east, however, they settled in such strength as to wholly Germanize some areas. Elsewhere Germans, peasants and others alike, remained, as were the Spaniards to remain in the Americas, as an alien minority, though a minority predestined to enjoy a far briefer hegemony. In 1400, for example, the ratio of native to German in Samland (Prussia) was perhaps three to five, but in Courland, Livonia and Estonia the towns alone were truly German (as were those of the Americas truly Spanish), whilst the countryside remained solidly native. Nevertheless, the presence of peasants profoundly affected the whole course and nature of German colonization. Their migration was inspired not by bellicose urges and ambitions, but by the simple desire to escape from the overpopulated countryside and social oppressions of the west. Unlike the *conquistadores* they expected, as did the English Puritans in North America, to work, just as they expected to find in the new lands those liberties denied them elsewhere – holdings with freedom of tenure and legal security (see pp. 46, 489). With land in the east abundantly available, comparatively easily accessible, and obtainable on liberal terms, German peasants, like the English smallholders in New England in the 1600s, were never impelled to undertake such epic searches as were the Scandinavians (see pp. 1–9 and 11, 14). Nor, with their wants so easily met, were they tempted to those heroic itineraries and prodigies of endurance into which the Iberians were drawn in their quest for gold and other riches, and so the extent of German endeavour is to be measured in thousands of square kilometres, that of the Spaniards and Portuguese in millions. Furthermore, with limitless amounts of potential agricultural land – uncleared forest and undrained marsh – to be had in the east, with equally extensive reserves of manpower in the west, and with lords eager to attract those who by their skills could most rapidly bring such territories into production, the agrarian economy of the colonial east – at least to begin with – only rarely, unlike that of Iberian America, depended on the forced labour of native peoples. Instead there emerged a free peasantry – free that is from the burdens of the manorial system of the west – of Germanic origin which in its heyday in the late 1200s was probably at least 500,000 strong. And, what is even more remarkable, there also emerged in some lands not heavily settled by Germans, but colonized by native princes with indigenous labour, a native peasantry enjoying comparable liberties under that 'German law' of whose benefits enterprising lords were clearly aware.

So there were opened up whole new areas almost as unknown to western Europe as were those discovered overseas in the fifteenth and sixteenth centuries, and, with consequences equally far-reaching, the bases of new states were laid. In Silesia 1200 villages were founded between 1200 and 1350, whilst by 1410 the Teutonic Knights alone had established a further 1400 on their Prussian demesne, quite apart from private foundations and the creation of something like 100 towns. And it was a colonization remarkably and perhaps uniquely systematic, often in the hands of specialist agents (variously described as promoters, locators or undertakers) who, like the later Genoese colonial companies, or the Portuguese *donatorios* undertook – though usually on a smaller scale – the settlement of some particular area at their own risk in exchange for fiscal and judicial privileges (see pp. 191, 247). Such professional skills are reflected in the careful integration in many places of urban and rural settlement. In thirteenth-century Silesia, for example, duke and developers established groups of villages, each centred economically and administratively, on a town. The system was an old and tried one, and was to be deployed to great effect by Spain in the Americas (see p. 329). No doubt the sense of security that colonists drew from the proximity of town walls was often misplaced. But at least association with a town did something to lessen their vulnerable isolation among an alien population, and gave an area a measure of political cohesion. In all this the Germans, like the Spaniards later, had the immense benefit of a long experience of conquest and re-settlement. In the course of generations of internal colonization, and during the penetration of Austria and the southeast, techniques had been developed which were now perfected and employed on an even larger scale. There were, for instance, a handful of basic municipal plans and codes ideal for indefinite, if not particularly inspiring, reproduction.

What, however, was so remarkable in German expansion was that territorial growth, impressive enough in itself, was accompanied by the creation, in even shorter time, of a commercial empire of a size and nature new to the north and, indeed, to Europe. The conquest and settlement of new territories, the quickening, often under German influence, of the economic life of the old, brought into being a vast northern world with products to offer and with needs to be met. In all empires new lands produce, in some measure, new trades, but rarely of the scale and significance of this Baltic economy, which by the sixteenth century had called into being, and was employing a volume of shipping equalling the total owned in the Mediterranean (*c.* 350,000t), and dwarfing that engaged in Europe's nascent trans-oceanic commerce (see pp. 342–4). It was an economy that was the basis of the wealth and power of the Dutch republic, just as in earlier centuries it inspired and sustained the growth of those German towns and cities of the Baltic littoral which had been so influential in its creation. Within a hundred years – and usually well within one hundred years – of their foundation these new towns were conducting a trade which at its height was to give them the virtual control of the economies of several northern countries, and which in its final stages, around 1600, was to embrace not only the Baltic and the seas of northwestern Europe, but also Iceland, Archangel, the Greek Islands and the New World of the Iberians.

Already in the 1200s German energy and influence flowed powerfully and purposefully in all directions to create as inflexible an informal empire as any. Norway, short of grain to feed a growing population, fell into a crippling dependence on Lübeck and the Wendish towns,[2] and well before 1300 German merchants were firmly entrenched with extensive fiscal and judicial privileges. The process was repeated, in varying degrees, throughout the rest of Scandinavia where the Germans encountered no developed political organization to resist them; where rulers, like those of potential colonial territories elsewhere, hoped for some advantage in favouring the alien; and where they met the competition of no appreciable native merchant class. Germans monopolized the Scanian herring fishery, dominated the trade of Copenhagen, and made up the bulk of the population of many other less celebrated Danish towns. In Sweden, where they played a large part in the founding of Stockholm (*c.* 1251), German merchants and craftsmen stimulated and shaped urban growth, whilst miners from the Harz mountains worked the country's rich deposits of copper.

In the west, with distance, densely populated lands and more sophisticated societies a barrier to mass migration, the German impact may have been less overwhelming, but was nevertheless of fundamental importance. Cities such as Cologne and Bremen had ancient commercial associations with England. In the 1200s, however, their merchants were joined by those of such new Baltic towns as Lübeck, Rostock and Riga.[3] For some considerable time there was friction between the two groups, but notwithstanding a series of internecine disputes, the same rapid acquisition of extensive privileges (see p. 67). Meanwhile German merchants were establishing themselves in the great and growing markets of the Low Countries. They appeared in Bruges where, by the thirteenth century, could be found the products of every part of Europe – wool for the textile industries of the Netherlands from Spain and the British Isles; fruits from the south; the wines of France; the riches of the Mediterranean and the orient brought by land and river across Europe, or in the galleys of Genoa and Venice by the long sea route through the Straits of Gibraltar. In this vital entrepôt there was a Lübeck Street and a Hamburg Street by 1300, and indeed German commercial enterprise seemed limitless. Germans traded at Tourhout, Ypres, Champagne and Troyes in the west; at Prague in the east. By the fourteenth century they had made contact with Cracow from Prussia, and thence with Lvow where they met Italian merchants from the Genoese and Venetian bases on the Black Sea. From Lübeck and Cologne they traded in the late Middle Ages with Venice via Augsburg and the Brenner Pass; with Milan and Genoa through Constance and the St Gotthard Pass. Of this land-borne commerce, which in the case of Lübeck may well have surpassed the value of the city's maritime trade, the traces are few. But far from obscure was the seeming ubiquity of ships belonging to the Baltic towns, and ships whose size and capacity, of an order new to the north, rendered their presence even more apparent. In the thirteenth and fourteenth centuries they virtually monopolized the trade of the Baltic and, working through the Skaggerak, of the North Sea. They were off the coasts of Poitou and Gascony by the mid-1300s, and of Asturias and Portugal less than one hundred years later. And by then they could be met sailing in fleets of a hundred or more to and from the ports of the French Atlantic littoral, and there was a German merchant colony in Lisbon by the mid-fifteenth century.

II *An empire of trade*

The causes of this expansion were as diverse and complex as the movement itself. It began in the early Middle Ages as Frankish and Saxon emperors pushed eastwards to extend and strengthen their frontiers; to conquer, convert and tax the pagan; and to implement assorted imperial (and potentially profitable) ambitions. It was resumed in the eleventh and twelfth centuries, when the enthusiasm of a reformed and re-invigorated Catholic church for the overthrow of pagan and infidel allowed St Bernard to divert (1147) a north-German crusade destined for the Holy Land into a similar (and abortive) onslaught against the Slavs. But more important than this, or other and equally bloodthirsty proceedings, was that at this time a number of able and enterprising north-German princes – in Saxony, Holstein, Meissen and Brandenburg – came to realize the possibilities of eastward expansion. They understood the prospects of trade, just as they understood the profits and power to be had, in a period of growing population, from the ownership and exploitation of more and better lands. Further-more, with imperial authority weak in Germany – the emperors in pursuit of various chimera in Italy or engaged in conflict with the papacy – and the country often in political turmoil such rulers enjoyed sufficient independence to pursue their own interests, yet at the same time were powerful enough to bring to their colonial undertakings all those advantages, as was later the case in Portugal, of purposeful support and direction (see p. 261). The same rulers were, moreover, able to turn to their benefit the land-hunger of the peasant population of north Germany and the Low

Countries. It was a land-hunger caused in part by inadequate technology and natural disaster so that, as a chronicler records, 'those living near the coast . . . suffered from the irruptions of the seas'; but it was caused in large measure by the pressure of an increasing population on limited resources, leading to the fragmentation of holdings, inspiring tales of the agrarian paradise to be found in the eastlands, and in the end provoking that massive migration already noticed (see pp. 40–3). Yet German peasant ambitions, like those of most later colonists, were more than merely economic, and there were hopes that in the east would come release from those ever-more onerous burdens and duties which political disorders had enabled, if not compelled, lords of the homeland to impose upon their men. But not even in its earliest phases was the German push to the east exclusively one of conquest and colonization. The very account of the founding of Lübeck suggests a determination to exploit that Baltic commerce in which the Germans were already in some degree engaged by the twelfth century, and within a matter of years they had traversed, with that same determination as brought the Vikings to Constantinople or the Portuguese to Malacca, the 1500kms of pirate-infested sea and river that led to Novgorod (see pp. 30 and 238–9). No more than with any other people was a voyage of this nature undertaken to acquire articles of common usage, but to bring into German hands, as was rapidly done, those luxuries which Novgorod had for long transmitted to the west (see p. 30).

   In pursuit of these objectives the Germans enjoyed all those advantages soon to be familiar in other phases of Europe's expansion. Some spectacular obstacles apart – Saxony in the early Middle Ages, Prussia later – they met on the whole with little organized or sustained resistance. In their initial advance they encountered in the north and east no developed Slav or Scandinavian states but instead, as did the Vikings in the west, only fragmented or inchoate groupings. Against such opponents they had, furthermore, the advantages of a military superiority conferred under the Saxon kings and emperors by heavy armour, and earlier by those Frankish swords as celebrated in their day as were those of Toledo in Spain's heroic age. Then, with the emergence in later centuries of Scandinavian, Slav and often Christian kingdoms and principalities, the Germans were encouraged and accepted by native rulers for those same reasons that were to make Europeans welcome to many native peoples and rulers in the New Worlds. They were, for one thing, powerful allies in internecine wars, and so early in the twelfth century a Christian Abodrite prince joined forces with the Saxons to attack the pagan Slavs of the island of Rügen, whilst some one hundred years later it was a Polish duke who invited the Teutonic Knights to help him subdue the independent Prussians. Nor was this all, for like those oriental and African chiefs who demanded weapons and artisans from the Portuguese and Spaniards, Slav rulers sought to benefit from German skills in government, commerce and agriculture (see p. 252). German officials were introduced into Bohemia; communities of German merchants – as at Danzig in the early 1200s – were granted privileges by local potentates; German peasants with their heavy ploughs, Netherlanders with their proficiency in diking and draining, were brought in to open up waste lands which the native peoples had neither the implements, skill nor incentives to exploit. 'God forbid', exclaimed a Slav princeling on one notable occasion, 'that the land should ever relapse into its former state, that we should drive out the German settlers and again undertake its cultivation.' With such support and encouragement, and with the advantage of commercial skills acquired by association in the west with the merchants of Flanders and northern Italy, German expansion was for a time irresistible. And it was an advance sustained by that same technological enterprise and adaptability as underlay virtually every other phase of Europe's expansion, an enterprise manifested in the development of ships which were to ensure German hegemony in northern waters for the best part of 200 years (see pp. 77–80).

So, like the Italian republics in the Mediterranean, or the Portuguese in the Indian Ocean, the Germans, or more precisely the towns of north Germany, could turn to their profit the opportunities of an existing pattern of commerce, and beyond this create, as the Iberians were later to do in the Atlantic, a whole new maritime economy (see pp. 327ff.). The growth of Europe's population in the twelfth and thirteenth centuries, of which German expansion in the Baltic and elsewhere was but one particularly dramatic expression, made the resources of the newly opened east in food and raw materials indispensable. At the same time the exploitation of these reserves created, or rather stimulated, a native demand for those things which the west either itself produced or acquired elsewhere. Initially, therefore, German merchants were not seeking to dispose of their own products in tepid or hostile markets, but like their Italian contemporaries in the Orient and the Portuguese in Asia later, endeavouring to buy or otherwise acquire what would satisfy the wants of their customers in the homelands. Thus it was that they had every incentive to penetrate widely and rapidly – to Novgorod for furs and eastern luxuries; to Bergen for fish; to Flanders for cloth. Hence the main currents of medieval northern trade came to run roughly between east and west along routes German controlled to begin with, and with German towns at most major halts or confluences with subsidiary streams of commerce. It was a pattern of domination – less extensive, more complex and more urban – resembling those established for similar reasons by other commercial powers such as Venice and Holland, or where, as with the Portuguese in Asia, an existing network of trades came into other hands (see pp. 236ff.). Its basis was an axis whose extremities were Novgorod in the east and Bruges in the west. In the centre, economically and politically, was Lübeck, vitally situated, as we have seen, at the neck of Jutland peninsula (see p. 40). Not only did it control, until the late thirteenth century, the flow of commerce between the Baltic and the North Sea, but also, together with Hamburg, Bremen, Wismar and Rostock, that to Scania and Scandinavia in the north, and to Saxony, Brandenburg and Mecklenburg in the south. By land it was in contact with Nürnburg, Frankfurt and Cologne, as well as with many towns of the Baltic and Netherlands coasts, whilst it shared with other north-German ports the resources of a hinterland served by the Rhine, Weser, Elbe and Oder. To the west Cologne – the largest city of medieval Germany – and its various satellites linked the Baltic towns with the Rhine Valley, with the Low Countries and – until a direct sea-route came into use – with England. And it was also through Cologne and the Netherlands that these towns were linked to the great trans-European route to Italy. Then in the north and east the Prussian ports, Danzig especially, gave entry not only to the surrounding territories, but to Poland, Lithuania and Hungary, whilst from Riga, Reval and Dorpat merchants traded to Livonia, the upper Dvina, western Russia and Novgorod.

So in their heyday the Germans of the north monopolized a commerce pre-dominately in bulk goods of relatively low value, unlike those trades in luxuries or bullion which elsewhere developed under Italian and Iberian control (see pp. 101, 327). From the Baltic littoral, and from the vast regions to which a galaxy of mighty rivers and their confluents – the Oder, Vistula, Dnepr, Bug, Dvina, Niemen – gave comparatively easy access, there flowed, as there was to continue to flow for centuries, food and raw materials. With no significant industrialized areas of its own to feed, and with its countless acres of rye, barley and wheat, the Baltic was from the late 1200s Europe's granary, and a granary, as population grew, of ever-increasing importance. Its resources, like those of North America in recent times, kept alive the peoples of industrialized, infertile or overpopulated regions, and were urgently solicited (as by England in the fifteenth and Portugal in the sixteenth centuries) in moments of famine or other crisis. In the 1200s Brandenburg and Mecklenburg were supplying grain to Norway, south Germany and the Netherlands. Three hundred years later the market had expanded to embrace France, Iberia and even Italy. It was in 1590 that representatives of the enterprising grand duke of Tuscany, who had already been at some pains and expense to ensure that the poor of his realms should be fed, despatched 'with great joy' eight shiploads of wheat from Danzig to Livorno where, three years later, the arrival of 16,000t is recorded.

With the passage of time the centres of production moved further south and east – from Brandenburg and Mecklenburg to Prussia, the major grower by the late Middle Ages, then to Lithuania, Poland and the Ukraine, whose hard-husked grains proved better able to withstand the rigours and delays of the lengthy sea-voyages common after 1300. But throughout it was Danzig that handled the bulk (about 75 per cent) of the trade, with Königsberg, Riga and Stettin taking the rest. Quite apart from its natural advantages and abundant shipping it was, as a fastidious Venetian observed, inhabited by persons richer and less barbarous than their neighbours, and by the 1500s offered financial facilities something like those to which Italian businessmen were accustomed. At the beginning of the sixteenth century it was exporting roughly 20,000 tonnes of rye a year, and by the middle of the following century well over 100,000 tonnes. Nor was this all, for there were similar increases for other kinds of grain, whilst in the half-dozen years after 1620 a relatively insignificant Stralsund merchant alone handled more than 1200 tonnes of assorted grains and flour.

Equally vital was high-quality timber. It was used in building, in the manufacture of furniture, and, with notorious lavishness and extravagance, in the construction of ships – all industries, that is, whose demands were more exacting when population grew or prosperity increased. With the sylvan resources of most of Europe either dwindling or in effect inaccessible by the late Middle Ages, those of the Baltic were indispensable. True, through the accidents of politics and geography, not all its immense riches were equally exploitable. But Danzig in particular, served by the Vistula and its tributaries and confluents, became the outlet for the timber of the great forests of Poland, Ruthenia and Lithuania which was floated down river for export. Quite apart from a sizable business in manufactured wooden products ranging from ships to chests and boxes it supplied, together with other Prussian ports, the oak balks from which the keels of ships were made, the beech and oak for planking, pines for masts, ash for oars, and the forestry by-products of tar and pitch used to stop (caulk) the gaps between timbers. And with the same prodigality the eastern Baltic provided, too, flax and hemp from which ropes and sails were made. So, from the 1300s assorted planks, balks and beams were being sent out to England, Flanders and Holland. In the following century they were to be counted in their thousands, with the single port of Newcastle-upon-Tyne taking about 3500 wainscots even in the depressed years of 1465–6. And by the 1500s Portugal, Spain and France had likewise become important customers as the increased volume of Europe's trade, its expansion into the oceans of the world, and the maritime ambitions of such rulers as the Habsburgs demanded, and cost, more shipping (see pp. 342ff.). The pace slowed in the sixteenth century, partly because of the competition of more easily available Norwegian timber, partly because the most accessible forests were exhausted and (in Poland at least), because of domestic demand and a concentration on the production of grain. But the flow of what were generically known as naval stores continued to expand. The more primitive economies of the Russian and Lithuanian lands of the Dvina basin, if not equal to the marketing of timber, were able to supply pitch and tar; and it was a region whose soil and climate were ideal for the cultivation of flax, which together with hemp accounted for 60 per cent of Riga's exports to the west in the early seventeenth century.

Yet Baltic exports were no more exclusively utilitarian than were those of Asia and the Americas exclusively luxuries (see p. 323). It was not grain and timber but furs, a business evocative of high and ostantatious living, and one in which the Scandinavians had long been active, which first drew German merchants to the east, and which remained throughout an important element in their prosperity (see pp. 30, 46). There was a brisk and widespread market in the west not only for the expensive sables, beavers and ermines needed to warm, comfort and adorn the affluent and their ladies, and to embellish the dress of assorted dignitaries, secular and ecclesiastical, but also for more mundane squirrel furs (for linings and trimmings), and those of otters and weasels. They were taken in abundance almost everywhere – in Livonia, Poland, Lithuania, Prussia and Sweden. The major supplier, however, was Russia, and in particular Novgorod, to where furs were brought from regions as remote as the Volga basin and the White Sea littoral, and then shipped out through Lübeck, Danzig, Reval and Riga from where, in 1405, three ships sailed for Bruges carrying between them the best part of 500,000. It was in fact a classic colonial trade: the exploitation, under primitive and arduous conditions, of the natural wealth produced by the simple economies of strange and distant lands. A celebrated piece of medieval German wood carving, the panels presented in the fourteenth century to the church of St Nicholas in Stralsund by the town's Novgorod traders, shows bearded Russians, armed with bows and sticks, pursuing their quarry in their native forests and offering their haul – in a scene which might well be from the later and more familiar trade of the backwoods of North America – to a merchant at the gate of the German *kontor*[4] in Novgorod. Once again it was a commerce of remarkable tenacity and longevity, but, being re-routed overland through Leipzig and Frankfurt in the sixteenth and seventeenth centuries, escaped from the control of the Baltic ports.

It was similarly from the great forests of the east that there came the wax used in the manufacture of candles both for domestic lighting and in the devotional practices of Christian Europe. And here, too, the Germans early established a monopoly – certainly by the thirteenth century – which they long and successfully defended, just as here, too, the volume of the traffic was, by current standards, imposing. By the late 1400s, when the sacrist of the cathedral of Durham was buying, simply for liturgical purposes, some 200kg of wax a year, the Germans were annually importing into England 100,000kg, and over six times this amount by 1525–9. In the same way, though they controlled no single major centre of production, German merchants were strategically entrenched in the supply of metals, and in particular of the increasingly important copper and iron. Iron was used not only for various tools and implements, but also in building, in the manufacture of fastenings and fittings for ships (anchors for example), and in the production of armour, weapons and (eventually) artillery. Copper – from which bronze and brass were derived – was likewise important for ordnance, for the church bells so dear to a pious age, and in the production of domestic and industrial utensils. Some came from the Harz – finding its way west through Cologne – some from Slovakia, exported either from Thorn and Danzig, or going overland through Breslau, whilst that of Hungary and Sweden was shipped to the Low Countries and England via Lübeck in a trade still flourishing in the early seventeenth century. Sweden was also a substantial supplier of iron, especially the high quality osmund, exported to the west from Lübeck and Danzig in a commerce which remained vital in the 1600s notwithstanding the competition of the more flexible Spanish iron.

In exchange for such products the Baltic towns took from the west primarily textiles: first those of Flanders, to which with characteristic conservatism they long remained loyal, then those of England and Holland. In the fourteenth century woollen cloths – and cloths of a bewildering variety, such as the forty different sorts mentioned in the papers of one Hamburg merchant – accounted for more than 75 per cent of the value of north German exports from Flanders. In the following century they made up 90 per cent of their exports from England, running at between 6000 and 12,000 pieces a year, and by the early 1500s the figure had risen to 20,000 to 30,000 a year. Still later a Stralsund linen-draper was handling, in the seventeenth century, textiles from Flanders, Holland, Pomerania, England and Germany. Most of these were throughout cloths of middling or relatively cheap quality, though a small but growing demand for the more elegant and expensive products of Italy and for those 'well-dyed and costly' cloths from England by the late Middle Ages, indicates upper-class taste and prosperity.

Here again we have the epitome of a colonial trade. The more advanced economies of the west extracted from the east, initially through the medium of a series of German outposts, food and raw materials produced by societies increasingly dominated, with the passage of time, by large estates worked by unfree labour and geared, like the sugar and tobacco plantations of the New Worlds, to meeting an external demand. In return, western Europe provided, as it was to provide to the Americas, those luxuries (spices for instance) and expensive novelties (such as clocks) demanded by the opulent, and those cheap manufactured goods which a concentration on primary products discouraged or prevented the native economy from supplying. In some cases it was the Germans themselves who endeavoured to maintain this colonial relationship, with the Novgorod *kontor* prohibiting, in the fourteenth century, the sale of cloths produced by a nascent Silesian industry in much the same way as Castile later attempted to cripple the manufacture of textiles in the Americas (see pp. 326–7). In other cases it was a powerful local interest, as with the dedication, in the 1500s, of the Polish aristocracy to the large-scale growing of grain for export, to the detriment of the rest of the country's economy (see p. 71).

These basic features are clear enough without further extending the catalogue of western manufactures – wine for instance – taken by the Baltic. But the trade, like most colonial trades, fits uneasily into the simple pattern developed by many theorists of the sixteenth and seventeenth centuries, in which a colony provided raw materials, the mother country manufactures. Such were western Europe's demands on the east, and such the imbalance in both volume and value of the trade, that from an early date some part of German purchases had to be paid for in silver. Already in the mid-1300s the accounts of one of the greatest Lübeck merchants show him buying grain, wax, furs and malt in Livonia and Prussia with, amongst other things, bar silver – acquired in either Bohemia or in Mansfeld (see p. 70). And so, also, three and four hundred years later some German (as other) purchases in Poland and Russia were paid for in silver, though now the silver of the Spanish Americas. Then again, the west itself supplied the Baltic with primary products. Of these by far the most important from the mid-fourteenth century was salt, consumed in heroic quantities in the preservation and titillation of food. Initially it came from Lüneburg through Lübeck. But this local salt was soon eclipsed by 'bay' salt, first bought in Flanders, and then in the later Middle Ages at the source of production, the Bay of Bourgneuf and Brouage on the French Atlantic coast.

In the early fifteenth century Reval alone was taking some 5000 tonnes a year, and thereafter demand grew at such a pace that in the 1620s the east was importing over 100,000 tonnes annually, with the resources of Iberia being tapped as well as those of France. Furthermore, the Baltic exported manufactures since, as in the European empires in Asia and the Americas, settlers quickly developed industries to meet their needs, to benefit from better or more abundant raw materials, or to exploit native labour (see p. 326). Brewing flourished in medieval north Germany, with its products much appreciated in neighbouring countries. It was largely concentrated in Hamburg, Wismar (with 200 breweries in 1460) and Rostock, which by the late 1400s was allegedly supplying a presumably permanently inebriated Sweden with 400,000 tonnes a year. Besides this there were wooden products, and the German Baltic ports became, as the Americas were later to become, considerable centres of shipbuilding, with Danzig, for example, meeting in the late fifteenth century not only local demand, but also constructing vessels for English, Dutch and even Italian owners (see pp. 80–1).

Sustained by, and sustaining, the great long-distance exchanges there were, as in other maritime economies, an infinity of local trades through which cargoes were assembled for despatch, and imports redistributed. True, the Baltic ports, handling basically the common products of a roughly identical hinterland, might appear to have dealt less with one another than say those of the Americas dealing in the resources of widely differing regions. Yet the very names of their merchant associations – the venturers to Bergen, Riga, Danzig, Stockholm, Gotland, Novgorod – suggest vigorous local exchanges. In the late fifteenth century Lübeck sent western cloth and wine to Danzig and Königsberg, Rostock exported beer through much of the Baltic, and Danzig re-exported bay salt, just as later Stralsund supplied Sweden with goods (sugar, rice, spices) of clearly exotic origins. Moreover, not only did the Germans maintain, to the best of their ability, and as long as they could, a commercial monopoly in the waters they controlled, but their shipping penetrated, when opportunity offered, intermediate trade routes – a rough parallel with the 'country trade' of the Europeans in Asia (see pp. 478ff). In the thirteenth and fourteenth centuries, for example, German ships were carrying English wool to the Low Countries. At the same time they came to dominate the run from Norway to England, and developed a triangular traffic, taking grain from Lübeck to Bergen, cod from Bergen to Boston and finally cloth from Boston to Lübeck. And in the later Middle Ages, exploiting the English loss of Gascony in the Hundred Years War, they successfully pushed into the shipment of wines from Gascony to England, whilst in the early 1400s their competition with Castilians in Spain's commerce with La Rochelle led in the end to war.

In all essentials this network of trades, and the hegemony in northern waters, and indeed in northern economies, that it reflected, was established by about 1350. Thereafter it was a matter of enlarging or maintaining privileges and of clipping the wings of rivals actual and potential. Yet the earliest stages of German commercial expansion had shown few of those characteristics displayed, in comparable circumstances, by the Spaniards in the Atlantic, and by the Portuguese and Dutch in Asia – the attempted imposition, that is, at the very outset, of a rigid commercial monopoly, enforced and extended by violence (see pp. 396ff.). Nor perhaps surprisingly, for in the Baltic there was to start with none of that immense wealth, easily controllable and immediately apparent, that inspires such behaviour. Then again, the initial German commercial penetration of the east was by merchants from a number of towns, old and new, under no overall control and direction, who far from subjecting all and sundry to their authority did no more than form associations among themselves in those places they were said to 'frequent' (i.e. in which they were not permanently established). Individual German towns, lacking at first the strength to do otherwise, admitted strangers, and ambitious princes, fostering new foundations, offered concessions to any willing to trade in them irrespective of nationality. But as the German towns of the east prospered and grew, a more familiar picture emerged. Already in the early 1200s Lübeck had expended much energy in trying to check the rise of Stralsund (sacked by a Lübeck fleet in 1249) and Rostock. And once on their feet the towns made all haste to be rid of the alien and of competitors, shutting Flemish, Frisian and English ships out of the Baltic well before the end of the thirteenth century. Then in 1323 the *kontor* of Bruges was established as the staple for the exchange of northern for other goods – just as Venice, Lisbon and Seville were to be the exclusive entrepôts in their respective colonial economies – beyond which, London excepted, southern vessels were not to trade (see p. 342). With the passage of time, as more extensive privileges were sought, as commercial arrangements became more complex, as client nations became more restive, and as rivals pressed more insistently, associations of merchants waned and, the German towns themselves drew together in formal groupings to protect and further their interests.

There had been leagues of limited membership and duration in the thirteenth century, and in 1284–94 that of the Wendish towns (Lübeck, Kiel, Wismar, Rostock and Stralsund), with some fraternal support had, by witholding supplies of food, and by rigorous naval blockade, compelled the luckless Norwegians to grant them even greater privileges than before. And by 1370 the redoubtable Hanseatic League, with Lübeck at its head, was in existence. Though it included the grand master of the Teutonic Order – which had conquered and created a sovereign Prussian state – and for a time the peasant community of Dithmarschen in Holstein, it was an association of towns, and perhaps the most remarkable urban phenomenon that western Europe has seen. It was a league quite unequalled in power, longevity and sheer size, with some 70 or 80 major towns and cities and about 100 or so lesser associates in the fifteenth and sixteenth centuries. And it was unique in that it was a league of non-sovereign towns, united only by commercial interest, and governed throughout their history – revolutions and upheavals notwithstanding – by merchants. Its strength rested on that commerce we have already examined, conducted through a network of trading posts (*kontors*, factories) covering northern and eastern Europe, and richly endowed with extensive privileges (see pp. 67–8). They were linked by routes, many of them sea-routes, all virtually monopolized by Germans and stretching from the Low Countries to Russia, from England to the Slav lands of the Baltic, and from Iberia to Germany.

Yet the Hanse was an association astonishingly nebulous and inchoate. Funds it could raise, irregularly and with difficulty, but it possessed nothing of the machinery of government of even the most rudimentary state. It had a general assembly (*Hansetage*) in which issues of moment were decided. But this met with increasing irregularity – barely annually in the fourteenth century, perhaps every three years in the fifteenth – whilst its deliberations were undermined by the non-arrival of many delegates and the early departure of others, and its authority and efficacy weakened by the growth of regional gatherings. Policies, nevertheless, the League had in abundance, and policies for long enforced with impressive success. It regulated the economic conduct of its merchants, it defined how they should live abroad, it decreed (1403) that its ships should not be at sea in the hard months between November and April. Clearly this was no equivalent to that comprehensive oversight of commerce and empire first displayed by Venice and subsequently by the Iberian kingdoms, and in essence the Hanse was concerned to secure for its members the most favourable legal and fiscal provisions in alien lands and, later, to defend such privileges and to destroy, or at least contain, its competitors. So, in the fifteenth century, it attempted to exclude foreigners from partnerships with Hanse merchants, to prevent their direct access to the native producers in the east, and to bar the Dutch from Hanse preserves by decreeing (1442), amongst other things, that only cloth bought in the German staple at Bruges could be shipped from the Low Countries to the Baltic.

Many of these xenophobic measures were, predictably enough, failures. All the same, and notwithstanding serious economic setbacks in the late Middle Ages, the Hanse was to fight and negotiate, often on all fronts at once, over long periods, and with remarkable resilience and success. Unlike the Vikings it had the commercial skills, the numbers and the volume of technologically superior tonnage (and so the force) to impose and defend a monopoly. It could put armies in the field. It could embarrass and intimidate, if not always subdue, its opponents by depriving them of food and materials through naval blockade. And it could deal, on more than equal terms, with sovereign states. Denmark, which for a decade had enjoyed a brief period of power and glory under Valdemar IV Atterdag – who having set his house in order took Scania in 1360, reconquered Gotland and destroyed a Hanseatic fleet of fifty ships sent against him – was brought to a humiliating peace in 1370 after Hanse squadrons had sacked Copenhagen and pillaged the Danish coast. The League's vital interests were safeguarded by the occupation of a number of strongholds controlling access to the Baltic and – as potent a manifestation of informal empire as any – by extracting from the Danes a promise that in the event of Valdemar's death the Hanse was to be consulted as to the choice of his successor.

But such vigorous and decisive expressions of will were to become rarer with the passage of time as an increasingly disunited Hanse faced increasingly powerful opposition, not only in the Baltic, but throughout much of northern Europe. In effect the League was nothing more than a confederation, or more accurately, an alliance with some rudimentary machinery for consultation and the making of policy. Such associations are fragile enough at the best of times. But where the basis was ostensibly material interest, and where a large number of towns of widely varying size, prosperity and development were involved, each naturally concerned to protect its own commerce, and all anxious to avoid any untoward expenditure, the bonds of unity were particularly tenuous. And to all the inherent disadvantages of government by committee – indecision, delay, faction – the League brought others of its own, since there was nothing to stop its members allying themselves to the princes and cities outside the association. So time and again agreed courses of action foundered through the divergent aims of the various members of the Hanse, and such differences were further aggravated as individual towns were themselves split by social and religious divisions. And the forces for disagreement and disruption within the League were indeed powerful. Its Baltic towns, enjoying common privileges abroad, engaged in much the same trade, and not constituting on the whole markets for each other's products, were in fact potential rivals rather than natural allies. By the late fourteenth century those of Livonia and Prussia – Danzig especially – were in direct maritime contact with Holland and England. They had no need, and a lessening desire, to accept Lübeck as the entrepôt on the east-west axis, a growing disinclination to follow her policies and an increasing will and ability to exclude her from the trade of Prussia and Livonia. At the same time the Teutonic Order, a large-scale and efficient producer of grain, was only too pleased – whatever the supposed interests of the Hanse in general or of its own Prussian towns in particular – to receive ships from England and Holland which brought in cloth and took out its produce. Similarly in the west the members of the so-called Rhenish group, of which the ancient and powerful city of Cologne was the most important, were primarily concerned with the well-being of their commerce with the Low Countries and England to which, in any crisis, all else was subordinate. Meanwhile, everywhere individual towns and cities sought to establish themselves as controlling absolutely, even against their fellows, their respective and generously defined hinterlands. In the 1400s Cologne complained of the restrictions Lübeck placed on its citizens wishing to trade in the Baltic; the commerce of the Wendish and the Prussian towns became in effect at this time that between Lübeck and Danzig; and a century later, after the loss of Novgorod, Riga, Reval and Dorpat aimed to monopolize the Russia trade.

Yet that such divisive forces were not necessarily conducive to self-destruction was shown by the history of the Dutch republic (see pp. 421–2). In states, as in persons, longevity entails more than the right constitution, and given economic or financial power, political organizations of an antique or inadequate nature can, like the Swiss in the contemporary world, survive and prosper. The problems of the Hanse were of a more fundamental order. Whatever the many weaknesses of the Dutch state it was of modest geographical dimensions and its experiences in the sixteenth century gave it a sense of unity the League never possessed. The very size of the Hanse – in numbers, in sheer physical extent – and the fact that after the mid-fourteenth century it contained no one city enjoying such obvious pre-eminence as did Amsterdam, Venice and Genoa within their respective societies, were all massive obstacles to any feeling of cohesiveness and the possibility of concerted action (see pp. 57–9). Furthermore, the League, and more especially its Baltic members, though they might produce beer, ships and linen, had no industrial hinterland comparable to those controlled by the Italian maritime republics, and by the towns of Holland (see p. 376). The urban patricians of the Hanse were powerful enough on the whole to suppress any artisan aspirations, and their resources, unlike those of their Dutch equivalents, were invested not in industry, but in emulating the tastes and behaviour of the predominantly aristocratic society among which, again unlike the Dutch, they were situated. So, like the towns of the Spanish Americas, those of the League lived – and they needed to do no more – without significant industries and on the demand for the natural products of the territory they controlled (see pp. 323ff.). And so the ever-present fissiparous tendencies of the Hanse were inevitably intensified as each town sought to guarantee its prosperity by ensuring its own unimpeded exploitation of its particular hinterland.

Hamstrung by these barely concealed weaknesses, the League was to attempt to defend a commercial empire which was hopelessly vulnerable. It consisted, as did others – those of the Italian maritime republics (see p. 116), or that of the Portuguese in Asia – deriving from the penetration or extension of a network of trade routes, of a string of towns, cities and concessions at focal points on these routes. Simultaneously to defend anything more than a handful of these, scattered along lines of communication which in many cases stretched across Europe and beyond would, had it ever been envisaged, have involved an impossible dissipation of resources. But the Hanse, like the far richer cities of Italy, was more and more unable to muster the naval and military strength that ebullient and aspiring monarchs could assemble, and increasingly unable to implement far less ambitious schemes. True, some of the threats to its hegemony that it identified, serious though they were, were more apparent than real, yet all were handled with an unsureness of touch that was to become ever more obvious with the passage of time. In the fourteenth century there was much alarm at the appearance of the ubiquitous Italians, particularly suspect in view of their superior commercial techniques and financial resources, In Hanse preserves. Pushing north along the routes that linked the Baltic with their colonies on the Black Sea and with Bohemia, Hungary and the Mediterranean, they eventually emerged, in the late 1390s, on the Baltic littoral itself. And here, the League's prohibitions against any dealings with such undesirable competitors notwithstanding, their advance continued. But though an Italian bank was established in Lübeck in the early fifteenth century, and though scattered Italian merchants were to be found in the maritime towns of the Baltic over the next two centuries, there was never any real danger of a large-scale migration of Italian interests to the north.

More formidable and persistent was the pressure from south Germany, enjoying in the fourteenth and fifteenth centuries a prosperity stimulated by the demand for precious metals – of which it was the natural supplier – and by the opportunities of the developing economies of eastern Europe. By the early 1400s merchants from Nürnburg were in Lübeck and had a substantial foothold in northern trade. Such encroachments were vociferously condemned, but to resist them was another matter. Lübeck had commercial interests of its own in the south, where it sold furs, amber, herring and even Icelandic falcons, and was accordingly open to reprisal. More than this, there was the feeling, not unusual in such situations, that since the competition was so powerful it made more sense to join it and share the profits rather than to resist in vain. Thus, through their own enterprise on the one hand, and with the encouragement, open or tacit, of important northern interests – including the Teutonic Knights – on the other, the south Germans spread quickly and widely through Hanseatic preserves. They opened a new route, linking Nürnburg with Frankfurt, Leipzig and Poznan, so undermining the role of the Hanse as the intermediary between east and west and (by virtue of its southern contacts in Bruges) between the north-east and the Mediterranean (see pp. 44–5). Instead of coming down river for shipment through Bruges, Lübeck and Reval, the products of central Europe could now bypass the Hanse network, as could those of Russia and Poland moving in one direction, and of south Germany and the Mediterranean moving in the other, with, for example, spices from Venice reaching Danzig through Nürnburg and Leipzig.

And whilst Nürnburg undermined the traditional commerce of the League at Bruges and in south Germany, south German competition and enterprise reached a climax with the manifestation in the north of the influence of the Augsburg family of the Fuggers, bankers to popes and emperors. They had representatives at Antwerp, Poznan and Breslau in the early 1490s, in Lübeck by 1496, and within a short time their trade had expanded to Stettin, Danzig, Hamburg and into Livonia. In 1515 the firm organized the despatch of copper from their mines in Hungary through Cracow to Danzig, and thence by sea for sale to the Portuguese in Antwerp. This was in direct conflict with the Hanse interest in the export of Swedish copper to the same market, and a massive infringement of their pretended control of the Baltic. Such, however, was the inefficacy of the League's – and especially Lübeck's – opposition, that supported by Danzig, Hamburg, Breslau and Cracow the Fugger empire continued to grow. They traded to Russia, buying furs in a Hanse market, for spice and silver, they provided the king of Denmark with warships and they were licensed to set up a copper mill just outside Lübeck. Unable to stem this advance the city ignominiously lifted its restrictions on the firm in 1538. Yet here again the League's salvation came not by its own works, but more or less by chance when the Fuggers redeployed their capital and endeavour in the Low Countries and Spain.

At sea, however, the Hanse was to meet in the Dutch and the English, opponents more single minded. Both, by the late Middle Ages, were major producers of woollen textiles for which, with the shrinking markets of a European economy in recession, they were eager to find new outlets. With no industry of its own, the Baltic was particularly attractive, the more so as it was known to the Dutch and English alike as a provider of food and raw materials. From an insignificant trade to Norway and Scania in the thirteenth century Dutch influence grew within the next two hundred years to replace the hegemony of the League in the Baltic with a monopoly even more extensive and exclusive (see pp. 375ff.). Against these pressures the Hanse offered, as against its other opponents, no united opposition, little effective resistance and few sensible policies. In the early 1400s, whatever others might say, the Teutonic Order refused to join an attempt to stop the flow of grain to Holland and the Prussian aristocracy repeatedly required that nothing be done to impair their relations with valued customers in the Netherlands. Characteristically the League thought to exclude the Dutch from the north by reviving the ancient Bruges staple, by insisting, that is, that expensive eastern goods must be shipped to Bruges for sale in the west, and that Low Countries cloth could only be exported to the Baltic through Bruges (see pp. 53–4). But with Bruges already in decline the move was doomed from the start, whilst trade, including that of many Hanseatic merchants themselves, was increasingly concentrated in Antwerp. Here again the League eventually proposed to reorganize itself, but in a style so grand, and with progress so leisurely, that the completion of the Antwerp *kontor* coincided in the end with the political and economic disasters of the city in the late 1500s (see pp. 73, 384).

The threat from the English was seemingly of a different order. They were, throughout the later Middle Ages, vigorously aggressive, even if, as was to recur in the sixteenth century, predatory zeal cost them economic advantage (see p. 476). And from an early date they were far from negligible at sea. English ships were in the Baltic by the thirteenth century, whilst in Prussia English merchants, with local encouragement, attempted to penetrate inland to their customers. For a time all went well. English vessels carried the goods of German merchants, and by 1388 the English had a factory in Danzig like those of the Hanse in alien territories. But such was their reputation and behaviour – bringing, for example, their families to Danzig – in contrast to the initially unobtrusive and exclusively commercial expansion of the Dutch, as to focus hostility on them. Then, however, with the disintegration of English government in the factional rivalries of the mid-fifteenth century, the country was deprived of any coherent direction and the interests of its merchants sacrificed to the private gains of powerful adventurers. The professed aim of the English merchants was to secure in the Baltic privileges similar to those enjoyed by the Hanse in England.

Little as the League welcomed such aspirations it welcomed even less the unimpeded looting of its shipping – the taking in 1449 by an English commander of a convoy of over 100 Hanseatic and Netherlands craft, and the capture nine years later of another Hanse fleet by vessels of the earl of Warwick. When, in the later 1400s, such clashes degenerated into open naval war the English, some notable reverses notwithstanding (as when the lord mayor of London was taken at sea), inflicted heavy losses on the League. But once again any advantage was destroyed by the accident of politics. Edward IV, momentarily driven from his throne, returned to England in 1471 with Hanseatic support, in exchange for which the League received a handsome indemnity and the restoration of all its privileges. From then on its trade with England flourished – by 1500 it was handling something like 25 per cent of the country's cloth exports – whilst the English were effectively excluded from the Baltic. True, individual ships appeared there – royal vessels on charter to London merchants in 1511, merchantmen from the east coast ports in the following two decades. But the hold of the Tudors on England in the first half of the sixteenth century was still sufficiently precarious to discourage them from any embroilments with the League.

The collapse, however, in the 1550s of the Antwerp market, where most of England's overseas trade had become concentrated, and subsequent English disagreements with the Spanish rulers of the Low Countries, brought renewed attempts to penetrate the Baltic, whilst Hanse privileges in England were an obvious target for governments sensitive to merchant opinion and desirous of tapping native mercantile wealth. And now the response of the League, with troubles enough elsewhere, was feeble. By the 1560s it had lost its former predominance in the export of English cloths to north-east Germany. Moreover, the situation in the Baltic meant that more than ever it lacked such unity of purpose as it had once possessed, and encouraged individual towns to ensure their own particular interests as best they might in the face of adversity (see pp. 60ff.) In 1567 Hamburg, despite the opposition of its fellows, granted the English a ten-year concession. And when this lapsed they were received in Elbing, where English cloths soon accounted for most of the town's imports. In the course of England's war with Spain in the late 1500s Hanse ships were regularly arrested for trading to Iberia, and when at length such behaviour brought the expulsion of the English from Germany, they speedily retaliated by ejecting the League from England in 1598 (see pp. 64). But this merely demonstrated what had long been clear enough: that politically the Hanse was now negligible, that its onetime dominance of the Anglo-Baltic trade had disappeared and that England itself had valuable, if somewhat precarious, footholds in northern and eastern Europe – supplying, for instance, a good half of Königsberg's cloth in 1581. And individual Hanse towns, ignoring the strictures of the League, made what they could of their opportunities. Stade came to terms with the English in 1601; Hamburg, to its great benefit, in 1611 (see pp. 64–5).

Thus the German commercial monopoly in the north and east, and the privileges of the League elsewhere in Europe, had inevitably attracted the hostility of other merchants, and a hostility that had intensified as during the economic recession of the late Middle Ages the struggle for markets had become more bitter, and as rulers in western Europe saw opportunities to extend their authority and increase their revenues by backing native against alien traders. At the same time the Hanse faced in the Baltic all those now familiar forces causing and reflecting imperial decline: the resurgence in subject territories of native political power, the demand of such societies to enjoy for themselves the profits of economies stimulated by alien rule or exploitation, their resistance to the implementation or continuance of privileges previously conceded to those who had held them in political or economic subjugation and the costly expenditure by such powers on the attempted maintenance of their former dominance, so engendering further hostility and resistance. Nor was this all. German commercial expansion northwards and eastwards had coincided with, and indeed reflected, a more general German expansion (see pp. 40–3). But the outflow of German settlers, once so prolific, dried up in the later Middle Ages as German population, like that of most western Europe, declined, and just as Slav and Scandinavian national consciousness became forces to be reckoned with.

All this received dramatic expression in the defeat and destruction of the Teutonic Order by the now powerful kingdom of Poland. By 1466 West Prussia was Polish and the Grand Master himself a Polish vassal. A century later the remnants of the Order in Livonia, threatened by the Russians, likewise became Polish subjects (1561). These upheavals were not necessarily inimical to the interests of individual Hanseatic towns. Those of Prussia were freed from the commercial competition of the Order, and Danzig in particular was cherished by its new Slav suzerain. But the Order had been, when so inclined, able to defend the needs and aspirations of the League through much of northern Europe. Now, however, as aristocratic or monarchical authority was extended and as that of the Hanse declined, towns or groups of towns increasingly came to look, from necessity or discretion, to the power of some neighbouring state or prince in moments of crisis.

The emergence from obscurity of Russia in the late fifteenth century brought further disasters. Its seizure in 1478 of the more or less autonomous republic of Novgorod – to which indeed German trade continued into the 1600s – was of an impact more symbolic than real, since much of Russia's commerce had been, or could be, diverted into other channels (cf. pp. 46 and 49–50). But under Ivan IV the Russians moved onto the Baltic coast, taking Livonia and the Hanse towns of Dorpat and Narva (1558). Dorpat they destroyed, but Narva was deliberately developed as a Russian port to break the stranglehold the German cities of Livonia (Riga and Reval) had imposed on the Russia trade, and a port open not only to Dutch, English and other merchants but also, despite the protests of their fellows, to those of the Wendish towns of the League. And at almost the same time English seamen, optimistically seeking Cathay, arrived on the Russian White Sea coast to establish within a few years yet another route to Russia outside

Hanseatic control (see pp. 472, 474). And once again, whatever the alleged interests of the League, its members had no scruples about deserting or competing with their associates, and before long ships from Hamburg and Bremen were working to Archangel.

But despite some momentary spasms of alarm in the West and some futile talk of a crusade against Russia, the Baltic was not to come under Slav control. As German influence dwindled it slowly emerged that, politically at least, it was to be replaced by that of the Scandinavians. In the early 1400s the Danish kings renewed their efforts to loosen the grip of the Hanse on their possessions, encouraging Dutch, English and native merchants, and imposing in 1429 a toll on shipping passing through the Sound. Just as earlier such unwelcome independence soon led to trouble, and as earlier there was the same pattern of momentary and spectacular Danish success followed by humiliating failure. In 1435 the Wendish towns secured themselves exemption from the Sound dues and once again the Hanse intervened to re-establish its privileges and to regulate the royal succession. For a time the situation remained delicate rather than dangerous, with Danish energies largely devoted to attempting to hold together a precarious union of the three Scandinavian kingdoms. Events, however, took a turn for the worse in the early 1500s when the able but unbalanced Christian II, possessor of a substantial navy, increased the Sound tolls and entertained visions of a great Northern Trading Company which was to have the monopoly of the commerce between Europe and the Baltic lands. Fortunately for the Hanse he was simultaneously endeavouring to reassert his authority in Sweden, soon seeking and obtaining its freedom under Gustav Vasa. But for a time the League – or rather Lübeck – handled the situation in the old imperial style. A fleet went to Stockholm (1522) and arbitrated between Christian and Gustav. The following year it helped to drive Christian from his throne and two new kings, Gustav I of Sweden and Frederik I of Denmark, both obliged to renew and extend Hanseatic privileges, reigned by the grace of Lübeck. But here the city's good fortune ended. Under a Protestant burgomaster, Jurgen Wullenwever, who had come to office in the social and religious upheavals of the 1530s, it attempted to instal an anti-Dutch regime in Denmark, to break up the kingdom itself to further its own economic interests, to exclude the Dutch from the Baltic – of necessity without the support and indeed to the detriment of, the Prussian towns (see pp. 55, 58) – and then, when things went wrong, at least to bring Denmark and Sweden to heel. Such ambitions ended, a sure sign of the times, with the capture and execution of Wullenwever, with the old polity re-established in Lübeck by Habsburg pressure and with Denmark ruled by a candidate likewise amenable to their will who, as Christian III, agreed in 1544 to exempt their Dutch subjects from the Sound toll (see p. 378).

Lübeck then had to contend with Sweden, now independent, reorganized and reformed in every sense of the word under her erstwhile client, Gustav I Vasa (1523–60). He too had a navy, its nucleus provided by Lübeck herself, and he too aimed to foster his country's economic relations with western Europe and to dispense, wherever he might, with Hanse and German middlemen. Amongst other things this encouraged him and his successors to envisage, with increasing optimism, Swedish control of the Gulf of Finland and so of trade to and from Russia. Reval was in Swedish hands by 1561, and its commerce fostered whilst Narva, the centre of Lübeck's dealings with Russia, was soon tightly blockaded. With no support from the rest of the League – unwilling to disrupt relations with Sweden, let alone to trifle with the awesome Vasas – Lübeck, in alliance with Poland and Denmark, made strenuous but futile attempts to protect her interests. She turned out a sizable naval force which bombarded Reval (1569). But Swedish men-of-war made the voyage to Narva a risky undertaking – as not only vessels from Lübeck but those of the English as well discovered. The town itself was Swedish by 1581, and by 1617 the Swedes had sealed off Russia from the Baltic, and thus had the remaining Hanse commerce with Muscovy at their mercy.

Later in the century Lübeck was able to negotiate some agreement with the Vasas to trade to Narva and elsewhere, but it was clear that for all practical purposes the Hanse as such was now defunct.[5] Access to the Baltic was controlled, with varying degrees of success, by the kings of Denmark. Its littoral was disputed among the Slav and Scandinavian monarchies – with occasional interjections by German potentates – which had absorbed, or were absorbing, by one means or another, former Hanseatic towns. Individual cities could and did prosper, but whatever their wealth and resources it was others, as with Venice and Genoa in the Mediterranean, who determined the pattern of events (cf. pp. 132, 203). All this was plain enough, but as ever it was easier to diagnose the ill than to prescribe its remedy. There were in the late sixteenth century various schemes to reform and regenerate the League: to find it a protector, to endow it with a permanent and professional administrator, to raise a common fund. And in 1557 a ten-year alliance – which was to survive in attenuated form into the 1600s – setting out the duties of its members was agreed by sixty-three towns. But administrative zeal, respect for the past, and other noble and proper sentiments were no substitutes for power. The alliance included many towns of utter insignificance, and a large number of others that joined soon withdrew. And its authority, such as it was, was openly flouted. Hamburg and Elbing made their own commercial arrangements with England and Bremen prosperously survived explusion (1563), only to be unrepentantly re-admitted (1576) on the orders of the emperor (see p. 59).

The final collapse came in the seventeenth century. The Baltic became the theatre of a violent struggle for supremacy involving Denmark, Sweden and Poland. The domestic rivalries of the various Hanse towns were, as in the previous two centuries, aggravated by the commercial ambitions of the Dutch and the English, by the momentary aspirations of the Austrian Habsburgs to establish imperial and Catholic power in the largely Protestant north and by French distribution of subsidies to any who would divert Habsburg attentions from their activities elsewhere. In all this complex interplay of diplomacy and war the Hanse cities, such as they were – and only eleven attended the assembly of 1628 – were individually and collectively impotent.

Their general wish, as in any community dependent for its survival on the flow of commerce, was for neutrality. But, as had already happened with Venice, they were hopelessly overshadowed by the power of more extensive territorial units (cf. pp. 132ff.). The majority of the towns had become embedded in states with mutually conflicting interests, and none had the manpower or the maritime resources to resist on the one hand the lavishly backed ambitions of the royal dynasts of the north, or on the other Dutch and English naval force. True their potential, had there been any means of deploying it, was still impressive, and in 1627 there was a Habsburg plan to overthrow the Dutch with the aid of the League. Its ships, under Habsburg protection, were to handle the commerce between the Baltic and Iberia, to the exclusion of those of the rebellious Netherlands. This would destroy the wealth of the republic, prosperous on the northern carrying trade, and thereby its will to resist Spain (cf. pp. 378, 381). It was a scheme barely feasible in the face of Dutch maritime strength – which could endanger the well-being of those many Hanse merchants whose business was confined to the Baltic – and it foundered on the objections of the cities to militaristic and Catholic entanglements, and on their realistic appraisal of the power of the Scandinavian monarchies, and the dangers inherent in any resurgence of imperial authority in the north.

But such dreams were in any case shattered by a new wave of Swedish ambition. Since 1617 Gustav II Adolf had been engaged in vigorous and profitable empire-building at the expense of Poland. Riga, Livonia and Prussia (Danzig excepted) all came into his hands, and their commerce (including that of Danzig) was taxed for his benefit, producing, in a good year, 50 per cent of Sweden's total revenues. Then in 1630 the conquest of Germany was undertaken. Hanse cities were either appropriated (like Stralsund and Wismar), or tactfully expressed (as did Lübeck, Bremen and Hamburg) benevolent neutrality. When the war ended (1648) Sweden was firmly established on the North Sea at Stade, and on the south Baltic coast, with Stettin, Stralsund and Wismar all Swedish. Thus happily situated, the Vasas milked the entire Hanseatic trade, drawing at times sums equal to those the Danes were meanwhile taking from the Sound tolls. So the wheel had come full circle, with those cities which had once so freely and successfully exploited Scandinavia now themselves dominated and exploited by the Scandinavians. The last *Hansetage*, attended by representatives of only eight towns, met in Lübeck in 1669 and there closed its proceedings with the pious hope that better times would come.

Yet though the power and influence of the League vanished once its commercial monopoly, established by the Germans as pioneers in much of the north and east, collapsed, individual Hanseatic cities continued, economically at least, to flourish. Some, indeed, did remarkably well. The late 1500s saw Iberia at war with England till 1604 and with the Dutch till 1609, and then again from 1621 to 1648. Enterprising Germans could thus handle – and were encouraged by Spain to do so – that vital flow of food, munitions and naval stores from the Baltic to Iberia, otherwise largely monopolized

by the Dutch. At the same time those – which meant in fact the English and the Dutch –
who wished to continue, wars notwithstanding, their commerce with the Peninsula could
do so in partnership with Germans, or in vessels of real or nominal German ownership
(cf. pp. 381, 496). Hence from the 1570s Hanse ships – especially those of Protestant
Lübeck, Bremen, Danzig, Wismar and Hamburg – carried in imposing numbers timber
(much of it Norwegian), grain, metals and munitions (some of them English) to Catholic
Iberia to repair Habsburg deficiencies in victuals, weapons and tonnage aggravated by
grandiose imperial ambitions and commitments (cf. pp. 293, 343). In exchange the
northerners received both the products of Iberia itself (wines and fruits for instance)
and those of the Spanish and Portuguese oceanic empires (such as sugar, spices and that
silver necessary for their east-European commerce). Such operations had obvious
dangers. German ships were arrested or harried by English and Dutch privateers, to
avoid whose attentions they took to sailing by the storm-ridden route round the north of
Scotland and to the west of Ireland to the Peninsula. And there they were all too likely
to be arrested for naval service, which brought some of them north with the Armada of
1588, to whose retreating commanders their masters like as not suggested the return
home by the now familiar way of what in seamen's parlance was the backside of England
(cf. pp. 468–9). Nevertheless the trade prospered until well into the early 1600s, with
English men-of-war intercepting, or reporting, Hanse fleets sixty or so strong bound
for Iberia. Once there, moreover, they could engage in local interport commerce, just as
German merchants could undertake to victual Spain's African strongholds, whilst
occasional Hanse vessels worked to the Portuguese Atlantic islands and even to Brazil.
Others, meanwhile, with Dutch competition muted if not suppressed, pioneered a new
traffic by carrying grain from the thriving Danzig to a Mediterranean – Italy especially
– short of food (cf. pp. 48, 143, 379ff.). The passage was frequently made, or attempted,
direct, as was the case with a victim of the English, the *Prussian Maiden*, who with her
consorts had set out in armed convoy for Genoa. And there in 1592 there were twenty-
six craft from Hamburg alone, with other German ships recorded at roughly the same
date in Malaga, Valencia, Livorno, Venice, the Adriatic and Crete.

Under such stimuli the League's tonnage in 1600 – perhaps 1000 vessels totalling
100,000t – was 50 per cent up on its level a century before.[6] Lübeck itself did
particularly well. English prize courts heard of vast ships – allegedly of 1000t apiece –
especially built there in the late sixteenth century for the Spanish trade, and in 1595 it
had a fleet, still growing, of 250 vessels (18,000t). Even more successful was Hamburg,
linked by the Elbe to the economies of central and southern Germany and governed by
men of remarkable perspicacity. It came to terms with England in the early 1600s, and it
welcomed refugees so that in the late sixteenth century it was vitalized by an influx of
the skills and resources of those Flemish Calvinists who had left the now Spanish
Antwerp, and by those of Portuguese *marranos* (converted Jews) from the same city
whose commercial, religious and family affiliations stretched through most of the
known world (cf. pp. 59, 344 and 384). Along such channels a nominally German trade

could flow largely unhindered by the accidents of politics. And thus it was that in the first half of the seventeenth century Hamburg replaced Lübeck as the maritime centre of north Germany, and emerged as one of the greatest seaports in Europe. It became the essential link between the Baltic and southern Europe, saw its fleet double in size, and its ships penetrate on the one hand to the waters of Iceland and the White Sea, and on the other to those of the New World.

Nor was this Hanseatic prosperity overthrown until the resurgence of the Dutch in the mid-1600s, notwithstanding the chaos of the Thirty Years War after 1618, and its ultimate disruption of the Spanish trade. In the 1630s Rostock was exporting twice as much of her celebrated beer as half a century before, and there were still some 1200 sailings a year to and from Wismar. But clearly this was not the commerce of the heroic centuries. Most of the voyages from Baltic ports were short hauls within the Baltic itself, turning German seamen, like their Venetian contemporaries, into inshore sailors (cf. p. 149). True, the tonnage of the Hanse was still growing at the beginning of the seventeenth century, giving the League one of Europe's largest fleets (cf. pp. 64, 148, 496). But it was dwarfed, as was its rate of growth, by that of the Dutch whose vessels more and more dominated the carrying trade after 1550, whilst the Hanse could muster nothing of the fighting power of the bellicose English or Iberians (cf. pp. 469). So *c*. 1600 it was merely one of the participants, and one of decreasing importance, in a commerce and a general prosperity increasingly benefiting others. And not even the good fortunes of German ships were necessarily those of German owners. It was said of Hamburg in 1609 – admittedly by the far from admiring Lübeck – that most of its business was in foreign hands, and it would in fact appear that much of its tonnage was Dutch owned. Nor, significantly, did the Germans hold many of the new trades that they penetrated. They were soon excluded (in the early 1600s) by Spanish intransigence from the Americas, whilst their lack of manufactures to sell, and their involvements in Iberia, brought their retreat from the Mediterranean. Indeed their momentarily impressive participation in the traffic to Iberia and the Mediterranean waxed and waned in a rhythm determined by the presence or absence of Dutch competition. When the Dutch were fighting Spain, as they were until 1609, and from 1621 to 1648, the Hanse did remarkably well. But when Holland came to terms with Spain, and the Dutch were able to devote themselves wholeheartedly to business – not, of course, that this had by any means been neglected even in times of war – it was a very different story. Thus, whilst in 1600 the Lübeck shipowner Rotger von Dicke was heavily committed to the Iberian trade, with shares in four large vessels, after 1608 the family concentrated on much smaller fry – even down to 20t – clearly intended for purely local working. However, with the renewal of the Spanish-Dutch war in 1621 there was a brisk reversion to earlier interests, and between 1627 and 1641 the von Dickes and their associates were involved in the construction of fifteen big ships – including the 600t *Hercules* – almost certainly destined for the Spanish and Portuguese trades. Their behaviour was by no means unique, and doubtless this flexibility says much for German business acumen. But at the same time it reveals a complete and abject acceptance of Dutch commercial superiority (cf. pp. 379ff.).

III *The Hanseatic legacy*

Of all the early maritime empires that of the Hanse is the most elusive, its influence and achievement the most difficult to assess. There are doubts on such fundamental matters as its exact extent and the precise size of its membership. Its general organization remained remarkably inchoate, and, like its business techniques, remarkably rudimentary. Individual cities had their proper pride, and by the ships displayed on their seals – as at Lübeck, Wismar, Stralsund, Danzig, Elbing – showed where they considered their power and prosperity lay. But the League itself produced no theorists of dominion or empire, not even an apologist to explain or justify its existence. Perhaps this merely reflects the discretion of its later years, or more probably the insignificance and irrelevance of such things in the eyes of the association. Yet though the Hanse had no messianic imperial urge like that of the Iberians or other monarchical or aristocratic societies, no sense of its destiny to conquer and subdue the east, its towns and merchants nevertheless long shared a more modest and rational feeling of national unity and common purpose. The authority of the German emperors had been defunct in the north since at least the thirteenth century, but citizens of the towns of the League described themselves none the less in the proud and resonant style of 'merchants of the Roman empire of Germany'. Such sentiments sprang from the institutional links between the various cities, and from the common origin and closely knit interrelationship of their ruling families. The new urban foundations in the east in the twelfth and thirteenth centuries took in general either the customs – the civic laws – of Lübeck (as did Rostock and Stralsund) or of Magdeburg (as did Thorn). This basic heritage, and the fact that a number of towns, like Elbing, were quite literally colonized from Lübeck produced a feeling of affiliation, though no guarantee of undying mutual support and loyalty, and in part explains that respect so long accorded to Lübeck. And the relationship was strengthened by the fact that many of the new towns were settled, and for many years dominated, by families from Westphalia – from one small area, that is, of Europe. So, for example, the Warendorps, a dynasty influential in Lübeck from the twelfth to the sixteenth century, appeared also – and often in positions of power – in Danzig, Elbing, Visby, Riga and Dorpat.

Clearly, however, some sense of cohesion and unity of purpose do not constitute an empire. But by its regulation of the affairs of a variety of countries, and especially by its domination of those whose economies were of a relatively primitive nature, the Hanse, without military conquest or political annexation, established, exercised and maintained, generally by economic pressure, an authority which may fairly be defined as imperial. Scandinavia was the earliest and easiest victim. In Denmark the League engaged in that same sort of king-making for commercial advantage as did those equally imperial maritime powers, Venice and Genoa, in Byzantium (cf. pp. 92, 160). So, too, when in 1284 the king of Norway attempted to restrict the activities of German merchants within his realm, the Wendish cities, assisted by some of their fellows from the North Sea littoral, imposed a tight blockade. Long since unable to produce sufficient food to feed her population, and unable to survive without Hanseatic grain, Norway was forced to an abject surrender. She paid the Germans a handsome indemnity, conceded (1294) their freedom to trade in all ports south of Bergen, to use their own ships and to carry on business inland exempt from taxation. From such a promising hold the German grip quickly tightened. Germans displaced many local artisans in Bergen, and the town's overseas trade came largely into the hands of Lübeck merchants. The situation in Sweden was marginally better, but here again such was the demand for German skills and products that, with the encouragement of the Folkungar dynasty, Germans were soon paramount in towns, mining and commerce, and by the 1520s Lübeck could confidently expect to be given absolute control of the country's trade (see p. 61). Such, indeed, was the German impact that it has left a permanent memorial, a real colonial heritage, in the large number of German words and derivatives – roughly 30 per cent of the total – still current in the Swedish language.

Less overwhelming, but none the less remarkable, was the Hanse position in England. Here, too, their power sprang from their monopoly of goods – timber, wax, grain, Rhenish wine – in vigorous demand. And here, too, royal favour, in the form of commercial and fiscal privileges in exchange for loans to the first three Edwards, assisted them. So whilst from 1347 English merchants had to pay 1/2d on each undyed cloth they exported, and less fortunate foreigners 2/9d, the Hansards paid only 1/-. Such advantages they defended tenaciously, refusing to submit to a further *ad valorem* tax, and not surprisingly by the late Middle Ages they accounted for a substantial part of England's overseas trade (cf. pp. 50, 59). The Hanse, therefore, was an imperial power not only in the sense that it subjugated, as in Scandinavia, states or economies to its needs, but also in that in lands to which its members penetrated it expected, as did other commercial empires, some measure of exemption from the normal operation of local law and custom, and the right to regulate its own affairs (cf. pp. 116, 183, 410). In various strategic centres the Germans established that they could form communities, hold assemblies and elect their own officers. The Steelyard in London is a familiar instance of this sort of concession, the equivalent of the colonial factories of the contemporary Italians and Portuguese, or the European treaty ports in Asia in more recent times, and an eloquent indication of Hanseatic strength. It was a walled enclave, initially leased by the Germans but eventually (1474) – as was also the case with their *kontor* in Bergen – recognized as their own private property. Here, by the late 1400s, they annually chose from among themselves an alderman who headed the governing council of their community, and there was in existence an organization capable of looking after Hanse interests in England, and of settling disputes between Germans and natives. All these great *kontors* – London, Novgorod, Bergen – were more or less autonomous, excluding local officials, and with courts empowered to determine actions between their members, and enabled to fine or imprison offenders, and indeed in Novgorod to sentence them to mutilation or death. And these were not the only manifestations of Hanse power, for along the littorals of northern Europe from Iberia to Norway there stretched a chain of Hanseatic factories – seven in England alone – smaller than, but juridically indistinguishable from, the *kontors*. In the west these trading bases were usually subject to a *kontor*, whilst elsewhere they looked to the town from which the majority of their merchants came, and some of the more important, like Oslo in Norway, or Boston in England, controlled, as did the *kontors*, their own territorial enclaves. From such strongholds the League sought and was generally able to secure, its maximum advantage. It everywhere demanded and obtained fiscal exemptions or favours, it required the closest definition of whatever its merchants were obliged to pay and it extracted assurances that these amounts would not be increased. It demanded that if a Hansard, and even one of illegitimate birth, died abroad his property should go, not, as was customary, to the local lord or sovereign, but to his own heirs. And it ensured that the sins of individual Hanseatic merchants in foreign parts could not be visited on the association as a whole, nor on the fellow citizens of the delinquent's home town. Such liberties incurred, hardly surprisingly, much odium and became increasingly difficult to maintain. But in acquiring them, and in imposing its will in other ways on a whole range of authorities, the Hanse had established northern Europe's first and most rigorously informal empire.

Nor was this by any means the full extent, or the most significant part, of its achievements. Its empire was an aspect, and a major aspect, of that German expansion in the north and east in the Middle Ages whose profound political and economic consequences – the massive increase in the territorial extent of Germany, the opening up of vast agricultural reserves, the founding, in the colonial lands, of powerful new states, the establishment there of a free peasantry of German origins, the frequent improvement in the lot of that of native stock – we have already noticed (cf. pp. 42ff.). To these achievements of princes and peasants, German merchants added the urbanization of the Baltic littoral and much of its hinterland, and an alteration in the whole nature and pattern of northern, and indeed of European, trade, changes more radical than those effected by the voyages of the Scandinavians, Italians and Iberians. The north and east were not without towns before the arrival of the Germans. Settlements, sometimes attracting cosmopolitan merchant communities, are known to have existed in Prussia (Truso), Mecklenburg, Pomerania, Scandinavia and Poland, where possibly half the medieval towns had pre-Germanic origins. A handful, such as Jumna (Wollin) were involved in a considerable and wide-ranging, long-distance trade (cf. pp. 30–1). But despite such stirrings, largely inspired by the Scandinavians, the economy of eastern Europe as a whole (the modern Bohemia, south-west Russia, Poland and the Baltic littoral) remained, *c*. 900–1200, primitive, its agriculture rudimentary, and most of its towns small agglomerations of craftsmen and petty traders sited by, and serving the needs of, fortified princely residences. And if the economic climate was not conducive to rapid and luxuriant growth, there was the further and related disability of the lack of any law protecting the business, interests and persons of merchants.

After two centuries of German endeavour the picture was very different. The north and east were studded with scores of towns and cities, not all names to conjure with, but of undoubted power and importance. Such a transformation might have come to pass in the fullness of time and without German intervention. But it seems unlikely, and it is clear that *c.* 1200 Slav and Scandinavian lords considered that the Germans had something to offer in terms of experience, technical skill and wealth that native wit and resources could not approach, and were prepared to run considerable risks to attract them. The Hanse then, or more precisely the Germans, may not in the strictest terms have created town life in northern and eastern Europe. But for all practical purposes, by their new foundations, by their revitalization of those already in existence, by their frequent domination of their government, and by the general stimulus of their commerce, they were responsible for the urbanization of the Baltic littoral and its hinterland in the same way that the Iberians were responsible for that of South America. And it was an urbanization of much the same order of magnitude, undertaken for comparable reasons, effected by much the same methods and producing very similar results. Many of the new towns became, as did some of those in the Americas, major entrepôts, just as many were in the same way centres, however modest, of culture and civilization. And like the Spanish cities of the Americas, those of the Germans on the Baltic were privileged communities ethnically distinct from the populations amongst which they were established. In the countryside of the Baltic littoral native peoples survived, and in many cases predominated, as they did in the hinterland. In the towns, however, with one or two exceptions, they were, like the Indians in the Americas, of no consequence, even though until the mid-fourteenth century Slavs were, by German custom, eligible for citizenship. But whatever freedoms they may have supposedly possessed were curbed at the onset of the economic recession of the later Middle Ages, and in view of the ominous indications of the growth of Slav power. But it was in any case Germans who in one way or another – by their wealth, their skills and usually by their sheer numbers – controlled the towns, as did the Spaniards those of the Americas. Between the Elbe and the Oder, and in Pomerania, the Slav urban population was insignificant by the fifteenth century. Further east, 90 per cent of that of Danzig and 70 or 80 per cent of that of Riga were German in the 1300s, and even at the very extremities of German expansion there was no doubt as to who was master. At Reval in the early 1500s only about 30 per cent of the inhabitants were German, but the ruling patriciate was exclusively so, whilst the lower orders were overwhelmingly Slav.

Of this German hegemony there is no more eloquent testimony than the towns themselves. Along the Baltic, and indeed throughout the whole region from Bremen to Riga, on the Lower Elbe, and in Brandenburg and Silesia, the Germans built towns and cities in a style as distinctly unique as were those of Spanish colonial America or imperial British India. They are conservative, austere and solid – the whole impression heightened by the almost exclusive use of brick in their construction – the very epitome of those characteristics peculiarly Hanseatic.[7] They are usually laid out on that chessboard plan found in other new towns of the Middle Ages, and introduced into the Americas by the Spaniards (see p. 329). At the centre is the square or market place, flanked by the town hall – the dominant secular building – increasingly imposing with the passage of time, and with municipal granaries and various other impressive edifices for business and pleasure added later. But here, architecturally at least, the parallel ends. Unlike those of the Americas, Hanse cities are walled, and their crowning glory is their merchants' churches. In the early centuries these were built in a style of French inspiration, but transmuted to a characteristic severity – little ornament, no rose windows – only in part imposed by the exigencies of working in brick. And typically the favoured style in the maritime cities in the late Middle Ages – as with the great Danzig church (1340–1502) – was a revival of one of romanesque origin: three naves of equal height, usually covered by one roof, no flying buttresses and a single lofty and imposing tower serving as a beacon for seamen.

But German power and commerce were to effect considerably more than the urbanization and adornment of a formerly remote and undeveloped part of the world. In Scandinavia, as we have seen, Germans were of paramount importance in the founding and organization of towns, and in Sweden in the exploitation of the country's mineral wealth, bringing, it has been argued, to those in contact with them a wider outlook on matters of state than that of the ordinary peasant. Meanwhile Holstein and Mecklenburg grew rich on the production of commodities (grain, livestock, beer) needed, or exported by, neighbouring Hanse entrepôts, their wealth, the ravages of wars notwithstanding, still recalled in the unmistakably Hanseatic gateways, churches, towers and walls of dozens of small towns. So also the undoubted development of Poland, Bohemia and Hungary in the 1200s and 1300s – their more intensive agriculture, the emergence of a seigneurial regime, its customs based on those of the Germans – clearly owed much to a relatively small number of German settlers. And in that area of eastern Europe where economic change was most apparent in the high Middle Ages – the region stretching from the Czech plateau to Transylvania, and embracing Silesia and Little Poland in the north, and upper Hungary in the south – the German presence was of prime importance. In Bohemia, until the Hussite revolt changed things, the great landowners and the urban patriciate were generally of German extraction. It was German miners, operating under German mining law, who opened up the rich Czech resources in silver, gold and copper, and to such effect that in the thirteenth and fourteenth centuries the Czechs were largely paying for their western textiles and assorted luxuries with precious metals, whilst by the late Middle Ages Hanseatic merchants from Prussia were handling Hungarian and Ruthenian copper and silver, and using bullion to buy Russian furs in Novgorod. Then again, the economies of Silesia and Little Poland were stimulated by, amongst other things, the flow of traffic along those great trans-European trade routes which crossed their territories, linking the west with the Italian colonies on the Black Sea, and the Baltic with Bohemia, Hungary and southern Europe. Through these channels Hanseatic cloth reached Hungary and the east. By the 1300s merchants from Thorn were trading in Cracow, the major outlet for the copper of Nowy Sacz, Gelnica and Smolnik. And until the route was disrupted by the Mongol invasions, and energies diverted to a more profitable commerce with the west, other Hansards were active in Lvow selling cloth, amber and herring to the Venetians and Genoese from the Black Sea in exchange for spices and silk.

It was similarly German influence that in the late Middle Ages affected the more primitive economies of Central Poland, Lithuania and western Russia. As was to happen with other European colonial regimes in Asia and the Americas, they were linked to an external demand more insistent and exclusive, and introduced to more sophisticated modes of payment or exchange (cf. pp. 283, 327). Hanse purchases of forest products and furs were often paid for in silver, so put into circulation with apparently beneficial effects in Poland and Lithuania in the fifteenth and sixteenth centuries. Likewise in Russia, first around Novgorod in the 1400s, and then over a wider area, the influx of money earned by sales to the Hanse (or its competitors) enabled peasants to pay some of their dues in cash. Further west Hanseatic merchants, emulating the Teutonic Order, took deliberate and successful measures to ensure a flow of grain and timber to the Baltic coast for export, advancing, for example, as Europeans were later to do in Asia, credits which producers were obliged to repay in kind (cf. p. 399). Before long the economies of Central Poland, the Ukraine and – to a lesser extent – of Lithuania and Livonia were profoundly influenced by these pressures. There emerged in the 1500s large-scale aristocratic estates, worked by serf labour and geared, in true colonial style, to the production of a limited number of cash crops. This certainly brought prosperity to the big landowners and to the merchants handling the trade. But such was the aristocratic drive for grain in sixteenth-century Poland as to depress the condition of the peasantry, often ruined by the imposition of the heavier labour services that an agriculture of this nature and order demanded. So peasant liberty and peasant purchasing power were destroyed, and thereby the market for many of the products of native industry. And in Poland it became considered aristocratic policy – explicit in an (unenforced) act of 1565 – to obtain manufactured goods from abroad, and without the intervention of native merchants. That there should eventually have appeared in eastern Europe societies and economies closely resembling those of the contemporary Iberian Americas was not the sole responsibility of German merchants and German cities. The demands and activities of the Dutch and the English from the fifteenth century onwards, and the subsequent impact of the Thirty Years War, all intensified these developments. Nor was eastern industry totally extinguished, with the manufacture of linens flourishing in Bohemia, Saxony and Silesia in the 1500s. Nevertheless it was the Hanse that had linked the resources of the east to the demands of Europe, so setting in train this whole process of change. And it is a sad irony that the German presence in the east, initially so strongly associated with freedom and opportunity, and benefiting the humble, migrant and native alike, should in the end have been instrumental in reducing many to a condition indistinguishable from slavery.

Of the enormous economic impact of the Hanse in the north and east of Europe there can, then, be little doubt. Nor, indeed, were these its limits, for it revolutionized, after roughly 1300, the whole nature and pattern of much of Europe's trade. Norway, once self-sufficient, or supplied from England, came to depend on Baltic grain, as did Flanders which had previously drawn on the resources of northern France and the upper Rhine. Throughout the west the timber and forest products of Scandinavia and southern Germany were replaced by those of the Baltic, which supplied the shipbuilding materials without which the maritime activity of much of Europe from the late fourteenth century could scarcely have been maintained, just as it provided the food without which many of the inhabitants of western Europe could hardly have survived. And in the markets of a more accessible and more prosperous east there emerged an extensive and vital outlet for the textiles of a succession of western manufacturers – the Flemings, the Dutch and the English. True, the Baltic and its littoral, and the routes linking their various peoples both with one another and with a wider world were known and used in pre-Germanic days (see pp. 28–31). But what was of such radical significance was the scale of German migration, the abundance of German resources and the quality of German skills. Their agriculture increased the rich potential of the east, their merchants, from towns and cities of a size and sophistication new to the region, exploited it and their seamen, with vessels capable of moving bulk cargoes, ensured its products reached the west in quantity.

Yet no other empire, whether equally or even more wholeheartedly devoted to the pursuit of profit, was to show such little curiosity about the countries in which it traded or ruled as did, its achievements notwithstanding, the Hanse. Of whatever they may have seen of primitive Russian or Scandinavian society its merchants left no account. The earliest descriptions come from other sources, and there are no Hanseatic equivalents to the great Iberian narratives, or – a juster comparison – to the geographical writings of the medieval Italian merchants and travellers. In part this reflects the character and nature of Hanseatic commerce, in part the quality of Hanse civilization. The early established and long-maintained monopoly of the League, and its intense conservatism, left its merchants with no need or desire to explore and describe remote lands. Nor, indeed, unlike the Iberians, Italians and Scandinavians were they explorers, since they penetrated Russia along routes already known, just as they followed the English to Iceland. And once established their policy was to avoid, as far as possible, undue familiarity and contact with the natives – intermarriage, for example, was discouraged – so as to escape any entanglement in local affairs, or the concession of any advantage to non-Hansards. Instead they aimed to live and trade under their own privileges in what, in some instances, were virtually self-contained fortresses. Thus their Novgorod *kontor* consisted of commercial and domestic premises enclosed within defensive walls. Russians were admitted to these precincts only during the day and at nightfall after their withdrawal, the gates were barred against them. Nor did this merely reflect some well-found Hanseatic appreciation of the limits of Slavonic goodwill, for even in the Netherlands there were in the mid-1500s schemes to reorganize in Antwerp, and in traditional ways, the large number of merchants who, having foresaken Bruges, were dwelling in unwholesome commercial and personal association with the locals. Married men were to withdraw with their wives and families to some Hanseatic town. The remaining bachelors were to live and do business in time-honoured style in a vast, expensive and specially constructed edifice, containing over a hundred bedrooms, together with dormitories, refectories, cellars and shops. Whatever the supposed commercial advantages of such a system, it was hardly calculated to inspire a lively interest in the countries and societies in which Hanse merchants traded. And in any case as men whose prime concern was with their business, and as monopolists actual or potential, they had no incentive or occasion to describe for the possible benefit of others the opportunities they encountered.

Moreover, such interest and curiosity presuppose that the agents of a conquering or colonizing power are the products of a vigorous civilization, and one that accepts (as in Scandinavia or Iberia) that heroic endeavour is worth undertaking and recording, or that (as in Italy or Iberia) the testimony of personal experience is, for some reason, of particular value (cf. pp. 33ff.). But these were not the assumptions of Hanseatic civilization. The increasing volume and complexity of northern trade had indeed produced, by the fourteenth century, a commerce in which account and letter books were known, and in which some merchants directed their enterprises from home by precise and factual letters addressed to agents or factors in distant parts, who replied in similar style. And to ensure that the requisite skills should be available the city fathers of Lübeck established, as early as 1300, four elementary schools to which they appointed the masters – notwithstanding the opposition of the cathedral chapter, which here as elsewhere controlled instruction – and so presumably provided an education in some degree determined by the demands of utility rather than by current clerical opinion.

But the simple ability to amass, and, should it be desirable, to disseminate useful information – and by the late 1400s almost all the major German Baltic cities had printing presses – is not in itself a basis for the description or appreciation of alien peoples and customs. Economic restraints aside, the Hanse cities lacked the powerful impulse that Antiquity gave to such interests in those of the Mediterranean, just as they lacked the soldiers and missionaries elsewhere eager to narrate their victories and tribulations (cf. p. 215). And when, in the early 1500s those humanist influences, which explain so much of the quality of Italian and Iberian depiction and evaluation of the unfamiliar, reached the Baltic, the opportunity had gone for the Hanse (cf. pp. 60ff.

and 75). Instead the popular culture of its cities produced in the late Middle Ages mystery plays of south German inspiration, whilst their patricians did their best to emulate the practices and tastes of the potent aristocratic world of the north. So, in the late medieval centuries, the paraphernalia of chivalry was much in evidence. Towns erected statues to the nine worthies – that incongrous band of heroes recruited from scripture, history and Antiquity, jousts were organized, societies of local notables met in their courts of king Arthur, and burgesses christened their children with names (Gunter, Paris) from legend and romance. There was, that is, little that could be defined as a Hanseatic culture – the style of the cities themselves apart – nor, given the intensity of these preoccupations, a culture that was sensitive or receptive. Hanse merchants were, it is true, patrons of artists. But though some of these, like Master Francke or Bertram of Minden (*c.* 1340–1415) were born or worked in Hanse cities, their woodcarving stemmed from a wider north German tradition, and their painting was much influenced by that of Flanders and Burgundy. And not even the carvings, sculptures and paintings of the much travelled Lübeck master, Bernt Notke (*c.* 1440–1509) scattered through the towns and churches of the League and of Scandinavia and Finland alike, reflected any German experience of strange and distant lands. A single, early and magnificent exception is the carving offered by the Stralsund Novgorod traders to the church of St Nicholas in the fourteenth century, with its fine portrayal of Russian hunters (see p. 50). But for the rest, there is no Hanse art or literature drawing inspiration, or even themes, from German travels among, or contact with, other peoples. There is no adequate record of Hanse achievement – not surprisingly since there seems to have been no sense of any such achievement, and no feeling, as with the Norse, of adventure and heroic endeavour, or as with the Iberians, of the fulfilment of some divinely appointed destiny. Even in the days of incipient German nationalism in the early 1500s there was no concern in the rest of Germany with what had been accomplished in the east. True, there was some pragmatic interest, by no means peculiarly Hanseatic, in the languages of peoples encountered, and in the early 1600s a Lübeck merchant, Tönnies Fonne, published for the benefit of fellow traders a manual of spoken Russian, now of considerable linguistic value (cf. pp. 212, 280–1). And like other merchants and seamen, those of the Hanse produced, when occasion demanded, collections of concise and accurate descriptions of places, events and natural phenomena (see pp. 16, 216, 280). The compilations of the fifteenth-century shipowner Caspar Weinrich are full of curious information about the maritime history of Danzig, whilst there appeared in the late 1400s a German volume of sailing directions adding to earlier Flemish material the fruits of an experience acquired by Hanse ships working in waters from Cadiz to the Gulf of Finland. But beyond this Hanseatic expansion resulted only in the production of a handful of town chronicles, of which the most extensive and useful are those of Lübeck, largely written, characteristically enough however, by clerics.

As in other empires, the spread of the language of the colonizing power accompanied the spread of its people and authority. Quite apart from the massive dissemination of German in the north and east by aristocratic and peasant settlement, the language of north Germany[8] – or more precisely of Lower Saxony – was carried as far as Narva by the Hanse and for a time into the towns of Poland, Denmark and Sweden. And the commercial and political pre-eminence of Lübeck meant that its own particular Low German dialect appeared (as did that of Magdeburg) wherever its law and customs were established. From the mid-fourteenth century onwards it was used both to record the decisions of the League's assembly and in a great deal of its diplomatic correspondence. But it was not to become, like Spanish, Portuguese or English, an ineradicable language of empire, for by the 1500s it was in retreat before the dialect of south Germany – that of the Protestant church and of such triumphal centres of commerce as Nürnburg and Augsburg.

Even if the League was not a powerful cultural force in itself it was, all the same, influential in the transmission to the north and east of the culture of western Europe. In this it was admittedly by no means the only agent, nor the most important, with, for example, sixteenth-century Renaissance fashions spread by the courts of the Vasas in Sweden, and the Jagellons in Poland. But in the medieval centuries it was through the Hanse cities that the styles of the ecclesiastical architecture of Westphalia and the Rhineland reached Scandinavia, just as in the 1400s some 300 German painted or carved panels were exported from Lübeck alone to Finland, Scandinavia and other parts of the Baltic. More important still was that the League, with its *kontor* in Bruges, was in close contact with the distinguished civilization of Burgundy and Flanders. It was in the Low Countries at the end of the Middle Ages that Hanse magnates, emulating the practice of high society there, had their portraits painted by south German or Flemish masters – Mathias Mulich of Lübeck by James of Utrecht, Georg Giese of Danzig by Hans Holbein (1532). And it was along the Bruges-Lübeck axis that there travelled to the north and the east the current tastes of Burgundian chivalry, such as translations of French and Flemish poetry. Then from Lübeck and Reval a series of German and Italian craftsmen, artists and doctors went to work in Russia in the fifteenth and sixteenth centuries, whilst in the 1600s painters, and gold- and silversmiths from Hamburg, reached the Muscovite empire through Archangel. Nor were such influences confined to matters of taste and fashion. The doctrines of the Protestant reformer Martin Luther were established, often to the accompaniment of violent political and social upheaval, in many Hanseatic towns in the early 1500s. From these they penetrated along familiar commercial routes, possibly to England, and certainly to Sweden, where Hanse traders were responsible for their introduction into Stockholm as early as 1521.

In more mundane matters the League had either no skills to transmit, or no desire to see such as it had in more general use. So in the development of business and financial practice it played no comparable role to that of the Italians or the Dutch (cf. p. 428ff.). Its commercial methods were in general primitive and its merchants by and large resolutely opposed, in its later years, to any innovation. They were indeed keeping written financial records by the fourteenth century, but of the crudest nature with debit or credit items simply crossed out when paid. Nor was the practice, such as it was, sufficiently widespread to encourage, as in Italy, the production of manuals of instruction, neither did the Germans, any more than other northern merchants, employ Italian-style double-entry book-keeping before the sixteenth century. As elsewhere partnerships were common, but again there was little to approach the size and nature of an Italian business firm – a more or less permanent institution with headquarters, branch offices, staff – until the appearance of the Loitz of Stettin in the 1500s. The one considerable exception was the Teutonic Order, active until the sixteenth century and, like the religious Orders in Iberian Asia and America, free from inhibitions as to engaging in trade, in which it employed a substantial capital and an elaborate organization. For the rest, however, the Hanse had no banking houses before the 1400s – and then only momentarily – no organized money market, and no insurance until the 1500s. Instead there was from the fourteenth century a resolute hostility to the use of credit – previously widespread – and the vigorous advocacy of trade by simple barter. In part this reflects that almost neurotic conservatism of the Hanse, and a conservatism that became more intense the more the League's monopoly was challenged and the stronger its desire to exclude competitors by any means. But it also shows how primitive much of the world with which the Hanse traded remained. Certainly purchases were made with coin or bullion in the north and east, and techniques of transmitting money and the use of letters of exchange were known. But the League faced the perennial problem of how to deal with a rudimentary economy, and it was the merchants of the towns whose interests lay in Russia who, like other Muscovy traders after them, opposed the granting of credit to natives because of the difficulties all too likely to ensue when the day of reckoning arrived.

Equally unremarkable, in comparison with most others, was the Hanse record in seamanship. Its vessels navigated in the medieval centuries by dead-reckoning (cf. p. 206), without charts – though in 1400 the Teutonic Order had a map of the Baltic – and by regular use of the sounding line (see pp. 15, 18). Nor, given that they were largely working in shallow European waters, had they much reason to do otherwise. In the seas of the northwest of the continent banks of sand, silt and shingle are constantly formed, shaped and reshaped by fast running tides and the flow of rivers, whilst tidal ranges (the difference between high and low water) are great, not to say in places astonishing. It was therefore vital that a seaman should know by sounding how much water he had under him, and the nature and lie of its bottom. True, the Hanse was by no means impervious to change. It soon took up the compass, with which, along with lodestones, its craft were equipped in the late Middle Ages – the League itself employed compass-makers as early as 1394 – and the German sailing directions of the fifteenth century give compass courses for the North Sea and the Baltic (see p. 18). But no more than in the techniques of art or business is there anything of specifically Hanseatic inspiration in all this.

Thus the League displayed most of the familiar features of empire – the control and exploitation of alien lands and the establishment there of the people, language, institutions and civilization of the metropolitan society. Yet characteristically the civilization it transmitted was not its own. And characteristically the profits its merchants made and the fortunes they accumulated were relatively modest. In its heyday the Portuguese trade to Asia could bring – though not always – clear gains as high as 2000 per cent (see p. 239). In the Baltic *c.* 1400 the average net profit was 15–25 per cent (with the chance of 60 per cent on herring), whilst 200 years later 14 per cent profit could be got on wax and 43 per cent on rye. And whilst the volume of these northern trades far outstripped that of the Iberian oceanic commerce a Hanse plutocrat of *c.* 1500 could muster roughly only 10 per cent of the capital of such global financiers and entrepreneurs as the Welsers and Fuggers of south Germany.

All the same the Hanse, whatever its technological, cultural and commercial shortcomings, produced, as did every other maritime empire, a ship peculiarly its own, and upon whose excellence its fortunes in large measure rested. This was its bulk-carrier, the cog, which to start with drove the lighter craft of the Scandinavians from the waters of the north (cf. p. 24). Its origins and early evolution are obscure. That it was of Norse ancestry seems unlikely, given the characteristics of Scandinavian vessels, though certainly some of the first Hanse ships show Scandinavian influences – prominent bow and stern posts, animal decorations. Nor is it very likely that it was of unsullied Germanic descent, produced to meet pressing needs with such urgency that contemporary building techniques had to be ignored or rejected, and ships put together in the same way as houses were built in Saxony. Most likely it was developed from some Flemish prototype by artisans working in a craft as avidly eclectic and imitative as the modern car industry. Flemish cogs, so described, were known in the Low Countries in the mid-twelfth century, and well before this the Frisians appear to have used large ships in their Baltic trade, where at Birka there was a 'cog haven' (*Kugghamn*) (cf. pp. 28ff.). Moreover, many of the earliest German colonists in the east were in fact Flemings, and in the seaports of the Baltic the usual term for a shipyard was the Flemish word *lastadie*. Like as not then the cog either came into the Baltic with the Flemings, or was familiar to the Germans in the Low Countries, so that when a large ship was needed they had an obvious exemplar to hand. But that it was modified in some unascertainable way seems clear enough. Possibly the demand for tonnage was such *c.* 1200 that hastily recruited and inexperienced builders, endeavouring to produce rapidly large numbers of craft of considerable size, attempted, without much success, to apply ordinary domestic carpentry to shipbuilding – merely nailing, for instance, planking to the outer faces of stem and stern posts rather than letting them in.

But whatever its precise ancestry it was as the ship of the Hanse that the cog was to be known, and even as early as 1197 its distinctive features off Beirut told Christian prisoners in the Holy Land of the arrival of German help. By contemporary standards it was, especially in its final form, a sizable vessel, commonly over 200t by the mid-1300s, and with an overall length (for a ship of 150t) of 29m, a beam of 7m, and drawing some

Fig. 4   Hanse cog, *c.* 1350, reconstructed from representations on the seals of Elbing and Stralsund and from remains found at Bremen. The reefpoints on the sail are debatable.

3m.[9] It thus differed radically from both the ungainly lines of the 'round ship', with its curved keel, and from the grace of the Viking craft (cf. pp. 18–21). Carrying capacity apart, it had a straight stem and stern (instead of the handsome curves of the Norse), a flat bottom (again suggesting a Flemish origin) and a straight keel which was to become so prominent with the passage of time that by the early 1500s a big German ship aground would fall over. Despite castles of increasing elaborateness at bow and stern the hull was thoroughly practical: it sat well down in the water, had plenty of freeboard,[10] was decked and had a covered cargo hold. The cog was rigged with a single mast set amidships, carrying one large square sail whose area could be increased by bonnets tacked along its foot. A sprit projecting over the bow – which first appears in the 1200s – carried rigging that enabled the yard and sail to be trimmed to various angles to the hull, allowing the ship to sail across the wind and if need be to attempt, like those of the Scandinavians, to beat against it (cf. pp. 19–20). And she was controlled, from the mid-thirteenth century, not by a steering oar – which would have been of unmanageable proportions – but, like other large northern vessels, by a rudder hung on the sternpost and turned by a tiller.

In build the cog was totally different from her Scandinavian predecessors. In these the skin – the planking of the hull – was assembled first and the ribs inserted later. But in the cog, because of her size, such methods were not possible, and the frames were erected first and the planks then secured to them, overlapping in clinker fashion (cf. p. 19). Possibly in the first innocent and experimental days it was usual to put the top plank on first, giving a sequence in which the lower plank overlapped the upper – the reverse, that is, of Scandinavian and modern practice. Be this as it may – and the evidence is doubtful – the techniques of cog building were not in themselves revolutionary. Building on frames was well and widely established, and by the thirteenth century there are representations of ships in which the heads of horizontal cross beams can be seen protruding through their sides. Nevertheless the cog herself was a revolutionary vessel. It soon became difficult, and eventually impossible, to find timbers of sufficient strength for masts of the size demanded, and by 1200 they were being made from two pieces fastened together. Moreover, because of her un-precedented bulk and depth, a cog could only work to and from deepwater harbours, and not, like Scandinavian craft, off open beaches (cf. pp. 19ff.). So her very appearance marks an advance towards a maritime commerce conducted on a regular basis through a limited number of clearly defined entrepôts. Then again, with her dimensions she could only practicably and economically be propelled by sail and not, with a consequent saving in manpower, by oars. Furthermore because of her depth – of an order new to northern Europe – the cog had a much better grip on the water than the light, shallow-draught Scandinavian craft. Before, or across, the wind these could travel at great speed, with some part of the fore-end of the hull lifting clear of the sea. When beating to windward, however, because of their lack of hold on the water, they would tend to drift sideways downwind. This potentially fatal weakness is less pronounced in deeper hulls which have, moreover, the considerable advantage of making better progress when heading into a rough sea, their deep bows cutting the waves and the momentum of their bulk carrying them along. The shallow-draught vessel, on the other hand, whatever its other excellences, quite literally bangs its way to windward, flinging itself onto the crest or side of a wave, and bringing up short and spectacularly in a cloud of spray with a jolt which may start the planking or bring down the mast. The advantage of momentum is particularly important when changing tacks. In anything of a sea the lighter hull is liable to lose speed in the act of turning, even – embarrassingly and perhaps dangerously – to stop altogether, and needs the use of oars to get it round. But the heavier and deeper vessel, provided it has sufficient initial momentum, will complete the turn – in its own good time – with the wind out of its sail (cf. pp. 20–1).

So with the cog there came enormous technological and economic gains: a seaworthy ship, tolerably manoeuvrable by contemporary standards, capable of lifting cargoes of unprecedented volume for the north, and sparing in manpower – with obvious saving of costs for owners – since it used no oarsmen. And with its high freeboard and its castles it was a vessel as easily defensible against low-set craft, such as those of the Vikings, as were its Mediterranean successors against the galley, whilst its fighting power was further enhanced by the League's practice of sailing its ships in convoy (cf. pp. 147, 149–50). These merits were widely and quickly appreciated. There were cogs in the Mediterranean by the early 1300s of Genoese, Venetian and Catalan build or ownership. And whereas (galleys apart) southern sailing craft of any size had formerly been two or three-masted, lateen-rigged and controlled by twin steering oars – one either side of the hull – there was now a rapid change to the more angular lines, single mast, square sail and stern rudder of the cog. Eventually these peculiarly northern lines and features underwent further and important modification in southern hands to produce, in the late 1300s, the carrack, which in its turn was taken up and employed all over Europe, and was to be the first big ocean-going sailing ship (see pp. 146, 194).

But the development of the cog did not mark the end of the inventiveness of Hanse builders, and in the fifteenth century they were constructing vessels, known by the unflattering name of hulks, of even more generous proportions than those of the cog which they soon replaced. Once again the pedigree is uncertain, and the ancestor of the hulk has been variously identified as a primitive, banana-shaped planked vessel without stem or sternposts, or more convincingly as a small, full and flat-bottomed craft. Then, either to reduce the high labour costs of the fifteenth century by working a bigger ship with a proportionately smaller crew, or to meet the demands of the movement of cargoes of salt, timber and Prussian grain, such features were fused with those of the cog to give a new and even more capacious (500t and above) bulk-carrier. It was rigged, to start with, like the cog, and had its familiar straight keel and straight or slightly angled stem, but was larger and beamier – big-bellied, as nautical jargon crudely but graphically puts it. The hulk, which remained into the 1600s the distinctive ship of the Hanse, as vast as she was slow by contemporary standards, was the last of the League's contributions to ship-design and construction. Yet even if by *c.* 1500 its shipwrights had nothing new of their own to offer they were – up to a point – prepared to accept modifications and techniques developed elsewhere. In the 1400s small masts were added at the bow and stern of big ships (cf. p. 194). Carvel building in Mediterranean style, with planks set edge to edge instead of overlapping, made its appearance, and in the late fifteenth century large (400t or more) three-masted *krawels*, deriving from Iberian prototypes, were being constructed in the Baltic (cf. pp. 262–3). So, too, before the end of the following century Dutch-style *fluits* were owned, and probably being built, in Lübeck.[11]

Indeed throughout the late Middle Ages and well into the 1500s German ships continued to be widely and highly regarded for their excellence in war and peace alike. Whatever the rest of the Hanse might have to say, Danzig built extensively for

Fig. 5   Hanse hulk, *c.* 1400, reconstructed fairly freely from the ship depicted on the seal of Danzig.

foreigners – English, Dutch, Italians. Gustav Vasa of Sweden bought the nucleus of his navy from Lübeck, whilst that of Henry VIII of England was reinforced with ships from German yards, or built in England on German lines, and the *Jesus of Lübeck* was to have a long and colourful career in English service. Nor was this respect ill-founded, for appraisals of Hanse vessels arrested by the English in the late 1500s show them – by the standards of the time – both well-armed and economically manned.[12] Yet though German shipwrights might accept occasional innovations from the outside they were in general – like most of their fellows elsewhere – opposed to change. They were organized in tight, conservative guilds. Their craft was governed by tradition; knowledge and skill were transmitted from master to apprentice. In the absence of anything approaching a science of shipbuilding, the normal practice was to copy some existing vessel which experience had shown to be satisfactory, whilst in any case the formidable cost of building a large ship was in itself sufficient to stifle rash thoughts of experiment. These failings, far from peculiar to the Hanse, were aggravated when, after about 1400, timber costs commenced to soar. The most easily accessible wood had long since been cleared, and the remaining resources had to bear the pressure not only of a growing demand for domestic and industrial fuel, but also for timber for building of every sort. In 1558 the council of Stettin ordered that no ships be constructed for strangers lest the city's reserves, particularly of oak, be completely destroyed. At the same time xenophobic reactions to foreign penetration of the Baltic led to attempts to confine building to the burgesses of the towns themselves, to destroy the competition of various small villages and to exclude alien, non-Hanseatic – in fact very often Dutch – labour. All this pushed up costs – in 1601 it was alleged that in Lübeck the shipwrights' wages alone came to more than the price of a new vessel in Hamburg – and what was worse, cut off German builders from potential sources of new technical information. Significantly enough it was Danzig, independent in this as in so many other ways, that in the late sixteenth century admitted alien, and in particular Dutch, workmen, just as 100 years earlier it had pioneered the building of carvels in the Baltic. But there is no clearer indication of the decline of German shipbuilding, and no more decisive corroboration of the waning of those qualities which had once ensured the maritime hegemony of the League, than when in 1577 the Danes proposed to measure vessels for Sound toll purposes by their deck-level dimensions, it was not the Hanse, but the Dutch who ingeniously produced a ship whose lines defeated the intention of the law. Now, indeed, the key to the Baltic was in other hands.

Bibliographical note

There are few of the literary and record sources of medieval and early modern northern Europe which do not have some bearing on the history of the Hanse, and it would clearly be impossible in a book such as this to attempt their survey. Nor is it practicable to give more than the briefest indication of the rich archives of the League itself and of its constituent members. These records are now housed partly in Göttingen, partly in the Central Archives at Potsdam and partly in the various onetime Hanseatic towns and cities. They include wills, municipal accounts, council proceedings, court books, the records of guilds and companies (such as those of the Lübeck tailors, 1447–1503), merchants' accounts (those of the Rodde for the seventeenth century, for instance, in the Mecklenburgische Landeshauptarchiv Schwerin), and the records of commercial and diplomatic relations with other states and communities (especially the extensive *Senatsakten, Externa*, of Lübeck with their self-explanatory classes *Ruthenica, Danica, Suecica, Hispanica*). Of especial value to maritime historians are the sixteenth- and seventeenth-century records of the Shipwrights' Company at Hamburg (*Staatsarchiv*) and of the Shipbuilders' (Shipcarpenters') Company at Wismar (*Ratsakten*). There are also *Pfundzollisten* (the accounts of a tax on a variety of exports and imports), commencing in the 1300s extant for Lübeck, Hamburg and Reval, many of which have been edited. Equally important are the *Pfahlkammerbücher* (recording taxes levied for the upkeep of harbours) of which Danzig has a broken series commencing in 1468 and other cities later sequences. For some towns, as for Reval for

1426–8, there are lists of ships. Documents of the preceding three categories are discussed by Johannes Schildhauer in *HGB*, 86 (1968), 63ff.

My figures for Newcastle's fifteenth-century Baltic timber imports come from the Particulars of Customs for the port (PRO Exchequer KR, E 122/107/57). For the renewal of English trade to the Baltic in the early 1500s I have used the records of the English High Court of Admiralty, Instance and Prize Examination Books (PRO HCA 13), vols 2 and 3. This class also contains, for the years in which the English intercepted Hanseatic trade to and from Iberia, much valuable evidence concerning the shipping and commerce of the League. Information about the consumption of wax in the monastery of Durham comes from the accounts of the Sacrist now in the Prior's Kitchen at Durham.

There is an excellent survey of the printed sources for the history of the League, as well as an ample bibliography in Philippe Dollinger, *La Hanse* (Paris, 1964). A revised and corrected edition of this sensible and balanced synthesis is available in German (*Die Hanse*, Stuttgart, 1966) and in English (translated by D.S. Ault and S.H. Steinberg, 1970). I have therefore added here only some sources overlooked by Professor Dollinger, some editions that have appeared since his work was completed, and a number of recent studies of particular value.

For the history of the Hanse, the Baltic and, indeed, much of medieval and early modern Europe the archives of the Teutonic Order are of the utmost importance. Their range and significance may be gathered from the *Regesta historico-diplomatica Ordinis S.Mariae Theutonicorum, 1198–1524.* Part I: *Regesten zum Ordensbriefarchiv, 1198–1510.* Part II: *Regesta Privilegiorum* which was published at Göttingen in 1948–50, ed. F. Joachim and W. Hubatsch. In 1973 there appeared, also from Göttingen, the *Index Tabularii Ordinis S.Mariae Theutonicorum, Regesten zum Ordensbriefarchiv*, III, 1511–25. Much valuable statistical evidence on the Hanse's English trade is assembled in E.M. Carus-Wilson and Olive Coleman, *England's Export Trade 1275–1547* (Oxford, 1963). In *The Port and Trade of Early Elizabethan London, Documents* (London Record Society, 1972) Brian Dietz edits the London port book for the fiscal year 1567–8 which throws considerable light on the commercial dealings of Hamburg and Danzig with England. There is still a great deal to be found on the English in the Baltic in the early 1500s in the *Calendar of Letters and Papers, Foreign and Domestic, Henry VIII*, ed. J.S. Brewer, J. Gairdner and R.H. Brodie (1862–1932).

The extensive flow of books and articles in all major and many minor European languages in any way concerning the Hanse is reviewed in meticulous detail in the *HGB*, issued twice yearly by the Hansischer Geschichtsverein. This also carries general and specialist articles on every aspect of Hanseatic history. The historiography of the Prussian lands is conveniently surveyed in the revised and extended *Bibliographie der Geschichte von Ost und West Preussen*, J.G. Herder-Institut, XII (Marburg/Lahn, 1972).

German beginnings in the East are succinctly analysed in Dollinger, *La Hanse*, and in such olders books as G. Barraclough, *The Origins of Modern Germany* (2nd edn, Oxford, 1947) and F.L. Carsten, *The Origins of Prussia* (Oxford, 1954). An even older account is resurrected in the *Cambridge Economic History of Europe*, ed. M.M. Postan (revised edn, Cambridge, 1966) vol. I. The many stimulating, if not always convincing, opinions of Fritz Rörig are available in *The*

Medieval Town (1967) which is a translation by D. Bryant of his *Die Europäische Stadt im Mittelalter* (revised edn, Göttingen, 1955). There is a magisterial survey of the Slav societies and civilizations of the Baltic throughout (and well beyond) the period examined here by Roger Portal, *Les Slaves* (Paris, 1965). Chronologically more restricted, but equally authoritative, and likewise not confined to political and economic matters is the fine study by Michael Roberts, *The Early Vasas: A History of Sweden 1523–1611* (Cambridge, 1968).

England's relations with the Hanse and trade to the Baltic are perceptively discussed in G.D. Ramsay, *English Overseas Trade during the Centuries of Emergence* (1957). The influence of the Hanse (and others) on the economy of the Slav hinterlands of the Baltic is examined in two important articles by Marian Malowist in *Ec. Hist. Rev.*, XII (1959), 177ff. and *Ec. Hist. Rev.*, XIX (1966), 15ff. Of especial value, and based on a great deal of previously unworked archival material, is the study of seventeenth-century Hanseatic trade by Karl-Friedrich Olechnowitz, *Handel und Seeschiffahrt der Späten Hanse* (Weimar, 1965). This covers in particular the commerce of Wismar, Rostock and Stralsund and Lübeck's relations with Russia. Local records are used to chart the German penetration of the Mediterranean in the sixteenth and seventeenth centuries by Maurice Aymard, *Venise, Raguse et le Commerce du blé pendant la seconde moitié du XVIᵉ Siècle* (Paris, 1966); E. Grendi, *Rivista Storica Italiana*, 80 (1968) and 83 (1971); and Alvaro Castillo Pintado, *Trafico Maritimo y Comercio de Importacion en Valencia a Comienzos del Siglo XVII* (Madrid, 1967). The impact of the Thirty Years War on northern economies and societies is outlined, from the secondary literature by Henry Kamen in *P&P*, 39 (1968), 44ff. The commerce of Stralsund is examined in detail by H. Langer, *Stralsund 1600–1630* (Weimar, 1970), and that of Pernau, Reval and Narva in the seventeenth century by A. Pijrimjae in *Skansborn*, XV (1970), 7ff., who demonstrates the survival of Lübeck's trade to Narva. Commercial profit rates in the early 1600s are calculated by Maria Bogucka in *Acta Poloniae Historica*, 23 (1971), whilst H. Zins gives a detailed if pedestrian account of Anglo–Polish trade in *England and the Baltic in the Elizabethan Era* (Manchester, 1972). In *HJ*, XV (1972), 385 ff., the present writer notices English investment in Hanseatic shipping during the Anglo-Spanish war of the late 1500s. The subject of the Hanse in the Mediterranean is re-opened in a richly documented essay by Pierre Jeannin in *Mélanges en l'Honneur de Fernand Braudel* edited by Edouard Privat (Toulouse, 1973), vol. I, 263ff., who, in his comparison of German failure with Dutch success follows the arguments of Braudel himself, whose great study of the Mediterranean, one of the outstanding works of modern historical scholarship, is now available in English as *The Mediterranean and the Mediterranean World in the Age of Philip II*, trs. by S. Reynolds (2 vols, 1972–3). The Dutch penetration of the Baltic in the late Middle Ages is explained, to the accompaniment of Marxist polemics, in generally accepted terms by Klaus Spading, *Holland und die Hanse im 15.Jahrhundert* (Weimar, 1973), whilst Walter Stark prefaces a useful statistical analysis of the commerce between Lübeck and Danzig with an even more tedious political harangue in *Lübeck and Danzig in der zweiten Hälfte des 15.Jahrhunderts* (Weimar, 1973). Of fundamental importance is Artur Attman, *The Russian and Polish Markets in International Trade, 1500–1650* (Gothenburg, 1973).

A wide variety of Hanseatic cultural relations with, and influences in, Russia are carefully established by N. Angermann in *HGB*, 84 (1966), 20ff., and more recently in his *Hamburg und Russland in Frühen Neuzeit* (Hamburg, 1972). The Hanseatic impact on Scandinavian art is somewhat abruptly identified by Volker Plagemann in *HGB*, 86 (1968), 13ff., whilst Pierre Jeannin examines the pioneer Slavicist Tönnies Fonne in *HGB*, 91 (1973), 50ff.

The organization of Hanseatic trade, and the League's economic policies and behaviour are discussed in their European context in vol. III of the *Cambridge Economic History of Europe*, ed. M.M. Postan, F.F. Rich, and E. Miller (Cambridge, 1963). The techniques of navigation employed in northern waters are, as already noticed (p. 37), most usefully and convincingly surveyed in E.G.R. Taylor's *The Haven-Finding Art* (1956), whilst in *Hist.*, XLI (1956) G.J. Marcus conclusively demonstrates that Hanseatic seamen were using the compass by the late Middle Ages. The impact of northern ship-design and rig in the Mediterranean is summarized by F.C. Lane, *Navires et Constructeurs à Venise pendant la Renaissance* (Paris, 1965), and some valuable detail on northern builds in the first modern centuries is added from the departmental archives of France by Jacques Bernard in *CIHM*, 5 (1966). Hanseatic vessels and their construction are authoritatively discussed in the light of new archaeological and other evidence by Ole Crumlin-Pedersen in *A History of Seafaring*, ed. G.F. Bass (1972). Material on manning rates is brought together by the present writer in *MM*, 56 (1970), 131ff.

3

The Venetian Republic

I 'The most triumphant city'

Whilst among the rigours of the north the Vikings and the Hanse prospered on trades reaching to the fringe of Europe and indeed to the ends of the known world, in the south a handful of Italian maritime cities, dominating the commerce of the Mediterranean, and intermediaries in the ancient trade between Europe and Asia, rose to a dazzling opulence and splendour. The Baltic, by the very nature and sheer volume of the goods it provided, could support a whole galaxy of entrepôts. But in the Mediterranean a traffic in small quantities of immensely valuable commodities was already in the 1300s contested between Venice and Genoa alone, and a hundred years later that of the Levant[1] was to all intents the exclusive preserve of the Venetians. And so there emerged an imperial pattern soon widely emulated, in which a trade considered vital or particularly valuable was conducted as the carefully defined monopoly of a single port. The wealth of Venice, like that of other urban and commercial empires (the Hanse and the Dutch) came in essence not from the creation of new trade routes and associations, but from the dominance of those already in existence by a combination of force and superior business technique and maritime technology. It was, furthermore, a wealth which unlike that of most imperial powers depended not on the exploitation of primitive peoples and economies but, at least for several formative centuries, on dealings with ancient, powerful and distinguished states and civilizations – Byzantine Greece, China and Persia. Thus Venetian trade in its great days was not, as that of the Hanse, in bulk primary products, nor, as that of the Spaniards in America or the Vikings in Europe, in precious commodities wrested from those powerless to retain them, but in high-priced luxuries, ranging from spices to silks and carpets, which reached the west only after a series of complex commercial transactions. And though in the Middle Ages individual Venetian travellers, like Polo and Conti, were to undertake epic journeys and to see and record the wonders of India and China in books that captured the imagination of Europe, and though in later centuries their less-celebrated compatriots might be found anywhere from England to Burma, only momentarily did Venetians penetrate to, and never did they control, the oriental sources of supply.

These were not the only individual features of Venice's commerce and policy. Its great trades, likes those of other cities, were controlled by a mercantile oligarchy. But it was an oligarchy which unlike those of the Baltic or Dutch towns included aristocrats, and which before long came to regard itself, whatever the scepticism of others, as an

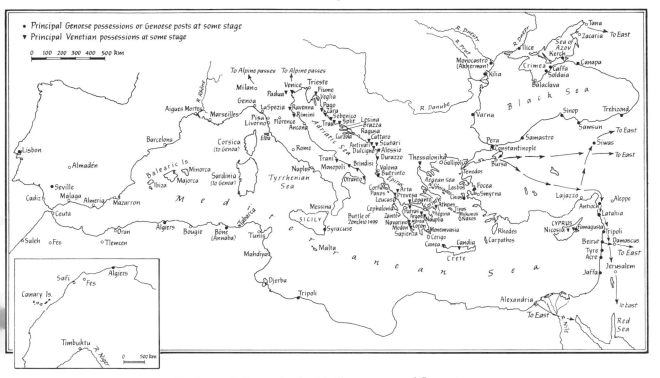

3 Venice and Genoa in the Mediterranean and Levant

aristocracy. Thus whilst Venetian patricians pursued commercial advantage as ruthlessly as the humbler rulers of any purely mercantile city, they also displayed, when occasion offered, a devotion as ardent as that of any Scandinavian chief or Iberian squire to the rewards of conquest and plunder. Venetian and Genoese trading stations indeed stretched from northern Europe into Africa and Asia. The rich littoral of the Black Sea was converted to a colonial territory to provide food, raw materials and slaves in much the same way that of the Baltic was exploited for the benefit of the Germans and the Dutch. But at the same time Venetian principalities appeared in the eastern waters of the Mediterranean, and a territorial empire was established on the Italian mainland. Such proceedings were justified, as they usually are, in terms of the defence of trade and other vital interests. Be this as it may, it meant that from an early date Venice, and to a lesser extent Genoa, were colonial and maritime powers in the fullest sense of the words, and to a far greater extent than the Germans were, or the Norse had been. Their prosperity rested on the profits of trade and the shipping it employed. By the high Middle Ages Venice, uniquely in Europe, possessed not only an impressive state navy, but also state-owned merchantmen and dockyards. Together with Genoa she controlled – and well into the 1500s – a substantial part of the west's naval forces, whose tactics and strategy were largely established by Genoese and Venetian commanders. Furthermore, from the eleventh century onwards both republics were engaged in the acquisition of factories in the lands to which they traded, and strategic bases from which to protect commercial routes they controlled or hoped to control. Such territories Venice, at least, by policies which strikingly anticipate those of the Iberian oceanic powers, was able to consolidate into a centrally governed empire, administered by officers of the state and contributing substantially to its revenues. And thus it was that the republic was lifted to a political and cultural pre-eminence which few western cities – those of Antiquity apart – have ever enjoyed. Its dominance and handling of the rich trades of the Levant inspired widespread envy and attempted emulation. Its arts, music and science profoundly affected the whole development of European civilization, whilst scions of its patrician families married royalty or became cardinals and popes. By the end of the Middle Ages, as legends as to the origins of its riches circulated, like its currency, in west and east alike, Venice, though still far from having attained its final architectural magnificence, seemed to a civilized northerner 'the most triumphant city I have ever seen'. It was one of Europe's greatest seaports, and with a population in 1500 of 120,000 one of its largest cities. Such was the scale of its commercial operations that in 1439 two of its great galleys could between them load something like 10 per cent of England's cloth exports. And even when past the apogee of its power, in the mid-1500s, its political stability, diplomatic acumen, social organization and economic skills were still admired by publicists as different as those of Catholic Portugal and Protestant England.

Yet the beginnings of this distinguished history are remarkably obscure. Nevertheless, notwithstanding the cherished beliefs of some medieval patriots as to the founding of their city by a band of dispossessed Trojans, it is clear that it owed its origins to no such single prescient act of policy. There was in Roman times a region at the head of the Adriatic described as Venetia. Its coasts, with their maze of islands, marshes, beaches and lagoons, made an attractive summer resort for the wealthy inhabitants of neighbouring cities, and supported a less affluent population of fishermen, boatmen and salt-makers. When, in the early Middle Ages, the western empire disintegrated under barbarian attack and its lands were taken by Germanic invaders, these comparatively inaccessible parts came momentarily under the authority of the Roman empire of the east – Byzantium, with its capital at Constantinople – which had footholds on the northern Adriatic at Ravenna[2] and in Istria. Renewed Germanic invasions of Italy in the sixth century brought a flow of refugees, many of considerable wealth, from the mainland to the security of the adjacent islands, including to those we now know as Venice.[3] From thenceforward, with the islet of Rialto emerging as its centre, the future republic throve. Like many similar if less illustrious communities it enjoyed the advantages of being sited where the peripheries of two different and usually hostile worlds – Orthodox Byzantium and the barbarian west to start with, Catholic Europe and Ottoman Islam later – met. It was nominally subject to Byzantium, from which,

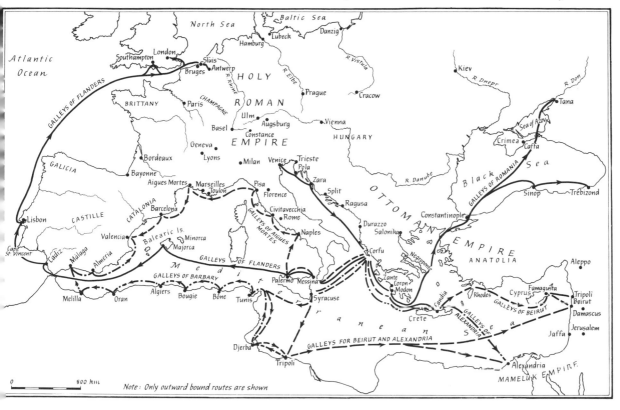

4   Venetian state galley routes in the fifteenth century

however, once Constantinople had lost (751) Ravenna to the Germanic kingdom of the Lombards, it was sufficiently remote to escape any untimely attentions, and to be able to slide unobtrusively into independence.[4] And with the Lombardic lands eventually absorbed into the Frankish empire, it was equally remote from the major centres of Germanic power in the west, and in any case difficult of access to those without maritime, not to say aquatic, skills and resources. So its inhabitants, more or less unmolested, could enjoy a modest prosperity derived from fishing and the making of salt. At the same time they could supply some of the wants, and tap some of the riches, of the great plains of north-eastern Italy, easily reached through a host of navigable rivers, just as they could ship such things as wine and timber along the coasts of the Adriatic.

Then, as with the Vikings, by a combination of technological superiority, predatory zeal and (like the Dutch later) commercial skill, the Venetians were able to penetrate, and ultimately dominate and extend, a far greater and more opulent maritime economy. Already in the eighth century their vessels were carrying Italian wine and grain,

Venetian salt and Dalmatian timber to Constantinople. A hundred years later it was Venice that was to supply the shipping for a Frankish imperial expedition in the Adriatic, and before long Venetian merchants were in Syria and Alexandria. Here, as at Constantinople, they could participate in that commerce which from time immemorial had linked east and west, with the orient supplying those luxuries, whether Asian spices or Levantine dancing girls, eagerly demanded to titillate the palates and passions of the wealthy of Europe. It was a trade which flowing west by a variety of routes (see pp. 101ff.) had, in the last centuries of Antiquity and at the beginning of the Middle Ages, passed from western into eastern hands – those of Jews, Moslems, Greeks and Syrians. Such a shift reflected the destruction or disruption of the economy of Europe by the barbarian invasions, and by Arab expansion in the Mediterranean. But as these incursions ceased, and as Arab, like Byzantine seapower, weakened the whole pattern was reversed, and by the tenth century control of the western extremities of the trade[5] was disputed by the maritime cities of a resurgent Italy – Venice, Naples, Pisa, Amalfi. This was not, admittedly, the sole source of Venetian wealth, and the local trades in salt, grain, timber and wine were, and remained – like the coastal shipment of coal in England's maritime economy in the eighteenth and nineteenth centuries – of fundamental importance. And it was the Venetians, too, who at this time supplied Christians and Moslems alike with slaves from the Slav hinterland of the Adriatic, just as with characteristic commercial disregard for the constraints of morality, they provided arms and munitions to Christian Europe's Moslem enemies. But it was the luxury trade, as the Venetians themselves repeatedly acknowledged, that was the essential basis of their prosperity. Indeed it was a trade to whose control the republic's fortunes were more intimately linked than were those of any other maritime power to the domination of any single route, or the provision of any single commodity, except for the Hanse's comparable dependence on the trade of the Baltic.

Venice's triumphant emergence – and already in the 800s contemporaries viewed with a mixture of hostility and incredulity those who so visibly flourished freed from the normal tedium and burden of agricultural toil – was one aspect of that re-emergence of western Europe, increasingly prosperous and populated, with the ending of barbarian depredations. And from such prosperity Venice was singularly well-placed to benefit. It had by sea and river access to the markets of Italy, economically the most advanced part of western Europe. Along the north Italian rivers, and through the eastern Alpine passes its imports could reach Germany, and conversely the celebrated metals of Germany – silver, copper, iron – could reach Venice. No doubt, like most of the successful, it owed much to sheer good fortune. Its site saved it from conquest. Its tenuous political association with Byzantium, with which to start with it could accordingly trade unimpeded as a Greek dependency, eased its establishment in the commerce in spices. The generally bad relations between Latins and Greeks, and between Christians and Moslems provided excellent scope for an intermediary. Wealthy immigrants perhaps supplied – and again quite fortuitously – some initial business capital. And pure accident conveniently removed some of Venice's potentially most dangerous competitors, like Amalfi, stifled in the eleventh century by incorporation into the Norman kingdom of Sicily. But what fate offered man improved. The dynasts of the early dogal families of the ninth and tenth centuries, striving to create a hereditary dukedom, gave to Venetian expansion that same purposeful direction that Portugal and Spain later received from the ambitions and convictions of their ruling houses. Comacchio, controlling the mouths of the Po, and supported by its Lombard and Carolingian lords, was sacked in 886 and once it showed signs of reviving sufficiently to dispute the trade of Venice, sacked again in the following century. Naval expeditions established Venetian maritime supremacy in the upper Adriatic, whilst in the year 1000, in that familiar style of more recent times, a fleet under the command of the doge himself, after destroying a number of pirate bases on the Dalmatian coast, returned home in a triumphant cruise to display the meaning of Venetian might. But no more than in the growth of other imperial powers was force everything, and it was a characteristically adept diplomacy, for which the republic was long to be celebrated, which enabled it to remain on good terms with the Greek and western empires alike, securing from both commercial privileges in the late 900s.

Thus in much the same way as that of Holland later, Venetian powers and influence spread. An increasingly prosperous Europe could absorb its imports. And as Byzantium grew feebler and its enemies more numerous and potent, Greek commerce came into Venetian hands, just as did that of Iberia into those of the Dutch in the sixteenth and seventeenth centuries. Venetian ships came to the rescue of the Greeks besieged in Bari by Moslems in 1002. With the arrival of the Normans in southern Italy soon after, aggressive as ever, and with ambitions in the Adriatic and indeed in Byzantium, such interventions were even more vital, both to sustain the Greeks and to protect Venetian interests. Hence in 1081 a fleet fought and defeated the Normans at Durazzo by, amongst other stratagems, dropping weights from its mastheads through the bottoms of the opposing vessels. For such services the rewards granted (or extorted) were equally remarkable, and by a series of treaties, each more extensive than its predecessor, the empire, with the significant exception of the Black Sea, was opened up to Venetian merchants whose trade was exempted from taxation (the rate for natives was 10 per cent), and who were granted their own quarter in Constantinople in 1082. And should the imperial gratitude not be expressed with sufficient alacrity, Venetian ships were turned against the empire itself until Venetian demands were met.

Nor was this all. Citizens of the republic had long traded to those former Roman and Byzantine lands of the Middle East, giving access to the wealth of Asia which since their conquest by the Arabs in the decade after 635, had been under Moslem control. But as a result of the crusades launched from the Catholic west in the eleventh and twelfth centuries to recover the holy places of Christianity, Venice's position was enormously strengthened. True, preoccupied with Byzantium and the command of the Adriatic, she was not initially so deeply involved in the transport of warriors to the Holy Land, or in attacks on Moslem fleets and strongholds, as were such maritime and commercial rivals as Genoa and Pisa. But once committed, Venice's interventions were decisive. Venetian forces defeated a Moslem fleet off Ascalon (1123) and took a vital part in the capture of Tyre the following year. As with Byzantium such services had their price, and the city – as indeed her competitors – received from the rulers of the new crusader principalities extensive concessions for trade and settlement in the ports of Syria. Meanwhile Venetian trade with Moslem Egypt – where pepper and alum amongst other things were obtained in Alexandria – had reached such a volume and value that the city successfully sought exemption (1198) from the papal ban on dealings with the infidel, on the grounds that only by such commerce could she survive. But whilst Venetian ships, like those of other Italian maritime cities, spread through the Mediterranean – with one despatched to Bougie or Ceuta in Moslem Barbary in 1177 – and whilst Venetian merchants, like other compatriots, penetrated overland to northern Europe[6] to market their goods, and to buy the textiles needed to pay for them (cf. p. 158), it was Byzantium that remained the basis of Venetian wealth. Notwithstanding growing Genoese and Pisan competition from the mid-1100s, Venice controlled much of the empire's trade both in the Aegean and in the Mediterranean. Venetian merchants were established in strength not only in Constantinople – where allegedly there were 10,000 by 1200 – but in colonies throughout many of the provinces, where they appear like the frontiersmen of other colonial societies, less primeval no doubt, but often married to local women, speaking the local language and knowing the local markets. It was men such as these who with their own ships handled much of the empire's long-distance and interport trade, acquiring in Constantinople the products of Asia Minor and the Black Sea littoral, supplying the capital with goods from the Ionian and Aegean coasts; shipping Greek oils and silks to the west, and bringing in return the spices and cottons of the Levant, and the textiles, metals and weapons of western Europe. Little wonder that one should call his ship *The Whole World*, or that when Venetian zeal in the pursuit of profit provoked the inevitable xenophobic reaction among the Greeks – the anti-Latin movement of the late 1100s – its impact in the republic was so disastrous. And little wonder either that in 1204 Venetian money and Venetian ships ensured the overthrow of the Greek state, and the setting up in its place of a Latin regime. Thus, as the logical culmination of several centuries of economic penetration, formal empire replaced informal control. Such policies were rarely envisaged – Holland's abortive venture in Brazil is another striking exception – by commercial powers lacking the territorial ambitions of aristocrats, squires or peasants (cf. pp. 386ff.). Nor were they effected by individual cities. Indeed the events of 1204 were eloquent testimony to the rewards of seapower and trade. Already in the late twelfth century, Venice, a single city with no subject territory, had been able to mediate between a defeated German emperor – from whom commercial concessions were characteristically obtained – and the league of Italian cities that opposed him. But now in Byzantium the republic not only intervened to establish an authority to its liking in an area of vital commercial interest – as did, but only at the apogee of their power, and as a more or less united force, the towns of the Hanse in the north – but embarked on the conquest and colonization of subject lands.

True, the overthrow of Byzantium was not directly engineered by Venice. A crusade was in preparation, destined admittedly for Egypt, and thus likely to disrupt one of the city's vital markets. It soon emerged, however, that its aristocratic leaders were unable to pay for the shipping – 200 transports and 50 fighting vessels – they had chartered from Venice to carry them to their destination. Astutely the city agreed to forgo the debt if the crusaders would assist, as they somewhat reluctantly did, in the subjugation of Zara,[7] a tiresome obstacle to Venetian pretensions to hegemony in the Adriatic through its ambitions to become an independent port. But then a contender for the disputed Byzantine throne enlisted crusading support – yet another instance of conquest effected as much through internal dissensions as external force – whilst to Venice's ruling magnates the instability of the empire, and the recent Greek attacks on western inhabitants and property, suggested the desirability of a radical solution, and one which would have the merit of providing an outlet for the city's surplus population, and for the ambitions of its politically restive lower classes. And possibly, too, there were hopes of unimpeded access to the riches of the east. Hence, notwithstanding considerable defections, the crusaders swept on to Constantinople to instal their Greek client. But the Orthodox inhabitants showed no enthusiasm for a puppet imposed by the force of Catholic arms, and in the end the crusade had to take the capital – unconquered since its foundation – by military assault. It was an operation in which the high quality of Venetian tactics and the redoubtable skills of Venetian seamen in siege operations were once again displayed. And from the ensuing looting of the captured city, Venice received, as did some Iberians from the pillaging of the Americas, an impressive accession of wealth, ranging from cash to the famous bronze horses which now decorate St Mark's, and an exquisitely housed fragment of the True Cross. Then, it having been found necessary to establish Latin rule in Byzantium, the republic adeptly ensured the election as the first emperor of the candidate thought most amenable to Venetian persuasion, whilst from the dismemberment of the old Greek state she acquired the rudiments of a territorial empire, strategically sited to protect her trade, and title to a great deal more. She was to have the islands of the Cyclades and the Ionian Sea (to which Crete was quickly added), part of Thrace, which was at least in the possession of the Latins, and an imposing list of lands in Epirus, the Peloponnese and Euboea. Potentially the approaches to the Adriatic, the Aegean, Constantinople itself (of which she was to receive three-eighths) and the Black Sea were in Venetian hands. Nor was this all: her ancient commercial privileges were confirmed and her rivals excluded from the reconstituted empire, or admitted only by Venetian favour.

The control of this rich heritage, and of the commerce with the Levant, were to be disputed with Genoa over the next two centuries in a series of bitter and intensive maritime and colonial wars. Like those of the European powers in the seventeenth and

eighteenth centuries for the mastery of far greater areas and resources, they were
marked by ambitious strategies aimed at destroying an opponent both at home and
abroad. And in the same way they were characterized by large fleet actions in distant
waters, by the exploitation of rivalries among native peoples and by the spectacular
military and naval achievements of more or less independent colonial pro-consuls (cf.
pp. 95–8). In the long run Venice was the victor, though hardly an unqualified victor
since, with Genoese connivance, the Greek empire was restored (1261), and since
Genoese colonies and trading posts flourished in the Black Sea, and were not eradicated
until, together with those of the Venetians themselves, they fell to the Turks (cf. pp.
169–70). Nevertheless for something like half a century Venice virtually monopolized the
commerce of the Black Sea with the West, and thereafter carried on a valuable trade
through her factories there. In Greece and the adjacent waters – as also in Italy – she
developed a strategically and economically important empire; and she eventually
dominated Europe's commerce with the Middle East. It was an achievement more
logically conceived, and through an admixture of commercial realism and patrician
ambition, more logically effected, than those of the Hanse in the Baltic or the
Portuguese in Asia. And if it was of a smaller scale than was that of the Spaniards in the
Atlantic so, too, were the resources involved.

To begin with, however, Venice, confronted with such opportunities, but as yet
innocent of colonial experience, showed the same indecision as any other incipient
imperial power. Defeated the Greeks may have been, but conquered they were not, and
in 1204 the republic – harassed, too, by Genoa – was far from being able to inherit an
empire as could the Spaniards those of the Incas and Aztecs after the campaigns of
Cortés and Pizarro. And whilst the city hesitated enterprising individuals in the East
took matters into their own hands. Magnates of the Venetian community in
Constantinople, some of whom like the Spaniards of sixteenth-century Peru entertained momentary visions of independence, elected their own leader without
reference to the metropolis (cf. p. 316). Others, like the patrician Marco Sanudo, who
set up in Naxos with the title of duke of the Archipelago, carved out their own holdings
in the Aegean. But then the city, with customary realism, abandoned what it considered
useless and set about, as its magnates had desired, the acquisition and pacification of
those lands thought to be of strategic importance. Here again the success was not
unqualified. Though Corfu, the key to the Straits of Otranto and so to the Adriatic was
taken in 1207 it was lost to the Greeks seven years later, whilst a Latin feudatory secured
the Peloponnese. But in the Aegean Venice had a substantial foothold once Negroponte
was conquered, and in Crete, astride the approaches to the Levant and the whole Aegean
basin, things went more, if not entirely, in the way the republic desired. The islets to the
northwest were taken in 1206–8, and after the ejection of a Genoese adventurer, the
island itself brought under nominal Venetian control. Then with that characteristic
devotion to her own commercial well-being that was to make her so suspect in simpler or
more idealistic eyes, Venice further reinsured her position. She continued to support her

erstwhile associates in the creation of the now visibly decrepit Latin empire. But at the same time agreements were negotiated with the Turks and with the Moslems of Egypt, peace was made with the Greeks who had established a new state in Nicaea and settlements reached with the city's commercial rivals (Pisa and Genoa) in Italy.

So, for a time, the tide ran strongly in Venice's favour, now, as one of its chroniclers wrote, 'made famous by honours and riches given by God throughout nearly all the world'. Its political, economic and territorial power spread, but without, in general, anything of that pursuit of indefinitie horizons so typically Scandinavian and Iberian. Instead, as with other merchant-dominated states or communities, it penetrated to those focal points in commercial networks beyond which, economically at least, there was no reason to go.[8] From Constantinople Venetian ships were soon into the Black Sea, reaching a world whose climates ranged from sub-tropical heat and rains (in the east), to the rigours of the Russian steppes, and whose rich natural resources had once been known to Antiquity. Moreover, it was possible to reach from its shores the plains of the Danube and of Russia, the Baltic, the Caspian and the Orient and (from Trebizond) Central Asia and Persian Gulf (cf. pp. 30, 102, 169ff.). And whilst Venetian vessels were off the Crimea (as they apparently were as early as 1206), or Venetian merchants penetrated to Kiev (where they are mentioned in 1247), the republic was opening a trade to Tunis and improving its access to the wealth of the east through the Levant – still the primary route – by obtaining concessions in Lajazzo (1201).[9] Furthermore, it ensured as best it could that goods acquired in the Black Sea, the onetime lands of Byzantium – the *Romania* of Venetian documents – the Levant, or elsewhere in the Mediterranean, should only reach Europe through its port, just as European commerce flowing in the opposite direction should similarly pass through Venice. Hence by a mixture of force and guile Ferrara was displaced as the entrepôt in which oriental products were exchanged for German silver and textiles, and the maritime commerce of such potential rivals as Ancona, Zara and the Apulian towns was curbed by Venetian seapower. So, also, much of the seaborne trade of the northern Adriatic was funnelled through Venice, and the salt and grain traffic of northern Italy monopolized by the city.

But naturally enough no more than with the Hanse in the Baltic, or the Iberians in oceanic commerce, did such ambitions go unchallenged (cf. pp. 56, 297, 363ff.). In the east there was the hostility of the surviving Greek principalities, and everywhere, and far more formidable, that of Genoa, a maritime and commercial republic in every way equal, and in many ways superior, to Venice (see p. 159ff.). With Pisa, their onetime common enemy in decline, the two cities now came face to face. In the Levant Genoa's earlier pre-eminence had been undermined by the arrival of the Venetians, and in the Black Sea a city of proverbial business acuteness was hardly likely to accept the overwhelming preponderance that the conquest of Constantinople had given her rival. Squabbles in Acre, a leading Christian market in the oriental trade and, until its loss, capital of what remained of the Latin crusading state, brought before long open war, and with it yet another demonstration of the maritime excellence of Venice. Genoa was crushingly defeated in the two sea battles in or off the port of Acre, in the second of which (1258) she lost half her fleet and 1700 men, and from which the Venetian commander – a Tiepolo – returned with still more artistic treasures to decorate St Mark's. But in the Greek lands it was another matter. By the mid-1200s all that remained of the Latin empire of the east was its capital, defended by Venetian ships. The resurgent Greek state of Trebizond,[10] needing naval support, and the Genoese eager to displace the Venetians, were thus natural allies. In return for a promise to assist in the Greek recapture of Constantinople and to provide (at Greek expense) vessels for its defence, Genoa obtained the most extensive concessions. The Venetians were to be expelled from the restored empire, and Genoese merchants were to be allowed to trade freely throughout its lands and in the Black Sea. Nor, as it transpired, was Genoa put to any such trouble as Venice had incurred in 1204, since the Greeks retook Constantinople themselves (1261) before the Genoese squadron even put in an appearance.

This was a reverse of an order that Venice had not experienced for centuries. Her prestige was shaken, her trade damaged and new commercial rivals (the Florentines and Catalans in particular) encouraged. Furthermore, the resultant wars, of a far greater scale and cost than hitherto, and the consequent disruption of trade, brought the city their own familiar sequence of difficulties. Food was often scarce, prices rose, many small merchants were ruined, magnates refused to pay their taxes and the republic was in turn unable to pay its officials. The ruling oligarchs fell out over the strategies and policies to be pursued, and the exigencies of war, strengthening their powers and demands, brought suspicions of despotism and in the end (in 1266 and again in 1310) open revolt. And from one disaster came others. The maritime war against Genoa in the mid-1200s was conventionally organized and conventionally fought. The honour and reputation of Venice were indeed vindicated in successful fleet actions – in which the behaviour of the Genoese was often marked by scandalous incompetence – but Genoa did increasingly well, at least financially, from raids on Venetian commerce. Nor was it merely from the rich resources of the Black Sea itself – its slaves, furs, timber, wax and grain – that Venice was in danger of exclusion. By the late thirteenth century an intransigently Moslem Egypt had Syria in its control – with the last Christian outpost taken in 1291 – and so those commercial routes to the east through the Red Sea. At this very time, however, the Mongol conquest of a gigantic empire stretching from the borders of Hungary to the Sea of Japan opened, or re-opened, as the epic travels of the Polo family dramatically revealed, other ways to the Far East. But the starting point of the route through Central Asia was on the Sea of Azov, and one of those for the way through Mongol Persia and the Indian Ocean at Trebizond – both, that is, accessible only by the Genoese-dominated Black Sea. The situation was not, admittedly, irreparable. Venice secured (1262) commercial privileges in Alexandria. Her merchants were in Tabriz in 1264, back in Constantinople a few years later, and in 1291 an agreement was made with the Kipchak Mongols, rivals of those of Persia who favoured the Genoese.[11] Nor was the picture of Venetian commerce, all its difficulties notwithstanding, one of unrelieved gloom. Whilst Genoa fought Pisa, Venice could enjoy spells of prosperity. And what rewards could be had is clear from the will of a former doge who died in 1268. A patrician indeed he was, but with over half his fortune in trade, and in a trade in which the capital and an average profit of 10 per cent could be recovered within a year. Nevertheless in the struggle for the mastery of that great oriental commerce now increasingly funnelled through the Black Sea (or through Lajazzo) Venice had been worsted. Her carefully assembled empire in the south and south-west Aegean protected a route to Syria and Egypt in danger of eclipse, whilst Genoa was supreme in Constantinople and Asia Minor. Nor were these her only problems. The political anarchy in Italy after the disintegration of German imperial power – internecine wars between a multitude of cities; the emergence of aggressive local despots – and not least her own ambitions, drew her into the politics of the mainland to ensure the safety of the trade routes leading to the north. At the same time Hungary threatened her hegemony in the Adriatic, the restored Greeks her positions in the Aegean and in Crete there was more or less continuous revolt from 1264 to 1299.

For a time the republic contemplated restoring Latin rule, and thereby her own commercial supremacy, in Constantinople. But for this there were needed the military resources and feckless ambition of some dynast, which as a commercial city Venice lacked. Her most likely allies were the French, established since 1266 in the old Norman lands of southern Italy. But they, like their predecessors, had ambitions of their own in the east, and were in any case soon embroiled in troubles in their Italian possessions. So Venice alternately fought and negotiated with the Greeks and with the Genoese. And between the two republics the rivalry intensified once Genoa had destroyed (1284) Pisan seapower; when Lajazzo became, after the fall of Acre to the Moslems in 1291 the only (legally) accessible entrepôt for Christians in the Levant trade; as Genoese power spread along the coasts of Asia Minor; and as Venice insistently pushed back into the Black Sea (see pp. 98, 161). Venetian negotiations with Trebizond precipitated in 1294 a war in which the strategies – attacks on colonies and trading posts; attempts to disrupt by naval blockade vital commercial routes – anticipate in all essentials those of later oceanic conflicts. It was, furthermore, a war which demonstrated that a faction-ridden Genoa was unable to exploit to the full the opportunities opened by the enterprise of her commanders, and that there had been a disastrous decline in Venetian competence at sea. Off Lajazzo (1294) a fleet raised by the Genoese colony of Pera (see p. 185), its ships lashed together in line abreast in Arab and Viking style, their masts down, defeated the Venetians caught in rising wind with their sails still set. And in another action in the Adriatic a large Venetian force was outsailed and outfought by a smaller Genoese fleet, with the loss of most of its ships and thousands of men, amongst them Marco Polo.

But this longest of commercial and colonial wars was to continue, interspersed with barely observed truces, for more than another century. The strategic aims of the two

republics were not merely, as were those of the Hanse, to secure the monopoly of a
particular trade, or the dominance of a particular area, but entirely to eradicate their
opponent – commerce, colonies, metropolis alike. And since in terms of maritime
resources they were, unlike the contestants in the oceanic wars of the century before
1650, more or less equal, not only was the conflict prolonged, but at times of a violence,
tenacity and bitterness comparable to that of the Anglo-Dutch battles of the later 1600s.
Ultimately the balance was to swing, partly by good luck, partly through her own
determination and diplomatic adroitness, in Venice's favour. Bases were acquired in the
Black Sea – at Soldaia in the Crimea;[12] at Tana on the Sea of Azov; at Trebizond which
gave access to Tabriz – where, by the mid-fourteenth century Venetian commerce was
at its peak. Yet whatever the weaknesses of a factious Genoa and its equally factious
colonies, Venice's success was no foregone conclusion. The 1350s saw the collapse of a
grand design for the destruction of Genoa, more naval defeats, one doge accused of
cowardice and another executed for treason. Then, a quarter of a century later, under
the rule of a divided and unpopular oligarchy, an attempt to secure the mastery of the
Dardanelles by occupying Tenedos – where a Genoese coup had already failed –
miscarried. The islet was fortified, but against Genoa and her impressive array of allies
Venice was hard put, at a time of demographic recession, to man her fleets, whose
morale, furthermore, was often poor. Defeat in the Adriatic enabled the Genoese to
trade there, and if, in 1379, there was some spectacularly successful commerce raiding
in the style of Genoa, there was the further disaster of the siege of Venice itself by a
Genoese fleet and its allied land forces (1379–80). But whilst pessimists gave the city up
for lost, it was saved by a supreme effort, some adept diplomacy and a providential
Genoese collapse. And by now the pattern of conflict was changing. The disintegration
of the great Mongol empire, the expulsion of the Mongols from China and the
disruption of Asia in the late 1300s by the armies of Timur (the Tamburlaine of
Western romance) meant that those routes once travelled by the Polos and others – that
Venetian recorded in 1317 as 'dead in the land of the Tartars', or those compatriots who
in 1338 set out for Delhi – were no longer safe, let alone profitable. Trade was indeed to
continue to the Black Sea, but a trade increasingly, like that of the Genoese, in local
products – grain to feed the population of Venice; alum for use in the manufacture of
cloth; slaves for the Egyptian and European markets – and not in those of the east (cf.
pp. 169–70). The post of Tana, destroyed in 1343, was soon re-opened to enjoy a
somewhat precarious existence for the best part of another century; a Venetian consul
appears at Varna in the mid-1300s; and the republic acquired commercial privileges in
Bulgaria. Moreover, from the weakening of the Kipchaks came new opportunities. The
way was now relatively clear from Poland to the Crimea, and, through the valleys of the
Prut and the Dnestr, to the mouth of the Danube and the adjoining coast. And here in
the 1430s Venetian ships were trading at Kilia – where earlier efforts had been thwarted
by the Genoese – and Monocastro (Akkerman), the Bessarabian port for furs and grain,
linked by land routes to northern and western Europe. Nor, with such resources at

stake, and with the needs of Constantinople still to be met, was there any slackening in the struggle for the control of these waters and their approaches. Genoa ensured that Venetian commerce in Kilia and Monocastro remained modest. Venice attempted (and failed) to take the vital Genoese base of Chios in 1432, whilst the following year the Genoese defeated a Venetian fleet in the southern Aegean, and attacked the republic's possessions there.

Nevertheless by about 1400 the bulk of the great trade from the east, diverted by the disorders in the Kipchak and Persian empires of the Mongols, and by the ravages of Tamburlaine's armies, was now flowing through Syria and Egypt. And so it was by this ancient route that Nicolo Conti, a Venetian even more intrepid than the Polos, journeyed to India and beyond (1414–39), leaving a remarkably lucid and perceptive account of what he saw. The association with Syria and Egypt Venice had never entirely abandoned, particularly after her setbacks in the Black Sea in the 1260s. And when direct dealings with the infidel were, if not impossible certainly difficult – as during the suppose papal prohibition of trade with Egypt following the fall of the last remnants of the Latin crusading principalities (1291) – then they could be maintained through some suitable entrepôt, whether Lajazzo (until this too was lost to the Moslems in 1347), Cyprus or even Tunis.[13] But with the re-opening (1302) of formal Venetian relations with the Sultan of Egypt, papal acceptance (1344) of such a traffic and with Genoa decreasingly effective Venice was – politically at least – at the height of her power by the early 1400s, and her citizens, as a far from friendly critic put it, 'the most powerful people on both land and sea'. Since the late fourteenth century Venetian merchants had traded to northern Europe by that maritime route through the Straits of Gibraltar opened up earlier by the Genoese (see pp. 124, 164). From the Black Sea they penetrated to central Europe. They traded to North Africa and throughout much of the Mediterranean, their commerce carried not only, as elsewhere, in privately owned shipping but, on certain routes, in those state galleys whose arrivals and departures were a matter of wonder in ports from the English Channel to the Levant. The Adriatic was recognized as a Venetian preserve where the republic's patrolling squadrons ensured, as did those of the Iberians in the waters of Africa and the Indies later, that this lordship of the sea was respected. There were Venetian trading posts and more substantial settlements in the Black Sea, Venetian factories in northern Europe, the Levant and North Africa, and in the eastern Mediterranean an important and growing territorial empire stretching from the Greek and Slav coasts of the Adriatic to Crete and later to Cyprus. Even more remarkable for a community of such a size was that the establishment of this overseas empire was accompanied – as was that of Spain's in the sixteenth century, though for very different reasons – by the acquisition of another in the metropolitan mainland (cf. pp. 119, 301).

It was, however, at this very time that Venice's eastern trade and possessions were threatened by the westward advance of the Ottoman Turks. Faced only by the decayed remnants of Byzantium, by the more or less autonomous fragments of the Genoese colonial empire, by the widely dispersed Venetian territories, and by an unimpressive assortment of Latin bases and principalities in Greece and the Aegean, these particularly redoubtable members of a redoubtable race, their aid often solicited by warring Christians, broke out of Asia Minor in the mid-1300s. In roughly a century they had taken Constantinople, overrun the littoral of the Black Sea, swept on into the Balkans, occupied most of Greece and landed in Italy itself. Against such a military power, invincible by the inept paladins of Christian chivalry, as a sequence of disasters from Nicopolis (1396) to Mohacs (1526) showed, Venice had neither the men nor the resources to stand. Nor indeed had she much incentive, since to begin with there was little call for those brave gestures rarely good for business. The Turks were initially more interested in military conquest, loot, tribute and slaving than in naval ventures and the deliberate destruction of Venetian maritime commerce. So the republic, long accustomed, whatever the strictures of moralists, to trading with the infidel, had no hesitation in negotiating commercial concessions as opportunity allowed. She gave little help to the various western expeditions sent against the Turk – almost without exception abortive, or like those of the fifteenth-century Albanian hero Scanderbeg, only too prone to attack Venetian interests – just as she adamantly refused to countenance any campaign against Moslem Egypt. But Venice was no quiescent victim. The republic maintained for a time its control of the commercial routes through eastern waters. The first tentative attempts of the Turks to take to the sea were decisively quashed in naval battles off Gallipoli in 1416 and 1429. Strategic bases in Greece and the Aegean, defensible by sea, were seized, bought or otherwise acquired in the face of the Ottoman advance. Turkish raids on Venetian trade or property were answered in kind. And there were characteristically Venetian efforts to mobilize against the Turks those who, like the Tartars, the rulers of Moldavia or the shah of Persia, might divert their energies.[14] But if such tactics might delay, they could not halt the Turkish advance, an advance, moreover, soon as much by sea as by land. As ever with Venice, something could be saved. The main artery of her commerce, that to Egypt, was as yet unaffected, and even though the Turks were in Constantinople (after 1453), trade was still possible – on their terms – with the onetime Greek lands. Nevertheless the Ottoman hold on the Hellespont meant the ultimate exclusion of Venice from the Black Sea, though naturally enough commerce died neither totally nor abruptly. Far worse, the emergence of the Turks as a formidable seapower, able by 1499 to defeat Venice in a regular engagement, involved the republic in the expense of maintaining a greatly enlarged navy, and in all the burdens of war, as both the lines of her seaborne trade and her very control of the Adriatic were threatened.

II   *The east in fee*

That Venice could withstand the attacks of the greatest military empire of the time is a measure of the talents and resources she could command. Her rise to this power and affluence – and by the 1400s the republic's annual income surpassed that of any Italian rival and like as not those of most European monarchs – began, as we have already noticed, with that resurgence of Italy, and indeed of western Europe, which commenced with the ending in the early Middle Ages of Arab, Viking and Hungarian raids and conquests. And it was at this very time, when the first Venetian entrepreneurs could direct into maritime enterprise the skills of a local fishing and river-going population, that the dominant seapowers began to weaken. In the southern Mediterranean Arab shipbuilding was dangerously dependent on the timber supplied by others. It is also possible, though by no means certain, that simpler Italian construction techniques produced lighter, cheaper, and thus more economical vessels, than those built in the Greek style, their planks fastened to one another by mortise and tenon joints.[15] But the matter was more than one of resources and technology. Under the control of a bureaucracy hostile to trade, Byzantium allowed its commerce to pass largely into alien hands, and its merchant shipping to decline. Yet for defence it was obliged to maintain, at considerable cost, a naval force whose vessels, however, unlike those of private Italian owners, could not be employed in what according to taste may be regarded as the accumulation of loot or capital. Meanwhile a favourable geographical situation, well-removed from the major centres of political power in east and west alike and sheltered from sudden seaborne attack by the long gulf of the Adriatic, ensured Venice's initial survival and allowed her subsequent commercial expansion. And it was the association with Byzantium which brought the city's establishment in those trades from which her wealth was to come.

The essence of this commerce was the import of oriental luxuries, especially spices, and their redistribution throughout Europe. By any standards, and especially those of the Hanse or Dutch bulk trades, it was in volume modest, even insignificant, and in 1400 amounted to the import of no more than 500t of spices a year. Nor, as in the later operations of the Portuguese and their competitors, were they carried over vast distances by Europeans, who in the Middle Ages generally penetrated no nearer to the sources of supply than Asia Minor and the eastern Mediterranean. But the value and importance of this commerce were immense. By the fourteenth century the cargo of a single Venetian galley could be worth a royal ransom, and spices were handled by a small group of influential plutocrats, commonly making 40 per cent profit a year on their investments, and whose speculations and financial dealings had an enormous influence on the medieval economy. The fundamental Venetian import, 'the very milk and nourishment' of the city's being, as it was dramatically put in a moment of crisis, was the pepper of India and Indonesia, accounting in 1400 for about 60 per cent of the volume of its spice trade. This was chiefly used, in a world without other techniques of preservation, to make palatable meat which had been salted down. In addition it was Venice and her competitors who for centuries supplied the green ginger needed for salads and preserves, and such other Asiatic spices as cloves and cinnamon. But spice was a vast and ill-defined generic which also embraced perfumes like incense and musk, medicines and drugs (the galingale of China and the aloes of Socotra), dyes, and the exquisite manufactures of the east, ranging from Chinese silk and porcelain to the carpets and tapestries of Persia. To these were added the products, as we shall see, of the Middle East – the glassware, for example of Damascus – and curiosities such as assorted exotic animals and birds, like that parrot whose persistent conversation with a corpse being shipped home for burial, confirmed the worst suspicions of a devout passenger in a Venetian galley as to what went on at sea.

These commodities Europeans acquired in the markets of Asia Minor and the Levant where there terminated routes from the Orient whose number and variety explain – together with its enormous profitability – the indestructibility of the Asian trade in the face of apparently incessant difficulties, just as they explain the successive shifts of Venetian interest in the Middle East. When, in the 800s, the city first emerges as of any commercial significance, one major flow of oriental commerce was across the steppes of central Asia to the Crimea, and another from Afghanistan and Persia to Trebizond. From these entrepôts goods were then carried by Greek ships to Constantinople, which in part accounts for the early Venetian concern with the penetration of both the Greek empire and the Black Sea. But with these routes disrupted after the eleventh century by nomadic invaders, ambitions were turned elsewhere. Byzantium, like its Moslem successors in Egypt and Syria, had a maritime link with Asia through the Red Sea and the Indian Ocean. When conditions allowed, which was the case after *c.* 1000, oriental goods were shipped to Jiddah, from where they travelled either to Damascus (and so to the coast), or to Cairo (for Alexandria and Acre) from Suez and Quseir. And further north, though in decline by the eleventh century, yet another route led through the Persian Gulf and Sinbad's home port of Basra to Baghdad and Damascus. So, to avoid the Greek monopoly of the dwindling long-distance trade through the Black Sea, the Italian maritime cities turned to the markets of the Middle East, their importance further enhanced by the establishment of the Latin crusading principalities. From these, once the urge to plunder had cooled, there was conducted a flourishing trade with the infidel in the same way, and to the similar scandal of zealots, that later Portuguese colonists in Asia dealt with, and even entered into partnerships with, Moslems (cf. p. 274ff.). From their bases at Acre and Tyre[16] (until lost to Egypt in 1291), Venetians shipped to the west local products such as cotton and sugar, together with those of the Orient brought up by native caravans from Egypt, or across Syria and Palestine. And in Egypt, a ready market for timber and metals, there could likewise be obtained not only eastern spices but the valuable alum, sugar and wheat of the country itself. Nevertheless the trade was not without its difficulties. In the Middle East Europeans faced no such fragmented opposition, and enjoyed few such technological advantages as did, to begin with, the Germans in the Baltic (cf. pp. 46–7). The Moslem sultans, rulers of a vigorous martial state that could defeat crusaders and Mongols alike, refused to allow foreign merchants through their lands and insisted on an Egyptian monopoly of the commerce of the Red Sea – a monopoly which, even had they wished, the Venetians were in no position to destroy by land, or circumvent by sea. Furthermore the great entrepôt of Alexandria was a fortified Egyptian city where Venetian, like other European merchants, traded at the mercy of the sultan's officers, especially so since the prevailing winds made westerly departures by ships difficult except in early spring or late autumn. Then, for a time (1291–1344) any such commerce was prohibited by the papacy. Ineffective the ban may have been, with private ships carrying cargoes from Egypt and Syria to Lajazzo or Cyprus to be picked up by the State fleets, but it further added to the attractions of those routes created, or re-opened, by the establishment of the Mongol empire.

This massive agglomeration of lands reaching from the Polar regions to the Indian Ocean, and from eastern Europe to the Pacific, conquered in the thirteenth century, blocked for one thing Egyptian access to the Orient. It further meant that under efficient Mongol rule the roads to the furthest east were open, and according to one contemporary expert 'perfectly safe whether by day or night'. And more than this, unlike the routes under Egyptian control they were, through Mongol tolerance, open to all who were willing to travel them. So the Polos reached China, whilst Venetian (and other) merchants traded to India and China, where in 1340 a Venetian woman died in Hankow (cf. p. 162). Catholic bishoprics were established in India and Samarkand, Peking became the seat of an archdiocese and Asia was dotted with mission stations. China could be reached by two ways. One was the so called sea route, running from either Trebizond or Lajazzo to Tabriz (cf. pp. 95–6). This Persian city was already known to the Venetians by the mid-1200s as an emporium for Chinese silk and was, an enthusiast claimed, 'the best place in the world for merchandise', his judgement endorsed by the creation there first of a Genoese and then (1324) a Venetian consulate. From Tabriz travellers went on to Hormuz on the Persian Gulf, and ultimately by eastern ships to India and south China – a marathon voyage taking in all about two years. But a second route was safer – in avoiding the sea – and quicker. One branch led from Tabriz to Merv, Bokhara and Samarkand, and the imperial posts which travelled this way could be in China within five or six months. From about 1300, however, this way was overshadowed by another, slow but convenient, which commencing in the Crimea crossed the steppes to Astrakhan or Sarai. From these towns merchants travelled by camel caravan over the desert to Urgench (from where India could be reached), on to Bokhara and Samarkand, through central Asia, and so into China.

It was the existence of these routes that explains the struggles between Venice and Genoa in the century and a half after 1260 for the mastery of the Black Sea, and for the establishment of bases there. From Trebizond Venice could reach the spices, precious stones and bullion that flowed to Tabriz; from Tana the riches of both the Black Sea hinterland and of India and China (cf. pp. 95, 98). So vigorous did these trades become that for a time old China hands were well-known in Italy and useful manuals describing the mechanisms and opportunities of the commerce of the Orient, and giving advice on everything from the tonsorial proprieties to the consolations offered by native women, were drawn up for the benefit of newcomers. And that the trade flourished is less colourfully shown by the fact that something like 60 per cent of the price at which state galleys were leased for eastern voyages came, in 1332–45, from those destined for the Black Sea. But by the mid-1300s the situation had once again radically changed, and with the routes through Persia and central Asia neither accessible nor safe, the Venetian spice trade swung away from the Black Sea and back to the markets of the Middle East – to Damascus, Tripoli, Amman, Cairo and above all to Alexandria and Beirut (cf. pp. 102 and 124). So between 1410–12 and again between 1443–56 it was ships destined for these two ports that accounted for roughly 80 per cent of the auction price of the eastern galleys. Here again there were problems. True, the collapse of Genoa (see pp. 168, 170) and the shift of Genoese energies to other endeavours left the trade through Egypt as a Venetian trade, and one whose flow became more predictable once the sultan brought Mecca and Jiddah under Egyptian authority in the 1420s. There were nevertheless other European competitors, those merchants from Naples, Ancona, Barcelona and southern France whose goods a pilgrim noticed in Cairo in 1395, and whose misdeeds, real or alleged, in a xenophobic Moslem state could rebound to Venice's disadvantage. But if with fellow Europeans there was some room for manoeuvre, far more delicate and difficult were relations with the sultan. It was by his licence that the Venetians enjoyed such rigorously defined privileges and footholds – notably their factories in Cairo and Alexandria – as they had in the country, and it was from him, as the self-appointed (in the 1420s) monopolist of pepper that they obtained the cargoes that were the basis of the republic's prosperity. Hence their unwillingness to give more than token support to those spasmodic attempts of western chivalry and piety to chastise the infidel, ideals being found, as they commonly are, detrimental to sound business. Even so, it was a situation that demanded all Venice's considerable diplomatic skills. The late medieval sultans were enmeshed in desperate economic difficulties, hypersensitive, as men in such crises frequently are, and only too willing to attempt to solve their problems by punitive taxation. In the late 1300s Europeans in Alexandria were paying dues of roughly 100 per cent the value of their goods in transit. In the 1440s there was the demand that pepper should sell at the Sultan's price and Venetian merchants were arbitrarily and violently imprisoned. Yet such was the European market for spices, and such the profit on the trade to the west, very largely (approximately 70 per cent) in Venetian hands,[17] that notwithstanding these obstacles – never diminished in the telling – the commerce throve. The amount of pepper exported from Syria and Egypt between 1400 and 1500 perhaps doubled, whilst in Venice its wholesale price fell 50 per cent in 1420–40, and was still lower at the end of the century than in its opening decades.

But spices were only a part, albeit the most important, of Venice's imports from the Levant. It was from the Middle East, taking the words in the broadest sense, that the republic had for centuries also shipped a great variety of other cargoes ranging from raw materials in bulk to such refinements as perfumes. From Egypt came grain, sugar and those delicious confectionaries that could, until recently, still be bought in Cairo and

Alexandria. Syria provided silken textiles, some of them made by native labour working in the Venetian enclave at Tyre, a city renowned for its silks since Antiquity. And from Syria, too, there came the vitrifiable sand used in the production of Venice's celebrated glass, together with cotton, increasingly in demand in the high Middle Ages with the growth of a major textile industry in south Germany. Such indeed was the scale and value of this traffic that it stimulated the development of special ships to handle it, and obliged the Venetian government to legislate for its regulation. By the 1300s there were laws to ensure that enterprising shippers filled only the holds, and not the decks, cabins and arsenals of vessels with cargo, and to prevent damage to ships and cargoes alike by the use of mechanical devices to compress the cotton to allow larger amounts to be loaded. Then, as we have seen, there were the Venetian imports from the littorals of the Black Sea and the Aegean – the silks of Thebes and Sparta; the alum of Asia Minor (used in the manufacture of cloth, glass and those distinctive Venetian mosaics); the grain of Thrace, Macedonia, Romania and southern Russia; the oil, timber, fish and furs of the northern hinterlands of the Black Sea (cf. pp. 95, 98).

To all these was soon added the considerable output of the Venetian possessions themselves – Crete, Cyprus, the lands in, and the islands off, southern Greece (cf. pp. 94 and 117). On a modest scale they in part fulfilled the classic colonial role of providing the metropolis with primary products. But they also became, under Venetian direction, the suppliers of manufactures in widespread demand, and, like members of other imperial economies, markets in some degree for one anothers goods (cf. pp. 283, 327).And with the passage of time, as Venetian needs grew, and as other sources of supply became less reliable or more difficult of access, the empire was of a still greater consequence. Its economy was developed with a skill perhaps unrivalled by any other early colonial power, to allow Venice to extract, by the careful fostering of local specialities, the maximum benefit from each minute territory. Crete, for example, a way station for shipping working to and from the Levant, prospered as an entrepôt locally distributing both western manufactures and oriental luxuries. As a stopping place for pilgrims bound for the Holy Land it enabled Venetian and local entrepreneurs to make money from feeding the pious – their appetites sharpened by a welcome return to land – and from such peculiarly Mediterranean home industries as the sale of souvenirs, and the organization of guided tours of wonders like the supposed Minotaur's labyrinth. Then there was the republic's purposeful encouragement, in the late Middle Ages, of the production of sugar. And with internal peace restored to the island, and with an abundant labour force of slaves and Armenian immigrants, the industry flourished until destroyed in the 1450s by the competition of that of the Portuguese Atlantic possessions (see p. 245). So efforts were diverted into the provision of increased amounts of Crete's sweet, potent and expensive malmsey wine, already exported to Flanders in the 1300s, and a century later being shipped to east and west alike – to Constantinople, Cyprus, Beirut, Bruges and London. Its appearance and acceptance in comfortable circles in the remote north-east of England can, for example, be traced in the accounts of the convent of Durham, where it is spasmodically mentioned in the 1470s and then more or less regularly until the Reformation. Such indeed was its popularity and ubiquity in the fifteenth century that the handling of the trade became a bone of contention between Venice and England, whilst northern gossips could assume that it was in a butt of malmsey that an English king had disposed of a troublesome brother. So successful were Venetian policies that with Crete supplying alum, grain, timber, sugar, wax, wine and the renowed scarlet dye (kermes); Cyprus providing salt, sugar and later cotton,[18] and Zante and Cephalonia those currants soon to enjoy enormous vogue in Tudor and early-Stuart England, the overseas territories were accounting for something like 16 per cent of the republic's annual income by the early 1400s. With this in addition to the profits of those great trades the empire had been created to defend, Venice was clearly an outstandingly successful imperial power.

The total value and volume of Venetian imports from the east over any substantial period of time are uncertain. Overall, perhaps, they constituted a commerce richer in quality and variety than the comparable oceanic trades of the Iberians, and than that of the Hanse. It was a commerce, furthermore, remarkable in involving the import of so many manufactures, reflecting, that is, Venice's dealings with developed economies in the Far and Middle East. But it was also a commerce characteristically colonial in its concern with primary products and with slaves. From the earliest centuries the Venetians, like the inhabitants of other Italian maritime cities, had been engaged in slaving, whigh largely meant selling Slavs taken from the Balkan littoral of the Adriatic to Italian and Moslem customers. Such activities, reduced in scale, continued into the fifteenth century, but with the opening of the Black Sea, and the rise of the slave-based Mameluke empire of Egypt, came far greater opportunities, and like their Genoese and Catalan competitors the Venetians emerged as formidable slavers in the eastern Mediterranean and Asia Minor. They had even fewer scruples than the Iberians were later to display as to the race, creed or colour of their victims, and their operations, by laymen and clergy alike, appear largely unimpaired by any qualms of sentiment or conscience (cf. pp. 268, 332). Sixteenth-century Venetian acts of manumission contain no such reflections on naturally bestowed liberty and humanly imposed bondage as do those – more numerous – from Genoa. And it is from Venice, too, that there comes in the early 1500s the 'Song of the Slave Merchant' telling of his wares, 'tall, agile and beautiful' awaiting 'sweet and dear servitude'. True, the buying and selling of slaves in the city centre was prohibited in 1386, and the trade in Christians condemned as being 'against God and the honour of our Lord'. Nevertheless in a society dependent on commerce, and accordingly resolutely and pragmatically devoted to the pursuit of profit, the traffic continued. Unlike that of the Iberians it was unimpeded by the idealism of powerful religious Orders and its nature and fluctuations were determined solely by the course of political events in the Levant (cf. p. 354). And though it was a trade that involved the buying and selling of Europeans and Christians, and the large-scale prostitution of young girls, it attracted neither then nor later nothing of the odium the Portuguese and Spaniards were to incur from their exploitation of the Amerindians and Africans.

Venice's major sources for slaves were the hinterlands of the Aegean and the Black Sea, and the Republic's activities were concentrated in two main centres. One was Tana, on the Sea of Azov (see pp. 98, 175, and 186), where in the mid-1300s Tartars, Circassians, Chinese, Jews, Mongols and Russians were being bought and sold. The other was Candia in Crete, where the native Greeks despatched their compatriots into slavery, the Venetians disposed of those who opposed their regime and Christian and Moslem merchants and corsairs marketed their captives. But what stimulated, shaped and finally destroyed this particular trade was the Ottoman advance to the west. Prisoners taken by the Turks could be sold by entrepreneurs, and thus the numbers and the ethnic origins of slaves available in Candia fluctuated according to the direction of the latest Ottoman thrust. After the 1380s the luckless Greeks, who had long formed the largest contingent, were reinforced by Russians, Tartars, Bulgarians, Wallachians, Albanians, Serbs and Hungarians, but with the races and nationalities from the Black Sea hinterland ultimately preponderant. Once, however, the Turks had subdued the southeast, and as their frontiers and their raids moved further west, they no longer needed the Venetian outlet. Deprived of this flow of prisoners, Crete by the late 1400s was conducting only a modest traffic, mainly in Turks and Negroes, whilst with the Bosphorus in Ottoman hands Tana was now virtually inaccessible (see pp. 100 and 170).

The volume of the Venetian trade is unknown, but with slave-owning so widespread in Mediterranean society it was clearly, in its heyday, considerable. From fourteenth-century Venetian Crete alone there are mentions of the slaves not only of the clergy (Catholic and Orthodox), officials and members of the professions, but of fishermen, and even of one belonging to a serf. So, too, a decree of the republic refers (1427) to cargoes of not less than 400 heads, and in Candia a single notary handled the sale of 58 slaves in ten months (1301–2), and another that of over 400 in the two years after 1381. Some of these slaves, bought (as at Tana) by Armenians, Jews, Tartars, Greeks and those Italians living, like the Portuguese were later to do in Africa (cf. p. 253), in the outback were intended for resale or service in the east. Girls became the servants and commonly the mistresses of, amongst others, European colonials with for example, a Venetian freeing in the early 1400s 'my Tartar, mother of my child'. Young males were shipped to Egypt to become fighting men in the sultan's army, or were taken for menial and agricultural labour in Crete, Cyprus and the surviving Latin possessions. At the same time Venetians, Genoese, Catalans and others were sending slaves to the west for sale along the Mediterranean littoral – in Africa, Italy, south Spain and southern France – where slavery in one form or another was to endure for centuries. These were almost exclusively girls in their early teens – many of them Christians[19] – used as domestic servants and concubines, their employment so common that in 1442 a Venetian gentleman could settle his debts to a shipwright by handing over a Russian girl to him.

The Venetian interest in the Levant was thus by the late Middle Ages complex, deep-rooted and accordingly tenacious, sustained not only by the legendary profits of the spice and luxury trades, but also by the exploitation of local markets and resources. The assorted products of these diverse economies were distributed throughout much of Europe. They went by sea from Venice to England and Flanders, to south Spain, France and Italy, by land to northern Italy, France, Switzerland, the Low Countries (should the maritime route be deemed for any reason unsafe) and an indeterminable area of the east of the continent and they were carried by merchants of Augsburg, Ulm and Nürnburg into Germany. And it was in these equally diverse markets that Venice found some of the things needed either to satisfy her own domestic demands, or to enable her to pay for her purchases in the Levant. From Spain she took, besides much else, wool, olive oil and silk; from Germany metal goods and precious metals; and from England woollen textiles, wool, hides and tin. In Bruges (and later Antwerp) she tapped not only the rich industrial resources of the Low Countries themselves, but also those of south and central Germany, and could acquire as well the products of that great Hanse economy whose nature we have already noticed (see pp. 44, 47). So in Flanders, whose prosperity and commercial associations usually assured a lively market for Venetian cargoes, the republic could buy anything from French or Flemish textiles to the assorted ironmongery concealed under the expressive generic of 'battery', or bowstrings destined for use by her own (and others') mercenaries. Like, however, all other European states trading to Asia until comparatively recent times, Venice had to contend with the problem of the imbalance between western needs and western purchasing power. For most of the medieval centuries the east had a great deal that Europe required, but Europe had relatively little for which there was any sizeable Asian demand.[20] The difficulty was, it is true, somewhat alleviated by the purely fortuitous fact that Venetian purchases of oriental goods were of necessity made in the Middle, and not the Far East, so allowing the resources of the Levant to be in some degree employed, though here too the limited market for European exports restricted what might be obtained. Venice was also able to use the earnings of her shipping industry, arising first from the transport of crusaders (as to Constantinople in 1203, when the freight charges came to about twice the annual income of the king of England), and then from the carriage of pilgrims to the Holy Land. This was a traffic more frequent than that resulting from the Scandinavian migrations across the North Sea and North Atlantic, and one of the largest, until the Iberian colonization of the Americas, involving the regular shipment of people rather than goods.[21] Such was its scale, and such the opportunities it offered the unscrupulous, that as early as 1229 it was the subject of detailed legislation by the republic. And when, from the narratives of late medieval travellers, something of its working can be seen, it appears like so many things

Venetian, as remarkably modern. There was a comprehensive organization to handle the needs of pilgrims: to assemble them on arrival in Venice, to house them, to assist them with their currency problems and to put them in touch with shipowners.

Most of the sailings were for Jaffa[22] (the port for Jerusalem), though there were some for Tripoli or Alexandria, from whence there was access to Mount Sinai. For the reasonably prosperous traveller there were two possibilities. He could go by galley – private, not state-owned – which meant a basically coastal passage with minimum exposure to the rigours of the sea, and plenty of stops for sight-seeing and refreshment. Or, by the end of the Middle Ages, he could go more cheaply by sailing ship, with, however, the intimidating prospect for many that the run was made direct and non-stop. For men of consequence, with whose families or countries the republic wished to remain on good terms, things were naturally more tastefully arranged. If no suitable private craft were to hand they might travel with the state galleys bound for the east, and if they were thought to be of special eminence they would be provided with a ship of their own. By the late Middle Ages this flourishing and rewarding traffic was handled exclusively by private owners, though the state intervened to ensure that the vessels employed were sound and adequate, to which end they were checked by officials in Venetian ports of call, or by Venetian naval squadrons at sea. Even so, travellers were eloquent on the shortcomings of ships, crews and owners alike. But given what the pious would endure for their faith, and what to return to the comfort of their homes, there was a seller's market for shipowners who could, for example, embark 600 pilgrims in one fleet in 1384.

There were, similarly, profits to be made in the Middle East from the sale of arms, or of the materials from which weapons and ships could be produced. So from the earliest date, with that same economic logic by which the Dutch were to provide their Iberian opponents with munitions (see p. 381ff.), the Venetians exported to the Levant the timber vital to a largely treeless Egypt, and the equally vital iron which in the later Middle Ages was sent indiscriminately to the Black Sea, the surviving Latin outposts, and to ports under Mameluke or Ottoman control. Then again there were the earnings of Venetian ships in various local trades in the eastern Mediterranean. Even so, the fundamental commercial imbalance of the west and east remained, and merchants of the Republic, like the Romans before them and the Portuguese, Dutch and English after them, were obliged to pay for some of their purchases with precious metals, either coined or unminted, for which there was an insatiable demand in certain Far Eastern economies (see p. 270). For the most part it was silver that was used, obtained from Germany, Bohemia (especially in the fourteenth and fifteenth centuries), Bosnia and Serbia. And to the silver of Europe there was added by the 1400s the gold of the Sudan and Abyssinia, acquired in Egypt, and that of North Africa which reached the south-Mediterranean coast by routes across the Sahara. Thus the Venetians were early established at Ceuta (probably from the 1200s), and were familiar with Tripoli, Algiers and Oran by the fifteenth century. A regular galley service to Barbary was instituted in 1440, and from then until the early 1500s there was a steady and substantial flow of

African gold to Venice. The volume and value of the republic's export of coin and bullion to the east is unknown, but it was clearly considerable – on the departure of the Levant fleet in 1464 the city was said to be without money since all its silver was 'sailing in the ships for Syria'.[23] Nor was this the rhetoric of publicists, for by the end of the century specie probably accounted for anything from 40 per cent to 60 per cent of the value of the cargoes carried by state ships to Syria and Egypt.[24] Not surprisingly, when the Portuguese arrived in Asia they found Venetian coins seemingly ubiquitous.

Some of the remainder of her imports Venice paid for with either high-priced natural products or with European manufactures. And such was the skill of her merchants, and such the range of economies upon which they could draw, that these comprised a larger proportion of her exports than they did of those of her Mediterranean rivals or, in the sixteenth century, of her Portuguese competitors (cf. p. 270). Hence alongside coin and bullion there appeared in Venetian cargoes quick-silver, amber and coral (further explaining the Venetian interest in Germany and North Africa), together with products of the city itself, like glass. Equally important were copper (which could be minted in Asia), tin and lead, which went out either unworked, or in the form of the metal goods and weapons of which south Germany was a major producer. But of the most far-reaching economic significance was the export of textiles. From silk brought in from all over the Levant and Asia Minor, Venice was in the late Middle Ages making cloths, some of which were shipped to Constantinople and Alexandria. Even more important were the woollen cloths, which already in the twelfth century Venetians – like other Italians – were buying in northern Europe, partly for domestic consumption, but chiefly for export to Africa and the Levant. By the early 1200s there was a substantial flow from Venice to the Middle East of an impressive variety of such textiles, with a tariff of 1265 mentioning thirty different Flemish and English sorts, all of them of high quality and price, together with some cheaper Italian brands. With the passage of time new industries developed – including in Venice itself from the 1200s – at the expense of the old, and the main centres of production shifted from northern to southern Europe and back again. But the increasing volume of exports to the Middle East meant that – intermittent crises apart – the pressure on coin and bullion was significantly eased, whilst European purchasing power was enhanced, so allowing a further growth in the demand for eastern luxuries (cf. p. 104). And at the same time, to meet the requirements of wealthy oriental clients Europe turned to the manufacture of those sumptuous fabrics, such as Milanese cloth of gold, that Venice was exporting in the fifteenth century.

Finally there were the earnings of Venetian ships able, as the long arms of Venetian enterprise stretched further through northern and Mediterranean waters, to work in interport trades. In the Black Sea they carried, for example, local grain and wine to Constantinople. The state galleys sailing to North Africa, attractive in their reputation for safety and reliability, were used by Moorish merchants for trade and travel between Tunis and Alexandria. Those on passage to the north called in Iberian ports to load such things as silks, fruits and dyes which they took to England so causing, the Commons complained in the early 1400s, English ships to be thrown out of work, and prices to be intolerably increased. Indeed, such was the efficiency of their operation that it was even worth their carrying German furs from Bruges to Southampton on their return south from Flanders.

Yet if these trades guaranteed the wealth and power of Venice, her control of the commercial empire they constituted is not to be explained simply in economic terms. Starting in much the same circumstances, and with much the same opportunities, her Italian rivals, Genoa especially, were unable to achieve the same results.

In part this reflects that same good fortune which in the early centuries had allowed the establishment and survival of the Republic. Until the rise of the Spanish and Ottoman empires Venice was never subject to the sustained pressure of powerful neighbours. Before that, dangerous though they might be, the cities and principalities surrounding her were for the most part small, and almost all chronically unstable. And at the same time imperial authority in Germany declined, and with it any serious threat from imperial ambitions in Italy, whilst Byzantium, from whose internal factional strife the city was indeed to benefit, sank into political insignificance in the later Middle Ages. But of fundamental importance was Venice's ability to exploit whatever chances were offered. Initially doges as able and forceful as Pietro II Orseolo (who enforced Venetian authority in the central Adriatic *c.* 1000), Sebastiano Ziani (who in 1177 mediated between pope and emperor), and Enrico Dandolo (who in his 80s extracted from the Fourth Crusade great advantages for his city), gave a vital and forceful direction to Venetian expansion (see pp. 91–3). Then the domination of the republic by a commercial aristocracy brought it a unique stability and meant that for something like 500 years its policies had a consistency of purpose and an efficacy in execution hardly paralleled elsewhere. Not that an interest in the conduct and well-being of commerce had not already long been present, and even when Venice was ruled like any other nascent dynastic principality by a duke (doge) and his councillors, such magnates were engaged in trade, with an aristocratic will of 829 showing besides landed holdings investments in shipping and commerce. And such concerns became paramount as power shifted to a more extensive patriciate, recruited in part from ancient landed families, in part from those of more recent mercantile origins.

Thus by the fourteenth century Venice was in the hands of a remarkable aristocracy, the object of much contemporary wonder and comment, its privileges conferred not by some grateful (or impecunious) sovereign for services given or expected, but by civic recognition of a wealth and standing achieved through commerce. To the accumulation of land, particularly in the republic's overseas possessions, some of its members were not averse, though few devoted much of their capital to the improvement of such acquisitions. But Venice and Venetian ambitions were unaffected by the whims of a predatory martial aristocracy, hankering for dynastic aggrandizement through military ventures. And no more than the equally mercantile Holland did Venice possess a class of bellicose squires and depressed peasants, who in more primitive societies could envisage and accomplish vast schemes of conquest and colonization. Like the Genoese or the Dutch, the Venetians might well seek to dispose of their commercial rivals by force. But equally like the Genoese or the Dutch only rarely – and for the most part relatively late in their history – did they turn to the extensive annexation of territory, to settlement, or to the exaction of tribute (cf. pp. 117, 184, 386). Instead the republic's ruling class endeavoured to protect and further its commercial interests. True, there were disputes as to how this might best be effected – not least as to the benefits of formal imperial expansion – whilst the unsuccessful pursuit of profit abroad could lead, as in the thirteenth and fourteenth centuries, to revolt at home. Yet Venice's troubles were nothing in comparison with those which in the end crippled Genoa, and her policies, whatever their defects, entailed no such dissipation of resources as did those, frequently mutually contradictory, of states such as England or Spain (cf. p. 470ff.).

The other major element in Venetian success was the city's astonishingly cohesive and stable society which, if it inspired few of its inhabitants to seek sanctuary or opportunity in distant lands, also freed it from many of the disruptions and distractions that affected other imperial powers. Venice had, as we have seen, no turbulent martial grandees or squires. Its economy was less specialized, and thus less precarious, than that of Genoa (see p. 196). Furthermore, regarded by its ruling oligarchs as a commercial entrepôt, it was never in the medieval centuries a manufacturing centre in the sense that textile cities such as Florence were, supporting a sizable population of workers and artisans, and thus vulnerable to the disorders arising from the industrial recession or dislocation. Moreover, as a predominantly maritime city, and particularly as the employer of large, oared vessels, much of its manpower – and presumably the most vigorous and adventurous – was often and regularly away from home in its merchant and war fleets, and so removed from the temptations and opportunities of concerted political activity (see pp. 126–9). The very involvement of Venetian patricians in trade – perhaps initially since other outlets for their energies were few; perhaps because the attractions of a commerce already flowing in the vicinity of the nascent republic were so obvious – may have helped to turn their tastes from violence. Possibly, too, their behaviour was tempered in the earliest centuries by membership of a community formed, unlike Genoa, in the authoritarian traditions of Byzantium, and demanding that individual interests be subordinate to civic requirements, just as it was coloured in later years by the revival of Roman ideals of public service. And Venetian aristocrats were in any case, from the very nature of Venice's beginnings as an island refuge, far more completely integrated into their city than were those of Genoa, who retained castles in the neighbouring and independent countryside to which, in the event of political defeat, they could withdraw for safety, and to recoup their forces. But magnates living in Venice were prevented by sheer lack of space from housing within their palaces those bands of retainers needed to stimulate and sustain factional war, just as they were obliged to dwell not in clan-dominated enclaves, but scattered throughout the city. And in a congested world of canals, bridges and squares they were, like Dutch patricians, far more exposed to public scrutiny – and potential hostility – than were the grandees of more conventional societies. Their presence within the city made them, unlike the Genoese magnates, frequently exiled or in foreign service, the eventual patrons of a distinctive culture. And though undoubtedly wealthy some of them were, it was not a wealth for the most part ostentatiously displayed or offensively concentrated in a few hands, and – most important – it was paralleled by an impressive non-patrician wealth. When, in 1379, the republic determined those who were of sufficient means to lend to the state, out of a total of just over 2000 nearly half were non-noble. Thus whilst foreigners might complain of the arrogance and rudeness of the Venetian aristocrats, 'inherited from their fishermen ancestors', with the inhabitants of the city remained in general popular, and their rule was never maintained by armed force.

All these advantages, however bestowed, were consciously improved. From the high Middle Ages the state was entirely controlled by the aristocracy – a class carefully and generously, though not finally defined in the late thirteenth century. Then, by limiting the powers of the most ancient families, and by giving access to office to the greatest number of the patriciate, many causes of discontent and disaffection were deftly removed. Cumbersome and complex the government of the city may have been, but its very profusion of councils and committees, and its convoluted electoral procedures, made it seem that all who wished might become usefully employed. Yet at the same time supreme power was wielded   and as expeditiously as anywhere if need be – by a mere handful comprising the doge, his cabinet, the influential officers of other councils and (later) a number of ministers with special responsibilities. So, though not without disagreements, the patricians could systematically and effectively implement those policies thought most beneficial to their own and the state's well-being. Inspired in part by the pragmatic realism of merchants whose wealth depended on dealings with non-Europeans, and often Moslems, and in part, from the fifteenth century, by classical ideals of good and just rule, they sought, as did the Dutch oligarchs, to ensure by fair and tolerant government that resources were fully exploited, useful talents not lost, and discontents allayed. In a spirit very different from that of such intolerant and non-mercantile societies as Habsburg Iberia or Tudor and early Stuart England they allowed, as was often remarked, considerable freedom of speech. They oppressed neither their colonial peasantry nor their metropolitan labour force, which was handled with a benign paternalistic firmness: the idle and unruly were punished and the widows and orphans cherished. In the empire, the Greek aristocracy of Crete, provided it showed itself co-operative, was allowed to retain its privileges, and native Cretan customs were – somewhat disdainfully – left unaffected. Slavery apart, this same modest liberalism in matters of race and religion was manifested in the city itself. After some difficulties, a Greek Orthodox community with its own church and cemetery was established, and there was likewise no violent reaction when in the early 1500s Lutheranism took a hold among both artisans and patricians in Venice.[25] Even the

Jews, almost universally persecuted in the west, were, by the standards of the time, well treated.

More than this, though much patrician money was from an early date in bonds and land, the Venetian aristocrats had the clearest views as to where wealth lay, and the will and power to implement their opinions as to how such opportunities were to be exploited and improved. The great and enormously profitable traffic in oriental luxuries became their prerogative, though a prerogative they would share with some members of that equally carefully defined, but less privileged class, the 'citizens'. Under their guidance, and for their benefit Venice was turned, in a way of which later mercantilist thinkers would have approved, into one vast entrepôt since, as a statute of 1363 explained with engaging frankness, 'nothing is better able to increase and enrich the condition of our city than to give to all the liberty and occasion that commodities be brought here and procured here rather than elsewhere, because this results in advantage both to the state and to private persons.' Hence the republic was to be the intermediary in Europe's trade with the east, for the more exclusive control of which Venetians were encouraged, not to say compelled, to join city cartels for the purchasing of oriental goods. Hence, too, the insistence that the commerce of its colonies be channelled through Venice, the republic's enforcement of its hegemony in the Adriatic and its economic and political ambitions in northern Italy. So, also, its seaborne commerce was to be carried only in Venetian ships – guarded, if need by, by Venetian men-of-war – or in vessels of the cargo's country of origin. For the defence and advance of these trades the odium of Christian Europe was incurred by accommodating behaviour to Jews, Moslems and other undesirables, a whole series of maritime and colonial wars was fought and those who, like the sultan of Egypt in 1430, impeded the life-giving flow of commerce were brought to heel by naval or economic pressure (see pp. 95–9 and 102).

But Venetian economic policy was not, in the republic's triumphant centuries, one of unintelligent and bellicose protectionism. Less adventurous than that of the equally commercially based Dutch state it may have been, yet it was still in general enlightened. Provided they accepted its terms all, including erstwhile opponents, were encouraged to trade in the city. On the whole medieval Venetians were not troubled by those restrictions on the taking of interest on loans which elsewhere hampered business, and money-lenders were not harassed before the fourteenth century, and then only for charging excessive rates. Dealing as they did with the advanced commercial economies of much of the Levant in the early Middle Ages, Venetian, like other Italian merchants, acquired new techniques of mobilizing and transmitting wealth. Trade deliberately directed through Venice the city could tax with ease. And unlike most other imperial powers it could also successfully tax its overseas possessions – many of them as onetime Byzantine territories accustomed to such exactions – prudently run on business lines (cf. pp. 93, 105–6, 122). In Venice itself a fiscal system was devised which, though of that common order by which the prosperity of the rich was ensured at the expense of the poor, was nevertheless without the fatal consequences of that of Castile, yet of enormous benefit to the ruling oligarchs (cf. p. 368). From 1262 Venice maintained a funded public debt to which all of substantial resources were obliged to contribute. In return they received bonds giving them interest – 2.5 per cent in the fourteenth century – paid from the imperial revenues, and from indirect taxes on things such as salt and wine. Until well into the 1500s the opulent received far more in interest than they contributed in loans, whilst at the same time the state's resources were, like those of the more fiscally equitable Dutch republic, adequate and it was never reduced to those desperate expedients the common lot of most monarchies (cf. pp. 273, 368, 428).

Furthermore, the well-being of Venice was ensured by the regulation of virtually every aspect of the political and economic life of the republic and its colonies on a scale not elsewhere attempted before the creation of the Iberian maritime empires (see pp. 276, 341). From the high Middle Ages the balance and flow of commerce were, as far as was possible, controlled. Shipping was diverted from unprofitable runs, and the over or under supply of tonnage redressed by adjusting the volume and cost of what was available. The payment of bounties was used to stimulate the construction of craft of the required size whilst periodic prohibitions of the employment of foreign-built vessels protected the native construction industry. It was the state that decreed what armaments should be carried by its own and private ships alike. It measured and recorded the carrying capacity of every vessel, attempted to ensure that this was not exceeded, insisted that adequate crews and gear were embarked and legislated to restrain the cupidity of masters who might otherwise, for private profit, overload their commands or simply sell their rigging. And whilst the smallest of private vessels could work unsupervised – as did also some large sailing craft in the late Middle Ages – the operation of any Venetian-owned ships carrying valuable goods was likewise under state direction.

Together with the creation of a Venetian navy, the acquisition of a strategically sited empire and the operation of a fleet of state-owned merchant galleys, these policies helped to ensure the solvency and stability of the republic and the prosperity of its ruling oligarchs (see pp. 118–29). The provision of state-owned ships allowed the concentration of merchant capital in trade, and it allowed, too, men of relatively modest means to remain in business since they were able to get their goods transported. In such ways the accumulation of vast individual fortunes was prevented, and with the resultant broad distribution of wealth, and through a judicious admixture of private and public enterprise, the possibility of economic and political unrest diminished. In its insistence on the monopoly of certain trades, and in its stipulation as to where commodities were to be shipped, and by whom they were to be handled, Venetian policy was fundamentally a more extensive and logical version of the measures commonly favoured by other commercial cities, such as those of the Hanse (cf. pp. 53–4). Yet it contrasted sharply with the liberal economic behaviour – in Europe at least – of the similarly based Dutch republic. It was in part a difference dictated by their contrasting social and political structures – the Low Countries barely constituting a state; their urban oligarchs without the authoritarian traditions of the Venetian patricians – in part by the very nature of the trades that brought and established their respective prosperity. The Dutch rose to power on the transport in bulk of grain, salt and wine. This generated a mass of low-cost tonnage, and was initially handled through a variety of small ports hardly needing, let along permitting, close regulation or elaborate protection (see pp. 375–8). The source of Venetian prosperity on the other hand was the shipment of insignificant quantities of high-priced luxuries, seasonally available at a limited (and decreasing) number of centres in the Levant, and transported to the west in a handful of vessels constituting a potential prize of a value unequalled until the appearance of the Iberian spice and bullion fleets (cf. pp. 270, 342). Even the Dutch themselves, ardent protagonists though they might be of the freedom of the seas in other waters, were in turn to operate their spice trade in much the style of Venice (see pp. 396, 407). But though other imperial powers might devote much of their energies and resources to the defence of some particular monopoly, with none, except Venice, did its running and protection become in effect the whole purpose of their being, with the state providing the ships for its operation and a navy and empire for its safeguard.

Like other commercial empires, that of the city was to start with a network of trading posts, the majority, however, in rich, cosmopolitan and ancient centres of international exchanges. In these, linked to Venice by routes dominated by her merchants and ships, the republic enjoyed a variety of vigorously maintained fiscal and jurisdictional privileges. Thus, as we have seen, there were Venetians early established in Constantinople, Greece, the Black Sea and the Levant, as later in the Low Countries, England and Persia. These concessions often entailed more than exemption from the authority of the local ruler, and in the Holy Land, for example, Venice owned either outright or in part 60 per cent of the villages in the lordship of Tyre. Nor were Venetian factories (*fondaci*) allowed by a purposefully governed parent society anything of the wayward individualism of those of the fissiparous league of Hanseatic towns.[26] Instead each was under the direction of a salaried Venetian patrician appointed not by his compatriots abroad – true colonials who were born and spent their lives overseas – but by the Venetian state, to which he took an oath of loyalty, and to which he eventually gave account of his conduct. Such consuls exercised jurisdiction over their fellow countrymen within a factory, handled Venetian relations with the local ruler and kept the mother city regularly informed as to the course of events.

Unlike, however, those other primarily commercial powers, the Hanse and Holland, Venice added to trading privileges the sizable acquisition of territory. True, no more than the Dutch had the city, as a prosperous and generally equitable business community, either the inclination or the resources in manpower to undertake any significant colonization (cf. pp. 66ff. and 389). And equally, like the Dutch, little talent or energy was directed to missionary endeavour. Hence in its imperial days Venice made no such mark on the societies and civilizations subject to its rule as did in the Americas the migratory and proselytizing Iberians. Its conversion to formal empire was characteristically cautious, slow and late. Initially in the east Venice sought freedom for its merchants to trade unimpeded, not to say unchallenged. Then, under the impetus of Genoese rivalry, and with Byzantium increasingly feeble, it attempted to ensure that its citizens overseas could control their own affairs and organize their own defence. Finally, in the early 1200s, it seized the opportunity to acquire lands and islands covering the trade routes to the Black Sea and the Middle East (see pp. 91–3).

The subjugation of some of these acquisitions, Crete especially, was to tax the abilities of a non-military state to the full. Though only some 300km long and 50km broad the island nevertheless dwarfed its potential suzerain. Moreover, behind its prosperous and densely populated littoral there lay great mountain ranges, their valleys blocked by snow in winter and scorched by the sun in summer, and supporting a determined and intractable people, Greek in speech and Greek Orthodox in religion. Thus between this essentially rural world, accustomed to the rule of a distant but nonetheless absolute and sacerdotal Byzantine emperor, and that of the urban, commercial, Latin and Catholic Venice there was an antipathy as complete as that between the Spaniards and the natives of the Americas (see p. 358). Individual Venetians might learn Greek and marry Greek women, but Latin and Italian were the languages of empire, and Greek society as a whole, and that of Crete in particular, were something outside the republic's interest and experience. There were on the island large numbers of small-holders and freemen, unwavering believers in the sanctity of hereditary possessions, determined enemies of any change likely to endanger their property, their natural hostility sustained by their Church. Above them were the great aristocratic landowners, with vast and growing ancestral estates. They had everything to lose by surrender to the Venetians and their wealth and standing made them the natural leaders of any opposition. Thus the situation was quite unlike that of the Spaniards in America later. The island was unconquered, the restoration in 1261 of the Greek empire strengthened its hostility, Venice had no military advantage and there was no support to be had from any disaffected class ready to rise against its rulers. Without the impetus provided in Iberia by the ambitions of martial squires, and in Germany by the hopes of an oppressed peasantry for the sanctuary and opportunities of some Utopia, and without the German experience of extensive colonization, the city thought at first merely to occupy a limited number of strategic posts (cf. pp. 42–3 and 388). Then, in face of native and Genoese opposition, it attempted to subdue the island, demanding the unconditional surrender of the native aristocracy. This, too, having failed it turned to conquest, but to a conquest to be undertaken by feudatories, and eased by agreements with amenable Cretan magnates. Reserving to itself the areas vital to its commercial policies, and granting to the well-disciplined and subservient Venetian church a suitably rich reward, the rest of the island was turned into fiefs – lands held, as was already the case in Venetian Tyre, in exchange for the discharge of military and other duties. Some were granted to members of ancient Venetian families, others to those of less distinguished origins, and a suitable population was provided by carefully selected settlers from the mother city. Unlike those of the Germans in the north-east, these were techniques of subjugation rather than exploitation, foreshadowing in detail practices soon to become familiar in the first oceanic empires (cf. pp. 42–3, 247, 392). Characteristically, Venetian policies entailed no such abdication of sovereign rights as did those of Genoa, or as was threatened or occurred in the vast colonies of the Iberians (cf. pp. 190, 248, 321). The tenure of fiefs was indeed hereditary, but no more than in Spanish America was there to be anything of the luxuriant feudal growth of early medieval Europe. Military forces were mustered by officers of the State, fiefs were held on clearly defined terms and patricians appointed as knights – the prime conquerors and defenders of the colony – were obliged to live in Candia where the state could watch their activities.

So the systematic subjugation of the island commenced, and by the mid-1200s the Republic had sent out 3500 colonists, an enormous sacrifice in manpower for a community of about 50,000. For a time, too, amicable relations were established with some Cretan aristocrats, until the restoration of the Greek empire in Constantinople (1261) again stiffened their resistance. Hence to the end of the century Venice had to struggle first with George Cortazzi – finally exiled – and then with Alexis Kalergis, who ultimately secured excellent terms for himself, including the recognition of his hereditary estates and liberties. Such concessions, however, whether formally granted or tacitly permitted, brought their own problems. There were complaints (1302) from Venetian families that unworthy natives flourished whilst those who were 'flesh of the flesh and bones of the bones' of the mother city were ruined. Overtaxed, short of labour, pressed by the incessant demands of the embattled state for money and supplies, and with their complaints unheeded, some of the Venetian colonial aristocracy eventually joined with Greek magnates in a revolt (1363) which took the republic three years to suppress.

And now, as the city became a deliberate and conscious imperial power, the whole nature of Venetian expansion began to change. In Crete the very magnitude of the problem, with the ominous emergence of an opposition compounded of Greek and Venetian discontent, demanded careful attention. Then there was the republic's consistent and realistic desire for some suitable return on current investment. But this explains neither the speed nor the extent of her territorial acquisitions both in Italy and the Levant. The final collapse of Genoa, and the chronic political instability of northern Italy could justify, as the prudent anticipation of impending dangers, the occupation of lands. Then again, the Ottoman advance persuaded assorted princelings to accept Venetian sovereignty, just as it enabled and encouraged the city to take strategic bases from which trade routes could be patrolled and enemies watched. Yet in Italy at least her conduct was not determined solely by such foresight. Imperial expansion took on that familiar momentum of its own, and as an increasingly aristocratic patriciate welcomed the opportunity to accumulate lands or secure office within the new possessions, Venice was drawn into areas well outside any logical sphere of interest or influence.

In Crete this purposeful imperialism meant strenuous efforts in the late fourteenth century to repopulate the island, to vitalize its economy, and to ensure its ability to pay its taxes. Similar policies were used elsewhere – in 1425, for instance, 300 families were moved from Athens to Negroponte – as territories old and new were brought under a tighter control. More than this, Venice showed itself magnificently adept in the deployment of every known technique of aggrandizement. Legal claims, however tenuous, were doggedly pursued, rulers – usually weak and insecure – were pushed into surrender, acceptable regimes were set up (as by the Hanse) where necessary and lands were bought, annexed or simply conquered. In 1378 there was an attempt to seize Tenedos, which controlled the access to the Dardanelles. Failure here was balanced by success elsewhere in the Aegean, with Negroponte finally under Venetian rule in 1383, as were the islands of Mykonos and Tinos, and the towns of Argos and Nauplia (in the eastern Morea) by 1390. Four years later Athens was annexed, and Thessalonika in 1423, whilst in 1431 Venice was trying, not for the first time, to get control of Chios 'the right eye of the Genoese' (see pp. 186–7). Aegina was conveniently inherited in 1451; the northern Sporades islands taken two years later; and Naxos at last acquired in 1494. Thus whilst Crete held the republic's trade with the Levant was secure, and the egress of hostile fleets from the northern Aegean could be, if not checked, at least observed. But that not all was governed by rational calculation was shown by the acquisition in 1489 of the former kingdom of Cyprus. Given its proximity to the Ottoman heartland, it was a move provocative rather than prudent. And characteristically enough sufficient title was found in the fact that the widowed queen was Venetian. That her husband had been a usurper, and that force was needed to revive her flagging loyalties to the mother city, were matters of no concern in such exuberant days.

Similarly, Venetian interests in the Adriatic were guarded by denying any undesirable power access to the sea and by ensuring that its shores never fell into the hands of a single hostile state. Hence the occupation in 1386 of Corfu, 'the very heart of the Venetian state by sea', and Paxo and Butrinto after the failure of earlier attempts. The Albanian bases of Durazzo, Alessio and Scutari became Venetian in 1392, and between 1411 and 1419 the towns and islands of the Dalmatian coast were conquered. Lepanto was obtained (1407), like as not by force, and in the Morea – which Venice for a time thought of annexing outright – Navarino was added (1417) to the existing strongholds of Modon and Coron. In 1482 the island of Zante was acquired to forestall the ambitions of the Aragonese in Naples, who showed every sign of emulating the earlier behaviour of the Normans and Angevins in southern Italy. And from a war against the Ottomans (1499–1503) Venice emerged with Cephalonia and Ithaca. So by the end of the fifteenth century she had an almost unbroken chain of possessions – some little more than rocks surmounted by castles – lining the entire eastern coast of the Adriatic and Ionian seas. The trade of potential rivals was controlled or suppressed, the Venetian monopoly ensured and extended and the ships of the republic sailed, as they are frequently portrayed, in armed strength through waters commanded by fortified Venetian strongholds. And to this overseas empire there was simultaneously added –

just as the Spaniards were to add, with less rational purpose, hegemony in Europe to the conquest of the Americas – another on the mainland, where by 1500 Venice controlled in Italy territories whose outposts stretched from the Tyrol to Apulia, and from the head of the Adriatic almost to Milan. With these her access to the vital markets of northern Italy by the valley of the Po was ensured, and she held the approaches to the Alpine routes leading through the Val Camonica, the Brenner Pass and the valley of the Piave to the vast commercial hinterland of Europe.

For the control of these possessions, or at least those overseas, there was created a clearly defined system of government, many of whose features were to recur in other imperial administrations. The colonies, whether commercial enclaves or territorial holdings, were regarded as parts of the commune of Venice, and were all administered in the same way. The supreme officers – the consuls in the factories, the duke in Crete, the castellans of the various fortified bases, the count in Zara – were the representatives of, and entirely subject to, the mother city, which both determined imperial policy and directed its enforcement. To this end power in the overseas possessions was divided between an individual (duke, consul, etc.) and a small executive council, this in turn assisted (and balanced) by a number of other councils representing the interests of Venetian residents and, to a lesser extent, of native inhabitants. And the effective functioning of these simplified replicas of the republic's constitution was ensured by regular inspection and investigation by the state.

The key figure of each colony, whether castellan, duke or consul, was a Venetian patrician appointed by the city, his duties, powers and qualifications defined with that same precision as was later displayed in Iberian imperial commissions. He was to be aged at least twenty-five and was to hold office for no more than two years. To ensure his impartiality and whole-hearted devotion to duty, he was to receive a salary and, together with his household, to refrain from private business until the closing weeks of his tenure. It was his responsibility to dispense justice fairly, to see to the defence of the territory entrusted to him, to ensure that taxes were collected, and to keep a record of his administration's income and expenditure. And to prevent anything other than these thoroughly practical and businesslike aims from being translated into action, Venetian colonial governors needed the assent of their councils to validate any decision. More than this, their behaviour, like that of the similarly circumscribed viceroys of imperial Spain, was subject to an ever closer surveillance. Their accounts were checked, their correspondence examined, and by 1400 a regular machinery of inspection had been evolved. Every five years two specially appointed officers were sent by the state to Crete, and two others to Durazzo, Corfu, Modon and Negroponte. There they looked into all that had taken place in the previous decade, participated in the deliberations of the local administration and within a year of their return reported in writing to the Republic on their findings. It was, if in miniscule, the essential pattern of the later and justly celebrated Spanish imperial government (cf. pp. 344–9).

Yet unlike the Iberians, apprehensive of any assembly which might allow or foster feudal or separatist inclinations, Venice with characteristic pragmatism was prepared to hear the opinions of at least some of its subjects resident overseas. The Venetian colonial aristocracy could offer administrative and commercial advice. Furthermore its members, sitting in the great council of their particular territory – a body chosen in the city's usual oblique and tortuous fashion – could appoint various minor officials. But their powers and ambitions were then judiciously constrained, in Crete at least, by the creation of yet another assembly to which the island's government could submit matters for debate and opinion. Even more remarkable was that with the passage of time Venice was prepared to admit native peoples to lesser local offices – the brother of the painter El Greco became, for example, collector of the customs in Candia in the late sixteenth century – to accept the traditional usages of the lands it ruled, and ultimately to listen to the grievances of its subjects, irrespective of their race or religion. In Crete some part of the hereditary Greek aristocracy was allowed to survive with its lands and privileges intact. So, too, the Jewish communities of the overseas territories did passably well, whilst Greek merchants were active in local commerce and some, together with other non-Venetians, were even admitted to the status and privileges of citizenship of the republic. The Greek Orthodox church in the colonies was handled with the same admixture of firmness and realism. It was not persecuted, its liturgical practices were respected and its members were spared the attentions of missionaries. Instead, following the disappearance or removal of the hierarchy during the Venetian conquest or occupation, the heads of local churches were nominated in consultation with the Latin archbishop, by Greeks, but the whole organization kept under the tightest Venetian control. Similar policies were used with the peasantry of the former Byzantine lands. Serfs loyal to the new regime were freed, unruly freemen reduced to bondage and the onerous fiscal system inherited from the old empire operated equitably, with the impoverished or unfortunate treated with consideration. In the same way, though newly acquired cities on the Italian mainland were put under Venetian patricians, their particular rights and institutions were preserved, frequently leaving them a substantial degree of autonomy. Such measures brought their own rewards. As the Turks pushed west in the late Middle Ages entire communities in the Greek lands and seas volunteered to join the Venetian empire. And in Italy, after the republic's disasters in face of a combined onslaught in 1509, the city soon benefited from the wish of the mass of the people of the subject territories to return to the blessings of Venetian rule after their experiences of the tyranny and excesses of their liberators.

The imperial record of Venice was thus, unlike those of other mercantile states, not one of indifference to the condition of peoples subject to its rule or influence. Nor, like that of the Iberians, was it a chronicle of the destruction of indigenous populations. The city's governing oligarchs were guided, from the fifteenth century, by a conscious sense of their duty to rule justly. Hence they never succumbed to such noble and impracticable ideals as those that briefly flowered in Spanish America, where there were hopes of endowing suitable Amerindian peoples with European institutions (cf. pp. 348, 354). In much of the world to which the Venetians penetrated, under Mameluke or Mongol domination, ambitions of this order were in any case impossible. And Venice, as a commercial city without extensive resources in manpower, a predatory aristocracy, a military caste or a zealot clergy, lacked the means of large-scale extortion and repression, just as it lacked the Iberian urge to save native souls and remodel native societies (cf. pp. 256, 354). It lacked, furthermore, that primeval Iberian – and Viking – urge for plunder. Constantinople it could indeed sack, but the city's trade was not ruined in the way the Portuguese were to ruin that of Malacca (cf. pp. 242, 274). In part this reflects the pragmatic commercialism of the Venetians who, to ensure the safety and flow of their trade, had no desire to see men outraged by innovation, injustice and oppression. In part it reflects a considered ideal of government and, not least, in the later centuries when Venetian colonial policies became increasingly accommodating, a desperate need for support – such as the Spanish *conquistadores* only briefly experienced – as Turkish pressure grew.

Yet these benign features notwithstanding, there was never any doubt as for whose benefit the empire existed or, as in the mother city, in whose hands power rested. Maritime and imperial matters were handled by a standing committee of the Venetian senate; the officers who ran, and who scrutinized the running of, the colonies were appointed by the state, as were those responsible for their defence. Venice determined the overall imperial strategy and established (in consultation with the local authorities) the naval and military needs of each territory, together with their individual contributions to the imperial forces. Hence by the late Middle Ages Crete had to provide from two to four galleys, Corfu one or two, Negroponte one and Coron and Modon one between them. The various colonies were similarly exploited for the benefit of the republic. Those overseas were rapidly encased in a network of discriminatory and protectionist legislation. All goods going to or from them had to pass through Venice, and their essential function was to supply the city with primary produce. In contrast with the inept policies of Spain in America, they were allowed no industries – with the insignificant exception of shipbuilding in Candia, and this under the strictest Venetian supervision – competing with those of the republic (cf. pp. 326, 365). But regional specialities such as wine and sugar were fostered. The best lands, especially in Crete, were soon in Venetian ownership, defended by carefully sited fortresses, and systematically worked with a meticulous attention to irrigation and an adequate supply of slaves, to ensure that from almost all its possessions, however unpromising, the city drew some benefit. And naturally enough in a state where colonial officials could be told (1396) to keep their accounts in a businesslike fashion, the empire, unlike most of the others with which we are concerned, was heavily, regularly and successfully taxed. The native Greeks were subject to a number of direct taxes the Venetians inherited from the fiscally advanced Byzantine state. The city further took levies on individual communities such as that raised each year – usually in every sense of the word – on the

Jews. And should it be thought necessary, others would be imposed on the entire non-peasant population ranging from the feudatories to the Venetian clergy. In addition, there was a formidable array of indirect taxes, some on trade, some in fact feudal services. Beyond these the state drew an income from its salt monopoly (in Corfu and Nauplia) and benefited from the grain which in Crete Greek landowners and Venetian magnates alike were obliged to sell at suitably modest prices. These imperial revenues were bluntly described as 'the money of our commune', and the surplus remaining after local needs had been met was transmitted home. Nor was it to be diminished on or before passage. No colonial governor could pay out any substantial sum without the republic's written consent. And the state, furthermore, appointed the colonial treasurers. These were salaried Venetian aristocrats, serving only short terms, and who, in addition to collecting dues and taxes, in Crete followed the local officials on their rounds the more closely to check their expenditure.

From such prudence and vigilance came solvency. Out of Venice's total income in 1432–5 and again in 1500 just over 40 per cent was from the mainland and overseas possessions, making the city a uniquely successful imperial power. Nor was this all. The Italian lands and towns may, as the advocates of expansion argued, have generated new commercial capital, just as in the late Middle Ages it was probably their resources that enabled the republic to sustain an increasing burden of defence costs. From the colonial territories the vital routes of Venetian seaborne commerce were protected, in their harbours vessels were revictualled and refitted, crews and passengers refreshed, and many of them were important suppliers of ships and men. Moreover, like every other empire that of Venice provided, in its plethora of offices lay and ecclesiastical, an outlet for the energies, and a reward for the ambitions of the influential – the city's patricians and citizens – to whom the greatest opportunities in imperial commerce and government were confined. And to these were added the rewards of private endeavour. True, not all of the empire did equally well. In 1415 Negroponte was unable to make ends meet, and like Spain and Portugal Venice had its disgruntled colonial poor whites. But Cretan-Venetian merchants prospered, like country traders elsewhere, in the interport commerce of the empire, and Venetian patricians assiduously accumulated land, holding, it was alleged in 1446, one-third of that around Padua, and occasionally turned, like the Corner with their sugar plantations in fourteenth-century Cyprus, to its intensive exploitation.

Along the sea routes of this empire there sailed in the late Middle Ages fleets of state-owned merchant galleys. These did not carry the whole of Venice's maritime commerce, nor did they constitute the bulk of her tonnage, and to and from the city there also worked, besides such foreign craft as were permitted, privately owned (and generally sailing) vessels operating either independently, or under state regulation or licence. But it was the communal fleets that transported those luxury goods that were the essence of Venetian wealth; that so dramatically symbolized the republic's opulence and prestige; and whose movements dominated the entire economy of the city with debts falling due and payments to be made on their arrival.[27] After some experiment, state ships were voyaging to Cyprus, Constantinople and the Black Sea in the 1330s, and to Egypt and Flanders in the following decade. They sailed for Syria and England in the 1370s, to Aigues Mortes in 1402 – and soon from there to Catalonia – to Barbary (the Mediterranean coasts of Morocco, Algeria and Tunisia) shortly after, and finally established a link between Tunisia, Libya and the Levant. This system of the regular despatch of interlocking fleets, operating what was tantamount to a liner schedule, reached its apogee in the fifteenth century. Seven galleys then left annually for the East in August, and after calling at Corfu and Modon went, sometimes under armed escort, to Crete where the fleet divided, part going (*via* Rhodes and Cyprus) to Syria, and part to Alexandria. For the return journey, roughly five months later, the ships in Alexandria would be joined by those inward bound from North Africa, and after picking up the Beirut flotilla the re-united squadron sailed westwards to reach Venice in December. A smaller fleet served the Black Sea and its approaches, leaving in the spring and working its way along the Greek coast to Negroponte. From here two galleys went to Constantinople, whilst the rest moved into the Black Sea, some making for Trebizond and the remainder for Tana. Another flotilla – three ships as a rule – after touching in Sicily crossed to Tripoli, coasted west with frequent stops to Melilla, and then, carrying Moors and their goods, worked its way along the south Spanish coast to Valencia, where it met the two Aigues Mortes galleys which had come out by Sicily, western Italy and south France.[28] Yet another fleet sailed from Venice to Tunis, shipping from there to Alexandria or Beirut Moslem-owned cargoes of anything up to 2000 black slaves, and returning with the main eastern squadron after completing two shuttles between Tunisia and the Levant. But the longest and most arduous run was that undertaken by the Flanders galleys, generally four in number. Departing in mid-summer they touched at Cadiz and Lisbon, and then – unlike other Venetian squadrons, rarely out of sight of land for any appreciable time – made a deep-water passage by compass course from Finisterre in Galicia to the western approaches of the English Channel. Having made a landfall on the Breton peninsula, or having identified their position from the nature of the bottom found by sounding, they turned for the ports of the great markets of the Low Countries (Bruges or Antwerp), and for Southampton and London for woollen textiles, wintering in England before returning home the following year.

Though the distances involved, the tonnage employed (and lost) and the hazards encountered, were all less than in the voyages of the subsequent and comparable Iberian fleets to Asia and the Americas, the Venetian system was more comprehensive, logical and complex. In origin it reflected the seasonal arrival in the Middle East of the caravans bringing oriental goods, and the need, in the course of the Genoese wars, to protect the vessels carrying them to the west. So, already in the thirteenth century Venetian ships – sailing craft, not galleys, and privately owned – can be found moving in convoy. But such tactical considerations were reinforced by others of greater weight.

Like Portuguese Indiamen of the ships of the American *flotas*, the Venetian state galleys had the monopoly of the transport of specified valuable commodities on specified routes (cf. pp. 269, 342). Whereas, however, the Iberian fleets were essentially to ensure a flow of spice or bullion for the royal benefit, Venetian aims were characteristically less crude. By creating a service of common carriers the republic prevented, as it consistently strove to do, any unfair advantage accruing to any individual Venetian, with all its potential political implications. Yet at the same time a body of prosperous oligarchs endowed themselves, like many a less scrupulous board of directors since, with the handsomest privileges. The movement of goods by fleets working to integrated schedules concentrated business in predictable periods of time, during which commodities could accordingly be sold quickly, and capital reinvested readily. The provision, from the public funds, of transport meant more private resources could be devoted to trade. Then a network of state consuls supplied commercial information, factories abroad allowed merchants a reasonable measure of safety, state shipping assured them priority in lading and the proverbial reliability and security of the Venetian convoys brought them a substantial advantage over their competitors. Moreover, the simultaneous arrival in, or impending departure from, a port of a fleet of the republic's ships gave the Venetian merchants using them enviable powers to dictate the terms on which they would buy and sell.

Hence the city's control of its galleys was close and purposeful. It built, maintained and repaired them to its own standards. As commercial strategy dictated, it decided when and to where they should sail, what cargoes they should load, the freights common to all shippers – to be charged, the routes to be followed, the number of vessels to be employed and the complements to be carried.[29] Yet though state-owned – unlike the ships of the Iberian spice and treasure fleets – the galleys were not state-operated. Instead, after much experiment in the early 1300s, they were leased for specified voyages to the highest bidders in an auction confined to patricians. Each vessel then came under the command of the aristocrat whose offer was accepted – providing he satisfied the state as to his personal suitability and the adequacy of his backers' financial resources. As the *patrono* he was licensed to operate his ship on behalf of a group of investors, and his duties and responsibilities were minutely set out in a volume with a suitably illustrated frontispiece. His deck officers the republic likewise selected, and he eventually sailed as a member of a fleet under the overall control of a state-appointed *capitanio*.

In response to the demands of the trades in which they were engaged, and of their policies for their domination, the Venetians developed, as did most other maritime powers, a particular and distinctive ship. This was the 'great galley', heavily manned, and propelled by oars and sail. It was designed to fight – either in its own defence or in pursuit of a prize – to work essentially coastal routes interspersed with frequent ports of call, and to carry rapidly, safely and reliably small high-priced and low-bulk cargoes. Its origins are obscure, but it was significantly the outcome of no such revolution as

Fig. 6   Three-masted, lateen-rigged great galley under oars and sail, *c.* 1445, reconstruction by R.C. Anderson.

produced the characteristic vessels of the Norse and the Hanse (cf. pp. 19, 77). Venice
neither invented nor particularly modified the galley, a traditional Mediterranean craft
with an ancestry reaching back beyond Antiquity. By the Middle Ages it was moved, as
circumstances allowed or demanded, either by oars or by sail, and with its shallow hull,
carvel build, long, lean lines and low freeboard,[30] it was fast and manoeuvrable. It was,
furthermore, by reason of its independence of the wind – rarely sustained or predictable
in the Mediterranean – both capable of disciplined evolutions and less likely to be
embarrassingly or dangerously immobilized. Already in the early twelfth century
Venice had large and powerful vessels known as 'cats', which carried oars and sails.
These may have derived from, and were possibly improvements on, a Byzantine
original (cf. p. 101). But initially the great galley, introduced according to Venetian
tradition in 1290 for the Constantinople voyage, was apparently nothing more than an
enlarged version of a normal craft, and probably a single-masted ship capable of lifting
about 50t of cargo, rowed with three oars to a bench,[31] and needing a crew of nearly
200.

  With, however, the passage of time such vessels, though retaining the basic features

Fig. 7   Venetian great galley, *c.* 1485, from a contemporary print.

of galley design and construction (cf. pp. 129ff.) took on a form and size peculiarly their own. Between 1300 and 1550 their cargo capacity roughly quadrupled to allow them to lift in the end nearly 300t. Of necessity they became larger, with a length of over 53m and a beam of nearly 9m in the late 1400s, and the state insisting by mid-sixteenth century that their maximum dimensions should not exceed 42m by 7. Thus by their sheer size, more comfortable lines, elaborate superstructures and accommodation, and increasingly complex rig the merchant galleys became as different from the republic's men-of-war, the 'light galleys', as had become earlier, by a similar evolution, the oceangoing vessels of the Norse from their fighting ships. They were steered by a curious adaptation of the northern rudder, curved to fit the lines of their sternposts, but yet retained auxiliary side-rudders, descendants of the old steering oars. In place of the traditional rig of a single mast setting a single lateen sail,[32] the great galleys had by about 1400 two masts, and, before the end of the century, three, of which the biggest was in the bow and the smallest in the stern – but all lateen-rigged – so giving them for a time the appearance, and perhaps something of the qualities, of the Portuguese carvel. Then towards 1500 there came another radical shift to a large mast stepped amidships, on which was set the main (lateen) driving sail, and with a small (square-rigged) mast in the bow and another (lateen-rigged) in the stern.[33] This was an arrangement part northern in inspiration and showed not only a lively Venetian appreciation of current developments, but also that the great galley had become to all intents a sailing vessel, rarely using her oars, and needing a rig that would assist in her control. And this was clearly the view of some of the republic's commanders who, with their ships sitting low in the water when fully loaded, regarded them as too heavy or too awkward to be rowed. They expected a tow when becalmed, put to sea only with a favourable breeze, and affirmed their convictions by either landing their oars, or using them for firewood.

Nevertheless oarsmen continued to be carried – 170 to a ship in 1412[34] – not only constituting an impressive fighting potential but allowing a galley to be propelled briefly by their labours at two to three knots. She could thus under oars keep moving, and hence maintain a schedule, in a calm. Should the wind fall or become foul, she could still enter harbour and so diminish the chances of wreck or piratical attack, just as she could pull away from a lee shore. She could, furthermore, reach difficult ports – London, for example, with its hazardous approaches and usually unfavourable winds – and in confined spaces she could manoeuvre with some measure of control, avoiding collisions and the retaliatory violence they might provoke. Nor was this her only strength. By the late Middle Ages a merchant galley would have on board anything from 200 to 300 men – up to 40 seamen, 20 to 40 crossbowmen (arquebusiers later), among whom were a number of young aristocrats from impoverished families learning the ways of the sea and business, and a large contingent of oarsmen who were not slaves but paid freemen. Such a crew, in its demands on space and food, limited a ship's cargo capacity and limited her range of operations before she needed to revictual. But this, no more than the vast capital employed in the transport of a modest volume of goods, clashed with neither the nature nor the pattern of Venetian commerce. And since the majority of this complement could be armed, should the need arise, and since the galleys themselves mounted artillery by the fifteenth century, a flotilla sailing in company constituted a force well able to defend itself. Maintained to the state's exacting standards, and moving only at propitious times, the great galleys of Venice enjoyed such a reputation for safety and reliability that in 1401 it could be argued that the goods they carried – and these of the highest value – needed no insurance. Nor was this irresponsible optimism. Between 1437 and 1495, though occasionally attacked or even captured by hostile squadrons, none of the Flanders galleys, working the exposed route to the English Channel, was lost by stress of weather. And in 1509, when their return was urgently demanded in the republic's hour of crisis, they made a direct run from Southampton to Otranto (about 4000km) in thirty-one days. In so doing, at an average speed of roughly 3 knots – equalling that of a good Viking ship on passage – they triumphantly demonstrated that they combined the performance of oared craft with the endurance of large sailing vessels (cf. p. 21).

Furthermore, whilst the carriage of the republic's most precious cargoes was so comprehensively and carefully organized, the security of its shipping and its political and commercial interests in the Mediterranean were protected by a regular navy. This was developed in the course of the lengthy struggles with Genoa in the 1300s to replace the assortment of private vessels previously hired or commandeered in time of war.[35] It did not comprise the whole of Venice's seaborne fighting power. In the years of economic depression in the fourteenth century, Greek and other foreign warships were hired, whilst the merchant galleys and privately owned merchantmen were commonly used as reinforcements. But its nucleus, and one of ever-increasing importance, was a body of specialist fighting ships, the 'light galleys', belonging to the state. The possession of such a standing force made Venice virtually unique in medieval western Europe, and for centuries the galley symbolized her seapower as once the ship of the line did that of Britain.

The light galley was not a Venetian invention, but the common fighting vessel of the Mediterranean deriving from an ancient tradition of maritime warfare. By about 1300 those of Venice had a length of 36m, a maximum beam of 4.5m, and measured no more than 1.5 or 1.8m from deck to keel. Unlike the equally low and rakish Scandinavian longships, to which the galley has some resemblance, the frames and ribs of the hull were erected first and the planking then added, with the planks themselves set to give a flush surface offering less resistance to the water than did the overlapping planks of northern vessels. The galley was rowed – briefly reaching seven knots entering battle, and cruising at four – by some 200 oarsmen sitting three to a bench, and with an oar to each man. Since she had only one deck, and all her oars were at the same level, considerable ingenuity was needed to ensure that her rowers could pull in unison and were neither lifted into the air nor flung down by the movement of the oars (8.7 to 9.7m long) they worked. Hence the benches on which they sat were divided by a central passage running the length of the ship. Along this they were set obliquely, with the outer edge further forward than the inner, presenting from above the appearance of a pattern of chevrons. Furthermore, the oars were weighted to balance them, and pivoted not on the hull itself, but on projecting outriggers extending down either side of the vessel to give the oarsmen adequate leverage. These same outriggers were continued round the remainder of the hull, affording the crew some protection, and serving to break the impact of an enemy ram. At her bow the galley had a spur used as a ram and boarding ladder against opponents, and a platform mounting various weapons for hurling missiles, lime to blind the enemy crew, and soft soap to impede their movement. The ship's fighting force was a contingent of armed men – known, with the true conservatism of the sea as crossbowmen long after the weapon was defunct – who operated from the bow platform, a castle in the stern, and the catwalk linking the two ends of the galley, and who were reinforced in battle until approximately the middle of the sixteenth century, by the oarsmen. As in the great galleys these were freemen, and not slaves seeking an opportunity to escape, and so could safely be employed, particularly since with naval warfare a matter of grappling, boarding and hand-to-hand fighting there was no further call for them to row once ships were engaged. The galley also carried a handful of seamen, usually about a dozen, who in addition to discharging the obvious duties handled her sail and served as helmsmen. She was steered to start with by an oar set aft on either side of the hull, ultimately replaced by a stern rudder. The usual rig was one mast (though two-masters were not unknown) setting a single lateen sail which in a calm sea and with a good following wind would move the ship at as

much as 12 knots, and whose great arched yard served besides as a gangway for assaults
on defensive walls.

The limitations of such a craft are clear enough. It could not be used on long voyages,
in the open sea or in bad weather. It had more than enough speed to overtake a 'round
ship' under sail, but with its low lines and exposed complement was rarely able to
grapple and storm large and high-built merchantmen. Even so, it was a powerful and
versatile vessel, far bigger and, by reason of its construction, stronger than the oared
fighting ships of the Norse. Viking tactics did not envisage, and rarely entailed,
engagements with an organized opposing force. But war at sea in the Mediterranean
involved battles between fleets consisting in part of galleys, in part of much heavier
sailing craft mounting missile-firing weapons. The function of the galley, alone capable
with its oars of rapid, precise and concerted manoeuvres, was to bring the enemy to
action, preferably by tempting him into a disorderly assault on the heavier ships which
would leave him disorganized, weakened, and vulnerable to counter-attack. And not
only could the galley quickly bring to bear an impressive weight of fighting strength,
but also she could, by reason of her shallow draft, close with, and engage land
fortifications. Then, moored stern to shore and lashed together, a line of galleys
presented a formidable defensive obstacle, whilst at sea, in fleets or squadrons, they
could maintain regular inshore patrols, move with alacrity to intercept opponents, or
carry officials and information swiftly and safely.

Hence within the centuries with which we are concerned the galley underwent no
more than superficial modification. She became marginally larger and there were
attempts to combine, in the aptly named 'bastard', her virtues with those of the great
galley, just as a number of smaller derivatives using fewer oars and men were
developed. Guns were added too, and in the hope of still better performance hulls
became even lower and sleeker, lines finer, and there was much experiment with the
arrangement of oars.[36] Meanwhile, however, the size, nature and deployment of the
Venetian fleet had all radically changed. To meet the threat of the vast seaborne forces
first of the Ottomans and then of the Spaniards it was rapidly enlarged – an increase
facilitated by the occupation of Dalmatia in the early 1400s, from where abundant
rowers could be recruited. In the fourteenth and fifteenth centuries the republic's navy
never amounted to more than about 30 light galleys, reinforced in war by private vessels
and the merchant galleys. In peace time ten or so of the light galleys were held in reserve,
whilst another ten patrolled the Adriatic, the waters around Crete and even as far as
Rhodes and the Dardanelles, escorting convoys, suppressing piracy and protecting
Venetian interests.[37] But by 1581 Venice had a fleet of 146 such vessels. It was now,
uniquely in the west, an almost exclusively professional force, since craft not built to
state specifications found difficulties in operating with state squadrons, and since the
crews of auxiliary merchantmen repeatedly showed little enthusiasm for action, and
their officers a disruptive individualism when it came to obeying orders. But most
remarkably it was the largest regular navy in Christian Europe, requiring with full

complements about 30,000 men. Such a figure was more in keeping with the resources of the maritime states of later centuries than of a single city and its dependencies, and gives a striking indication of both the extent of Venetian commitments and ambitions, and the skills of a government that could assemble and sustain any such force. Not all these ships were normally in commission and a reserve – put at fifty in 1525 and one hundred later – was established, once again reflecting the sophistication of the Venetian state and the efficacy of its administration. Vessels in reserve were laid up ashore in the Arsenal, their seams uncaulked (that is there was no filling between the planks of the hull, which would naturally shrink when dry), and with their weapons and gear in store. How rapidly they could be mobilized was demonstrated in 1574, when to impress the king of France a galley was launched and prepared for sea in an hour. No doubt as with other displays for the delectation of visiting dignitaries such spontaneous efficiency rested on careful preparation, but when in 1570 Cyprus was in danger 100 galleys were put into commission within approximately seven weeks.

All this was done in the Arsenal, the state dockyard, yet another organization unique in the west[38] and already in the fifteenth century regarded as one of the sights of Europe, producing in those who witnessed its operation that same awe as the wonders of industrial Britain later inspired in earnest visitors. In 1436 a fascinated observer described how a galley being prepared for service was towed down a narrow channel running between a series of warehouses. As it moved forward, as if on a production line, weapons, munitions, gear and supplies were loaded on to it through their windows, and when it reached the end of the channel it was ready for sea. As its name indicates, the Arsenal was originally a place where weapons and equipment were stored, though from the earliest times it had built some of the warships owned by the city. But to ensure the satisfactory construction of the communal merchant galleys and the vessels of the standing war fleet it was converted into a full-scale state dockyard. By the sixteenth century it was, as was said, the 'very heart of Venice' – a complex embracing docks, slipways, powder mills and a rope factory, all under the republic's immediate control, and with its workers recruited and paid as the city directed. The Arsenal built and repaired the state-owned ships, produced, assembled and stored every sort of gear, weapons and munitions and maintained the reserve fleet. In addition it ran a salvage service, supplied the auxiliary depots throughout the empire, lent or sold timber to private shipbuilders, and in general exercised a powerful control over the whole of Venice's shipping industry.

Expansion on this scale brought a growth in its size and complexity. To the Old Arsenal there was added (1303–25) the New, and in 1473 the Newest, with the whole then inclosed within defensive walls. In the fifteenth century covered slipways were constructed capable eventually of housing as many as eighty galleys.[39] Hence not only could work continue on vessels irrespective of the weather, but their timbers were kept – in the same way that those of the war galleys of Antiquity had once been – as dry and thus as light as possible. Equally remarkable was the labour force employed. It included every type of specialist from shipwrights to female sail-makers, rose in the 1500s to a total strength of between two and three thousand – making the Arsenal Europe's largest single industrial enterprise – and operated under a recognizable factory discipline, with the workers summoned in the morning by the ringing of a bell, and their arrival and departure checked by timekeepers. Nor were these the only intimations of modernity. The whole undertaking was of an imposing size, concentrated on a single site, state-owned, its fixed capital investments high, and its labour force of the customary lavish order. Even more significantly it produced vessels of a standard design, fitted in some degree with interchangeable standard parts.

III   *Prolonged recessional*

Strength, however, is never more than relative, and impressive though the resources of the republic and the skills of its administrators undoubtedly were, after roughly 1500 Venice was confronted, and often simultaneously, by monarchies far larger, controlling reserves of manpower far greater, and ruled by sovereigns whose ambitions were untrammelled by a concern for solvency or the well-being of commerce. So, unlike the empire of the Hanse or those of many recent colonial powers, Venetian hegemony collapsed less through the reactions of subject peoples or the resurgence of subject economies, than through the weight of external pressure. True, her history and reputation and the sheer opulence and grandeur of the city itself long enabled Venice to exercise an influence out of all proportion to her real strength. And as with Britain in the last half century, her hesitations and blunders often seemed to simple or over-subtle observers signs of superior intelligence and superlative cunning. But that the world had changed was dramatically shown when after their defeat at Lepanto the Turks were able to make good massive losses in men and ships within a year, whilst the triumphant Venetians remained chronically short of crews (see pp. 134, 148ff.).

The first military threat to the republic itself came as France, briefly revived from the disasters of the Hundred years War by its Valois kings, repeatedly intervened in Italy in the half century after 1494, heading in 1509 a coalition which defeated and momentarily humiliated the city. More dangerous was the appearance, in response to French designs and in pursuit of its own ambitions, of Spain. From the early 1500s Castile was the centre of a Habsburg world empire, Europe's greatest military and maritime power, and the universal opponent of heretic and infidel. She controlled Milan – Venice's near neighbour and ancient enemy – which gave access to Habsburg possessions in northern and central Europe, Sicily which supplied her with vital grain, and Naples. Thus from the toe of Italy the Habsburgs could, as the defenders of the Christian west, and rulers in south Spain of a recently converted and restive Moorish population, challenge the Turks and cut, should they wish, the arteries of Venetian seaborne trade. But ominous enough though Spanish power was, particularly once freed from Valois competition with the collapse of France into civil war in the second half of the sixteenth century, the immediate threat to Venice was the relentless advance by sea and land of the Ottomans. The situation was handled with customary Venetian adroitness. French military assistance was enlisted against Castile and Spanish seapower against the Turks, which meant that in the course of a turbulent century the republic was only engaged in two brief naval campaigns. But such brilliance concealed little. The Venetian factories in the Black Sea were lost to the Ottomans by 1484, most of her onetime possessions in Greece, and many in Albania, by 1503. Thereafter the Turks swept on not only to the gates of Vienna but to overrun Syria (1516) and Egypt (1517), turning the eastern Mediterranean, which in the previous four centuries if not always Venetian had at least been Christian, into a Moslem lake. The city's ships indeed continued to sail and her trade to flow, but there was now no doubt as to who was master. Worse still, the early 1500s saw the emergence of the Ottomans, reinforced by the maritime resources and skills of the conquered Greeks, as a naval power second to none, and their advance by sea as rapid and dramatic as their previous triumphs by land. They took Rhodes in 1522, established a foothold in North Africa (1529) and in 1538 defeated a combined Genoese, Spanish and Venetian fleet in the Ionian Sea, so opening the way to the western Mediterranean for their corsairs and regular squadrons. Meanwhile Venice lost more possessions in Greece and Dalmatia, Ottoman galleys penetrated beyond Ragusa in the Adriatic and raiding parties from the sultan's armies came within striking distance of Venice itself.

But if the difficulties of moving an army from Constantinople through the hard terrain of south-eastern Europe in the course of a summer campaign were to save the republic from the Ottomans, as they had once saved it from the Greeks, there was no respite for its shipping. Neither the Spaniards, their kinsmen in Austria, nor the papacy were willing to accept the Venetian claim that the Adriatic was her exclusive preserve, and that her dominion of the sea was justified – as the Portuguese defended similar pretensions in Asia – by the lives it had cost to establish it. Nor did the bellicose and intolerant Spaniards view with any enthusiasm Venetian devotion to the pursuit of profit – especially when it involved such accommodating relations with Jews, Moslems and heretics – and the republic's reluctance to sacrifice its resources in the interests of Spain. And so the Habsburgs dealt with Venice much as the Protestant powers of the north dealt with the Habsburgs. Venetian ships, goods and fortresses were attacked not only by regular naval forces based in Sicily and Naples, commanding the approaches to the Adriatic, but by pirates and privateers from Iberia and southern Italy. With the passage of time the situation deteriorated even further. The commercial association of Venice with Spain's enemies, Holland and England, in the late sixteenth century was added provocation. Then the decline of Spanish and Ottoman power in the Mediterranean allowed their proconsuls almost limitless scope. In the late 1500s the viceroy of Sicily was operating the suitably named *Golden Lion* and *Silver Lion*, which between them took, it was alleged, 'unbelievably rich prizes', whilst other royal servants – and even the wife of the viceroy of Naples – sent out ships or flotillas in raids on

Venetian commerce which only died down when in the seventeenth century there was little of the city's shipping left to plunder.

Meanwhile Moslem piracy had spread throughout the Mediterranean. Turkish warfleets entering or leaving Constantinople, and of necessity crossing the main lines of Venetian trade, were accompanied by bands of corsairs. Moreover, the Ottoman advance to the west brought their bases nearer to Venice itself. So from lairs on the Adriatic coast or in the Greek islands – sheltered; too numerous for any peace-keeping force to patrol adequately; adjoining major commercial routes – pirates, often Greek or Albanian in origin, operated in conjunction or competition with those from Anatolia and North Africa. Against them the republic had even less success than did the Spaniards against intruders in the Caribbean (cf. p. 364). There the problem was one of geography, and the Spanish lack of ships and men; with Venice it was primarily political. She could hardly challenge the might of the Ottomans, nor in general had she much inclination to do so. A state that lived by trade could afford neither the diversion of resources nor the disruption of commerce and the consequent loss of revenue that counter-measures entailed. Yet if the city did nothing her reputation suffered, and the Turks blamed her besides for the ravages of Christian pirates. Should, however, she take any vigorous action then they complained that their sovereignty was infringed since the control of Ottoman subjects was their prerogative.

Nevertheless Venice was far from humiliated and intimidated by the Turks with whom, for much of the time, she conducted a lively trade. She fought and lost at Zonchio (1499) and Prevesa (1538), just as she fought and won at Lepanto (1571), a battle which characterized more sharply than anything her changed position. Here, in the Gulf of Patras in southern Greece, in the last and greatest galley action, a combined Catholic fleet defeated that of the Ottomans. The Turks had already taken most of Cyprus, and it was the ambition of their admiral to open the way to the capture of Crete, the Ionian islands, Dalmatia and more besides. No doubt the behaviour of the republic in the years before and after the battle – suspicions of her allies, negotiations with the enemy – left much to be desired. But Lepanto itself was a different story. Over half the Christian galleys present – 110 out of 208 – were Venetian, their captains amongst the most tenacious advocates of bold tactics. The strategic positioning of the city's heavy craft in advance of the western fleet, and the weight of their gunfire, did something to break up the Ottoman formation, and contributed to a victory which cost the Turks 30,000 men either killed or captured, and left them with only 30 galleys out of their original force of some 230 ships. But the man who is remembered – the hero even of Venetian popular song – is the flamboyant Spanish commander, Don John of Austria. And though Venetian ships constituted the largest contingent, their complements – such was the city's lack of men – had to be made up from Spain. Moreover, this famous Christian victory ended with Venice surrendering Cyprus and lands in Dalmatia to the Turks, and paying them an indemnity as she hastened to strengthen her defences against Spanish Milan. There were indeed to be no more Ottoman conquests from the republic for a further three generations. But this was small tribute to Venetian strength. Turkish, like Spanish, energies were employed elsewhere, and there remained in any case little more except Crete – which the Ottomans took in the seventeenth century – for the city to lose.

As one opponent weakened or was held, however, others sprang up. Even in Venice's most jealously guarded preserves in the northern Adriatic there appeared in the sixteenth century those Uskoks whose activities were to cost the republic much time, money and impotent wrath. In origin they were Slavs who had fled before the Turks – the word means fugitive – and established themselves in Senj and Fiume. Here they were Habsburg subjects, since the remains of the kingdom of Hungary had been inherited by Charles V after its conquest by the Ottomans in 1526. But they were conveniently distant from their nominal rulers in Austria just as, like Venice, they were protected by impassable country from the arrival of Turkish siege artillery. Even more conveniently, they were within easy reach of both the main axis of Venetian maritime trade which ran, as the wind systems dictated, along the north-east Adriatic coast, and a vigorous local seaborne commerce especially between Venice and the Balkan lands. Never more than about 1000 at most, and using small, fast and heavily manned open rowing boats which could avoid or outpace patrolling Venetian warships, they attacked all and sundry, Christian and Moslem alike. They worked from a coast of islets, rocks and creeks which afforded superb shelter to those who knew it, and offered every hazard to the unwary attempting pursuit. In Venetian Dalmatia – a haven amongst other things for refugees from the republic – they found support and recruits, whilst agents in Venice informed them of the movements of potential prizes. Against corsairs operating with all the advantages of the inshore pirate – local bases, local knowledge, local backing and short voyages in small craft equipped and run at negligible cost – conventional counter-measures, such as blockade and punitive raids, had little effect. Nor, despite the possibility that the Turks, who held Venice responsible for their losses to the Uskoks, might intervene to protect their commerce, could the republic proceed with uninhibited vigour for fear of repercussions in her Dalmatian territories. And if Venetian seamen, in no danger of enslavement by Christian Uskoks, saw no reason to fight when attacked, their commanders, desperately short of crews, willingly pardoned any renegades they took who were willing to serve with them. Moreover, whatever resolution Venice might make about Senj and Fiume, behind them was the flourishing market of Trieste sustained by the flow of Uskok and other loot, and protected by its Habsburg suzerains who had no desire to see either their profits from such a trade dwindle, their nominal subjects harrassed, or relations between the Ottomans and Venice improved. Hence notwithstanding increased Venetian efforts, expenditure and eloquence the situation grew worse. By the end of the sixteenth century Uskoks were operating as far south as Ragusa (Dubrovnik) and after 1615 – in the course of a Habsburg-Venetian war – throughout the Adriatic with Spanish encouragement and assistance. Dutch troops were unavailingly tried against them in 1617, and continuing

Uskok depredations were amongst the reasons for the rerouting of the city's trade to the east through Split and overland (see p. 142).

Yet Uskok raids, destructive enough though they were, were only a local manifestation of that piracy which in the century and a half after *c.* 1500 became not only ubiquitous in the Mediterranean but, it would seem, of an unprecedented violence and intensity. No doubt the impression is heightened by the more abundant references to losses in the increasingly extensive records of more sophisticated states, and by the graphic descriptions of the hazards of life at sea, such as those of Cervantes, for the first time preserved and widely disseminated in printed books. Nevertheless the volume and value of potential prizes was greater in the flourishing European economy of the sixteenth century than in that of the depressed 1400s, as were the opportunities and the forces – those of such new or resurgent predatory maritime powers as the Ottomans and the English – for their capture. By reason of her geographical location, and through her tactful accommodations with the Turks, Venice had been spared the full impact of Islamic seapower when in the years between their victory at Prevesa (1538) and their defeat at Lepanto (1571) Ottoman fleets could move without hindrance. But after Lepanto, and as the Spanish and Turkish empires first turned their energies elsewhere – Spain to the Atlantic, and the Ottomans for a time to the east – and then slid into decline there was no dominant power in the Mediterranean. Into a sea which was a *mare liberum* in the unhappiest sense of the words there came pirate craft of every sort. Some were owned by individuals or groups of individuals in the nominal service of the decaying empires, such as the Spaniards of southern Italy or the Moslems of North Africa. More formidable were the organized squadrons operating from those regular pirate bases – Tunis, Algiers, Malta, Livorno – to which the maritime initiative had now passed. From Malta the galleys of the Knights of St John – rehoused after the loss of their base at Rhodes to the Turks – ranged at will, pushing into the Levant to carry on their war against the infidel and at the same time helping themselves to whatever seemed fitting. And indeed nothing appeared more financially and morally suitable than the rich trade of Venice with the Moslem east. So Venetian ships were plundered, Venetian strongholds bombarded and Venetian supplies seized, whilst such stirring enterprise was soon emulated by the Tuscan Knights of St Stephen whose vessels, the republic complained in 1601, entered her ports 'with excessive licence and violence'.

Finally and fatally there were the ships of the Atlantic maritime powers. Such northern incursions into the Mediterranean were not new. Viking and Hanse craft had appeared at the time of the crusades and earlier, and Iberian and even English vessels had passed the Straits of Gibraltar in the fourteenth and fifteenth centuries. Nor was their re-appearance simply the outcome of insatiable predatory urges. Already in the 1300s occasional Biscayan ships were working the great commercial route from Europe to the Levant. The Portuguese appeared in the fifteenth century to market the sugar of their Atlantic islands; the English only a little later to acquire the products of Venetian colonies and ex-colonies and to find an outlet for their cloth; the Dutch and the

Germans in the 1500s to meet a southern demand for grain. But what was new was that although the Iberians were to turn away to their oceanic empires, the northern powers had, by the late sixteenth century, permanently established themselves in the commerce of the Mediterranean (cf. pp. 64, 143, 379, 494). Nevertheless their penetration was not merely economic. They sought an easier route to the east than that used by the Portuguese and they hoped to find amongst the Habsburgs Moslem enemies not only customers but allies against the omnipresent Spaniards (cf. pp. 381, 474). And, to the misfortune of Venice. they employed convoys of heavily armed sailing ships against which galleys were little use, and which fought, as did Spanish, French and German troops in the Italian wars, with a ferocity that shocked Mediterranean susceptibilities. Moreover, even if primarily engaged in trade, they were only too willing to make some incidental profit by attacking any likely looking victims encountered en route, and since they needed return cargoes, had no scruples as to how or where they found their freights. The English, it was complained, regarded everything they met as fair game, 'without distinguishing friend from foe'. And so they did. In 1580, for instance, the *Bark Row*, prepared for all contingencies, had a French licence to trade with the Turks and a Maltese licence to fight them. A little later another English ship took an Ottoman vessel off Crete, and then went on the demonstrate its impartiality by landing a party to sack Venetian property. And besides those who had some connection, however tenuous, with commerce were the pirates and privateers. In the late 1500s some English privateers operating against Spain and finding suitable victims increasingly scarce and elusive in the Atlantic, moved into the Mediterranean (see pp. 468, 471). Then when in 1604 the Anglo-Spanish war ended, there were those who to continue in their calling, established themselves in Greece, Tuscany and especially in Algiers and Tunis which, with the aid of other renegades, both Christian and Moslem, they soon converted to the major centres of European piracy.

Of the depredations of these and other enemies Venice, attacked from east and west alike, was eloquent. Yet the true impact of piracy on her economy is hard to assess. Such assaults were nothing new, and throughout the Middle Ages Venetian ships had been lost to Turkish, Catalan, Genoese and other corsairs. Then again merchants – as elsewhere – were ingenious in re-routing trades, or passing off ships as belonging to others, so that the true volume and extent of their commerce is often uncertain, whilst losses, particularly if there was any prospect of reimbursement, were never diminished in the telling. Nor, in economies where occasional high profits could support considerable runs of loss, do we know at what point the continued operation of a particular route was considered to be no longer worthwhile. All the same the damage done to Venice was hardly negligible. The attacks on her trade were more general than those endured by any other maritime empire, and were directed, as happened only with Portugal, against a seaborne commerce which was the basis of her prosperity – indeed existence – whilst the state was no longer capable of containing the onslaught in the way it had managed earlier, and less serious, piratical threats. So by the late 1500s there were over 2500 Venetian subjects imprisoned in various parts of the Mediterranean, and between 1592 and 1609 300 ships sailing to or from the city were attacked or taken by pirates. True, more were lost by stress of weather, and if on average 40 disappeared each year from one cause or another, over 700 voyages were safely accomplished annually. But such figures mean very little. They are based on contracts of insurance and thus give no indication of the true rate of loss since many voyages were uninsured. Nor do they distinguish between the size of the ships involved, or the value of their cargoes. It redounded little to the prosperity and less to the standing of a leading maritime power to become – as happened to the Portuguese in Asia and the Hanse in the north – the centre of a coasting trade whilst its long-distance traffic foundered (cf. pp. 65, 142, 272ff.). Nor indeed did Venice's handling of the problem in the sixteenth and seventeenth centuries enhance her reputation. She withdrew from trades – such as the carriage of Moslem goods in North Africa – found to be especially provocative, whilst her ships acquired the reputation of surrendering without a fight, and hence being the choice victims of pirates. So confidence sagged to the extent that in the traffic with Syria insurance rates rose from a nominal sum to 25 per cent in 1612, and Venetians themselves preferred to use alien vessels.

This sad record was an indication rather than an explanation of Venice's increasing inadequacy as a seapower. Not only was she faced by states commanding greater resources, but the whole commercial basis of her existence was undermined, and she was at the same time obliged to contend with economies if not necessarily more vigorous, certainly more flexible than her own. Such problems were no novelty. After the rapid growth and resultant prosperity of the 1200s had come a long recession, and not even by the early 1400s had Venetian wealth and trade the extent and volume of the great days of the thirteenth century. Even so Venice had emerged from these troubles as the virtual monopolist of the commerce in spices. But by 1650 this control had been destroyed and the republic's merchants and ships driven from the other trades they had once dominated. Already in the late 1400s the competition of sugar cheaply produced in the Portuguese Atlantic islands, and brought to Europe in Genoese and Portuguese ships, had destroyed the industry of the Venetian colonies. Soon after, from the same new oceanic economy, there came the dyes of Brazil to replace those formerly imported from India through the Middle East, and Mexican cochineal to eclipse the kermes of Venetian Crete and the Morea (see pp. 245, 323). More fundamental, though, was the disruption of the spice trade, and the weakening of Venice's hold on it. Her struggles with France and the Ottomans at the end of the fifteenth century, and the consequent cessation of the sailing of her galleys, allowed much of this commerce to come into the hands of such long-standing competitors as French, Catalan and Ragusan merchants. Then as the Mameluke state decayed there were further setbacks. Arab marauders halted the caravans from the Red Sea and Venetians trading in Egypt were harassed by the sultan's rapacious officials, with the galleys fleeing from Alexandria under fire in 1505 and all business being suspended. And it was in these already difficult years that

Vasco da Gama's epic voyage (1498) opened to the Portuguese a new oceanic route round the Cape of Good Hope to the riches of the east (see pp. 233ff.). Venetian reaction to this magnificent achievement was that characteristic response of a complacent oligarchy; indifference followed by panic. There were, to start with, hopes that the route would be economically impracticable, but then, as imports of spices began to flow, came predictions of the ruin of Venice. Nor surprisingly. The Portuguese disrupted the shipment of spice from Asia to the Levant, thus further weakening the Mamelukes, and consequently provoking renewed disorders. Hence prices rose in the Middle East – pepper nearly threefold in Cairo in 1496–1505 – and at times, as in 1504, no spices were to be had in either Beirut or Alexandria. Moreover, whilst purchase prices were pushed up for the Venetians, the Portuguese were selling their own imports in Venice's traditional European markets – Flanders, England, even (1518) in the republic itself – and thus depressing prices in the west, where Venice was for a time in that unhappiest of all situations of selling cheap what had been bought dear. Nor was this all. With the Turks established on the Black Sea, Polish and Ottoman merchants could import oriental produce as could, too, through Turkey and Persia, those of Russia using for their purchase the bullion acquired in Muscovy's trade to the west (see pp. 51, 71).

From this predicament Venice was saved in part by her own skill, but largely by Portuguese ineptitude. The Ottoman conquest of the Middle East in the early 1500s replaced the unpredictable Mamelukes with a power both well able to control its subjects and, like the Venetians themselves, vitally interested in the continuing prosperity of the Red Sea route. Thus whilst to the benefit of Venice the Turks radically reduced the taxes on the trade with the east it was, according to the Portuguese – and not implausibly – the perfidious Venetians who aided and abetted Ottoman expansion into the Indian Ocean. Meanwhile in Asia the Portuguese were unable either to impose or maintain for any length of time a blockade of oriental commerce to the Red Sea. They could hardly interfere with the trade of those Asian communities whose goodwill, for political or economic reasons, they needed. Nor, simultaneously committed as they were to other ambitious schemes, had they the men, ships or bases for so grand a strategy. Already in 1507 there were complaints that the Venetians were receiving, by the old ways, as much spice as ever before, and (1508) or the impossibility of checking the trade through the Levant. And even when Portuguese ships were on station things were hardly better. Wily Orientals dodged the blockade with false papers or thinly disguised cargoes (pepper under a covering of rice) and impecunious Portuguese officers – 'who can only in this way make a living' as the Venetians appreciatively remarked – were easily bribed, or were themselves actively engaged in the very trade they were commissioned to suppress. So native shipping continued to sail, and a vigorous contraband traffic flourished handling, naturally enough, only spices of the highest quality. Then, a further bonus to Venice, Asian seamen quickly opened a direct maritime route from Indonesia to the Red Sea (*via* the Maldives), avoiding the

Portuguese bases in the Arabian Sea (see pp. 272, 283). By 1566 twice as much pepper was reaching the Levant, according to Portuguese calculations, as they were carrying round the Cape, and shortly after (1569) attempts to close the Red Sea were abandoned. Nor was this the end of Venetian good fortune, for it was equally impossible for the Portuguese to blockade the Persian Gulf, through which Asian trade also flowed to the west. This rich commerce could indeed be taxed or pillaged, but not destroyed whilst Portugal had hopes of enlisting the shah of Persia as an ally against the Ottomans. Hence the Venetians were able to obtain spices imported through the Gulf in Beirut – usually a more stable market than Alexandria – and, after the Turkish conquest of Iraq (1534–5), in Aleppo (see pp. 242, 272).

So favoured, the republic had re-established her ancient position in the spice trade by the mid-1500s, and was importing up to 600t a year through the Red Sea alone, including as much – and often more – pepper as in the pre-Portuguese era. Whilst Portuguese publicists urged the reform of the state on Venetian lines, Venetian spices returned to old, or captured new, markets – Poland and Russia amongst them – and once again, as in the days of the Polos Venetian merchants penetrated to the Far East. By the late sixteenth century not only were they living and trading in such familiar centres as Aleppo, Alexandria and Cairo, but also in Hormuz, from where they were in contact with Portuguese Goa and could, it was alleged, usurp the best of India's commerce with their tricks. Such were the ramifications of their operations that they handled the official Iberian mails to Asia, improving their understanding of events, it was said in 1585, by opening their clients' correspondence.[40] And in pursuit of profit – actual or anticipated – Venetian merchants made their way through much of the east in the late 1500s, appearing in Diu, Burma (of which Gaspar Balbi left a penetrating account), south China and (1610) Agra.

Such was Venice's success that in 1563 the Portuguese were reduced to (vainly) seeking permission to trade to the east through the Red Sea. Then, with some 80 per cent of Asian pepper imports to the west coming via the Levant by the late 1500s, there were equally futile Iberian schemes to ruin the republic by resurrecting a reinvigorated Portuguese monopoly. Even more improbably the Habsburgs, having annexed Portugal, offered Venice in 1584 the handling of the Lisbon pepper trade – imports to be sold through a European cartel; the Venetian Levant traffic to be abandoned – which, after much debate, the republic refused. But these triumphs reflected less Venetian strength manifested in sapient decisions, than Iberian commercial innocence and incompetence. In Asia Portugal had not only no monopoly of – for example – ginger, but increasing difficulty in acquiring adequate supplies of other spices. Furthermore, her bases were remote from the major Indonesian centres of production, so that Portuguese cargoes reached Europe only after a long, expensive – costs were about five times those of the traditional routes – and dangerous voyage, in the course of which, according to connoisseurs, their quality deteriorated. Venice, on the other hand, enjoyed all the advantages of an established trade, and one in which risks were lessened by the transport of goods in a series of short hauls by a succession of merchants. And she had, too, the further advantage that Portugal could only with difficulty supply Asia with those Levantine products – such as saffron and opium – it demanded, and the west with the silks and cottons of the Middle East. Finally Venice's resurgence was aided by the Protestant attacks on the commerce and empires of the Iberians in the late sixteenth and early seventeenth centuries, disrupting sailings from the east, inflating costs and even deflecting some Portuguese imports into the Mediterranean (see pp. 270–4, 294, 380).

This good fortune was not, however, to last and the same formidable northern seapower that destroyed the Iberian maritime economies destroyed with equal ease that of Venice. Established in Asia and the Middle East in the early 1600s the Dutch, with their vast resources in shipping and their ruthless policies, virtually closed the ancient spice routes to the west. Traditional markets dried up – spices were to be had in Aleppo in 1605 it was reported – cargoes came instead by the Cape of Good Hope in Dutch vessels, Amsterdam and Hamburg were the new entrepôts, the redistributive trade of Venice was overthrown and by mid-seventeenth century the republic was getting her spices, like her sugar, from the English and the Dutch. Yet Venice was not beaten out of this trade in the way that the Hanse lost control of that of the Baltic, or the Iberians those of Asia and the Atlantic, to the economically more efficient Dutch. Instead her position was undermined by the opening of an alternative route over which she had no control and which, by reason of her geographical location, existing commitments and the nature of her shipping, it was hardly feasible for her to employ. And a similar element of ill-luck explains some other Venetian misfortunes. The Valois alliance with the Ottomans (1536) secured French merchants parity in the Levant with those of the city. The Turkish advance destroyed alike Venice's empire in the Middle East, much of her trade with it, and the best part of her dealings in slaves. Political changes and accident likewise disrupted the republic's customary supplies of bullion. Moslem and Iberian wars diverted that of North Africa to the Atlantic, the rising price of Venetian spices in the early sixteenth century reduced the amounts coming from Germany and only relatively late did the city have direct access to that of the Americas which rivals such as the English, French and Dutch could obtain by trade or force from Spain (see pp. 107, 133, 359, 377–86, 466ff.).

Nevertheless the republic was no innocent victim of circumstances, and flexible and enterprising though her merchants often showed themselves, they were driven all the same from most of their traditional trades within the Mediterranean itself. Even in the Adriatic, for centuries Venice's jealously guarded preserve, Ancona emerged in the sixteenth century as a flourishing entrepôt in the traffic between east and west. And closely associated with it was Ragusa. By the early 1500s this onetime Venetian protectorate was to all intents independent and able, once the Ottomans controlled the Balkans, to supply the Middle East overland with such western products as textiles – thereby weakening Venice in whose trade cloth was of vital importance – and to receive in exchange oriental goods then shipped westwards in Ragusan vessels. Thus instead of that virtual monopoly of the import of spices from the Levant which she had once enjoyed, by the mid 1500s Venice only accounted for about 50 per cent of the trade, and by the beginning of the seventeenth century her Syrian commerce was equalled by that of the French. Then again, the manufacture of woollen textiles in Venice, carefully fostered in the mid-1500s as increasing purchases of spice demanded greater resources to pay for them, and whilst the English industry was in disorder, grew at an impressive rate. In the early sixteenth century annual output was no more than 2000 cloths; a hundred years later it had risen nearly fifteenfold. But with the Levant spice trade dead in the early seventeenth century, and faced with the competition of the Dutch and the English, vigorously seeking new markets for their cheaper products, imported directly in their own ships, the Venetian industry collapsed (cf. p. 380). In the same way the city was driven from the silk and cotton trade of the Middle East. Venetian practice was to obtain these materials in exchange for other goods. But with the Ottoman world in monetary chaos *c.* 1600 the city's merchants were at a disastrous disadvantage in competition with those from the west who could use bullion. Thus whilst the English took cotton from Smyrna, and dominated the silk trade of Aleppo the Germans, once Venice's best customers, turned to France and Holland for the cotton needed by their textile industry. Similarly Venetian production of expensive silk cloth dwindled under the pressure of the industries of the neighbouring hinterland, geared to German demand, and of England, to which Venice ultimately became merely the supplier of raw materials.

Decline, as moralists well know, has a momentum of its own. The less Venice could provide the less custom she attracted, and with the collapse of her trade came the decay of her shipping. The sailings of the great galleys to North Africa ended in 1532; to northern Europe by 1535; to Egypt in 1564, and of this once elaborate system all that remained by the end of the century was a service to Split from where, emulating Ragusan enterprise, goods travelled to and from Constantinople by land. Venetians, it is true, continued to own and operate a considerable tonnage of sailing craft, but now only in the face of powerful competition. Some came from within the Mediterranean, from France and especially from Ragusa, independent, neutral and owning by 1570 over 50,000t of shipping, some working to Venice itself or – when the republic was at war – on routes which would otherwise have employed Venetian craft. Far more damaging, however, and reflecting a shift in the whole economic balance in Europe, was the penetration not only of the Mediterranean, but of Venetian waters by the ships of those Atlantic maritime powers which, it was incorrectly alleged, had never in the past come further south than to the Straits of Gibraltar (see pp. 136–7). Some – the Portuguese and Biscayans – soon turned to other opportunities, but the advance of the northern Protestants was irresistible. Into the Mediterranean there came, after hesitant beginnings in the late Middle Ages, English merchantmen, warships and privateers, among them some of Europe's most formidable fighting craft, products of the country's long devotion to piracy and allied pursuits, and intended, after England's breach with

Spain in 1585, to be able to force their way through the Straits. Intimidated by none, invited in the late 1500s by the ruler of Tuscany (whose port of Livorno was yet another of Venice's rivals), soon in contact with the Ottomans and other Moslem states and welcomed by the inhabitants of the republic's onetime colonial possessions, English ships were soon carrying Aegean wine and raisins to the north, English textiles to the islands, trading between Venetian ports and bringing the produce of Asia and the Americas into the Mediterranean. By the end of the century, whilst English merchants were firmly established in the Levant, at the very heart of Venice's commerce, such was the reputation of their ships, that in pirate-infested waters Venetians were willing to pay their high freight charges to enjoy the security they could provide (see pp. 468, 497). And what the English could accomplish by force the Dutch, their energies similarly freed in the early 1600s from war with Spain, achieved by economic superiority. They displaced the Hanse as the suppliers of northern grain to the south, traded to the Levant, shipped its products directly to northern Europe and penetrated throughout the Mediterranean (see pp. 379–81). By the mid-seventeenth century they monopolized, with the English, Venice's trade to the north, and had reduced the role of the republic's shipping to that of assembling, by a coastwise traffic, cargoes for despatch.

Such reverses reflect Venetian weaknesses as much as her adversaries' strength. The city's overseas empire, like those of other commercial powers, was a string of highly vulnerable posts spread out along trade routes, and for the most part accessible from Venice only by sea. The westward advance of the Ottomans cut off Venetian islands from a Turkish-controlled mainland, and Venetian ports from a Turkish hinterland, so depriving them, in the event of war between the Sultan and the republic, of a market for their produce and access to supplies of food. Unlike the European colonies in South America, able by the late 1500s to tap immense agrarian reserves, the Venetian islands – Corfu, Crete and Cyprus in particular – their agriculture directed to the production of commercial crops, were in danger of starvation unless relieved by the mother city (cf. pp. 105–6, 249, 323). But such relief was not easily effected. It depended on Venice's increasingly uncertain control of the sea, and on her possession of a surplus of food. And for much of the time the city, always a substantial grain importer, was herself short, as in the sixteenth century her own population grew, and since her traditional granaries – southern Russia, Egypt, Greece – had come under Turkish control and were, if not inaccessible, unreliable with their harvests likely to be taken to feed Ottoman populations or victual Ottoman armies.

Hence by the late 1500s few of Venice's remaining overseas possessions were in any condition to help themselves. Many were short of food. Their defences, some massive Venetian expenditure on re-fortification notwithstanding, were in general inadequate to resist the formidable Turkish siege artillery. And the very number of the republic's outposts – once so easily accumulated – meant that, as with the Portuguese in Asia, military and naval resources were dissipated among a multitude of tiny and often useless garrisons, such as the seventy-five men entrusted to hold Split (cf. pp. 240, 296).

Surrounded by Ottoman seas and territories, the Venetian colonies were thus not only at the mercy of the sultans' fleets and armies, but more frequently the prey of Moslem slavers, assorted pirates and local bandits. From such depredations many of the native population fled, and those who remained, ill-fed and ill-defended, had little inclination to strive for the continuance of Venetian rule, whatever benefits it might have offered in the past. Friction continued, indeed was intensified, between rulers, Italian and Catholic, and ruled – Slav, Greek and Orthodox. Opportunities the republic provided for some of her colonial subjects – the prospect of working in the city itself or studying at the Venetian controlled university of Padua – but for many they were eclipsed by those to be found in Ottoman service, in an empire tolerant in religion and in which, with its desperate shortage of skilled men, the humblest could rise to the highest office. With the Greeks neither conquered nor dispossessed, the Venetian imperial minority was accordingly far more precariously established than were the Spaniards in the Americas, where relatively primitive regimes were overthrown and adapted to Spanish needs, and where there were no other alien intruders to whom the native survivors might turn (cf. pp. 310, 321). Already in the mid-1400s the republic had renewed doubts as to the reliability of Crete. And in Cyprus a bad situation was made worse by the nature of the Venetian exploitation, with wine, sugar and cotton produced by an oppressed native serf labour force for the benefit of Italian plantation owners, and to the detriment of the island's ability to feed itself. When in 1570 the Turkish assault came the Cypriots, Venice complained, gave the defenders no help but remained asleep in their beds. Years later an English sailor was shown the ruins of the Venetian palaces, their inhabitants, he was told, rightly massacred by the Ottomans for their evil ways.

Equally fundamental were the shortcomings of Venice herself, with her conservative economy and many uncompetitive industries. After the vigorous expansion of the 1500s her woollen textile industry – its high costs and resistance to change largely induced by a well-organized, urban and consequently expensive labour force – was unable to compete with those of the Dutch and English. In the seventeenth century new lighter textured northern cloths captured the Italian market and the cheaper varieties those of the Levant. Nor was this the only instance of a tenacious and even foolish conservatism. Venetian merchants, accustomed like those of the Hanse to a prosperity sustained by the operation of a rigorously controlled entrepôt, and with their long-established practices and associations, showed little of the enterprise of those competitors struggling to establish monopolies of their own. The English (1604) and the Dutch (1610) were refused permission to trade through Venice, by which means the ancient spice route might at least have been kept alive, even if in other hands. So, too, the republic's rigid insistence on the use of Venetian ships in its commerce with the Levant inevitably diverted much cargo into other safer and more efficient vessels and to other ports. Then again, with the unthinking routine of habit, Venetian merchants continued, in the sixteenth century, to export eastern mohair to Antwerp although the market was saturated with a superior local product, just as in the Middle East they continued their business in time-honoured and leisurely fashion, whilst the Dutch and English, to cut costs, kept their ships in eastern waters for as short a time as possible. Similarly in finance the republic's techniques lagged well behind those of the Florentines and Genoese whose monetary expertise was clearly regarded by many as something far removed from 'true and honest' commerce (cf. pp. 177ff.).

Indeed in business and financial practice the city, like the Hanse in its latter days, displayed at times an almost neurotic conservatism, prohibiting, for example, the use of cheques in 1526. Nevertheless its economy, less specialized than that of Genoa, and so potentially more flexible, was not impervious to change. Unlike the towns of the Hanse Venice, safe and tolerant, had, or could easily attract, abundant skilled labour and was not dependent as they were on some powerful neighbouring industrial region for manufactures (cf. pp. 50–1 and 56). Hence in the sixteenth and seventeenth centuries there was a considerable shift of Venetian capital and energy not only from commerce into industry, but from one industry to another. And there was at the same time an increasing flow of patrician money into land. Admittedly this was nothing new but now, by the early 1600s, mainland estates had come to account for over 30 per cent of aristocratic incomes. In part this reflects, as in associations for the reclamation of land, or projects for the draining of the lagoons themselves, a sensible reaction to a growing domestic demand for food. But it reflects even more an admission of difficulties and defeats elsewhere. Nor was it the only one. Faced by English and Dutch competition in Italy and the Middle East the Venetian woollen industry retreated to the manufacture of a cloth acceptable to less-demanding Balkan purchasers, just as some of the city's silk producers were reduced to making a poorer material to sell to the equally unexacting Poles (see p. 142).

Thus the city avoided rather than confronted opposition or competition. Capital was diverted to industries producing for less-disputed markets; opponents were placated; flexibility and adaptability meant not the bold seizure of new opportunities but a prudent will to survive. But it was survival at a price and nowhere was this more graphically shown than in Venice's decline at sea. In 1335 26 great galleys (totalling nearly 4000t) sailed from its port; in 1557 only 4 of 1000t in all. Even so, the city had kept the galley in long-distance commercial service far later than any other maritime power. Nor, in a sense, was this unreasonable. As long as it could move luxury goods quickly and safely there was little point in experimenting, as Genoa and the Hanse had to do, with vessels capable of carrying a greater cargo (cf. pp. 77ff. and 194ff.). Nor was there anything to be gained, and a great deal to be lost, by concentrating a mass of valuables in a ship of larger capacity. And neither, unlike the Genoese, whose vessels were sailing directly from the Levant to the English Channel in the late Middle Ages, had the republic any incentive to develop a craft of greater endurance. Far from it, for it insisted – to ensure that all trade was taxed, and to reduce risks by moving goods only in short hauls – that each branch of its seaborne commerce be kept separate, and that all cargoes should come in the first instance to Venice for re-despatch by land or sea. But as, from about 1500, sailing ships became (with smaller crews) cheaper, faster and (with heavier armaments) safer than galleys, and as her commerce was increasingly one of bulk cargoes which galleys were unable to handle, Venice was obliged to change (see pp. 147ff.). Nor were the reasons simply economic. With much of her trade in the sixteenth century dependent on the goodwill of the Ottomans and their satellites, and with not even a squadron of great galleys capable of repulsing fleets of Turkish or Spanish men of war, it was not only risky but provocative to continue the sailing of the state galley convoys. Even so, something could be salvaged. The great galley, already armed with guns in the mid-1400s, had long been used to reinforce the navy. Now, as the galleass, it re-emerged in the late sixteenth century as a regular and – as its performance at Lepanto showed – momentarily formidable fighting ship (see p. 134). It could mount, as the light galley could not, a considerable weight of guns – seventy by 1600, the heavier pieces at the bow and stern, the lighter ones along its sides in northern style, interspersed between the oars. But these hybrid dreadnoughts had crippling limitations. Notwithstanding efforts to improve their performance they were slow, not to say immovable under oars; their seakeeping qualities were modest – they were so low in the water it was complained in 1605 as to be continuously awash, and with their vast crews they were both inordinately expensive, and difficult to man. A handful lingered on into the eighteenth century, but sailing ships slowly became an increasingly important element in the Venetian war fleet, accounting for about 30 per cent of its strength by the middle of the seventeenth century, the rest being made up from light galleys.[41]

Meanwhile with the disappearance of the state-built and operated great galleys, privately owned and constructed sailing craft came by the late 1500s to constitute the bulk of Venice's seagoing merchant tonnage. For centuries much of the city's trade outside the galley monopoly had been carried by sailing ships of one sort or another, their ancestry as venerable as that of the galleys themselves, and none of them of a peculiarly Venetian origin. Already in the thirteenth century the republic owned a variety of such vessels, some over 38m long and with a beam of 14m. Among them were the *bucius* – which might be as big as 500t and could, by reason of its height repulse the attacks of galleys – and the smaller *taretta*.

The *bucius* had, unlike a galley, two or three decks, was built up at the bow and stern, rigged with two or three masts each setting a lateen sail, and controlled by a steering oar on either side aft. In the late thirteenth century, as the volume of trade increased, there were attempts to improve the capacity and performance of these ungainly craft which, shallow and beamy, dangerously resembled floating dishes. But local enterprise was eclipsed by the appearance of the northern cog, with its square sail, deep draught and stern rudder, on whose lines large Mediterranean vessels were being constructed by the early 1300s (cf. p. 80). Hence there developed in Venice, as elsewhere in the western Mediterranean, a succession of big ships – first the cog, then in the fourteenth century the carrack, and finally in the 1500s the galleon – combining features of both northern and southern rig and design. Carvel-built, steered by stern rudders, in part square-rigged, they were alike more controllable, safer and less extravagant in manpower than their lateen predecessors. The excellencies of the lateen sail are indeed many. Its spar holds its leading edge firmly into the wind, so ensuring that it sets well, and in a following breeze it has, by its sheer extent, enormous driving power. Nevertheless, to swing the foot of a lateen yard behind the mast and reset the sail on another tack when the ship is beating to windward requires considerable strength and consequently a large crew, and should the sail break loose during the manoeuvre the vessel might well be laid on her side. The squaresail, on the other hand, its yard pivoting on the mast, turns easily to the required angle and can, with less hazard, be reduced (by reefs) or increased (by the lacing on of bonnets), whereas in a lateener any substantial change in the strength of the wind entailed the setting of a new sail (cf. pp. 19, 78). Thus with ships demanding smaller crews – and for a 240t vessel the complement was halved between the thirteenth and fourteenth centuries – Venetian freight rates for some bulk cargoes dropped as much as 25 per cent in the late Middle Ages. Furthermore, ships of such design could be built far larger – reaching even 2000t *c.* 1500, a size not surpassed in Europe until the eighteenth century – to operate more profitably in old trades, such as the carriage of Levantine cotton, or new, like the shipment of Cretan wine. Nor were these the only changes. The lines of the hull were improved, the castles at bow and stern moulded into the vessel's contour, and a satisfactory rig combining square (northern) sails with those (lateen) of the south devised. Something of this was possibly of Venetian inspiration, for the city had in the mid-1300s two-masted ships setting a square mainsail on the foremast and a lateen on the after. But in the fifteenth century the two-masted cog was displaced by the multi-masted carrack, which by the mid-1500s was rigged – perhaps an Iberian refinement of further Mediterranean experiment – with four masts, the forward pair each setting three square sails and the after pair a lateen each (cf. pp. 194, 263). This subdivision of the sail area allowed it to be reduced quickly in bad weather and made the handling of individual sails less difficult. Other improvements, such as square sails set on a sprit at the bow to help turn the ship[42] meant that craft of this design and rig were in the end faster, cheaper and handier than their predecessors, and more seaworthy than galleys. Equally important, they were well able to defend themselves since, unencumbered with oars they could carry in broadsides (i.e. along their sides) the greatly improved guns of the sixteenth century. So the sailing ship triumphed, penetrating routes once the exclusive preserve of the galley. It was employed in the Syrian, Greek and Black Sea trades by 1400, was carrying spices from the Levant before the galley monopoly was finally abandoned in 1514, and was making the long run to northern Europe in the late Middle Ages. Venice instigated few if any of these fundamental developments yet nevertheless accepted them with – for her – alacrity, and by the mid-sixteenth century owned forty such vessels of 240t and above. At the same time the city attempted to combine the power of the carrack, conferred by its artillery and high freeboard, with the speed of the light galley. One such hybrid was the galleon, possibly a cross between a derivative of the Portuguese carvel and a Venetian river craft (see pp. 263, 279). It appeared in the early 1500s, and though some of this class were successful others, with their high-built and narrow hulls, and with their guns mounted well above water level were unstable, and did more credit to Venetian ingenuity than Venetian competence.

Such mishaps, though hardly reassuring, were certainly by no means peculiar to the republic, and were not in themselves evidence of irrevocable maritime decline. Even so, Venice failed to hold her position as a seapower. Her onetime flourishing private shipbuilding industry, which had provided her sailing craft, contracted. It was crippled from the fifteenth century by a growing shortage of timber – oak in particular – consumed in vast amounts in ambitious state naval projects, and in the construction of big merchantmen. So shipwrights sought other work, certain types of vessels were no longer built, owners shifted their favours elsewhere, prices rose – and at such a pace that in 1581 it was reckoned none could afford the luxury of a big Venetian-built ship; and the quality of the products of the city's yards deteriorated. Even more fundamentally, Venetians refused to invest in ships on the scale of their competitors, notwithstanding the offer in 1627 of subsidies to those willing to buy craft of foreign origin. Once again the process had its own momentum. A declining building industry produced poorer vessels, equally indifferent it was said in 1603 in fighting and sailing. Those purchased abroad – about 40 per cent of the city's tonnage in 1600 – were inevitably not the pick of the market and included at this date a 20-year-old and much-repaired English ship.[43] With trade falling there was an unwillingness and inability to meet the costs of naval protection and fewer vessels meant fewer experienced seamen and these, as their generally sad record against their bellicose northern opponents showed, hardly the most enterprising. True, some Venetian merchantmen continued to sail, but largely in a coasting traffic and as representatives of a minor commercial state whose tonnage dropped from 80,000t in 1450, to less than half in 1605, whilst the fleets of the Hanse, the Dutch and the English were all growing (see pp. 64, 373, 496). By 1650 it was reported of the city, most of its trade now carried in foreign craft, that 'ships are not made here and very few bought'. Such was the Venice which in the Middle Ages had been in the vanguard of navigational and cartographic innovation, and which was still in the 1500s experimenting with the use of mathematics in ship-design (see pp. 206ff.).

This mercantile decline was accompanied by a less dramatic naval decline. Admittedly, the problems were not all of Venice's making, but problems they nevertheless remained. By the sixteenth century war fleets were of such a size that although the republic controlled on the Italian mainland a population of about 1,500,000 – roughly equalling those of Portugal or Holland – it was unsuitable and insufficient to provide the vast crews needed by galleys, which remained vital fighting ships in the often windless Mediterranean. And whilst the Ottomans and Spaniards commanded far superior resources in men and timber the relentless Turkish advance further weakened Venice by depriving her of many of those colonial possessions which had once provided ships and men. Furthermore, the Ottomans, whose oarsmen were slaves, could easily augment or replenish their crews by raids, whereas the republic, using freemen and anxious not to endanger the well-being of its commerce, was unable to resort to such crudely effective measures. Thus already by the mid-sixteenth century it was reported that she could only man one-third of her war fleet, and the problem was never thereafter adequately solved. From 1539 guilds[44] were made obligatory for virtually all the city's craftsmen, since whatever their influence in ensuring high wages for their members, they undertook to provide oarsmen for the navy. Then peasants from the mainland territories – embarrassingly eager to be home for harvest time – were tried, also conscripts and (after 1545) convicts with whom, by the end of the century, an entire squadron was manned.

Moreover, as her maritime commitments contracted, the Republic inevitably became less effective as a seapower. After roughly 1550 the Ottoman advance confined her sphere of naval operations to the littorals of Dalmatia, Ionia and Crete, turning the Venetian fleet into a coastal defence force whose seamen consequently lacked the range of experience and the skills of their opponents. Significantly enough, a direct passage between two places was known to sixteenth-century Venetians as 'the French way'. So by the 1600s the republic found herself in that familiar impasse of possessing the vestiges of a navy designed to meet the problems of the past, but too elaborate and inflexible for those of the present, as its failure against the Uskoks and other pirates clearly demonstrated. And though this fleet remained for centuries one of some strength – with, for example, thirty light galleys in commission in the 1600s – for most of the time it was divided into a number of small squadrons patrolling waters in which the republic retained an interest, and none with the strength, mobility or endurance[45] to effect anything of consequence.

Nor were these the only flaws in Venetian naval power. The city, conservative though it was, was never totally opposed to change or innovation. To meet new commercial opportunities it had in the 1200s radically speeded up the sailing of its merchant galleys to the east, just as in later centuries it employed Atlantic-style carvels in various local trades, and experimented with the use of artillery at sea (cf. pp. 128, 130, 263). Nevertheless, it remained resolutely committed to the galley as its principal fighting ship until well into the seventeenth century. But good as the galley was against craft of the same type, and necessary as it was since retained by the republic's main Mediterranean antagonists, it was at a grave disadvantage with the appearance in southern waters from the 1500s of high-built northern sailing ships deploying heavy artillery along their sides. Low and open, the galley afforded its crew little protection against their fire, could not operate, as they could, in bad weather, nor, because of its oars and limited freeboard, could it carry anything like their weight of artillery, or carry it in broadsides. Instead, with its bow-mounted guns, the galley itself had to be turned to bring its weapons to bear and was, furthermore, generally unable to give them sufficient elevation to allow their shot to destroy the weapons and crews of high-charged ships. Moreover, if pieces of any weight – as were those of the Venetians by the late fifteenth century – were carried at the bow, a vessel would naturally tend to bury her head in the sea when running before a strong wind, a failing aggravated as builders in pursuit of better performance made their ships narrower, sleeker and even lower in the water. Worse still, Venetian galleys were by the sixteenth century frequently outclassed by those of other Mediterranean powers. Despite the generally admitted excellence of their artillery, they were more lightly manned than Spanish craft, slower under oars than those of Turks and Spaniards alike and dangerously unseaworthy since, with their sails of a heavier cloth than that used elsewhere, they heeled over with the direst consequences should these become wet. Equally ominous in a state which had once prided itself on its business-like efficiency, was that by the late 1500s Venetian galleys with their free oarsmen were up to 30 per cent more expensive to operate than slave-rowed Spanish vessels.

All this reflects the declining quality of Venetian government, a decline further displayed in the behaviour of the city's naval commanders who, notwithstanding their performance at Lepanto and in other fleet actions, were in the sixteenth and seventeenth centuries increasingly reluctant to fight marauders. Maybe, as was suggested at the time, this caution – to put it charitably – simply stemmed from Venice's refusal to allow her ships to pillage opponents. There had been similar complaints in the Middle Ages and the city, her trade particularly dependent on the goodwill of others, had consistently refused to license privateers for fear of the retaliation their activities might provoke. Instead she insisted, as only a highly developed State could, that disputes be solved by diplomacy, or by the use of her navy, and so fostered no tradition of piracy and privateering. Her patrician commanders, governed by precise instructions – which they disregarded at their peril – were unwilling to be drawn into unprofitable and potentially disastrous brawls, and had little of the aggressive individualism of commanders from less highly organized and complex societies whether, as amongst those of the English and the Turks in the sixteenth century they were seamen of humble origins who had risen by their skills and merits, or as with those of medieval Genoa and Catalonia, they were bellicose minor aristocrats (cf. pp. 157, 466). And all these ills were aggravated by the changing outlook after about 1550 of the patricians who monopolized naval command in Venice. Instead of that traditional devotion to public service – real enough even though often better displayed in theory than practice – incompetence, folly and idiosyncracy were given the fullest rein by a network of family interest and influence among the ruling oligarchs, which ensured that the errant incurred no punishment or indeed criticism. So aristocratic officers fed their crews on biscuit and water, and charged the state for soup and wine. They frequently refused to sail in anything but the latest vessel, or expressed their individuality by having their ships withdrawn from service to be ostentatiously decorated or modified at public expense. And should they get to sea they commonly refused to stay there but – like the blue-blooded elsewhere – abandoned their posts to return to the comforts and delights of metropolitan society.

Such behaviour reflected the character of the Venetian state in the centuries after 1500. Its government, always complex, became ever more so in response to new commitments and problems, and was conducted by boards and committees which admirable though they were in accumulating facts and opinions rarely excelled in purposeful direction. Office continued to be the prerogative of the elderly, not to say the senile, but the ruling oligarchy was now both smaller – only in 1646 opening its ranks after nearly 200 years to such as could afford the privilege of joining them – more parochial in its interests, more powerful with the collapse of an embryonic party system in the early 1600s, and more aristocratic in its tastes. The economic difficulties of the sixteenth and seventeenth centuries widened the gap between a minority of rich patricians and the many poor members of their class, whilst the teachings of the disciples of a revived Antiquity, and the behaviour of the grandees of Spain and France presented plutocrats with a new mirror of fashion. Men of consequence were to live with dignity – on rents, that is, not on the vulgar profits of trade or industry – and with style, lavishing their wealth on the arts. And there were more powerful if less ethereal reasons why patricians should not, as in the past, risk their money in commerce or expend their energies in public service. The trades of Venice's greatness were by 1600 largely in other hands, and as the empire contracted the number of prestigious and profitable posts it could offer declined, just as those that remained were increasingly hazardous and unrewarding to accept. Hence whilst impoverished Venetian patricians sought an income from minor office, or simply from the sale of their votes, the wealthy, barely troubled by direct taxes, turned from the traditional fields of commerce and finance to live on the income from their holdings in the public debt, to more extensive investment in land – and by the early 1600s about 40 per cent of that around Treviso, Padua and Polesina was owned by Venetian nobles and citizens – to building or to the management and conservation of their existing assets. Economically this meant that the standing and practice of commerce was further depressed; politically, a conservatism that refused to change, or even to admit the need for change, disastrously manifested by the defeat in 1610 of a proposal to make Venice a free port. It also meant, in a class hardly prone at the best to self-doubt, downright irresponsibility, with patricians refusing to pay taxes or to take office, or, if they did, demonstrating that enthusiasm and efficiency in its discharge were considered signs of a lack of wealth and breeding.

IV   *A new hegemony*

At the beginning of the sixteenth century Venice, though not unchallenged, was the leading maritime state in the Mediterranean, whose aid even the formidable Spaniards sought after their overwhelming defeat by the Ottomans at Djerba (North Africa) in 1560. A hundred years later the republic was, by the standards of Holland and England, a minor naval and commercial power. Yet unlike the more primitive Spain and Portugal, Venice did not ruin herself in the defence of her supposed interests but turned, or was perhaps rather propelled, into others, less arduous to sustain. Nor was her eclipse sudden and total. Some Venetian merchantmen continued to sail, particularly when, in the seventeenth century, Mediterranean piracy dwindled as the Dutch and English concentrated on commerce, and Venice's own trade was insufficient to tempt predators. So, too, her fleet continued to fight, boldly cutting a Barbary squadron out of Valona (Albania) in 1638, and in mid-century – significantly using a large number of Dutch and English sailing vessels – engaging the Turks in some brave and successful actions in the long and futile war to save Crete from them. Nor were these the only signs of life. In the 1600s agriculture flourished in the fertile mainland territories; the city's population, momentarily diminished by plague in the 1630s, soon returned to its former level of about 120,000, Venice was free from debt by the early seventeenth century and in the mid-1600s possessed deposits which, in terms of silver, were worth more than twice those held by Amsterdam.

True, the empire had been largely lost and the great trades of the medieval centuries had collapsed, but with some entrepreneurs, if not the ruling oligarchs, displaying a flexibility and adaptability far superior to that shown by the Hanse and the Iberians in similar circumstances, Venice continued to flourish (cf. pp. 56ff., 76, 294ff., 365). It became, as other onetime imperial capitals have become, a centre of high finance through its age-old connections and associations. It became also, set as the north German cities were not, in a region of distinguished civilization, a centre of high culture and high living. And through its wealth, and a security and tolerance that few other states could equal before the eighteenth century, it attracted and maintained luxury industries – the production of furniture and of magnificent and ornate glassware, the printing, by the Aldine Press, for long one of the most celebrated in Europe, of books. And even if seaborne trade was now largely in other hands, the volume flowing through the port showed few signs of flagging before the end of the seventeenth century, whilst Venetian merchants handled an extensive overland commerce to Frankfurt and Leipzig, and maintained one with Austria and south Germany which not even the Thirty Years War destroyed.

Nevertheless though the city could impress visitors with its wealth and splendour it could no longer protect its political and commercial interests. Most of its overseas possessions were lost in wars, it was unable to contain attacks on its shipping and its voice was of decreasing significance in European affairs. Its port sank from an international, to little more than a local, entrepôt, and Venice was embarked on a process, reversing the whole course of economic development, which ended with her as the supplier of such primary products as rice and maize. Yet in the century and a half after roughly 1500 she became, as did no other dying imperial power, pre-eminent in the arts. No longer was she the Venice whose doges overthrew empires and whose fleets subdued cities, but of the painting of Titian and Veronese, the music of the Gabrielis and Monteverdi, the architecture of Palladio, the mathematics of Galileo (cf. pp. 210ff.). In her fall, as in her longevity – some 600 years of maritime pre-eminence – the city was unique.

Bibliographical note

Venice, like Genoa, has been less studied than other major Italian cities, and more in decline than in growth. It would be pointless to add here an extensive bibliography in view of the appearance of Frederic Lane's *Venice, A Maritime Republic* (Baltimore, 1973). This crowns a lifetime of research by the city's most distinguished historian writing in English, and contains an admirable discussion of the sources and literature. Additional detail as to the scale and scope of the archives of Venice is given in Fernand Braudel's *The Mediterranean and the Mediterranean World in the Age of Philip II* trs. S. Reynolds (2 vols, 1972–3). I have therefore merely noticed some books and articles which have been issued since the publication of Lane's magisterial study or which were not used by him.

W.H. McNeill, *Venice, the Hinge of Europe, 1081–1797* (Chicago, 1974) is a brief and stimulating general survey. A large number of articles of varying quality are brought together in A. Pertusi (ed.), *Venezie e il Levante fino al Secolo XV* (2 vols, Florence, 1973). They include an important discussion by Ugo Tucci of, amongst other things, the attempts to improve large Venetian ships prior to the introduction of the cog ('La navigazione Veneziana nel Duecento e nel primo Trecento'). Valuable, too, is the contribution by Alberto Tenenti, 'Venezia e la pirateria nel Levante' explaining the republic's lack of a tradition of privateering. New material on Venetian imperial government is added by Manoussos Manoussacas in 'L'Isola di Creta sotto il dominio Veneziano'.

Portuguese reflections on the merits of the Venetian state occur in J. Wicki, SJ (ed.), 'Duas relacões sobre a situacão de India Portuguesa nos anos 1568 e 1569', *Studia*, 8 (1961), 163, 203.

Information on the nature of patrician wealth and investments in the mid-thirteenth century comes from Gino Luzzatto, 'Il Patrimonio Privato di un Doge' in his *Studi di Storia Economica Veneziana* (Padua, 1954).

The Venetian penetration of the Far East is discussed in Leonardo Olschki's *Marco Polo's Asia* (Berkeley, 1960). The survival of the city's commerce with Ottoman-occupied lands in the late Middle Ages is shown by F. Thiriet, 'Les lettres commerciales des Bembo et le Commerce Vénetien dans l'empire Ottoman à la fin du XVe Siècle' in Guido Astuti *et al.*, *Studi in Onore di Armando Sapori* (2 vols, Milan, 1957). The same author also demonstrates the shifting pattern of Venice's eastern trade in the Middle Ages and the redeployment of the commercial galleys in 'Quelques observations sur le traffic des galères Vénitiennes d'après chiffres des incants, XIVe–XVe Siècles', in vol. III of *Studi in Onore di Amintore Fanfani* (6 vols, Milan, 1962).

For the Venetian slave trade I have used in addition to the literature cited by Lane the articles by Charles Verlinden in vol. II of *Studi in Onore di Gino Luzzatto* (4 vols, Milan, 1949–50), and in vol. III of A. Guiffrè (ed.) *Studi . . . Fanfani*. I have also used material from F. Thiriet's edition of the *Délibérations des Assemblées Vénitiennes concernant la Romanie*, I, 1160–1363 (Paris, 1966) and the important contribution by Alberto Tenenti, 'Gli schiavi di Venezia alla fine del Cinquecento' in *Rivista Storica Italiana*, 67 (1955), 52ff.

The survival of the ancient spice routes in competition with that opened by the Portuguese is described in the letters of early sixteenth-century Portuguese viceroys and officials in Asia some of which are printed in vol. 4 (section I, part I) of A.B. de Bragança Pereira, *Arquivo Português Oriental, Nova Edição* (11 vols, Bastora-Goa, 1936–40). See also the information in Wicki's edition of the 'Duas relações . . .', p. 158. The transmission of information about the east through Venice to Portugal is recorded, amongst other places, in Gaspar Correa, *Lendas da India*, ed. R.J. de Lima Felner (4 vols, Lisbon, 1858–64), vol IV, 142. Ugo Tucci examines the activities of sixteenth-century Venetian merchants in India in an important paper 'Mercanti Veneziani in India alla fine del secolo XVI' in vol. II of *Studi . . . Sapori*, and the ending of the Venetian spice trade through the Levant is discussed with a wealth of detail by Niels Steensgaard, *Carracks, Caravans and Companies: The Structural Crisis in the European-Asian Trade in the Early Seventeenth Century* (Copenhagen, 1973).

4

The Genoese Republic

∞

1 'Genoese and therefore a merchant'

Throughout much of the Middle Ages Venice's most formidable and persistent rival was her fellow maritime republic of Genoa. Genoese merchants disputed her commercial ambitions; Genoese fleets commanded by some of the most illustrious names in the long history of galley warfare challenged her naval aspirations and, indeed, for a time threatened her very existence. Between the two cities the antithesis was complete. Venice, whatever restrictions islands and lagoons might impose on her, still had all the space of the Adriatic and the Po Valley to hand. Genoa, hemmed in by mountains, and huddled on a narrow coastal fringe, was already in medieval art a city without gardens or squares, dominated by skyscrapers, and with its population confined by the 1400s within a walled area only one-fifth the size of that of Ghent. Torn by factional strife, and for long a byword for political instability, Genoa succumbed to alien rule in the Middle Ages whilst Venice, to the admiration of publicists, preserved her independence until modern times. The Genoese state was territorially insignificant, feeble and fragile, yet the economy of Genoa was the most glowing testimony to the blessings of free enterprise before the rise of industrial Britain. Venice on the other hand was strong and centralized with almost every detail of social and economic life controlled by a ruling class equally remarkable for its prudence and sense of duty. And if Venice, its patricians housed in elegant palaces, was to produce in architecture, art and music one of Europe's most distinctive and influential cultures, Genoa, whose embattled magnates owned urban fortresses, was to be remembered as the very apotheosis of the business ethos. 'Genoese and therefore a merchant' it was said in the medieval centuries, and, to many, such merchants were energetic philistines unwholesomely dedicated to the pursuit of profit. They were, wrote a Portuguese chronicler of the fifteenth century, men who never invested their capital without the certainty of gain, whilst another equally high-minded Iberian dismissed them as persons 'of a sordid mercantile mentality'. And it was that true son of Genoa, Christopher Columbus, who having in his will nobly spoken of the need 'for every man of rank and property to serve God', characteristically went on to remind his son that the Bank of St George in their native city paid 6 per cent on deposits.

As an imperial power in the accepted sense of the words Genoa was never anything but insignificant. Unlike Venice it had a population of probably at best (c. 1300) no more than 80,000, falling as low as 45,000 by the 1400s.[1] It was unable and unwilling to emulate Venetian policies in northern Italy, and overseas it controlled – and tenuously at that – merely a handful of possessions. Yet for centuries it exercised a financial, commercial and maritime influence far greater than that of the Hanse or Venice. By the late 1200s there were Genoese experts advising and serving alike the Capetian rulers of France and the Mongol khans of Asia; Genoese plutocrats monopolized vital trades; Genoese ships and seamen were working the waters of the known world from the Atlantic to the Indian Ocean. When in the sixteenth century the Portuguese arrived in Abyssinia the Genoese were already there – some so much at home as to have set up house with native women – and before long they had established themselves in many parts of the Asian and American empires of the Iberians. Meanwhile that same ruthless energy and unbridled individualism that destroyed the republic provided not only naval *condottieri* famous throughout Europe, but some of the greatest names in oceanic enterprise from the enigmatic Vivaldis in the thirteenth century to Columbus at the end of the Middle Ages. And the lands they were influential in discovering the Genoese were equally influential in exploiting, so that to a disgruntled Spaniard they appeared in the late 1500s as men to whom the prospect of running the world presented no particular difficulty. Indeed by this time, just as Genoa's political standing and influence were at their nadir, so extensive was the city's economic power, and such its grip on the finances of the Iberian Habsburgs – rulers of the first world empire – that it has plausibly been argued that the 100 years after about 1550 should be called the Genoese century (see pp. 177ff.).

The city's origins are as distant and obscure as those of Venice. In Antiquity it was a Roman port of no great distinction, which then in the early Middle Ages came – as the Venetians never did – under direct barbarian, Byzantine and eventually Lombard rule, before re-emerging in those same circumstances as allowed the growth of other Italian maritime cities (see pp. 90, 101). But Genoa emerged more slowly since, by its very geographical location, it was further from the rich opportunities of Byzantium, was without Venice's invaluable association with the Greek empire, and was dangerously near to Spain and North Africa, the seats of a still formidable Moslem power in the west. It was, moreover, situated on a proverbially inhospitable coast, where mountains overshadowed a meagre littoral gashed by rivers quickly turned to impassible torrents by rains falling, like those of Portugal, in the spring. Thus, backed in the early medieval centuries by a primitive and isolated hinterland, and surrounded by restive feudal lords whose wants and ambitions so wretched a country could barely support, Genoa was in no such position, and without any such incentive as Venice, to aspire to the hegemony of the Gulf at whose head it stood. Still worse, the city had virtually no contact with the outside world by land. Its encircling mountains were, even in the fifteenth century, crossed by only two major (and difficult) routes leading north, whilst the disintegration of the Roman roads along the Mediterranean coast and across the Apennines deprived Genoa of access to the ancient Via Francigena which ran from the plains of Lombardy to the heart of Italy. Nevertheless so harsh an environment brought its own rewards. It ensured a steady flow into the city of refugees from the rigours of the Ligurian climate and terrain. Internecine strife over such meagre resources and opportunities as it offered in some measure diverted aristocratic energies and talents, as in Viking Scandinavia, to war, plunder and commerce abroad. And being, as even its admirers admitted, set in a land which produced virtually nothing Genoa, if it was to survive, had to seek its food elsewhere, just as if it was to grow it was obliged, like Portugal, to do so by sea (see pp. 259ff.).

Without any of Venice's geographical and political advantages, and harrassed by the seapower of the Moslems of the western Mediterranean, the city emerged from obscurity only in the eleventh century to begin a cycle of expansion which was of roughly the same nature, and followed much the same course, as that of the Venetians. But Genoa turned initially not to Byzantium but to Africa and the Middle East, and throughout most of its history it combined to a degree hardly approached elsewhere that wholehearted pursuit of profit characteristic of other predominantly commercial powers – displaying a zeal only subsequently equalled by the Dutch – with those bellicose ambitions typically aristocratic. Unlike that of the Hanse or Holland, Genoa's expansion was not confined to the domination or extension of existing commercial networks but was accompanied, as was that of the Iberians and Vikings, by piracy, violence and looting. In alliance with the equally redoubtable Pisans, the Genoese first drove the Moslems from Corsica and Sardinia (1015–16), stormed (1088) their base at Mahdiyah (near Tunis) in North Africa – soon bartered back to its ruler in exchange for an indemnity and commercial privileges – and then turned to the pleasing prospects opened in the Middle East by the crusades. Here their intervention, like that of the Pisans – and later the Venetians – was vital to Christian success. They controlled a substantial volume of shipping, they had wide experience of Moslem seapower, they were well aware of both the quality of the opposition and the chances of gain and unlike the Venetians, with their investments in and commitments to Byzantium, they had no inhibitions about infringing alleged Greek interests. So in 1097 Genoese ships carried the horses of the first crusade to the east, and Genoese siege engines played a decisive role in the taking of Antioch (1098) and Jerusalem the year after. Such services were repeated in subsequent crusades, and when Moslem resurgence threatened the Holy Land it was the Genoese who were to help to save it – the pope warning the faithful in 1186 of the dangers of offending so powerful a potential ally – just as when it was lost it was on Genoese aid that schemes for its recovery counted. For support either rendered or anticipated the city, like its fellow maritime republics, was generously – not to say rashly – rewarded with extensive territorial and commercial privileges by the rulers of the Latin principalities (cf. p. 184). So Genoa's wealth, power and reputation grew. In a way that Venice never allowed, the aristocratic family of the Embriaci was able to found an independent principality in the Holy Land (see p. 192). Genoese shipowners profited from the carriage of troops, pilgrims and goods to the Middle East, Genoese merchants exploited its rich trading opportunities, so that by the mid-1100s dealings with the Levant probably engaged the best part of half the city's commercial capital, and the Syrian trade was handled by an oligarchy of wealthy plutocrats commonly making an average annual gain of at least 100 per cent.[2]

To market eastern luxuries, to obtain the bullion required for their purchase, to acquire those commodities in demand in the east and to protect or control the routes along which this traffic flowed, the Genoese rapidly and forcefully extended their influence and authority. They appeared in Sicily, which both dominated the maritime approaches to Africa and the Levant, and was besides a major market in its own right and an important supplier of grain. The de Giovi pass was opened through the mountains north of the city to bring contact with the thriving world of Piedmont, Lombardy and beyond, and before long goods were entering and leaving Genoa by those mule convoys which were to become so large and malodorous a feature of its economy as to necessitate the construction of special pathways for their passage through the streets. Agreements were negotiated with Antibes, Marseilles and elsewhere to ensure that north European textiles coming from the fairs of Provence could reach the city by the Rhône valley, just as later in the twelfth century Genoa got the best terms she could from the duke of Burgundy – then hoping to take ship for the Holy Land – for her merchants travelling through his lands to the fairs of Champagne. At the same time she strove in one way and another to monopolize the seaborne commerce of the south French and northwest Italian coasts as did Venice that of the littoral of the northern Adriatic, to stamp out neighbouring feudal rivals, to control the Apennine passes and to guarantee her access to the Lombard plain and the rich trades it served.

Nor were these the limits of Genoa's ambitions. In maritime wars forshadowing those soon to come against Venice, the city fought Pisa for supremacy in the great islands of the Tyrrhenian Sea, suppliers, like Sicily, of food and raw materials, and strategic posts on the routes to Africa and the Levant. Genoa struggled long and hard (1119–33) with her erstwhile ally for Corsica – eventually establishing a colony and fortress – and for Sardinia, where there were hopes of setting up a puppet king. The bitterness and intensity of these conflicts reveals what was now thought to be at stake, and the scale of operations the impressive naval resources – 80 galleys and 63 other craft on one occasion – the city could deploy. Much the same happened in southern Spain – Moslem since the days of the great Arab conquests of the early Middle Ages – where in exchange for promises of commercial concessions Genoa first supported the attempted Christian reconquest, and then obtained similar privileges from the Moorish princes of both the mainland and the Balearic Islands. So, too, in North Africa[3] – a market for textiles, spices and metal wares, and the provider of slaves and that gold particularly essential to Europe's trade with the Middle East once papal prohibitions impeded the sale of munitions to the infidel – footholds were established and extended (see pp. 90, 103,

109). The Genoese were in what is now Algeria and Ceuta (on the Straits of Gibraltar) by the mid-twelfth century, and after a display of force in the early 1200s acquired a chain of *fondaci* stretching along the coast from roughly Algiers to Tripoli.

Thus by about 1150 the Genoese were trading throughout most of the Mediterranean, their privileges specified and recognized in treaties with the rulers of the Catholic Holy Land and Moslem Africa alike, and their city had risen from the obscurity of a fishing village to become a major entrepôt. Genoese merchants sold spices in Nürnburg and bought, like the Venetians, textiles in northern Europe. Genoese ships worked in not only the great traffic between Europe and the Middle East, but from Byzantium to Egypt, or carried African grain and slaves to Alexandria so, to the disgust of the pious, linking and sustaining the two halves of Islam. Such were the rewards of these activities that the republic enjoyed a favourable balance of trade with the Levant, and such the prowess of her ships and seamen that unknown as a maritime power 150 years earlier Genoa was by the mid-1100s equalled in Italy only by Pisa and Venice, and by the end of the century the former had been surpassed and the latter overtaken. Meanwhile on the mainland Genoa, like Venice, profited from the endemic wars of popes and emperors and – momentarily at least – from the decline of the imperial authority (see pp. 92 and 111). No more than the Venetians were the Genoese troubled by the ambitions of the emperor Frederick Barbarossa who, amongst other things, intended to bring to heel the urban communities now in Europe's booming economy proliferating and flourishing in northern Italy, and – though without a fleet   to subdue Sicily. Hence in 1162, in exchange for a promise of naval assistance, the commune of Genoa secured imperial recognition of its autonomy – the very liberty the emperor so adamantly denied other cities – and of its supremacy in Liguria, together with commercial privileges in Sicily when, with Genoese aid, the kingdom had been taken.

Successes on this scale reflected something more than superlative business skills. Not indeed that these were lacking, and in the 1180s, by economic manipulation as adept as that of any subsequent exponent of informal empire, the republic obliged the debt-ridden young king of Sardinia to acknowledge its suzerainty. But to a far greater extent than that of Venice Genoa's initial wealth and power were founded simply on force. Loot figures largely in the accounts of the city's earliest achievements; its division is a prominent feature of any agreement involving Genoese assistance. As recorded by a civilized observer in the twelfth century, the behaviour of the Genoese is indistinguishable from that of the Vikings: 'they dominate the sea, they build galleys with which they go forth to pillage the most distant regions, returning home with their spoils.' Indeed such was their unrestrained individualism and violence, untouched by any of those Byzantine traditions which perhaps coloured the early evolution of Venice, that like the equally resolutely independent Iberians they attempted to avert disputes by defining and recording in notarial deeds their liberties and responsibilities, even down to such fine details as the precise degree of sexual freedom a husband might enjoy in the course of a sea voyage. And it was these same qualities that in large measure ensured the republic's stormy political development. After its obscure beginnings as an appanage of the Lombard and Carolingian kingdoms, Genoa came under the control of a commune in the eleventh century. This was an organization of a nature common in Italian towns and cities as the economy revived and imperial power foundered. It was in Genoa's case a sworn association apparently – and characteristically – of military origins, recognized as the effective ruling authority by Barbarossa in 1162. It was no democratic assembly of merchants but together with its officers – consuls – the tightest of oligarchies: a small group of magnates who owned fortresses within the city, who possessed lands around it, yet who had nevertheless some interest in trade. Such a regime was not to enjoy the stability of that of Venice. More or less sovereign lords continued to live in Genoa; other communes survived in the surrounding countryside. Then as the republic prospered others, not members of the dominant minority, were enriched, their ambitions fired and their interests as they saw them either sacrificed or ignored. The commune's expansionist policies brought financial chaos and the fall of one patrician clan, and in the early 1200s, in a city already notorious for its 'many hatreds and dissentions', consular rule was abandoned.

Nor were these the least of Genoa's troubles. The Christian footholds in the Middle East, and with them her factories, fell to the Moslems in the twelfth and thirteenth centuries (see p. 96). As trade with the orient through Syria and Egypt became, because of papal and Islamic intransigence, more difficult, the attractions of Byzantium accordingly grew. Here, however, though the Genoese were already established in some strength in the 1100s – with 300 merchants mentioned in Constantinople in 1162 – and where they had obtained imperial privileges, their position was far weaker than that of the Venetians and Pisans. And, as we have seen, Venetian primacy was decisively asserted by her overthrow of the Greek empire in 1204 (see pp. 92ff.). With the profits of her Eastern trade disastrously dwindling to a mere 50 per cent by the early 1200s, Genoa was forced to look for new ways to the wealth of Asia. She turned first to Syria – there opposed by her old enemy the emperor Frederick II, now titular king of Jerusalem, and far more effectively by the Venetians – to Christian Armenia, from where her merchants reached the eastern basin of the Black Sea, and to the Black Sea itself, to which her traders had long sought to penetrate and where, as Venetian prosperity showed, the greatest opportunities lay. So in 1261 she hastened the collapse of Venice's puppet regime in Constantinople and supported the restoration of the Greeks. Promises of naval assistance secured the republic's freedom to trade throughout the resurrected Byzantine empire and in the Black Sea on the most advantageous terms, together with the exclusion from these preserves of Venice and other undesirables (see pp. 95ff., 185).

Triumphs of this order ensured that to her age-old maritime and commercial struggle with Pisa, Genoa now added that with Venice. From the coasts of North Africa to the waters of Greece they were rivals – their antipathy as total as that once between Rome and Carthage – for the same rich trades, disputed into the fifteenth century in wars which soon merged with even wider conflicts in Europe, and between west and east. In these the republic's performance, often impeded by violent internecine strife, was characteristically more wayward and erratic than that of Venice. No adequate system of public finance was developed to sustain its naval and military endeavour and outraged or exiled Genoese admirals led the fleets of their city's mortal enemies, such as those of the emperor Frederick II who sought to re-assert imperial authority there. Such was the lack of any overall direction that the republic's colonial possessions displayed a remarkable, not to say at times irresponsible, independence and initiative, with Pera (Constantinople), for example, setting out a squadron of its own which defeated the Venetians off Lajazzo in 1294 (see p. 97). And if Genoa mounted a largely successful privateering campaign against the vulnerable commerce of Venice, its profits did little more than enrich the shipowning magnates of the city. Even so, the republic made astonishing and spectacular efforts, mustering 200 galleys and over 40,000 men in 1295. Nor in vain. True, the Venetians were not excluded from the Black Sea, but Genoese authority was re-established in Sicily following the death of Frederick II (1250), and the area around Syracuse colonized. More impressively, Pisa was humbled by the crushing Genoese naval victory at Meloria (1284) and her ambitions in Corsica, Sardinia and Elba scotched. Unable to shake the carefully deployed Venetian power in the Aegean – where Genoese privateers nevertheless continued to operate, and where control of Crete was for a time disputed – the Genoese assured their trade to the east by an agreement with the sultan of Egypt before Catholic Acra was lost. They also prudently established themselves in Lajazzo, Cyprus and along most of the littoral of Asia Minor from the Isthmus of Suez to the western shores of modern Turkey in the thirteenth century (see pp. 102ff.). Above all the city was after 1261 firmly entrenched in Constantinople and the Black Sea, whose already vast economic importance were further enhanced by the establishment of the Mongol empire.

From the Greek capital Genoese merchants penetrated to Macedonia and perhaps even Albania in the west. At the same time Genoese magnates monopolized the alum trade of Asia Minor and married into the Byzantine imperial house, whilst the ships of the republic entered the Black Sea in strength. A colony, virtually autonomous, at Pera (Constantinople) ensured for a time that the Bosphorus was closed to unwanted competitors, allowing the Genoese, their energies and resources concentrated by setbacks elsewhere, to reach on the one hand the mouths of the Danube and the Dnestr, and on the other the Crimea, the key to the Sea of Azov and so to Russia (see pp. 95, 98). On this strategic peninsula – as indeed on the rest of the Black Sea littoral – Genoese settlements quickly appeared, and already by 1290 Caffa displayed all those familiar features of later European outposts of empire (see pp. 185f.). In it there were established in style, with their lands and houses, members of some of Genoa's most illustrious families, served by native slaves and artisans and trading with local merchants and entrepreneurs. They imported luxuries from the Far East and tapped the resources of an almost limitless hinterland – the caviar of Tana; the salt of Caffa itself; the alum, silver, iron and timber of Trebizond. Through the Bosphorus they brought in, in true colonial fashion, European manufactures, chiefly textiles, whilst primary products – grain from the Ukraine and southern Russia, furs from the north, wax, hides and honey – were collected for re-export to destinations as distant and diverse as Tunis, Genoa, Syria and southern Spain. Nor were these the only opportunities. Food was shipped from the Crimea to Constantinople and Trebizond, and slaves from the Georgian and Caucasian coasts to the Levant and the western Mediterranean.

But quite apart from its own many attractions the Black Sea, like the Americas in the eyes of later colonial theorists, had the further merit of being a stepping stone to even better prospects, since with the establishment of Mongol rule in Central Asia the Italian bases on its shores became points of access to Persia and the East. Already in 1224, before the great push to the Orient was under way, a company had been formed in Genoa to promote trade with India. Whether it did so or not is unknown, but within a few years the enterprising were to be found throughout much of the Far East. The Genoese had a concession in Siwas[4] by 1280 and were active, as Marco Polo discovered, in the great Persian entrepôt of Tabriz, from where they sent silk to Europe and to their Black Sea stations (see p. 103). By the early 1300s they were at Hormuz on the Persian Gulf and in central Asia, India and China, where in 1338 a Genoese gift of 'horses and other marvels' so delighted the grand khan as to be lauded in verse and depicted in the summer palace in Peking. Naturally enough expeditions of this nature, seeking in the face of great difficulties and intense competition profits of a legendary magnitude, left Europe furtively, and commonly only came to light through some dispute or difficulty, as when a Genoese merchant brought to the west news of the massacre of a Catholic mission near Bombay in 1320. But clearly, even if the majority of the republic's merchants went no further east than Tabriz there were still nevertheless many either in, or familiar with, the Far East. One such, who had lived in India for 15 years, turned up in Cyprus in the mid-fourteenth century to beguile the by no means innocent locals with his wondrous stories, whilst to Boccaccio the Genoese were the authorities on all things oriental.

Their expansion, however, unlike that of Venice, was not confined to the penetration of existing commercial routes. Instead they pushed on in voyages and enterprises hardly less heroic than those of the Vikings and the Iberians. In 1290 they were providing naval support for the khan of Persia in the Black Sea, whilst Marco Polo noticed that their ships had reached the Caspian. This they had probably done by an arduous journey through southern Russia – across the Sea of Azov, along the Don and then overland and down the Volga – but once established there the Genoese could move goods on the routes to and from the East more cheaply, rapidly and safely than by caravan. Hence the Caspian remained the scene of assorted Genoese maritime endeavour – trade, piracy, even projected opposition to Tamburlaine – until at least the beginning of the fifteenth century. Nor did their ambitions and achievements stop here. In 1290 a grandiose scheme was devised, apparently by the Mongol khan of Persia, to ruin Mameluke Egypt by diverting its eastern trade into Persian ports. To this end he took into his service a large number of Genoese seamen – 900 according to one oriental source – who were to build and man the two galleys which would blockade the Red Sea. But although the ships were successfully completed in Baghdad, on arrival in Basra their crews fell out and massacred eath other instead of their intended victims. Disappointing though its outcome may have been, the episode reveals the presence, or availability, in the east of appreciable numbers of skilled Genoese men to whom the Arabian Sea and its approaches were clearly no obstacle. And undeterred by the spectacle of Genoese indiscipline and fratricidal inclinations, one idealist proposed (*c.* 1300) to employ the republic's sailors – 'unequalled in their skills and their zeal for profit' – to blockade the Red Sea from the Indian Ocean and so ruin both the infidel in Egypt and those unscrupulous Christians who persisted in trading with the Mamelukes notwithstanding papal prohibitions (see pp. 99, 103). But although this pious strategy came to nothing, an incidental reference by its author – a missionary with first-hand experience of what he was describing shows that at this very time there were Genoese ships operating in the Indian Ocean 'in the hope of gain'.[5]

Similar motives presumably lead to the despatch into the Atlantic in 1291 of an expedition under the Vivaldi brothers, bound for 'the parts of India'. The voyage was organized by distant relatives of the celebrated Genoese admiral Benedetto Zaccaria (see p. 192), protagonist of an alliance with the Mongols against Egypt, but beyond this its purpose is as obscure as its outcome. It may have been an attempt to gain some advantage over Venice – and so a precursor of the voyages of Columbus and da Gama – or it may have been intended, like the abortive scheme of the khan of Persia, to break the Mameluke stranglehold on the Red Sea spice trade. The Egyptians did indeed prohibit direct European access to the Orient, but this the Genoese already enjoyed by the routes through central Asia. And in any case, ecclesiastical fulminations notwithstanding, their position in Egypt was far from desperate. They had come to terms with the sultan in 1290, their colony in Alexandria was not recalled after the papal ban on dealings with the Mamelukes the following year and many of the city's most influential families were opposed to a breach with Egypt. So before long the republic was once again selling military supplies to the sultan, and such were their relations that in the early 1300s a Genoese observer could write that he understood 'from our merchants that the Ethiopian road (i.e. to India *via* Abyssinia and East Africa) is open to any who wish to take it'.[6]

What the Vivaldis perhaps intended therefore was to reach compatriots thought to be already sailing in eastern waters. It may have been their intention to accomplish this by a westward passage round the world – generally accepted by men of learning to be spherical – or more likely by a circumnavigation of Africa (see p. 229). Whether such a voyage, through blazing equatorial heat, along coasts where fevers were endemic and supplies scarce, was practicable in heavily manned oared craft is doubtful, though it is not certain that such vessels were used. What became of the expedition is unknown. Part may have been lost in Guinea, whilst the rest perhaps reached the Cape of Good Hope, and there may be some trace of its wanderings in that one of the Canary Islands, discovered by the Genoese, was given the name of a Vivaldi ship. It is also possible that the mysterious disappearance of the brothers coloured Dante's description of the fate of Ulysses, 'swallowed by the seas on the threshold of a new hemisphere,' just as it gave rise to rumours persisting through the medieval centuries of the sighting of survivors or their descendants in various parts of Africa.

With her energies concentrated on the opportunities of the Black Sea and on the maritime struggle with Venice, Genoa made no further attempts to find a new sea route to Asia. But her sailors were far from deterred by the fate of the Vivaldis from undertaking other lengthy and hazardous voyages. In the twelfth century they were already on the Atlantic coast of Morocco, and by 1250, if not earlier, were as far south as Safi. Here, in exchange for European silver, gold vital to the west's trade with the Orient could be had, brought in by caravan from Timbuktu (see pp. 170, 251). And as in the late thirteenth century demand and competition increased, enterprising Genoese merchants pushed inland towards the sources of supply in the Sudan along those trans-Saharan routes terminating in Morocco. By 1291 one had penetrated to Sidjilmassa, in the very heart of the desert, and on a Genoese map of *c.* 1320 information about the interior of Africa is said to have been provided by a citizen of the republic who had lived in the same township. Even more remarkably, difficulties encountered by the Genoese on passages along the African coast may have lead them, like the Portuguese later, to stand out to sea and so to discover a number of Atlantic islands (cf. pp. 228, 245ff.). A search for the unfortunate Vivaldis brought to light the Canaries, once known to Antiquity but long since forgotten, and by the early 1300s one had become Allegranza – perhaps after the brothers' ship of that name. But more was involved than chance, the investigation of classical intimations of paradise or the fate of the city's men and money. That one expedition displayed spices to the natives that they might reveal where similar things could be obtained shows what hopes there were. Nor were they merely of commerce. Petrarch – who was born in 1304 – could remember his parents talking of the departure of a Genoese war-fleet for the Canaries, and it was not the last, since in the 1330s a force under Lanzarotto Malocello – a member of a Genoese family long influential in Ceuta – having coasted the Saharan littoral, conquered the island which still bears his name. Then in 1341 a Genoese captain was involved in a cosmopolitan armada launched against the Canaries by the Portuguese. And although this too came to grief there was much other Iberian and Italian activity among the islands 'newly found' and now, as Petrarch wrote of the Canaries in 1337, familiar 'from the information of travellers who are constantly going there'.

Meanwhile other Genoese vessels, perhaps following routes pioneered by the Catalans, had been pushing northwards eventually to appear (1277) in the English

Channel. And thus there was opened after hesitant beginnings, a more or less regular seaborne trade from the Mediterranean to England and Flanders, with Genoese galleys and sailing vessels bringing in spices and – increasingly – the oils, dyes and mordants used in the manufacture of cloth, and taking out wool or woollen textiles, besides working their way, like their Venetian rivals, into various northern interport traffics (cf. pp. 110–11). But no more here than elsewhere could Genoese energies be confined to commerce, and the republic's fighting ships were to make their presence felt on many occasions, sacking, for example, Southampton in French service in 1338. Nevertheless the city's fundamental achievement was the establishment of a new and major commercial route – supplementing, rivalling, but never eclipsing those across the Continent – and so permitting an increased flow of goods. There had indeed been spasmodic direct maritime contact between the north and the Mediterranean in earlier centuries, but the new link was permanent, and even if in the end it was controlled by others its inception was in its way a revolution as great as the opening of a Cape route to Asia in the 1500s, or that through Suez in the nineteenth century. No more than the great Viking or Iberian voyages can it be explained in technological terms – the introduction of new methods of navigaton or the construction of vessels of greater endurance – since Genoese craft had been in the Atlantic and the Bay of Biscay (La Rochelle for instance) for something like half a century before they appeared in the Channel. But now there were new incentives and new opportunities, since by the late 1200s Genoa was able to exploit the resources of the Black Sea (see pp. 161–2). She had at her disposal a greater amount of eastern goods, she needed more textiles and bullion for their purchase and, increasingly prosperous, she developed a larger and livelier domestic market of her own. So, on the one hand, the Genoese pushed down and into Africa for gold, and on the other attempted to ensure their easier and unchallenged access to the manufactures of northern Europe. It may well be that the merits of the sea were initially recommended by the disruption of the transcontinental routes during the Franco-Flemish wars of *c.* 1300, and by the city's own relative proximity to the Atlantic. But the despatch of her merchantmen through the Straits of Gibraltar essentially reflected a wider economic reorganization. Previous policies were indeed maintained, with the city continuing her expansion in Liguria – where, for example, La Spezia was acquired in 1276 – to protect her interests and to stifle competition. But now textiles were drawn in by land and sea from an ever-increasing range of producers, and Genoa herself became in the late 1200s a considerable manufacturer of high quality woollen cloth and consequently a bulk importer of wool from England, Spain and North Africa.

II *A Genoese age*

Thus by roughly 1300 the republic, like Venice and the north German cities, had reached a peak of commercial prosperity, but one which, unlike them, she was never to re-attain (cf. pp. 53, 64). Between 1214 and 1274 the volume of goods she handled doubled and then, in the next nineteen years, quadrupled, with their value at its maximum in 1293. In all essentials her trade was identical with that of Venice, with the city importing oriental luxuries, slaves and local products from the Black Sea and the eastern Mediterranean, and paying for them with an admixture of western manufactures – ranging from textiles to weapons – and bullion. In addition Genoese, like Venetian, shipping transported Christian pilgrims and warriors, and penetrated local interport trades in east and west alike by its efficiency and reliability (cf. pp. 101–11 and 193ff.). But to the rewards of such normal commercial operations the Genoese added, as the Venetians did not, loot from privateering, and the earnings of those war fleets supplied to both European and Asian rulers (see pp. 00–0). So, also, the city's rise and affluence were due to those same causes that allowed the emergence of other maritime republics in the Mediterranean and the north: the absence of opponents commanding overwhelmingly superior resources; the increasing weakness and technological sterility of the formerly dominant seapowers; the ending of the barbarian and Islamic invasions; the stimulus of Europe's increasing population and reviving economy (cf. pp. 89ff.). To exploit these opportunities Genoa, an early rival of the far better placed Pisa and Venice, seemed for a time almost uniquely well suited. Already in the twelfth century virtually all its inhabitants were to some degree engaged in commerce, property and liquid capital were soon equally divided between the bourgeoisie and urban nobility and before long not even the official chronicler could define the rank of his city's men of consequence, grouping them instead under the obliging generic of 'the quality'. Such a society was unreservedly dedicated to the pursuit of profit, its policies and behaviour, like those of the Dutch – and, to a lesser degree, of Venice – pragmatically liberal. To become a citizen of Genoa, and so theoretically entitled to participate in public life, involved none of the difficulties encountered in Venice, but simply a promise to fulfil the obligations of citizenship. Unlike their fellows elsewhere, Genoese merchants showed little inclination to withdraw from business to the delights of a country seat – perhaps for no better reason than the reluctance of the local landed aristocracy to associate with them. In Genoa Jews were rarely subjected to violent persecution, alien artisans – heretics included – were willingly accepted, religious enthusiasms inimical to the flow of business were coolly received and money was not expended on lavish building in the style of the Hanse, let alone of Venice (cf. pp. 69–70, 210f., 219). Then to such prudent virtues there was added the drive provided by the ambitions and energies of the landed magnates living in and around the city. As with Venice their resources backed some of its earliest ventures and a few, like the Fieschi and Spinola were to remain in business for centuries. They were, however, no Venetian patricians. Defeated in interminable feuds at home, they were often driven, like Viking chiefs, to seek new opportunities abroad. And even in the happiest times loot and land concerned them more than trade, with the Embriaci accumulating titles and possessions in Sicily and the Holy Land in the 1100s, and later compatriots establishing principalities in Asia Minor and off the West African coast (see pp. 164, 182, 192).

But the end of the Middle Ages brought Genoa none of Venice's so visibly manifested triumphs. Instead, crippled by those very forces which had ensured her initial success – that uncontrollable individualism and almost frenetic energy – she lost both her commercial pre-eminence and her independence. Even by the standards of the times Genoa's political instability was remarkable – 'always changing, always in flux' as a pope somewhat platitudinously observed of a city that endured fourteen revolutions between 1413 and 1453. Urban patricians struggled to thwart the political aspirations of the unprivileged; the interests of a new banking plutocracy conflicted with those of merchants; aristocratic factions pursued their ancient vendettas. As a result the city was in foreign hands for much of the fourteenth century before becoming a client first of the French, and then, in the early 1500s, of the Spanish crown. Nor was this surprising. Neither socially nor territorially did Genoa attain anything of Venice's cohesion. Bellicose local feudal magnates, consolidating their own authority, had no intention of allowing the city to become stable, powerful, or under any rule from which they might suffer. And with their urban holdings, their armies, and their fortresses often commanding vital routes – as did those of the Fieschi the Apennine passes – they were well able to look to their interests. Then, within Genoa itself, was the city's own equally factious aristocracy, an amalgam of old and new families, numbering by the mid-1400s some 800 individuals. With their material and political preponderance they were the nearest approximation to Venice's patricians. Their power, however, was not sustained by generally acceptable policies, or the adept manipulation of potential opposition, but by the clans (*alberghi*) to which they belonged. These, which emerged in the thirteenth century, were groups of nobles, not necessarily related by blood, but all having, often by formal agreement, the same name. They were in essence associations for mutual protection. Their strength was based on the ownership of an urban fortress, and their consequent predominance in its neighbourhood, from which with the backing of their clients and retainers they could ensure, as a Doria put it on the occasion of his kidnapping of an heiress, that none should meddle 'in our affairs'. Opposed to these were the inappositely named 'people', whose ranks embraced anything from mercantile grandees to textile workers and who, as a party, were weakened by the rift between the artisan class which grew as industry developed, and the merchants who, like aristocrats, formed clans of their own.

Confined in a crowded city, unimpeded by the restraints that topography imposed on faction in Venice, barely weakened by any substantial and permanent migration, such divisions intensified and proliferated. Hence late medieval Genoa possessed not so much a constitution and form of government as a series of rival authorities, private and public, the victories of various factions recorded in agreements detailing in characteristic Genoese fashion the exact extent of their entitlement to power. On the one hand there was a group of increasingly aristocratic councils, of which that of the 'elders' was the most important, directing the running of the republic in normal times and supervising, through other assemblies, such matters as maritime and colonial affairs (cf. pp. 190, 198). On the other hand, however, there was the doge,[7] who as nominal head of the city controlled its army and held its castles – usually with greater tenacity against his subjects than their enemies. Then, independent to all intents, were the aristocratic *alberghi* and the great financial corporations, with the Bank of St George intervening in public affairs as and when it felt necessary (cf. pp. 188, 191).

Such divisions ensured, as indeed they reflected, Genoa's failure to establish a mainland empire like that of the Venetians, notwithstanding early efforts to dominate the Ligurian littoral and the mountain cantons. Neighbouring and competing ports – of which Savona was the most dangerous – survived, often under aristocratic patronage; the holdings of local magnates and of the city's alleged feudatories flourished unsubdued amongst its possessions. With so fragmented a basis of authority Genoa produced no fiscal system comparable to that of Venice. Its Ligurian territories perhaps provided about 25 per cent of its revenues by the 1500s – roughly the percentage Venice drew from its mainland possessions – but its salt monopoly, unlike that of the Venetians, was imperfect and Genoese ships avoided the payment of customs by working from nearby ports.[8] Thus with no public revenues to speak of the republic was already obliged in the twelfth century, and to a greater degree later, to raise capital or to attempt to meet its debts, by mortgaging state assets, and even colonial possessions, to private persons or institutions (cf. pp. 190–2).

Equally damaging, the city was for much of the late Middle Ages in the hands of alien rulers to whom its commercial well-being was of small concern. And whereas outside Italy Venice had in the west little more to contend with than the decayed German empire, Genoa, further crippled by the general economic recession of the fourteenth century, had the ill-fortune to have as neighbours not only the restive Florentine and Milanese states but the French and the Aragonese as well, who from the late 1200s were formidable opponents in both the Ligurian and Tyrrhenian seas, and the waters of the eastern Mediterranean. And here the Greek empire, so opportunely and effortlessly restored with Genoese connivance in 1261, soon showed itself fragile and unstable, all too susceptible to Venetian and ultimately Ottoman pressure, or apt in moments of energy and effectiveness to regret and resist Genoese tutelage.

Hence unable to formulate, let alone implement, sustained policies and more often than not internally in chaos Genoa eventually failed against Venice, and in particular against Venice in the Levant, even though battles and campaigns enough were won. In the renewed struggle for the Black Sea, which commenced in 1350, Genoese intrigues against the Aragonese now established in Sardinia brought an alliance of Venice and Aragon against them. Yet the outcome was no worse than stalemate. Each in the end agreed to respect the other's interests in the Black Sea, and it was accepted that Venetian warships were to keep out of the Gulf of Genoa and those of the Genoese out of the Adriatic. The next round, precipitated by a clash over mastery of the Dardanelles, started in much the same way. At sea the Genoese were defeated in the Tyrrhenian but then went on to a resounding victory over Venice off Pola (1379). Hard on this they moved against the city itself, and for a time Genoese ships were stationed at the very entrance to the lagoon, where Pietro Doria occupied Chioggia. But Venice rallied and Genoa collapsed. Thereafter her efforts were decreasingly effective and as Venetian authority was reinforced and extended in the Levant that of Genoa declined (cf. pp. 98, 118). Her colonies were either mortgaged or, prosperous themselves, doggedly pursuing their own interests, often in open defiance of the mother city. At the same time the disintegration of the Mongol empire eventually destroyed western trade to the east through the Black Sea, as the fall of roughly 700 per cent in the value of the Genoese customs at Pera between 1334 and 1423 dramatically shows. Nor as the transcontinental routes declined had Genoa the will and ability to challenge Venice's preeminence in Syria and Egypt, to where the bulk of eastern commerce now flowed (cf. p. 104). In face of the Mamelukes, and later the Ottomans, one – and perhaps the only solution – was, as Venice demonstrated, to establish a territorial empire and to so organize business that discrete pressure could be applied, and potential provocations arising from individual enterprises, however brilliant or original, in some measure obviated (cf. pp. 114, 123). But that the Genoese were incapable of such designs was – no more than their political misfortunes – not necessarily synonymous with economic ruin. Thus whilst the Venetians accumulated possessions in the eastern Mediterranean, the Genoese turned instead, but as private persons and not as a political or economic community, to spectacular business and financial operations in western Europe and the Atlantic (cf. pp. 163ff. and 177ff.). State direction might produce, as with Venice or the Iberians, the most visible manifestations of empire, but it was economic domination – informal empire as practised by Genoa and Holland – that brought the greatest accretions of individual wealth and power.

Nevertheless old-established trades were neither suddenly nor totally abandoned. In the Levant individual Genoese merchants continued to compete with the Venetians and even in 1364 dealings with Alexandria still accounted for 50 per cent of the value of Genoa's commerce. In the fourteenth century Genoese merchants could obtain spices in Cyprus, whilst in the 1440s a number of the city's magnates were trading in Beirut and Damascus. Then, in the later Middle Ages, there was an important route from the Orient to the Ottoman-held Bursa (Sea of Marmara), from where some eastern goods continued to reach the west by a variety of ways. They might be taken to the Genoese base at Chios in the Aegean, in direct maritime contact with the western Mediterranean and northern Europe (see p. 173); they could be shipped to Pera, and from there to Caffa, and so by land and river to the Polish market of Lvow for re-despatch; and after the loss of Caffa to the Turks they could go from Pera along the Dobrogean coast to the Dnestr, and so again to Lvow. These, however, were now the least of Genoa's trades in the Black Sea. Its own potential had long been appreciated, and as access to the Far East became impossible the Genoese turned (and with greater energy and success than the Venetians with their major interests elsewhere) to the exploitation of the rich and varied natural resources – grain, furs, fish, slaves – of an ever-growing area of eastern Europe and Asia Minor accessible from posts established or developed at the outlet of the

Dnestr route (Akkerman), in Bulgaria (Varna), at the mouth of the Danube (Kilia Vechia) and in the Crimea (cf. pp. 98–9 and 185–6). Caffa became a vigorous regional market, scarcely any longer in commercial contact with its parent city. Its inhabitants shipped wine from Bulgaria, fostered viticulture in the Crimea, dominated the fisheries of the Sea of Azov, and traded with a hinterland that reached from the littoral of the Black Sea to northern Russia, and from Greece to Caucasia. Yet these pleasing opportunities were likewise doomed. With Tamburlaine's destruction of the Kipchak khanate warring native principalities threatened Genoa's possessions in the Crimea, Wallachia and Moldavia blocked Hungary's approaches to the Black Sea, Poland was attracted to the Baltic as Hanseatic control weakened in the north and in the end Genoese, like Venetian colonies in the east were isolated, taxed and finally overrun by the Ottomans (cf. pp. 99–100). Even so, such was the variety of routes, and such the pertinacity of the Genoese acquisitive urge, that trade continued to flow even as the Turkish net closed. In the late fifteenth century Pera and Caffa could be reached from Genoa by lengthy overland routes along which, moreover, other openings – farming the Polish customs for instance – were to be found. By Ottoman licence Genoese ships still exported grain from the Black Sea after the fall of Constantinople just as, by Ottoman licence, the colony at Pera, which had not resisted the conquest, retained most of its privileges. But the sultan's mercy was not infinite. Caffa fell to his armies in 1475, and Akkerman and Kilia shortly after (1481).

These reverses, and Venice's domination of the spice trade, brought a change in the area and nature of the republic's commercial and imperial interests as radical as the later diversion of Portuguese enterprise from Africa to Asia, or that of the British from North America to India (see pp. 251ff.). Genoese energies increasingly turned from trade to finance, and from the Levant to the west. In some cases this meant no more than the vigorous resumption of former practices, as when in North Africa Tripoli was sacked (1355), Djerba occupied (1388) and Mahdiyah unsuccessfully assaulted (1390) (see p. 157). But in general relations with the African contintent, where by the late Middle Ages Genoa had footholds from Safi in Atlantic Morocco to Tripoli in Libya as well as in the interior – at Fes for example – were less bellicose. North Africa was an excellent market for the produce of southern Spain, where the city's economic power was rapidly spreading, just as its Algerian littoral was a major supplier of grain, which in the early 1400s the Genoese were shipping out in bulk – up to nearly 4000t at a time. From North Africa, too, there came the gold which travelling by caravan eventually reached, through the Saharan market of Timbuktu, such Mediterranean outlets as Oran, Tlemcen and Honein. Hence when some of these traditional routes were disrupted by the Portuguese invasion of Morocco in the fifteenth century (see pp. 251–2), and as Genoa's growing trade with southern Spain demanded more bullion, the Genoese renewed their earlier efforts to reach the sources of supply. By land they penetrated to Touat (1447) and Timbuktu (1470), whilst their seamen, vainly seeking another world as a German chronicler put it, were off the Senegambian coast in the mid-1400s.[9]

Meanwhile Genoese merchants were establishing an ever-tightening grip on the economies of Iberia, dominating the sugar trade of the new Portuguese Atlantic islands, and monopolizing alike the Castilian mercury mines at Almadén and the export of fruit from Moorish Granada. At the same time the nature of Genoa's northern commerce was changing. The fairs of Geneva, and then of Lyons, replaced those of Provence and Champagne as markets for the purchase of English and Flemish goods, and the sale of Genoese exports. Through Milan and the Alpine passes (the St Gotthard and the Splügen) there was in the fifteenth century a vital trade with south Germany, the upper Rhine and the great international commercial centre of Cologne (see p. 171). And though Genoese vessels still worked to the English Channel they were no longer galleys but carracks – some seven or eight a year in the early 1400s – carrying to the cloth-producing centres of the Low Countries and England impressive quantities of alum, brought direct from Asia Minor, or Lombard woad (1300t in 1467) shipped from Genoa itself.

True, even at this date some former ambitions still remained, and at the very moment of the first great wave of Iberian oceanic expansion two Genoese merchants undertook through the Middle East and Red Sea a commercial voyage to the Far East (1493–9) which ended in disaster, and is known only from the cryptic account of the survivor, Girolamo di Santo Stefano, who reached Sumatra. And equally futile were Paolo Centurione's schemes in the 1520s of penetrating to Asia through Russia, as the English were later to try (see p. 474). Nevertheless, with little of the support that the comparatively stable oligarchies of the Hanse and Venice accorded to their merchants, and with few of the restrictions that they likewise imposed upon them, the Genoese – their wits often further sharpened, like those of Portuguese traders in Asia later, by political disaster – were more flexible and resourceful in the face of difficulties than were the Venetians or Germans. So by the early 1500s the republic, to judge from the evidence of its customs records and the ubiquity of its citizens, was in touch with the widest of worlds, vigorously extending its interests westward into Iberia, the Atlantic and the newly discovered Americas, yet still doing business in Pera, Alexandria and Asia. From England, where there was an important Genoese colony in London, the city continued to take, as for centuries past, metals and the woollen textiles destined for Italy, Africa and the orient. In exchange it supplied some of those eastern luxuries once so important in its northern trade, but basically Mediterranean alum, fruits and wines, and the manufactures of south Germany and northern Italy (see pp. 166 and 176). If, however, these cargoes went by sea it was no longer in Genoese ships, but in either English vessels working through the Straits of Gibraltar or – and more important – in an astonishing variety of craft which carried them to Lisbon or Cadiz for re-shipment north or south. For the rest, it was a trade conducted, like that with Flanders, overland across Europe, so that even African or Asian pepper coming through Lisbon to Antwerp could eventually reach Genoa via Lyons.[10]

But the decline of the old Genoese sea route to the north was in some degree redressed by the opportunities of the Iberian Atlantic islands – the Spanish Canaries, Portuguese Madeira and São Tomé – from which the republic's ships (seventeen in 1495 alone) were soon taking sugar into the Mediterranean, either to their home port or to Chios, for redistribution throughout the Levant (see pp. 182, 186). Then from Portugal itself, either directly or by way of Cadiz and Marseilles, Genoa imported such local products as fish (the celebrated tunny in particular) together with pepper from Portuguese Asia, and slaves and ivory from Portuguese Africa. In exchange the republic supplied manufactures, some (paper and velvet) its own, others (metal goods) from Lombardy and south Germany, together with those things which might reinforce the reality and image of Portuguese imperial power, such as, on one occasion, 1500 galley oars and a sizable load of black marble.

Of much the same nature, though of far greater economic consequence, was Genoa's trade with Spain, which in 1537 accounted for about 50 per cent (by value) of its imports. From the southern ports of the peninsula, and generally in Spanish ships, the city acquired for – amongst other things – grain and industrial goods an admixture of colonial and native products ranging from fish, silk, oils and fruit to the alum of the Genoese-controlled mines at Mazarron, and those leather articles for which Spain was renowned. But by far the most important was the wool of Castile and Aragon, the raw material of Genoa's textile industry, brought from Tortosa and Cartagena often in big Genoese craft, and in the 1520s constituting the bulk of the republic's imports of wool. Nor – opportunities in banking and high finance apart – were these Spain's only attractions. By sea its south-western coast was in contact with northern Europe, North Africa, the eastern Mediterranean and the Americas, so that in Cadiz there were to be found things as different as English and Flemish textiles, Irish cattle, Atlantic sugar and American hides and dyes. Hence from here in 1495, for example, some of Genoa's most illustrious families were shipping sugar and cloth to Chios.

Roughly similar were the republic's dealings with the ancient market of southern France where Marseilles, tapping a rich hinterland, provided vital primary products (grain, salt, honey), manufactures such as paper, and was besides an entrepôt of some consequence in the Spanish trade. It was, furthermore, a port from which Genoese vessels regularly worked to North Africa – Oran in particular – taking out as many as 20,000 French cloths at a time in the 1490s. The equally long-established and fundamental connection with southern Italy also persisted and flourished. Naples provided some Levantine goods left by ships on passage down the Mediterranean and brought north by coaster. It also provided wine, and silk in such quantities that in 1535 Andrea Doria alone had thirteen galleys engaged in its carriage. To pay for these purchases Genoa exported English woollen cloths, together with its own velvets, silks and cottons, adeptly exploiting its advantage as banker to the Spanish Crown to press for preferential treatment and the destruction of local competition.[11] Even more colonial was the relationship with Sicily, the other major provider of raw silk for which, and for Sicilian grain, Genoa paid largely with bullion. The long-standing Genoese commerce with North Africa, which for centuries had supplied gold and a rich variety of natural products, had lost much of its importance as Iberian incursions not only deflected the flow of bullion but unleashed Christian ardour against Genoese ships carrying, like those of the Venetians, Moslem goods and passengers along the North African coast. Even so there was something to be retrieved. In Morocco Portuguese officials made use of Genoese financial skills, Portuguese garrisons needed weapons and Africa continued to take European textiles, and to provided alike dates for England and Moorish carpets for Iberia.

But of the great trade to the eastern Mediterranean, once the basis of Genoese prosperity, little remained. With Constantinople, formerly the point of access to the riches of Asia, Asia Minor and the Black Sea, such contacts as survived were indirect, and in that resurgence of the Levantine trade from which Venice so handsomely gained Genoa had no part (cf. pp. 139–41). Relations with Egypt and Syria were fitful – eight voyages to Alexandria between 1520–31; six to Beirut 1507–26 – yielding some spice, silk and precious stones. Yet notwithstanding the Ottoman advance and Venice's commercial pre-eminence, amongst western powers, in Egypt and Syria, Genoese merchants continued to trade in the Levant from the republic's base in Chios. More or less in the centre of the Aegean, on the very border of the Moslem and Christian worlds and in vigorous contact with both it was, like Macao or Hongkong later, a magnificently sited island from which, whatever the state of international relations, the enterprising could effect something of profit. Here slaves taken by Moslems and Christians alike were sold, and from here Genoese financiers invested in Christian Rhodes, whilst Genoese merchants re-exported Iberian fruit to Islamic south-eastern Europe for the purchase of grain. In the early 1400s it was sending cotton and alum from Asia Minor direct to western Europe – with nine ships sailing for Southampton and Flanders in 1445 – together with silk of its own and that from further east. To pay for such goods Chios took from the west textiles, coral, sugar and that silver needed to balance its commerce with Syria and Central Asia. Nevertheless it was no Phoenix risen from the ashes of Genoese ruin. The loss to the Turks of the alum mines of Focea (1455) soon ended the seaborne commerce to the north, whilst by the end of the century Chian trade with Iberia was mainly in Portuguese ships, and that with the republic itself handled by no more than five vessels a year (cf. pp. 136, 261–3).

Thus, simply, in terms of commodities Genoese trade in the early 1500s, and even later, was still recognizably that of the Middle Ages. The city continued to re-export European textiles to Spain, North Africa and the rest of Italy, and to provide Iberia with weapons and other manufactures, just as it remained a major importer of wool, even if no longer that of England, but of Africa, the Balkans and Spain, which in 1521 alone provided over 6000 sacks. It likewise remained a vital centre of the bullion trade, but instead of the African gold of which it had once been Italy's most important supplier, it was by the late 1500s transmitting across Europe, as the agent of the Spanish Crown, American silver to the Habsburg Netherlands (cf. pp. 179, 359). So, too, deprived by the Ottoman conquests of the alum of Asia Minor, Genoa found other sources in Castile and in the Italian mines at Tolfa, exploited from 1541 by companies in which the republic's influence was usually strong.

But nowhere was the continuity of Genoese interests and the flexibility of Genoese techniques more clearly displayed than in slaving. In the medieval centuries the city's trade was in general of the same nature as that of the Venetians, conducted from a homeland in which slavery was accepted and directed to Moslem and Greek states in which it was endemic (see pp. 106–8). But Genoese slaving was pursued more ruthlessly, proved more enduring and eventually affected a far wider world than did that of Venice. An early trade in Moslem prisoners taken in the western Mediterranean was eclipsed with the opening of the Black Sea. Here, like their Venetian and Catalan rivals, the Genoese were soon handling not only such remote and unfortunate peoples as Circassians, Tcherkesses, Alans and – in increasing numbers by the late 1300s – Tartars, but as opportunity allowed, Bulgarians, Georgians, Russians and Greeks, who were Christians, even if of the wrong persuasion (see pp. 106–8). And once the restored Greek empire allowed Egyptian commerce through the Bosphorus (1263), the Genoese established themselves as the major suppliers of the harems and armies of the Mameluke sultans.[12] Nor was Egypt their only market. Male slaves were sent to the Genoese alum mines at Focea or to work the land in the city's possessions in the Levant. The rest were shipped west to be used, amongst other things, in agriculture and industry in the republic, which meant that some, like African slaves in the Spanish Americas, could become so integrated into European society as occasionally to acquire specialist skills, including even those of the artist (cf. p. 334). For women the usual fate was domestic servitude in southern Europe or in Genoa itself where by *c.* 1400 perhaps as much as 10 per cent of the population was unfree, and in whose colonial possessions bishops were amongst the owners of slave girls. So, as with the Venetians, much of the Genoese trade was in young women, their colour carefully recorded (black, white, brown, olive) for the benefit of buyers in an age often wrongly thought innocent of such distinctions and discrimination, and the best prices commanded by the well-favoured – the handsome and striking Circassians in particular – and virgin.[13]

It was a traffic conducted with the same brutality as that across the Atlantic, soon to engage Genoese skills and capital (cf. pp. 175, 255). In a ship sailing from the Crimea to Chios in 1455 30 per cent of the slaves on board died. Genoese law accepted that a master could beat his slave to death, whilst for the rape of a female the punishment was merely a modest fine combined with the obligation to compensate her owner for the damage to his property. Against such proceedings few protests were raised, except that in the early fourteenth century Genoese ruthlessness, and indeed slavery itself, were condemned by brother William Adam who, like las Casas in the Spanish Indies later, had seen what he denounced. But this was to no avail. With their trade to Egypt the Genoese profited, as the Iberians, whatever their iniquities were never to do, from supplying troops to a formidable enemy of Christendom. And such was their reputation that even in the 1430s they were suspected of selling baptized Christians to the Mamelukes and were still, notwithstanding the opposition of the city's magistrates, enslaving Greeks.

For much of the late Middle Ages the main centres of this traffic were the Black Sea ports of Caffa and Tana. In or from these bases slaves could be bought from peoples amongst whom servitude was endemic or from those who, in the desperation of famine, sold their offspring, with the balance made up from prisoners taken in Genoese raids and piracy in eastern waters. From the Black Sea shiploads of such wretches were then despatched either direct to the west or, in Christian and Islamic vessels alike, to Egypt, with the entrepôt of Cyprus being used if for any reason free access to Moslem lands was impeded. Only with the loss of Constantinople to the Turks, ending the Greek – and hence Genoese – relationship with Egypt did the trade, which had once involved the shipment of two or three hundred slaves at a time, falter. For a while it continued from Chios, with the harvest of victims from the Black Sea littoral first augmented, and then eclipsed, by an influx of Christians enslaved by the advancing Ottomans, and who were sold in North Africa, Asia Minor and Italy.[14] But the Turkish conquest first of the remaining Genoese stations, and then of Egypt itself ended both this and an overland commerce through Moldavia and Wallachia.

Such, however, were the demands of the domestic market, and such the profits of the trade, that as supplies failed in the east old sources were revived, and new ones discovered, in the west. In the early fifteenth century the Genoese – papal condemnations notwithstanding – were dealing in Guanches from the Canaries whose homeland they helped to subjugate and exploit (cf. pp. 164, 180, 182). To these were soon added Moors taken in the Castilian reconquest of Spain, prisoners from Portuguese Morocco, and Jews expelled from Spain in 1492. By the early 1500s the Genoese were also shipping cargoes of 200 or so slaves – generally white Berbers, but including some black Africans as well – from Tunis to either Chios or to their home port. And at the same time Negroes obtained by the Iberians in West Africa were brought to Genoa from Cadiz or the ports of Mediterranean Spain, usually in modest numbers but occasionally – 1522 for example – in cargoes of nearly 200. And whatever the pious reflections in acts of manumission on the natural freedom of the human kind the victims were primarily, as in the old Levant trade, young girls.

But this domestic traffic was by no means the limit of Genoese endeavour, since the republic's colony in Seville found in the needs of the new Spanish settlements in the Americas yet another outlet for its skills and capital (see pp. 180ff.). When, in the earliest days, the export of slaves to the Indies was regulated by royal licence the Genoese quickly discovered the gains to be made from speculation in permits. When, however, returns began to drop some, like the Vivaldi and Centurione commenced (1514) to ship Africans to Hispaniola. Better still was to come, for after the emperor Charles V had granted a monopoly of the trade to one of his favourites (1518), it was the Genoese who handled it, making a twelvefold profit from the sale of licences and from forcing up prices by a judicious regulation of the volume and frequency of shipments. When, as a result of the shortage of slaves in Hispaniola, the monopoly was abolished, the same merchants successfully turned to the competitive trade (1526), with the Vivaldi specializing in providing labour for the expanding West Indian sugar industry (see pp. 181, 321). And as demand, prices and opportunities increased so did the scope of Genoese activities. A Lomellini and his associates were licensed to export 900 slaves in 1542 – mainly for the estates of Hernán Cortés – whilst others dealt not only in Africans but also invested in the vessels used in their carriage such as the inappositely named *San Salvador* of the di Negri.[15]

Yet whatever the elements of continuity the republic was by the sixteenth century no longer, as in the past, a major entrepôt in the trade between the east and west, its shipping was for the most part employed in short-distance interport traffics and its commerce was becoming, like that of Venice later, of a nature nearer to that of the Hanse (cf. pp. 48, 152). Nowhere was this more apparent than in the city's relations with the north. In the twelfth and thirteenth centuries the Genoese had obtained, first through the fairs of Provence and then of Champagne, French, Flemish and English cloths brought south overland, and largely paid for with oriental luxuries. But with the opening of an Atlantic sea-route in the late 1200s the volume and variety of this commerce increased, and to the cargoes of eastern goods carried in Genoese vessels sailing for the Channel were added such products of the Mediterranean as the fruits, wine and grain of southern Spain and North Africa. When, however, access to the markets of the orient became increasingly difficult for Genoa, whilst the northern textile industry flourished, the republic, unlike Venice, turned from the luxury trade to concentrate on the export from northern Europe of wool and woollen textiles paid for – some jewelry, spices and other such items apart – basically with those materials needed in the manufacture of cloth, and which the city could obtain with comparative ease (cf. pp. 172–3). Thus from Italy the Genoese shipped woad and wood ashes; from Asia Minor the alum of which their control of Focea (1275–1455) gave them a virtual monopoly; and from Spain oils and soaps. In a commerce of this nature – which could, as in 1445, involve the movement of 3000t of alum at a time – the city employed not galleys, but bulk carriers eventually capable of making the direct passage from the eastern Mediterranean to the Channel, and of such efficiency that they could, to the disgust of patriots, oust English vessels from the country's trade to Flanders (see pp. 194–6). Yet by the 1400s these operations were in trouble. There was the momentary competition of a galley service provided by the energetic and capable Florentines. But even when this faded the difficulties remained. In England the economic advantages which large and relatively lightly manned Genoese sailing craft might have enjoyed were denied them by the xenophobic natives who, in the commercial depression of the early fifteenth century, showed a natural reluctance to share what little trade there was with foreigners. And by the late 1400s, with royal encouragement and with that of the Florentines who had in the meanwhile dropped out of shipping, the English had opened their own seaborne commerce with the Mediterranean (see p. 460). Hence, whereas in the early 1400s several big Genoese ships might reach England in a year, by the end of the century there were no more than one or two. The trade to Flanders, where Genoese interests were increasingly concentrated, continued in the face of powerful Iberian maritime competition, but by the sixteenth century, though occasional Genoese ships might appear in the Channel, they had in general withdrawn not only from English waters, but from those of northern Spain and even from south-western Iberia. Thereafter Genoa's northern commerce was conducted either overland or, directly or indirectly, in the shipping of other ports (cf. pp. 171, 202).

This collapse reflects the inability of big Genoese ships – and they were amongst the largest in regular use at the time – to compete, like those of the Venetians, either economically or in terms of security, in seas then particularly infested with pirates and privateers (see pp. 133ff.). Moreover, vessels called into being by long-distance bulk trades were restricted by their very characteristics – their size, depth and limited manoeuvrability in confined waters – as to the routes on which they could work or the harbours which they could enter. Thus Genoa, ultimately crippled by that indifference to technological change characteristic of commercial and industrial decline, and supporting a fleet not easily redeployed once the demand for its especial qualities had disappeared, was unable to compete with Biscayan, Portuguese, English and Ragusan owners with their less imposing but more adaptable vessels (cf. pp. 142–3).

Nor, by the late fifteenth century, could it easily supply those commodities its ships had once carried. The Ottomans dominated the eastern Mediterranean and controlled (after 1455) the alum of Focea, whilst the woad of Lombardy was replaced by that of Toulouse for which the natural outlet was Bordeaux. And in any case the Genoese had by now found in neighbouring southern Spain an ample supplier of their own requirements and a limitless outlet for their ambitions.

Equally radically, Genoa moved away from commerce and came by the 1500s to rank with Florence, Milan and Venice as a major centre of manufacturing. It produced paper, coral goods, a considerable amount of cottons and, from the thirteenth century, woollen textiles. But of the greatest value was its silk industry, described with confused enthusiasm by a patriot in the mid-1500s – before high wages and a reluctance to accept current fashions brought its speedy demise – as 'not the right eye but the life and soul of the republic'. And in many ways it was. Its demands involved the import of raw materials from much of the Mediterranean – with southern Italy and Spain of increasing importance as the Turkish advance cut off traditional eastern markets – and on such a scale as to account for about 50 per cent of the value of the city's incoming trade in the early sixteenth century.

Yet all this was insignificant compared with Genoa's emergence as a centre of international finance and its economic colonization of Iberia. The attractions of the peninsula became increasingly apparent, as in the Levant the city faced the commercial hegemony of Venice and the military and naval supremacy of the Ottomans and in northern Italy the strength of Florence. The power of Spain, which for centuries had pressed on Genoa – as first Sicily (1282), then Sardinia (1325), Naples (1455) and ultimately most of Italy and parts of North Africa came under Spanish influence or control – was by the early 1500s ubiquitous, and Genoa itself a client of the Spanish crown from 1528. But Iberia, quite apart from the produce it could supply to replace that of the eastern Mediterranean, and the political support it could offer, held even greater promise in that it was, at the very moment of its rise to world domination, commercially and financially relatively undeveloped (see pp. 337, 368). It thus provided a particularly congenial outlet for the skills and resources of Genoese plutocrats whose native city had, unlike Venice, little land to attract patrician investment, few offices either at home or abroad to satisfy their ambitions, and inspired in them no sense of public duty and civic responsibility likely to impede their success in international financial speculation (cf. pp. 167–8). Hence in the sixteenth and seventeenth centuries the Genoese re-enacted in some measure in Iberia their former achievements in Byzantium. But they were not, like the Venetians in Greece, or the Hanse in Scandinavia, to be engaged in the making and breaking of dynasties, nor, confronted by comparatively well-organized states, had they much reason or opportunity to seek such liberties as they had once enjoyed in the loosely governed east (cf. pp. 54, 92). Not only were the Iberian monarchies too powerful, and able, if they wished, to find other entrepreneurs, but the Genoese hold on the peninsula was not the outcome of the ruthless enforcement of a coherent policy by some organized political or economic entity, but simply the manifestation of the influence of individual Genoese merchants and financiers, many of them domiciled and even naturalized in Iberia. Their influence was thus less dramatic but none the less potent as in exchange for their services they exacted financial, commercial and industrial privileges, dominated and vitalized by their skills and resources whole sectors of the Iberian economy, and exercised in short an extensive informal empire.

The ancient association of Genoa with Spain, going back to at least the early 1100s, had strengthened in the Middle Ages. The Christian reconquest of the country from the Moslems allowed the foundation of Genoese colonies, such as that at Seville (1248) in the recovered lands, and the opening of the sea route to the north, with Genoese vessels touching in Iberia on passage to and from the Channel, further and rapidly enhanced the importance of Spain and Portugal in the city's economy (cf. pp. 164–5). Hence by the early 1500s Genoese merchants and financiers were established throughout much of the peninsula, including even Biscay, and engaged in operations ranging from financial dealings in Seville and Andalusia to trade with the Atlantic islands, and from the export of silk, wool and oil from Spain, to the acquisition in Andalusian ports of the products of northern Europe and the Iberian colonial empires (cf. pp. 172 and 180ff.). And this already close relationship was finally sealed by political accident. In the early 1500s Genoese financiers, citizens of a client state of Spain, were conveniently situated to handle the pay of the forces the Habsburgs maintained in the Mediterranean, as their ambitions and possessions in the south were threatened by French and Ottoman hostility (see pp. 134, 364). Even more important, in the second half of the century, at the very time – and indeed for this very reason – that Philip II of Spain was attempting to suppress the revolt in his Netherlands patrimony, the sea route from Iberia to the north was cut by Protestant privateers. Faced with this difficulty the Spaniards found after some experiment that if their troops in the Netherlands were to be paid – which was admittedly not often the case – the safest way was to ship bullion from (as a rule) Barcelona to Genoa and then carry it by the long and difficult overland route to the north.[16] This traffic commenced about 1570 and continued for as long as Spain held any part of the Low Countries, but it was at its most vigorous in the late sixteenth and early seventeenth centuries when precious metals were shipped from Spain in convoys of up to twenty galleys, many of them Genoese.

But this was only one manifestation of the city's financial strength and importance. Long experienced in lending to royalty, Genoese magnates commenced to lend to the Spanish crown. They began in Naples where by the beginning of the sixteenth century they controlled the fiscal system as security for advances. Then in the mid-1500s they were operating in Spain itself, replacing the great south-German bankers, and with the size of their loans increasing rapidly in the late sixteenth century as Habsburg commitments and needs grew, and as merchant capital sought new outlets when seaborne commerce was disrupted by the Spanish-Protestant wars (cf. pp. 363–4). In 1573 there were thought to be representatives of one hundred major Genoese banking houses at the Spanish court, where by the end of the century the Spinola and Centurione were advancing the government massive amounts. These loans, on which the interest was already 13 per cent in the mid-1500s, were induced by grants of monopolies of one sort or another, or secured on such imperial resources as the bullion of the Americas. Hence to cynics it appeared that the empire had been founded less for the glory of God and Spain than for the benefit of Genoa, and to wags that wealth was born in the Indies, died in Spain and was buried in Genoa. But far from being interred the profits from these transactions were, to the further distress of patriots, invested in trade, lands and rents either in Iberia itself or in Italy. Furthermore Genoese financiers obtrusively advanced the money that enabled some Spanish subjects to pay their taxes, Genoese merchants blatantly monopolized whole Iberian trades and the Genoese in Andalusia were prominent in the establishment and exploitation of Spain's American empire.

Already in the fifteenth century the city's ancient interest in the Atlantic, re-invigorated by news of gold in West Africa, had revived (see pp. 163, 170). From the ports of south-western Spain Genoese merchants traded with Portugal's possessions in Guinea in the 1400s and 1500s, notwithstanding the supposed monopoly of the Portuguese, or their seizure of a joint Castilian-Genoese interloping expedition in 1453. Then in the Iberian Atlantic islands – some indeed first discovered by the republic's seaman – the Genoese found other profitable and less hazardous opportunities. These were colonies of a size to which they were long accustomed in the eastern Mediterranean, and ideal for the production of sugar in which they were expert (cf. pp. 184ff. and 188). Thus they assisted the establishment in the Portuguese and Spanish islands of those slave-worked sugar plantations soon to characterize the European settlement of much of the New World (see pp. 245, 248). They backed the conquest of Las Palmas (1492) and Tenerife, and before long were exploiting land in the Canaries granted in exchange for their services, importing slaves, raising cattle and shipping sugar to Seville.

From such dealings to more ambitious ventures seems, given the nature of earlier Genoese history, a natural enough step. Yet in the great Iberian oceanic voyages of the fifteenth and sixteenth centuries the city took a relatively modest role. Christopher Columbus apart, Genoese himself and a onetime employee of the Centurione, direct Genoese participation amounted to little more than a Fieschi commanding the smallest vessel in the fourth Columbus expedition (see p. 305). Like any other businessmen they were unmoved by the expensive ideals of visionaries, and only interested, as they explained to the emperor Charles V on one occasion, in investing in trade, not conquest. They might therefore finance voyages of exploration, even those with the most improbable objectives, provided there was some chance of profit. Thus the Genoese in Spain – the Rivarola, Doria, Catanei, Spinola, Pineli and Centurione – put up money for all the Columbus voyages, yet other than these exceptional dealings with a persistent compatriot they were rarely, if ever, the major investors in such ventures, sharing with the equally financially conscious and realistic Dutch, in later years, a scepticism as to their value (see p. 402). Nor – two fiascos apart – were any of the great oceanic voyages after those of Columbus of direct Genoese inspiration. To their regret the Seville community backed the disastrous attempt of the hen-pecked and vacillating Cabot to open a short route to the spices of the Moluccas (1526), and they backed the equally disastrous attempt of Orellana to find in South America the land of El Dorado (1545) (see pp. 317–18).

But once the riches of the Americas were known and a Spanish oceanic commerce established it was a different story, and by the mid-1500s the Genoese in Seville – the focal point of the new Spanish Atlantic economy – were lending money to would-be settlers in the Americas, to merchants hoping to trade there, to shipowners fitting out vessels, and even occasionally to empire-builders such as Hernando de Soto (see p. 318). Whatever the strictures of church and state, rates of interest were anything from 50–90 per cent, and the market in sea loans – where the lender carried the risk of the enterprise – was dominated by the Genoese, with seven bankers alone providing more than 50 per cent of the capital advanced on goods in one six-month period of 1507–8. Besides this the Sevillan Genoese themselves traded with the Americas, supplying in the early years such necessities as the wine, cloth and domestic animals which in the heroic days *conquistadores* had neither the time nor inclination to seek, and then with the emergence of a prosperous colonial society, the European luxuries it demanded (cf. p.

327). Such was the scale of this commerce that as early as 1504 the governor of Santo Domingo was complaining that most of the trade of Hispaniola was in Genoese or other alien hands. And when at the end of the sixteenth century opportunities in insurance and money-lending in Seville contracted with the growing wealth and sophistication of the native business community, the Genoese there took an increasing interest in shipowning, and by *c*. 1600 controlled a dozen vessels regularly working to Spanish America (see p. 176). They were besides early engaged in providing African slaves for the Indies, in importing sugar from the islands – to which it had been introduced from the Canaries by Columbus in 1493 – and indeed in producing it themselves in the west (see pp. 175–6). Already in the early 1500s three of the most successful mills in Hispaniola were Genoese-owned, one belonging to a Castello who in so encouraging an environment soon had a hand in everything from stock-raising to speculation in land. And by the end of the century men of such parts, merchants as a rule, had in the style of the Genoese past penetrated to every corner of the empire from the Caribbean to Chile and Peru – to which significantly enough a Vivaldi proposed (1536) to sail from Mexico *via* the Straits of Magellan.

In Portugal and the Portuguese empire the picture was much the same. Here, too, the association was of long-standing, reaching back to at least 1287 when 'don Vivaldo, genovês' – perhaps he of the abortive Far Eastern voyage – was present in Lisbon (see pp. 163–4). And here, too, the association intensified as Genoa's position in the eastern Mediterranean deteriorated, and as the full potential of Iberia became apparent. In Portugal as in Spain there was access to the possibilities of West Africa; there was an ambitious crown and aristocracy, neither particularly skilled in the arts of raising money and there was land and a climate suitable for the growing of sugar together with a market for its consumption. By the beginning of the fifteenth century the Genoese were producing sugar in the Algarve[17] and before long familiar names appear – often, as in Spain, those of Genoese families living or naturalized in the country – their penetration of the Portuguese economy charted by complaints from the Cortes[18] in the later 1400s as to their undesirable ubiquity. Between 1456 and 1484 the Lomellini and their associates monopolized the export of cork, just as in the early 1500s the coral used in Portugal's Asian commerce had to be bought from another member of the same family who farmed the Spanish North African fishery at Tabarca (cf. p. 270). The Genoese similarly controlled (1490) the export of Portuguese woad and – into the seventeenth century – alum, besides shipping grain to the Portuguese forts in Morocco and engaging in Portugal's trade with northern Europe.

Furthermore, Genoese capital, skills and experience were of decisive importance in the earliest and comparatively modest stages of Portugal's overseas expansion (see p. 245). Early in the fourteenth century king Dinis took into his service Manuel Pessagno, one of the many Genoese naval *condottieri* then in foreign pay, and a member of a family widely influential in European high finance and politics. As admiral, and with twenty compatriots 'expert in things of the sea', he was, amongst his other duties, to advise the crown in maritime matters. That with his arrival Portuguese penetration of the Atlantic commenced is probably no mere coincidence, and it was like as not in his entourage that there came to Portugal the Malocello who discovered and conquered Lanzarote (see p. 164). After various upsets – including expulsion by a native revolt – the *conquistador* was granted land in the Canaries (1370) which apparently he eventually managed to subjugate and settle. Indeed it may well be that the rapid and remarkable growth of knowledge of the whole area of the Canaries, Madeira and the Azores in these years was due to Italian, and particularly Genoese, activity inspired or directed by the then admiral of Portugal (1367–83), Lanzarotto Pessagno. Nor did this Genoese endeavour lapse with the disappearance of this influential dynasty, since some of the Cape Verde Islands were discovered (1460) and colonized by a compatriot, Antonio da Noli.

But, as in Spain, it was in the exploitation of these colonial possessions, established in the course of the fifteenth and sixteenth centuries, that the talents of the Genoese found their fullest expression. It was they – already present in the islands in the early 1400s – who introduced sugar and cotton into the Azores and Greek vines to Madeira, soon a major producer of malmsey wine (cf. pp. 105–6). And if the Madeiran sugar industry may not have been the creation of citizens of the republic it was nevertheless they who before long owned the largest mills in the island, and monopolized the export of their produce. Such was their grip on the trade, and such the depressed level of the prices they paid to the growers of cane, that in 1469 there were thoughts of a royal monopoly to improve the situation. What, however, emerged (1470) was a joint Portuguese-Genoese marketing organization with one of the Lomellini most in evidence in its affairs. And as the trade flourished, with shipments made after 1472 direct to the Low Countries, and as markets widened – to include, for instance, the eastern Mediterranean (see p. 162) – other powerful families arrived to enjoy the benefits. By the beginning of the sixteenth century the Doria, Spinola, Lomellini and di Negri were all established in the island, one of the Catanei was the contractor for the sale of royal sugar (1500) and a Genoese consortium was set up (1503) to handle the north-Italian market.

Nor did this exhaust Genoese energies and resources. From the fifteenth century they were trading in Portuguese Africa, where in the mid-1400s Antoniotto Uso di Mare – who had learned his business with the Bank of St George, a colonizer at Caffa – was taking slaves in Gambia (cf. pp. 191 and 253). By 1500 there were Genoese merchants farming assorted colonial revenues and monopolies from the crown, whilst others were exporting the sugar of São Tomé to Europe (see p. 246), ignoring often enough the royal requirement that such cargoes were to be carried only to Lisbon. They appeared, too, in Brazil, colonized by the Portuguese in the later sixteenth century, and where surveys of the captaincy of Bahía show sugar mills belonging to the Adorno (1587) and Doria (1662). Nor were these recent acquisitions for it was an Adorno who in the 1570s was to supply the English with sugar (cf. p. 465). Earlier still, in the mid-sixteenth century, three Genoese (including an Adorno and a Doria) occur in a heresy trial, and, whatever their spiritual misdemeanours, they were clearly prosperous, the Adorno house having its own chapel.[19] But in Portugal's expansion to the east, involving some of the longest and most arduous maritime voyages as yet undertaken, the role of the Genoese was, as in the oceanic ventures of the Spaniards, modest. There were certainly many Genoese seamen and gunners in Portuguese service in Asia, but of the backers of expeditions only a Salvago who invested in that of Cabral (1500), and who belonged to a family whose interests in Portugal ranged from sugar to royal finance, was of any significance (cf. pp. 233ff.). Once, however, an Asian commerce was established the di Negri characteristically appear amongst that handful of plutocrats who in the early sixteenth century were engaged in the lucrative if hazardous business of selling Portuguese spices in northern Europe. In this trade the focal point was Antwerp, from where, by the mid-1500s, this Genoese – or perhaps Jewish[20] – family, reputedly amongst Antwerp's richest, conducted, together with other compatriots, extensive commercial and financial operations. Meanwhile although elsewhere in the north – as at Bruges where in the fifteenth century the Genoese colony built themselves a magnificent hall – native xenophobia and organized states ensured that the privileges enjoyed by citizens of the republic were, like those of the Hanse, never too generous, their power was still impressive. There were complaints from England in the mid-1400s that Genoese merchants dominated the commerce of Southampton, and that Genoese ships were even competing in the port's trade with the Low Countries. In London, where the Genoese had been favoured by the crown in the fourteenth century – with the astute and influential Antonio Pessagno imprudently rewarded by Edward II – the Grimaldi were associates of Henry VII's notorious official Edmund Dudley, and the Vivaldi and Lomellini active in finance under Henry VIII. And though the direct involvement of their parent city in maritime enterprise might have been flagging, it found yet another outlet in marine insurance, and was in the 1560s and 1570s covering sailings from Italian ports to northern and western Europe, and from Iberia to the Atlantic islands and the Americas. Genoese merchants may no longer have been the acknowledged experts on Far Eastern commerce, or Genoese admirals Europe's major naval *condottieri*, but that the republic's power, now more subtly exercised, survived there could be little doubt.

III   *A microcosm of empire*

To protect and further their interests the Genoese had for centuries engaged in activities which may legitimately be described as imperial. Not surprisingly, however, in a city always notoriously unstable, and which evolved from a pirate community to a centre of international banking, such policies – more varied and ingenious though they may have been than those of the Hanse – had nothing of the systematic comprehensiveness of Venetian or Spanish imperial rule. Genoese merchants, like those of Venice and the Hanse, acquired assorted privileges in regions through which their trade passed (cf.

pp. 67–8, 91, 116). These were usually, though by no means exclusively, fiscal and might be so extensive as to erode the sovereignty of the state in whose territory they were exercised. Then in some areas – such as Byzantium, where, as a Greek writer lamented in the mid-fourteenth century the republic controlled all the empire's wealth and most of its revenues – Genoa enjoyed like the Hanse an economic supremacy so overwhelming as to reduce them to the level of the republic's satellites. And characteristically Genoese were the conquests and acquisitions of individual Genoese citizens, many of which came ultimately into the republic's hands, whilst in the earliest centuries of Genoese expansion there had been obtained in North Africa and the Levant a series of bases similar to those of the Venetians and other Italian maritime cities overseas, or to the concessionary ports of the western powers in Asia later. From these commercial monopoly could be enforced and protected, the flow of Genoa's trade ensured and that of rivals if not destroyed at least restrained.

The extent of the lands controlled by the republic was admittedly never impressive. In Liguria, hemmed in by equally formidable mountains and opponents, it was never able to acquire, as did Venice, a substantial and reasonably cohesive territorial basis. Abroad it was primarily concerned with commercial advantage generally to be found in countries of a size or strength that rendered conquest impracticable. Even so, Genoese aristocrats founded, like those of Venice, occasional principalities, and the republic itself eventually turned to the annexation of territory and the manipulation of regimes on the grounds of economic necessity, just as it engaged in their exploitation for its own benefit. Nevertheless of all maritime empires that of Genoa was, in the purely territorial sense, the smallest and the least united. And by the late Middle Ages what few possessions Genoa still tenuously held in the Mediterranean were hardly to be saved from the Spaniards in the west, or the Ottomans and Venetians in the east by a faction-ridden city lacking public resources in money and manpower – those of private individuals were another matter – and in any case more interested in other less arduous imperial opportunities (cf. pp. 167ff., 177ff.).

Yet initially the republic appeared to be well on the way to becoming a considerable and formidable colonial power. For their services in the crusades the Genoese – more often groups of merchants rather than representatives of the republic itself – were handsomely rewarded, and in the course of the eleventh and twelfth centuries established themselves in Antioch, Jerusalem, Tyre, Acre, Latakia, Tripoli, Jaffa (Tel Aviv) and indeed in all the principal places of the Holy Land, exempt from commercial dues and with the right of self-government (cf. pp. 157–8). In the towns they had their own particular sectors, soon embellished with Genoese buildings, public and private; in the seaports they collected customs on non-Genoese trade; and from their rural holdings they took the cotton and sugar provided by native labour. Nor were these the only manifestations of the imperial urge. With characteristic insensitivity the Genoese set up in the Holy Sepulchre a notice recording their achievements and privileges, and aroused further hostility by persistent attempts to subject to their authority all the inhabitants – irrespective of race or religion – of their lands.

Meanwhile, to ensure maritime access to Africa and the Levant, footholds were obtained in Sicily, Corsica and Crete, and before the Holy Land and its Genoese bases were finally lost to Islam in the thirteenth century the republic had created for itself a new and greater empire in Byzantium. Here, like other Italian cities, Genoa already possessed by the mid-1100s some concessions in Constantinople to which there were added in the early thirteenth century further privileges in Greece and Cyprus. Then with the republic's promised aid in the overthrow of Latin rule in Constantinople (1261) came lavish grants from the Greeks. The Genoese were to trade freely throughout Byzantium whilst their opponents (the Pisans excepted) were to be excluded from the Black Sea (cf. pp. 96, 160). In addition Genoa was to have Smyrna, together with self-governing enclaves in various Greek territories including the still unliberated Crete and Constantinople. Thus for no more than the promise of naval assistance the republic had the prospect of controlling key points on a galaxy of major commercial routes. In the Aegean and its approaches Venice ensured that Genoa accomplished little, but in the Black Sea it was a different story (cf. pp. 161ff.). Here, until the Ottoman conquests, Pera, across the Golden Horn from Constantinople, and occupied from 1265, was the main Genoese centre. But initially it was no treaty port. Many citizens of the republic continued to live elsewhere in the Greek capital just as Greeks continued to live in Pera. Nor, despite a considerable artisan and cosmopolitan population, was it merely a centre of relentless commercial endeavour. Settled in such evocative surroundings, amongst the vestiges of powerful civilizations, and without the solace of female compatriots, the Genoese, like other Europeans in similar circumstances, succumbed to their new environment (cf. pp. 290, 416). Married to Greek, Slav, Tartar or Caucasian women they lived a life more oriental than occidental, dwelling in houses surrounded by gardens and vineyards and furnished with baths and carpets, and wearing baggy eastern trousers (*shalvars*). But a combination of Greek decrepitude and Genoese strength eventually turned a one-time suburb into a substantial, fortified and self-governing area in which all the republic's citizens in Constantinople were to live, and over which the Greek state eventually (1303) surrendered its sovereignty. Thus ultimately the Genoese governors of Pera, rulers of an independent stronghold and backed by Genoese seapower, could deal with the emperors of Byzantium as with equals, if not indeed inferiors.

The other major centre of the republic's power was the Crimea where there quickly developed what was to become the walled city of Caffa. Here, too, on a concession probably obtained from the Tartars there was soon an organized government (*c.* 1280), and before long a large and opulent community – allegedly 100,000 strong by the early 1400s – sufficiently affluent to send out its own war fleets. Within the city, whose port handled 200 ships at a time in its heyday according to an Arab visitor, there was a remarkable concentration of Genoese wealth and talent, with most of the republic's great commercial families represented by the late 1200s. Here, too, life was orientalized – eased and enriched by such ungodly luxuries as baths and fountains – and cosmopolitan in a town inhabited, amongst others, by Italians, Tartars, Hungarians,

Armenians, Greeks, Bulgarians and Romanians. And here, too, there flourished the familiar pragmatic tolerance of a mercantile community. Not only had Caffa churches of every Christian persuasion, but mosques and synagogues as well. Genoese citizens married, moreover, oriental women and lived amongst Moslems – with whom the Dorias had apparently especially close relations reflected in the presence at the battle of Meloria (1284) of three of the clan named respectively Turco, Soldan and Hassan. So, also, like Pera the city became virtually independent, establishing direct diplomatic relations with the rulers of Poland, Moscow and Wallachia in the fifteenth century, and enforcing its own policies in the neighbouring Black Sea littoral.

Besides these vital entrepôts, the republic also held in the Crimea Soldaia (fortified in 1414), Balaclava (seized in 1357) and the coastal lands (Gotia) linking it to Caffa, in which Genoa appointed some officials of its own. Genoese trade in the Sea of Azov was handled by stations at Tana (at the mouth of the Don) and Kerch, whilst on the Black Sea's Kuban and Caucasian coasts there were further Genoese posts at Anapa, Anakira and Lentina and, after the loss of Caffa, a settlement inland at Kutaisi further south. By the late Middle Ages the Genoese also held Akkerman, at the outlet of the great Dnestr route, Ilice at the mouth of Dnepr, a fortress near Varna, and Kilia Vechia at the Danube mouth as well as settlement at Suceava in Moldavia (cf. pp. 169–70). On the southeastern littoral of the sea, giving access to the riches of the Far East and Persia alike, they were established in Greek Trebizond by the 1290s, where soon after they had their own privileged and fortified enclave. Beyond this there were Genoese footholds of indeterminate status in Turkish territory at Samsun, Sinop and Samastro in the fifteenth century, whilst earlier (1341) the republic had recognized the right of its citizens in Tabriz (Persia) to govern themslves.[21]

Of the rest of the eastern empire the longest lived member and most determined survivor was the island of Chios commanding – as the lengthy struggles of Genoa and Venice for its control testified – the Black Sea approaches. Though the republic was granted concessions there by the Greeks in 1261 Chios was not occupied until seized – and this on his own initiative – by the redoubtable Benedetto Zaccaria in 1304. Twenty-five years later it was retaken by a momentarily resurgent Byzantium, and then once again by the Genoese in 1346 in whose hands it remained until lost in 1566 to the Ottomans (cf. pp. 99, 119, 192). Though increasingly under pressure as the Turks overran the Middle East, obliged to meet their sudden and arbitrary demands – for the provision of skilled shipbuilders for instance – and tactfully disowned by the republic to avoid difficulties, it was of considerable economic importance for a time in the late Middle Ages. It became a useful entrepôt, was the centre of Genoa's eastern slave trade, and was the base from which alum was shipped to the west, as well as being the producer of the much sought after mastic with which oriental ladies whitened their teeth and sweetened their breath (cf. p. 173).

Thus Chios developed, even if in miniscule, as a colony of the sort increasingly common in the European dominated wider world of later centuries. It handled and employed slaves. Trade in its most valuable products was the monopoly of an alien ruling power. Its agriculture was so concentrated on the production of silk, wine and mastic for the commercial benefit of the parent community that grain had to be imported to feed the populace and – anticipating subsequent Dutch practice in the Spice Islands – the Genoese burned any surplus mastic to keep up prices (see p. 409). Furthermore the island was deliberately colonized, with fiscal privileges offered (1428) to those Genoese and Ligurians who would settle there, take a wife – foreshadowing this time later Iberian policies – and a mastic farm. So large tracts of Chios came into the hands of Genoese rentiers whilst its resources, like those of Spanish America in the sixteenth and seventeenth centuries, supported a sizable body not only of landowners and merchants from the parent state, but of artisans, lawyers and officials (see pp. 330ff.). And no more than elsewhere was colonial rule established for the benefit of the natives. There might be some measure of that inevitable fusion of races present in all empires as Greeks married Latins, or Latins entered into commercial partnerships with Greeks, but free or slave Greeks were supposedly excluded from office, and an alien and Catholic minority lorded it over an Orthodox populace. And, like many other colonies, the island was regarded by the metropolitan ruling class as a haven for what were described as their 'delinquent, disobedient and insolvent sons', whose modest talents were often as not employed in extorting whatever they might need from the indigenous population. Not surprisingly in 1548–9 the Chians offered themselves and their homeland to the duke of Tuscany.

Nor were the Genoese any more successful elsewhere in the east, and of their imperial shortcomings there is no more eloquent testimony than Genoa's failure in the Catholic kingdom of Cyprus as compared with Venice's success in Byzantine Crete (cf. pp. 105, 117). An initial Genoese interest in the island's sugar, cotton and wine was sharpened by the prospect of using Cyprus as an entrepôt in the trade with the Mamelukes (see pp. 99, 103). Hence a base was established in Famagusta, and by the mid-fourteenth century a virtually independent and privileged Genoese community was flourishing under its own officials. Such ostentatious supremacy provoked native and Venetian reaction, leading in turn to a further and forcible extension of Genoese influence. A private company (founded in 1373 and renewed in 1403) sent out an army of 14,000 men and a fleet of 42 vessels. After the sack of some of the island's principal towns, the seizure of Famagusta and the sequestration of its revenues, a Genoese commercial monopoly, and what indeed was tantamount to a Genoese protectorate, were imposed in Cyprus. Officials from the republic lived in regal splendour in buildings embellished with the works of Italian artists, their rule sustained, as a local chronicler lamented, by 'oppressive tyranny and rapacious ferocity'. But a commercial company's zest for such expensive proceedings faded when the island's economic importance dwindled through loss of contact with Persia, and as Venice monopolized most of the western spice trade through the Mameluke empire (cf. p. 104). After a succession of failures the Genoese entrepreneurs, lacking the determination of the

Venetian state, gave up the struggle and handed over their surviving Cypriot possessions to the Bank of St George (1447). But not even this powerful organization could do much better, and by 1489 the island was Venetian (cf. p. 119). True, Genoa had faced a delicate and difficult situation in dealing with a Catholic sovereign and his feudal aristocracy, from whom, nevertheless, some of her citizens did remarkably well, securing lands and revenues in exchange for loans. And a number did equally well as planters and investors, specializing in grain, indigo, sugar and the island's famous camelot textiles. But these were private ventures, involving no obligation to, or support from, the city whose Levantine interests flagged in the later Middle Ages. Hence the island, where even in the period of so-called Genoese rule the Venetians had continued to trade, was never of much consequence in terms of direct economic relations with the republic. And in any case Genoa – bemoaning its misfortunes in singularly unimperial style in 1462 – lacked the political stability and financial resources to emulate Venetian behaviour in Crete.

Equally unimpressive were the republic's colonial proceedings in the western Mediterranean, where for centuries it had vainly struggled to secure the vital island of Corsica – planted, indeed, like Sardinia, with Genoese strongholds and settlers – against first Moorish and then Spanish power (see pp. 157, 178). The undertaking was formidable enough – a wild and fierce terrain inhabited by equally wild and fierce people – and made worse by Genoa's lack of money, purpose and method. As in Cyprus its possessions, now reduced to a few coastal fortresses, ended in the hands of a private company (1378) and ultimately in those of the Bank of St George (1453). This contended to the best of its ability with the Spaniards and with a revolt of what were fastidiously described as the 'ferocious and savage natives' before selling its claims to the duke of Milan (1464), only to be obliged to re-attempt the conquest of the island in 1482. But the sum outcome of intermittent imperial endeavour and ill-advised financial demands on a poverty-stricken and overpopulated land was to fill the ports of the Mediterranean – Algiers in particular – with Corsican exiles united in their hatred of Genoa. Moreover, once the republic became in the early 1500s so closely and clearly identified with Spain the disaffected island was a convenient lever for those – the French especially – eager to embarrass the city and its patrons (see pp. 178, 199). For a time the Genoese coped successfully with an almost impossible situation. But the worst was to come with the bloodthirsty revolt of Sampiero Corso and the equally bloodthirsty attempts to suppress it (1564). With French aid Corso acquired such a hold on the island that the king of Spain considered it yet another potential victim or ally of the Ottomans. Nor were things improved by the assassination of Corso in 1567. Nevertheless the Spaniards, prudently assessing the hazards and expense of campaigning in such a country, did nothing to help Genoa, just as with equal prudence they rejected the city's bequest of the island, so leaving the struggle to drag hopelessly on.

Significantly more successful was the republic's exploitation of the coral fisheries of the North African coast. Having obtained (1451) a monopoly of that near Bône

(Annaba), a joint-stock company involving some of Genoa's most powerful families was set up to work it. And here, as in the later north European fisheries off Newfoundland, the flag followed trade. Vessels taking coral needed to put in for repairs or to refresh their crews, and before long the Genoese had a base in Africa of the pattern already well-known in the east, with dwellings, warehouses and a harbour enclosed within defensive walls.

The government of these possessions, ranging from simple commercial factories (*fondaci*) in Africa to independent communities in the Levant, had little of the system and order of Venetian colonial administration (cf. pp. 120ff.). In all Genoa's major territories or concessions overseas her citizens were under the exclusive jurisdiction of officers whose appointment and functions the republic had – initially at least – some pretensions to control, and whom she made some attempt to incorporate within a comprehensive imperial organization. By the end of the twelfth century there were Genoese officials in Latin Syria supposedly in overall charge of the city's possessions in the Levant. Later the governor (*podesta*) of Pera both watched over Genoese interests in Constantinople and exercised a general authority over the rest of the republic's colonies – Caffa excepted – in Asia Minor and on the Black Sea. Like a Spanish viceroy or the Venetian duke of Crete, he was a man of considerable consequence, recruited from amongst Genoa's richest and most powerful families, and entrusted with office for only the briefest period – usually no more than a year (cf. pp. 120 and 346). He took high precedence in the Greek imperial court, headed Pera's judiciary, and regulated the entire commercial, social and religious life of the community. With the passage of time his authority became less paramount, not so much because the republic had, like Venice or Spain, a conscious policy of counterbalancing the power of such magnates, but through the growing wealth and influence of his colonial compatriots. Hence from the thirteenth century he was aided or restrained by two councils (one of 24 members, the other of 6) and a general assembly which met from time to time. Obscure though the details may be, it is clear enough that Genoese Pera was a self-governing entity, enjoying its own laws and customs which by the early 1300s were sufficiently numerous and diverse to be collected, codified and submitted – though simply as a formality – for imperial Greek approval. These laws were administered by the court of Pera – which had its own officials and records – and the entire governmental and commercial organization was housed in a building (the *loggia*) whose bold, opulent and distinctive architecture so aptly characterized, as in Cyprus and Chios, imperial Genoa.

The situation was roughly the same in Caffa where, however, even if the city had formal supremacy over the republic's other possessions in the Crimea and on the Sea of Azov in the fifteenth century, the Tartar khan nevertheless retained a tenuous sovereignty. Here, from 1316, the governor was a consul ruling with the aid of councils of 24 and 6, and heading an administration of some elaboration. He, too, was elected annually in Genoa, was debarred in Venetian style from engaging in commerce whilst in office, and likewise obliged to give account of his proceedings on retirement. And as in the Venetian empire the growing difficulties of the late Middle Ages brought, in the hope of placating them, concessions to the indigenous peoples who were allowed if not office at least representation in the colony's government.

Yet neither in imperial nor in any other matters was Genoa merely the triumphant exponent of *laissez-faire*. Within its own bounds, and from an early date, it both legislated on the conduct of business and the quality of goods, and ensured that its citizens were fed in times of hardship. Like its fellow maritime republics it intervened in the operation of seaborne commerce, established monopolies – most notably that of salt in the Tyrrhenian – attempted, by boycott, to protect its interests against those endangering them, and endeavoured like every other seapower to monopolize whatever long-distance trades it could.

Such duties and aspirations came to be the responsibility of a series of corporate bodies: the *Officium Maris* (see p. 198); the *Officium Mercantie*, which dealt with matters relating to trade; and the *Officium Gazarie* (i.e. of the Khazars or Crimea), which from 1313 to 1441 handled the city's overseas possessions. Yet despite this superficially elaborate, logical and impressive organization relations between Genoa and its colonies were never particularly close. And with the passage of time, though the republic might occasionally intervene with vigour in a particular crisis, the association grew even feebler as Genoa's own many misfortunes, chronic poverty, and consequently increasingly corrupt and debilitated administration, deprived it of the will, let alone the authority, to act imperially. Thus nominally Genoese colonies behaved with the same independence as the individual *kontors* and members of the German Hanse which equally came to lack the will and means to implement any overall control (cf. pp. 54, 62). And like the Hanse Genoa produced no apologist for its imperial behaviour and achievements, most of which were, like those of the Norse, the outcome of individual initiatives, or, like those of the Dutch and English, of company enterprise (cf. pp. 2ff., 402ff., 497). Hence of all maritime empires that of Genoa was, with the possible exception of the Norse, the most loosely knit, and with the possible exception of the Dutch, the most blatantly devoted to the pursuit of profit. True, the Genoese backed some modest and unsuccessful missionary endeavour among the Moslems of Ceuta in the early thirteenth century. But for the most part their only concern, as was most notoriously shown in the mishandling of Cyprus, was with commercial and financial reward and advantage. And this indeed they carried to imprudent lengths. Not only did they provide the Mamelukes with much of their manpower, but in the fifteenth century Genoese colonials repeatedly supplied the advancing Ottomans with ships, weapons and food, and even transported their troops across the Dardanelles – blockaded by the Venetians – in the campaign that culminated in the Turkish victory over a Christian army at Varna (1444) (see pp. 169–70, 174).

The logic of good business similarly meant that at some time or other the republic leased most of its overseas possessions to groups of private entrepreneurs. Such farming out of assets or liabilities, actual and potential, was a universal expedient in a world in which communications were poor, administrative resources negligible and a modest sum of ready cash preferable to distant prospects of larger amounts. It was early Portuguese practice to allow private persons to discover and exploit at their own expense new territories abroad, just as the Dutch East India Company later came to enjoy virtually sovereign authority (cf. pp. 248, 403). The Genoese associations, however, did not as a rule pioneer colonial ventures nor, with smaller resources and without consistent state backing, could they undertake policies as ambitious as those of the Dutch company in Asia. Instead they relieved the city not so much of going concerns as of embarrassing or expensive liabilities, so that in the fourteenth century Chios, Cyprus and Corsica all passed into the hands of Genoese joint-stock companies (*mahones*) (cf. pp. 187–8 and 204). That of Chios (founded in 1346 and reorganized in 1362) was a consortium of those who, in return for supplying the republic with a fleet for which it was unable to pay, were allowed to undertake the island's reconquest. For an annual rent – soon overlooked – the company was given a more or less free hand, first for a limited term and then, with Genoa's inability to clear its debts, indefinitely. The city did indeed reserve its sovereignty over the island and participate in both the appointment of its governor and the scrutiny of his behaviour. Nevertheless it was the *mahona*'s agents who ruled, defended, taxed and exploited Chios. Their policies were often – economically at least – shrewd. Settlers were brought in, a highly specialized commercial agriculture was developed and neighbouring lands and islets – such as Focea with its alum – subordinated to the island. But as shares were accumulated in the hands of a single family the company became a corrupt, arbitrary and oppressive monopolist. Major offices were openly bought and sold, taxes were imposed at the governor's whim and the predictable reaction to attempts to restrain such practices was open rebellion.

Elsewhere when the situation became desperate the republic sold its colonial rights and possessions to the Bank of St George which, integrated as it was in the city's government and with ships and men of its own, was considerably more than a financial institution. It was the Bank which took Cyprus on a twenty-nine-year lease (1447), just as it accepted the surviving Black Sea colonies after the fall of Constantinople, exercising from Caffa an authority complete and sovereign. It established forms of government reminiscent of those employed by Venice, forbidding its chief servants – a captain in Cyprus and a consul in Caffa – to engage in trade, having their behaviour investigated in Cyprus and Corsica by commissions on which the local populace was represented and in the Black Sea attempting to curb a destructive particularism by insisting that consuls governing individual communities be appointed in Genoa and not locally. Its rule was also in general as thorough and efficient as circumstances allowed, with the nature and possibilities of Corsica's resources investigated and Caffa supplied (1464) with artisans. But neither in east or west, as the Bank's imperial misfortunes demonstrated, was such prudence the answer to armed strength.

Thus, notwithstanding its ambitious beginnings, the maritime empire of Genoa was territorially small and lacking, some brief interludes apart, any unity or cohesion. Both in its domination by merchants and in the intransigent individualism of its members it reflected all too faithfully the characteristics of its parent society. To its government the republic brought, the maximization of profit aside, little that might be described as a colonial policy, and like the equally commercially conscious Holland the city was impelled by no sense of duty or obligation to indigeneous populations (see pp. 414, 419). Yet with the same pragmatism as the Venetians the Genoese often left local society and institutions intact and even occasionally consulted colonial populations – or at least, in 1395, Chians 'from the most distinguished families' – whom they proposed to tax. And in the same way, whilst the slave trade in the eastern Mediterranean was pursued with ruthless vigour and the Chian Orthodox church subjected to their authority, the Genoese were nevertheless prepared to accept local styles of dress and domestic usage, and to intermarry with eastern peoples.[22]

But Genoa's imperial and colonial enterprise was not confined to what the city itself accomplished or to the enormous economic influence of its merchants and bankers, for like Viking chiefs its aristocrats acquired lands, powers and titles wherever they could. The Cavo became lords of Rhodes for a time in the thirteenth century; in the 1300s Francisco Gattilusio founded an Aegean dynasty soon related to the Greek imperial house; and in the fifteenth century compatriots momentarily established principalities on the shores of the Black Sea. Even more remarkable were the doings of a number of families who combined to a degree rarely equalled in other empires military, naval and business skills. Already in the heroic days of Genoa's expansion many of its interests in the Holy Land were monopolized by the Embriaci, who by the mid-twelfth century controlled not only their own holdings but also the republic's concessions in Latakia, Antioch and – in exchange for timely financial assistance – Acre. Such was the extent of their authority that they could grant fellow citizens freedom to trade within their jurisdiction, and such their independence that Genoa was reduced to seeking papal aid to persuade them to obey its injunctions (1186). Then in the following century there came the spectacular rise of the Zaccaria dynasty. It was largely the work of that Benedetto Zaccaria who was one of the Genoese commanders in the victory over the Pisan fleet at Meloria (1284), who as admiral of Castile crushed the Moroccans at sea and who organized and directed the galleys of France in northern waters. In the east, where he married the sister of the Greek emperor, his career was even more colourful, embracing everything from diplomacy to piracy. He conquered Tripoli, negotiated commercial treaties with Persia and Armenia, secured control of the mastic of Chios, and the alum of Focea and northern Asia Minor, and exported in his own vessels – amongst them the aptly if arrogantly named *Riches*. At Pera, where they had long been established, the family recruited labour for their mines and troops to defend their investments. They had their own factory at Caffa and some more extensive possessions on the Sea of Azov, where there appears on early maps, like those European names later scattered across the world by proconsuls of empire, the area of *Zacaria* to the south of

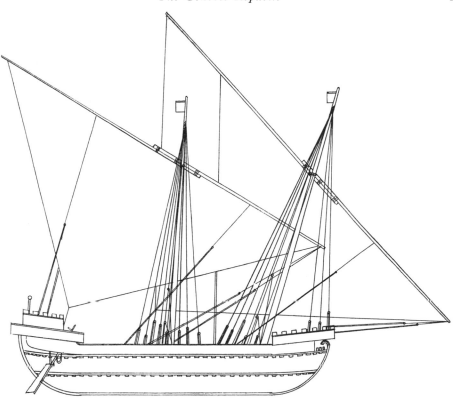

Fig. 8   Lateen-rigged Genoese *navis* of the mid-thirteenth century, employed for troop
or horse transport. This reconstruction is by J.E. Dotson.

the Gulf of Taganrog. And for a time the dynasty lived in regal splendour in Chios,
where with his own fleet and army Benedetto's grandson reigned as king and despot of
Asia Minor until his tactless alienation of Greek and Turk alike led to his overthrow
in 1329.

   Equally individual was the evolution of the Genoese shipping industry and the
organization of Genoese seapower. In the early centuries the city's luxury trade with
the Levant was, like that of Venice, handled by galleys, as was much of its more local
commerce – with south Spain and southern Italy for instance. And like the Venetians
the Genoese had long employed a variety of large and generously proportioned sailing
craft. Prominent amongst these by *c.* 1200 was the *bucius* or *navis* which might have
ports cut in its hull to allow the easy embarkation of horses, or which might mount
weapons capable of hurling 14kg-stones and other fearsome missiles.[23] Such vessels,
widely employed in military operations, in the Syrian and North African trades and in
the transport of crusaders and pilgrims, had in the twelfth century two, and by the

thirteenth century, with the increase in business, three decks. The lower (or lowest) was used for either horses or the less opulent passengers, whilst the bow and stern castles, in addition to their military functions, could house well-born travellers in appropriate style. By the early 1200s some of these ships were, like those of the Venetians, portly vessels of a considerable size – roughly 37m long, with a beam of 10m and capable of carrying 200 horses and 600 men or an equivalent number of pilgrims.[24]

Nor were these the only big ships owned in the republic, where in the early 1300s there appear *dromons*, able to work to England, and, as elsewhere, cogs.[25] But from the late fourteenth century all these were eclipsed by the carrack, the product of a fusion of Baltic and Mediterranean traditions, and already at this date a vessel of up to 1000t (cf. pp. 146–7). And before long it became even bigger as Genoa was driven, or turned to, the exploitation of the natural resources of the Black Sea and Asia Minor, and to providing northern Europe with some of the raw materials used in the manufacture of woollen cloths in exchange for wool and woollen textiles (see p. 176). The ships required to carry these bulk cargoes – ever the begetters of ungainly size – were soon too large to enter many harbours, whilst the distance between markets and sources of supply made it desirable and prudent that they should sail direct and accordingly lengthy runs between terminal ports. Thus by the early 1400s carracks on passage from Chios to Southampton normally avoided Genoa itself and instead coasted along the North African littoral – though some touched in southern Italy or Majorca – before crossing from Honein to Almeria or Malaga in south Spain. Then, after clearing the Straits they sailed directly from the Guadalquivir to the English Channel, keeping, as far as is known, well clear of the Iberian coast. Though more ambitious than that of the north-bound Venetian great galleys, the run was not, it is true, a feat of oceanic seamanship (see p. 124). It was not unbroken and the vessels were only intermittently out of sight of land, with the longest leg made in the Mediterranean, where even if the weather can be as formidable as in any other sea, navigation is relatively simple. Nevertheless the distance covered (a round trip of over 11,500km) was impressive, and the route was worked throughout the year, showing once again, as with the Norse Atlantic voyages or those of the English to Iceland, the ability of medieval ships to cope with long and arduous passages (cf. pp. 2ff., 460).

By the mid-fifteenth century carracks at times as big as 2000t were employed to take cloth south and to bring woad, alum – first that of Focea and then, after its loss, of Italy and Spain – and other such materials north. These were ships now ingeniously rigged with three masts setting two square sails on the foremast, another two on the larger mainmast and a lateen on the small mizzen. As in Venice this amalgam of northern and southern rigs – though where it was pioneered is uncertain – made vessels easier to control[26] and with its subdivision of the sail area into safer and more manageable units allowed smaller crews to be carried. With her generous capacity provided by a broad-bellied hull which tapered away to narrower upperworks, her great freeboard giving relative immunity from assault by boarding, and her ability to sail from England to

Fig. 9   Carrack, *c.* 1470, possibly Genoese, from a contemporary
Flemish print.

Genoa, stops included, in just under eight weeks, such a ship, it was generally agreed, was a paragon, 'the best in all the world' according to an enthusiastic Spaniard in 1435. Some years later (1470) her particular virtues were more precisely explained in simple terms by experts to a would-be pilgrim to the Holy Land, innocent of sophisticated criteria. Should he wish to travel in winter he was advised to sail in a Venetian galley which in the event of storms could quickly make for shelter. But should he go in the fair weather of the summer, then it could only be by Genoese carrack. She offered her passengers plenty of room – so lessening the chance of contracting diseases spread through overcrowding – and she carried an abundance of food and a powerful defensive armament.

Such indeed were the attractions of the carrack that by the last decade of the fifteenth century ships of this type accounted for about 90 per cent of Genoa's total tonnage. Specialization of this order, unusual if not unknown before the appearance of the liner, oil-tanker and bulk-carrier fleets of recent times, had important repercussions. There were many ports which large and comparatively unwieldy sailing vessels could not easily enter or leave, and so in England Genoese ships came to use Sandwich and Southampton instead of London with its lengthy and difficult approaches. Then because of their sheer capacity and the nature and balance of the trade between northern and southern Europe it was impossible to provide carracks outward bound from the English Channel with full ladings, and thus they took to stopping in south Spain and North Africa to complete their cargoes for the eastern Mediterranean. Moreover, with so much Genoese capital and manpower invested in ships of such a size, the republic's local seaborne commerce passed into the hands of foreign owners – Portuguese and Spanish for the most part – using much smaller craft. Thus by the end of the Middle Ages the highly specialized Genoese shipping industry was dangerously dependent on a limited range of commodities carried over an even more restricted range of routes, so that when the great northern trade failed the reign of the Genoese carrack – unlike the Venetian – ended abruptly (cf. pp. 147–8). It was, however, an abdication hastened by those same forces that were shortly to cripple Venice – growing piracy; the competition of smaller, more adaptable and more powerfully armed northern craft; the shortage of seamen and shipbuilding materials (see pp. 133, 148). So in 1518, after some vain attempts to revive enthusiasm for big ships by offering subsidies for their construction, the city came to the reluctant conclusion that 'smaller vessels are more necessary and more suited to our needs'. But that owners had already reached this conclusion is clear enough. In the late 1400s small craft accounted for no more than 10 per cent of Genoa's tonnage; by the mid-1500s, however, their share had risen to nearly 70 per cent. And whereas in 1460 the republic had thirty carracks a century later it had only two and the biggest a mere 800t.

Such specialization in cargoes and ships had also entailed in Genoa, as was not the case with the more diversified Venetian economy, the eclipse of the galley as a merchantman. It was, however, an eclipse neither permanent nor total. In the early sixteenth century galleys worked in the Neapolitan silk trade – a trade that is for which they were particularly suited, involving the rapid carriage of a valuable commodity over a short distance – just as they were employed to transport troops, officials and ambassadors in similarly brief and urgent voyages. And in the late 1500s they were used to move bullion from south Spain to Genoa for transmission overland in an operation as much military as commercial, for as a fighting ship the galley long survived and flourished in the republic as elsewhere in the Mediterranean (cf. pp. 130, 148–50).

Genoa, like Venice, carefully and closely specified the dimensions of the galleys built within its jurisdiction; like Venice, too, it ordered a number (though much smaller) from time to time for its own use; and as in Venice they were classified as 'light' or 'great'.[27] In general, though the city came to own some powerfully armed galleasses (see p. 146), its oared ships were designed above all for speed – naturally enough in a port so devoted to privateering and allied pursuits, and where individual owners had an obvious interest in the ability of expensive vessels briskly to engage, and if need be equally briskly to disengage, the enemy. Thus after the early fourteenth century Genoese great galleys which had opened the sea route to the north, were not merchantmen but fighting ships. As such they became by the mid-1400s small (40m in length and so no more than the city's own light galleys), narrow (with a beam of only 4.96m), and hence in comparison with their counterparts elsewhere low-set, sleek and rakish craft.

In the same way Genoese light galleys developed as smaller and more heavily manned – already in 1298 rowed with three men to a bench – than those of the republic's main rivals and competitors. In the early fourteenth century they were roughly the same size as their Venetian equivalents (cf. p. 129). But whilst their length remained more or less constant over the next 200 years they became relatively less beamy (4.4m) in the fifteenth century and then broadened out to 5.5m in the 1500s, probably in an attempt to get the room and stability necessary to mount artillery (cf. pp. 149–50). At the same time, presumably to provide the power to shift a greater weight at greater speed, the number of oarsmen was increased as was – with more seamen to handle more sail – the total complement. So whilst in 1552 a Doria galley had a company of 350, of whom 150 were oarsmen, in 1573 a similar craft had 390 men on board, of whom 280 were oarsmen. This was a lavishness Venice could rarely afford and reflects Genoa's characteristically less squeamish solution of the manning problem (cf. pp. 148–9). The city's rowers were either volunteers, convicts or slaves. Of these the volunteers – free men working for pay – were the least important, occupying nothing like the role of those of Venice. Genoa had few possessions in which suitable men could be found, and significantly enough attempts to impose a quota system on the mainland territories met with little success. No doubt the lack of opportunity and employment in the Ligurian hinterland did occasionally produce a flow of those willing to serve. But more often than not the recruits were too few, too feeble or too unreliable. Nor were convicts much better, for though readily available the majority were unfit. Hence slaves characteristically came to be regarded as the most suitable, and, particularly in the sixteenth century, those hardy and experienced oarsmen taken in battle with North African corsairs.

Such was the demand for these rowers, and such the difficulty of meeting it, that there grew up in Genoa a well-organized industry run by contractors who sold or hired to owners entire complements, and whose capital was prudently safeguarded by fining those who caused, 'through excessive floggings', the death of any slaves they provided.[28] Maybe if the property of just and considerate masters, such wretches might be, by the tenets of statistical logic, better off than free men elsewhere. Yet, as the republic's own legislation would suggest, the lot of such Genoese oarsmen was even worse than that of their most depressed Venetian counterparts. Their food was of a lower standard, consisting in 1552 of a daily issue of biscuit, with soup (rice or bean) twice a month, wine after a hard row, and meat (together with rice and wine) twice a year. The Venetians on the other hand got bean soup every day – and more than one dole – about 0.5kg of bread each evening, and wine after a hard row. True, with the increasing difficulty in obtaining – and no doubt in keeping alive – oarsmen, there came in the 1600s a somewhat more adequate diet including fish and meat. Even so, the life, such as it was, of the Genoese galley slave remained intolerably hard. If they were allowed ashore it was under guard and in pairs chained together. Nor did the winter, when their ships were out of commission and out of the water, bring any relief, since then they could be set on tallowing the hull, a task regarded if anything as more exhausting than rowing.

Unlike Venice, Genoa characteristically maintained no state fighting fleet of any consequence and operated no state-owned merchantmen. But though the Genoese shipping industry, like so much else in the republic, commenced, developed and remained firmly in private hands, individual enterprise did not blossom untrammelled. Through the *Officium Maris* and – from the 1440s – the *Officium Gazarie* (cf. p. 190) the Genoese state concerned itself in the later Middle Ages with the condition and operation of its ships. And though its concern was spasmodic, and not on the Venetian scale (see pp. 115, 125), it nevertheless sought – as indeed it had long sought – to ensure that maritime contracts were honoured and that crews discharged their duties. When necessary it ordered that vessels should sail in convoy, it specified alike the dimensions of galleys, the pay of seamen and the size of complements and it checked that craft arriving or departing were suitably rigged and equipped and that waterlines (marked by nails) were duly observed. As elsewhere such interventions were largely related to the pressures of political or economic difficulties. Hence in the hard years of the fifteenth century, to ensure, amongst other things, that its ships could defend themselves the republic laid down that – with remarkable lavishness – those over 380t should have one man to every eight tons and smaller craft one man to seven tons.[29] And in the early 1500s there were attempts to encourage the building of big ships, to maintain – like the Hanse and Venice – an adequate supply of skilled labour, and to protect slender resources in timber (cf. pp. 81–2, 115).

But often the state did no more than try to moderate or control the wilder excesses of Genoese individualism. Thus commanders about to sail were required (1437, 1481) to swear that they would neither attack vessels belonging to allied powers, enter foreign service nor sell their ships abroad. Indeed in the early modern centuries it was these same powerful private interests, looking to their own benefit in the most obvious and direct fashion, who were behind schemes to regulate the republic's entire shipping industry. In 1490, and again in 1526, Genoese shipowners succeeded in imposing on the city an organization to control all the crafts engaged in the building, repair and running of vessels on the familiar grounds that their irresponsible behaviour had led to an unacceptable rise in prices. And after some further experiment the same group re-emerged in charge of the new machinery set up in 1602 to oversee all maritime affairs.

As such behaviour testifies, the antithesis between Genoa and Venice was total. In Venice there was certainly a powerful private shipping industry, but there was also, in the late medieval and early modern centuries, both a state-owned merchant service and a large and efficient state navy. That of Genoa, on the other hand, began and remained negligible. And this insignificance, according to doge Matteo Senerago at the end of the sixteenth century – echoing the opinions of many other commentators on the striking discrepancy between public poverty and private wealth in the republic – was the outcome of the activities of a rich minority 'who are the true masters of this city and do here as they please'. True, in time of need Genoa could, like other rudimentarily organized states, usually muster an impressive fleet from the vessels of individual owners. But it rarely possessed more than a dozen galleys of its own, housed like those of Venice in a state arsenal which, though by the 1400s a fortified area within the city walls, accommodated at best only 20 ships. Nor did the growing difficulties of the sixteenth century bring, as in Venice, any significant changes. The state fleet remained at between six and eight galleys which did, however, like the Venetian flotillas, carry out organized patrols against pirates. And in the later 1600s there was a tardy and ill-managed attempt to introduce, as the Venetians were doing, northern style men-of-war – known locally as galleons – to provide a state convoy system. But the inevitable lack of co-operation from private owners, and a timorous anticipation of French reaction soon finished the experiment, and the last of the squadron was paid off in 1684.[30]

But this puny and largely ineffective force was as little an indication of Genoa's maritime power and skills as was her territorial empire an expression of her economic and financial strength. Not only did Genoese shipwrights build ships, or Genoese admirals – Benedetto Zaccaria for example – organize and command fleets for whoever would pay them, but many Genoese owners controlled what often amounted to private navies, engaged from at least the time of the first crusade in large-scale commercial and martial operations. It was such magnates who, for instance, in the second half of the thirteenth century supplied the bellicose French monarchy with many of the vessels needed for its various crusading expeditions. In the early 1300s, whilst one of the Pessagni was providing the Portuguese crown with expert maritime advice, another was victualling the armies of Edward II of England with grain, fruit and wine brought from Iberia and North Africa in Genoese ships. And at the outset of the Hundred Years War there were twenty galleys belonging to the Doria and the Grimaldi serving the French in northern waters.

Nor was the importance of these *condottieri* much diminished with the passage of time, and at the very moment that a patriot was lamenting the overthrow of Genoese seapower the whole naval balance in the Mediterranean was affected when the Dorias, a family long influential at sea, transferred their allegiance, resources and skills from France to Spain. In this the prime mover was Andrea Doria who had accepted the old French alliance until, in 1528, disgruntled by France's encouragement of the rival port of Savona, by French resistance to his own political schemes and not least by their dilatoriness in matters of pay and privilege, he went over to the Habsburgs. Such was his own and his city's standing that he could command impressive terms – a substantial advance of money: a fief in Naples; appointment as captain-general amongst other things – and such the weight of his forces that it may well be that the withdrawal of his ships left the French so weakened as to oblige them to accept the Turks as the only adequate counterpoise to the now reinforced imperial fleets. And this Doria and Genoese influence was to be long-lasting in Spain. Musters of some of the Habsburg galley squadrons in the Mediterranean in the mid-1500s show that anything up to 70 per cent of their strength might be from the republic, and Doria admirals were still commanding Iberian fleets in the seventeenth century.

But as in other societies where central government was weak and aristocratic and private interests strong, owners often saw their greatest opportunities in overt or thinly disguised piracy. Almost the first major manifestations of Genoese seapower – the assaults on North Africa and the Holy Land in the eleventh century – were as much plundering raids as anything else, and once Genoese colonies were established in the eastern Mediterranean they fought for centuries a largely self-sustained maritime war with those of the Pisans, Venetians and other powers irrespective of relations between the parent communities (cf. pp. 159, 185). That, as was later the case in the West Indies, peace at home was no obstacle to war abroad is an indication both of the fragility of metropolitan authority and of the profits at stake – profits, as investors in a privateer of the Malleone family were promised in 1251, of 50 or 100 per cent on their capital according to the luck of the cruise. So throughout the early Middle Ages there were Genoese pirates and privateers working the waters of the Levant, Italy, North Africa and Iberia. Unlike Venice, which refused to countenance such proceedings, their depredations were encouraged by the republic as an economical form of warfare, and their pursuit of prizes was so vigorous and indiscriminate as to oblige Genoa to establish in 1296 a special tribunal to hear the complaints of strangers as to the misdeeds of her citizens. By the late 1300s there was a Genoese pirate in the Caspian, and in the following century Paolo Fregoso, erstwhile doge and archbishop, his political and spiritual careers having foundered, took to the sea so successfully with four ships and 500 men that not even a regular naval expedition could subdue him. Nor was this by any means the end, for in the early 1600s Genoese privateering against Savoy reached such a pitch as to provoke reprisals.

This irrepressible free enterprise, far removed from the careful and systematic policies of the Venetians, gave to Genoese maritime and colonial endeavour much the same character as that of the Norse in the early Middle Ages or of the English under Elizabeth and the first Stuarts. Vikings, Genoese and English were all widely regarded as pirates, their achievements were largely the outcome of un-coordinated private initiatives and they were commonly inspired by an admixture of expectations of loot and hopes of escape from the oppressions of the mother country (cf. pp. 1–12, 465ff., 481ff.). Wasteful in resources such behaviour undoubtedly was, and conducive to endemic internecine strife. But it could also produce, as with the Genoese voyages into the Atlantic, Genoese interventions in Asian waters or the impressive achievements of a Benedetto Zaccaria or a Christopher Columbus, a boldness and originality notably lacking in tightly controlled Venetian commanders (cf. p. 150). And significantly enough Doria galleys of the mid-sixteenth century were named in that same purposeful and idiosyncratic manner – *Wealth*, *Victory*, *Fortune* – favoured by Elizabethan seamen.

IV *Eclipse*

Until almost the end of the sixteenth century Genoa was of prime importance in the maritime life of Europe, opening in the late 1200s a sea route from the Mediterranean to the north, dominating with the Norse the earliest stages of the continent's oceanic expansion, and exercising directly and indirectly an influence out of all proportion to her resources. It is not, however, an importance easily demonstrated statistically, for with the city's indifferent administration and with many of her ships and seamen regularly absent either on piratical cruises or in foreign service it is impossible to know the volume of tonnage owned in the republic at any given moment. When, for example, in the 1490s the port allegedly possessed no more than 20 vessels, Genoese owners were none the less able to provide the king of France with a fleet of some 100 ships, including not only galleys but carvels and oared galleons which were craft of the latest fashion and style (cf. pp. 00–0 and 00–0). Nor were such concentrations of naval power anything unusual. The republic's maritime resources may not have been as extensive as reported by credulous or patriotic chroniclers, but throughout the medieval centuries Genoa regularly assembled fleets of anything up to 200 vessels manned by several thousand men – fleets, that is, which in numbers of both ships and complements roughly equalled those of the Christians at Lepanto or the Spaniards at the outset of the Armada campaign.[31] As late as the mid-1500s the city could still muster 91 vessels totalling roughly 30,000t, and even at the end of the century a single member of the Lomellini clan alone controlled 15 ships.

Nevertheless by then the greatest days of Genoese seapower were well passed. The republic had made a far poorer showing against the Ottomans than had Venice; great families dropped out of shipowning in the course of the sixteenth century; and that long and remarkable succession of Genoese seamen, admirals and *condottieri* failed. More than this Genoa, whose tonnage by the late 1500s amounted at best to an insignificant 12,000t, was short of ships – particularly those of the size and lines favoured by the English and the Dutch – and of men to build them. True, there were in the first half of the seventeenth century plans to create a fleet of northern-style merchantmen, and plans of an even more ambitious nature – witness the establishment in 1647–8 of the Company of the Indies – to enable Genoa to participate in the profits of the expanding economy of the North Atlantic. But little came of such dreams. Nor were the once renowned Genoese war galleys any better off. Timber for their construction – which even in the fifteenth century had been coming in by river and sea from as far away as Dauphiné – became, as in Venice, rarer and more expensive. At the same time a massive drop in the city's population – reduced by dearth and plague from perhaps 75,000 in the 1630s to 38,000 in 1660 – combined with smaller hauls of prisoners as naval activity contracted, meant that the republic found it increasingly difficult to recruit oarsmen. Such indeed was the situation that by the mid 1600s it was possible to hire a large (450t) and fully armed and manned northern sailing ship for the monthly wages of a complement of free rowers.

These problems were not peculiar to Genoa, and even if her notorious political turbulence denied her an eclipse as dignified and fruitful as that of Venice she displayed in decline more enterprise than her ancient rival, declaring herself a freeport in 1608 and endeavouring to attract trade from the now flourishing Livorno and Marseilles. Some of her troubles, such as war, pestilence and famine in the 1530s, or a dearth of grain in the late sixteenth century, though assuredly crippling, were at least only momentary. But Genoa's maritime decline reflected a more general decline, and like that of Venice the shift of economic and political power to the north. Yet in the early 1600s the city remained rich and ebullient, and its population, after falling in the late Middle Ages, was back to roughly the level of the republic's greatest days at the end of the thirteenth century. In the same way the port itself, following the general economic recession of the fourteenth and fifteenth centuries, was by the mid-1500s once again handling a trade of a value approaching that of the late 1200s, and fifty years later, with an average of thirty ships arriving each month, it was well on the way to eclipsing Livorno. But for all its efforts Genoa in the end fared little better than Venice. Much of this new and booming commerce was that of foreign merchants carried in foreign vessels – Ragusan, Hanseatic, Dutch – with northern ships arriving by the mid-seventeenth century in such strength as to account for 80 per cent of the traffic using the port, and to provoke a crisis in its operation. Furthermore these vessels brought mainly grain and salt – a commerce which inevitably contracted as Genoa's population fell towards the 1650s – and took out little produced by the city's decaying industries, whilst the rich trades, such as that of the Levant went either to north European ports or to Livorno and Marseilles (see pp. 64, 142–3).

In part these reverses reflected, as did those of the Venetians, the unchallengeable supremacy of northern seapower. But they also reflected the weaknesses of the Genoese economy: first its highly specialized shipping industry and then the dangerous concentration of the city's capital and skills in lucrative enterprises in Iberia (see pp. 176, 196). Hence Genoa lacked the scope enjoyed by the less-developed Venice to re-deploy its resources. And hence, too, when Spain sank the republic sank with it, for its commitment to the Habsburgs had been so complete as to involve (after 1528) not only the exclusion from the city of those to whom the pro-Spanish Doria regime was unacceptable, but ultimately a dedication to high finance to the virtual exclusion of all other economic activity. At the same time the city, like Venice, was overshadowed by increasingly powerful opponents against whom its modest and decreasing resources in men and materials were of little avail. To its great detriment the duke of Tuscany developed the neighbouring port of Livorno in the late sixteenth century, just as the duke of Savoy encouraged that of Nice in the early seventeenth. Then Genoese shipping was attacked, as was that of Venice, by the Moslem and Christian pirates ubiquitous in the Mediterranean. More disastrously still the republic suffered from the persistent and eventually successful attempts of its erstwhile client, the now formidable and ambitious French monarchy, to create a navy of its own, and from the growing debility of its onetime Spanish protector. And indeed trapped between France and the Spanish colonies of Naples, Sicily and Majorca the city was singularly unfortunate. Bourbon and Habsburg were mortal rivals in the seventeenth century, and every time that Spain and France fought Genoese vessels were convenient prizes, especially for undiscriminating Spanish corsairs working from Finale – a Spanish enclave in the very heart of Genoese territory – and for French and North African craft operating from Genoa's own island of Corsica.

So between the twelfth and sixteenth centuries the republic's possessions in the eastern Mediterranean – independent, self-willed and more or less left to their own devices – were effortlessly swept away by Saracens, Mamelukes and Ottomans, with Chios, the last survivor, falling to the Turks in 1566 (see pp. 183–8). Meanwhile in the west her tenuous territorial empire was eventually reduced to the doubtful asset of the ungovernable Corsica. And finally the rewards once reaped in Iberia dwindled as the economy of the peninsula decayed, and as in the early 1600s Spain sank further into financial chaos, making the risks of lending to the Spanish crown increasingly unacceptable (see pp. 178ff. and 366ff.). In 1626, with yet another financial crash impending, the Genoese refused to act, and the Habsburgs opened dealings with a syndicate of Portuguese Jewish bankers. Not that this was the end of the city's Spanish connection, and even as late as 1670 its merchants were taking about 17 per cent of such American silver as was recorded as reaching Spain – and doubtless more that was not – and handling at roughly the same date approximately 25 per cent (by value) of the Spanish-American trade.

But by this time neither Spain nor Genoa were what they had once been, and unlike Venice with its distinguished civilization and its long struggle for Crete, the republic showed little signs of any final surge of political or cultural energy. The last vestiges of its empire had gone and its merchant fleet and navy were negligible. Indeed such was Genoa's decline that it could be argued in a city once famous for the quality and pugnacity of its seamen that to build warships would only invite embarrassing demands from Spain for their hire, whilst Genoese commanders afloat fled at the approach of the enemy to avoid what were described in the discrete language of diplomacy as 'encounters damaging to the prestige of the Most Serene Republic'.

v *Imperial imprint*

'Of all those who have enlarged man's knowledge of the world', wrote a Venetian in
1543, 'none have contributed more than the inhabitants of this city.' Nearly 400 years
earlier, with equal pride and markedly less grace, the Genoese had informed the
Emperor Frederick Barbarossa that so effectively had they defended the shores of
Europe that all 'from Rome to Barcelona' could now sleep peacefully 'which is more
than the (German) empire could have accomplished at the cost of 10,000 silver marks a
year'. Yet even if the achievements of Genoa and Venice were less than those claimed in
this haughty imperial rhetoric, impressive enough they still were. Genoese financiers
were amongst those whose wealth supported the follies and ambitions of the kings of
England and France in the high Middle Ages, and whose resources were a major prop of
the Habsburg monarchs of Spain in the sixteenth and seventeenth centuries. Like the
Norse before them and the Iberians after, the republics by an admixture of downright
violence and commercial enterprise extended, even if only momentarily, the world
economy. And like the Hanse and the Dutch they stimulated or modified in varying
degrees by their skills or demands the economies with which they came into contact.
They opened for a time a direct European commerce with the Far East, and by one
maritime route brought the Black Sea into close and regular association with western
Europe, and by another established a tighter and more vigorous relationship between the
north and south of the continent. Besides this they and their fellow maritime powers –
the Pisans and Catalans especially – created in the Middle Ages a western commercial
empire in North Africa and the Levant. And their eastern trade provided, as did the
later Iberian conquests, new or more extensive markets for European textiles, so
stimulating their manufacture, affecting the qualities and styles of the cloths produced,
and by the sheer volume of their export enhancing western prosperity and purchasing
power. No more than with other imperial expansion were these influences inevitably
and universally benign. Greek islands were converted to the economic satellites of
Venice; peoples of the Black Sea were drained into the harems and armies of Mameluke
Egypt. Yet it may have been the invigorating flow of Genoese commerce through such
bases as Kilia Vechia that assisted the future Romania to resist the Ottomans, just as
German penetration of medieval Poland and Hungary from the north and west was
balanced, and in some degree limited, by that of the Genoese spreading inland from the
Black Sea (cf. pp. 70–1 and 169–70).

   So, too, partly as a result of their own experiences and partly from their early
association with economically advanced societies, Genoa and Venice developed or
acquired sophisticated commercial and financial techniques often, in the course of time,
transmitted to other areas of Europe. The *mahona*, that peculiarly Genoese contribution to the ways of financing imperial expansion, and perhaps with its freely
transferable shares the precursor of the big joint-stock companies of the north, took its
name if not its form from the arabic *ma ̄ina*.[32] Brokers, the agents with whom in many

medieval states and cities alien merchants were obliged to deal, appear in Genoa and Venice in the 1100s as *sensali* or *sanseri* (Arabic *simsār*) and subsequently elsewhere in Europe. Genoa was likewise among the pioneers of marine insurance and of double-entry book-keeping – the oldest surviving accounts displaying its fully developed form being those of the city for 1340 – to which the Venetians in turn added further refinements. And the great Genoese monopoly corporations of the late Middle Ages, comparatively long-lived associations of two dozen or so shareholders dealing in, for instance, alum or coral, anticipated, in their complete control of a commodity from production to sale, later Dutch commercial practice (cf. pp. 405ff.).

Yet many of these techniques, such as the use of partnerships and other relatively elaborate methods of raising capital, were known elsewhere. Nor did Genoa and Venice, generally employing only short-term or family associations, attain the sophistication of Florence where by *c.*1300 there had developed vast companies bringing together large numbers of investors for long periods of time. But in all things maritime, as the owners of the largest and most powerful agglomeration of naval and commercial shipping in western Europe before the sixteenth century, and as experts in the control and exploitation of colonial possessions, their influence was unique and decisive. In the early Middle Ages they modified and brought into general use in the Mediterranean Byzantine and Arab naval tactics – the employment of seaborne projectile-firing weapons, the protection of ships against incendiary and explosive missiles, the deployment of large numbers of oared vessels lashed to one another for close engagements. Together with Pisa they demonstrated their superiority by destroying the last vestiges of Greek and Moslem seapower. By piracy and trade they acquired a strength without which the Crusades are hardly conceivable. Genoa, Pisa and Venice provided most of the vessels that carried Christian armies, pilgrims and supplies to the east, and on occasion rescued the crusaders from difficulty or danger. Thereafter their naval supremacy was for centuries unchallenged. They excluded intruders from the Mediterranean, and their fleets crushed those of Islam with the same ease and frequency that Saracen, Mameluke, Mongol and Ottoman armies crushed the forces of Christian chivalry. Genoese admirals took a prominent role in the initial stages of Portugal's oceanic expansion, and commanded Castilian squadrons that defeated the Moroccans in the thirteenth century and the English in the fourteenth. Meanwhile the maritime strength of Venice, still preponderant at Lepanto, long contained Ottoman naval ambitions in the Mediterranean.

This supremacy was furthermore one of technology, and throughout the Middle Ages Genoese (and to a lesser extent Venetian) shipwrights – who were used, for example by Henry VIII of England – were widely employed to build vessels of the types for which their cities were celebrated. The Genoese provided the galleys with which the Castilians defeated Moorish pirates at the beginning of the twelfth century. In the high Middle Ages they supplied alike the kings of France, the khan of Persia and the emperors of Greece with ships, and constructed arsenals at Seville for Alfonso the

Wise of Castile and at Rouen for Philip the Bel of France. They were in Ottoman service soon after 1400, with the Tuscans and Catalans in the early 1500s, and at the end of the sixteenth century the arrival of Genoese artisans in the Spanish Netherlands was viewed with apprehension by the English.[33] Nor was this respect for such skills mistaken. The great galley was the excellent Venetian answer to the long-distance transport of precious commodities, and the multi-masted carrack, Europe's first big ocean-going sailing ship, the equally satisfactory, and like as not Genoese solution to the carriage of bulk goods.

But the influence of Venice and Genoa went far beyond matters of war and trade. In the course of the Middle Ages the Mediterranean was responsible for three major navigational innovations. There was produced the first comprehensive volume of sailing directions;[34] there appeared the first maritime charts; and there was developed a technique enabling a navigator using compass, chart and sailing directions to calculate his position at sea with some confidence. Not all these advances can be attributed exclusively to Venice and Genoa. Nevertheless it is significant that the pioneer collection of sailing direction, the famous *Compasso da Navigare*, describing the whole Mediterranean littoral and probably compiled *c.* 1250, deals not only with the African Atlantic coast as far south as Safi, then well known to the Genoese, but also with the Black Sea, hotly disputed between the two republics (see pp. 95, 164). So, too, the first clear reference to the use of a chart afloat relates to Genoa. In 1270 some of the city's ships transporting the king of France and his army to Tunis were obliged to run before a storm, and the royal alarm was only allayed when the king was shown, on what his biographer describes as a map, where his pilots believed themselves to be. Furthermore, what the surviving charts depict is the area of Genoese and Venetian seaborne commerce. The earliest, the *Carta Pisana* of *c.* 1275 and perhaps of Genoese origin, whatever its other merits, is hazy as to the shape of the coast of western Europe beyond Cape St Vincent. But once the ships of the two republics began to work regularly to the north the quality of the information mapped rapidly improved. Charts produced in fourteenth-century Venice, Genoa and Majorca portray accurately the littorals of the Mediterranean and the Black Sea, together with parts of the Atlantic seaboards of Europe and north-west Africa. Only when they deal with regions, such as the Baltic, outside the range of Venetian and Genoese experience do they become unsatisfactory.

Unlike the previous fantasies of the medieval mind these *portolans*[35] were based on direct observation and on the use of the compass. Admittedly they are not like the charts on which modern navigators plot routes and positions. They make no allowance for the curvature of the earth's surface, they have no parallels or meridians and in the earliest versions different regions are recorded on different scales. Yet the outlines of Europe they established were accepted with only minor modifications by cartographers until well into the 1700s. And their vital innovation was that they gave distance and, by compass bearings, direction. A compass of sorts, nothing more than a magnetic needle pushed through a piece of wood and floating in a basin of water, had been used at sea since at least the twelfth century. But with a form so primitive and impracticable it was only employed to get a direction when all else failed. About 1200, however, there came fundamental changes, probably inspired, as were contemporary experiments in ship-design, by the longer routes and busier trades now worked by Genoese and Venetian vessels.[36] The needle was mounted on a pivot, and not long after attached to a compass card. This revolved freely in a box fastened in line with the ship's keel and thus indicated her course. Bearings could therefore now be taken relatively easily and rapidly, the horizon could be divided more minutely and directions could be given more precisely. Exactly where and when these advances were made is unknown, though clearly it was at some time before the construction of the *Carta Pisana* in *c*. 1275. From thenceforward it was possible to indicate direction on a chart and so allow a navigator to use it to get his bearings. This was done in an ingenious, though to the modern eye confusing, way. For mapping purposes the Mediterranean was divided into two halves. Then two circles were drawn with their rims just touching, and from the centre of each sixteen rays were projected representing directions – named in the early *portolans* after winds and not compass points. Where these lines of direction met the circumferences of the circles, windroses were inserted, consisting of four quarter winds (i.e. directions) on either side of the central ray and extended to the opposite side of the circle. Thus a nagivator wishing to find the bearing between his point of departure and his desired destination could put a ruler on the chart and join the two. Then with dividers he searched for the line of bearing (the rhumb) parallel with his ruler and thus established the direction he needed.

But only on the rarest occasions can a ship hope to make an unbroken run in a straight line, and with the increasing distances being worked by Genoese and Venetian vessels the probability was even remoter. Hence there came a further refinement enabling a pilot to reckon, by the simplest trigonometry, how far he had travelled in the desired direction if for any reason he lost his compass course, and how far he needed to sail to recover it. Perhaps not surprisingly the oldest surviving copy of the tables used in these calculations, the *Tavola de Marteloio*, comes from a Venetian treatise of the early 1400s – though they were probably already known in the late thirteenth century – and the first explicit reference to them from a Genoese inventory of 1390. Obviously more scientific than that of the Norse (cf. pp. 15ff.), and equally obviously impracticable for lengthy oceanic passages, this new nagivation turned on a knowledge of the compass and an understanding of arithmetic far from peculiar to Venice and Genoa by the thirteenth century. Even so, the Venetians or Genoese are its most likely devisers and were certainly amongst its most successful practicioners, with their ships regularly working on long runs.

In the later Middle Ages, after momentary eclipse by the Catalans, the two cities regained much of their former pre-eminence as centres of geographical knowledge and cartographic skill. Rumour had it that information obtained in Venice inflamed Portuguese ambitions to reach Asia, and Venetian and Genoese cartographers demonstrated their excellence in a series of attempts to depict the world in maps reconciling the authoritative views of Antiquity revealed in Ptolemy's newly recovered *Geography* with information obtained from merchants and seamen. It was probably in Genoa that there was produced in 1457 what its author described as 'a true account of the world from which all frivolous tales have been removed'. It is a carefully drawn map, generally leaning heavily on Ptolemy, but for Asia incorporating a great deal which had come from the Venetian traveller Nicolo Conti. It records, possibly for the first time, the Moluccas and, defying Ptolemy, has one of the earliest representations of an open Indian Ocean. Meanwhile in 1448 the Venetian Andrea Bianco had plotted – also probably for the first time – Portuguese activities in West Africa as far south as Cape Verde, and such was the reputation of Venetian cartographers that in 1457 Fra Mauro, one of the most celebrated, was commissioned by the king of Portugal to draw a map which would guide his subjects down the African coast to Asia. To this end he was furnished with Portuguese charts recording the fruits of their exploration of the Atlantic. Fra Mauro, however, warming to his work with true scholarly zeal, produced instead an important world map,[37] based, as he explained, on 'many years of investigation and intercourse with persons worthy of credence who have seen with their own eyes what is now faithfully set out'. Admittedly the result left much to be desired. Quite apart from the inadequacies of his projection and the inescapable influence of Ptolemy, Fra Mauro had, as he acknowledged, no idea of the size of the earth and consequently no clear understanding of how much of it he was depicting. Nevertheless he knew the accounts of Polo and Conti and possibly some Arabic and Ethiopian sources too. In his map Jerusalem – after apologies – is not represented as the centre of the world, the Indian Ocean is not enclosed by land, the relative longitudinal extents of Europe and Asia are more or less right, a fair knowledge of China and Abyssinia is displayed and Sumatra appears for the first time.

Thereafter cartographical pre-eminence, like maritime supremacy, passed to Iberia and ultimately to northern Europe. Venice, however, still by trade and politics in touch with the widest of worlds, and with its civilization approaching its apogee, was to remain influential in recording and publicizing the whole course of the greatest age of Europe's expansion overseas. Charts such as those of Grazioso Benincasa (drawn 1465–74) and Cristoforo Soligo (drawn *c.* 1490) set out much of Portugal's penetration of the Atlantic. The Contarini map of 1506 was the first printed to show any part of the New World, whilst seventy atlases published between 1527 and 1564 by Battista Agnese alone have survived. Then in the mid-1500s there appeared the three magnificent volumes of the *Voyages and Travels* (*Navigazioni e Viaggi*) of Gian Battista Ramusio, systematically assembling a mass of material relating to the geographical discoveries, and by their example inspiring others elsewhere – Hakluyt, de Bry, Purchas – to attempt similar undertakings.

But the contribution of Venice and Genoa to Europe's discovery and eventual domination of the world went far beyond publicizing the achievements of others. The experience gained and the techniques developed in the course of the establishment and exploitation of their own overseas possessions were in some measure transmitted to other empires in the sixteenth and seventeenth centuries. It may well be that the Spanish *Casa de la Contratación*, set up like as not on Genoese advice to handle the trade and maritime affairs of the Americas, was modelled on the republic's *Officium Gazarie*. In general terms the organization of the Iberian Asian and American monopolies resembled that of the jealously regarded Venetian luxury trade, whilst the overall structure of Spanish imperial government had close affinities with the much-admired Venetian colonial institutions. The appearance of the familiar Italian-style slave-worked sugar plantation in the American colonies of Spain and the Atlantic islands of Portugal was no accident, and it is possible, too, that Genoa's use of the *mahona* to exploit colonial territories was followed – initially at least – by the Iberians when they rewarded explorers with grants of their discoveries to allow them to recover their expenses. Indeed Genoese practice may have suggested the policy subsequently employed in northern Europe of leasing or entrusting overseas possessions to specially created companies, just as the *mahona* itself is a possible ancestor of the joint-stock associations commonly used (cf. pp. 269ff., 345–9, 402ff.).

Yet if some of these affiliations are perhaps tenuous, of the direct and powerful influence of Venice and Genoa on Europe's early expansion there is no doubt. The Venetians Polo and Conti reached and described in glowing terms the Far East; Genoese ships and commanders pioneered the west's penetration of the southern Atlantic and the Indian Ocean. And even these achievements they soon eclipsed. America was discovered by the Genoese Columbus and his less successful contemporary John Cabot – probably Genoese by birth and Venetian by choice – was associated with renewed English exploration of the north-west Atlantic. And it was Sebastian Cabot – John's son and pilot-major of Spain at one stage of a turbulent career – who in English employment was influential in the reorganization and redirection of Protestant maritime endeavour in the mid-1500s. These, however, are merely the most familiar names amongst many others less celebrated yet still important. Genoese seamen and merchants were involved in the early stages of Portuguese exploration of West Africa, whilst in 1454–6 Ca da Mosto, discoverer of some of the Cape Verde Islands and one whose expertise, as a Venetian, in the matter of spices was highly esteemed, was also serving Portugal. Nor was he alone, for he had been recruited by a compatriot apparently employed by the Portuguese to interest his fellows in the business opportunities of their new possessions. And such influences endured into the later phases of Iberian, and indeed European, expansion, with the Venetians trading to Portuguese Asia in the sixteenth century and the Genoese deploying their resources and skills in the Iberian colonies in the west (cf. pp. 140 and 180ff.).

Achievement on this scale naturally enough gave to the citizens of Venice and Genoa a proper sense of their merits and consequence. In the days of the Latin crusading state the Genoese had set up in the Holy Sepulchre a record, inscribed in letters of gold, relating all they had accomplished. Meanwhile the Venetians, established in Constantinople, had come to see themselves as the true heirs of Constantine, and such intimations of immortality were soon, and powerfully, reinforced by further imperial success and by the growing influence of the rediscovered classics. The euophoria of triumph, of wealth gained, of lands subdued and peoples conquered was certainly nothing peculiarly Italian. The medieval literature of Iceland reflects clearly enough an awareness of the epic achievements of Scandinavian seamen, whilst the conquests of the Iberians were to intensify in the Spaniards and Portuguese the belief that they were God's chosen peoples. But Venice was the first colonial power since Antiquity consciously to record and idealize in art and letters its imperial triumphs, and upon whose culture empire made so direct, visible and splendid an impact. That this should have been so is to be explained, in part at least, by the very fact of Venetian expansion into an area of the eastern Mediterranean (Byzantium) so replete with the magnificent remains of the Roman empire of the east. Yet this experience, and the resultant wealth, were shared by Genoa which produced no equivalent glories, and what was even more potent in Venetian development was the intellectual climate of Italy in the late medieval and Renaissance centuries, with its adulation of Antiquity. The imperial ideal, that is, and reactions to discovery and conquest were formed and conditioned by ideas already existing in the mother country rather than induced by the novel experiences of empire. And significantly enough, the only colonial or imperial power amongst those with which we are concerned upon whom acquaintance with new lands, new peoples, new opportunities and new responsibilities produced so little effect was the culturally undistinguished Hanse (see pp. 72ff.). Thus in a world of reviving classicism the Venetians saw themselves by the fifteenth century as the new Romans, if not indeed as their superiors. History was tastefully rearranged to give the city a suitably impressive ancestry; patricians had pedigrees concocted to show their Roman origins. As in Antiquity the virtues and rewards of patriotism and heroic achievement were splendidly recorded, and the state itself in good neo-Roman style commissioned works – imposing civic buildings, historical and allegorical paintings – demonstrating its wealth and triumphs, and depicting the benefits of its rule.

Nor, like less sophisticated builders of empire, had the Venetians any inhibitions as to more forthright expressions of the simpler satisfactions of success and power. The Lion of St Mark, symbol of the republic's rule, was proudly emblazoned on colonial buildings. That men of consequence might know of the city's achievements there was set up in the Dogal Palace a great world-map recording the travels of eminent Venetians, and to ensure the appreciation of a wider audience the Aldine Press published (1543) a collection of Venetian voyages with a preface extolling the republic's primacy in geographical discovery. The naval victory at Lepanto was to have been immortalized in a painting (unhappily lost) by Tintoretto, and if Venice had no Elgar or Kipling to crudely trumpet its praises nothing expresses better the grandeur and self-esteem of its oligarchs than the vast and voluptuously coloured canvasses of Veronese.

And in many other ways the impact of empire was clear and direct. Seaborne commerce and rule inspired the first truly maritime art, and from the time of Vittore Carpaccio in the late fifteenth century Venetian painters recorded with minute accuracy, as did Dutch marine artists later, the features of the ships that sustained the wealth and security of their society. Then again, war and trade brought the Venetians and Genoese into contact with a whole range of states and civilizations previously either entirely or largely unknown. Already in the twelfth century there were Hellenized Venetians in Byzantium, and Genoese officials in Acre who spoke and wrote Arabic. Over the next 300 years citizens of the two republics were to penetrate to China, central Asia, India, Persia, Abyssinia, the islands of the north-east Atlantic and to the interior of north and north-west Africa. Moreover, by the end of the Middle Ages Venice and Genoa had themselves become, like other entrepôts before and since, centres to which were drawn or brought peoples from an infinity of races, and where, if the strange speech of slaves was cause for fashionable mirth, their great numbers and uncertain loyalty were matters for concern.

So from the experience and record of travel, and from contacts formal and informal western man's knowledge of the world was enlarged and improved. Thirteenth-century Genoese map-makers came to know from Oriental savants in the service of the Mongol rulers of Persia something of the geographical lore of the east. Information about the Far East from Polo and Conti appears in late medieval European maps, and the travels of a Venetian in Burma were recorded (1608) by the Dutch cartographer Blaeu. Nor was this access of fact merely geographical. The customs and habits of many alien civilizations, whether those of the generally admired Chinese or the widely disliked Corsicans were observed and noted. And with the revival of the classics merchants and clerks inflamed by scholarship visited the pyramids (recommended by Herodotus) or counted the statues cast down in Knossos. Furthermore, through trade, conquest or natural curiosity there came to medieval Europe, as there came to the continent from the Americas in the sixteenth century, new commodities, fashions and words. Just as the Spaniards looted Aztec and Inca treasures so the Venetians enriched and beautified their city with the spoils of Constantinople, whilst to a fourteenth-century traveller Genoa appeared to be 'wholly made from Athens'. The less strenuous endeavour of the two republics introduced, or brought into more general western use, an enormous variety of refinements in diet, dress and taste. By the late Middle Ages the wealthy of even the darkest corners of Europe – northern England for instance – were accustomed to sugar, pepper, cloves, ginger and cinnamon. Magnates and their ladies in Venice and elsewhere dressed in comfort and splendour in expensive oriental materials – Chinese and Persian silks; cloths of Damascus (*damasks*), Aleppo (*alepini*) and Mosul (*mussolas*). Exotic styles and customs were adopted both by Italian colonials – like those Genoese of the Black Sea territories dressed in Turkish or Asiatic fashion – and by the relatively poor of the metropolitan cities who in Venice took to the *bernous* and *kaftan* (cf. pp. 185–6). Similarly by the late Middle Ages opulent dwellings in Venice and elsewhere were graced and enhanced by Oriental carpets. Until the early 1600s the most splendid were those supposedly from Damascus – though made in fact in Egypt – when there appeared the superb products of Persia with their interwoven silver and gold. And naturally enough with the import of exotic goods or the emulation of exotic institutions there came into western usage – though not always immediately recognizable – their vernacular names. From the Arabs were taken, amongst much else, *mahona*, *arsenal*, *bazaar* and *fondaco*.[38] Even more influential were the Greeks, many of whose fiscal practices Venice continued in the onetime Byzantine lands she acquired. Hence the city's dialect came to abound in words of Greek origin and constructions of Greek usage.

But as in other empires linguistic borrowings went far beyond those occasioned by the formal contacts of war, politics and commerce. True neither Venice nor Genoa, ruling no extensive populations of previously unknown speech and innocent of all urges to convert the pagan and infidel, had any of the interest of the Iberians of the sixteenth and seventeenth centuries in the systematic study of indigenous languages. Yet the routine demands of business produced, as they later produced in the Hanse, some practical aids for the merchant trading in distant lands, and most notably a lexicon (probably Genoese and *c.* 1300) of Persian, Latin and Couman, 'the language spoken and used throughout the empires of the Tartars, Persians, Chaldeans, Medes and Cathay'. Moreover, so intense were the relations of Venice with the east, and such the number of her citizens with some experience of the Levant in particular, that by the sixteenth century orientalisms were freely and naturally used – with the obvious expectation of being widely understood – in literature, popular drama and private correspondence. So the writer of a letter can, like other colonials and expatriates of more recent vintage, greet his friends with a smattering of some eastern tongue. Yet this, like the spicing of nineteenth-century English with Indian words, was only the most obvious and superficial aspect of a more general exotic influence on the culture of imperial societies and indeed on that of the west as a whole. Already in the twelfth century a Venetian text can cynically compare a woman without malice to the riches of India. Treasures looted from Constantinople in 1204 profoundly affected Venetian culture, whilst from the early Renaissance centuries eastern topics, eastern themes (real or imagined) and ultimately eastern figures appeared in Italian and eventually Venetian art. There are Chinese and Tartars in the work of Giotto and Andrea di Firenze. About 1440 Antonio Pisanello drew a superbly intimidating Mongol Archer, and in the sixteenth century there comes, probably from Veronese, the reception of a Persian embassy in Venice. With some artists experience of the east was direct and personal. At the request of the sultan himself Gentile Bellini was sent from Venice in 1479 to portray the formidable conqueror of Constantinople, Mahomet II, and it is like as not from Bellini too that we have the magnificent painting of the arrival of a Venetian delegation in Cairo.

To paint or draw the east more or less accurately or realistically was one thing, but the real exoticism was to idealize it; to ape its customs and conventions; to collect its artefacts; to attempt to convey what, rightly or wrongly, was thought to be its atmosphere. Such aspirations were not strong in Venice, and the collections accumulated by connoisseurs in the sixteenth and seventeenth centuries contained nothing truly exotic. Yet this essentially modern taste was not entirely absent. Islamic and Chinese designs appeared in textiles alongside those of local and Greek inspiration. In the 1400s, whilst men of wealth and sensibility were collecting Chinese porcelain, Venetian bookbinders were decorating their work with Persian motifs, using at times meaningless Sufic characters for effect. And in the sixteenth century oriental-style metal goods were being produced in the city.

But probably the major external influence on Venetian culture and one of the most potent in medieval Europe was that of Byzantium. The Greek empire, embodying even in ruins a superb civilization, was the scene of Venice's initial commercial triumphs and the victim of her first territorial ambitions (cf. pp. 91–4). From these associations the culture of the republic was to receive a stimulus which in its directness and intensity entirely eclipses that exercised by any other civilization on a colonizing power since Antiquity. The pomp and ceremony of the Venetian State was that of Byzantium. From onetime Greek lands came the bodies of saints to be housed in churches of eastern dedications, and to be the object of Venetian cults. And to this massive Greek influence there is no more striking testimony than the great church of St Mark itself. Begun in the eleventh century with the help of Greek artists and workmen it was lavishly embellished in the 1200s from the loot taken at the sack of Constantinople, which provided amongst other things a hundred precious relics. In every way, externally and internally, the predominant influence is Greek, whether in the motifs, colours and mosaics or in the appearance of those peculiarly Byzantine six-winged cherubims. Nor was this all. The decorations in looted Greek manuscripts served as models to Venetian sculptors and the much-admired horses from the Hippodrome of Constantinople which now adorn St Mark's were triumphantly adopted as imperial symbols.

With the passage of time, and particularly with the westward advance of the Turks, there grew up in Venice a sizable Greek community reinforced by those Greeks from the Venetian possessions drawn, like other hopeful colonial subjects before and since, to the heart of the empire. By the late fifteenth century they numbered perhaps four or five thousand, and by 1580 as many as 15,000, making Venice, it was remarked, another Byzantium. They were not, as were so many of those brought to Europe by later oceanic expansion, slaves or prisoners, nor were they, unlike the inhabitants of most great seaports, absorbed into a polyglot society, but maintained instead, with the republic's consent, much of their own way of life. Many were artisans, seamen, soldiers or *madonneri* – craftsmen who painted traditional Greek icons of the Virgin. But there were also amongst them – from Crete especially – artists of genius of whom the most celebrated was Domenikos Theotokopoulos (El Greco) working in the deliberately unnaturalistic style of Byzantium.

So, too, it was to Venice, capital of a largely Greek empire, that Byzantine scholars exiled by the Ottoman conquests turned, or through Venice that they travelled to seek preferment in the West. For his timely comparison of Venetian government with the best practice of the Ancients, George of Trebizond was taken into the republic's service; and as a token of his gratitude for the sanctuary granted him Cardinal Bessarion, most eminent of all Greek refugees, left the city his library (1468). Venetian enthusiasm for Greek antiquity may have been slow to develop, and perhaps initially owed more to the needs of the city's printing industry for textual specialists to assist in the publication of the classics than to pure scholarly zeal.[39] Nevertheless in the fifteenth and sixteenth centuries Venice established herself as one of the leading centres for the dissemination throughout the west of a knowledge of ancient Greece. Such was the output of classical Greek texts from her presses that probably no other individual city has ever transmitted a comparable body of literature in so short a period of time. The printing of Greek was indeed neither initiated nor monopolized by Venice. Yet the flow of scholars and manuscripts to the republic, its standing in Greek eyes and its tolerant acceptance of a talented Greek community largely explain the remarkable success of Aldo Manuzio's press which with a Cretan Greek as principle editor, and with others as compositors, produced the first of a long succession of Aldine texts in 1494–5. And so it was that Venice made available to the west the original texts not only of Greek writers – Plato and Aristotle – long if imperfectly known, but also those previously either partly or wholly forgotten: Thucydides, Sophocles, Pindar.

Similarly in the empire Venetian culture was influenced, though with less momentous repercussions, by such vigorous indigenous civilizations as that of Crete. Like the great Iberian historians of Asia and the Americas later, a Venetian scholar writing of the island's past at the turn of the fourteenth and fifteenth centuries felt impelled to employ local vernacular sources. Then through the use of native craftsmen in their construction the Catholic churches of Venetian Crete displayed, like those of the Spaniards in America or the Portuguese in the east, an admixture of metropolitan and traditional styles, as in the characteristically Greek colouring of the frescoes and the equally characteristically Greek iconography at Candia and Rettimo. And such was the quality of the island's own civilization that by the sixteenth century many Cretan feudatories of Venetian origin were not only Orthodox in religion but, like other colonists faced by powerful indigenous cultures, had to all intents and purposes adopted the local way of life.

Yet the massive impact of Antiquity apart – one aspect in any case of a more general European recovery of knowledge and understanding of the civilizations of classical Greece and Rome – there is little to suggest that in Venice or Genoa, or indeed in any other imperial power, experience of strange lands and unknown peoples fundamentally affected the ways in which Europeans thought or behaved. Imperial success might well inculcate attitudes and aspirations far different from those that had occasioned it, turning Viking seamen into farmers and Venetian merchants into landed magnates. But these are scarcely matters of changing sensibility. Then again, if Venetian and Genoese enslavement of Christians was occasionally condemned it was far more widely accepted. Its demise, moreover, was largely due to changing political circumstances – the Ottoman conquests; a western interest in reunion with the eastern church – rather than to any heightened moral revulsion. Nor in either Venice or Genoa did the enslavement of peoples of widely differing races give rise to any serious speculation as to the theological or ethical justification of such proceedings. And no more than with the Hanse could a rich experience of the alien world by itself endow Genoa with a vigorous and distinctive culture (cf. pp. 106ff. and 174–5).

Nevertheless the vast commercial and maritime expansion of the high Middle Ages had other than political and economic repercussions. From Venice and Genoa, as from elsewhere in Europe, there came close and careful descriptions of alien societies displaying in their dispassionate precision all those virtues often assumed to be the peculiar products of later centuries. Whatever his weaknesses – his indifference to music, art and religion, his lack of curiosity about customs and institutions, his Baedeker-like passion for architectural remains – Marco Polo, who from 1273 was for nearly a quarter of a century in the service of the Mongol grand khan, was an acute and on the whole remarkably objective observer of the eastern world, relating as he claimed what he knew from his own direct experience or 'from those in whom he could put faith'. Nor was he by any means unique. The contemporary Catholic missions to the Orient often equalled and sometimes surpassed his achievement, whilst in the fifteenth century the Venetian Conti produced an outstanding and perceptive account of Indian civilization. Yet there is no reason to assume that the clarity, precision and objectivity of much of these writings were induced in their authors by the shock or surprise of encountering the peoples and societies they described. For one thing the growing influence of the classics from the twelfth century onwards encouraged the appeal to observation and experience even to the extent that some thinkers, such as Albert the Great, were led to reject the opinions of Antiquity itself on these very criteria. Meanwhile in the visual arts such assumptions were reinforced by other powerful influences. The illustrations of books of empirical science – classical and Arabic in inspiration – intensified in its demand for the accurate depiction of natural phenomena that interest in the realistic representation of plants and animals long present in medieval art. And not unreasonably when patrons commissioned paintings of persons or places, as they did in Italy from the 1300s onwards, they expected to receive identifiable likenesses.

Moreover, these same qualities were inculcated and stimulated by the even more practical demands of commerce and seafaring. Merchants who hoped to prosper and seamen who aspired to sail again had of necessity to be capable of careful, concise and accurate descriptions of anything from landfalls and the run of coasts to the demands and opportunities of markets. And this was increasingly the case with the development of long-distance commerce, such as that of the Genoese and Venetians to northern Europe and the east. Business was no longer decided by the skill and acumen of an itinerant merchant, but was now commonly directed from home with the whole enterprise dependent on frequent and detailed written communication, the keeping of records, and the transmission of accurate information and precise instructions.[40] Merchants were accordingly exhorted to write – 'never spare the pen' the thirteenth-century tyro was urged – to describe, to keep their books in order. But more than this they were encouraged to write on particular things in a particular way. In Genoa in the 1300s a master could be hired to teach the young 'merchant style'; in Venice the putative business man could learn, like his modern counterpart, to improve his memory to enable him to recall with greater facility facts and figures. Hence the flow from the thirteenth century onwards of books of 'merchant practice' describing the opportunities and conventions of various markets, and hence, too, the flow of charts and sailing directions so carefully compiled and corrected. Little wonder, as Boccaccio observed, that merchants wrote to each other 'not so much letters as volumes'. And little wonder either that those trained in such traditions, like Polo and Conti, could write as they did on the worlds that they saw, or that the reports of Venetian ambassadors should come to enjoy the reputation they did.

Thus as a result of the changing nature and pattern of commerce the tendency towards realism, accuracy and even objectivity already existing in European civilization was powerfully reinforced. The observant, tolerant and receptive nature of Venetian and Genoese culture needs, that is, no extra-European explanation – and indeed, as in any other empire, these very qualities were all too prone to evaporate when entrepreneurs were presented with the opportunity to exploit native peoples. 'This is a land of beasts' wrote a Venetian of Syria in 1506. And when alien or for that matter western societies were judged, either implicitly or explicitly, the terms of reference were naturally enough European, which is to say inherited by some route or other from Antiquity. Primitive peoples who failed to meet the political criteria established by Aristotle were therefore, as were Africans and Amerindians to many Iberians later, barbarians or worse, unacquainted with civilized human life and to be treated accordingly (cf. pp. 327, 362). To Polo the inhabitants of the Nicobars appeared as 'wild animals' living without laws or organization. And with the passage of time the classics spoke with increasing authority. The Corsicans – fierce and ungovernable – were to a Genoese of 1470 'in a state of barbarism'; the Portuguese, according to a Florentine in 1486 were laudably engaged in leading the benighted Africans 'from bestial towards human existence';[41] in 1543 an eminent Venetian expressed the view that his compatriots had long dealt with many 'barbarous nations'.

Yet if experience of alien societies hardly affected medieval man's way of thinking, the voyages of merchants, missionaries and scholars capable of accurate and reasonably dispassionate observation led to the appearance of a considerable volume of geographical literature. Even this, however, like its better known counterpart of the sixteenth and seventeenth centuries, made remarkably little impact on European civilization (cf. pp. 282, 361). True, the geographical information gathered and recorded strengthened belief in the possibility of reaching Asia by circumnavigating Africa and eventually influenced – and with important consequences – cartographic representations of the world. Ultimately and momentously, too, Polo's glowing description of the east was to fire the imagination of Christopher Columbus (see p. 302). Moreover the discoveries of medieval travellers appeared to confirm a classical assumption as to the existence of inhabited lands antipodal to Europe. But any suggestion of regions unknown and peoples unexplained was unacceptable to the Catholic church which held all humanity to be descended from Adam and Eve and that the teachings of Christ had reached the ends of the earth. Hence to accommodate the new geographical information theologians argued that there existed a landmass unbroken by oceans, and thus totally accessible, yet so vast that peoples of a common origin could inhabit its opposite extremities in mutual ignorance. But such metaphysical triumphs marked no overthrow of traditional modes of thought – the very opposite in fact – and the authority of the church was no more weakened than was that of the classics, even though a scholar in the bliss of discovery might maintain (1448) that as a result of Conti's journeys many of the opinions of Antiquity about India had become untenable.

Some of the literature of travel was indeed to enjoy a remarkable popularity. Over a hundred manuscripts of Polo's narrative have survived, and his was the first vernacular book by an Italian author to pass (in translation) into general European circulation. But its appeal was not that of a work of erudition but of a collection of those *mirabilia* – fantastic and unusual happenings – so dear to the medieval mind, as the enormous success of Sir John Mandeville's mythical travels showed. Less colourful descriptions of voyages or exotic lands were on the other hand lost, forgotten or ignored. Nor was this merely the inescapable reward of dullness, for not even Polo made a serious impact in artistic and literary circles. Dante ignores him completely, drawing his Asia from Pliny and those two unequalled collectors of astonishing information, Solinus and Isidore of Seville. So, too, Boccaccio is more indebted to learned tradition for his opinions on the east than to the experiences of those contemporary merchants, with whom he was clearly well-acquainted, who had been there. And Chaucer, as realistic as any concerning his fellows, writes vaguely and conventionally about India, whilst d'Ailly, in his *Imago Mundi* (written *c.*1400 and published in 1483) reiterates traditional fantasies as to the wonders of the east. Meanwhile – and hardly surprisingly – the discoveries were largely ignored by the authors of that courtly literature in which for centuries there had luxuriated the richest growth of improbabilities about the Orient. Writers might occasionally embellish their plots with some suitable incidentals from Polo or Antiquity, but as the realities of the east became better known to their readers they simply substituted purely fictional settings and equally impossible marvels, as when in Ariosto's *Orlando Furioso* a hero departs for the moon from Ethiopia.

Such resolute indifference to alien societies was not peculiarly medieval. The same attitudes re-appeared in sixteenth-century Iberia leading some humanists, such as the Portuguese historian Barros, to castigate their compatriots for their lack of curiosity about the New Worlds (cf. p. 282). Nor was the situation substantially different in imperial Britain in the eighteenth and nineteenth centuries. In general man is most concerned with the most apparent, and whatever the marvels reported from strange places they can rarely compete, at least for long, with more pressing local matters. At the same time new facts and new opinions have to contend with established conventions of thought and taste, which in the late medieval and early modern centuries meant a respect for the classics, an obsession with law and religion, and a delight in chivalric and other fantasies. In these tales of wonder and imagination the east, like the paradises of other fertile minds elsewhere, abounds in all those things so sadly lacking or unhappily prohibited in Europe (cf. pp. 8, 40). It is the land of immeasurable wealth and limitless promise; the home of man in the primeval bliss of the Golden Age, where were freely practised among women of superlative beauty and ready availability all the forbidden pleasures of the flesh – nudity, polygamy, incest, eroticism. Compared with this, reality, even as depicted by Polo, had little to offer.

Nor was the impact of the west on the east any more profound. The Chinese possibly acquired, as a result of the commercial expansion of the high Middle Ages, some idea of the geography of Asia Minor. A handful of Indians, Tartars and Chinese were momentarily converted to Catholicism, though Christianity in some form or other was already well known in the Far East before the appearance of the European missions of the thirteenth and fourteenth centuries. But in the politics of Persia, India and China the west had no influence. Individuals like Polo might serve the Mongols, but not even as communities did western merchants have the numerical strength or resources to affect, had they so wished, the course of events. Nor, as far as can be seen, was the economy of the east in any way altered as a result of European demand, or through the penetration to Asia of European merchants. Venice and Genoa did not create some new economic relationship between east and west but rather reinvigorated, and in some degree re-routed, a trade already centuries old. Similarly, though the activities of the two republics hastened the decline of Arab and Greek commercial and maritime power in the Mediterranean, they did not in themselves cause it, no more than they were in the long run responsible for the collapse of the Byzantine empire and the westward advance of the Ottomans. Elsewhere their impact was more evident. They converted much of the littoral of the Black Sea to a supplier of primary products to the west, whilst by providing the Mamelukes with slaves they assisted the growth of the Egyptian military state. Yet vigorous and efficient though their slaving was, it was the continuation of a commerce both well established before their arrival and long enduring after their departure. Then again, the intensive agrarian exploitation of their colonial possessions in the eastern Mediterranean by the Venetians, and to a lesser extent by the Genoese, brought a radical change in the agriculture of a limited area. But neither the crops nor the techniques were new and the overall economy of the Levant was barely affected.

Nevertheless the very presence and behaviour of Italians in onetime Byzantine lands both exacerbated relations with indigenous populations – to the point that by the 1500s most of the colonial peasantry were willing to welcome the Turks – and inspired among many literate Greeks a feeling if not of nationalism certainly of loyalty to Byzantine traditions (cf. pp. 144, 187).

The most enduring memorial of empire, however, is not political or economic but cultural – the transmission to, and survival in, colonial territories of the architecture, language and customs of the imperial power. Thus in Chios and the Crimea there appeared – as were later to appear in Latin America buildings in the Iberian baroque and in British India those in English neo-gothic – characteristically Genoese fortifications and private dwellings. In the Venetian possessions there likewise spread, particularly during the sixteenth century, the city's grand imperial styles. Venetian fortifications can still be seen in Cyprus, Candia had a ducal palace and Padua a Venetian-inspired clock tower. At Verona, Belluno and elsewhere there were set up not only impressive defence works but also those massive Venetian gateways like triumphal arches which dramatically proclaimed the republic's rule. Nor were these the only cultural repercussions of subjection. Where, as in Crete, there was a vigorous and Christian indigenous civilization; where Greeks and Italians intermarried; where colonials studied in the universities of the ruling state – as Cretans did at Padua; and where in towns differences of race and social standing were obscured, there appeared that same fusion of cultures which in differing degrees had occurred or was to occur in other empires (cf. pp. 290 and 353). Already in the early 1400s Crete had in Leonardo Dellaporta a poet Italian in name yet Orthodox in religion and outlook, who wrote in Greek works in which themes of biblical and patristic inspiration mingled with those drawn, not to say lifted, from Byzantine history and romance. And by the sixteenth century there were Cretan authors who, under Italian influence, could compose alike pseudo-Senecan tragedies or Venetian comedies. In art the Venetians introduced to the island themes formerly unknown to vernacular painters, possibly modified the rigid forms of Cretan tradition and gave to Greek icon painters new western settings for customary Orthodox figures. Nor were such fusions only at the level of prosperous eclecticism, for in one Cretan dialect alone there are even now something like 1000 words of Italian origin.

But as with Rome in Antiquity, or Britain in the nineteenth century, the influence of Venice and Genoa penetrated far beyond the regions under their immediate control. Merchants, seamen, entrepreneurs and adventurers spread their language, techniques and customs far and wide. Italian came into general use for commerce in the Mediterranean, whilst the Venetian dialect influenced indigenous speech in Cyprus and the Slav lands of the Adriatic and the Balkans, besides providing Turkish and Byzantine Greek with many of their nautical terms. Similarly Venetian styles affected the art of Dalmatia and Serbia, and indeed whole areas of the Mediterranean and southern Europe took on in some degree or other a Venetian or Genoese appearance.

Long before the taste of the continent was dominated by Italy, the architecture of
Germany, from Augsburg along the Lech, was that of Venice – reflecting the closest of
economic ties. Along the Wertach, and for similar reasons, it was that of Genoa. In the
Greek-speaking Ionian islands and the Slav world of the eastern Adriatic, upper-class
life was very largely modelled on that of Venice. So close was the emulation of Italian
precept in the independent republic of Ragusa by the 1500s – children educated at
Padua; the native ruling oligarchs furnished with bogus Italian pedigrees – that the city
was to all intents Italian: Italian in appearance and Italian in practice, with its business
conducted in Italian and its records written almost exclusively in Italian. And even after
Cyprus had been lost to the Turks and repopulated with Anatolian peasants, the
inhabitants, a visitor remarked in the mid-seventeenth century, 'both men and women,
were dressed in the Italian way'. Such was the indelibility of the imperial imprint.

Bibliographical note

There are few archival and literary sources for the history of medieval and early modern Europe
– those of the south and Iberia especially – which do not throw some light on Genoese activities.
The former republic's own archives – the Archivio di Stato di Genova, briefly described in *Atti
della Società Ligure Storia Patria* n.s.3 (1963), 276ff. – are of a wealth and abundance that have
so far discouraged historians from attempting their extensive exploitation. The Archivio
Notariale is the most ancient collection of notarial minutes in Europe. The earliest (1154–64)
alone record 1300 Acts and the series extends, in 17,500 volumes, up to the nineteenth century.
With its precise and detailed information on shipping, trade, finance, political organization and
every aspect of social life this notarial evidence is of immense value. Its nature, the difficulties of
handling it and the results it can yield are indicated in the works of G.I. Bratianu (see p. 221),
in vol. I of R. Doehaerd, *Les Relations Commerciales entre Gênes, La Belgique et L'Outrement*
(3 vols, Rome-Brussels, 1941), and also in the introduction to P. Argenti, *The Occupation
of Chios by the Genoese and their Administration of the Island, 1346–1566* (Cambridge, 1958, I).
Many notarial minutes and instruments have been published in the *Atti della Soc. Ligure*.

In the section *Manoscritti* of the Archivio di Stato there is material relating to the
administration of the medieval republic (*Reformationes*) and to the affairs of various patrician
families. In the Archivio Secreto there are treaties (*Politicorum*) and details of relations with
neighbouring powers (*Confinium*). Of outstanding value to the maritime historian is the
Archivio di San Giorgio. From this the *Gabella Marinariorum* (1482) records details of ships,
voyages and crews. Similar material for 1485 occurs in the *Gabella Securitatis*, whilst for 1423
there is a register of cargo manifests of imports (*Caratorum Sancti Georgii Registri; Sala* 38 no.
543), and another of customs levied on vessels arriving in Genoa in 1458 (*Sala* 38/54, no. 1553).

In addition to the rich resources of the Archivio di Stato there are the records of the Archivio
Civico di Genova and the Archivio dei Padri del Commune, amongst which (*Filza*, I, no.3) are
listed ships held for debts in Genoa. In the Biblioteca Universitaria di Genova there survive
ordnances relating to shipping (B VI.15; *Officium Gazarie*).

As well as selections of archival material some of the early, if less remarkable, literary sources for the history of the city have been published. The *Registrum Curiae*, drawn up in 1143 and later amplified, which contains details of the commune's liberties and titles to property was edited in 2 vols by L.T. Belgrano (Genoa, 1862, 1887). He also edited the important *Annali Genovesi di Caffaro* (2 vols, Rome, 1890, 1901), the officially compiled record of events in the city taken to 1163 by Caffaro and to the end of the twelfth century by continuators who were eyewitnesses of much they report. The *Liber Jurium*, a thirteenth-century compilation intended to preserve Genoa's most ancient archives, was published together with other early material, by C. Imperiale, *Codice Diplomatico della Repubblica di Genova* (3 vols, Rome, 1936–42). Guiseppe Felloni discusses a census of the city for 1531–5 in *Atti della Soc. Ligure* n.s.4 (1964). This journal, published in Genoa, prints articles and documents in Genoese history, as also does from time to time the *Rivista Storica italiana*. Since 1958 the University of Genoa has produced collections of essays (*Miscellanea Storica Ligure*), some dealing with topics of Genoese or more general maritime history (see p. 223).

Genoa lacks a modern general history equalling Lane's magisterial survey of the Venetian past. It has, however, been the subject of a number of excellent if less ambitious works. G.I. Bratianu, *Recherches sur le Commerce Génois dans la Mer Noire au XIIIᵉ Siècle* (Paris, 1929) is a study by an outstanding east-European scholar whose career was tragically ended in the political upheavals of the post-war world. It covers a great deal more than its title suggests, and by an imaginative use of the city's notarial records presents a vivid and detailed picture of Genoese commercial policies, organization and activity in the east. R.S. Lopez, *Storia delle Colonie Genovesi nel Mediterraneo* (Bologna, 1938) is a brief, vigorous and patriotic survey of the whole field of Genoese expansion particularly enriched by the author's knowledge and use of the archives of his native city. The economic and political history of the republic is briefly outlined in the introduction (vol. I) to Doehaerd, *Les Relations*. In *The Cambridge Economic History of Europe*, M.M. Postan and E.E. Rich (Cambridge, 1952) vol. 2, R.S. Lopez enthusiastically evaluates the role of Genoa in the economy of medieval Europe. Erik Bach, *La Cité de Gênes au XIIᵉ Siècle* (Copenhagen, 1955) – a book of many bold and stimulating hypotheses – attempts to establish, by a close analysis of Genoa's earliest notarial collections, the nature and pattern of the city's commerce and the political and economic organization that sustained it. R.S. Lopez presents yet another brief and scintillating appreciation of Genoa's history and achievements in 'Le Marchand Génois', *Annales*, 13 (1958), 501ff. Notwithstanding its title vol.I of Argenti, *The Occupation of Chios by the Genoese*, based on exhaustive archival researches, covers the whole history of the republic in the late medieval and early modern centuries. The major modern work on medieval Genoa, dealing with every aspect of its economy and society is the magisterial survey by Jacques Heers, *Gênes au XVᵉ Siècle* (Paris, 1961). Many aspects of the city's later history are penetratingly discussed in F. Braudel, *The Mediterranean and the Mediterranean World in the Age of Philip II*, trs. by S. Reynolds (2 vols, 1972–3).

The commercial expansion of medieval Genoa is discussed in Doehaerd, *Les Relations* and more provocatively by V. Magalhães-Godinho, *L'Économie de l'Empire Portugais aux XVᵉ et XVIᵉ Siècles* (Paris, 1969). This remarkable, valuable and singularly ill-organized work is also available in a more luxurious and extensive format as *Os Descobrimentos e a Economia Mundial* (2 vols, Lisbon, 1963–5). The rise of the Italian maritime republics, and the course of their wars and rivalries, are excellently treated in Frederic Lane's *Venice, A Maritime Republic* (Baltimore, 1973). Genoese penetration of the Black Sea is discussed by Bratianu, *Recherches*, and further lines of inquiry are indicated by H. Bibicou, 'Sources Byzantines pour servir à l'Histoire Maritime', in *CIHM*, 4 (1962). Genoese commercial and political behaviour in the Levant and Asia Minor are examined by Anthony Luttrell, 'The Crusade in the Fourteenth Century', in *Europe in the Late Middle Ages*, ed. J.R. Hale, J.R.L. Highfield and B. Smalley (1965), and in important and stimulating papers by M.R.H. Bautier, M.J. Richard and M.M. Balard in *CIHM*, 8 (1970).

The arrival of the Genoese (and other Italians) in Asia is brilliantly outlined by R.S. Lopez in *The Journal of Economic History*, 3 (1943), 164ff., and the nature of European commerce with the Far East searchingly examined in papers by M.R.H. Bautier, M.E. Baratier and M.J. Richard in *CIHM*, 8 (1970).

For the medieval bullion trade and Genoa's role in it I have relied on the already cited article of A.M. Watson, 'Back to Gold – and Silver' in *Ec. Hist. Rev*, XX (1967). Genoa's penetration of the Atlantic is examined (for the north) by A.A. Ruddock, *Italian Merchants and Shipping in Southampton, 1270–1600* (Southampton, 1951), and (for the west and south) in R. Mauny's brief but important *Les Navigations Médiévales sur les Côtes Sahariennes antérieures à la Découverte Portugaise* (Lisbon, 1960).

In addition to the information in the general works already noticed, Genoa's political and social evolution are usefully discussed by Diane Owen Hughes in *P&P*, 66 (1975), 3ff. The republic's commerce in the late Middle Ages and early modern centuries has been the subject of a number of important studies based on the city's rich archives. Its general nature and pattern are established by Heers, *Gênes*. The period 1495–1537 is minutely scrutinized by Domenico Gioffre in *Studi in Onore di Amintore Fanfani*, V (6 vols, Milan, 1962) and the alum trade by Jean Delumeau also in A. Guiffrè (ed.) *Studi . . . Fanfani*, vol. IV. Genoese slaving is examined, with a wealth of statistics, in Domenico Gioffre's *Il Mercato degli Schiavi a Genova nel Secolo XV* (Genoa, 1971). Relations with south Spain are briefly noticed by Alvaro Castillo Pintado, *Trafico Maritimo y Comercio de Importacion en Valencia a Comienzos del Siglo XVII* (Madrid, 1967). Genoas' role in the Spanish slave trade to the Americas in the sixteenth century is established by Ruth Pike, *Enterprise and Adventure: The Genoese in Seville and the Opening of the New World* (Cornell, 1966).

Genoa's economic colonization of Spain from the fifteenth century onwards is discussed in Heers, *Gênes* and Pike, *Enterprise*. It is usefully outlined in John Lynch, *Spain under the Habsburgs* (2 vols, Oxford, 1964–9) and most perceptively by Braudel in his indispensable *Mediterranean*. Of fundamental importance is the contribution of Felipe Ruiz Martin, 'Las Finanzas de la Monarquia Hispanica y la Liga Santa' to G. Benzoni (ed.), *Il Mediterraneo nella seconda meta del 500 alla luce di Lepanto* (Florence, 1974). Genoa's role in the early oceanic expansion of Spain is examined in detail by Pike, *Enterprise*, and re-assessed by Heers in *CIHM*, 5 (1966). The part played by Genoese skills and experience in shaping the nature of Spain's control and exploitation of her oceanic possessions is stressed by Charles Verlinden, *Les Origines de la Civilisation Atlantique* (Paris, 1966), re-stating the conclusions of the author's many earlier papers. Genoa's influence in the Canaries is examined by Manuela Marrero in *Studi . . . Fanfani*, vol V and the presence of the Genoese in seventeenth-century Peru is noticed by Marie Helmer in *Jahrbuch für Geschichte von Staat, Wirtschaft und Gesellschaft Lateinamerikas*, 2 (1965).

Genoese economic influence in Portugal is outlined by Charles Verlinden, 'La Colonie italienne de Lisbonne', in *Studi in Onore di Armando Sapori* (2 vols, Milan, 1957), 615ff., and its persistence demonstrated by J. Gentil da Silva, *Stratégie des Affaires à Lisbonne entre 1595–1607* (Paris, 1956). The significance of Genoa in Portugal's early imperial expansion is argued by Verlinden in *Congresso Internacional de Historia dos Descobrimentos*, *Actas* III (Lisbon, 1961) and more cautiously by Virginia Rau and J. Gentil da Silva in *CIHM*, 5. The importance of the Genoese in the economy of the Portuguese Atlantic sugar islands is demonstrated by Virginia Rau and Jorge de Macedo, *O Açúcar da Madeira nos Fins do Século XV* (Funchal, 1962) and in Brazil and the Angolan slave trade by F. Mauro, *Le Portugal et l'Atlantique au XVIIᵉ Siècle, 1570–1670* (Paris, 1960). There are many references to the Genoese in Portugal and the Portuguese empire scattered through Godinho, *Os Descobrimentos*.

The rise of Genoa as a maritime power is traced in Eugene H. Byrne, *Genoese Shipping in the Twelfth and Thirteenth Centuries* (Cambridge, Mass., 1930) which uses to good effect the city's notarial archives. There is important material on the changing nature of the Genoese shipping industry and the evolution of the carrack in the late Middle Ages in Heers, *Gênes*. A mass of new and important information on every aspect of Genoese shipping is brought together in the articles collected in *Guerra e Commercio nell'Evoluzione della Marina Genovese tra XV e XVII Secolo*, published in *Miscellanea Storica Ligure* (Genoa, 1970). The construction and appearance of medieval Genoese ships are convincingly re-examined by J.E. Dotson in *MM*, 59 (1973), 161ff.

Genoese policies in eastern Europe in the republic's declining years are examined by G. Musso, 'Nuove ricerche d'archivio su Genova e l'Europa centro-orientale nell'ultimo Medio Evo' in *Rivista Storica Italiana*, 83 (1971), 130ff. The changing fortunes of the port of Genoa in the sixteenth and seventeenth centuries, the volume of its trade and the growing predominance of north-European shipping are detailed in two important articles by E. Grendi in *Rivista Storica Italiana*, 80 (1968) and 83 (1971).

The business methods of Venice and Genoa and their influence on those of the rest of Europe are usefully studied in vol. III of *The Cambridge Economic History of Europe*, to which should be added the article of Alfred E. Lieber in *Ec. Hist. Rev*, XXI (1968), 230ff. The important Mediterranean contribution to the development of navigational techniques is splendidly explained in E.G.R. Taylor, *The Haven-Finding Art* (1956). Cartography is briefly and authoritatively surveyed by G.R. Crone, *Maps and their Makers* (1962). To these two works should be added such specialist studies as those of Messrs Beaujouan and Poulle in *CIHM*, 1 (1957), Commandant Denoix in *CIHM*, 3 (1960), and Comandante Teixeira da Mota in *CIHM*, 5 (1966).

My discussion of the importance of Genoa and Venice in the changing culture of late medieval and Renaissance Italy and Europe has drawn heavily on D.F. Lach's massive *Asia in the making of Europe* (2 vols, Chicago, 1965–70); the brilliant *Imperial Age of Venice, 1380–1580* (1970) of D.S. Chambers; John Larner's equally outstanding *Culture and Society in Italy, 1290–1420* (1971); Oliver Logan, *Culture and Society in Venice, 1470–1790* (1972); and Lane's *Venice*. I have also, in the matters of Italian views of alien societies and the fusion of cultures, made extensive use of the articles by Jacques Le Goff and M. Cortelazzo in M. Cortelazzo (ed.), *Mediterraneo e Oceano Indio* (Florence, 1970). I have likewise greatly benefited from the many writers who, in *Venezia e l'Oriente fra Tardo Medioevo e Rinascimento*, ed. Agostino Pertusi (Florence, 1966) illuminate the cultural relations of Venice with the east.

5

Portugal

∞

I *The empire of India*

In 1483, wrote the learned chronicler of the great city of Nürnburg, a Portuguese fleet sailing down the West African coast crossed 'the equinoctial line to enter another world for which the Genoese had for years searched in vain'. The detail is disputable but the message true enough. In the mid-1400s the Portuguese had no more than some fragile footholds in a number of Atlantic islands and on the littorals of West and North-west Africa. Half a century later they had rounded the Cape of Good Hope, penetrated to India and – probably by accident rather than design – touched on the coast of Brazil, so laying the foundations of an empire which at its brief zenith stretched from South China to the backlands of the Brazilian Matto Grosso, and embraced possessions or rights of some sort in every habitable continent except Australia. Yet in a sense this astonishing feat was merely the fulfilment of medieval Italian aspirations. Like contemporary Castile, and like Venice and Genoa earlier, the Portuguese in the decisive years of their empire-building were largely driven on by hopes of direct access to the riches of Asia and Africa. And their achievement was equally medieval in that together with the maritime expansion of other Atlantic powers it marked the culmination of that steady extension of European influence and authority which had already taken the Norse to America and the Germans to Russia, and which ultimately – in the early seventeenth century, at the very time the Iberian empires were at their apogee – was to bring the Russians themselves to the Pacific.

But as the Portuguese were well aware, there was much more to what they had accomplished than this. Like the Venetians they were conscious imperialists, and the first in modern times to deliberately plan and undertake sustained expansion outside Europe. The growth of their empire was, in comparison with that of the Spanish in America, slow and spasmodic, yet Portuguese colonial rule was to outlive, in however attenuated a form, that of most other European states. Moreover, their voyages and conquests marked the beginning of that European subjugation and exploitation of most of the rest of the world which was to last into the twentieth century, just as the establishment of their power in Asia ended that age-old pattern in which the east – whether Arab, Mongol or Turk – was a threat actual or potential to the west. And together with, and indeed overshadowed by the Spaniards, the Portuguese were responsible for the last great mass conversions to Christianity. Often enough, they employed downright violence, following that biblical precept 'compel them to come in'.

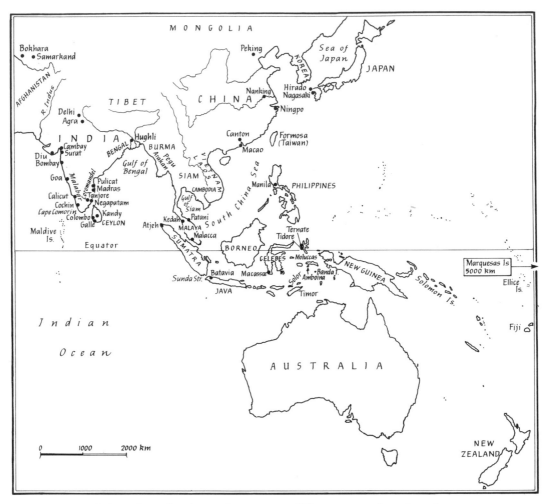

5   Asia *c.*1600, showing major centres of European trade and settlement

Nevertheless the behaviour of the Iberians was unique in that unlike most would-be conquerers of distant lands – the Germans in eastern Europe in the early medieval centuries and the Latin crusaders apart – they were in some degree inspired by a desire to spread the Christian religion, and remarkably successful in doing so. Furthermore if Asia, which absorbed most of Portugal's energies until the late sixteenth century, was by no means unknown to medieval western Europe, the knowledge was to say the least imperfect, and the contacts fragile. But after 1500, as the result of Spanish and Portuguese voyages, not only Asia and Europe, but almost the whole world was brought into enduring association. To Iberian men of letters, steeped in the marvels of

Antiquity, it rightly seemed that here at last the achievements of Greece and Rome had been eclipsed.

The roots of Portuguese expansion lay in those Christian assaults on a weakening Moslem power in the early Middle Ages, and the later and largely Italian penetration of Africa and the North Atlantic (see pp. 163ff.). The Portuguese attacked Ceuta in the twelfth century, other parts of the Moroccan coast in the following 200 years, and backed or participated in some of the mainly Genoese voyages to the Canaries in the early 1300s (see p. 164). Then in 1415, after a lull as Genoa turned to other interests and Portugal herself was involved in dynastic and European difficulties, a Portuguese army took Ceuta, so beginning in characteristic style an association with Africa only recently dissolved. What underlay the attack is unknown. Through war and trade with the Moors of the north, and from Christian contact with Moslem and Jewish merchants and scholars in reconquered Spain, European knowledge of Africa had been growing since the twelfth century. The Genoese had in some fashion mapped the interior of the continent in the early 1300s, the importance of the Niger basin as a supplier of gold was known and recorded by a Majorcan cartographer in 1339, a direct passage to this 'River of Gold' was attempted by a Catalan seaman a few years later and the caravan routes from North Africa to Negro Guinea were shown in the great Catalan Atlas of 1375 (see pp. 164, 170). Whether the Portuguese knew much of this and of the growing African commerce of Venice and Genoa is doubtful. They may indeed have had their hopes of gold and of access to the rich agricultural resources of the Maghreb. But there was little in their subsequent behaviour in Morocco to suggest that this insignificant and backward kingdom was inspired by any such purposeful imperialism. More likely Portuguese hopes were of a less sophisticated order – an opportunity for the royal princes to be knighted in battle against Islam; prospects of plundering infidel commerce and seizing infidel hostages for ransom; the diversion of aristocratic delight in violence and loot into some conveniently neighbouring, but happily alien, land.

Then, *c.* 1419, there commenced a series of voyages down the West African coast which by 1460 had brought the Portuguese some 4000km south to Sierra Leone, and seen their discovery and colonization of Madeira, the Azores and the Cape Verde Islands. These were by no means unknown waters, notwithstanding stories of terrors that deterred all seamen. On some of them, including probably those of the Saharan coast, the Genoese had sailed in the thirteenth and fourteenth centuries. The Normans were in the Canaries and on the adjacent mainland in the early 1400s, and by 1415 there was some knowledge, probably from Iberian fishermen, of what lay beyond Cape Juby (see pp. 163–4 and 148). Even so, the Portuguese undertaking was formidable enough. The low-lying north-west coast of the vast African continent offers the sailor little shelter – and along its Saharan fringe small prospect of food and water – and its few recognizable features are usually obscured by spray from seas breaking on off-shore banks. Then from Senegambia – with its estuaries and towns – to the modern Freetown the coast is lined with islets, rocks and shoals. After Freetown comes a succession of lagoons and swamps, briefly relieved by the sandy beaches of Ghana, before more lagoons and swamps culminate in the gigantic morass of the Niger delta.

Why the Portuguese should have so doggedly contended with such hazards, in voyages which for a quarter of a century offered them little more than a few slaves and some sealskins and oil, is uncertain. The pious may have dreamed of souls to be won for Christ, or of a meeting with the supposedly mighty Christian potentate, Prester John; the rest of wealth so clearly lacking at home. But there is little to suggest that the voyages were undertaken as a result of information acquired in Morocco, where the Portuguese spent most of their time in pointless skirmishing and looting. Yet here they could have learned not only, as they did, of the commerce linking the Maghreb with lands south of the Sahara, but also – through the Middle East – with the orient. This eastern trade was, however, still unknown to them in the late fifteenth century, and only reported as a matter of wonder from the Red Sea in the early 1500s (see pp. 232, 234). With no real reason for their continuance, and indeed with many against, the voyages might well have been abandoned but for the determination of prince Henry (the Infante Dom Henrique) an enigmatic and elusive figure, unsuccessful alike in politics, war and business and who, though he never sailed on an expedition of discovery, has ironically become known to posterity as 'the Navigator' through the admiration of a nineteenth-century English scholar. Yet though the prince was personally responsible for probably no more than a quarter of the African voyages made before his death (1460), it was he who financed the discovery and colonization of Madeira (*c.* 1420) and the Azores (1427), and who sustained the initially unrewarding exploration of the African coast (see pp. 245ff.). But once, from the 1440s, it was clear that West Africa offered gold, slaves and similar delights the interest of others was aroused, and the pace of advance quickened.

Even so, there was no inexorable drive down the coast. Cape Bojador (in fact probably the modern Cape Juby) was not cleared till 1434, and Cape Verde not until the 1470s. In the 1430s such chimerical ventures were opposed at the Portuguese court on both practical and moral grounds, and Portuguese energies in any case diverted into a campaign against Tangier in 1437. Nor were these hesitations and inconsistencies, reflecting the course of high politics, the only obstacle. In the tropics uncontrollable disease killed men on shore, and the fearful heat decimated overclad crews crowded into tiny ships. Then expeditions sailing inshore to explore the coast encountered beyond the Canaries winds and currents setting roughly south, certainly speeding the outward passage, but giving ships with a poor windward performance a hard and prolonged struggle to get back home. Though, as later Canarian fishermen showed, it is possible to beat northward through these waters by a careful use of prevailing and land breezes, the Portuguese eventually found – in roughly the mid-1400s – that by standing well out to sea they could pick up following winds for Europe. And in the same way it was appreciated by the 1480s that on a southern passage the calms south of Cape Verde could be avoided by holding across to South America – as yet unknown – for a favourable wind.

By the time of Henry's death Portuguese persistence had thus been vindicated. The Atlantic islands were in profitable cultivation, and a trading base had been established (1443) at Arguim, in what is now Mauritania (see pp. 245ff.). Better was still to come. The purposeful direction once provided by the Infante was in the ensuing decades supplied first by Fernão Gomes – merchant, soldier and admiral in the style of Benedetto Zaccaria – to whom the king leased responsibility for exploring the African coast (1469), and then by the outstandingly able and vigorous prince John (João), the future king John II. Portuguese ships were off the Ivory Coast in 1470, crossed the equator in 1473, sighted the island of São Tomé the following year, and by 1483 had entered 'that most powerful river', the congo (see pp. 253ff.). Meanwhile, with equal determination, Portugal secured from the papacy extensive rights in and beyond Africa, and in a bloodthirsty war at sea scotched a growing Spanish commerce with West Africa, obliging the Spaniards to recognize (1479) – at least on paper – her monopoly of the whole trade of the West African coast (see pp. 301–2). Such successes brought even grander ambitions, and the wealth to sustain them, and by the 1470s, if not earlier, the Portuguese were seeking a route to Asia.

The wealth and splendours of the east, and the existence there of Christian – albeit unfortunately Nestorian – communities were widely known in the later Middle Ages. They were described in missionary narratives of the thirteenth and fourteenth centuries, and in the aimiable nonsense of the mythical Sir John Mandeville, reinforced by garbled reminiscences of the geographical lore of Antiquity and reports of the colourful travels of the Venetians Polo and Conti (see pp. 99, 215). At the same time Catholic Europe's search for an ally against Islam, and the papacy's brief enthusiasm for oecumenicism in the early fifteenth century, brought a sprinkling of oriental Christians to the west. From this sprang discussion as to the nature and whereabouts of the realms of the Christian emperor Prester John, sited anywhere from Ethiopia to between Africa and 'Middle India', or envisaged as stretching from eastern Africa to the Niger.[1] Asia itself appears in a recognizable form in the Catalan Atlas of 1375 and, as we have seen, in subsequent world maps (see p. 208). That, as was understood by missionaries in the early 1300s, it might be accessible by sea, was increasingly admitted, the voyages of Polo alone suggesting that this must be the case. Men of learning knew the world to be round, and in the 1200s Ramon Lull wrote of the possibility of a westward passage to Asia – perhaps attempted by the Vivaldis – whilst in the following century Mandeville explained how the earth could be circumnavigated (see pp. 163–4).

These influential opinions were reinforced by a growing acquaintance with classical learning, and in particular by the re-discovery in the early 1400s of some of the works of the geographers of Antiquity. Aristotle was reported to have written that the ocean crossing from Spain to the Indies was a matter of days, and Strabo recorded with equal authority that only a want of resolution had prevented its accomplishment. The world as depicted in Ptolemy's compendious *Geography* – known from about 1410 – admittedly left much to be desired. Outside Europe he has a broad and truncated Africa, an even more abbreviated India, and Ceylon enormously enlarged. Beyond

India is the huge peninsula of the Golden Chersonese, a vast arm of the sea ('The Great Gulf') to its east, and further east still, the land of the Sinae. The Indian Ocean is indeed land-locked, with southern Africa joining the country of the Sinae. But India and Asia are stretched eastwards, Africa, reaching south of the equator, is presumed habitable – as some medieval sages had already concluded – and the size of the earth is grossly underestimated. Equally encouragingly, Strabo had the entire shores of Asia washed by the Ocean Sea and India projecting into the Atlantic. Contemporary theologians were similarly accomodating. Constrained by biblical authority to deny the existence of lands harbouring humans of any other species, subtle exegesists postulated a world landmass (island of the earth) either so great as to encompass the entire globe, or so small as to be limited to the northern hemisphere, leaving the rest of the world water interspersed with insignificant islands (cf. p. 217). One way or another, therefore, across the Atlantic or round Africa – held by many in the mid-fifteenth century to be circumnavigable – Asia could be reached by sea.

How this was to be done, and with what degree of danger and difficulty, was less certain. In the early 1400s Cardinal d'Ailly, a man of massive if indiscriminate learning, argued on one occasion for the near proximity of Morocco to eastern Asia, and on another for an eastward voyage lasting about a year. Similar views are implicit in many of the great world maps drawn after 1415 (see p. 208), and in 1474 the Italian cosmographer Toscanelli – scion of a merchant house dealing in spices rather than pious hopes and colourful fictions – informed a representative of the king of Portugal that the great Chinese city of Quinsay lay on the same latitude as Lisbon, some 5000 nautical miles (roughly 9260km) westward. Even better, it could be reached in a passage conveniently punctuated by agreeable stopping places – those many islands with which medieval imagination had peppered the Atlantic. The celebrated Behaim Globe of 1492 tells much the same story, and in the following year an erudite German vainly urged the Portuguese to undertake the voyage – which, of course, Christopher Columbus, seeking intimations of the grand khan of China in the Caribbean, thought himself to have accomplished (see pp. 302ff.).

The impact of these ideas in Portugal is uncertain. Prince Henry's own geographical learning was characteristically none of the latest, even if other members of the dynasty were less conservative.[2] According to contemporary and near contemporary sources, one of the Infante's most cherished ambitions was to learn 'of the Indies and of Prester John', and to open a sea route to those lands where there dwelt 'Indians who are said to worship the name of Christ'. This, and other scraps of evidence, suggest hopes of India itself – where the tomb of the Nestorian apostle St Thomas had long been visited by European pilgrims – rather than some desire for a closer acquaintance with the homeland of those Ethiopian Christians who could be met in the Portuguese capital from the 1450s (see p. 229). On the prince's instructions an expedition of 1456 or 1458 carried an interpreter expert in what is unhelpfully described as 'Indian', the Mauro map prepared in Venice for the Portuguese crown shows a ship sailing eastwards

Fig. 10   Heavily-armed galleon, possibly Iberian, from the engraving, *c.* 1565, by H.
Cock of a painting by Pieter Breughel showing shipping at Messina.

off southern Africa and in 1459 the Portuguese were in contact with Toscanelli, the
arch-protagonist of a maritime route to Asia (see p. 208). More significantly still, in
the second half of the fifteenth century their ships ascended as best they could the great
rivers found in West Africa, seeking a way round or through the continent.

But only in the 1480s, under the forceful direction of king John II (1481–95), were

Portuguese ambitions clearly and closely defined. By then westward voyages into the Atlantic were apparently futile (see p. 246), whereas Africa, and what was thought to lie beyond, were increasingly attractive, with an amicable ruler discovered in the Congo, and rumours from Benin of some great Christian potentate inland (see pp. 253–4). Equally important, the Portuguese also knew from the experience of their merchants and seamen now regularly trading well into the Mediterranean – victualling Genoa; bringing in sugar from the Atlantic islands – something of the basis and imposing extent of Venetian wealth. Hence in 1487, as part of a uniquely systematic and co-ordinated reconnaissance, a fleet was sent out under Bartholomeu Dias. Its instructions, which have not survived, were presumably to find Prester John and the sea route round Africa to India, both now assumed to be near at hand. Nor was this all. The ships carried – as had earlier expeditions – stone columns to be erected to proclaim Portuguese sovereignty, and half a dozen kidnapped Africans to be put ashore on the unknown coasts of their native continent with samples of gold, silver and spices in the hope that like would attract like. Dias, one of a galaxy of exceptionally able early Portuguese commanders, worked down West Africa, reached and passed – without sighting it – its southern tip, and then followed (1488) a coast running east and north-east until halted, somewhere near the Great Fish River, by incipient mutiny. Thus prevented, as a contemporary put it, like Moses from entering the Promised Land, he turned back, this time identifying and naming the great southern cape Good Hope 'for the prospect it gave of the discovery of India'.[3]

At the same time as this voyage which, dwarfing the scale of all previous maritime endeavour, had brought the Portuguese roughly 11,000km south, there were overland expeditions to Asia. The first failed (1485 or 1486) from an elementary lack of Arabic – although the Portuguese had been trading in the eastern Mediterranean for several decades, and fighting in Morocco for several more (see pp. 251–2, 261–3). Then in 1487 came a more realistic attempt. Two members of the royal household, one (Covilhã) a diplomat, the other (Paiva) a former spy, and both fluent in Arabic, were to travel east to learn of Prester John 'and whether he bordered on the sea', and to discover the origins of the pepper and cinnamon which came to Venice 'through the land of the Moors'. In disguise, and fortified by the learning of Portuguese scholars who claimed to know – probably from Arabic sources – of a sea passage linking Ethiopia with the west,[4] the pair made their way to the Red Sea. Paiva disappeared, but Covilhã, travelling the ancient route from Aden, finally reached the western coast of India and then, possibly after visiting East Africa, returned to Cairo in 1490 or 1491. From here, so he later claimed, he sent the king a detailed account of India, including how the Indian Ocean might be entered by sailing through 'the seas of Guinea and making for the coast of Sofala'. This done, he once again set out eastwards on royal orders, only to end in captivity in Ethiopia, where his compatriots eventually found him living in admirable style.

Subsequent Portuguese behaviour – surprise at the wealth of the Moslem cities of

East Africa, an unfortunate confusion of Hindu temples with Christian churches, and an even more unfortunate failure to provide appropriate gifts for Indian rulers – suggests that this invaluable information was not known when Vasco da Gama's fleet sailed. This, however, was not until 1497. In the meanwhile there had been many other difficulties. Money was short, which perhaps explains the curious attempt to persuade the Fuggers to back a voyage to China (1493). John II died (1495) in the midst of a prolonged struggle with Spain over the division of the recently discovered New World, and there was by now strenuous opposition in Portugal to any such costly and potentially dangerous undertakings, only overcome by the determination of the new ruler, Dom Manuel I (1495–1521) (see pp. 261, 307). Da Gama's expedition was meticulously planned. It included several of the country's most experienced navigators, and its four ships were carefully prepared under the supervision of Bartholomeu Dias. In customary Portuguese style the commander was a man of suitably elevated birth from the royal household, a soldier and diplomat – fierce, formidable, and in behaviour anything but diplomatic. His commission was not for conquests, but to seek out the Christian sovereigns of the east, and to establish Portugal in the great trades of the orient. To this end he carried letters addressed to the ruler of Calicut and to Prester John, together with samples of the spices, gold and pearls so ardently desired.

Sailing from Lisbon, the fleet called at the Cape Verde Islands and then, clearly knowing the wind systems of the Atlantic, worked south-east and south before making a wide sweep westwards to reach the zone of the variable and westerly winds which blow beyond 20°s. Due east – or so they thought – of the Cape of Good Hope the ships turned and ran down the latitude.[5] After a passage of some 6000km, lasting ninety-three days out of sight of land, they found themselves off the southern extremity of West Africa. Da Gama had indeed failed to double the Cape, but in its boldness, difficulty and duration – roughly three times that of the first Columbus voyage – his achievement was a superlative feat of seamanship, unequalled till the circumnavigation of the globe begun by his compatriot Magellan and completed by Elcano (see p. 319). There followed disappointing encounters with yet more primitive peoples, a hard struggle past Good Hope, and a slow progress up the south-east African coast before the Portuguese touched, in the southern Indian Ocean, the fringe of the world they had long sought.

It was, however, no great realm providently subject to some magnificent and well-disposed potentate. Instead the Portuguese found an infinity of states, and a vast, ancient and complex commercial system whose extremities were Europe in the west and China in the east. Subsistence agriculture barely supported gigantic populations periodically and drastically reduced by disease and famine. But for its more fortunate and opulent minorities there was little, as the Portuguese soon discovered, that the east could not itself provide. It had the esteemed luxuries of China; spices of every sort, from the pepper of western India and Sumatra to the nutmeg of Banda and the cinnamon of Ceylon; the fine textiles of north-west India and Bengal. From East Africa, where a chain of Swahili city states – Arab and Moslem – lined the coast of a Negro hinterland, there came, the Portuguese rejoiced to find, gold, ivory and slaves. And through the Red Sea and the Persian Gulf the Orient had access to the resources of the Middle East – Arabian horses, Persian silks and silver amongst them – and of Europe (cf. pp. 90 and 101ff.).

Across the seas and oceans of this immense world there flowed a multiplicity of trades, both local and long-distance. In the ports of western India, some in touch with East Africa, the Red Sea, the Persian Gulf and Malaya, merchants from the Middle East exchanged European metals and bullion for Indian and imported spices. North African Moors traded to Malaya. Indian textiles were sold for gold and ivory in East Africa. With distances so vast – from western India to East Africa is over 4000km, and from southern Malaya to western India about the same – commercial currents so many and varied, and the peoples and natural conditions encountered so diverse, the major trades had over the centuries come to be handled through a number of entrepôts. These were cosmopolitan ports of transhipment at which, usually for geographical or climatic reasons, vessels were obliged to stop. Nowhere was this clearer than in the Indian Ocean itself, where the monsoons blowing from the north-east (November–April) and the south-west (May–October) rigorously determined the movement of shipping. Hence in southern Malaya, where the wind system of the Indian Ocean met that of the China seas, Malacca had by 1500 emerged to eclipse all predecessors. The wealth of this 'richest place in all the world' was to strain Portuguese resources in metaphor and simile. It was 'the mine of spices' to which all Asia was drawn as surely 'as rivers flow to the sea'. Here were to be found alike merchants from Tunis and China; ships from India; junks from Okinawa. It gathered in Chinese silks, Indian textiles, East Indian spices, Sumatran gold, and European goods that had travelled the long route from Cairo and Aden. It was, in short, the collecting point for all the products of the Far East, and the focus of trade between the Orient, western Asia and the Middle East. Far less inviting, but equally important, was Aden, strategically sited – on bare rock and in stifling heat – at the juncture of the Red and Arabian seas. It controlled, the Portuguese later reported, 'an unbelievable commerce', re-shipping spices to Cairo and Damascus, exporting African gold, choice opium (to induce, amongst other things, refinements of sexual delight), Arabian horses, Yemeni dyes and European cloths to the east. Handling a very similar trade, and enduring a very similar, if not worse, climate was Hormuz, at the mouth of the Persian Gulf. It stood on a barren island producing only salt and sulphur, and to which even water had to be fetched. Yet here again the Portuguese were to find a stylish city, rich on what was channelled through it. It more or less monopolized the commerce between India and Persia – where spices were alleged to produce in their consumers such thirsts as to make them 'even drunker than Germans' – and its coins of gold (*xerafims*) and silver (*larins*) circulated widely in Asia.

The business of such entrepôts was carried on by merchants and seamen of an astonishing variety of races and religions. Some were Christians, trading from the

Malabar coast of western India to East Africa. Many, as in Coromandel (southeast India) were Hindu, whilst in Gujarat (northwest India) even Hindus of high caste were merchants and shipowners. But on the whole, though low-caste Hindus were commonly sailors, the problems of defilement through association with the impure on board ship meant that their high-caste co-religionaries generally confined themselves, if merchants, to land-borne commerce. Hence to their disgust the Portuguese discovered that in the Indian Ocean, as indeed well beyond, most seamen and traders were Moslems. In the west they were Arabs, ancient enemies in Iberia and Morocco, in the east Indians, and all loathsome *Mouros* professing a faith unhappily in the full vigour of triumphant expansion. Equally distastefully to European intolerance, peoples of such diverse races and religions lived on the whole amicably together. In Hormuz there were Christians, Jews, Moors and Turks; in Hindu Calicut, alien Moslems (*Pardesi*) of anywhere from Tunis to Arabia, alongside native Moslems (*Māpilla*).

Into this complex world da Gama intruded with rude energy, moving up the East African coast in search of a pilot. Scufflings in Mozambique led to his bombardment of the city; at Mombasa gracious gifts were repaid with cheap beads. Only in Malindi, whose ruler had hopes of assistance against neighbouring Kilwa, could a pilot be found, and by a strange irony he was Ibn Majid, the most distinguished Asian navigator of the time. Under his guidance the Portuguese made a fast passage to western India, eventually reaching (1498) Calicut, a major centre for the production of silk textiles, and the collecting point for the spices of the Craganore coast. Here da Gama's proceedings produced much the same results as in East Africa. Attempts to enter the spice trade were impeded by a lack of suitable goods to trade, and the initial goodwill of the Hindu raja (*samorin*) was quickly dissipated by arrogant Portuguese disregard for the elaborate formalities of oriental custom. More fundamentally still, the dominant Moslem merchants, informed of Portuguese behaviour in Africa, had no desire to see their commerce destroyed, nor was the raja prepared to forfeit their goodwill and the revenues their presence ensured by favouring piratical strangers.

After further debacles and misunderstandings – misguided Portuguese worship at Hindu shrines; Indian seizure of Portuguese goods; da Gama's kidnapping of some locals – the remains of his fleet left for home with a lading of pepper and cinnamon. They arrived in Lisbon after an absence of two years, and on the completion of a voyage which had involved 300 days at sea and cost the lives of more than half the company. As a feat of human endurance and seamanship it was superb. All the same da Gama, honoured and rewarded for his services, had not, as had been hoped, concluded any alliance, or secured any commercial concessions. Nor had he reached the source of the most valuable spices, but had naturally enough been led by his pilot into the heart of the redistributive network of the Indian Ocean. And having ensured the hostility of the Moslems, the most powerful maritime interest there, he had returned to Europe convinced that those Indians who were not followers of Mahomet must be worshippers – errant ones maybe – of Christ.

However in Calicut the Portuguese took into their service a Tunisian Moslem and a Spanish Jew resident in the East, from whom they learned both something of the nature and extent of the Asian economy, and how it might best be turned to their advantage. Its subjugation was begun without delay, not with the spontaneous and disorganized vigour of earlier Viking expansion in the north but, like Venice in the Mediterranean, in accordance with carefully defined state – which in this case meant royal – policy, and under the closest state direction (cf. pp. 115, 261, 269). Attempts in the early 1500s to find a less arduous westward passage to the now visibly enormous riches of Asia were abandoned and Portuguese energies and resources concentrated on the routes opened by da Gama. The essential ambition was as commercial as that of the Hanse or Venice in Europe, but its realization was commenced by a dynasty, aristocracy and gentry as predatory as any, their native violence and rapacity further inflamed by religious bigotry (see pp. 261, 266, 276). Impressed by da Gama's reports of the ubiquity of Moslems, of whom it was naively remarked there were 'more between Malacca and Hormuz than in the kingdoms of Fes and Tunis', and the intensity of their hostility, the king determined to divert their monopoly of the spice trade of the Indian Ocean into Portuguese hands by 'cruel war with fire and sword'.

And so it was, with cities bombarded, ships pillaged and sunk, and appalling cruelties – the slicing off of noses and ears – inflicted on enemies real or imagined. Yet whatever the material or other advantages of the Portuguese, these familiar recipes for imperial success might have produced little but for the lack of any sustained opposition, and a Portuguese exploitation, as adept and pragmatic as that of the Spaniards in South America, of the opportunities presented by the disunity of their opponents and the nature of their societies (see pp. 339f.). Neither in the Indian Ocean nor the seas east of Ceylon was there any dominant power, and particularly any dominant naval power. The Chinese, long employing in their vessels such refinements as compasses and axial rudders, and owning junks the equal of most ships in the west, might well have filled such a role. In the fifteenth century a brief spasm of curiosity about the outside world had brought their fleets to India, East Africa and the Persian Gulf. But by 1500 they had once more relapsed into their normal xenophobic isolation and their naval force had largely disintegrated. The Ottoman Turks, most formidable of all Moslems, were at the time of the Portuguese beginnings in the east engaged in a victorious onslaught on Europe, whilst their co-religionaries, the once redoubtable Egyptian Mamelukes – through being without timber never of any maritime consequence – were in irrevocable decline. Even with a European stiffening, their fleet together with that of the Gujaratis was no match for the Portuguese who in 1509 destroyed the fleet off Diu.

Then partly by accident and partly by design the Portuguese gained some advantage, and hoped for more, from the religious and political rivalries and enmities in the east, such as the endemic wars between Moslems and Hindus. Moreover, finding Islam divided between Sunni Ottomans and Shia Persians they entertained for a while expectations – illusory it soon transpired – of aid from the 'Grand Sophy' of Persia against their mutual arch-enemy the 'Great Turk'. Fortunately, too, their preoccupation with seaborne commerce and downright piracy meant they had little contact with the land-locked and momentarily dormant Moslem power of northern India, or with the even more inaccessible Hindu empire of Vijayanagar in the south (destroyed by the Moslems in 1565). Hotheads accordingly leapt to the conclusion that India was a country inhabited by dolts (*bestas*) who, unlike the Turks or Venetians, could easily be subdued. Such astonishing arrogance is at least explicable. The western coast of India was in the hands of a number of petty princelings, Moslem (like the sultan of Gujarat) as far down as Goa, Hindu (as were the samorin of Calicut, the kings of Cochin and Quilon and the raja of Cannanore) in the south, where mountain ranges and tropical forests effectively excluded the authority of Vijayanagar. Few of these rulers had anything of a commercial or maritime policy, and none the means to effectively enforce one. Nevertheless the revenues brought by trade were not beneath their lordly concern, and the presence of the Portuguese offered pleasing opportunities. The Mahomedan governor of Diu abandoned the 'league of all Moslems', which was to have overthrown the Portuguese, to get the best commercial terms he could from them (1508), whilst the king of Cochin welcomed the Portuguese rebuffed by his fellow Hindu, but ancient rival, the samorin of Calicut.

So by an admixture of luck, diplomacy and force, and arrogating to themselves ever grander titles, the Portuguese quickly secured bases and fortresses in western India – Cochin, Quilon, Cannanore – and East Africa – Kilwa, Sofala, Mozambique – giving them a substantial hold on the trade of the Indian Ocean. Next (1505) there was established, at least on paper, the 'State of India'. But even if there was no Portuguese territory in the sub-continent this was no invisible empire. The flow of Asian spices both 'to the lands of the sultan' (of Egypt) – and thence largely to Venice – and through the Persian Gulf was to be stopped, and they were to reach Europe only in Portuguese ships sailing by the Cape route. In the spice markets of India the competition of Moslem merchants, who bought from Hindu producers with goods, was to be destroyed by the Portuguese offering bullion. Trades which provided commodities or revenues valuable or useful for the acquisition of spices were to be diverted into Portuguese hands. But the crown's imposing economic strategy, which was to have endowed it with 'gold enough to fill a tower', was impossibly ambitious, and could never, over such a huge area, be more than partially or momentarily implemented. Asian tenacity and ingenuity were too great; Portugal's commitments too many; her resources too few; her naval forces insufficient, and their officers inspired by no Venetian-like sense of duty to the state such policies demanded. Apart from a brief occupation of the inhospitable Socotra, she found no forward base from which to blockade the Red Sea. There were indeed thoughts of taking Jiddah, and an ill-organized (and unsuccessful) attack was made on Aden (1513). Sanguine minds envisaged the destruction of Islamic wealth by the diversion of the Blue Nile, whilst a bold if futile raid, which penetrated to within sight of Suez (1541), was mounted from India. Nevertheless eastern commerce was once again passing through the Red Sea within less than a decade of da Gama's voyage – though now under spasmodic Portuguese surveillance – and on such a scale that by the 1560s they had hopes of being allowed to participate in it themselves.[6]

Elsewhere Portuguese pressure was more effective. Calicut came to terms in 1513. After campaigns of a fearful violence Hormuz, the key to the Persian Gulf, was secured (1515) and eventually annexed (1543). In the economically vital north-west India, Bassein was acquired in 1534, and as a result of help promised against the Moguls, a stronghold obtained at Diu the year after. And with Afonso de Albuquerque's capture of Goa (1510) Portugal made her first military conquest in the east. But though this was on Albuquerque's initiative, his role was not that of a Cortés or a John Winthrop, determining the character of a whole cycle of imperial growth and policy. He was the royal governor of India (1509–15), an aristocrat like the Spanish viceroys of the Americas, or the major Venetian colonial officials, and his other most celebrated exploits – the seizure of Malacca (1511) and Hormuz – were undertaken in wayward fulfilment of explicit royal instructions (see pp. 310ff. and 490). One of the handful of supremely able men who ensured the establishment of a Portuguese empire, he was cast in the familiar mould of the *conquistador*. He was of fearsome energy – dictating from horseback to secretaries in hot pursuit – and unscrupulous ingenuity, persuading the heir-apparent of Calicut to poison the Samorin who obstructed Portuguese ambitions. Brutal, vindictive, and apt in moments of fury to express himself in graphic and wounding language, he could nevertheless hold the loyalty of his troops by his affability and personal bravery – notwithstanding his introduction of Swiss officers to lick them into shape.[7] Nor was he an intolerant bigot, but with a smattering of humanist learning and the pragmatism of a man of the world, he found talents and ideas where he could. In Goa local dancing girls, musicians, war-elephants and mercenary troops were all brought into Portuguese service, and the very capture of the city was suggested by the Hindu captain, Timoja (see p. 267).

Thus by the mid-1500s the Portuguese held most of the major entrepôts in the Indian Ocean. A royal monopoly of trade with certain ports and in certain goods – most notably spices – had been established, whilst in theory Portugal regulated the whole commerce of the ocean, exacting dues on designated cargoes from eastern shipping obliged to call at Goa, Hormuz and Malacca (see pp. 296ff.). With resources infinitely inferior the Portuguese were attempting to impose over far greater areas policies much more ambitious than those ever envisaged by Venice in the Mediterranean or the Hanse in the north. Outside the Indian Ocean their penetration along ancient trade routes was more rapid, the control they exercised more superficial, and their behaviour marginally more tactful. The first viceroy of India had been instructed (1506) to seize and fortify Malacca with or without local consent, the matter being urgent since the Spaniards were thought to harbour similar ambitions, and as the king wrote, pithily summarizing a notable theory of empire, 'possession gives us good title'. But only under Albuquerque was this accomplished and the long-projected investigation of what lay further east commenced when, in 1511, three ships were sent from Malacca – in one of them the future circumnavigator Magellan – to find and open dealings with the Spice Islands. All reached Amboina and Banda, from where two returned, whilst the captain of the third, having lost his own vessel, pushed on to Ternate in a commandeered local craft. Here, at the source of clove production, the Portuguese were initially welcomed by the ruler for the assistance they could give against his rival in the equally miniscule Tidore. But then there commenced a familiar sequence of imperial history. The Spaniards were drawn to Tidore (1521), and the indigenous populations became the victims of wars which ended with Spanish withdrawal (1529) (see also pp. 319–20). Thereupon Ternate fell into the hands of the most ruthless Portuguese adventurers who, freed from any serious European threat, and with no prospect of royal control from distant India or Malacca – let alone the mother country – turned its history into a melancholy sequence of revolts, mutinies and palace revolutions until their expulsion in 1575.

At the same time, and in much the same style, the prospects of China were investigated. By now this once great and remarkable empire and civilization was in decline, politically weak, and much troubled by the coastal raids of Japanese pirates whose behaviour reinforced an already intense Chinese xenophobia. The emperor, theoretically a despot, remained isolated in his palace, surrounded by court eunuchs who, along with the imperial provincial officers, were the real men of power. Trade was little regarded, foreign merchants prohibited, and the life of the empire, administered by an intensely scholarly bureaucracy, basically agrarian and intellectual. Rumours of Chinese wealth and splendour soon reached the Portuguese, and an early (and abortive) expedition to Malacca (1508) was ordered to discover all it could of the country and its inhabitants, 'whether they are weak or warlike, whether they have weapons or artillery, what clothes they wear, and whether they are big in body' – always a sore point with the small and undernourished Portuguese. Nor, once Malacca was taken, did events belie expectations. Trading ventures brought profits of 2000 per cent and not surprisingly reports of this 'very good people'. But then, meeting only the pacific agrarian society of the south, the Portuguese began to behave as they did on the coasts of India and Africa. Whilst an official embassy was in the imperial capital, another expedition set about the construction of a fortress at the mouth of the Pearl River, accompanied by the usual excesses of demands for commercial monopoly and the exaction of forced labour. The outcome was the speedy expulsion of the 'men with beards and big eyes' from China (1521), and the defeat of Portuguese ships in clashes with Chinese naval patrols. But the bonds of profit are not so easily broken. Many Chinese were willing to trade, and in those heroic days the Portuguese were not easily deterred. Not by royal direction, but on their own initiative, groups and individuals continued to do business. At first this was on offshore islands, in suitably obscure Chinese ports, or through Malay or Siamese intermediaries. But before long it was largely conducted from a base at Macao,[8] with the Portuguese the indispensable middlemen in dealings with the Japanese who, as a result of their piratical depredations, were banned by the emperor from China.

Nor was this the limit of Portuguese endeavour. Japan itself was found, Viking-style, purely by accident when a party of would-be China traders was blown there by a typhoon (1543). To their delight they encountered people less haughtily contemptuous of foreigners than the Chinese and with so avid a desire for the products of Europe and China as to make their country 'one of the best and most suitable . . . for gaining profit'. Earlier the Portuguese had reached Siam and Burma, besides establishing posts in eastern India. Some uncertain authority also came to be exercised over Ceylon, rich in cinnamon, elephants – used in war and ceremony in India – and precious stones. Straddling the shipping routes from the Arabian Sea to the Bay of Bengal and southern Asia, and politically weak, it appeared to bold strategists the ideal base for privateering, and the possible seat of a great eastern realm.

These fanciful dreams were not realized, and by the mid-1500s Portugal's Asian empire had reached its fullest extent. Individuals were indeed to penetrate further still, merchants or seamen to Manila, New Guinea and the Seychelles in the later sixteenth century; missionaries to Vietnam and Tibet in the early 1600s. At the same time local hostility, European competition, and the ever-growing power of Islam brought a search for new bases and new allies. Nevertheless the essential character of the empire remained unchanged. Whatever the grandiose titles concocted at home, or the bellicose language of imperial correspondence, the Portuguese were notoriously not, as were the Spaniards in America, rulers by conquest of subject millions. Their territorial possessions were few; colonization – in face of a hostile climate, organized and populous Asian societies, and their own demographic weakness – was insignificant. Instead, Portugal's eastern empire was a string of fortresses and factories – the very worst to defend – sustained by, or potentially controlling, maritime trade routes. In this, though the product of a remarkably non-mercantile society, it resembled those of the Hanse and Venice. Similarly, as in their empires, long-distance trades were complemented, and often overshadowed, by local 'country' traffics. And, as with Genoa, the fragile authority of the parent community and the limited opportunities it offered, encouraged individuals to trade where the flag of the mother country could never hope to follow, and ensured that Portuguese commerce long survived the demise of Portuguese rule. But Portugal enjoyed nothing of the economic hegemony of the German or Italian cities. Her commercial monopolies were less effective, and her empire – isolated survivals apart – far shorter lived. Simply a seapower of modest strength, she controlled no inland bases, and stimulated no such spate of urban foundations as the more intensively commercial Hanse. And reflecting its peculiarly monarchical and aristocratic origins, Portugal's empire was largely geared to plunder, and to the conduct of a trade even more exclusively devoted to luxuries than that of Venice (cf. pp. 101ff.).

At its brief zenith, lasting only until the early 1600s, it comprised a number of distinct but interlocking economies. The remotest centred on Macao, the only Asian city truly created by Portugal. Here, presumably with the connivance of suitably rewarded Chinese officials, and without the knowledge of either the Chinese or Portuguese governments, a settlement grew up. By 1600 it was one of the most important in the east, prosperous, to all intents independent, and enjoying privileges conferred by both China and Portugal. The city housed in style between 400 and 600 married males of Portuguese birth or descent. Together with their children, wives and mistresses – gorgeous Orientals, Africans or Indians, visitors enviously noted – their slaves and retainers, they made up a total multi-racial population of about 20,000. Macao handled a commerce of insignificant volume, but impressive value, its basis the monopoly of trade between China and Japan.[9] Chinese gold – abundant but little esteemed in its own land – and silks were exchanged for Japanese silver at a rumoured overall profit of 150 per cent simply on bullion. But dealings quickly grew more complex. To meet Chinese demand silver was brought in from countries as far apart as Persia (through Goa) to South America (*via* either Europe or Manila in the Spanish Philippines). And besides silver – of which Japan alone provided 26t a year by 1600 – Indian spices and textiles, together with such European novelties as prisms and lenses, were also sent to Canton. Chinese silk, Indian and European goods, were shipped to Manila,[10] and the exquisite products of China – porcelain, carvings, lacquer-work and silks – exported to Goa for redistribution in India, Africa and Europe. In Japan, in addition to gold, the Portuguese sold spices, silks, and European manufactures. Missionary zeal, and the ability to provide such things as the latest weapons highly prized by the bellicose Japanese, brought Portugal in 1571 a base at Nagasaki, in the fief of a newly converted Christian feudatory (see pp. 286f.). Here business moved at an agreeable pace, with Portuguese merchants opulently passing the best part of a year in this 'land of Cockaigne', and soon engendering there a thriving Luso-Japanese community. And from Nagasaki they also traded to Manila, exchanging foodstuffs and weapons for bullion (Chinese gold and Mexican silver), Chinese silk, and Spanish goods that had come the long route across the Atlantic and Pacific (see p. 328). But though by the early 1600s the greatest days of Macao's commerce were gone its prosperity was far from ended. Hopes of a direct trade to South America may have been thwarted, but the Portuguese nevertheless successfully repulsed the attempts of Spain – by whom Portugal and her possessions were annexed 1580–1640 – to trade from the Philippines to Macao, and when expelled from Japan found themselves new openings in Timor, Macassar, Indo-China and Siam (see pp. 287, 295).

Roughly 3000km further south the Portuguese held Malacca until its loss to the Dutch in 1641 (see p. 400). Here they had no need, as in Macao, to develop new trades, but instead they enthusiastically entered to start with such as they wished of those already flowing through an established entrepôt. Thus with Indian textiles, rice and grain they purchased south-east Asian spices for resale in Europe, India and – at profits of reputedly 400 per cent – China. for the rest they used this magnificently sited base, controlling the waters of Malaysia and Indonesia, to tax and plunder whatever they could. But their position was never more than precarious. So fragile was their authority that the seamen of Atjeh (Sumatra) diverted fellow Moslems away from Malacca, sailed directly to the Red Sea with cargoes of spice, and attacked Portuguese vessels in the Bay of Bengal and the Andaman Sea (cf. p. 242). Moreover without – as in India and Japan – the benefit of missionary influence to persuade local rulers to exclude European competitors, Portuguese trade was damaged by the Spaniards who from Manila carried Asian products across the Pacific to Europe (see p. 328). And unconcerned, unlike in Macao, to retain the goodwill of a powerful eastern state, Portuguese depredations were on such a scale as to drive the best part of Malacca's Asian commerce elsewhere. Hence as much from necessity as from enterprise new trades came to be opened. Spices were shipped not only to India and China but also – together with slaves – to Manila, whilst those evading the royal monopoly of commerce between China and Japan did business in Vietnam with Chinese and Japanese merchants. And even after the successive loss of Ternate, Tidore and Amboina, and with the Dutch dominant in Indonesia in the early 1600s, the Portuguese could still purchase cloves (and diamonds as well) in Macassar in return for Chinese silk and Indian textiles (see pp. 295, 408). But the very existence, amongst the countless islands of southeast Asia, of so many potential suppliers encouraged and enabled the Portuguese to dissipate their resources. Their fortresses at Ternate and Solor were hopelessly isolated. Malacca, at the heart of a maritime economy largely controlled by Portugal's old enemies, the Moslem Gujaratis, was vulnerably dependent on local suppliers for its food, and engaged in a decreasingly successful struggle with the sultans of Johore. By the beginning of the seventeenth century what had once been one of southern Asia's most flourishing markets seemed to visitors to be virtually deserted.

Yet another – and larger – string of coastal fortresses and factories constituted the heart of the grandiosely named 'State of India'. There were Portuguese enclaves in the textile regions of north-west India – where in Cambay relations with the Gujarati merchants were so cordial that trade continued even in times of war – and in Coromandel. The west coast strongholds gave the Portuguese, whatever their insignificance in the sub-continent's internal affairs, some opportunity to licence and tax local shipping even in the seventeenth century, largely since the rulers of martial and aristocratic Indian states cared little for the sea or the misfortunes of those engaged in commerce. Similarly control (until 1622) of the great market of Hormuz, then of Muscat (till 1650) and Sind, enabled them both to trade to the Persian Gulf and the Middle East, and – so long as Hormuz was held – to tax and plunder native seaborne commerce. The imperial capital – and indeed the only imperial territory of any significance apart from that in Ceylon, and a strip of palm and rice-growing lands between Chaul and Daman in north-west India[11] – was Goa. Built like Macao on an island, it was a walled city, housing a larger but equally polyglot population, totalling perhaps 60,000 in the 1580s. Amongst these there were, fifty years later, some 1000 male Portuguese householders, together with their Asian or Eurasian wives, and their families, mistresses, slaves and retainers of assorted race and colour. Until the arrival of the Dutch, Goa prospered as a centre of colonial high life, intrigue, finance and corruption, and on a trade surpassing even that of Macao in its rich variety of luxuries. Spices from India and Malacca were re-shipped to Europe, the Middle East and Manila. Bullion and manufactures ranging from playing cards to Venetian glass were imported from Europe; Indian textiles sent to East Africa to be exchanged for ivory and slaves. From Cambay came diamonds and linens, some destined for Europe, others for Indonesia. Bengal provided superb cloths, Coromandel those cotton fabrics whose delicacy and transparency so seductively revealed the charms of Goa's Eurasian women, and which, it was said, were the only textiles acceptable in Java and Malaya. Burma supplied gold and precious stones, Ceylon elephants and cinnamon. And besides countless other such trades – whether the export of oriental luxuries to Europe, the sale of Persian and Arabian horses in southern India,[12] or the furnishing of Macao with silver, slaves and spices – Goa sustained a network of local commerce. It redistributed European and Asian products along the neighbouring coast, collected spices – most notably Cochin pepper – and imported from the Maldives palm wine, coir for ropes, and other necessities.

Rich on trade and loot, Goa in the halcyon days of the sixteenth century was a handsome city of great houses and fine churches. The epitome of Portuguese imperial aspirations, it was, however, no oriental Venice or Amsterdam. By commerce it lived, yet in the viceregal palace there hung heroic portraits of former governors, and visitors were received to the blare of Indian military music. Nor was its leisurely, luxurious and philistine life that of a western commercial city. The climate was oppressive; trade was virtually stopped for three months every winter when the offshore monsoon hindered the arrival of ships, and for another three months every summer when the onshore monsoon hampered their departure. But in any case a reasonable profit – 10 per cent 'without risk' as late as the 1620s – could be had on local loans, and fortunes made by fraud. Effort was thus superfluous. By the 1630s the vast bulk of the capital invested in the city's commerce belonged to non-Christian Indians, and even in happier times it was observed – not without envy – that with shipping absent on lengthy voyages, Portuguese merchants could single-mindedly devote themselves to the pursuit of pleasure. A large half-caste population discharged the many functions too demeaning for Portuguese attention. Even simple artisans owned two dozen or so slaves – mostly Africans – and the wealthy several hundred. In the eyes of stern moralists the city was another Babylon, but to men of the world it was a paradise where, with beautiful Eurasian girls readily available, life was a ceaseless round of amorous assignments and sexual delights.

II *The Atlantic and Africa*

These astonishing achievements in Asia were accompanied by the equally remarkable creation of an empire in South America, Africa and the Atlantic, which entailed in turn

6   Africa *c*.1600, showing major centres of European trade and settlement

the growth of wholly new maritime economies. In the highest latitudes of the Atlantic
the Portuguese accomplished relatively little. They probably knew as much as any of
medieval rumours of islands to the west of Europe, but showed little inclination to
investigate them (cf. pp. 246, 302). Nor is there any convincing evidence that they
forestalled Columbus in America, or that in the fifteenth century they were aware of the
existence of Greenland, and Norse survival there (see pp. 7–8). But with hopes,
perhaps, of an easier passage than that round the Cape to Asia, and with the English
taking an interest in the north-west and possibly infringing Portuguese rights under the
Treaty of Tordesillas (see pp. 308, 461), there came a series of northern voyages *c*. 1500.
Greenland, Newfoundland and Labrador were reached, and there was an attempt in
the 1520s to establish a settlement on Cape Breton Island – the first by Europeans in

North America since Viking days. But though all these ventures came to nothing a valuable fishery, employing fifty ships by 1578, was developed off Newfoundland.

Further south the Portuguese achievement was impressive and enduring. The islands on Africa's northwestern shoulder, previously known to, and in some degree colonized by, Italians and Iberians, were rediscovered and permanently settled (cf. pp. 164, 182). The Canaries, partially conquered by the French in the early 1400s, were lost to Spain (1477), but in the Azores, the Cape Verde Islands and Madeira the Portuguese established their earliest, and some of their most successful colonies. There were no troublesome indigenous populations; the climate was in general tolerable; the land virgin; markets readily accessible. Invigorated by Italian capital and business skills, the islands were governed and exploited by that admixture of feudal grants and commercial concessions favoured by Genoa, and later employed in the empire at large, and their economic evolution foreshadowed in miniature subsequent developments in Portuguese and Spanish America. Madeira, rediscovered (*c.* 1420) and colonized at the instigation of Prince Henry, soon became a flourishing producer of wheat and sugar, and thus the first European oceanic colony indisputably to prosper, and the first uninhabited land to be transformed into a vital member of the European economy. By *c.* 1500 it was producing about 1000t of sugar a year, exported at such prices and in such quantities to many parts of Europe as to destroy the old Mediterranean industry. Output on this scale led to the growth of sizable plantations, whose heavy labour requirements were met by the use of African slaves.[13] In the late sixteenth century, in face of the sugar of the even more favoured Brazil, the industry declined, and the island turned to the production, on smaller holdings, of dyes and that rightly prized sweet wine with which its name is most familiarly linked. Madeiran and other merchants imported the European manufactures demanded by prosperous islanders, and exported wine to the Old and New Worlds alike. Outward-bound vessels called in Madeira for wine, with which tobacco, sugar and Peruvian silver could be acquired in Brazil, and from there shipped either to the island itself or to Europe.[14] Unlike that of the isolated Norse oceanic settlements, the population of Madeira grew, and by the early seventeenth century had reached about 30,000 whites – black slaves having largely disappeared with the decline of sugar planting. Elsewhere the pattern was much the same. The wind-swept Azores, discovered in the course of a search for the mythical islands of St Brendan (1427), were populated at the insistence of princes Henry and Pedro. But only with difficulty. Portuguese peasants expected more from emigration than the prospect of re-enacting in a new and dour setting the familiar domestic routine of clearing and tilling the soil. The islands therefore had to be colonized with less-demanding Flemings and Bretons, reinforced as need be with criminals – murderers included. Like Madeira, the Azores enjoyed, albeit briefly, prosperity as producers of sugar and wine, before becoming (*c.* 1600) major suppliers of wheat and woad.[15] And with the growth of the Iberian maritime empires in Africa, India and the Americas they were for a time vital as a way-station. Fleets on the long homeward passage re-formed, revictualled, took on meat – livestock having been introduced into the islands on the instructions of the provident Prince Henry – and topped up cargoes of spices or bullion with grain. Crews were meanwhile rested, and their spirits raised by the profits of illicit trade, particularly in American silver.[16] With the rapid increase in their population, the Azores also became, like Norse Iceland and the Spanish Caribbean islands, bases from which the ambitious or discontented migrated, and from where new ventures were mounted. In the late fifteenth century Azoreans searched for northern lands, and for the non-existent Lovo and Capraria. Many later went to Brazil, and the imperial annals are full of the heroic deeds of others in Asia.

Very different was the evolution of the islands in the tropics, where heat and endemic disease killed most Europeans. São Tomé, in the Gulf of Guinea (discovered *c.* 1470), was initially peopled with anything from convicts to forcibly converted Jewish children; the Cape Verdes (discovered and settled 1456–60) with, amongst others, New Christians[17] and lepers. Both were soon producers of sugar, with São Tomé especially successful until crippled in the late 1500s by enemy raids, slave revolts, and Brazilian competition. And both were accordingly integrated into the Atlantic economy, importing European goods, owning ships,[18] trading with each other and with the New World. The Cape Verdes enjoyed a further prosperity as a way-station where Brazil-bound craft took on fish and the redoubtable local salted goat meat, or where African ivory and American silver were surreptitiously and profitably landed.[19] But above all they flourished, together with Príncipe (Gulf of Guinea) and São Tomé, as entrepôts in the early Atlantic slave trade (see pp. 255ff.). From the end of the fifteenth century they sent Africans – bought on the Guinea coast for horses, cotton, or Canary and Madeiran wines – to Iberia and the Canaries, and, from the early 1500s, directly to the Americas. Such pursuits in such climates produced societies radically different to those of the peasant-cultivated Madeira and Azores. Slaves and slaving were ubiquitous, whilst from African wives, mistresses or prostitutes there was sired a large mulatto[20] population. Nor were these the only intimations of the nature of future tropical colonialism. In São Tomé mulattos fought with whites, and slave revolts were so frequent as to hasten the collapse of the sugar industry. Yet in climates where most Europeans died, the population became predominantly negroid and, as was rarely the case elsewhere, free Africans and mulattos prospered as merchants – slavers especially – and were even able, in the absence of other candidates, to hold secular and ecclesiastical office.

But the apogee of Portuguese colonial achievement in the Atlantic was the discovery of what is now the gigantic state of Brazil. First seen as little better than a potential penal settlement, it became eventually, with its sugar and gold, the pillar of the Portuguese economy. It was found by accident when Cabral's expedition to India swung too far westward (1500)[21], and was then virtually ignored for over a quarter of a century, notwithstanding that its Atlantic shoulder was easily accessible by a route largely free from such hazards as fogs and icebergs, and served by the favourable north-east trade winds. Of other attractions, however, it was notably devoid. Its climate combined tropical heat and deluges with capricious droughts. Millions of square kms of the Amazon basin were dense equatorial forest; the fine grasslands further south could only be reached – other than along the valleys of the São Francisco or Parnaiba – through mountains and yet more forest. Much of the coast was similarly thickly afforested; there were no roads, as in the Aztec and Inca empires; few westward-flowing rivers, and none between the dangerous and unpredictable Amazon and the Río de la Plata that were navigable for any distance. Given sufficient incentives such obstacles, as the Spaniards showed, would be brushed aside. But Brazil had nothing to compete with the far less arduous attractions of Asia – no rich cities whose trade might be tapped; no readily available supplies of precious metals; no indigenous empires to be manipulated; not even animals or men fit to be used as beasts of burden (cf. pp. 310ff., 339–40).

Instead the Portuguese met only tribes of primitive Tupí-Guarani Indians. Noble savages they might have been to philosophers, but to settlers and traders their main occupation seemed to be painting their bodies and decorating themselves with feathers. They knew nothing of weaving, pottery or the working of metals, and were sustained by the labours of their women and the hunting and fishing of the males. Their polygamy, nudity, head-hunting and addiction to washing established their immorality in Christian eyes, and after some initial admiration of their physique it was discovered that they were unsuited to enslavement. Hence Portuguese colonization in South America was of a different pattern to that of the Spaniards. As in Africa, and like the Norse and English in North America, they were pinned to the coast. There, with nothing to draw them inland, they became, as producers of sugar and exporters of timber – bulk commodities most easily moved by water – still more firmly rooted, and with their transport and communications, as in Asia, almost exclusively, and vulnerably, by sea (see pp. 8f., 240, 481ff.).

It was the discovery that the country was rich in brazilwood – source of the red dye in demand in Europe's booming textile industry – that first aroused Portugal's imperial urge and gave the colony its name.[22] Under royal licence timber was bought from the Amerindians for such things as shirts and mirrors, and a thin scattering of coastal trading posts and settlements grew up. Even more influential was the realization that Brazil's meagre assets might well fall into other hands. Spaniards from Peru made the epic journey down the Amazon. The French – who persistently tried to settle – the English and the Dutch all traded to Brazil in the sixteenth century. By the early 1600s the English were attempting to colonize the lower Amazon, and the Dutch to annex part of Brazil itself (see pp. 386ff.). So Portugal came to take a livelier interest in its colony, and one further sharpened by the hope that, like the Spanish Americas, it might contain treasure, or at least give access to that under Spanish control. The French were, with difficulty, ejected and Portuguese settlement begun. As in the Atlantic islands it was to be done German and Genoese style, at little cost or trouble to a state with modest resources (see pp. 43, 191). The country was divided (1534) into fifteen captaincies.

These were granted to *donatorios* – usually gentry or middle class, unlike the more humbly born conquerors of Spanish America – who at their own expense were to occupy, populate and exploit them. In exchange they received enormous fiscal and political privileges such as were never conceded to the holders of *encomiendas* in Spanish colonies (see pp. 321f.). Their grants were hereditary, free from royal jurisdiction, and carried the right to found towns, to bestow lands, to retain a percentage of the taxes levied, and to enslave the Indians. Even so, and notwithstanding royal intervention (1549), colonization was slow and difficult. The attractions of Asia were never stronger, Portuguese manpower was insufficient and only the captaincies of Pernambuco in the north and São Vicente in the south grew.

But the colony's future was ensured, and its whole subsequent development determined, by the introduction, with royal encouragement, of sugar planting. The soil of Brazil's Atlantic littoral was virgin and rich, the climate was such as to give a crop in six months without the cost and labour of irrigation and a European market was near to hand. By the early 1600s Pernambuco alone had more than 100 plantations producing over 17,000t of sugar a year. Demanding a large labour force and expensive crushing mills, it was no crop for peasant cultivation (cf. p. 245). Thus the Brazilian captaincies evolved into great estates, with the land not required by the *donatorios* themselves farmed out to other large-scale and virtually independent entrepreneurs. These worked their holdings directly, except for what they leased to share-croppers obliged to clear an agreed area for cultivation. For long it was assumed that enslaved Amerindians would provide the labour, to be used, an Elizabethan visitor wrote, 'as we do horses to tyll the grounde'. But like other primitive peoples in similar circumstances, the Tupí – forced into unaccustomed clothes, the whole pattern of their nomadic life disrupted – either fled, revolted or committed suicide. Others were killed by overwork, misusage or European diseases to which they had no resistance (cf. pp. 349ff.). 'No one could believe', it was remarked with astonishment in 1583, 'that so great a supply could be so quickly exhausted.' Another, though hardly insuperable obstacle to the continuing use of Amerindians was the lively concern of the missions, and the occasional anxieties of the crown, as to their well-being. The Jesuits attempted to protect and convert the Tupí by congregating them in villages, and secured in 1570 the limitation of enslavement to those captured in war or known to practice cannibalism.[23] Undeterred, the colonists raided the settlements, seized the inhabitants so conveniently assembled, and momentarily secured the expulsion of the Order from São Paulo and elsewhere (1640–53).

Nevertheless the growing shortage, and obvious inadequacies, of Amerindians eventually obliged the planters to look elsewhere for their labour, and from the mid-1500s Africans were increasingly used. They cost five times as much as Tupí slaves, but a thriving industry could bear the expense, particularly since 'good pieces' – that is young males 'neither blind nor dumb' – were known from the experience of the Atlantic islands to be capable of enduring long hours of hard manual toil. To start with they were brought from Guinea, but later from the Congo and Angola, with some admixture of East Africans when the Portuguese lost control of the Atlantic outlets to the Dutch. By 1600 there were about 60,000 in the country, and for the next half century they continued to arrive at the rate of four to eight thousand a year (see pp. 253–6). Those from Guinea were largely concentrated in the vicinity of Bahia, whilst the smaller, less volatile, and (to Europeans) less dangerous Congolese and Angolan Bantu were most numerous around Pernambuco. But whatever their origin or destination, the lot of the Africans was the most wretched. They were irrevocably isolated from their homeland. Their tribal affinities were deliberately destroyed. Their misfortunes elicited little concern from missionaries who themselves possessed Negro slaves (cf. pp. 356f.). But no more than the Amerindians did the Africans accept servitude as their natural destiny. As in Spanish America large numbers escaped into wild country (see p. 334). There they imposed some authority on local peoples, consoled themselves with their women, and under their own leaders – often aristocrats vanquished in African tribal disputes – set up independent communities, and even states, such as Alagôas which survived till 1694.

By roughly the mid-1600s all the essential features of Brazil's economy and society had been established. A small white population – some 30,000, but growing rapidly once opportunities in Asia dwindled – was mainly centred on the Atlantic littoral. From São Paulo *bandeirantes*[24] – frequently Tupí-speaking offspring of Portuguese males and Indian women – had penetrated to the Amazon on the one hand, and to the foothills of the Andes on the other, in search of slaves and loot. In the north, Pará and Maranhão were occupied, the São Francisco valley opened up, and a settlement made at Manáus (1674), over 1200km from the mouth of the Amazon. Apart from schemes to exclude other European powers, little of this was on the initiative of the Portuguese crown, whose authority was exercised through a governmental system far looser than that of the Spanish empire.[25] Characteristically, when in the first half of the seventeenth century the Dutch attempted to annex north-east Brazil, they were ultimately defeated by the colonists themselves with little or no help from the mother country (see pp. 386ff.).

The basis of Brazilian wealth and power was sugar, needing 300 ships a year to carry it, legally and otherwise, to much of Europe. With sugar came rum, mostly sent to Angola where with fine impartiality it killed or paralysed alike free and slave, black and white. And with sugar there also came stock-raising – especially in the São Francisco valley, and on the great plateaux of the southern hinterland – supplying oxen to work mills, horses for war and transport, and beef for food. The export of brazilwood continued, whilst with the same enterprise as the Spaniards elsewhere in the continent, the Portuguese exploited native crops and introduced new ones to make the country a producer of rice, citrus fruits, wheat, cotton and tobacco (see p. 323). Nor were these its only attractions. The north, it was vainly hoped, would become a way-station for Central America. In the south, however, long but relatively easy routes led overland from the Río de la Plata to the rich and isolated Spanish Peru and Chile. Here there developed, from the mid-1500s in Portuguese and Spanish hands, a number of large-scale and valuable trades, usually illicit and always unquantifiable. In Buenos Aires Angolan and Brazilian slaves destined for Spanish possessions were sold for Peruvian silver, in turn spent in Brazil on sugar then shipped to Europe. At the same time local and imported products (Madeiran wine and English cloth amongst them) in demand in Chile and Peru were bought in Brazil with American bullion which eventually found its way to Africa, the Atlantic islands and Europe.[26]

This economy sustained a basically agrarian and patriarchal society far more rural than those of Spanish America or German-colonized eastern Europe (see pp. 38ff. and 329ff.). Notwithstanding the characteristic ubiquity of slavery and miscegenation, its nature – the tiny islands of the Gulf of Guinea apart – was quite different from that of the rest of the Portuguese colonial empire. It consisted of an admixture of subsistence agriculture and intensive monocultures. Modest estates and small-holdings – producing either sugar or tobacco – Brazil indeed possessed. But its essential feature, especially in the north, was the vast sugar plantation. This commonly had crushing mills of its own to which other growers were obliged to bring their cane, but in any case it was of a size and importance equalled only in the American empire of Spain (see pp. 322, 332). Over the greatest there presided, in the style and with the powers of the magnates of medieval Iceland, the 'lord of the mills', surrounded by his slaves – a hundred or so – his black and Amerindian mistresses, his freedom, his artisans, retainers and assorted offspring (see p. 3). But unlike Scandinavian Iceland or Protestant North America, Brazil was to an even lesser degree than Spanish America a centre of intellectual endeavour and high culture. It produced no such universities and printing presses as those of Mexico, Peru or Germanized east Europe (see pp. 73 and 330). Missionaries apart, it attracted few outstanding Europeans, and a combination of isolation and easy opulence made it, like Goa, a land of philistine luxury for the dominant minority. Civilization was represented by ostentatious ecclesiastical architecture, by the occasional import of paintings and by such curiosities as a thirty-piece Negro band under a French conductor.[27]

Beneath a planter aristocracy and landowning church sustained by the enforced labour of Africans and Amerindians, there flourished, as in Spanish America, a substantial community of soldiers, merchants and artisans – some of the latter freed Africans (see pp. 330, 333). Without the lucrative opportunities presented by the numerous cities and elaborate administrative machinery of the Spanish colonies, Brazil attracted few lawyers, whilst in a way unthinkable in the Spanish empire, some of its soil was tilled by European peasants (see p. 332). Of all colonial societies it was perhaps the most polyglot. The planter hierarchy included Flemish, Italian and even English blood. Settlers recruited from convicts and vagabonds were reinforced with the passage of time by Portuguese, Madeiran, Azorean and Irish peasants; most merchants were for long New Christians who had fled from persecution in Iberia. And as everywhere else within the Spanish and Portuguese colonial empires miscegenation was practised on a gigantic scale (see pp. 266, 351). Marriage to native women, however, was rare. The Church lacked the organization to enforce it. To the upper classes it was socially degrading, and to the rest a needless burden and expense with indigenous women so freely available. The ubiquity of such unions needs no elaborate explanation. They may indeed have been a particularly effective way for a small country to populate a large one, though there is no evidence that dedicated fornicators were conscious of their imperial obligations. As in all Portugal's colonies European women were scarce – scarcer than in any other except those of the Dutch – since, as a legacy from the country's Islamic past, Portuguese females were largely condemned to a secluded and static life (see pp. 415ff.). Amerindian women, however, were plentiful, and it requires little imagination to see the attractions for a settler, like as not an outcaste from Europe, of naked native girls unable, as a missionary coldly observed, to say no to anybody. And with the arrival of the far less primitive African there developed, on a perhaps even larger scale, similar associations with Negresses, whilst many Amerindian women found the extrovert and ebullient African male much to their liking. Thus there evolved a population of extraordinarily diverse origins, but with the precise degree and nature of its non-white blood always carefully and disobligingly defined by the Portuguese. As elsewhere occasional *mestiços*[28] – like the *bandeirantes* of São Paulo – and mulattos – like that hero of the Dutch wars, João Fernandez Vieira – might be persons of consequence. But for the most part the offspring of European males and Indian or African women were no more acceptable to whites than in other colonial empires, and the more negroid their blood and features the less their desirability (cf. pp. 352f.). From such a racial and cultural admixture there sprang an equally polyglot civilization. In all essentials – religion, dress, social organization, language – it was Portuguese. But since Portugal neither conquered Brazil, nor established there a white society as self-contained as that of the Spaniards in America, indigenous influences persisted (cf. pp. 331f.). Brazilian Christianity, like Brazilian Portuguese, was full of African and Indian elements. From Africa came a taste for highly seasoned food and violently rhythmic music; from the Amerindians, amongst other things, a knowledge of the benefits of the hammock and an understanding of the vital arts of jungle war and survival.

It was not, however, in the Americas that the Portuguese empire was to begin and end. Its initial and final ventures were with the vast, rich, and largely unknown continent of Africa. The first footholds were in Morocco – Arab, Berber and fanatically Moslem. Here, after their capture of Ceuta, the Portuguese found themselves confronting organized societies and advanced economies. The country contained large and prosperous towns, was a producer of grain and livestock, and was one of the outlets for gold mined on the upper reaches of the Senegal, Niger and Volta rivers and brought north, from Timbuktu, by trans-Saharan caravans (cf. pp. 164, 170). Such opportunities the Portuguese could appreciate. Tribute was exacted, trading posts established, and a commerce opened with the inland market of Sus. There were attempts to monopolize the traffic in gold, and even, in 1444–5, to penetrate overland to the sources of supply.

Slaves were taken in holy war against Islam – or less arduously in times of famine, when young girls especially could be had by the hundred – whilst Morocco came to provide grain and textiles used in new Portuguese maritime commerce with West Africa (see p. 253). In Atlantic Morocco, aided by tribal rivalries and local support, a protectorate was established over a number of coastal cities in the fifteenth century, leading to their annexation in the early 1500s. But Morocco was no isolated Mexico or Peru to be overthrown by the destruction of its ruling class (cf. pp. 338ff.). It was part of the flourishing Islamic world of the Mediterranean, able to call on the redoubtable Turks, and soon with military resources equal to those of the Portuguese who had, in any case, no adequate policies for its subjugation. Poor, predatory and bellicose they could bring no such commercial advantages as made the Genoese welcome, and occasional agrarian settlements apart, their energies were largely devoted to raiding for food, loot and prisoners. Such behaviour, together with their deflection of much Saharan gold to Portuguese West Africa, intensified Moroccan hostility and at the same time weakened the country's economy, and thus its ability to meet Portuguese demands (cf. pp. 170, 173, 253). Worse still, there appeared in the first half of the sixteenth century the powerful Chorfa dynasty, soon controlling the gold of Timbuktu, and hence able to raise an impressive army. Portuguese coastal bases, cut off from their natural hinterlands by spreading Moslem power, were for a time, and with difficulty, supported from home and then, in 1549–50, evacuated. A ludicrously inept attempt at reconquest ended with the death of the unhinged king Sebastian of Portugal at the battle of El-Ksar El-Kebir (1578) – the last of a long succession of Christian crusading disasters in North Africa – where most of his nobles were either slain or captured. The few remaining Portuguese possessions were lost, surrendered or abandoned in the course of the seventeenth and eighteenth centuries.

Dealings with Ethiopia were even briefer. Long idealized by western publicists as the ruler of a mighty Christian state, the emperor of Abyssinia controlled in fact a large, weak and primitive country (cf. p. 229). Threatened by Moslem neighbours, its civilization in decay, it was basically sustained by a simple pastoral economy and the export of some gold, slaves, and natural products. These inconvenient truths were only understood after the return in 1526 of an embassy which found the Ethiopian devotion to cowdung sauce unappealing and discovered the emperor to be no Prester John whose military power could be joined to Portuguese naval strength to defeat Islam, but an impecunious and peripatetic chieftain embarrassingly eager for European tools and weapons. Eventually, in 1541–3, the Portuguese saved Abyssinia from the Turks in a remarkable campaign mounted from India. But they established no authority over this remote and isolated land, inhabited by Coptic Christians regarded as heretics, and offering nothing worth the taking.

Elsewhere, however, their hold was more tenacious. The descent of the West African coast, if it brought increasingly arduous conditions the further south the Portuguese pushed – high temperatures, dense forests, lethal fevers – brought also the happy prospect of gold, slaves and pepper. Through their fortified trading post at Arguim (Mauritania), which survived until taken by the Dutch in 1638, they obtained slaves, and gold in sufficient quantities to allow the minting (1457) of a golden coin (the *cruzado*) in Portugal (see pp. 227ff.). In exchange they supplied the North African grain, cloth and horses formerly brought in overland. Faced by an organized society, and sufficiently distant from the mother country to be spared those crusading urges excited in the royal house by the proximity of Islamic Morocco, the Portuguese soon learned, as in Asia, that there was no prospect of conquest, and little sense in sacrificing profit to principle. After a short interlude of skirmishing they settled down to normal commercial relations with Moslem merchants, and showed only a momentary interest in penetrating inland.

But Arguim was eclipsed when, in the mid-1400s, the Portuguese reached Senegambia, the most highly developed part of Negro Africa – urban, Moslem, politically advanced, culturally distinguished – and with moreover, access to the gold of the interior. Military defeats at African hands, and the reduction of their always modest numbers by the uncontrollable ravages of disease, induced generally amicable Portuguese relations with the local peoples. Their ships worked as far up the Gambia as Cantor – about 700km inland – and some hardy individuals perhaps reached Timbuktu. But once again no control or occupation was attempted. Instead, in creeks and rivers along the coast from the Senegal to Cape Palmas, Portuguese merchants sold, in competition with overland traders from North Africa, Barbary horses, iron and cloth, for gold, ivory, slaves and *malagueta*.[29] But besides this more or less conventional commerce, uncertain numbers of adventurers were absorbed into indigenous societies, as was later the case in Asia (see pp. 274f.). These *lançados* were fugitives or exiles – often Jews, persecuted in Iberia – for whose talents there was no outlet in the mother country, and who settled in African villages inland, adopted local ways, and, whilst evading Portuguese authority and exactions, became invaluable intermediaries in trade.

Better still were the prospects of the littoral of the Gulf of Guinea, discovered in the second half of the fifteenth century. On the Gold Coast – Negro and pagan, but less politically advanced than Senegambia – the Portuguese were able to establish castles and posts at Mina (1482) and Axim (1503), and even to contemplate colonization. There quickly sprang up an impressive trade in *malagueta*, gold – officially put at over 400kg a year by the early 1500s – slaves, and such curiosities as ostrich eggs. In exchange the Portuguese gave beads, shells, textiles – some of them Indian – and metal goods improbably ranging from shaving mugs to chamber pots, making for a time, so it was alleged, profits of more than 500 per cent. And to these pleasing opportunities there were added, from the late fifteenth century, those of the Niger basin, with its ivory, slaves and high-quality pepper. But with the rise of Chorfa power, drawing bullion back to the old overland routes to North Africa, Portuguese gold exports declined from the mid-1500s, and the pepper trade was abandoned to protect that with Asia (see pp. 269ff.). Even worse, European competitors appeared – with the Spaniards as far south as Benin by the 1470s – forcing up prices in Africa and driving the Portuguese to the burden and expense of defending their commerce. Nor was their hold on the region in any case firm. They had no more than a handful of undermanned coastal fortresses, and such were relations with local peoples that no *lançados* penetrated inland, and miscegenation was so rare as to oblige the crown to order the provision (1529) of four white women to satisfy the sexual demands of Mina's fifty-six European inhabitants 'without preference or distinction'. Defeats by Africans in the late 1500s were followed by the loss of Mina itself to the Dutch (1638), who eventually secured the entire Gold Coast (1663) and control of its trade (see pp. 301f., 390).

Further south the pattern of empire was different. In 1483 the Portuguese reached the Bantu kingdom of the Congo,[30] an established realm, and like those of Upper Guinea, of a high political and cultural level. Partly through missionary influence; partly through Portuguese respect for a society governed, it was admitted, 'by reason'; partly through the genuine interest of the Congolese royal house in Christianity and those western skills likely to be useful in resisting primitive neighbours; and not least since, to start with, the Congo had no obviously exploitable resources, relations were for a time remarkably amicable. The king who reigned as Dom Afonso I (1506–43) was so perceptive a convert to the white man's religion as to demand (1516) that as a Christian ruler he should enjoy the monopoly of the slave trade in his own lands.[31] Congolese aristocrats were educated to such good effect in Portugal that their intelligence and elegant Latin impressed visitors. Meanwhile the Congolese royal court was reorganized on Portuguese lines; reform of the Congolese diet was mooted; skilled Portuguese workers were imported; a Congolese church was established and a royal Congolese bishop enthroned. But the Congo was to receive no such lasting stimulus from the Portuguese as eastern Europe had gained from the Hanse (see pp. 68ff.). Tropical disease destroyed limited resources in men. Missionary zeal waned, and Portuguese energies were either increasingly directed elsewhere or, in the Congo, and notwithstanding royal Portuguese and Congolese objections, turned to slaving. Portuguese continued to be spoken and written there well into the seventeenth century, and some form of Christianity survived even longer. But the Congolese were by then, and hardly surprisingly, amongst Portugal's most determined enemies.

High ideals flourished more briefly still in Angola, which the Portuguese knew from about 1520. This Bantu kingdom was far less advanced than the Congo and rumoured, moreover, to possess silver which inspired persistent searches for treasure, culminating in an attempt (1607) to find that of the headwaters of the Zambesi. By this time, too, such liberal views as had ever been held on the conversion of Africa had largely evaporated in the face of widespread missionary failure there. So the country was to be conquered and colonized (1571). But its history was not to be one of simple peasant settlement and agriculture as first envisaged. The demands of Iberian America for African labour, and Angola's easily accessible and vast human resources – 'such as will last to the ending of the world', it was optimistically reported – quickly established it as the pillar of the Atlantic slave trade. With this came the inescapable corollaries (cf. pp. 246 and 352–3). The intercourse of white males with African females produced a race of mulattos, unbeatable oppressors, like their Brazilian counterparts, of their non-white compatriots, and prime agents in slaving. With a ready market for prisoners, tribal warfare was exacerbated. The very intensity of the trade led to African risings, provoking in turn punitive expeditions which, combined with European-transmitted disease, brought a drastic fall in Angola's population by the late 1600s. Nevertheless the profits of slaving supported in style a small and wealthy colonial community. The city of Luanda – Portugal's only major urban creation in Africa – was founded in 1576. Some years later it was reported to house 'in costly and sumptuous buildings' the slavers and their half-caste minions who here, with white men so few, were able, as in the tropical West African islands, to rise to office (cf. pp. 246). But as usual it was a feebly based opulence. The Dutch, French and English all forced their way into the slave trade in the early 1600s, and the Dutch, supported by Portugal's onetime allies, the Jaga and the Congolese, occupied Luanda and Benguela from 1641–8. Though these were restored in 1663 a Dutch post remained at Loanga and Portugal's dominance of slaving had gone (see p. 390).

The intervention of Portugal in Africa disrupted established economies – diverting, for example, much of the ancient overland commerce between North and West Africa to the sea and into Portuguese hands – created new trades, and modified or extended old ones. Nowhere was this more clearly or notoriously the case than in slaving. Yet though they took and used slaves almost universally the Portuguese were not the original begetters of slavery, which *c.* 1500 was endemic in Africa, much of Europe and most of the recently discovered New World. Initially the Portuguese provided southern Europe with African slaves to supplement, and eventually replace, those of other races already long-employed there (cf. pp. 106ff., 172, 174ff.). Then, from the late 1400s, there came a massive expansion of the trade to meet the requirements of the Atlantic islands and America, where indigenous populations were either unavailable, insufficient or unsuitable for various fatally arduous tasks, particularly the large-scale production of crops commanding valuable markets in Europe. The Atlantic slave trade was thus both of a greater volume than its predecessor in the Mediterranean, and of a different pattern, dealing less in girls than in males for manual labour (see pp. 107–8 and 175).

These slaves, like those of the Genoese and Venetians, were not as a rule obtained by Viking-like European raids. Such operations indeed there were – in the Canaries in the early 1400s, in Morocco soon after, and most notably in Angola from the late sixteenth century. Here expeditions comprising mulattos, African slaves, and Portugal's allies, the cannibal Jagas, were capable of rounding up several thousand victims. But in a continent where in times of famine people sold themselves into slavery to stay alive, and where chiefs had prisoners, rivals and delinquents of every social class to dispose of, slaves could be much less arduously acquired. Some the Portuguese took as tribute, the rest they obtained by barter or purchase, using *lançados* as intermediaries in

Senegambia, and Africans and mulattos in Angola. North of the Gold Coast the horse was the best currency. To the south, where it was unable to survive, shells, trinkets, weapons and cloth were employed.

The volume of this traffic is uncertain. In the early years the crown farmed out stretches of the African coast to contractors. These supposedly sent their cargoes to Lisbon, but there was occasional permission for direct shipments to Spanish America, and the farmers themselves licensed other traders. With the union of Spain and Portugal (1580–1640) there appeared (1586) the *asiento* system, whereby contractors, usually Portuguese Jews or Genoese financiers, agreed with the king to provide a given number of slaves over a specified period in stipulated markets in the New World and Europe. But they too licensed others, and quite apart from the sale of slaves in Africa itself – bartered, for instance, at Mina for gold – there was a massive illegal traffic from Africa to America. Moreover, what were known in the language of the trade as 'pieces' were not necessarily individual humans. A 'piece' was a prime male aged between 15 and 25, but if younger or older three slaves were needed to make up two 'pieces'. Nevertheless the traffic was clearly a very substantial one. By 1540 some 10,000 slaves were probably being taken from West Africa every year, and between 1580 and 1640 about 500 000 were shipped to the Americas. They came, to start with, from Guinea, supporting, by 1500, a commerce of greater value than those in gold and pepper, and later from Angola which in *c.* 1600 was annually supplying 8000 to Brazil, 5000 to the Spanish Main and the Caribbean, and 1500 to Buenos Aires.[32]

Assembled and fattened up in coastal barracoons, slaves were shipped from Africa in horrifying conditions. Naked, the males chained for fear of revolt, they were crammed 500 at a time into the airless holds of ships cynically labelled floating coffins (*tumbeiros*) by the Portuguese. Hastily baptized and christened, they were despatched on a journey lasting (from Angola to Rio de Janeiro) up to fifty days, and on which 40 per cent of those embarked could be expected to die. Even so, whilst pedantic bureaucrats were exercised as to the eternal well-being of the souls of Africans unhappily transported in Protestant vessels, slavers reputedly reaped profits of several hundred per cent. The traffic was not, therefore, one likely to flag. The death rate of negro field hands was high in the Americas, their reproduction rate low, and colonial demand insatiable. Nor in a Europe where vagrants were branded and religious dissenters tortured or burned to death was there any serious objection to treating Africans in the same way. And least of all was a trade in which Portuguese clergy and royal princes alike were engaged in any danger of suppression. The wholesale enslavement of Negroes brought no such qualms to the Iberian conscience as did the treatment of the Amerindians. It was denounced by the Portuguese author of a treatise on naval warfare (1555), and criticised and condemned by some Iberian Jesuits and ecclesiasts in the sixteenth and seventeenth centuries. But only one writer of any consequence, the Spaniard Bartolomé de Albornoz, attacked its injustice and immorality in a work predictably enjoying little popularity (1573). Not till the end of his life did las Casas, the redoubtable Spanish protagonist of Amerindian rights, extend his compassion to Africans. To others of similar views the Amerindian was to be saved by enslaving the Negro (see pp. 333, 362).

Slavery was to be the Africans' lot since they were of the race that carried, as the Book of Genesis recorded, the burden of Noah's curse on the offspring of Canaan, son of Ham, and so destined to toil for ever in the service of others. They were supposedly captured in what were considered to be 'just wars' against societies of evil practices – though in fact most were acquired from pagan or infidel dealers. Their enslavement was accordingly legitimate, and the price they had to pay to become Christian. Crude prejudice reinforced this convenient erudition. Africans looked and smelled differently to Europeans, and were commonly and offensively naked. Above all they were black, the colour that proclaimed the enormity of their ancestors' sins, and the colour popularly identified with evil in a civilization already conscious of the superiority of whiteness (see p. 174). An urbane Italian merchant of the late sixteenth century freely admitted the admirable qualities and beauty of West African women, 'except', as he wrote, 'for their colour'.[33] Moreover, the most powerful societies the Portuguese encountered outside Europe were almost invariably ruled by peoples white rather than black – Moslem North Africa, Ottoman Turkey, Japan, China, Mogul India. But Africans the Portuguese had known as slaves since Moorish times, and had been bought as such from Arab traders as early as the thirteenth century. Next they were encountered during Portugal's expansion around and into Africa, very often living as people whose cultures and tribal societies apparently violated contemporary European criteria – basically those of Aristotle – as to what constituted civilization, and accordingly stigmatized them as natural inferiors. Faced, in Senegambia and the Congo, by organized African powers, the Portuguese were prepared to deal with them as with European states. For the rest, Africans were, as was said, merely animals 'fit to be used for any kind of work'.

Slavers the Portuguese might be in West Africa, but conquerors they were not, and whatever the exploits of individual missionaries and frontiersmen they remained, like other Europeans before the nineteenth century, on or just off the continent's coast. Yet if their military resources were inferior to those of Spain they were still sufficient to raise expeditions the size of those that overthrew the Aztecs and Incas (see pp. 309ff.). Nor was there a lack of potential allies in Africa. But here, as elsewhere, the general practice of the Portuguese, coming from a homeland where communication was easier by sea and river, was to penetrate, like the Vikings, along coasts and along riparian and maritime routes. And Africa was in any case no easy prey. Its highest cultures, outside Ethiopia and the Moslem north and east, may only have been of the iron age, but its inhabitants were more numerous, militarily stronger, and better able to defend themselves than were the Amerindians. Moreover, its cool highlands, unlike those of Mexico and Peru in which Europeans throve, were well inland and difficult to reach, condemning the Portuguese to the tropical heat and deadly fevers of coastal swamps and estuaries. There they rarely survived for long and so produced no *mestiço* population through miscegenation with local women, such as explains the tenacity of their hold on Brazil. And whilst for Spain the prospects of America seemed ever better, for Portugal those of Africa rapidly deteriorated as it was overshadowed by the riches of Asia, and harassed by European attacks from which the Far East was still relatively sheltered.

Much the same happened in East Africa. It was eventually realized that those 'infinite quantities of gold' reported by the first expeditions to India came from the Negro lands of the North Transvaal, Manica and the Matabele plateau. From there, together with slaves and ivory, they were transmitted through Moslem middlemen to the Arab merchants of the great ports of Kilwa, Mombasa and Malindi, and so entered the commerce of the Indian Ocean. Bold strategists saw no obstacles to establishing direct relations with the Negro producers, setting up yet another Portuguese monopoly, and destroying Arab commerce. Nor were such schemes wildly improbable. There was no unity among the Arab and Islamic coastal cities, and gold was provided by territories under the nominal suzerainty of the decaying Monomotapa empire. By force, fraud and luck the Portuguese secured fortresses and factories at Sofala (1505), Kilwa (1505) and Malindi. Mozambique became, through its strategic site, a way-station at which the crews of outward-bound Indiamen were rested, but where, the anti-scorbutic qualities of its coconuts notwithstanding, they died in huge numbers. With gold and ivory obtained through neighbouring ports it flourished as the centre of a trade with western India, which in the mid-1500s – when perhaps as much as 8t of gold were exported annually – was one of the most profitable in Portuguese hands.

In the course of these operations, and in the hope of further windfalls, the Portuguese explored part of the coast of Madagascar (1506), climbed Table Mountain, and took Mombasa (1528). Antonio Fernandes made his way into what was later southern Rhodesia (1514), and until defeated by the climate and Arab opposition Portuguese pioneers moved inland to trade with the Bantu, eventually reaching the southern shores of Lake Malawi. The killing of a missionary brought the momentary subjugation of Mashonaland, and between roughly 1575 and 1640 territory in the hinterland of Sofala was occupied, with the Portuguese perhaps pushing as far up the Zambesi as the Kariba Gorge, and founding posts at Sena, Tete and elsewhere. Even more remarkably, with the failure of the paramount chieftaincy of the Makalanga confederacy, white, Goan and mulatto adventurers received, or took for themselves, in the seventeenth century, lands of Zambesian sub-chiefs. Replacing these, even to the extent in some cases of exercising ritual functions, they became the virtually absolute rulers of territories as vast as the greatest estates of Iberian America, commanders of armies of free and enslaved Africans, and the recipients of wealth obtained from plunder and a trade in gold, ivory and cloth.

Nevertheless Portugal's hold on East Africa was of the usual precarious nature. There was, indeed, until the mid-1600s a substantial export of gold and ivory to western India, and the commerce of the Arab littoral was seriously damaged. Yet the

Portuguese monopoly was rarely more than nominal. Their manpower, again depleted by disease, was hopelessly inadequate to control the innumerable outlets for African gold. The Arabs drove them off the coast north of Cape Delgado in the seventeenth century, and in Mozambique and the Zambesi valley it was the familiar story of West Africa. Friendly relations grew up with a number of potentates, some of whom were converted to Christianity, but whatever their initial ambitions the Portuguese came to accept local sheiks, headmen and merchants as the intermediaries in their trade.

III *Motives and methods*

The startling paradox that a country so small and poor as Portugal should found an empire that heralded the onset of some five centuries of European attempts to subjugate the rest of mankind admits no simple explanation. The beginnings of Portuguese expansion were inspired by no such hopes of sanctuary as led to emigration from Viking Scandinavia or seventeenth-century England. There is no reason, either, to believe that, as in medieval Norway or Flanders, demographic pressure drove men abroad, and indeed the large-scale importation of slaves in the fifteenth century, when Europe's population was in general falling, suggests the very opposite. Nor, at least by the standards of the time, was food in short supply. Portugal admittedly occasionally imported grain in the early 1400s, but she also exported it, and whatever the undoubted rigours of their homeland the Portuguese showed, in the early and crucial years of empire, a marked reluctance to leave it. Colonizers were obliged to raise settlers from wherever they could, and the state to ship convicts to its new territories (cf. pp. oo–o).

Neither, to begin with, were there any commercial ambitions. The first Portuguese voyages had no such clearly defined objective as Columbus' search for Cathay. Nor was there any intention, as with the Italian and German cities earlier in the Middle Ages, of penetrating and dominating an established pattern of trade (cf. pp. oo–o and oo–o). An expedition to the Canaries in 1341, involving Venice's mortal enemies the Genoese, had hopes of spices.[34] But this interest only re-emerged in the course of the Portuguese exploration of West Africa, by which time, with their ships trading down the Mediterranean, they presumably had some appreciation of the basis of Venetian wealth. Moreover their attack on Morocco – hardly in any case likely to yield spices – was launched when the amount of pepper available to the west was increasing, and its price in Egypt falling.[35] Possibly, too, like other regions of Europe in the late Middle Ages, Portugal was in urgent need of bullion. But whilst this could be of pressing concern to a commercial power it was of lesser moment in a more rudimentary economy, and notwithstanding the obvious and timeless attractions of gold, the Portuguese were notably slower in attempting to control its flow in North Africa in the early 1400s than they were the movement of spices in Asia a century later (cf. pp. 251f., 236ff., 269). More than any such rational calculations their first assaults on Morocco reflect that same urge of martial aristocrats and squires for loot and glory as explains so much Viking, Genoese, English and subsequent Portuguese behaviour (cf. pp. 11, 159, 465, 482). It was an urge probably further sharpened by the falling rents and food prices of the fifteenth century, making the maintenance of proper style, and the liberal reward of followers, increasingly difficult. And with the end of the war with Castile in 1411, and ambitions in Europe barred by the Spanish kingdoms, Portugal's only outlets were to the south and west.

Humanist Portuguese chroniclers, however, recognized no such base motives. A great venture was inspired by Prince Henry, and he by a thirst for knowledge. But if genuine curiosity moved some of his royal successors – King Manuel instructing his captains 'where you come upon something new, send it to me'[36] – there is little sign of it in the Infante. Preoccupied with religion, astrology, honour, chastity and his own authority, his intellectual interests were limited, and his geographical learning modest. He knew nothing of Ptolemy or of such compilations as that of d'Ailly, let alone the works of the great Arab writers (see pp. 229f.). Excluded from high politics, his energies were turned, not like those of many other medieval magnates to factional strife, but to the support of the earliest and unrewarding African and Atlantic voyages, which might otherwise have been abandoned. But his ideals were those of a long tradition of courtly literature – to reward faithful retainers, convert the pagan, smite the infidel, seek out Christian princes. Nor did such aims ever entirely evaporate. In the early 1500s pious laymen could hope to hear Mass in the mosques of Morocco. For centuries the religious Orders were to labour to gain souls. In 1508 the hearts of oppressed eastern Christians were to be gladdened by tidings that relief was at hand, and even Albuquerque, pragmatist in most things, took a personal interest in the education of young Indian converts to Catholicism.

Nevertheless from the very beginning the Portuguese overseas, whatever their class, showed a remarkable zeal to do business with all they encountered, Moslems included. Already in the mid-1400s papal privileges combined commendation of missionary zeal with licence to trade with the infidel and grants of commercial monopoly. The amalgam of piracy, slaving and exploration in the first African voyages shows how early and strong such material urges were, and the ever-impecunious Prince Henry was soon himself engaged in the slave trade, whilst, like some Viking chieftain, distributing lands known and unknown to his retainers. The better the prospects, the livelier and more widespread the interest. Merchants who ignored the profitless Saharan littoral were willing enough to deal with West Africa; peasants could hope for land in Brazil or wealth by an infinity of ways in Asia; ever more splendid opportunities for plunder and extortion opened to aristocrats and knights in the east (cf. pp. 229 and 274–5). The crown itself aspired to monopolize Asia's richest trade, urged the subjugation of realms capable of rendering tribute and the discovery of those likely to produce profit.[37] Yet there was more, if not much more, to the empire's growth than the tireless quest for riches condemned by moralists. It grew in part by accidental finds (as with Japan), in part, like all others, by its own momentum (as in the interior of East Africa). It grew also, as with the taking of Malacca and the colonization of Brazil, to protect vital interests and forestall rivals (cf. pp. 238–9 and 247). And in Asia, Albuquerque and his admirers reiterated, conquests were to be made to overawe local rulers, and to enhance the power and glory of the kings of Portugal above that of all others.[38]

For the realization of these ambitions the country was, at first sight, poorly endowed. It comprised, *c.* 1400, some 89 000 square km of mostly barren, uncultivable or mountainous land. Its population, chiefly engaged in a primitive agriculture, numbered roughly one million at a time when that of India was perhaps a hundred million, and contributed little to Europe's commerce beyond salt, cork, fish and olive oil. Yet this impoverished and rural economy had its advantages. Aristocrats and squires, bred in the traditions of the reconquest of Iberia from the Moors to spurn menial toil, were ready seekers after riches overseas; peasants supplied the manpower for colonization. Poverty further freed Portugal from such wealthy cities (Lisbon apart) as troubled more opulent neighbours, and smallness allowed the growth of a sense of national identity and the effective exercise of royal authority. Nor was this by accident. Between 1385 and 1580 the state was ruled, largely in peace, by a succession of able monarchs of the Aviz dynasty, whose energies, denied an outlet in Europe by Portugal's geographical situation, were devoted to colonial endeavour with a singlemindedness unparalleled in any other royal house. The influence of princes Henry, Pedro and John was decisive in the earliest stages of expansion (see pp. 228–9, 245). Later, Manuel I both ensured that the enterprise of India was not abandoned, and in a ceaseless flow of instructions – embracing everything from the conduct of fleets at sea to the siting of fortresses ashore – directed his commanders to what were considered vital objectives. Under this close and purposeful supervision, and in search of goals identified from information carefully gathered and appraised, the initial Portuguese advance in Asia was impressively rapid.

But more was involved than the qualities of the ruling house and its servants. No European country, except Spain, was geographically closer to Africa, and none better sited to be a base for oceanic voyages. Most early ships, with their clumsy hulls and ill-cut sails, went to windward badly, making excessive leeway and changing tacks reluctantly. Hence they preferred such beam or following breezes as blow off Portugal, where to the south-west the prevailing winds set down the West African coast, and towards the nearby Atlantic islands and the shoulder of Brazil (in turn giving access to the equally favourable systems of the south Atlantic). For the return to Iberia following westerlies could be picked up in about latitude 35°n off North America. Portugal was admirably, though not exceptionally, suited to profit from these opportunities. Her kings had possessed a fleet since at least the thirteenth century, refurbished at one stage under Genoese supervision, and as in other aggressive maritime powers there was a vigorous tradition of aristocratic shipowning (cf. pp. 199ff., 337, 458). Fisherman worked from most of the country's lengthy coastline, and by the 1300s Portuguese ships were to be found anywhere from the Canaries to the English Channel. They penetrated

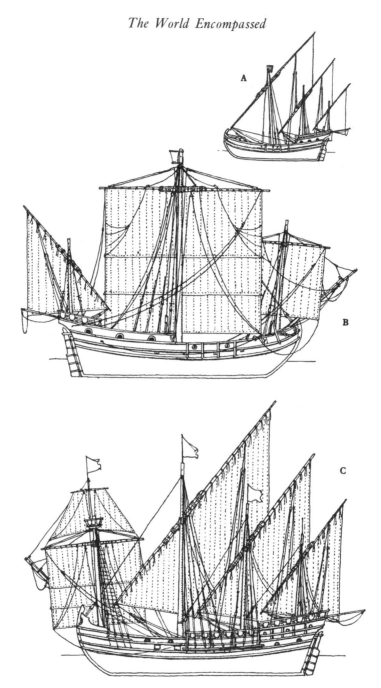

Fig. 11   Types of Iberian carvels, *c.* 1500 (A and B) and 1545
(C), reconstructed by Björn Landström.

the Mediterranean in the early fifteenth century, and besides entering local trades were soon carrying sugar direct from the Atlantic islands to the waters of the Levant.

To these considerable advantages fertile imaginations have generously added others, seeing the oceans opened to mankind by the Portuguese development of a particular vessel, the carvel, whose lateen rig and stern-rudder made her to all intents independent of the direction of the wind. But this she never was, as Columbus found when in 1494 his carvels gained only 51km in twenty-five days of tacking. However admirable the lateen is for sailing on or near the wind, or for long runs in favourable breezes, it can be a dangerous liability on short beats (cf. p. 147). Certainly by 1500 the carvel, after some three centuries of evolution, was an impressive craft – small (60–140t), rakish, and with her flush planking and fine lines, fast. She might be rigged with the traditional two masts – the larger amidships – both setting lateens. Or she might have one or two forward masts – the larger still amidships – carrying square sails, and another one or two aft with lateens. In part this reflected Mediterranean experiment, in part an evolution determined by the demands of oceanic voyaging, as when Dias suggested that da Gama's ships should be square-rigged (cf. pp. 147, 194). No more than the distinctive craft of the Norse or the Hanse did the carvel spring forth fully-fledged to permit the beginning of a particular cycle of maritime history (cf. pp. 18f., 77f.). In fact the first Portuguese explorers sailed in more or less whatever came to hand, whilst a celebrated pilot told John II that the Guinea voyage could be made by any good ship, and an intrepid compatriot returned from India in one only 5.5m long.

Nor did some especial Portuguese navigational skill permit these pioneers to find their way freely about the globe. Instead, as with the Norse, such techniques were the consequence, not the cause, of oceanic sailing. The first West African voyages demanded only seamanship of a high order since they were coastal passages made by craft which examined shores by day and anchored by night. They were indeed said to have been undertaken by crews recruited from northern trades who, unlike the best Mediterranean navigators, 'were unable to use either compass or chart'.[39] Once, however, lengthy runs had to be made out of sight of land – initially to avoid foul winds and currents – and new lands had to be located and mapped, something more was needed than the ancient practices of dead-reckoning (see p. 15). Like the Norse before them, and in much the same way, the Portuguese called the heavens to their aid. Navigators learned to calculate how far north or south they had travelled by observing the changing altitude of the Pole Star above the northern horizon. Further, by marking its elevation at a known place on an astrolabe or quadrant they could, on subsequent occasions, sail on until the particular reading was recovered and then turn for the desired landfall.[40] Near, or beyond the equator – reached by the Portuguese in the 1470s – where the Pole Star was invisible or too low, a pilot calculated his latitude from observation of the mid-day sun and, with the aid of tables, established the distance and direction to be sailed to arrive on that of his intended destination, along which he would then run. Though the problem of longitude was never solved the achievement was none the less impressive. But it was no revolution. The fixing of latitude by celestial observation was the application to the sea of skills long employed on land and far from exclusively Iberian. Unbeknown to the rest of Europe it had earlier, if more crudely, been practised by the Norse. Its potential maritime use was understood by Peter Peregrinus in the thirteenth century, and in 1429 the commander of a Florentine galley fleet on passage to the English Channel took the height of the Pole Star with his astrolabe.

Portugal shared something of the European scientific culture and the rich heritage of Judeo-Arabic mathematical and cosmographical learning that underlay such experiments. From the time of Prince Henry, who took into his service the cartographer Master James of Majorca, the ruling house employed distinguished specialists like the Venetian Fra Mauro or the Salamancan mathematicians Diego Ortiz and José Vizinho. Under the crown's direction their skills solved such urgent problems as, in the 1480s, the fixing of latitude south of the equator. But this intelligent royal use of an often foreign knowledge is no indication of some unique Portuguese precocity. Nor was the conversion to new ways sudden and total. There is no clear evidence of celestial determination of latitudes at sea by the Portuguese before the 1480s – by when the course of expansion was well advanced – and even as late as 1500 a learned pilot sailing for India could write of his colleagues 'only when we reach the Cape shall we know who goes better, they by chart (i.e. dead-reckoning) or I by chart and astrolabe.'[41]

Another alleged ingredient in Portuguese primacy was the country's association with those international merchants and bankers alone supposedly able to bear the vast expense of voyages of discovery. Certainly the country had its merchants both native (including an important Jewish and New Christian element) and foreign, who might, as did the Italians, dominate much of its economy (cf. pp. 181ff.). But for them to invest in going concerns was one thing, to put their money where risks were high and profits unlikely, quite another. The earliest Portuguese voyages aroused little interest, were largely sustained by the ruling dynasty, and were usually financed by loans from Jews, the church, the royal exchequer or well-disposed grandees. Nor did expeditions consisting at best of two or three small, unladen, vessels commanded by retainers of the house of Aviz require lavish backing. But once the potential of the discoveries was appreciated, the picture swiftly changed. A Lisbon merchant controlled the exploitation of the Guinea coast in the mid-1400s, and Genoese financiers were investing in the Atlantic islands (see p. 182). By the early 1500s many of the greatest names in European business were engaged in the new imperial commerce. From Portugal celebrated Florentine houses traded to Africa, Brazil and the east, with a Serigni enrolled to help with the 'discovery of Malacca'.[42] Cologne and Antwerp merchants dealt in wine and sugar; the Haros of Burgos supported the exploration of the Río de la Plata (1513) and farmed the commerce of Sierra Leone (1514); Welsers and other south-German plutocrats were prominent in trade with Asia. But though such magnates clearly speeded the exploitation of the Portuguese discoveries – indeed with such zest and success that it soon seemed that, like those of Spain, they had been made for their exclusive benefit – this is not to say that they had made those discoveries possible.

Outside Europe the Portuguese, as the pioneers of Europe's expansion, enjoyed the benefit of surprise. Like the Spaniards in America or the Germans in the north, they rarely encountered any sustained or substantial opposition, and their success in Brazil and Africa, a contemporary sourly remarked, was scarcely conceivable but for tribal disunity. In Asia the enormous diversity of race and religion, and the structure of commerce brought them allies and eased their penetration of an established and flourishing economy (see pp. 236–7). Their puny numbers were reinforced in war by slaves and local auxiliaries, and their fighting power occasionally enhanced – though never to the extent of that of Spain in America – by the use of cavalry against peoples unaccustomed to the horse (cf. pp. 337–9). And to their great good fortune they never directly faced any major naval or military power. More important still, it has been argued, were Portuguese guns and the ships that carried them, ensuring the defeat of nations innocent of such technological refinements. True, even in Asia (China excepted) there was little artillery of any size when the Portuguese first arrived. Nor, since the planking of eastern vessels (those of the Chinese apart) was sewn together and not, as in the west, nailed, could they have fired such weapons without disintegrating. But this imbalance was more apparent than real. Gujarati shipbuilders emulated European techniques of construction, whilst the Portuguese frequently employed both local craft and local weapons. By capture or purchase Asian peoples soon had guns, and taught by European renegades quickly became expert in their use and manufacture. Diu alone had over 100 pieces salvaged from Portuguese wrecks by 1508, and later in the century visitors admired the proficiency of Sinhalese musketeers.[43] Certainly European guns could, on occasions, overawe or demoralize those unaware of their notorious fallibility. But in the downpours of the tropics, with their powder wet and their temperamental reluctance to fire, they were often as not useless. Neither in Asia nor anywhere else was empire the inevitable corollary of technological superiority.

Imperial expansion was one thing. Simultaneously to govern and exploit possessions as different as uninhabited islands and thriving oriental entrepôts was something new to the experience of post-classical Europe. For two centuries, with a flexibility inspired in part by desperation, in part by the determination of an aristocratic society to reap the maximum reward for the minimum effort, the Portuguese experimented with every known form of colonial control. Lands peopled and unpeopled alike were settled with those unwanted at home. Whole territories and trades were handed over, in the manner of the Italian maritime cities, to individuals or companies (cf. pp. 190ff.). Venetian-style commercial monopolies were employed in Asia and Africa, and the success of the great Dutch and English trading corporations eventually inspired the setting up of Portuguese replicas for Asia (1628) and Brazil (1649). But as in any empire the simplest form of exploitation was downright plunder. Whilst kings called for the accomplish-

ment of martial feats and bellicose clerics demanded the fulfilment of Portugal's
crusading destiny, energies were devoted – particularly in the earliest decades in the
east – to looting. Captains expatiated on treasure found or expected; viceregal
instructions detailed the distribution of prizes; temples of even friendly Indian rulers
were sacked; commanders remiss in the pursuit of riches were abandoned by their men.
Not all wealth had to be so strenuously amassed. To high-born predators the maritime
commerce of Asia was a magnificent hostage to be either pillaged or subjected to
demands so extortionate as to destroy the prosperity of Hormuz and Malacca. What a
less primitive state could achieve in similar circumstances was shown by Genoese and
Venetian behaviour in Constantinople (see pp. 94, 161). Of much the same order was the
repeated Portuguese demand for tribute – grain from Morocco, cinnamon from Ceylon,
pearls from Hormuz. Occasionally this extended to the imposition of sovereignty, but
displays of force notwithstanding – often against relatively insignificant powers –
Portugal's empire was not, as was that of Spain in America, one of conquest (see pp.
308ff.). Both in Africa and Asia its essence was the attempted diversion into Portuguese
hands of existing trades. In the face of hostile climates, vast continents and powerful
civilizations this involved for so miniscule a state little of that colonization that had
earlier accompanied similar German achievements in the north (see pp. 38ff.). The
exceptions were Brazil and the Atlantic islands, deliberately populated by feudatories
and contractors in ways long familiar in Europe. In many cases convicts, not to say
desperados guilty of 'most hainous crimes and incestuous acts',[44] were used, just as
they were often landed, with a promise of freedom, to learn local languages and gather
information. This view of empire as a repository for the unwanted – far different from
that of the Spaniards – echoing though it does well-established traditions of
banishment, was Portugal's characteristic and influential contribution to the technique
of colonization (cf. p. 341).

But what might serve for desert islands and tropical backlands would hardly do for
Portuguese Asia. To this, too, emigration was under royal supervision, with unmarried
males (*soldados*) supposedly constituting a military reserve, and the married (*casados*),
exempt from such obligations, the living proof of Portuguese sovereignty and
permanence. The wives of these rank and file colonial citizens were generally
indigenous or half-caste women. Already in Africa the crown, appreciating that empire
entailed settlement, had ordered the marriage of some convicts to Negresses, and in São
Tomé provided bachelors with 'native girls for breeding'. The practice received a
notable extension after the capture of Goa through the enthusiasm of Albuquerque,
keenly aware, like others touched by resurgent classical influences, of Roman teaching
on the virtues of colonization (cf. p. 341). Female Moslem and Hindu prisoners were
converted, given doweries – often raised from the ransoms of their fathers or
husbands[45] – and married off to Portuguese men who were rewarded, like ex-Roman
legionaries, with grants of land and the prospect of a trade. There was no question of
racial equality or indifference to colour. The policy was strenuously opposed in

Portugal – 'the mating of slaves with trash' was one view[46] – and defended by its protagonists on the grounds that Moslem and high-caste Hindu girls were more or less white. Nevertheless by regularizing those unions which Portuguese, like most other expatriates, eagerly formed with local women it ingeniously attempted to alleviate the usual shortage of European females overseas, and its continuance ensured Portugal a tenacious colonial population she could not herself have provided (cf. pp. 250ff.).

Such proceedings characterized a willingness, peculiarly Iberian, to turn to profit, with as little effort as possible, whatever came to hand. In Africa Negro and mulatto intermediaries supplied slaves, just as in America Indian chiefs collected tribute for their Spanish masters (cf. pp. 255ff., 322, 351). In Asia native allies (Moslems included) were to help found an empire;[47] native troops defend it; native women populate it; and native skills benefit its lords. The use of Asian seamen in the royal ships was already being urged in 1505, and before long shipwrights in western India were building both inshore and ocean-going vessels for Portugal. In Goa, until growing religious intolerance largely scotched such pragmatism in the late 1500s, the Portuguese employed not only the system of labour organization they found, but also the whole machinery of revenue collection and administration. Moslems were still farming various monopolies in the mid-sixteenth century, and a hundred years later many sources of government income in Goa, Cochin and elsewhere – customs, taxes on cloth and tobacco – remained in the hands of Hindu lessees on whose financial assistance the Portuguese regularly called.

Then, as the Spaniards were even more clearly to demonstrate in Mexico and Peru, European weakness in manpower could be remedied, and European blood spared, by the use of local martial skills and resources. To take and hold Moslem Goa Albuquerque had the help of some 40 Hindu captains from the city and its vicinity, their troops ferociously assiduous in decapitating the enemy.[48] Over the next few decades, under their own officers – those *naikwaddis* who might also be village headmen – Goan and Malabar infantry and archers in their thousands served with the Portuguese anywhere from Malacca to Aden. Before, in mid-century, religious bigotry checked their use, Hindu mercenary commanders were well-known, well-regarded and well-rewarded figures. Timoja suggested to Albuquerque the attractions of taking Goa, served in the campaign which led to its capture with about 2000 men, and thereafter briefly garrisoned the territory and farmed its revenues. He was succeeded first by Melrao, and then by the wealthy and influential Brahmin, Krishna, who provided not only infantry and gunners, but money as well. For such notable services he was knighted and appointed, amongst other things, chief officer and 'captain of the native soldiers' in Goa. Taken prisoner on a diplomatic mission (1544), he was replaced by his son, and later by a Brahmin convert to Christianity who 'being very rich was found most acceptable'.

This dependence on Hindu, and even occasionally Moslem[49] arms, had obvious disadvantages besides outraging zealous churchmen. To Albuquerque's chagrin

Timoja, no intrepid warrior it transpired, flouted his authority and finally deserted with his rent for Goa unpaid, whilst Krishna was rumoured to be likewise swindling his masters. There was, moreover, the ever-present danger that the Portuguese might end as little more than clients of their own employees. Yet royal injunctions and ecclesiastical fulminations notwithstanding, necessity was a powerful argument for the continued acceptance of that local collaboration which everywhere eased the establishment of European empires, and the continued use of troops willing to serve for about half the pay supposedly received by Portuguese fighting men. Indians were employed in campaigns on the west coast of the sub-continent in the 1530s and 1540s; local auxiliaries fought in Malaysia; Abyssinians garrisoned posts around the Indian Ocean. What little strength Portugal had in Ceylon was largely Sinhalese, and for a time (1610) the Captain of Malacca had a Japanese bodyguard. In the west needs were still greater and scruples accordingly fewer. Negro head-hunters helped to repulse the Dutch from Mina in 1625, and in Angola – where subject chiefs were expected to provide warriors and bearers – the bulk of Portugal's African auxiliaries were Jaga cannibals. In Brazil Amerindians 'armed with shot and other weapons' were serving the Portuguese in the 1580s.[50] Tupí tribesmen were used against Dutch invaders the following century, and Paulista bands usually consisted of no more than a handful of Europeans and *mestiços* accompanied by thousands of Indians (cf. pp. 249 and 255).

Even more fundamental to the Portuguese, as to the Spaniards, were slaves who abroad and at home – where Moors and Africans worked as everything from artisans to manual labourers – were to perform the countless tasks considered menial. Such assumptions were not peculiarly Iberian, but a common heritage from time immemorial of much of the world. So empire and slavery were to be synonymous, and all, whether Berbers or Japanese, their particular aptitudes noted, were to make their contribution to the wealth and comfort of the Portuguese. Africans were used everywhere from South America to China, the women as servants and mistresses, the men as labourers, craftsmen, sailors and – especially the redoubtable warriors of Guinea – as infantry. In Brazil the Portuguese did their utmost to enslave the indigenous populations (cf. p. 248). In Asia they bought unwanted Chinese girls from their parents and accepted those who, like the Sinhalese, were driven by poverty to sell themselves into servitude. They enslaved prisoners, male and female, taken in war; shipped slaves to Europe; sold them to fellow Europeans in the east. Slaves built fortresses; served as interpreters and translators; made gunpowder; carried (men and women alike) their lords' weapons in war; transported the spoils of victory; manned Portuguese ships to ensure 'our men will not die from overwork'.[51] Girls attended to their masters' every need, and in Goa added what they earned from prostitution to their owners' income. Such was the ubiquity of female slaves as concubines and mistresses that, as was pithily remarked of Albuquerque's alleged monopoly of the charms of a galaxy of beauties captured in Goa, 'not even Mahomet had it so good'.[52]

Yet however much the empire depended on the services, willing or unwilling, of non-

Portuguese peoples, and however great the abrogation of royal authority its exploitation entailed, it was one in which, according to contemporary theorists, the power of the house of Aviz was absolute. Kings spoke, in the same language used by Castilian monarchs of their American possessions, of 'our rights of ownership'. These were held to stem from papal grant – from such privileges as the monopoly of commerce and navigation from Cape Bojador to the Indies conferred in 1455, from military conquest and its costs and from the simple fact of primacy. The African seas, John III declared in 1534, 'discovered by me with such great labour, are closed'. The oceans of the east, the historian Barros explained, having been subdued by the Portuguese, could only be navigated by those peoples they permitted. Hence, in the fifteenth century, a whole series of African trades – in gold, pepper and slaves – were declared royal monopolies. In the Indian Ocean commerce was to be brought under Portuguese control – with passes issued to approved vessels, and the rest, together with their cargoes, impounded – taxed, and the spice trade with the west reserved to the king and his subjects.

Wags mocked 'silly Portingales' who, unfit in their commercial innocence even to buy bread in the market, made such arrogant and ludicrous claims.[53] Yet the royal house successfully engaged in commerce – dealing, for example, in São Tomé sugar in the fifteenth century – and Albuquerque himself acknowledged that a crown monopoly would exclude profit-hungry merchants and give the king the best chance of immediate reward, as was indeed the case for a time (see pp. 272, 277). Nor was the attempted imposition of monopoly a peculiarly inept Portuguese ambition. It was in such style that the Hanse aspired to handle the trade of the Baltic, and Venice – as also later England and Holland – to deal with that in spices (cf. pp. 114, 405ff., 477ff.). Moreover, given that in the Indian Ocean the Portuguese encountered a rich and highly organized maritime economy, virtually monopolized by Moslems, it was neither improbable nor implausible that a bellicose Catholic monarchy and its aristocratic retainers should seek not to re-order it, but, like some castle-holding lord on a European trade route, to exact a profit. They had no wish to become growers of pepper or ginger. But the diversion from infidel control of so lucrative a commerce was, like the taking of tribute and loot, an occupation suitable for Christian gentlemen. And for a brief while such policies were effective. Fleets cruised in eastern waters, checking passes and ensuring the payment of dues. To the distress of Venice, the flow of Asian spices through the Levant was disrupted, whilst in the mid-1500s allegedly none were available in central Asia because of Portuguese control of the sources of supply.[54]

This monopoly was established, after some experiment, in 1505–6, when the import of spices, drugs and dyes, and the export of the commodities required for their purchase, became matters for the crown alone. The entire trade was to be conducted through the newly established India House[55] in Lisbon, which also forwarded the royal spices to the crown factor in the great entrepôt of Antwerp, which had the exclusive right of their sale in the north. But with the growth of piracy in the English Channel, and the influx of silver – vital in any dealings with Asia – from the Americas to Iberia, operations became centred in Lisbon by mid-century. Here the king's spice was sold in gross to Portuguese merchants and – increasingly – to German, Italian and New Christian plutocrats working either independently or in partnership. In Asia the crown acquired some of its spices through agreements with local rulers, but the rest were bought in the open market by agents from its factories competing against indigenous traders, and sometimes against each other as well. In the great days spice, as in Venice's trade, largely meant pepper. This was mainly purchased in Malabar, and for a time imports, eclipsing those of the Venetians, amounted to 1500t a year out of a total annual shipment of 3500t of spice (see pp. 101, 140). In exchange Portugal exported roughly the same things as Venice, and rarely any of them her own products. Copper came (via Antwerp) from south Germany; coral from North Africa; quick-silver from Spain; textiles from Italy, England and the Low Countries. But by far the most important element, and of relatively greater moment than in the Venetian trade, was coin and bullion, which in the earliest years might account for 75 per cent of the value of outgoing cargoes, and which by the 1580s, with China's thirst to slake, entailed the annual export of 32t of silver alone. At first this, too, came from southern Germany, and then, through Seville, from Spanish America, and in such quantities as to provoke complaints that Portugal was consuming the entire wealth of the Indies (see pp. 359f.). Purchasing power was initially – but briefly – reinforced with loot, and then strengthened by shipping from Africa the gold demanded by Malabar pepper merchants. After some innocent hopes of buying with Middle Eastern opium or Malaysian tin, the Portuguese turned to gathering still more bullion in the east – Persian and Japanese silver; Indonesian and Chinese gold – and to raising vital capital by interport trading in Asia.[56]

With its royal monopoly, direct royal engagement in trade, overseas factories and central metropolitan entrepôt, Portugal's commerce with the east was organized on the model of that with Africa, where various commodities, assembled by *feitorias*, were – in theory – introduced into Europe only through the House of the Mine (*Casa da Mina*) in Lisbon. The general pattern was one of ancient usage in Europe's long-distance trades, and later employed by Spain in the Atlantic and Pacific (cf. pp. 327–8, 342ff.). The Portuguese monopolies, involving state intervention and participation in business, and the creation of special offices for this purpose, bore a strong and probably deliberate resemblance to the way in which especially important trades were handled by Genoa and Venice. But that in spices, with purchases and sales made in the royal name, was characteristically more ambitious than any of its precursors, and equally characteristically less comprehensive in practice, since the king of Portugal had little effective say in either the buying or selling of his spice.

Similarly in the spirit, if hardly the style of Venice, Portuguese state authority extended for a time to the shipping employed in the trade to Asia and – less systematically – to Africa and Brazil (cf. pp. 123ff.). By the mid-1500s the annual Indies fleet – Portugal's only maritime link with the Far East – consisted of five or six vessels,

Fig. 12   Contemporary drawing of a Portuguese light galley coming to anchor off
western India in 1539. Asian sailors – or, more probably, African slaves – are shown
furling the main sail. The bearded figure at the stern is thought to be D. João de Castro
(1500–48), humanist, seamen and ultimately viceroy of Portuguese India.

some royal, some private, fitted out under the supervision of the *Casa da India*, and
commanded by those of suitably elevated birth either nominated or approved by the
crown. The ships used were fewer and larger than those that sailed between Spain and
the Americas. Some were galleons, but the majority the bigger carracks of 500–1000t,[57]
whose voyages to and from India, dictated by the pattern of favourable winds, were the
longest and most arduous regularly undertaken by European sailing craft before the
nineteenth century.[58] With trumpets sounding and guns firing the fleet left Lisbon in
spring to catch a fair wind for the Cape Verdes. There it turned towards Brazil to find
another fair wind with which it cleared, without sighting, the Cape of Good Hope.[59]
Working up the East African coast the ships then picked up the westerly monsoon
which brought them to Goa between August and October.[60] Late arrivals in the Indian
Ocean, however, would pass outside Madagascar in the hope of catching the last of the
monsoon, or, if they failed, turn back to winter in Africa. The return from India with
the north-east monsoon commenced any time from November to January, and if all

went well the fleet would be home in the following summer or early autumn, escorted in from the Azores after a round trip of at least 54,000kms lasting some 18 months.

This fearsome voyage was, as a rule, made with only one stop (Mozambique) outwards, one or two (Mozambique or St Helena, and the Azores) inwards, and – astonishingly – sometimes with none at all. Ships fell apart on passage, sank through stress of weather, or were lost through the invincible ignorance and incompetence of their officers. In those that remained afloat such was the overcrowding, filth and disease that it was nothing unusual for half the 1000 or so humans crammed into a vessel 50m long and with a beam of 14m to die on the outward run. But these were the hazards of a seafaring life anywhere, and conditions were not invariably so hard. Officers took prostitutes with them, rich passengers gratefully or apprehensively provided livestock and fruit for crews and in 1582 a knowledgeable Italian thought it less dangerous to sail from Lisbon to India than from Barcelona to Genoa. Nevertheless the Portuguese lost about a quarter of the vessels employed in the *carreira*[61] between 1500 and 1635, with, from the 1580s, Dutch and English attacks added to the many perils of the sea. Yet this reflects no especial ineptitude, for even in the eighteenth century the much better placed English East India Company was still losing roughly 10 per cent of its tonnage annually. And with officers and seamen alike vigorously engaged in every sort of private trade, and with spices selling at a profit of 90 per cent clear in the west, and pearls at 200–300 per cent, the toleration of this debilitating haemorrhage was no blind folly.

Such were the attractions of monopoly that the crown sought to extend it further. Between 1522 and 1535 there was an abortive royal monopoly of Moluccan cloves. From the mid-1500s the immensely profitable voyage from Goa via Macao to Nagasaki was limited to an annual ship under a commander appointed by the king. Even in the early 1600s there were still dreams that the riches of Ceylon could best be tapped by a crown monopoly. But by this time it was increasingly clear that such schemes were impracticable, since neither in theory nor in fact could these monopolies be made absolute. The Portuguese were never able to exclude Gujarati rivals from the many spice ports of the Malabar coast, and only momentarily did they close the Red Sea, through which, as through the Persian Gulf, spices and other goods continued to flow in ever-growing amounts in the sixteenth century (cf. pp. 139f.). Systematic blockade was beyond their administrative and naval resources, and already in 1508 it was recognized that there was little prospect of intercepting craft from Atjeh (Sumatra) which, coming to the Red Sea by a long southern route from Indonesia, passed outside the range of Portuguese patrols.[62] Neither was blockade always diplomatically feasible. The Persian Gulf could hardly be shut – though inevitably its traffic was taxed and pillaged – whilst the shah was a potential ally against the Turk. Nor, given Portugal's need for Gujarati textiles for her commerce with East Africa and Indonesia, could the Gujaratis, let alone her Indian allies, be excluded from the Red Sea. Moreover, as this ancient seaway revived, Portuguese officials profited from its resurgence by selling permits to ships bound for Red Sea ports, and on such a scale that by the early seventeenth century it was earnestly argued that if the route was opened and their sale abandoned Portuguese India would be ruined.

Furthermore, to raise cash, pay their servants and reward the influential, the kings of Portugal granted licences for the import of spices, just as, like other European monarchs, they sold office, titles and privileges. Combined with fraud imposing in its scale and effrontery this meant that in Asia most spices ended in private, not royal hands. It could then be smuggled to Europe, sold in Malacca, Goa and Hormuz to eastern merchants, or shipped in partnership with them to the Red Sea. Not surprisingly, by the late 1500s only about 20 per cent of the pepper, and less than 50 per cent of the remaining spices reaching the west came by the royal Cape route. The crown accordingly turned to the well-tried expedient of farming out to others what it could or would not do itself. It thus both obtained a revenue and relieved the country's primitive administration of an onerous burden. In such ways had medieval rulers and magnates rewarded followers and pacified creditors, and so had the impecunious republic of Genoa disposed of troublesome colonies (see pp. 190ff.). From the very beginnings of Portuguese expansion the discovery or exploitation of lands had, by feudal grant, simple lease, or commercial contract, been entrusted to private individuals. With the passage of time, and the growth of empire, the practice became, as in the possessions of Spain, ever more widespread. *Donatorios* were made responsible for huge territories in Brazil; command of the Macao carrack was auctioned to the highest bidder; the African slave trade was leased to contractors (see pp. 248, 256). So, too, from 1578 a sequence of German, Italian and Iberian capitalists, usually already deeply involved in royal finance and in the marketing of Portuguese spice in Europe, agreed to provide given quantities of Asian pepper. But whatever the subtlety of their business methods they could neither, in the face of Dutch, English and Asian competition in the east, provide what they promised, nor in Europe impose satisfactory prices. By the end of the century the monopoly was back with the crown, in whose care, notwithstanding some talk of free trade, and the brief establishment of a public company (1628–33), it eventually expired.

As through Dutch and English pressure and her own commercial inadequacies Portugal's dealings in spice foundered – with pepper imports falling to only 500t a year in the late 1500s – the whole pattern of Portuguese Asian commerce changed. With a zeal and resource reminiscent of the enterprise of Genoese expatriates in the Black Sea earlier, energies, private rather than public, turned to the opportunities of the local 'country' trades of the east (cf. pp. 169–70, 185–6). Shipments to Europe, like those of other western powers later, were increasingly of precious stones (diamonds, pearls, rubies), raw materials, such as Japanese copper, and oriental manufactures ranging from Indian cottons and carpets to Chinese porcelain, silks and beds. New conditions affected the nature and operation of Portuguese shipping. For a time some vessels for the *carreira* were provided by contractors. Others were constructed in India from the country's magnificently durable teak, just as in the Spanish empire large numbers of ships were built in the Americas for the Atlantic and Pacific trades (see p. 326). On all these routes vessels became fewer but bigger, with some Portuguese Indiamen – 2000t and the enormous draught of 9m – re-attaining, despite royal prohibition, the dimensions of earlier Genoese or Venetian leviathans.[63] But their generous proportions reflected hopes of comfort and security, not an appreciation of the economies of scale. Outward bound, less than half their carrying capacity was used for freight; on the return journey they were commonly so grossly overloaded as to be lost. To improve powers of resistance to enemy attacks convoys, sometimes with escorts – already tried on the Guinea route – were introduced in both the long-distance and interport trades in the late 1500s. Less successful were subsequent attempts to impose some similar organization on the numerous smaller private craft working between Portugal and Brazil's many harbours.

Royal trade, however, with its much-publicized difficulties, was only a part, and like as not the least important part, of a commerce conducted by the Portuguese anywhere from Japan to Peru. In the east they participated in indigenous trade, and carried on one way or another a vast private commerce unquantified and unquantifiable. The royal monopoly extended neither to such things as Asian textiles, porcelain or precious stones, nor to the 'country' trade, in which, it was soon discovered, more money could be made by selling spice than by shipping it to Europe. Hence whilst in Portugal's earliest days in Asia bellicose idealists were writing of ungodly realms cast down, the crown envisaged its subjects entering – as it did itself – into commercial partnerships with Asian, and even Moslem merchants.[64] Not that here, or anywhere else, were they easily restrained from such practices. The physical impossibility of controlling possessions so widely dispersed; the inability of the king to pay his servants; the magnitude and range of opportunity offered by Asia, allowed and encouraged every form of enterprise from honest trade to downright pillage. Already in 1508 royal officers were said to be too immersed in their own business affairs to attend to those of the crown. Some profited by selling the weapons and the equipment of royal vessels; others supplied the king with his own timber at top market prices.[65] In flat contravention of royal orders the captains of Hormuz traded to India and the Persian Gulf in their own ships. Whatever they needed, it was remarked in the late 1500s, they took at their own valuation. They forced their stock on reluctant purchasers, suppressed competitors and licensed supposedly prohibited commerce. With only three years – the usual term of service – to make their fortunes, exactions reached such a pitch that, as in Malacca, trade was driven elsewhere.

Not all enterprise was so crudely predatory, nor was it exclusively secular. As in the empire of Spain the clergy were, individually and corporately, busily engaged in laying up treasure on earth, with the Jesuit Order indiscreetly prominent in dealings in everything from bullion and silk in the east to sugar and slaves in the west (cf. pp. 286f.). At the same time Portuguese settlers, seamen and ex-soldiers – white, black, *mestiço* – penetrated most of the maritime economy of Asia. Virtually independent, firmly and prosperously integrated into local commerce and society, they largely survived the destruction of the *Estado da India* in the seventeenth century by the Dutch and English who were keenly aware of the competition from what were described as 'these sharp operators'. Trading in ever remoter parts as pressures grew, these pioneers were the equivalent of the *lançados* of Africa, of the trappers and the like found on the fringe of any empire, and more particularly of those entrepreneurs who flourished in regions under Genoa's equally fragile colonial rule. Like the conquerors of Spanish America, or many celebrated Elizabethan privateers, they were commonly men of humble birth to whom the oppressively hierarchical society of Europe offered no opportunity (cf. pp. 309ff. and 314ff.). But in Asia they found a rich and cosmopolitan commerce, and an infinity of small redistributive trades, all easily able to absorb, with pragmatic tolerance, a few thousand neo-orientals of modest means who constituted no political threat. The technical and commercial skills of these Portuguese were not such that they could propose, like the Germans in northern Europe, to attempt to isolate themselves from indigenous peoples (cf. pp. 72–3). Indeed, insignificant, barely under western rule, with little intention and less prospect of returning to Portugal, they had no scruples as to emulating local practices. They took local women as wives or mistresses; joined local enterprises. In the seventeenth century Francisco Vieira de Figueiredo, soon known as one better disposed to Hindus than to Christians, became the close associate of the Moslem sovereign of Macassar and a business partner of the ruler of Golconda. A trade of this nature, often continued by wives after their husbands' death, and with no identifiable and therefore vulnerable central organization, was remarkably tenacious. That its rewards were considerable is clear from the magnificent buildings of Goa and Macao in the 1600s, from the many stories of high living and from the financial assistance the Portuguese Asian communities accorded one another as Protestant attacks intensified. Nor surprisingly. Goan traders, it was reported in the late sixteenth century, imported Persian silver coins at a profit of about 10 per cent, sold them to the incoming fleet from Lisbon for Spanish silver currency at up to another 25 per cent profit and then sold these to China merchants for a further 25 per cent gain. Ordinary Goan *casados* were able, though rarely willing, to lend large sums to the ever-impoverished imperial government. And when, in 1615, the crown in its desperate need for money sold all office in Goa, the capital available in the city, even after a run of particularly difficult years, equalled that of the English East India Company.

IV *Birth and death of a new age*

The establishment of world-wide empire was, to many Portuguese, an incomparable achievement. Poets sang of the dawn of a new age with man at last shown to equal, and even surpass the heroes of Antiquity. Kings of the house of Aviz arrogated to themselves grandiose titles and new powers, whilst learned sychophants lauded their superiority to all other monarchs. But to these predictable fruits of imperial triumph the Portuguese added, like the Spaniards, the arrogant assumption that such success demonstrated the degeneracy of their victims and opponents. To primitive peoples their attitude was at best one of stern paternalism. For those without martial aptitudes a bellicose aristocracy and zealous clergy had – unlike the pragmatic merchants of Genoa and Venice, who aired few opinions on the natural inferiority of the vanquished or enslaved – nothing but contempt (cf. pp. 106ff., 174ff., 358). Kinder views were not indeed unknown. Slaves were frequently freed. Moslem and pagan Asians were admitted to be rational beings, and for a brief time around 1500 Portuguese kings believed that Christian baptism largely eradicated the profoundest differences of race and culture amongst their colonial subjects. But others thought otherwise. A proconsul of empire spoke of the Catholic king of the Congo as 'an infidel dog'. To most Portuguese expatriates Brazilian Amerindians were 'merely fit for labour and service', black Africans 'brutes without intelligence or understanding' and Indians 'poor, miserable and cowardly'. Faced only by those considered so despicable it seemed to some that there was no limit to what the Portuguese might achieve. There was talk of the conquest of Africa and Asia, the discovery of a greater India, and – as Messianism became obsessive in the years of Spanish annexation – of Portugal's divine mission to bring the world to Christ. As with Spain, pride in the initial achievement, the subsequent impact of reformed Catholicism, and the ultimate struggle to defend an empire against the combined assaults of heretic and infidel, led to the eclipse of the relatively enlightened humanism of the early 1500s, and the growth of that introspective intolerance of the seventeenth century (cf. p. 358).

But this was merely one aspect of a larger process. Hitherto isolated and insignificant, Portugal was more profoundly influenced by empire than states with other economic interests and political ambitions. The power and prestige of the monarchy were spectacularly enhanced by the success of the imperial expansion in which it had played so important a role. As in Spain papal grant and royal determination brought the crown absolute authority in the colonial church (cf. pp. 358–9). By the mid-sixteenth century the king nominated all bishops, enjoyed the patronage of all posts and livings, administered taxes, collected tithes, and had the oversight of all missionary activity. The government and exploitation of the empire were likewise matters for the crown alone, which endeavoured to regulate everything from the organization and protection of commerce to the licensing of nautical chart and instrument makers. Such ambitions inevitably entailed the creation of a more extensive administration. In the early 1500s the maintenance and victualling of the Moroccan strongholds were handled by a special department. The *Casa da Mina* and the *Casa da India* were established to control commerce and navigation with Africa and India. There was a secretary for imperial affairs from 1568, councils dealing with the economic and ecclesiastical problems of the colonies, and, after 1604, under Spanish influence, a Council of India – later the Council of Overseas Matters – responsible for the bulk of the empire. Power in Asia was from 1505 delegated to a high-born viceroy, aided – or more commonly opposed – in the course of time by the municipal councils of the eastern cities, and by his own exchequer, judicature, chancery and council. In Brazil there appeared first, in the mid-1500s, governors-general and captains-general, and ultimately (1640) a viceroy assisted by a series of financial and legal functionaries. It was a form of colonial administration resembling in general those of Venice and Spain, but without their elaborate provision for inspection and control, and lacking, in a feebler culture, their nucleus of dedicated and responsible administrators (cf. pp. 120 and 344–9). Dealing with similar problems over even greater distances, and with far inferior resources, it was of all imperial governments the most nebulous and least effective.

Nevertheless for a time the profits of empire, and of commerce with exotic lands, enriched Portugal to a degree equalled only in Venice and Genoa (cf. pp. 101, 166). The slave trade, it was reported in the mid-1400s, 'brought more gain than the taxes levied on the whole kingdom'.[66] The revenues of John II (1481–95) were doubled by the gold of West Africa, and in the mid-1520s half those of John III came from the trades of Asia – with profits of 200 per cent clear on pepper – and Africa. By the 1540s the *Estado da India* was buying spices on the proceeds of the oriental interport trade, and paying its way from its own resources. The following century the growing wealth of Brazil helped free Portugal from Spanish rule and from the economic stagnation that afflicted most of southern Europe. Nor was this all. An increase in European trade focused on Portugal as the entrepôt for colonial commerce meant a larger customs yield, whilst empire became as usual an excellent security for loans and a seemingly limitless reservoir of office and title with which to reward the influential and (less commonly) the deserving (cf. pp. 273 and 348). With their income augmented, their creditors reassured and many of their most ambitious or undesirable subjects abroad, kings could rule without recourse to the Cortes for money and support. So this representative assembly which had met 25 times under John I (1385–1433) came together only 4 times in the 26 years of Manuel I's reign (1495–1521) and 3 times in the 36-year reign of John III (1521–57). As in Spain, empire sustained the absolutist ambitions stimulated by its creation (cf. pp. 358–9).

Furthermore Portugal was lifted by imperial success from its previous obscurity and isolation to become a state whose alliance exotic potentates sought and whose policies publicists acclaimed. Initially, too, the metropolitan economy was, as always, vitalized (cf. pp. 88 and 360). Over 50 per cent of the spice sold in the *Case da India* in 1509–11 went to Portuguese merchants. Fortunes were made in trade, war and pillage in distant parts, and observers noticed the kingdom's wealth whilst moralists lamented the eclipse of martial virtue by commercial zeal. From the late fifteenth century onwards Atlantic sugar, Asian spices and coins minted from African gold were distributed widely throughout Europe, allowing Portugal to buy grain in Sicily, or weapons in the Netherlands, and firmly integrating her into the continent's economy. At the same time new sources of subsistence were found, with fisheries opened off north-west Africa, Brazil and Newfoundland – whose cod the Portuguese consumed in heroic quantities – and South American maize grown in many parts of the kingdom by

1600. Old industries likewise boomed – shipbuilding in particular with the incessant demands of world-wide seaborne war and trade to meet – and new ones were created. For a time Portugal produced Moroccan-style cotton cloths for sale in West Africa, and sugar refining developed on such a scale in the vicinity of Lisbon as to require regulation (1559). Of the contemporary architectural expressions of this brief age of opulence few have survived. But the grandeur of Tomar bears impressive witness to the pride and riches of the house of Aviz, as do the elegance of the Torre de Belem and the glittering magnificence of the church of the Jerónimos – built as thanksgiving for the success of da Gama's voyage – to the splendour and wealth of Renaissance Lisbon.

Empire indeed made the capital. Whilst the population of Portugal as a whole remained static, or only slightly increased, that of Lisbon rose from about 70,000 in 1528 to perhaps 165,000 a century later, establishing it as the biggest city in Iberia and the third largest in Europe. Like Seville, for a time focus of Spain's Atlantic empire, and for much the same reasons, its growth was at the expense of those many little ports which had initially sustained the peninsula's maritime expansion, and whose fortunes were in Portugal only restored by the growth of the Brazil trade in the seventeenth century (cf. p. 360). The country's political centre, and endowed with a superb natural harbour, Lisbon became the seat of various royal commercial monopolies and the official gateway to empire. Here were concentrated the bureaucrats who administered the imperial possessions, representatives of the merchant houses handling their trade, visitors from exotic lands and those slaves – mostly Negroes, but also Asians, Japanese, Chinese, Arabs and Berbers – who by the 1550s accounted for about 10 per cent of the city's population.

More complex was the intellectual impact of empire. Experience of a wider world combined with the problems of acquiring and controlling territories overseas must, it was once argued, have revolutionized men's ways of thinking, turning them from myths and fables to a wholesome concern with reality and accuracy. Much of the detail is indisputable. By 1650 whole oceans, countries and continents – India, Africa, Brazil, Japan, China – previously totally or largely unknown had been found. Many were perceptively described, particularly by merchants and missionaries, and many were mapped with impressive accuracy in this golden age of Portuguese nautical science and cartography. Improved techniques for the determination of latitude at sea were developed, the cross-staff, possibly of Arab inspiration, was produced for celestial observation[67] and sailing directions for most of the known world, together with a spate of works on navigation, were issued. In the early 1500s the geographical pattern of magnetic variation was noticed and recorded, and attempts made to use it to establish longitude. At the same time the mathematical prodigy Dr Nunes demonstrated that when a vessel followed a fixed course she described not a straight line, but a curve cutting successive meridians at a constant angle. The geographical discoveries – 60,000km of new coast alone by 1560 – were plotted on charts of an original and distinctive nature. Drawn with great care and precision they contained, perhaps under

Majorcan influence, an abundance of cosmographical information. They indicated, unlike their Italian precursors, latitudes by 1500, crude longitudes a little later, and were by the 1520s regularly corrected for magnetic variation. This excellence was maintained into the seventeenth century, with the crown requiring ships at sea to log everything of navigational consequence they encountered, and the information thus gathered then incorporated into revised charts. So, in essence, Portugal had advanced the art of navigation as far as was possible until, with the invention of the chronometer in the eighteenth century, longitude could be established accurately. In the meanwhile seamen had tolerable representations of the world in which they worked. Out of sight of land they sailed by dead-reckoning, checked and supplemented by observed latitude. They recorded with some confidence their 'height' (latitude), and recognized, if they knew their business, that on a long voyage they could be hundreds of kilometres out in their east-west account.

Clearly, too, Portugal as Europe's first oceanic imperial power faced new problems. There were lengthy exchanges on whether the empire of the east was one of conquest or trade, and as to how, like the African possessions, it might best be held and defended. Yet the terms of reference, like the solutions projected, were European. Colonies were controlled and exploited in ways long familiar, the emulation of Venetian or Spanish practice was urged and commanders wrote of the lessons to be learned from European wars. In the same way there was in navigation and ship-design a vast utilization of existing skills and practices. Of the ships of the heroic years of Portuguese expansion both the carvel and the carrack were of impeccable medieval ancestry. Nor was the renowned galleon – a fast, low-built fighting craft, smaller than the carrack and first mentioned in 1519 – without forerunners. Though possibly of Venetian inspiration, she probably derived from the bigger versions of the carvel, whose admixture of square and lateen rig she retained (cf. pp. 148, 263, 343).

There was, furthermore, no significant speculation on the justification of imperial rule or the responsibilities of imperial power. Notwithstanding the denial by a succession of medieval thinkers of the pope's unconditional authority over pagans and Moslems, Portugal, with characteristic conservatism, based her title on papal bulls – conceding everything from commercial monopoly to the right to enslave heathens, infidels and Moors – and priority of possession.[68] There were indeed occasional doubts. Princes Pedro and John were in the early 1400s concerned that the forcible conversion of Tangiers Moors contravened biblical precept, and the Crown itself sought the opinions of Italian legists on the lawfulness of its African policies. Thereafter the royal house spasmodically attempted to restrain the indiscriminate enslavement of peoples other than Negroes, the religious Orders defended the Brazilian Amerindians, and from time to time members of the Portuguese church condemned the maltreatment of Africans. In the later sixteenth century classically educated reformers advocated responsible imperial rule, and the desirability of treating Hindus and Moslems with reason and justice, whilst isolated voices even queried the right of Europeans to be in

Asia. But in a country lightly and briefly touched by humanistic learning, and whose expansion was accompanied by no such conquests as those of Castile in the Americas, the subjugation and exploitation of indigenous peoples was neither defended nor condemned with anything of that vigour and erudition similar themes evoked in the Spain of Charles V (cf. pp. 248, 256, 361ff.).

Yet as always the intellectual impact of empire was at first sight profound (cf. pp. 214ff., 360ff., 455ff.). Art, life and letters abound with references to, and themes from, distant lands. Local usages of dress and cooking were widely adopted by the Portuguese abroad, who in Asia ate rice, and to the amazement of fellow Europeans washed and bathed regularly. The first conscious exoticism appears in the *Travels* (1614) of Fernão Mendes Pinto. Savants like João de Castro sent home oriental plants and archaeological fragments. Chinese books, silks and porcelains; Indian carpets and textiles; Japanese lacquered wares all came into Portugal, whose language was enriched with words of oriental derivation such as *veniaga* (merchandise, from the Malay).[69] The unfolding of the country's imperial destiny was immortalized in *The Lusiads* (1572) of Luis de Camoës, and the omnipresence of the sea in the shells and ropes of Manueline architecture.

More than this, men were moved, as indeed they had been in other countries and at other times, to describe strange lands and their inhabitants. But in Portugal this writing was on a scale and of a quality equalled only in contemporary Spain, as for some two centuries after 1450 missionaries, merchants, officials and chroniclers produced a flow of accounts of states and civilizations as different as China, Japan, India, the Congo and Brazil (cf. p. 361). Many of these works were of the highest quality, reflecting an insistence on personal knowledge as opposed to that acquired from traditional authority, and the deliberate efforts of civilized minds to attain accuracy through the critical handling of evidence. The historian Diogo do Couto (1543–1616), in his attempts to ascertain the setting and sequence of Lusitanian triumphs in the east, used not only the testimony of compatriots, but questioned Sinhalese princes, Mogul diplomats and learned Brahmins. Nor were such virtues the prerogative of scholars. 'We have here been through everything and experienced it', wrote Tomé Pires of his description of the South Asian economy (1515), whilst to the alarm of the local populace fellow-countrymen measured and recorded monuments and fortifications in China and Ethiopia. Nevertheless such attitudes were neither new nor necessarily sincere, and even those allegedly writing from first-hand experience were not beyond easing the labours of composition by incorporating manifest hearsay. A competent account of the navigability of the Senegal (*c.* 1505) descends to nonsense on serpents 'a quarter of a league long' and the elusive satyrs of Sierra Leone, of whom little is said 'to avoid prolixity'.

The roots of a concern for accuracy and detail were, as we have seen, lengthy and complex (cf. pp. 215–16). Together with the Spaniards, the Portuguese indeed pioneered the study of non-European languages, approached more systematically than those with which Italian merchants had concerned themselves (cf. pp. 212 and 361). In India the English-born Fr Stephens SJ (1549–1619), composed a Marathi-Konkani version of the scriptures. Missionaries learned alike Chinese and the Ki-Mbundu of Angola, and dictionaries or grammars of Tamil, Konkani, Japanese and the tongues of the Brazilian coast were produced. Their object, however, was not to permit European appreciation of the felicities of the vernacular, but to ensure mastery of the languages with which the natives could be lead to Christianity (cf. pp. 285ff.). So, too, commanders of the expeditions, navigators and emissaries were required to 'keep a book' of their voyages, enabling the king to know the nature, extent and profitability of his new possessions, and allowing subsequent fleets to find them. That the crown so repeatedly demanded detailed reports – closely specifying what was to be investigated – suggests that dedication to careful inquiry was neither widespread nor profound.

But this is not to deny the genuine curiosity, in the sixteenth and early seventeenth centuries, of a handful of remarkable men who might search for the site of the Jewish crossing of the Red Sea or speculate on the origins of Congolese circumcision rites. Nor is it to overlook that at a time of increasing intolerance in Europe there were those who were willing to admit the merits of the inhabitants of other lands, and to accept that their customs were something more than expressions of folly or depravity. In the mid-1500s a Jesuit conceded, not without embarrassment, that the seductive transparency of the garments of Hormuz ladies was justified by the fearful climate in which they lived. This enlightenment had a twofold origin. On the one hand there was the powerful impact of resurgent Renaissance classicism, both that of Italy and the strongly Christianized humanism of Flanders (cf. pp. 214–15). Portuguese, like Spanish students, graduated from Louvain, Florence and Siena; humanists were established in royal and private Iberian households; the universities of Alcalá, Salamanca and Coimbra became centres for the dissemination of humanist doctrine. To see man and life whole and dispassionately was to obey, as in so many other things, the precepts of Antiquity. Quintilian proclaimed the merits of personal observation;[70] Livy supplied the model of majestic apologia for empire; the Dutch humanist Erasmus, particularly influential in early sixteenth-century Iberia, inculcated the virtues of writing with a high moral purpose – of history, fact, truth. Men trained in this atmosphere and tradition approached the world with what now appears as such refreshing honesty and enthusiasm, condemning, like Damião de Góis, the follies of intolerance, or declaring, as did his compatriot the Salamanca-educated botanist Garçia d'Orta, 'I have nothing to say but the truth and what I know.' Equally potent was the pragmatic tolerance of such as officials, seamen and merchants, which though often enough inspired by nothing more than the need for some sort of indigenous aid, could develop into genuine respect and even friendship. In India Portuguese notables wisely employed Hindu physicians, and to the disgust of the church Christians were to be found firing salutes at Moslem feasts and lending jewelry to participants in Hindu festivals.

Yet these qualities were not suddenly induced by experience of extra-European worlds, and toleration was most readily accorded to societies and practices resembling those of Europe (cf. pp. 216 and 257). Nor was the urge to record, assess and understand the concern of anything more than a minority, and a minority whose influence was, as in Spain, soon destroyed (cf. pp. 293 and 358). But in any case the discoveries were a matter of indifference to the majority of Portuguese even in the most liberal days. Men of learning were often less exercised to evaluate the present than to spot, with misapplied erudition, phenomena supposedly mentioned in the all-powerful classics. Eastern religions are lost in clouds of Greco-Roman learning; the natural scenery of the tropics barely noticed. Speculation on whether the tribes of South America represented man in a state of pristine bliss, and on matters of larger significance, were left to others. Distinguished pieces of geographical writing languished unpublished until the 1800s, and many, as in Spain, were forgotten or lost (cf. pp. 355, 455). This reflected no prescient policy of withholding Portuguese secrets from unworthy eyes, but, as the sixteenth-century historian Barros complained of his compatriots, a lack of curiosity, and significantly enough *The Lusiads* of Camoẽs only became a national epic during the decades of Spanish rule. Indeed, of the books published in Portugal in the sixty years after 1540, little more than 10 per cent were concerned with Asia, the very heart of the empire. For the rest taste was dominated by more urgent domestic themes – by politics, classics, religion and the nonsense of popular romance (cf. pp. 216ff., 361, 455).

Thus as everywhere the imperial impact was essentially economic and political, bringing new riches, enhancing royal authority and inflating national pride. But literature, art and religion went on their own individual ways, and new facts were either ignored or accommodated within the existing mental framework. Pedro Nunes, who in the early sixteenth century contributed so much to the advancement of nautical science, meditated on the prospect of his compatriots reaching the Terrestial Paradise, whilst they in turn searched for that countless wealth with which the imagination of a poverty-stricken and disease-ridden Europe had endowed distant lands. Not surprisingly, neither India nor Africa attained any prominence in Portugal's rich and varied folk-lore.

Very different was the influence of Portugal overseas, albeit an influence exercised by societies of widely differing character, seemingly united only in their numerical insignificance. The annual rate of Portuguese emigration in the sixteenth century was probably no more than 2000–4000, mostly males, and with a good part of these either dying on passage to, or soon after arrival in, the tropics. Nevertheless, like that of the Norse in the Atlantic or the Germans to the eastlands, it was an emigration of those destined to remain abroad (cf. pp. 2f., 42f.). And royal policy, the rumoured opportunities of distant realms, and the known hardships of the mother country combined to ensure a continuing flow of members of every section of Portuguese society from bellicose aristocrats intent on plunder to luckless prostitutes shipped to Angola. Furthermore, the fragility of the crown's authority allowed the survival in Portuguese territories of influential groups of aliens, such as those Spanish-speaking Jews, openly practising their religion, remarked by a visiting friar in Cochin and Goa (1605).[71] Thus with empire an outlet for latent talent and a refuge for dissidents, and with the loosening of the bonds of convention that comes with emigration, Portuguese communities overseas not so much reproduced the features of their parent society, but, as reflected in the usual sharpened focus of colonization, its salient qualities. The well-known Iberian horror of manual labour reached its fullest expression, as with Spain, in the slave-worked plantations of the new Atlantic economy. A world imbued with aristocratic ideals produced the neo-feudalism of Brazil and East Africa, where private individuals controlled vast domains.

Yet though there might be little more than 1500 Europeans in the whole of the *Estado da India* by the mid-1600s they, like their compatriots elsewhere, constituted a powerful force for the dissemination of Portuguese influence. It was, however, clearly not a political influence. Portugal's disruption of the commerce of the Red Sea in the early sixteenth century indeed hastened the collapse of Mameluke Egypt. The sultan of Malacca was dispossessed and in the 1540s Portuguese intervention saved Ethiopia from the Turks. But unlike the Venetians in Greece, or the Spaniards in America, Portugal overthrew no great empires and established no new balance of power. Nor, unlike the Germans in north-eastern Europe, did she achieve such success as to encourage extensive indigenous emulation of her political and social institutions and organization (cf. pp. 0010 and 00–0). Ironically, in view of her avowed intentions, Portugal's economic impact was far more profound. In the Atlantic a whole new economy was created, its members linked to each other, to Europe, America and Asia. In the east a part of the ancient spice trade to the Levant was diverted round Africa, and a commerce between China and Japan revived and invigorated (cf. pp. 241, 286). Though Asian agrarian life as a whole was unaffected, many regional and local economies were modified. Portuguese demand led to the extension of clove production from Tidore and Ternate to the Bandas and elsewhere. Macao and Nagasaki rose from obscurity to become major entrepôts, whilst Portuguese imports of bullion brought its wider use as currency. In the early 1600s the Javanese, previously innocent of such practices, expected to buy cottons in Malacca with silver, and in south China it became the accepted medium for the payment of taxes. The flow of silver to India, 'where coyne is beried . . . and goeth not out', possibly inflated Mogul prices and, together with Portuguese cloth purchases, may have stimulated the whole commerce and industry of Gujarat and Hindustan. Probably, too, Portuguese demand encouraged copper and silver mining in Japan, just as in parts of southern China their need for silks and their silver imports perhaps resulted in the growth of handicraft industries and textile production at the expense of the cultivation of rice. Such changes naturally affected existing patterns of trade. Portuguese policies and behaviour impoverished Hormuz and Malacca, led the Achinese to develop a direct maritime route to the Red Sea, and brought about the rise of Brunei as a rival market for cloves and nutmegs to Portuguese-dominated Ternate. In West Africa the Portuguese for a time drew to the continent's Atlantic coast much of the gold – probably about half by 1500 – that had formerly found its way to Egypt or North Africa. By so doing they weakened those powers (Mali, Songhay) the trade had once enriched, whilst states on the littoral (such as Cayor), now able to serve as entrepôts, flourished (cf. pp. 253ff.).

Nevertheless, as in other empires, the most profound and enduring impact was cultural, with the language, tastes, architecture and religion of the mother country scattered across the world (cf. pp. 69ff., 74ff., 219ff.). Portuguese fortresses can still be seen from Dahomey (West Africa) to Diu (western India). Africa abounds in Portuguese names – Sierra Leone (The Lion Mountains); Cape Verde (Green Point); Zaire (like Angola a Portuguese corruption of a vernacular word). Portuguese became and remains the language of Brazil, and continues in general use in Mozambique and Angola. It was once systematically taught, and widely spoken and written, in the Congo, besides being for centuries the lingua franca of the upper Guinea coast, with a patois even now surviving in places. It was introduced with astonishing success into Japan in the early 1500s, and before long was employed alike in Lourenço Marques and the Philippines. Such was its ubiquity that it became usual for English and Dutch East Indiamen to carry Portuguese interpreters. Nor was their language confined to those regions where the Portuguese themselves settled or traded. Eurasians, intensely conscious of their Europeanness, kept alive the speech of their supposed motherland long after its empire had vanished; their adopted tongue was introduced by Portuguese-speaking slaves into Dutch Batavia and South Africa, and Portuguese folksongs survive in some form or other from Indonesia to the Brazilian outback.

Equally pervasive, if less durable, was the acceptance of Portuguese social convention, either imposed by the church as a necessary adjunct to conversion, or emulated by those seeking the elixir of European power. In Brazil formerly naked Amerindians were put into some semblance of European clothing. On the Limpopo an African potentate was encountered in the early 1600s 'bravely dressed in Portuguese fashion, with a doublet inside out, a pair of baggy trousers back to front, and a hat upon his head.' Such adornments were not, however, mistaken for the substance of white strength. The Christianized rulers of the Congo not only reorganized their court in Portuguese style, but demanded artisans and gunfounders, and began the construction of stone buildings and defences. Soon, as in the Spanish empire, a whole range of European technology had been widely assimilated. Asian peoples acquired guns; Indian Ocean shipwrights took to fastening the planking of their craft with nails, as was the usage in the west. And nothing is more eloquent testimony to the respect for Portuguese skills, and the extent of Portuguese influence, than the survival – as from seventeenth-century Macassar – of vernacular tracts expounding Portuguese practice, or that leavening of oriental languages – Gulf Arabic especially – with Portuguese nautical terms, just as the Norse had earlier enriched the maritime vocabulary of Europe. Like Spain, Portugal was responsible, moreover, for introducing European plants and animals to new lands, taking the sugar cane, horse and ox to Brazil with enormous repercussions (cf. pp. 248–9 and 323). And with almost equally extensive consequences the Portuguese brought manioc, sweet potatoes and maize from the Americas to become acclimatized as vital staple crops in Africa.

But to the Portuguese, the spread of their language apart, these were accidental, and indeed in the case of the alien acquisition of European weapons, unwelcome developments. Only in their desire to convert pagans and infidels to Christianity did they have what might be termed a positive cultural ambition. Such aspirations were nothing new, but not since the crusades and the German push eastwards had they been a major factor in Europe's expansion. And the task was now entrusted – not to say abandoned – by the papacy to the Iberian monarchies, which between them effected the last and largest extension of the bounds of Christendom. Portuguese pronouncements depicted the establishment of empire as a great Christian enterprise, and the dissemination of the Faith as the country's peculiar responsibility. By the mid-1500s bishoprics had been instituted from Brazil to China, the imperial church, like that of Spain, was under the closest royal direction and, by papal bulls, the conversion of colonial subjects, native allies, and – with what today seems impossible arrogance – the entire east, had become the exclusive prerogative of the kings of Portugal (cf. pp. 276 and 341). How they were to discharge these duties in a state intellectually un-distinguished and with little experience of such endeavour was another matter. An indifferent secular church, its clergy often openly devoted to nothing more than the rapid accumulation of wealth, began the task. It was soon reinforced and eclipsed by such traditional missionary Orders as the Franciscans, and by the newly founded and cosmopolitan Jesuits, able to recruit, particularly from the vigorous culture of Italy, men of outstanding excellence. In Asia the church faced powerful and ancient civilizations, complex religions, which whatever their seeming resemblances to Christianity commonly held beliefs diametrically opposed to its tenets and languages and scripts radically different from those of Europe. And Islam, backed by Ottoman strength, and pragmatically recruiting talent where it could, proved more likely to attract Portuguese renegades than respond to Christian advances.

In India little was accomplished in the early 1500s beyond the superficial conversion, often by questionable means, of some members of the lowest castes of Hindu society. Later in the century the pace became notably brisker with royal patronage of the Jesuits, and with the growth of Portuguese intransigence, reflected in hostility to the Nestorian communities of the west coast, and in attempts to dispense with the employment of non-Christians, and to eradicate the open practice of their religions from the crown's possessions. In areas of direct Portuguese sovereignty, most notably in and around Goa, the majority of the inhabitants were converted by Franciscan and Jesuit endeavour. Elsewhere, though by 1610 the Jesuits had established 169 churches, they had no more than 100,000 converts in a population numbered in tens of millions. This brought, as in Japan and China, a fundamental change of tactics. Instead of

demanding a neophyte's immediate and total rejection of his former evil ways, the
Order attempted to understand, accept and Christianize existing society, recognizing
caste with all its restrictions and inequalities, and allowing the continued practice of its
rites. Such methods gained the Faith some 250,000 further souls in southern India by
1676, but also brought their own problems. When Fr Roberto de Nobili SJ – who by
his acceptance of Brahminical ways and his erudition in Brahminical literature had
gained admission to the caste – appeared before the archbishop of Goa (1618) in
Brahmin robes there was alarm that Catholics were being converted to Hinduism rather
than Hindus to Catholicism. The secular church was hostile, as were other missionary
Orders that regarded such methods as a denial of the very essence of Christianity. But
though these concessions – the Malabar Rites – were condemned by the papacy (1645),
the Jesuits continued their policies until the suppression of their Order in the
eighteenth century.

In China – where in the late 1500s Fr Ruggiero SJ became to all intents a Buddhist
bonze, and Fr Ricci SJ impressed mandarins with his demonstration by textual
criticism of the distortion of Confucian thought by glossators – similar methods
brought similar results, and ultimately similar vicissitudes. Nor in Japan, despite a
period of dazzling triumph, was the eventual outcome any better. Arriving in 1549 the
Basque saint, Francis Xavier SJ, promptly recognized in the country's proud, bellicose
and enterprising inhabitants another race of Spaniards who, once trained, could
convert the Orient unaided. It was a perceptive and realistic view, since briefly, and to a
degree not encountered elsewhere, there were then present in Japan all the
preconditions for successful proselytization. The country was totally accessible, with
one language understood throughout. There was widespread dissatisfaction with
existing creeds – decadent Buddhism in particular – combined with a willingness to
hear arguments and accept appeals to reason or faith. After some false starts the success
of the Jesuits, to whom the mission was exclusively entrusted by the crown, was
overwhelming. Admired for their dialectical skills, the fathers were in turn attracted by
the beauty of Japan, adopted its dress and etiquette, and respected warriors educated in
ways as spartan as their own. Furthermore, to such affinities of mind and spirit the
Jesuits added the ability to provide vital supplies. Until the late sixteenth century
Portugal was the sole commercial intermediary between China and Japan, and the sole
importer of European goods. With the authority of the emperor and his generalissimo
(*shogun*) in decay, power was in the hands of feudal lords (*daimyo*), only too glad to
welcome whoever could supply them with the gold – always a conveniently portable
form of wealth in times of trouble – and weapons invaluable in internecine strife.
Portugal's trade was accordingly initially directed to the domains of lords willing to
permit evangelization, before Nagasaki became both the Portuguese entrepôt and the
Jesuit headquarters (cf. p. 241). The Order drew extensive revenues from its
participation in the commerce between Macao and Japan, in which the fathers adeptly
established themselves as the indispensable agents of Japanese feudatories. Friendship

with Odo Nobunaga (1534–82), triumphantly engaged in restoring central authority, meant that uniquely in Portuguese experience a mission had the effective secular backing vital to success.

With Japan the prime field of Jesuit effort, the Order had made some 300,000 converts out of a population of about 20,000,000 by the early 1600s. Japanese Christians visited Rome, and ambitious plans were laid for the recruitment of a native clergy. But these brilliant prospects faded as rapidly as they had dawned. Re-unification of the Japanese state brought the inevitable resurgence of patriotism and traditional values. There were fears that Iberian arms might support Christian revolt, distaste for Portuguese slaving – which the crown attempted to check – and revulsion from the unrestrained destruction of Buddhist and Shinto shrines and temples by over-zealous converts. The arrival in the late 1500s of Spanish friars, followed by papal revocation (1608) of the Portuguese monopoly of the Asian mission, led to unseemly squabbles and to a dissipation of effort. Worse still the whole economic basis of Jesuit power was destroyed. Portuguese merchants entered the commerce between Japan and Macao, the Japanese themselves began to trade abroad in their own ships and finally the Dutch and the English appeared in Japan (cf. pp. 397, 477). Thus neither the Jesuits nor the Portuguese were any longer indispensable. Nor indeed were they desirable, and fears that the missions were the forerunners of a military conquest of Japan, assiduously intensified by the English, brought the prohibition of Christianity in 1614. Its adherents were persecuted, tortured and martyred with appalling cruelty. A rising by survivors was stamped out in 1638, and the Portuguese expelled the following year.

The picture was little better elsewhere. Africa, whose peoples were generally regarded as fit only for enslavement, offered nothing of the challenge of the Far East, nor, like America, the prospect of saving survivors from a Golden Age, and before the seventeenth century attracted few able clergy. In the north and east little impression was made in the face of Islam, whilst elsewhere the Portuguese were confined to territories inviting to only the most rugged individualists, or to fever-ridden lands where such missionaries as penetrated rarely survived. Success in the Congo was largely destroyed by European indifference to the lot of the Negro, and by that devotion to slaving shared by the church itself (cf. pp. 254–7 and 362). Only Brazil – where the Jesuits worked from 1549, joined by other Orders later – called forth an effort comparable to that made in the east. To protect the Amerindians from the white colonists, and the better to wean them from their reprobate ways, the Jesuits, like their Spanish colleagues elsewhere in South America, gathered onetime nomads into villages over which they attempted to exercise complete authority (cf. p. 355). But the obstacles were formidable. Acolytes tenaciously resisted, here as everywhere, the imposition of a sedentary clothed and monogamous existence. Defence of Indian freedom combined with the cheap production of sugar and tobacco earned the Order the hostility of the planters, who harassed it, prevented its ministering to their slaves, and recruited labour by raiding its settlements (see p. 248).

Yet the paradox is not that so little, but that so much, was accomplished. The Portuguese missions, spread out over an enormous field, and from a small and backward country, were only locally of the quality, and never of the size, of those of Spain. There were no more than 137 Jesuits in Japan even in 1597, whilst on less healthy stations there might be as few as half a dozen missionaries. For these to transmit the complexities of Christian belief in languages imperfectly understood, or through unsympathetic interpreters or equally unsympathetic or uncomprehending audiences, was an undertaking of immense difficulty, resulting in a Congolese sovereign confusing the immortality of the soul with that of the body. Frequently there was total antipathy between the Christian message and prevailing creeds and customs. Missionary insistence on pre-marital female virginity was as generally unacceptable as the doctrine of monogamous marriage dissolved only by death. In China and Japan, where the poor and insignificant were understood to be so from their breach of human and divine law, the idea that the son of God should have worked on earth as a humble carpenter and then suffered crucifixion was particularly repugnant. And to many adherents of major oriental religions – contemplative, passive, stoic – accustomed to rigid class societies and carefully defined etiquette, the apostles of Christianity often seemed strident, volatile and tasteless. Equally inimical to their success was the open European violation of the very essence of the faith supposedly being spread. The Orders engaged in trade, initially to finance their work, but before long for the benefit of their members, and on such a scale as to provoke the hostility of lay compatriots and, as in Asia, the distaste of peoples who held commerce in contempt. There were acrimonious disputes, as in the Spanish empire, between the Orders themselves, and between the missions and a secular church soon notoriously immoral and corrupt. All these troubles, long familiar in Europe, were further aggravated by opposition to the Portuguese royal monopoly, first from the Spaniards, to whose friars the pope opened most of Asia in 1608, and then from the papacy itself, which from 1622 sought to control all missions (cf. pp. 274 and 356ff.).

Moreover, whatever the church might preach was only too obviously not practised by the many Portuguese priests and laymen living overseas in ostentatious immorality. Nor in any case was the Christian message as interpreted by the missions always inviting. Apologists for a faith whose exponents were universally active in slaving spoke of enslavement as the inescapable lot of Turkish, Moorish, infidel and Negro captives, and of the beneficial effects of slavery in preparing primitive peoples living in 'bestial idleness' to receive the word of God.[72] Nowhere, royal injunctions notwithstanding, were local converts accepted as equal to Europeans, and the unfree, it was agreed, should remain so. Indians and half-castes were excluded from the Orders in the east, and confined to the lower ranks of the less exacting secular church. Japanese Christians were so reluctantly ordained by the Jesuits as to alienate many high-born lay brothers on whose services the fathers were particularly dependent. But such folly and insensitivity might have been immaterial had Portugal enjoyed, like Spain in America, freedom from external intervention, and that authority that comes from outright conquest. As it was, her power in Asia was inadequate for any grand ambitions, but sufficient to arouse suspicion and hostility.

Hardly surprisingly, then, conversion, as in Spain's empire, was not to what was always immediately recognizable as Christianity. Enormous concessions were made by the Jesuits to Hindu and Confucian usage. Many African neophytes were merely summarily baptized and incomprehending slaves were soon practising in new homelands vestiges of traditional tribal rites, whilst to stabilize and extend Portuguese influence the Faith was often spread, as in western India, by force, bribes,[73] or discrimination against non-Christians. Converts, moreover, were frequently attracted less by the message of Christianity than by the material benefits its exponents could provide, whether tools for Brazilian Indians, or military assistance for African rulers. Even so, the missions were not failures. Throughout much of the world Catholicism took deep and enduring root. A Christian tradition was established among the Dembos of Angola and on parts of the Guinea coast, where, as in Japan, it survived until the nineteenth century. In the east, from Mozambique and Goa to Vietnam[74] and the Moluccas, there were by 1600 perhaps a million converts, whose descendants were for centuries, and in some places still are, strenuous upholders of Portuguese ideals.

But essentially empire meant, with Portugal as with any other power, the establishment of Europeans amongst indigenous peoples, with the inescapable corollary of their oppression and exploitation, the disruption of their way of life, and, combined with the ravages of European-borne disease, the destruction in whole or part of entire communities. It also entailed the almost universal miscegenation of Portuguese males with local women. Unlike that of the Norse before them, or of the Puritan English after, Portuguese emigration was not in general of families or larger social groups but, to an even greater degree than from most other countries before modern times, predominantly masculine. Coming from a state which, unlike Spain, made no attempt to ensure that husbands were accompanied, not to say pursued, by their wives, and from a civilization in which, as in the rest of Iberia, female slavery was known and fornication with unmarried women considered no sin, pioneers naturally enough turned their desires, and frequently their affections, to whatever females they encountered (cf. pp. 2ff., 330ff., 488ff.). Those sufficiently white, like the Chinese girls of Macao, they were willing to marry. The rest – particularly pure-blooded or half-breed Negro women, so generally available and irresistible to Iberians – became mistresses and concubines in a harem society of a voluptuousness unapproached in any other empire. Furthermore, the Portuguese shipped their servants and slaves from continent to continent, where – like that Christian Kanarese[75] happily living in East Africa in the early 1600s with two wives and twenty children – they took such consolation as was offered. But though the large and polyglot populace so engendered was often tenaciously Portuguese in outlook and behaviour, its members were, like all non-Europeans, considered inherently inferior. The precise degree of their indigenous parentage was defined with the same precision as in Spain's colonies; the same unshakeable conviction reached that the darker their skin and the more negroid their features, the lower their standing. Political accident, as in the Congo, or – as in Angola and the Cape Verdes – a lack of white settlers, might subvert this natural order. But the principal remained untouched, and in 1545 the crown debarred those of mixed race from its service in India.

Such miscegenation inevitably brought cultural fusions of varying intensity and permanence. The extent to which the Portuguese, or indeed any other European people, were affected by indigenous civilizations depended on the number of settlers, on whether or not they came as conquerors, whether European women accompanied them, and the vigour of the cultures in contact (cf. pp. 25, 185, 353, 416). Isolated Portuguese males in the midst of flourishing alien civilizations simply, as in parts of West Africa, succumbed to them (see p. 253). Something of the same happened in southern Brazil, though in general the Portuguese arriving in relative strength, in a better climate and amongst primitive peoples, largely destroyed Amerindian culture. Even so, the Brazilian, African and mulatta women with whom they so gladly mated, influenced though they were by European ways, passed on to their offspring many of their own customs and traditions. In the east, with European women even fewer, the Portuguese, unlike the self-contained white society of Spanish America, were strongly affected by powerful indigenous civilizations (see pp. 251, 280, 330–1). And where high cultures met there could be impressive, even if only transient, cross-fertilization. In the late sixteenth century the Japanese were building ships whose design conflated European and oriental features to the extent of setting a square (western) topsail over a junk (oriental) mainsail. In India in the early 1600s, artists at the court of the Mogul emperors, impressed by the realism and perspective of European painting, known to them from exemplars provided by the Jesuits, took to working in a style unmistakably Indian, yet perceptibly western. At the same time, though more for commercial than aesthetic reasons, Portuguese themes and patterns were incorporated alike into Japanese picture screens, Chinese porcelain, and Indian carpets and textiles. But perhaps most satisfying was the execution of western designs in a vernacular tradition, as when at Macao Chinese and Japanese craftsmen decorated, under Jesuit supervision, a church of Italian inspiration, to produce a building of unique and widely admired beauty.

v *A chronicle of disaster*

'The empire in the east', wrote a Portuguese reformer in the mid-sixteenth century, 'is like a ship that is sinking. Everybody shouts we are foundering, but nobody pumps the water out.' And having set the scene with this revealing and favourite Iberian simile, he went on to depict the condition of the *Estado da India* in the gloomiest terms. His jeremiads could well have been applied to the empire as a whole. Exports of gold from West Africa were declining, the crown monopoly of Asian spices was in difficulties and by the 1630s investment in the commerce between Goa and Lisbon, which had once reached two million *cruzados*, was down to 3000 (cf. pp. 272ff.). As trades flagged, or were lost to others, so the royal revenues deriving from them dwindled, and before long the kings of Portugal, earlier apparently marvellously enriched by the profits of imperial commerce and the income from overseas possessions, were heavily in debt. In the 1550s the crown owed three million *cruzados* – chiefly in Antwerp – and by 1560 was bankrupt. But worse was to come as Portugal, like every other imperial power, ultimately had to face ever-increasing responsibilities with rapidly diminishing resources. To the burden of maintaining the perilously situated North African outposts there was added the far more onerous problem of the eastern empire which, with its demands for military and naval assistance on the one hand, and the untrammelled private enterprise of its officers on the other, was running at a loss from the mid-sixteenth century. The Atlantic islands could as a rule pay their way, and even contribute to the imperial revenues, whilst Angola and Brazil were capable of producing substantial surpluses. But all these, and more besides, were consumed in the struggle against the English and the Dutch from the late 1500s, with Angola laying out approximately 220,000 *cruzados* in 1655 against an income of only 130,000 (cf. pp. 297–8).

Not that a shortage of money was anything new to Portuguese rulers or their servants. King Manuel agreed in 1512 that it would be an excellent thing for his troops in India to be paid, 'though not at our expense'.[76] And clearly he was as good as his word, since from the very outset there was an unbroken flow of complaints from the east as to the lack of weapons, supplies and pay. Seamen and soldiers accordingly mutinied, deserted, entered the church, set up in business, or made what profit they could by selling royal property to the local populace. By the 1560s the English, so it was reported, considered the Portuguese too feeble to trouble them, and twenty years later the Spaniards thought them unable to take the offensive in Asia. More disastrously still, for an empire so fundamentally maritime, was the decline, not to say exhaustion, of Portuguese seafaring skills and resources. At the beginning of the seventeenth century the country was desperately short of ships, and had little over 6000 seamen with which to carry on the trade, and ensure the safety, of a world-wide empire under attack from the formidable power of the Dutch. Nautical science, in which Portugal had once been pre-eminent, was by the early 1600s in such a state that its only teachers in the kingdom were foreigners. Already, however, in the 1530s, according to a distinguished contemporary, the smallest Portuguese craft in India were fit merely to terrify their crews, the galleys were inferior to those of the Moslems, and the biggest vessels so indifferent that it took most of the day to hoist their sails. Nautical anecdotes of this order are never wanting, but of the unsatisfactory nature of much Portuguese shipping, even by the unexacting standards of the day, there is unambiguous evidence. From the mid-sixteenth century onwards there are well-attested stories of the loss of Portuguese Indiamen not only through the incompetence of those navigating and sailing them, but, as with other empires in decline, through the poor quality of the ships themselves (cf.

p. 148). They foundered when caulking fell out of the seams in their planking, when old fittings broke, or because massive deck cargoes illicitly embarked for the homeward passage hampered their working. Furthermore, Portugal, a backward country with no metallurgical industry, did not manufacture artillery, and the majority of her vessels were inadequately armed. Some in Asia were still without guns in the 1630s,[77] and even supposedly powerful Indiamen commonly had no more than about 20 small pieces, whereas English privateers might already mount twice this weight in the 1580s. So Portuguese fleets were defeated, and Portuguese ships lost, captured or sunk at such a rate that from *c.* 1600 the empire's great and rich trades were largely handled by alien, and especially Dutch, vessels (cf. p. 386).

The paradox is not, however, that this should happen – as it was also to happen to the better-endowed, if even more burdened Spain – but that it did not happen earlier. Widely dispersed, largely established in lethal tropical climates, Portugal's colonies made exorbitant demands for settlers, officials, clergy and – most urgently – fleets and troops, on her sparse human and material reserves. In 1515 there was talk of stationing 7000 men in Asia, supported – at a time when the infinitely wealthier Venetian state probably had a total of one hundred fighting ships – by forty vessels and 1500 pieces of artillery (cf. pp. 130–1). Morocco took, or hoped for, 5000 soldiers in the 1530s, whilst soon after squadrons were needed to protect trade with West Africa and, by the end of the century, with Brazil. Nor was this the whole story. Men died at sea from disease at an appalling rate, or succumbed to the endemic dysentry, fevers and malaria of the tropics with, on one occasion, a force of 1100 at Malacca reduced in no time to 200.[78] And to the constant, if vain, attempts at replacement was added the drain of emigration, totalling roughly 250,000 in the sixteenth century, and these mostly able-bodied and unmarried young men. This was approximately the equivalent of the country's adult manpower in any one year, and naturally enough included many of Portugal's ablest and most enterprising inhabitants, few of them destined to return to the mother country. In relation to a population of at best one and a half million before 1650, and this decimated by plague and epidemics in the late sixteenth and early seventeenth centuries, men left Portugal on a scale unequalled in any previous overseas migration (testimony alike to the hardships of metropolitan life and the attitudes of a state that could tolerate such an exodus) and at a rate eclipsing contemporary Spanish emigration to the healthier Americas (cf. pp. 282 and 368). And besides these, many sought their fortunes outside the possessions of Portugal. They appeared in the Spanish Canaries in the late 1400s, and in Spanish Mexico, Panama and Peru – where they constituted the biggest foreign community – in the sixteenth century. In Asia they deserted in alarming numbers, and were soon found in Persian, Mogul and Japanese service, whilst by the early 1600s Habsburg authorities viewed with distaste their ubiquity in the Americas and their dedication to smuggling and clandestine trade (cf. pp. 249ff., 344).

So an ever-widening gap opened between Portugal's resources and commitments. She was incapable of providing the volume of shipping her empire required. From soon after 1500 crews had to be made up from pressed and inexperienced landsmen, and from foreigners and slaves. In Asia German and Flemish gunners were used.[79] By the end of the century such military force as could be mustered in the east consisted of convicts, criminals and children, and many nominally Portuguese vessels had no more than a single European officer on board. In Portugal itself there was a shortage of labour. It may have been momentarily checked by the widespread use of slaves, but their very presence in strength in the country – and in the south in particular – probably depressed wages and diminished opportunities, so further encouraging emigration. But clearly the country's agriculture was in difficulties. Rarely, since the late Middle Ages, self-sufficing in grain, Portugal found it impossible simultaneously to meet her own and her colonies' demands, let alone their requirements of other foodstuffs. Hence, in the same way as Spain, and for the same reasons, Portugal became dependent on others, the Dutch especially, not only for weapons, textiles and metal goods, but for food itself. In 1558 ninety French ships laden with grain arrived in the Tagus in three days alone, and by the mid-1600s 30 per cent of the vessels entering Lisbon were carrying grain, chiefly from the Low Countries (cf. pp. 381ff.).

But more was involved than insufficient labour and overwhelming demand. Empire absorbed ability, and diverted, with its prospects of easy wealth, energies and resources from any lively concern with agricultural improvement. At the same time that intolerance and intransigence springing from imperial success, and intensified by Counter-Reformation and (after 1580) Spanish influences, led to attacks on the New Christians and Jews who provided much of Portugal's commercial skills and wealth. Many fled abroad, and those in Lisbon were reported by a London merchant in 1626 'not to keep much of their estate about them for fear of the Inquisition'.[80] Equally perniciously, the growth of an empire largely dependent on slave labour, dedicated to the ideals of conspicuous consumption, and sustained by the profits of plunder, peculation and office-holding, quickened that already vigorous Iberian contempt for any form of demeaning toil. Slaves – first from the Mediterranean, the Canaries and North Africa, then, after mid-fifteenth century, chiefly from West Africa – were abundant. By the 1550s they accounted for about 10 per cent of the population of Lisbon and the southern provinces and permeated the entire economy of Portugal to a degree unknown elsewhere in Europe (see pp. 268f.). Not surprisingly there was, as a northern visitor remarked, a general Portuguese reluctance to 'learn any occupation'. Empire promised affluence; provided servile labour; demanded and justified the non-productive callings of priest and bureaucrat, so that in the 1600s the city fathers of Lisbon attributed the lack of manpower to a surfeit of 'schools, colleges and seminaries'. Thus by its very society and economy Portugal was, like the equally bigoted and repressive Spain of the seventeenth century, increasingly unable to control, let alone benefit from its overseas possessions. Aristocrats and squires, without the sense of duty of their Spanish equivalents, or the business experience and ideals of public service of Venetian patricians, were, like their Viking or Genoese counterparts, better at founding than running an empire (cf. pp. 2ff., 111ff., 183ff.). A country whose nobility underwent no such military training as that of Spain accepted that in the east armies – inevitably inadequate – should be raised by mustering, as occasion demanded, whatever *soldados* could be found, and by the mid-sixteenth century was on the point of allowing the cavalry, 'without which we are of no account to our neighbours', to be disbanded.[81] Less profoundly affected by Renaissance influences than Venice or Spain, and in general ruling no such conquered or subject peoples as to provoke reflection on imperial obligations, Portugal produced no equivalent to the conscientious bureaucracies of the Venetian republic and Habsburg Castile. Viceroys refused to mar the prospects of a joyous homecoming by interfering with the doings of the well-connected in Asia, nor was there any machinery to ensure that they should. In an empire commonly regarded as one vast reservoir of tribute, officials made fortunes, whilst opportunities for royal gain were either unenthusiastically pursued, privately annexed, or inexpertly exploited. Hormuz, it was reckoned in the late 1500s, was leased at less than one-third of its potential value. By 1627 the royal spice monopoly failed to cover even its transport costs. This was not entirely due to Portuguese shortcomings. Islamic strength and hostility increased, and the Mogul re-opening of land routes to Persia and China sharpened demand and competition, and contributed to a rise of spice prices in Asia of about 400 per cent in the second half of the sixteenth century. But Portugal did nothing to improve the situation. The royal monopoly was imperfectly enforced. Large Portuguese imports of Gujarati textiles diminished their purchasing power in the spice markets of Malabar and the flood of Spanish silver into Asia, in some measure resulting from Portuguese dealings, stimulated a local demand they were unable to meet. Hence when the Dutch arrived in the east they entered the spice trade in part by downright force, in part by paying in Indonesia and the islands not in cloth, as the Portuguese did, but in bullion (which their seapower and commercial sophistication allowed them to acquire one way or another), sometimes at three times the accustomed Portuguese rate (cf. pp. 404ff.). Against such stratagems, which sent pepper prices in western India up 40 per cent between 1610 and 1632, Portugal had neither the skills nor the resources to compete. Unlike the Dutch monopoly company, the Portuguese crown held no trading capital in the east to be deployed as the situation demanded, but insisted instead that the goods and bullion it provided were used only in the purchase of spice (see pp. 269ff., 405–6). Furthermore, the enormously valuable interport trade was left in private hands, and indeed the whole *Estado da India* took on, like any other colonial possession, but with greater speed and to a greater degree, a life of its own. By the late 1500s it behaved, and was regarded, as an independent entity, often making considerable profits from customs and taxes, but transmitting none of these to Europe, and – as did Spain's American colonies – expecting the burden and cost of defence to be met by the mother country.

Elsewhere it was the same. Whole areas of the economies of Portugal and her new Atlantic possessions were by the late fifteenth century controlled by the Genoese (see pp. 181–2). From 1514 the import and marketing of Asian spices came to be largely dominated by great Italian firms. To these there succeeded south German bankers – Fugger, Welser, Rem, Ehinger – able to supply alike the grain needed by Portugal, the money required by her rulers, and the metal goods essential to her colonial trades. Such was the scale and nature of their operations that in the 1530s they took 500t of spice in repayment of royal debts, the Herwarts of Augsburg possessed a diamond too expensive even for the ruler of Spain's world empire, and profits ranged from 150 per cent in the best years to 45 per cent at the close of the century. By this date also, with spices handled by German-Italian consortia, Italian merchants allegedly naturalized in Portugal were conducting a vigorous commerce to Africa, South America and India, and one magnate was simultaneously the monopolist of Asian pepper and the trade of the Gold and Ivory Coasts of West Africa.[82] Meanwhile Portugal's commerce with the Netherlands was dominated by the Dutch, who in the early seventeenth century attempted as well to convert their preponderance in Brazil's carrying trade to the political subjugation of the colony (see pp. 386ff.).

But the collapse of Portugal's power and prosperity was neither sudden nor total. By land and sea the Portuguese fought long and hard, mustering at times, and in the most desperate circumstances, appreciable resources in men and materials, often in Goa financed by loans from indigenous merchants. The Dutch, though they took most of Portugal's Asian colonies and trade, were repulsed from Mozambique and cleared in the mid-1600s from Angola and Brazil in a war largely sustained by taxes levied locally on sugar (cf. pp. 388–90, 393ff.). Well into the seventeenth century Portuguese ships continued to give good accounts of themselves, impressing the English at Surat in 1612, defeating the Dutch off the Cape of Good Hope the following year, and breaking their blockade of Macao in 1627.[83] And if the dolefully entitled *Tragic History of the Sea* provides abundant evidence of Portuguese maritime ineptitude, it also records instances of seamanship of the highest order, and of the remarkable ingenuity of survivors in improvising tools, shelter and transport.

Moreover, whatever the misfortunes of the crown's Asian possessions and commerce, the interport trade was still thriving in the early 1600s, estates in the Indian Province of the North prospered until the end of the century, and defeats at Dutch hands turned the Portuguese to the opportunities of Vietnam, and to seeking spice in Macassar and copper in Solor.[84] Losses in the east were, furthermore, in some measure redressed by the growing wealth of the west, with sugar accounting for half the yield of the Lisbon customs in 1627. Nor was Portuguese merchant shipping driven from the seas. Even as, in the early seventeenth century, a scholar sought to revive, with abundant classical erudition, his compatriots' understanding of naval architecture, Portuguese craft were handling much of Valencia's commerce with Atlantic Iberia, fishing, as they had long done, off Newfoundland, and trading not only to Italy but to Spanish America. Many, particularly those working to Brazil, were tiny, sometimes no more than 25t.[85] But the weaknesses of Portugal itself were in part compensated by the appearance of vessels owned in colonial ports – sixty-five at Goa alone in 1620 – a further indication of that shift in Portuguese, as in Spanish dominions, of wealth from Europe to the overseas territories (cf. pp. 322ff., 365).

Yet whatever its successes against the Dutch, or in breaking free from Spain after 1640, the Portuguese empire was indisputably in decline by the mid-1600s. It was in essence a chain of posts along a series of maritime commercial routes. Over these Portugal's authority was only briefly absolute, and in the east climate, distance, geography and her own limited resources meant there were always alternatives open to Asian merchants and seamen. Stretching across the oceans of the world, Portugal's possessions entailed an impossible dissipation of her few ships and men. In many parts of Asia, moreover, her presence depended less on her own strength than on local goodwill or indifference. Her empire was, therefore, at the mercy of any major seapower. Its focal points, easily accessible, invited attack by their convenient concentration of wealth, and except for Brazil, presented few of the obstacles and expense involved in the attempted conquest of overseas mainland territories settled by Europeans. And at this crucial time Portugal lacked that able royal direction which had been so important in her years of expansion. The death of king Sebastian in Morocco (1578) led to the annexation of Portugal and her colonies by Spain (1580). The disadvantages were quickly apparent. Spain's formidable enemies, England and Holland, now attacked Portugal (cf. pp. 384ff., 475ff.). Portuguese resources were, it was complained, squandered on Spanish interests, whilst those of Portugal were neglected by the Spaniards, whose truce with Holland (1609) attempted to exclude the Dutch from America whilst giving them a relatively free hand in Asia (see pp. 396, 516). Meanwhile peoples such as the Congolese and Japanese, disenchanted with Portugal, turned to her European rivals. A combination of arrogance and ineptitude led to the expulsion of the Portuguese from Ternate, and, in the early seventeenth century, to strained relations with China. In Ceylon their overthrow stemmed from belated and ill-prepared attempts to subjugate the kingdom of Kandy, which brought Dutch intervention and ultimately military disaster, with the defeat and death of the Portuguese captain-general himself (1630). Equally fundamental was that general Islamic resurgence manifested alike in Portuguese retreat in Morocco and Ottoman intervention in Asia (see p. 252). By the early seventeenth century Achinese fleets regularly threatened Malacca and the Moguls drove the Portuguese from Bengal in 1632. Portugal's mishandling of Persia, combined with military and naval weakness, cost her Hormuz (1622), whilst the Omani Arabs expelled the Portuguese first from Muscat (1650) and then from the East African coast north of Cape Delgado by the end of the century (see pp. 242, 259). In western India, too, Portugal was under repeated and commonly Moslem attack. Chaul and Goa withstood a concerted assault in 1570–1, and in the mid-1600s Goan territory was taken by neighbouring Ikkeri, which controlled the sources of much of the imperial city's rice.

Not only, as the ubiquity and tenacity of these attacks indicates, was the opposition to

Portugal widespread and growing, but in the east, where at best she had no more than 10,000 Europeans in the sixteenth century, she was unable to damage, let alone destroy, her opponents. The bazaars of Calicut, it was reported in 1569, were full of Portuguese goods taken by local pirates. As with all empires, problems eventually became too many and resources too few. And as with any empire not based on the subjugation of primitive populations, or whose establishment had not entailed the destruction of indigenous peoples, European technological advantage was sooner or later eroded. Western firearms were quickly acquired or emulated in Asia. Ships and galleys 'equivalent to our own' were already being built in northern India in 1508, according to the first Portuguese viceroy.[86] The Omanis were using European-style craft in the mid-1600s, and some years earlier the English noticed that those of the Achinese – always a thorn in Portuguese flesh – mounted 'very good brass ordnance: demi-canon; culverins; sakers; minions', a full range, that is, of western artillery.[87]

Yet it was not resurgent indigenous strength that deprived the Portuguese of their empire, but European powers whose individual, let alone collective, maritime skills and resources, Portugal could never hope to equal. Spanish ships were off West Africa by the mid fifteenth century. The French, their 'well-gunned and well-equipped' vessels enviously appraised by Portuguese commanders, were soon after everywhere from Senegambia to Brazil and the Indian Ocean. In the mid-1500s the English seized Portuguese craft in the Channel, traded to West Africa, and before the end of the century were plundering Portugal's shipping in European, Atlantic and Asian waters alike. In the ensuing decades they attacked Portugal's bases in the east, disrupted her oriental commerce, and commenced to trade both in Asia itself and between Europe and the east (cf. pp. 440, 463, 475). Nevertheless neither England nor France was wholeheartedly dedicated to maritime expansion before 1650, and it was the Dutch who very largely destroyed Portugal's seaborne empire (see p. 393ff.). Against their crushing superiority in everything from ships to wealth Portugal had no redress. Holland's forces were more numerous, better trained, better led and better disciplined. They were also recruited, the Portuguese marvelled, from well-built and well-fed northerners. From 1595 the Dutch pushed into the Indian Ocean and the seas of Indonesia and South China. Worsted in their later attacks on Angola and Brazil, they none the less inflicted crippling losses on Portugal in the Atlantic as well, taking most of the 300 vessels working to Brazil in 1647–8. It was the triumph not only of maritime strength, but of commercial sophistication. In West Africa, a Jesuit father remarked, the Dutch bought and sold 'what we hold of little account'. As in Europe their shipping undercut that of competitors. Their grip on the maritime economy of Spain brought them bullion and those same advantages in Asia they enjoyed against Venice in the Mediterranean (see pp. 141–2). So for Portugal the later seventeenth century was a chronicle of disasters largely inflicted by the Dutch, against whom she struggled into the 1660s – apart from an ill-kept truce in 1641–52 – whilst from 1640 attempting, and in the end successfully, to secure independence from Spain. The Dutch destroyed the

Portuguese spice trade to the west, much of Portugal's Asian interport commerce, her power in the Persian Gulf and her lucrative position in Japan. They deprived her of many of her possessions in West Africa, and all those in the east except Goa, Macao and such lesser outposts as Solor and Timor (see pp. 393ff.). 'A bitter reminder', it was said in 1663, when the futility of empire seemed only too clear, 'of the little we now have.'

Bibliographical note

The magisterial survey by C.R. Boxer of *The Portuguese Seaborne Empire, 1415–1825* (1969), together with the information there given on the archives of Portugal and of her colonial, or former colonial, possessions renders any extended bibliography superfluous. I have accordingly listed below only some recent works, or those illustrating particular points. A comprehensive examination of the sources relevant to the history of Portugal in the Indian Ocean in the sixteenth and seventeenth centuries is also to be found in N.M. Pearson's excellent *Merchants and Rulers in Gujarat* (Berkeley, 1976). There is a general survey of materials relating to Latin America in *Itinerario*, I (Leyden, 1977). Documents on Portuguese colonial history are published in *Boletim da Filmateca Ultramarina Portuguesa* (1954–71) and *Studia: Revista Semestral* (1958–   ). This carries as well important articles, as does the *Revista Portuguesa de Historia* (1942–   ).

A number of outstanding papers on the Orient at the time of the arrival of the Portuguese, and on their early history in India, Persia and Ceylon, have appeared in *Mare Luso-Indicum* (Paris, 1971–   ). There is a fundamental, but difficult, examination of Portugal's Asian trade in Neils Steensgaard's *Carracks, Caravans and Companies: The Structural Crisis in the European-Asian Trade in the Early Seventeenth Century* (Copenhagen, 1973). P.-Y. Manguin, *Les Portugais sur les Côtes du Vietnam et du Campa* (Paris, 1972) discusses Portuguese activities in Vietnam. There is an excellent summary of the history and functions of Macao by C.R. Boxer, 'Macao as a Religious and Commercial Entrepôt in the Sixteenth and Seventeenth Centuries', *Acta Asiatica*, 26 (1974), 64ff. Pearson's *Merchants and Rulers in Gujarat*, covers more ground than its title indicates. It describes the maritime economy of the Indian Ocean in the sixteenth and seventeenth centuries, and throws a whole new light on indigenous response to Portuguese policies. A.R. Disney outlines the history of 'The First Portuguese India Company, 1628–33', in *Ec. Hist. Rev*, XXX (1977), 242ff.

Early Portuguese voyages in the North Atlantic are discussed with vigour and authority in S.E. Morison, *The European Discovery of America: The Northern Voyages* (Oxford, 1971), and with greater subtlety by D.B. Quinn, *England and the Discovery of America* (1974). The rise of the Madeiran sugar industry is analysed by Virginia Rau and Jorge de Macedo, *O Açúcar da Madeira nos Fins do Século XV* (Funchal, 1962), and that of São Tomé by Virginia Rau, *O Açúcar de S. Tomé no Segundo Quartel do Século XVI* (Lisbon, 1971). There is an admirable brief introduction to Portugal in Brazil in Richard Konetzke, *Die Indianerkulturen Altamerikas und die Spanisch-Portugiesische Kolonialherrschaft* (Frankfurt a/Main, 1965). For the trade between Brazil and the Spanish possessions in South America, see A. Jara, 'Estructuras de colonizacíon y modalidades del trafico en el Pacifico Sur Hispano-Americano' in *CIHM*, 7 (1965). Valuable new information on the Brazilian war against the Dutch is assembled in Evaldo Cabral de Mello, *Olinda Restaurada: Guerra e Açúcar no Nordeste, 1630–54* (Rio de Janeiro, 1975).

There are many stimulating hypotheses on the origins of Portuguese expansion (and on the role of the carvel) in H. and P. Chaunu, *Séville et l'Atlantique, 1504–1650* (8 vols, Paris, 1955–9), vol. VIII, I. Portugal's position in the European maritime economy *c.* 1500 is sketched by A.H. de Oliveira Marques, 'Notas para a História da Feitoria Portuguesa na Flandres no Século XV', in A. Guiffre (ed.), *Studi in Onore di Amintore fanfani*, (6 vols, Milan, 1962), II, 439ff. The activities of Portuguese shipping in south European waters are illustrated by Domenico Gioffrè, 'Il Commercio d'Importazione Genovese alla luce dei Registri del Dazio, 1495–1537', ibid., vol. V, 115ff. That Portuguese success was due to superior artillery and ships is briskly argued by Carlo M. Cipolla, *Guns and Sails in the Early Phase of European Expansion, 1400–1700* (1965). The evolution of the carvel is judiciously traced by Commandant Denoix in *CIHM*, 5 (1966), where there are also several valuable papers on the role of foreign capital in Portuguese expansion. My discussion of Portugal's dependence on indigenous collaboration in India draws on P. Pissurlencar, *Agentes da Diplomaçia Portuguesa na India* (Goa, 1952), and the unpublised researches of Dr P.J. Bury, whose Cambridge PhD thesis I have used. The organization of the Portuguese spice monopoly in northern Europe is described by J. van Houtte, 'Anvers au XVe et XVIe siècles', *Annales*, 16 (1961), 248ff. For the operation of the Portuguese India fleets, see in addition to the discussion in Boxer, *Portuguese Seaborne Empire*, the article of Virginia Rau, 'Les Escales de la Carreira da India', *Recueils de la Société Jean Bodin*, XXXIII (1972). There is a shrewd, colourful and entertaining appraisal of Portugal's empire (and much else besides) by the Florentine merchant Francesco Carletti, who recorded his travels between 1594 and 1606 in his *Ragionamenti*, of which there is an English translation by Herbert Weinstock, *My Voyage Around the World* (1965). Portuguese decline in Asia is admirably discussed by A.R. Disney, *Twilight of the Pepper Empire: Portuguese Trade in Southwest India in the Early Seventeenth Century* (Cambridge, Mass., 1978).

There is a convenient summary of Portuguese achievements in cartography in G.R. Crone, *Maps and their Makers* (1962), to which must be added the invaluable and definitive studies of Comandante Teixeira da Mota, especially in *CIHM*, 2 (1958) and *CIHM*, 5 (1966), and those produced since 1961 in Lisbon by the Centro de Estudos de Cartografia Antiga. For Portuguese navigational practice and innovations see E.G. Taylor, *The Haven-Finding Art* (1956), and the magisterial work of Commander David W. Waters, *The Art of Navigation in England in Elizabethan and Early Stuart Times* (1958). There are important analyses of Portuguese thought, and of 'the imperial dream' in the early sixteenth century in M. Bataillon, *Etudes sur le Portugal au temps de l'Humanisme* (Coimbra, 1952). The influence of empire on the culture and society of Portugal is examined by the present writer in *HJ*, XII (1969), 389ff.

Portugal's impact on the various economies of Africa in this period is briefly discussed by Raymond Mauny in *CIHM*, 7 (1965), 175ff. European intervention in Asian commerce, and in particular the effect of bullion imports to the East and the stimulation of Oriental economies, have of late received much attention. Of especial value are the articles of A. Kobata, 'The Production and Uses of Gold and Silver in Sixteenth and Seventeenth Century Japan', *Ec. Hist. Rev*, XVIII (1965), 245ff; C.R. Boxer, 'Plata es Sangre', *Philippine Studies*, 18 (1970), 457ff; Seiichi Iwao, 'Japanese Foreign Trade in the Sixteenth and Seventeenth Centuries', *Acta Asiatica*, 30 (1976), 1ff.

For the role of aliens in Portugal's imperial economy in this period, see the papers in *CIHM*, 5 (1966), and H. Kellenbenz, 'Os Mercadores Alemães de Lisboa per volta de 1530', *Revista Portuguesa de Historia*, 9 (1960), 125ff. My evidence for the survival of Portuguese merchant shipping into the seventeenth century comes from Alvaro Castillo Pintado, *Trafico Maritimo y Commercio de Importacion en Valencia a Comienzos del Siglo XVII* (Madrid, 1967) and PRO HCA Examinations.

6

Spain

1 *Hispania Victrix*

In 1552 the author of *Spain Triumphant*, proudly surveying the imperial achievement of his compatriots, adjudged it 'the greatest event since the making of the world, apart from the incarnation and death of him who created it'. And certainly no empire was more extensive or more swiftly established. None was acquired in such a sequence of voyages and campaigns, and none occasioned such searchings of conscience as to the nature of imperial obligations and the rights of subject peoples. Before 1492 Spain's only possessions of any consequence outside Europe were the Canary islands. By mid-sixteenth century she controlled most of the Caribbean, huge areas of the American continent, footholds in Africa and had penetrated by sea from the New World to the Far East. Even more astonishingly, this expansion was accompanied, as was that of no other people, by the establishment of hegemony in Europe. Largely by a series of politically felicitous marriages the Habsburg dynasty accumulated a territorial heritage un-equalled since the days of Charlemagne, or indeed Rome.[1] Under the emperor Charles V (1519–58) its power embraced the Spanish kingdoms, Germany, the Low Countries and much of Italy. Part of this rich patrimony was lost with the emperor's abdication. But to many the surrender of German titles and pretensions was more than compensated by the annexation (1580–1640) of Portugal and her colonies (see p. 296).

Unlike that of the Portuguese, dispersed and peripheral, Spain's overseas empire was in essence limited to one continent, and unlike its predecessors, based on the subjugation and Christianization of large and relatively highly developed states. Yet the beginnings were unimpressive. The Spanish kingdoms had, like Portugal, participated in that medieval search for the sources of African gold, and in the conquest and colonization of the Atlantic islands (see pp. 164, 227). The Canaries were ultimately, and with considerable difficulty, brought under Spanish sovereignty (1478–93). Their Guanche population was converted and reduced to servitude, and a seigniorial economy instituted, geared mainly to the production, Portuguese-style, of wine and sugar (see pp. 245f.). In the decades after 1450 there were also voyages, some backed or approved by the Castilian crown, from Andalusian harbours to the rich Portuguese preserves in West Africa, together with various generally unsuccessful attacks on Portugal's African trade and possessions. Hence in 1479 Spain was obliged to acknowledge Portuguese dominion in West Africa and the Atlantic islands, whilst

Portugal accepted, at no cost, Spain's title to the unsubdued Canaries (see p. 229). Spanish ships nevertheless continued to work the valuable fishery between Bojador and the Cape Verde Islands, and Andalusian and Canarian merchants continued to take slaves and do business on the shores of the Gulf of Guinea. But Spanish energies were largely concentrated on the destruction of the last Moorish strongholds in Granada and the pursuit of royal ambitions in Italy. Only with the arrival of Christopher Columbus in Iberia – yet another Genoese following a familiar path – did Spain turn, and then with nothing of the single-mindedness of Portugal, to oceanic exploration.

Born in 1451, Columbus was a man of humble origins who had worked his way up to become a factor for the great Genoese commercial house of Centurione, in whose employment he eventually reached Lisbon (1476). Here he became a chartmaker, and from here he sailed as an agent in Italian and Portuguese service to (possibly) England,[2] and to Madeira and West Africa. By his early thirties he had his own command, and had married a scion, albeit an illegitimate one, of an old Madeiran family. It was in these years that he became unshakeably conviced that Asia could be reached by sailing west. He may have heard from his wife's relatives of expeditions from the islands to seek lands to seaward, whose existence was popularly accepted, and whose presence a sharp observer might deduce from the nature of the flotsam cast up in Madeira. In Lisbon he could see the obvious rewards of Portuguese maritime persistence, and interpret by mental processes of peculiar convolution, the evidence of his own voyages and the experience of his Portuguese colleagues. And like any true convert his faith was continually reinforced. He knew, among much else, Polo's tales of the Orient and d'Ailly's *Imago Mundi*, which happily concluded that between Morocco and Asia there was an ocean 'of no great width' (see p. 230). From the words of the apocryphal Second Book of Esdras (vi, 42) 'six parts hast thou dried up', he deduced that waters covered only the remaining seventh of the earth – they cover in fact 70 per cent – and by misreading a medieval Islamic geographer he reduced its size by about a quarter.

Hence in 1484 he proposed to the king of Portugal to sail westwards to Ophir, Cathay, Cipangu (Japan) and various other lands. This in the light of contemporary knowledge and achievement, though bold, was neither improbable nor impossible. The best guesses underestimated the size of the globe and the ratio of water to land. Scholars – most notably the Florentine cosmographer Toscanelli, with whom Columbus eventually corresponded – accepted that such a voyage was feasible and the Portuguese themselves may have earlier toyed with the idea (see p. 230). But in his timing and his advocacy Columbus was unfortunate. Portuguese exploration of the African coast was increasingly promising, that of the Atlantic ever-more disappointing. Now an obscure Genoese seaman suggested an expedition which on his own reckoning involved a passage (from the Canaries to Cipangu) of over 8000km with only uncertain prospects of some resting place en route. Worse still, he demanded, contrary to Portuguese practice, that he should be paid by the king. And in putting his case he added to that family facility for living in strained relations with their fellow men the stridency of the insecure which later led him to describe himself as 'a captain of Spain' on the strength of a brief visit to a siege in the last stages of the *reconquista*. His arguments were rejected by, amongst others, the learned Diego Ortiz (see p. 512n4), and Portuguese tradition records that John II found him 'a vain boaster'.

Rejected in Portugal he turned to Spain, but here again he was unsuccessful (1486), and only after lengthy delays and further vain searches for support in France and England, did the Spanish sovereigns agree to back him (1492). The reasons are far from clear. To some, particularly the pious queen Isabella, his mystic religiosity may have been attractive, especially according with the euphoria inspired by the final overthrow of Moorish rule in Iberia.[3] But what was decisive was his own determination, and the fortuitous willingness of a royal official and some of Columbus' Genoese compatriots to finance him, thus relieving the ever-impecunious Crown of any expense (see p. 180). So he was appointed to the command of an expedition whose outcome has long and rightly been regarded as a turning point in the history of the world. Just past 40, he was, like many others freed by the tide of fortune, to reveal abilities of which his earlier years had given little indication. Ambitious, self-taught and self-made he pursued his ideas with fanatical tenacity. He wavered only momentarily from his belief that he had reached Cathay, and was increasingly convinced that the Terrestial Paradise – a pleasing figment of medieval imagination – was sited on the Orinoco, on a bulge on the earth's surface 'like a woman's nipple, this protusion being highest and nearest the sky'. Yet, as is not uncommon, such apocalyptic excesses and personal instability were accompanied by acute realism. No contemporary Portuguese, and no subsequent Spanish commander, acquired such lavish privileges as did Columbus in 1492. If successful he was to be ennobled, to be viceroy and governor-general of his discoveries, and to enjoy, as Admiral of the Ocean Sea, similar rights to the Admiral of Castile, which office was to be hereditary in his family.

He sailed from the insignificant port of Palos, on the Gulf of Cadiz, on 2 August 1492. His fleet consisted of two small carvels (see p. 263) – one lateen and one square-rigged – which local shipowners had reluctantly provided, and a 100t vessel from Galicia. Their crews were from Andalusia, and particularly from those Niebla harbours long engaged in war and trade in West Africa (see pp. 301–2). Compared with a major Portuguese undertaking the preparations were casual. Many of the company showed little enthusiasm for the venture, and their commander was to complain bitterly of the poor quality of his men and materials. But his Spanish pilots kept an impressively accurate record of the fleet's outward progress, just as Spanish seamanship ensured its survival on the return. Columbus, whose commission contained assertions of Spanish suzerainty over the ocean of the same ambitious order as those advanced by the Portuguese, was empowered 'to discover and acquire certain islands and mainlands in the Ocean Sea'. He carried a letter to be presented to the grand khan, and was accompanied by an interpreter through whom he would converse (apparently in Arabic) with the Chinese. Other documents spoke of 'the regions of India', and the gold, gems and spices to be obtained, of which he was to have one-tenth tax free.

He first made for the Canaries, from where he thought to sail with a favourable wind along the latitude which would bring him to Japan. The navigational practice was common enough, but never was its outcome so unexpected (see p. 263). After little over a month at sea, often in idyllic conditions and climates 'soft as April in Seville' Columbus found himself in the Bahamas (12 October). A deep-water voyage of a distance and duration unequalled since Viking times revealed not the brilliant civilizations of Polo's Asia but, as the Spaniards were to find elsewhere in the Antilles and the Caribbean, the simplest of primitive peoples. To the admiral, ever Genoese in such matters, the Tainos, naked, unarmed, pacific and adorned with gold ornaments, seemed ideal for enslavement.[4] Then, in pursuit of China, the fleet moved on to discover Cuba and Hispaniola (the modern Haiti and Dominican Republic) where, since one ship had deserted and another was wrecked, Columbus founded a settlement, the first in the west by Europeans since the Vikings. On 8 January 1493, the remaining vessels, now reunited, left Hispaniola and worked north to what was thought the appropriate latitude for Spain. The homeward passage, not surprisingly for the season, was a wild one. The ships lost company, and Columbus, despairing at one stage of survival, eventually arrived in Lisbon. To his own satisfaction he had returned from the east. Cuba was Japan, and he had indeed sent an emissary to negotiate with a local chief optimistically identified as the grand khan. Others had their doubts. The Portuguese first regarded him as a poacher on their African preserves, then as the discoverer of yet more Atlantic islands. Even the Spaniards ultimately settled for his revelation of 'distant lands in the west'. But what the voyage had incontrovertibly demonstrated, like those of the Vikings and the Portuguese, was the range and endurance – a round trip of 224 days – of medieval European ships, and the potential of relatively crude navigational techniques. It had also equally clearly demonstrated the strengths and weaknesses of Columbus himself – his obsession with Asia; his ability to describe his discoveries accurately and perceptively; his excellence in dead-reckoning navigation; his outstanding seamanship that allowed him, by a characteristic combination of skill and good fortune, to find the most satisfactory transatlantic route (cf. 21ff., pp. 263–4, 342).

Whatever his own views of his achievements, reports of possible slaves and converts, gold and naked women were more than enough to inspire widespread enthusiasm for a further expedition. But no longer was it a modest private venture mounted from an obscure haven. As Admiral of the Ocean Sea and Viceroy of the Indies Columbus was commissioned to convert the Indians,[5] establish a trading post, and to continue, almost incidentally, his search for the Orient. Seventeen ships, carrying some 1500 men – a colonizing force of Viking or early Germanic proportions – were assembled by Crown officials at Cadiz, and the whole company, gentlemen volunteers apart, was in royal pay. The fleet made one of the fastest passages ever achieved by a convoy, discovered sixty or so islands great and small in the lesser Antilles, and arrived (27 November 1493) off Hispaniola to find that insatiable Spanish lust for gold and women had provoked the Indians to destroy the original settlement and slaughter its inhabitants. A new colony was hastily founded on a totally unsuitable site, and before long, in what was to become the distinctive Spanish style, regular military expeditions were despatched inland to overawe and rob the natives. Columbus himself searched in vain for China, exploring the coasts of Cuba and Jamaica, and loosing, in equally distinctive Spanish style, great dogs against their peoples (see pp. 337–8). Meanwhile the Hispaniola settlement had collapsed. Spanish *hidalgos*, many of them soon revealed as the most ruthless of conquerors, found no land to support a gentleman in proper style, and no docile natives to supply them with treasure. Instead there was widespread and growing indigenous hostility. The insupportable prospect of manual labour to provide food threatened, and authority was all too obviously concentrated in the hands of the alien Columbus and his numerous relatives. In a futile bid to vindicate himself the admiral embarked on the subjugation of the island, rounding up slaves and imposing a tribute in gold. As with the Portuguese in the Indian Ocean the progression from exploration and trade to conquest was short and swift (see pp. 233–6). But whereas in Portugal it was made under royal direction, in Hispaniola it was in flat contravention of royal instructions. In Spain, to which he returned in 1496, Columbus' achievements raised little enthusiasm and many doubts. But that the discoveries offered some prospect of profit was clear enough, and the crown accordingly revoked the admiral's monopoly and licensed other expeditions.

After such setbacks Columbus was unable to raise men and to get to sea again before 1498. This time the fleet divided in the Canaries, part taking the well-tried route to Hispaniola, the remainder, under the commander himself, continuing south, possibly on account of what he knew of English finds in the North Atlantic (see p. 461). Beyond the Cape Verdes he turned west, expecting, as current orthodoxy taught, to encounter some landmass counterbalancing Africa, and in whose equatorial regions there would be, as in those of Africa, gold. On the northern coast of South America he discovered the island he named Trinidad, passed through the dangerous Gulf of Paría, touched in the future Venezuela – rightly identified as 'a great mainland' – and encountering the massive outflow of the Orinoco felt the Terrestial Paradise to be at hand. But in Hispaniola he found only chaos, and quickly made a bad situation desperate by a combination of incompetence and unbalanced behaviour. Such were the reports of his doings that a royal officer was despatched to the island (1500), from where he summarily shipped the admiral and his brothers home in chains.

From this ignominy Columbus was swiftly released, and though removed from the governorship of Hispaniola he was nevertheless allowed by the crown to retain his other titles. But never again was he given any office of responsibility, and not until 1502 was he entrusted with the command of another expedition. Then, with the spectacle of Portuguese success in Asia, he was given a small flotilla to attempt once more the westward passage to the orient (cf. pp. 233ff.). He carried instructions detailing his behaviour in the event of a meeting with the Portuguese, orders regulating the handling of any gold, silver and spices obtained, and was accompanied by an Irish wolfhound to quell recalcitrant natives. His intention was to seek the elusive strait in the western

Caribbean, and from there open a way to Jerusalem, whose recovery from the infidel increasingly exercised him.

Denied access to Hispaniola, he weathered a hurricane which destroyed less prudent seamen and crossed the Caribbean to discover the island of Guanaja, off the Honduran coast. In these waters he met a large canoe, the character of whose cargo, crew and passengers suggested the nearby presence of cultures of a higher level than any so far encountered. Faced with the most plausible contenders as yet for the role of subjects of the grand khan, Columbus disregarded a lead which might have brought him to the Maya or the Aztecs. Instead he commenced a laborious easterly beat to windward along the coasts of Honduras, Nicaragua, Costa Rica, Veragua and Panama. Ophir was not far, and the Ganges within easy reach. He was, of course, debarred from the Pacific by a narrow, but unbroken and formidably difficult isthmus, and indeed on Christmas Day 1502 was off the entrance to the modern Panama Canal. But not understanding the significance of his discovery, with no sign of a strait, and with the morale of his crews and the conditions of his ships deteriorating under the stress of incessant headwinds and rain 'like another deluge', he turned back to establish a post at Belén. The decision could scarcely have been worse, since he had neither the men nor the materials to set up or sustain a settlement in the rain-soaked jungle of Veragua, amongst hostile primitive peoples. But by now, verging on nervous breakdown, and given to alternate bouts of indecision, mystical fulmination and abject self-pity, he was barely able to handle either men or events. An attempt to recruit aid from the Caribbean islands ended with the company marooned in Jamaica, from whence the admiral eventually returned to Spain. Here his voyage was largely ignored, and his death shortly after (1506) passed almost unmarked.

But his last years were not spent in poverty and shame. After the usual difficulties in any financial dealings with the Spanish crown he obtained a share in the riches accruing from his discoveries, and his son Diego not only succeeded him as admiral but married into the royal house. He had not, it is true, fulfilled his dreams of opening a western sea-route to Asia, let alone strange ambitions of freeing Jerusalem and discovering the Garden of Eden. Ultimately he accepted, as did others more rational, that he had found 'another world' – a group of islands unknown to Ptolemy, and sited near the Malay Peninsula.[6] As a commander he was increasingly disastrous, prickly and consumed with outrageous messianic impulses. He had none of the personal or political skills of a Cortés, and he laboured under the enormous disadvantage of being a foreigner – worst still a Genoese – of humble extraction, serving a country obsessed with blood and status. But he was an outstanding seaman and navigator. No doubt, like many others, he had trouble with celestial observations, obtaining some grotesquely improbable results. Yet on the return from the second voyage, after six weeks sailing, and most of this tacking, his dead-reckoning was superbly accurate. His expeditions, apparently so easily accomplished, were into waters and weathers unknown and unpredictable, undertaken in vessels (chiefly carvels – see p. 263), which, whatever their merits, had little margin of safety and less of comfort. Yet he lost only one ship at sea, established, almost immediately, the most satisfactory transatlantic routes, and set up times for an outward passage never improved by his Spanish successors. Such excellence admirers have elevated to the superlative, arguing that already in 1492 the admiral had detected or deduced the pattern of winds in the northern Atlantic, and was to able to ensure the easiest courses for his first expedition. That he knew of offshore winds from the Canaries is likely enough. That he realized he would find them fair for Europe in the height of the Azores is more doubtful. He reached the latitude by accident, and in 1496 demonstrated the gaps in his knowledge by attempting a rhumb-line route home from the West Indies which took him straight into a belt of headwinds. But none of this detracts from his achievements. He inspired and accomplished four voyages which revealed, however unwilling he was to admit it, a new continent. He discovered more unknown territory than any other navigator, gave some idea of the true size of the Atlantic, and set in motion, as did no other individual, a staggering sequence of exploration and conquest.

Well before Columbus' death, royal disenchantment with the admiral, and the appreciation by his former companions of the possibilities of what he had found, inspired a succession of rival expeditions. They were mounted, like those of Columbus, from Spain, but now directed to the mainland. Ojeda and la Cosa reached the Guianas in a semi-piratical cruise (1499) and coasted past the mouth of the Orinoco to the Gulf of Maracaibo in Venezuela – so named by the Spaniards since the local villages were built Venetian-style on piling in the water. Others explored the shores of northern Brazil, Colombia and Panama, whilst the Florentine Amerigo Vespucci, a man of taste, learning and enviable literary style, claimed to have preceded the admiral in America. Such were his powers of exposition that in northern Europe his story was accepted, and the new lands accordingly became America. But to Spain, as to Columbus, they remained the Indies.

Thus within little more than a decade the run of a continental coast from Honduras to beyond Pernambuco had been traced, and all the major West Indian islands, apart from Barbados, discovered. To these lands, and to others still unknown, Spain established her title with that admixture of guile and force that earned Machiavelli's admiration. Two papal bulls were obtained in 1493, enunciating Spanish sovereignty in the Columban discoveries, and in other non-Christian territories yet to be found in the occident. A third privilege, the codicil to Adam's will, as Francis I of France bitterly put it, defined the donation as lying beyond a meridian drawn north/south 100 leagues out from the Azores and the Cape Verde Islands. At a stroke, and probably at Columbus' suggestion, any Portuguese claims in the west were destroyed, whilst Spain retained the right to reach the east by circumnavigating the globe. Portugal's objections were countered by even more extensive concessions from the pro-Spanish pope Alexander VI. Spain could explore to the west and the south, India was open to her, and all that lay beyond her reach were the actual possessions of Christian princes. This potential world hegemony the Portuguese averted, and in 1497 it was mutually accepted that the respective spheres of influence of the Iberian powers should be determined by a meridian 370 leagues west of the Cape Verdes. By accident or design Spanish claims were, on paper, much diminished. But the starting point for the measurements was uncertain, and the distance itself, given the age's notorious shortcomings in such matters, was never agreed. Moreover, whatever sacrifices Spain might supposedly have made in the west, she assumed, with enormous consequences for the future, the line would be projected round the world into Asia (see pp. 319–20).

Title and foothold established, and unimpeded by the presence of any powerful and organized indigenous society, Spain set about the exploitation of her new possessions. Hispaniola was conquered, forts constructed, resistance crushed, and Europeans – 5000 before 1500 – came flooding in. To provide gold the native inhabitants were parcelled out in what was indistinguishable from slavery, and when they died, as they did at an appalling rate, there were raids on neighbouring territories for replacements, and calls for the importation of African slaves to work the ranches and sugar plantations introduced as gold failed (see pp. 320–1). In search of similar or better opportunities, Spaniards disappointed in Hispaniola joined expeditions to the surrounding islands. Jamaica was occupied in 1511, Cuba subdued in 1511–14, and Puerto Rico subjected to the fearsome regime of Ponce de León, a former soldier in the *reconquista* and gentleman volunteer with Columbus. Next, with the growing influx of Europeans, the destruction of aboriginal populations, and the exhaustion of their accumulated stocks of gold, came attacks, first from Hispaniola, then from Cuba, on the mainland coast between the Orinoco delta and the foot of the Isthmus of Panama. Best known, and most readily accessible, was the Darien littoral of what is now Colombia, a region of difficult terrain and worse climate, inhabited by bellicose primitive peoples. A base was eventually created on the Gulf of Urabá (1509), where, before long there arrived, concealed in a barrel to escape his creditors, Vasco Núñez de Balboa. Able, ferocious and ruthless, of the sort to whom only war or revolution provide sufficient opportunity, he established himself, anticipating the tactics of Cortés in Mexico, as *alcalde* of his newly founded city of Darien (see p. 311). One of his superiors he cast adrift to drown, another he shipped out, and then, in fact and in law in command, commenced a search for gold and slaves. The Indians were subdued, as were his compatriots, by an admixture of blandishments (including the *conquistador*'s marriage to the daughter of a local chief) and violence (including pursuit by hunting dogs). To accomplish the great feat which would justify his behaviour to the crown, he marched through tropical forests, swamps and lakes to reach – the first Spaniard to do so – the Pacific (1513), claiming it and all adjacent lands, for Castile. But this epic ended with the arrival of a royal governor, Pedro Arias de Ávila, an aristocratic veteran of wars in Europe and Africa. In what was to become a familiar sequence Balboa was outmanoeuvred, seized, and in 1517 publicly executed (see pp. 312, 316). Then came a foretaste of what the continent could expect. The country was pillaged for gold and pearls, the hands and noses of un-cooperative Indians chopped off. Discovery and settlement were pushed ahead with the same ferocious energy, with Nicaragua and Honduras penetrated, and part of the Pacific and Caribbean coasts of the Isthmus explored. Panama was founded in 1519, from where expeditions pushing south soon heard rumours of the riches of Inca Peru. Such was Ávila's reputation that he was alleged to have been responsible for the death or enslavement of two million Indians, and would-be conquerors prudently kept well clear of his domain.

So in less than twenty years the Spaniards had subjugated, and commenced the exploitation of colonial territories more extensive than those acquired by the Portuguese in the best part of a century, or by the Norse and the Italian republics in the whole course of their expansion. But as yet they had no understanding of the true potential of the enormous American continent, once briefly and incomprehendingly touched by the Scandinavians, and perhaps earlier, but with no better knowledge by some of the peoples of the Far East. Here separated and isolated by every obstacle of climate and terrain – distance, forest, jungle, swamps, mountains – was a huge diversity of societies and civilizations. Some regions, like the Matto Grosso, were virtually uninhabited. Elsewhere, as in the south of the modern United States, there were embryonic stone-age civilizations, and in the high plateaux of the Valley of Mexico and the Andes, embracing about 80 per cent of the continent's human resources, there had evolved the impressive cultures of the Aztecs and Incas. Within two decades their empires were overthrown in campaigns which not even the feats of the heroes of contemporary epics of chivalry could approach. Yet victory was achieved not by armies of the size or nature of those employed in Europe, but, in the face of overwhelming numerical odds, by small bands of Spaniards, some accompanied, even across the Andes, by their women and children. Few were professional soldiers, though many had campaigned in Africa and Italy and – of far greater importance – had experience of slaving and Indian fighting in the islands. From these bases, and from Panama and Nicaragua, they moved on as opportunities diminished, and as in Scandinavian Iceland, feuds consequently intensified. Their expeditions were under royal licence, but not under royal direction, with the leaders responsible, as they had been in the *reconquista* and the subjugation of the Canaries, for raising men and money. The wars were fought with an intensity unknown in Europe, where, it was explained 'there is some fellow feeling between Christians and Moors, and both sides, in their own interest, spare their prisoners for the sake of the ransom'. They were equally remarkable in that nearly all the Spanish commanders were men of modest, not to say obscure, origins, drawn from that same great reservoir of ability as produced many of the enterprising merchants of Portuguese Asia and seamen of Tudor England, and normally untapped in a world according pre-eminence to rank, birth and connection. And remarkably too, many of the participants, most notably Hernán Cortés and Bernal Díaz, wrote like the great soldiers of classical Antiquity of their experiences to produce narratives of military history unsurpassed in any language.

First to fall was the empire of the Aztecs, situated in the Valley of Mexico and its vicinity. It was of comparatively recent origin, and its imposing capital, Tenochtitlán, larger than any contemporary European city, dated only from the fourteenth century. But a history of vigorous martial expansion in Middle America had culminated with the conquest (1502) of the tribes of the Gulf coast of Mexico. Alone among the major political units of the continent the Aztec empire was still growing when the Spaniards appeared, and fragile though it may have been it was in their eyes a thing of wonder. 'They lived', wrote Cortés, 'almost as we do in Spain, and in as much harmony and order, and considering they are barbarous, and so far from the knowledge of God, and cut off from all civilized nations, it is truly remarkable to see what they have achieved.' And indeed it was. They had a considerable culture in engineering, architecture, mathematics and astronomy, together with a body of tradition, history and poetry transmitted orally and by pictograph. A centralized government was headed by an emperor advised by a council of aristocratic relatives. Beneath him was a nobility, whose estates – former tribal lands – were exempt from taxation; a privileged merchant class; tenant farmers; peasants who worked state properties; serfs and slaves. With a population perhaps four times that of Spain, with its great cities and temples, its organized military forces, its populace rendering tribute to their rulers, lords and priests, and providing communal labour for their support, it was an impressive structure, generally conforming to European preconceptions as to the proper ordering of life. But it was a society imbued with a profound pessimism and sense of insecurity, reflecting an environment of marshes and volcanoes, with man driven to feed the gods with the blood of human sacrifice to assuage their wrath and persuade them to permit the sun to shine and the rain to fall. And it was an empire in process of evolution from a tribal to a monarchical and urban basis. Even in 1521 it still comprised over 700 tribes, many of them only recently and partially subdued, and willing for one reason or another to support the Spaniards.

The assault on Mexico was unwittingly set in motion by Diego Velázquez, governor of the now restive Cuba, where there was neither sufficient lands nor Indians to meet the expectations of a growing white population. Between 1516 and 1518 he sent out expeditions to reconnoitre the coasts of the Yucatán (reached by Ponce de León in 1513) and the Mexican Gulf, already known to slavers. Their reception was hardly encouraging, but there were clear indications of wealth of an order long and vainly sought elsewhere. Hence Velázquez commissioned Hernán Cortés to explore, trade and search for Christian captives in the Yucatán. A onetime notary in Hispaniola, Cortés was then thirty-five, and had been employed since 1512 as the often colourful secretary to Velázquez. He had no formal military training or experience, and only the most rudimentary formal education. But he was to prove an outstanding soldier, politican and writer. His justly celebrated letters describing the conquest reveal a lawyer's stock-in-trade of wise saws, something of the uncertain and obtrusive erudition – like that of Columbus – of the self-taught, adept projection of his own importance, and a magnificent narrative style. Of uncompromising independence he was nevertheless willing to do himself what he demanded of others, and able, when he wanted, to display an affability and charm which ensured the support of his men and brought him the favours of numerous ladies, Spanish and Indian alike. His energy and determination were formidable, and like every great commander he was quick and ingenious, willing to risk, and able to accomplish, bold and imaginative strokes. Impecunious, and on poor terms with Velázquez, he somehow secured a command – perhaps since his abilities were already recognized, perhaps because he obtained, in ways unknown, the financial backing of a local merchant and one of the governor's officers.

In 1519, with a few pieces of artillery, 16 horsemen and about 400 infantry recruited from amongst the poor whites of Cuba, he made for the nearest harbour to the Aztec capital. There he disavowed Velázquez's authority and persuaded his followers to undertake the conquest of Mexico. At his prompting they constituted themselves the *cabildo*[7] of the new city of Villa Rica de Vera Cruz, who, as 'good men of the land', were legally entitled to set aside laws, and from whom, as the proper representatives of the crown, he accepted supreme command. He wrote to his sovereign, Charles V, seeking confirmation of his title, and artfully combining descriptions of the ungodly ways of the natives and his 'just war' against heathens and their tyrannical ruler, with an account of their great wealth and his desire to spread the Christian faith and Spanish dominion. Then, to effect like Balboa the deed which would vindicate him, he left a garrison to hold Vera Cruz, and struck out for the Mexican capital, irrevocably committing his men by destroying the ships which had brought them. He marched through awesome terrain, much of it still inaccessible, taking over three months to cover about 300km, along a route determined by advice – initially from a Spanish survivor, subsequently from Indians – as to where he could recruit aid, and where the Aztecs were most vulnerable. He won the support of the Cempoalans, and then, after a sharp struggle, of the Tlaxcalans. Thus with native allies, native guides, native porters and native interpreters, and with their appetites inflamed by the rich gifts innocently sent by the Aztecs to persuade them to withdraw, the Spaniards advanced on Tenochtitlán through a land 'that seemed like the enchanted things they speak of in the book of Amadis'.[8] They found (1519) the lake-girt capital to be a city of great towers, temples and houses all built of solid masonry, and with its streets straight, clean and unsullied by animals. Their reception by its ruler, Montezuma, was courteous, and their quarters, where the inquisitive opening of a concealed door revealed hoarded treasure, magnificent. But in fact they were trapped in an island fortress, where the spectacle of human sacrifice indicated all too plainly their likely fate.

The situation was retrieved by Cortés in characteristic style. With breathtaking audacity the emperor was seized, so paralysing the Aztecs and reviving the flagging enthusiasm of the Spaniards' Indian allies. Then, whilst the imperial administration was employed to amass loot for the conquerors, Cortés withdrew to defeat, in a lightning move, and to appropriate to his own use, a force sent against him by

Velázquez. In his absence the ceaseless demands of his men for food and riches stirred up an Aztec hostility which broke into open war on his re-appearance with yet more troops (1520). The captive emperor died, or was killed; the Spanish survivors withdrew to Tlaxcalan territory with heavy losses and after a hard struggle, the loyalty of their allies, it was rumoured, only sustained by promises of land, booty and freedom from taxation. Nevertheless during the retreat a large and confident Aztec army was decisively defeated by the Spaniards, now fighting without the few firearms they had once possessed. Refreshed and reinforced, partly by European deserters from less rewarding expeditions, but largely by Indian auxiliaries, and accompanied by a puppet prince of the Aztec blood royal, the Spaniards returned to take Tenochtitlán in 1521. Once again Cortés' tactics were bold and original. A flotilla of small sailing vessels was built by native labour and launched on the waters surrounding the capital to seal it off from supplies and assistance. And in the final assault, perhaps at the suggestion of one of his Indian allies, the advancing troops systematically levelled all buildings, so that of Tenochtitlán and its lake there now hardly remains a trace in the Spanish city whose construction Cortés ordered on the site.

Thereafter Spanish power spread rapidly through and beyond the former empire – to North and South Mexico, to Central America, and to the Pacific, where in the 1530s and 1540s the coasts of Lower California were explored. The littoral of Vera Cruz was reconnoitred in 1519–23, and Guatemala – its capital founded in 1524 – brought under some measure of control. Honduras was secured when in 1526 Cortés made an astounding march across the base of the Yucatán, through dense rain forest and over abrupt mountain ranges, to suppress the attempt of one of his officers to establish an independent holding there. Such achievements brought, in 1522, his appointment by Charles V as governor and captain general of what was now described as New Spain. But his violence in Honduras led to a royal inquiry into his behaviour, and thereafter, though showered with lands and honours, he was, like Columbus, never again entrusted with political authority. Mexico became a viceroyalty in 1535 under a soldier from one of Spain's greatest aristocratic houses. For a time Cortés devoted himself to the exploitation of his magnificent properties before retiring to live off his wealth in Spain (1540). There, though the author of *Don Quixote* might rank him with the heroes of chivalry, he was, as Columbus had been, ignored by the government.

Whatever the blunders of his later years, Cortés gave Spain one of the largest accessions of riches and territory ever brought by an individual to a modern state. For Mexico's future he advocated a policy which was sensible and, in echoing the wishes of the crown, realistic. It was to be colonized by married men who, so restrained, would settle down to farm instead of stripping whatever resources there were and then departing, like the footloose bachelors of the Caribbean islands (see pp. 308, 330). His presence and personality ensured that New Spain suffered no such civil wars as did Hispaniola and Peru. He endowed it with a superb capital, and inspired and directed further exploration, so that by 1540 Mexico City was the metropolis of Spanish lands stretching from Central America to, and perhaps beyond, the Gulf of California.

The colony in turn engendered further expansion as, in familiar style, men sought new sources of booty and to escape the restrictions of imperial rule. But as effort was diffused, and as the lands and peoples encountered were far less tractable, the pace was slower. In northern Mexico, rich in silver, primitive and bellicose tribes long resisted the Spaniards, notwithstanding their use of every expedient from 'cruel war' to Christian kindness. Under viceregal direction, as the state increasingly did itself what had once been left to others, fleets explored the Pacific coast (1542), possibly reaching as far as the southern boundary of the modern Oregon. Meanwhile an expedition searching for further opulent realms of mighty native rulers pushed north to find only the primeval inhabitants of what is now Arizona in their 'cramped little villages', the intimidating barrier of the Grand Canyon, and (1542) the great plains southeast of the Rocky Mountains. With distances so vast, costs so great, rewards so few, and the population so hostile, subsequent endeavour was no more than intermittent, and the Spanish advance northward a long drawn out, hesitant and spasmodic process.

The going was equally arduous to the south of Mexico where, after struggling through dense forests, the Spaniards encountered in the Yucatán (1523–4) the remarkable civilization of the Maya, with its imposing cities and equally imposing virtuosity in mathematics and astronomy. Armed with little more than wooden weapons, and undeterred by European guns, the Maya defended their well-sited strongholds with the same determination they had already shown against the Aztecs. Absence of a unified Maya state allowed the invaders to exploit local rivalries, but it also obliged them, as they were to find elsewhere, to overcome each community individually. Undertaken with a ruthlessness which shocked even seasoned campaigners, and further delayed by its leader's departure to fish in the troubled waters of Peru, the conquest of the Yucatán was a prolonged and hard guerilla war, not completed till 1545. By then the victors were, as their prospective brides from Spain complained, a collection of maimed and battered veterans.

But the most staggering feat of Spanish arms, accomplished in a series of marches unparalleled in military history, was the overthrow of the empire of the Incas, lying 3000 to 4000 metres above sea level in the Andes. Here, since the twelfth century, the Quechua had been developing a state which at the time of its conquest was the most advanced in the Americas, and reached from what is now central Chile to the south of the modern Colombia, west to the Pacific, and east to the forests of the Amazon. It was paternalistic, highly organized, and better able than most European countries to count its population, then some 7,000,000 strong. Through an administration that provided roughly 13 officials to every 100 inhabitants, and a postal system capable of transmitting messages 200km a day, it ensured that its peoples were fed, defended and taxed. They in turn were obliged to work the land – much of it state-owned – to support themselves, and the nobles, priests and absolute emperor, the lineal descendant of the sun, who ruled over them.

Throughout the empire were sizeable cities 'of the Spanish manner', and great temples and fortresses of a massiveness recalling ancient Egypt, built with sophisticated engineering techniques under state direction. And to the immense benefit of the invaders, Peru was bound together by a network of roads comparable to those of the Romans. Tunnels were driven through hills, causeways taken across marshes, and rivers spanned by bridges. 'Should our great emperor wish a similar thing', wrote a Spaniard conscious of his homeland's notorious shortcomings in such matters, 'we could not build it.' Despite their geographical isolation and lack of any external stimuli, the Incas had developed a civilization richer than any other in America. In textiles, ceramics, the working of precious metals, engineering, architecture and medicine – with trepanning and amputation successfully practised – they were outstanding. They were, indeed, like the Aztecs, without knowledge of the wheel, the arch and writing, but traditional lore was passed on verbally, whilst with the aid of the strings and knots of the *quipu* ideas could be expressed and facts recorded.

Nevertheless the bases of Inca culture and power were fragile. Peru had few crops – of which maize and the potato were the most important – and few domestic animals, so producing, like the rest of the continent, a diet deficient in protein for its population. Inca religion, much given to omens and portents, was as pessimistic as that of the Aztecs, and its rigidly disciplined adherents fatalistically docile. Though far better equipped than any of Spain's previous American opponents, the large Inca armies rarely fought with the determination of the Maya or the Aztecs. And like Mexico, Peru was still far from unified and even more fatally flawed. Not only were recently subdued tribes still imperfectly absorbed, but a war of succession between the two sons of the emperor Huayna Capac had momentarily ended, when the Spaniards arrived, with Atahualpa's capture of his rival, Huascar. 'Without this division', a chronicler admitted, 'it would have been impossible, or at least very difficult, to conquer this land.'

Like most of their associates, the two Spanish commanders of this improbable venture were of humble birth, and both reasonably prosperous in Panama after long and varied careers in Indian fighting. They were, as were many of their fellows, in late middle age, both unmarried and both illiterate. Francisco Pizarro was an illegitimate member of the minor gentry, a chronically poor horseman, but none the less a soldier of well-attested parts. Equally so was his companion in arms, Diego de Almagro, who, a refugee from justice in Spain of the obscurest origins, had by his energy and affability established himself in Darien. And financing, and often reconciling the pair, was Gaspar de Espinosa, a lawyer and general entrepreneur in Panama, where, amongst other things, his fertile mind envisaged the digging (by 2000 Indians) of a canal from the Caribbean to the Pacific.

Rumours of some great realm to the south had circulated in Panama long before the abortive attempts of Pizarro and Almagro to enter Peru from its Pacific coast in the mid-1520s. But despite the fearful climate and hardships encountered, what they saw, and the threat of being forestalled, were sufficient to make them try again. To Almagro's chagrin his partner returned to Spain where, in the euphoric years of ubiquitous Habsburg military success and the triumphs of Cortés in Mexico, he secured for himself the governorship of Peru for life. Accompanied by troops from his native Estramadura, and by his four brothers, Pizarro was back in Peru by 1531 to found the town of San Miguel on the Pacific coast, just south of the equator. Then with 62 horsemen and about 100 infantry – among them veterans of wars both in Europe and Mexico – he set out in a campaign even more audacious than that of Cortés for the imperial capital of Cuzco. The Spaniards marched up the western cordillera of the Andes through passes as high as the Alps. Outnumbered, as in Mexico, and in trouble in close fighting on foot, they deployed their cavalry – notably more numerous than in Cortés' original force – to the same devastating effect. Equally adeptly, Pizarro persuaded either side in the civil war of his goodwill, so gathering native allies, and as in Mexico progress was eased by tribal revolts against the parent state.

Finally, at Cajamarca, where a tiny Spanish force confronted Atahualpa at the head of 30,000 troops, Pizarro, with a daring and aplomb which terrified even his compatriots, seized the emperor. Spanish morale was boosted and Inca resistance broken. 'By having this man in our hands the entire realm is calm', it was reported. To save himself and his throne, Atahualpa offered an enormous ransom, whilst at the same time ordering the secret execution of his imprisoned rival. Such was the nature of the Inca state that though captive and humiliated his commands were promptly obeyed. Huascar was strangled, and in two months there was assembled what seemed such a mass of gold and silver 'as never before had been seen anywhere in the world'. With over 11,000kg of gold objects alone melted down there still remained, after deduction of the royal fifth (see p. 341), sufficient bullion for every cavalryman to receive 41kg of gold and twice as much silver. Then Atahualpa, though impressive in adversity and now a Christian, was executed and the army marched on Cuzco to set up a puppet ruler (1533) and to ransack the city – one it was conceded 'with the manner and quality of greatness' – and torture its inhabitants in the expectation of further booty.

With the empire seemingly overthrown, the newly founded Lima, easily accessible by sea, was named capital of what was to become Spain's largest and richest overseas colony. But not for some time. Inca armies were still in the field; the Inca state still intact; and already dangerous dissensions among the Spaniards were soon aggravated by the arrival of ambitious compatriots from elsewhere in the Americas to share in the spoil of what Espinosa described as 'this vineyard of the Lord'. An invasion from the Yucatán was repulsed by Almagro and the erstwhile donkey-herd, Benalcázar, who then (1534) set himself up as virtual proconsul in Quito. The following year, leaving Peru to the now ennobled Pizarro, Almagro sacked and pillaged his way into Chile with an army accompanied by some 12,000 Indian auxiliaries and various Inca aristocrats. He went across the highest and bleakest part of the Bolivian plateau, over the Andes – his men and horses freezing to death, his Indians dying by the hundred – and down to the Pacific. Finding nothing to please him, as the inhabitants avoided open battle and wisely concealed such wealth as they had, he eventually returned (1537) after marching the full length of the Atacama desert.

During his absence, whilst adventurers flooded into Peru from the Isthmus and the Caribbean islands – where in Puerto Rico it was feared that 'not a single citizen will be left unless they are tied down' – and expeditions were projected in Antwerp and Seville, the puppet emperor Manco rose in revolt. Cuzco was besieged (1536), a relieving force massacred, and the isolated Spanish garrisons between the city and the sea wiped out. In desperation Pizarro called for aid from the neighbouring colonies, but before it could be of any use the Incas were beaten. Their armies were unable to keep the field for any time – supplies were inadequate; men had to be withdrawn for the essential tasks of agriculture – just as they were unable to contend with cavalry. With the rising suppressed, and the country overburdened with unemployed reinforcements, the return of Almagro without honour or profit brought open conflict with Pizarro. For over a decade there raged a war of pitched battles between Europeans – 'the most fearful and cruel ever seen', according to one chronicler – watched by astonished Indians, and fought with native aid. It entailed epic marches, provoked Inca insurrections, and led to the strangling of Almagro (1538), the murder of Pizarro (1541), and the death in action of the royal viceroy (1546). For a time it seemed that Peru, like some Norse colony, might break away from the mother country. Most of the old Inca empire, together with the vital maritime approaches and focal points of access to Europe fell into the hands of Pizarro's brother, Gonzalo. And when royal policy appeared to the settlers offensively favourable to the Indians, there was talk of his marrying an Inca princess, becoming king, and rewarding his supporters from the wealth of the recently opened mines of Potosí (see p. 325). But no more than Columbus, Balboa or Cortés was Gonzalo a match for the servants of the Spanish crown. He was captured and executed (1548), and the country brought under control. In 1572 a vestigial Inca state, surviving unsubdued in the wild and remote Amazonian jungle below Cuzco, was destroyed as its inhabitants commenced to display alarming skill in the use of European arms.

Thus whilst Mexico had been taken in less than five years there had been the best part of half a century's fighting in Peru, much of it amongst the Spaniards themselves. Geographically the Inca empire was no easy victim. It stretched about 5000km from north to south. Its heartland lay in gigantic mountains whose atmosphere rendered physical exertion exhausting to Europeans. Its approaches were guarded by the deserts of the Pacific littoral and the jungles of the eastern cordillera. To these intimidating obstacles the Spaniards added others of their making. The leadership of the assault was divided – in itself a sure recipe for disaster – between two men who, outstanding though they were as soldiers, had nothing of the political or personal finesse of Cortés, and indeed the illiterate Pizarro's obvious dependence on his secretary alone gave widespread offence. Unlike that of Mexico, the invasion encountered no sustained resistance to unite the Spaniards whose dissensions were intensified by the influx of adventurers to whom Peru appeared to offer the last chance of those riches which had so far eluded them.

Nor were they wrong, for the unprovided and superfluous were now driven into undertakings increasingly arduous and profitless. A hold was established in Chile, but vigorous resistance from the primitive Araucanian tribes, who soon had the measure of their would-be conquerors, obliged the Spaniards to fall back in the mid-1500s – their first withdrawal in the New World. Expansion continued nevertheless across the Andes into the modern Argentine, and the country developed a thriving agriculture. South of the Bío-Bío river, however, the Spanish position was long to remain precarious. Meanwhile from northern Peru expeditions were launched down the Andes into the limitless forests of the Amazon, performing prodigies of cruelty and endurance, hacking their way through undergrowth, struggling for months in incessant rain across saturated and broken terrain. But though Gonzalo Pizarro marched from Quito into Amazonia and back through Ecuador (1541), and his associate Orellana descended the 5000kms of the Amazon to the Atlantic in improvised boats (1541–2), they found none of the expected realms of cinnamon and gold. More fortunate was Quesada who in the late 1530s penetrated from the Caribbean, through the jungles of the Magdalena valley, to the uplands of Colombia to find there the Chibcha, rich in emeralds and gold, and to forestall rivals from Venezuela, and the redoubtable Belalcázar, who marched up from Quito, over the vast and untravelled heights of the central Andean cordillera, and through dense trackless forests.

Elsewhere expansion was sustained by adventurers' tenacious pursuit of assorted chimera, by prosperous colonies searching, in that familiar pattern of imperial growth, for new markets and outlets and by the attempts of the Crown to protect its own interests and damage those of its rivals. On the Atlantic coast of South America the Río de la Plata, entered by the Portuguese early in the sixteenth century, was examined by Solís in 1516 and by Sebastian Cabot, commissioned by the emperor in 1525 to reach the Spice Islands and Cathay through the strait recently discovered by Magellan (see pp. 319–20). Pilot-major of Spain, and a distinguished if controversial figure, Cabot was, like many of exalted intellectual achievement or pretension, of modest competence in the handling of his fellow men. An acrimonious crossing of the Atlantic led to a purposeless attempt to find 'gold, silver and precious stones' on the Río de la Plata, and a more valuable exploration of much of the Paraná and Paraguay rivers. His advocacy produced some efforts to colonize the Plata estuary, which achieved little against the fierce aboriginals who had already eaten Solís, and who with their *bolas*[9] could bring down horsemen. But after an exiguous existence the chief city of Buenos Aires was saved by the opening of a commercial route from the Atlantic to the expanding Andean colonies, and by the growth of Paraguay, where, at Asunción (founded in 1537) the settlers, aided by native allies, fought the various Chaco peoples, and in the style of the Portuguese in East Africa established themselves by martial and marital prowess as local chiefs (see pp. 249–50, 258, 328).

To the north progress against the bellicose primitive inhabitants of the fever-ridden swamps of Venezuela was long uncertain, and only with the occupation of the site of Caracas in the late sixteenth century were the rich pearl-fishing regions of the east linked to the lands of the Gulf of Maracaibo. For a time (1528–41) the colony was pledged to the German banking house of Welser, who graphically demonstrated, as the Genoese had already done and the Dutch were to do later, that few could outstrip the excesses of merchants in pursuit of a proper return on their investment. Under the motto 'whosoever resists, hangs', slaves were hunted down, the Spanish settlers driven to revolt, and a series of raids, conducted with sadistic brutality, fruitlessly despatched inland to find El Dorado, the gold-painted ruler of the supposed city of Manoa. Equally futile were the attempts of others to reach this promised land by ascending either the Amazon or the Orinoco. Accompanied, incredibly enough, by his young wife for whom this awesome journey was to serve as a honeymoon, Orellana, who had come down the Amazon with the survivors of Gonzalo Pizarro's expedition, returned (1545) in the hope of retracing his epic voyage. The enterprise ended, as did most of its successors, in total and disastrous failure.

After a cursory search, and some embittering experiences, the Spaniards accepted that the North American landmass offered no more than a harsh climate, intractable peoples, and resources more easily obtained elsewhere. Encouraged, however, by French discoveries in Canada, there were early hopes of a strait to Asia, intermittently sought by expeditions from both Europe and the Caribbean. The St Lawrence (see pp. 443ff.) – whose fisheries were soon worked by the Basques – was examined in 1525, and colonies were briefly established on the shores of North and South Carolina. The veteran *conquistador*, Ponce de León, searching the coasts of Florida (1513) for the fountain whose waters bestowed eternal youth and virility, found only unprepossessing and hostile aboriginals. In pursuit of other medieval fantasies Hernando de Soto, governor of Cuba and a lieutenant of Pizarro's at Cajamarca, marched in the old familiar style – cavalry in full armour; a train of manacled native porters – from Florida (1539) into Arkansas and Oklahoma. But as the failure of Gonzalo Pizarro's trek through the Amazonian forest likewise showed, the days in which handfuls of the bold could overthrow rich empires had gone. With their commander dead, and little prospect of life, let alone wealth, the survivors returned down the Mississippi. Interest in Florida later revived with the appearance there of the French, threatening the safety of the treasure fleets which passed outward bound with the favouring Gulf Stream through the straits at the tip of the peninsula. The intruders were massacred – 'with entire justification and prudence' wrote the king – and a settlement made at St Augustine (1566) (see p. 439). But the colony led a tenuous existence, kept alive only as a mission base, a refuge for the shipwrecked, and to prevent hostile penetration of so strategic an area.

The ultimate extension of Spanish power brought, in feats of superlative seamanship, the first circumnavigation of the world, and the opening of the Pacific. Access to the Far East became an urgent objective of Spanish policy in the early 1500s when Portugal was seen to be reaping the rich harvest of the spice trade, and Castile only the modest rewards of the Caribbean. There were thoughts of challenging the

Portuguese on the Cape route, and rumours of Spanish preparations precipitated Portuguese attempts on Malacca (see pp. 238–9). With the exploration of America came new possibilities for, and new obstacles to, the westward passage envisaged by Columbus. Balboa had revealed the existence of the Pacific; after Solís had reached the Río de la Plata the huge southern sweep of the continent was appreciated, as was, following prolonged searches, the absence of any strait leading to Asia (see pp. 308, 317–18). One – though hardly of the anticipated character – was found in maritime voyage without equal, initiated and commanded by the Portuguese Fernão Magelhães (Ferdinand Magellan). Convinced, after a long and not particularly distinguished career in Africa and the east, that he was slighted in his own country, and that the Moluccas lay in that part of the globe allocated to Spain by papal grant and subsequent diplomacy, he determined to place their wealth in his own and Habsburg hands (see pp. 307–8).

In 1519, with five ships and a cosmopolitan but largely Spanish company – amongst them the Italian, Pigafetta, who left a superb account of the expedition – he sailed in Spanish service to open a western route to Asia, or failing this, to go by the Cape of Good Hope. To the accompaniment of mutiny, disaffection and desertion he searched the estuary of the Río de la Plata and the Gulf of San Matías for the strait already confidently recorded by some cosmographers. He discovered it over 1000km further south, in that hostile passage with its reefs, tidal rips and unpredictable and furious winds which still bears his name. He was through in only thirty-eight days (1520), to enter a sea which in comparison seemed so tranquil that it was named, with ironic innocence, the Pacific. After working north for some 2000km he turned westward into an ocean which, it was bitterly learned, was 'so vast the human mind can scarcely conceive it'. Ninety-eight days out from the straits the survivors, living on rats and sawdust, made (March 1521) Guam (in the Ladrones or Robber Islands, so called from the uninhibitedly taking ways of their inhabitants), and then what are now the Philippines. Following Magellan's death in a futile skirmish ashore, the two remaining vessels finally arrived in the Moluccas and obtained ladings of spice without difficulty. One attempted to recross the Pacific, only to be beaten back by the foul winds of those latitudes to surrender to the Portuguese. The other, under Elcano, having sailed directly from Timor to South-East Africa to avoid Portuguese Indonesia, eventually (1522) reached Spain with only twenty-one of her crew alive. Thus, in the most remarkable feat of navigation ever achieved under sail, revealing the intimidating size of the earth and the even more intimidating size of the Pacific, was the dream of Columbus fulfilled.

With the prospect of Spain's control of the spices of the Orient, expeditions were sent out in the later 1520s to find easier routes either through the Isthmus of Central America or by the north of the continent. Fleets sailed from Spain both by the new straits and the Cape of Good Hope to fetch spices and establish Spanish power; others were despatched from Mexico, where Cortés wrote in 1526 of his intention of conquering and colonizing the Moluccas 'and many other islands' (see p. 312). But all to no purpose. Spain had no such forward base as Portuguese Malacca, winds blowing unceasingly from the east precluded any crossing of the Pacific from Asia to America and to follow in the tracks of Magellan was commercially, if not humanly, impossible. Hence, financially embarrassed in Europe, and with seemingly untold wealth available in America, Spain sold her claims on the Moluccas to Portugal (1529). Not that the Pacific was abandoned. More islands were found, and the Philippines, with their commercial links with Asia, conquered (1542–65). Their value became apparent when Urdaneta discovered that by working up to 39°50′n, and sailing in a wide northerly arc it was possible to get fair winds for America, so allowing the introduction of a regular traffic across the Pacific. The resultant wealth, together with the annexation of the Portuguese empire, soon refuelled Spanish ambitions. In the rich and cosmopolitan Philippines of the late 1500s there was wild talk of subjugating China, Japan and Taiwan. A start was made on Ternate, Cambodia and Siam; merchants demanded access to China and Japan, whatever the Portuguese might claim; visionaries anticipated the destruction of Islam in Asia. In South America similar urges inspired voyages to seek the great southern continent of Inca and European tradition. The Ellice, Solomon and Marquesas islands came to light, and the survivors of an attempt to found in 1605 a New Jerusalem in the unpropitious setting of the New Hebrides, returning to the Philippines, established that New Guinea was an island, and in passing through the straits named after their commander, Torres, perhaps sighted Australia. More mundanely, the incursions of European rivals into the Pacific brought Spanish exploration of the west coast of America up to 43°n to eradicate any threat to the trans-Pacific route, and re-exploration of the passage in the extreme south (1619) through which the Dutch under le Maire had entered the ocean.

II *Spain in America*

The initial impulse to the creation of Spain's global empire had been the desire to seize from Portugal the riches of West Africa, and to share in, and before long to dominate, Europe's trade with Asia. For a brief moment, under Columbus' influence, Spanish expansion was directed, as a commercial community would have wished, to the control of an existing trade. But Spain, triumphant in war, convinced of the paramountcy of military prowess, and over-endowed with an impoverished gentry or would-be gentry, was no Venice, and the Americas no Cathay. Once it was appreciated that in the New World there were precious metals and lands for the taking, and a docile labour force accustomed to menial toil, the Spaniards settled to the exploitation of their heritage with a predatory vigour reminiscent of that of the Norse. In a few years the Caribbean islands were stripped of bullion – much of it spent, since the colonists refused to demean themselves by working the land, on the purchase at inflated prices of provisions imported from Spain. Within a few decades the Taino peoples,[10] upon whose labour the production of gold depended, had been destroyed. The Spanish reaction was to abandon some areas, to import (into Hispaniola in 1502, for example) African slaves, to turn, as the crown had repeatedly urged, to agriculture and to engage in the ruthless exploitation of other natural resources. Balsam and brazilwood were exported from Hispaniola. Cuban copper was mined from 1545, and the Cubaguan pearl beds fished so relentlessly as to be exhausted by 1530. The fortuitous proliferation of European livestock loosed into the rich vegetation of the islands allowed fortunes to be made in ranching – not least in the equipping and victualling of expeditions to the mainland – whilst sugar, perceptively introduced by Columbus, was soon being produced in Hispaniola, Puerto Rico and Cuba on slave-worked plantations of a style long familiar in the islands of the Iberian Atlantic.

The same story was even more extravagantly enacted on the mainland. In Mexico, Peru, and to a lesser extent Colombia, not only was there seemingly limitless wealth in precious metals, but states whose subjects rendered tribute to their lords and worked as they directed. Royal lawyers might envisage them living henceforth as freely under the Spanish crown as the inhabitants of any of its European realms, but the conquerors knew better. Almost immediately Aztec and Inca institutions were geared to Spanish requirements. 'The chiefs and natives', wrote Cortés in 1522, 'will serve the Spaniards in all they may require . . ..' Groups and tribes were accordingly parcelled out in *encomienda* – committed to the care and keeping of one of the victors. Similar policies, which had roots reaching back to the early days of European feudalism, had been employed in the *reconquista*, the subjugation of the Canaries, and the exploitation of the Caribbean islands, where Indians were distributed amongst the colonists to be employed as required, and so, like the primitive victims of the Portuguese, to be weaned from vice and prepared by the blessings of regular toil to receive the Christian message. But the scale was now unprecedented. In the Valley of Mexico alone, Cortés distributed 180,000 Indians among 30 *encomiendas*, and most of Peru's 500 *encomenderos* could in the mid-1500s enjoy the services of at least 5000 Indians. They, in exchange for protection, education and conversion supported the *encomendero*, who was thus free to fight, with his retainers, in their defence and that of the empire. In regions of high culture this meant that they supplied him and his entourage with food and renders of bullion. Elsewhere more primitive peoples gave 'what little they could manage' – as was said of the Philippines – which generally meant labour.

In royal eyes there was no surrender of authority by the crown. With such abundance and opportunity on hand there was no need to attract settlers by the lavish measures employed by the Portuguese state in Brazil (cf. pp. 247–8). Nor had kings, well aware of the dangerous ambitions of landed magnates, any intention of allowing the growth of a similar caste in America. Grants of *encomienda* were of limited duration, the Indians supposedly continued to own their lands and the crown allegedly exercised jurisdiction over its new subjects. But men who had prostrated two great empires saw themselves, like the heroes of the *reconquista* and the paladins of chivalry, as feudal lords set over vast estates and native vassals. With their retainers they lived in grand aristocratic style in town houses, dominating, as mayors and councillors, the new imperial cities. They demanded whatever tribute and labour they saw fit, sought control of, and the right to reside in, the territories whose inhabitants were commended to them, and pressed for hereditary succession to what they regarded as their inheritances. When refused, or otherwise offended, they rebelled in Peru and plotted revolt in Mexico (1565) (see p. 316).

Even by the generous patrician standards of the times those few who secured *encomiendas* were uniquely fortunate. Tribal chiefs responsible for the collection of tribute might take many times more for themselves than for their masters, yet *encomenderos* still obtained all the necessities of life free, and accumulated, without effort, capital from renders in bullion and the sale of surplus tribute. Forced labour built them imposing dwellings at no cost, and provided them with valuable manpower which could be sold or leased. In exchange *encomenderos* rarely did anything to benefit their charges. But this unconstrained realization of the imperial dream was not to last. From the mid-1500s the crown insistently defined the length of grants, the nature and extent of tribute, and ensured that its officers, and not the settlers, governed the Indians. More fundamentally still, the whole basis of this parasitic economy was eroded by the fall in the indigenous population, and its consequent inability to meet Spanish needs (see pp. 349ff.).

But as by the late 1500s *encomienda* decayed into little more than royal grants of annuities based on the tribute of specified areas, new and equally acceptable opportunities emerged. A rapidly growing European population scattered across the enormous American continent demanded those familiar foods of the mother country which it was no longer physically or economically possible to supply from Europe. New urban and mining communities provided markets too extensive, and customers too capricious, to be satisfied with local produce, in any case increasingly expensive with the contraction of Indian agriculture. The pattern of settlement accordingly changed, and within the former Inca and Aztec empires Spaniards took possession of Indian lands, to be worked, according to the nature of the terrain, as pastoral or arable estates (*haciendas*). These they acquired and consolidated by anything from royal favour to downright extortion. Indians were harassed and forcibly resettled; boundaries were established by the casual wanderings of grazing livestock; men of influence secured grants for their clients who dutifully surrendered them to their patrons. By mid-seventeenth century the bulk of Mexican land was Spanish owned, and throughout the areas of relatively dense and sedentary native population of the Americas there appeared the great estate, its centre the residence of its white proprietor, the survival of his line and property ensured by entailed primogeniture. The authority of the *hacendado* was supposedly less extensive than that of his Brazilian counterpart (cf. p. 250). His land was not formerly virgin and his Indian labour force, which because of royal policy and the shortage of indigenous manpower he had to attract by wages, was supposedly free. But the parallel with Brazil was none the less close, and by advancing wages or goods to their workers, who came from neighbouring or even annexed Indian townships, many *hacendados* kept them in debt, and thereby in a subjection barely distinguishable from slavery.

No more than in contemporary Europe were such latifundia created for purposeless ostentation. Iberian and other crops ranging from indigo to barley and from wheat to citrus fruits were introduced, and often, as with vines and olives, so successfully cultivated as to sustain industries soon undermining those of the mother country and the empire's supposed economic dependence on Spain. In some areas, as in the vicinity of Trujillo (Peru), producing grain, cotton and sugar by the use of irrigation and guano fertilizer, agricultural technique was of a high order, and elsewhere, as on those estates in the Valley of Mexico which after some experiment with wheat switched (1580–1630) to maize, the farming clearly efficient. In addition there were the natural products of America itself, many to be had for little more than the taking. In Mexico there was cochineal – 'as valuable as gold' – and in the Yucatán brazilwood, dyes both in urgent demand in Europe's textile industries. Cod and whales were caught off Newfoundland; walrus[11] and furs obtained in the St Lawrence estuary; pearls fished along the Venezuelan coast. Some indigenous crops, notably cotton and tobacco, were eventually grown on a large scale, and so fashionable did chocolate (*cacao*) become as a drink as to create a ruthless monoculture which, after exhausting the rich soils of Guatemala and El Salvador, was concentrated in Venezuela. Nor were the markets of Europe and white America the only ones. Indian use of the narcotic *coca* (cocaine) had been restrained by the Incas, but with their downfall and the degredation of their former subjects the habit was soon again widespread. To meet this demand the Spaniards in Peru grew the drug on plantations along the Andean fringe of the tropical rain forest. Though their use, at a fearful cost of life in so hot and humid a climate, of forced labour from the Peruvian high plateaux was repeatedly condemned, the planters justified their behaviour with the convenient argument that *coca* was a gift from God, dulling the sense of hunger and thirst, and so enabling the Indians to endure the otherwise insupportable rigours of toiling for the benefit of Spain in the silver mines of Potosí (see p. 325).

Equally acceptable to Spaniards, amongst whom the ownership and management of flocks and herds were traditionally esteemed noble pursuits, were the opportunities and rewards of pastoral farming. Loosed into the lush, virgin and often unpopulated pastures of the New World, the domesticated animals of Europe ran wild and reproduced at an astonishing rate to provide, and again at little or no cost, a massive reservoir of easily exploitable wealth. Pigs were ravaging the native agriculture of the Caribbean within months of the Spaniards' arrival; horses multiplied so quickly in Hispaniola that their import from Spain was prohibited in 1507. Mexico soon had so many sheep that flocks spilled over northwards into the lands of nomadic Indians, whilst in the early 1600s a Dutch expedition marvelled at their proliferation around Valparaiso – producing suet enough to load 'whole ships'.[12] The grasslands of Mexico came to support gigantic herds of cattle, periodically rounded up for slaughter. Their cheap and indifferent meat was either abandoned or sold to the Indians, their tallow marketed locally and their hides shipped to the great leather industry of Spain in such quantities as to constitute (by volume) the largest item in the cargoes of the homeward-bound Indies fleets. Horses were profitably supplied first for war, then for the proper conveyance of gentlemen; oxen were in demand for use in agriculture and bulk carriage; mules were needed by the thousand to move bullion from, and provisions to, mining sites as remote as Zacatecas, or as difficult of access as Potosí. Already in the mid-1500s the profits of ranching in lands where Indians were few, primitive or nomadic, were of an order to make it a suitable occupation for the many aspirants to rank who were without *encomiendas*. It demanded not capital, but enterprise, skill and bravura. Herds flourished through nature's munificence, not man's providence, and animals – like bullion, labour and tribute – were taken with no heed for the future. 'They do not count the number of their mules and asses', it was said of Chile in the late 1500s, 'and whoever wants them goes into the country and catches them.'

Feckless the agrarian economy of the Spanish colonies undoubtedly was, yet there had been established, in a surprisingly short time, a relatively complex and specialized agriculture, more varied than that of Portuguese Brazil, sensibly utilizing the wide range of climatic conditions encountered, and shaped by local and regional demand. Though initially based on, and long sustained by, unfree or slave labour it came to employ many who worked for wages, and it was developed and directed by a society considerably more adaptable and less parasitic than its antecedents and original behaviour would have suggested. It was not, however, for such bucolic pursuits that the Spaniards had left Europe, and for long their energies were strenuously directed to the search for wealth in its most acceptable form, the bullion whose discovery determined the fate of the Aztec and Inca states. Gold was disappointing. It was first found in Hispaniola, where by pillage and tribute the inhabitants were stripped of whatever had been accumulated over the centuries, and then set, in effect as slaves, to pan for alluvial ore. The techniques were inefficient and the labour force rapidly destroyed, so that by 1530 the cycle of island gold was over. Finds in Chile were unexploited through wars and the absence of any amenable indigenous labour, and those in Colombia (Buritica) were mined with decreasing success into the 1600s as Indians became fewer, and the most easily accessible veins were exhausted. Overall perhaps 300t of gold were shipped from the Americas to the mother country between 1500 and 1660.

With silver, 'the blood of the body politic' to contemporary publicists. it was a different story, with 25,000t sent to Europe alone within the same period. To ensure its safe arrival became one of the prime objects of imperial strategy, its interception the ambition of Spain's opponents and its impact in the homeland a matter of contention then and ever since. Throughout the sixteenth, and well into the seventeenth century, there were major finds in the desert or semi-desert regions of northern Mexico, where if Indian nomads were hostile, ore could at least be extracted without the danger of flooding, against which early technology was helpless. But Mexico was eclipsed by Potosí (worked from 1545), where, 5000 metres up in the Peruvian Andes, it was possible to tunnel into solid mountains of silver with even less chance of meeting water. Mexican production reached its maximum in the early 1600s, that of Peru somewhat sooner, when at Potosí there were 13,000 men on the site, over 4000 of them underground at a time, and in shafts of such depth – 200 metres or more – as to oblige them to stay down for several days on end. With Spanish technology poor, the work arduous, and the ore-bearing regions so bleak and remote, exploitation was difficult. The crown leased mines to venturers who worked them with capital borrowed from neighbouring landowners or merchants, paying the king one-fifth – later reduced to one-tenth – of their takings. Technicians were often aliens, and the recruitment of labour – given the Spaniards' insistence on the primacy of bullion and their equally adamant refusal to mine it themselves – a matter of much experiment and debate. In Mexico impressed Indians, small numbers of expensive African slaves, and even Spaniards were used for a time. Then, after plans at the end of the sixteenth century to draft oriental immigrants and freed Africans into the mines, entrepreneurs had, as in agriculture, to attract labour – mulatto, *mestizo*, Indian – by the offer of wages. At Potosí, many workers were initially provided by *encomenderos* investing the tributary labour of their Indians as capital. But with the massive fall in the indigenous population, and the equally massive growth in Spanish demands for American bullion, there came more drastic measures, and from the 1570s an ever-widening body of Indians was compelled to serve in silver and mercury mining. Their use was justified on those familiar grounds of the overriding needs of the state and the moral benefits conferred on the uninitiated by regular toil. Eventually the tribal tribute (*mita*) once rendered to the Inca crown was converted to the taking, in rotation, of workers from all the Indian communities of the highlands between Cuzco and Tarija, 4000 serving for four months at a stretch. But with the consequent disruption of the entire native economy, and as men fled, avoided service, or died, the Spaniards – after the usual talk of putting footloose Africans and undesirable half-castes down the mines – settled for using a measure of wage labour.

Industrial undertakings of this scale anticipated in many ways subsequent developments in Europe. Substantial settlements appeared in the remote areas whose natural riches supported them, profoundly affecting – with their needs for food, labour and manufactures – local economies. By 1650 Potosí was the biggest city in Christendom, displaying in its brash materialism – 'I am Potosí, treasure of the world and envy of kings' – its brothels, dance halls and gaming saloons, all the unlovable features of later mining and industrial centres. The American mines were worked with characteristic improvidence of a society as devoted as that of the aristocrats and squires of Portuguese Asia to the exaction of plunder. Advanced refining techniques employing mercury were not used at Potosí before 1573. Ore was not hauled to the surface, but carried up on men's backs, and neither at Potosí nor the mercury mines of

Huancavelica, with their lethal dust, was there any heed for the lot of the Indian workers, maimed or killed by disease, disaster and the rigours of the climate. Yet such behaviour was not peculiarly Spanish, and was occasionally combined, as in other endeavour, with surprising enterprise and ingenuity. To provide hydraulic power for ore-crushing mills at Potosí, 32 artificial lakes, 16km of sluices and 18 dams were constructed in the late 1500s.

Nor were the Spaniards concerned only with those primary pursuits which were to characterize so much of the history of Europe's overseas expansion. From the beginning men of every class were, like the Portuguese in Asia, active in assorted business adventures (cf. pp. 274–5). Initially there were openings in the provision of things that could no longer be obtained from Europe, then came the exploitation of local resources and opportunities. An important – and by the end of the sixteenth century highly specialized – shipbuilding industry developed, able to draw alike on the timber of central and equatorial America and the copper of Chile. Havana (Cuba) constructed vessels for the Atlantic, supplying by 1650 about one-third of those working to Spain. Men-of-war were built at Cartagena, ships for the Pacific at Guayaquil (Ecuador) and in the Philippines, made from the renowned local teak, the celebrated Manila galleons (see p. 328). Not all were replicas of European prototypes. Venezuelan shipwrights devised shallow-draught bulk carriers suitable for the waters of Maracaibo. For the long beat to windward from Panama to Callao (Peru) there was produced a special hull – no superstructure, a broad bow tapering to a narrow stern – which, as Protestant seamen found in 1600, could 'outstrip them exceedingly',[13] just as the English had earlier learned that the lightly sparred, generously canvassed and heavily armed fighting ships of the Pacific could outperform the best Elizabethan craft.[14]

Equally typical of Spanish methods and assumptions was the history of the woollen textile industry in the Americas. It was established to help to meet the needs of a growing white population, and to assist in clothing those Indians now forbidden to offend God and man with their nakedness – in short to reduce a colonial demand dangerously inflating textile prices in Europe. Merino sheep were introduced into Mexico to provide high-quality wool, and by 1600 there were twenty-five cloth and ten hat factories in the vicinity of Mexico City alone, part of a large and successful industry satisfactorily complementary to that of the mother country, and not, like the short-lived manufacture of silks, in competition. The picture was a familiar one – an economy of some regional specialization; industrial enterprise of an unexpected order, its products of such excellence as to arouse an Englishman's doubts for the future of his compatriots' textiles in America (1572);[15] the usual ruthless exploitation of indigenous labour. To a visitor to sixteenth-century Mexico the Indian cloth workers appeared no better than slaves. Nor indeed were they. Some were provided from forced labour quotas, but the majority had been sentenced, legally or otherwise, to penal servitude. And whether recruited by such means, or enticed by the promise of wages, the Indians became prisoners, locked – sometimes 700 together – in their factories under the guard of African slaves. But by the seventeenth century the industry, though still flourishing in southern Mexico, was generally in trouble. Indians became fewer, their sentencing to factory servitude was (in theory) prohibited in 1601 and mill-owners were obliged to bring in expensive Negro slaves. At the same time opposition grew in Spain to an industry now visibly competing with its decayed counterpart in the mother country.

Elsewhere the Spaniards were restricted by the climates and peoples they encountered. Even so their imperial economy was a remarkable and unique achievement. Its basis was the carriage to Europe of American bullion in amounts which only in the early 1600s showed signs of flagging. The wholesale exaction of valuable commodities from subject territories was nothing new, no more than was their accumulation by downright plunder. But never had a parent society – not even the Norse – been able to acquire, on such a scale, at so little cost, and by no recognizable commercial process, such quantities of gold and silver, convincing many publicists that here at last was the recipe for profit and power. But Spain also drew from the New World substantial amounts of goods like hides and dyes, whilst in return wealthy colonists demanded food, wine and household necessities in the early years, and then, as the American economy developed, African slaves, assorted luxuries – from books of the latest vogue to clothes of the latest fashion – and raw materials, like Baltic naval stores, needed by their own industries. Thus the range and nature of Europe's commerce was enlarged as perhaps never before. Products of a hitherto unknown world were carried to the homeland and European goods given new and extensive markets. An oceanic economy of imposing wealth and scale was created, employing a far greater volume of tonnage than previously used over such distances, and with the opening of the Pacific, and the close association with, and ultimate annexation of, the Portuguese empire, Spain came to control a network of trades embracing the entire globe. And as American silver flowed to China, Chinese silk to Spain, and African slaves to the Americas, there also developed a series of vigorous and interrelated regional economies. Nicaragua supplied Peru with livestock; Peru shipped sugar to Panama and wine to Central America; Mexico sent Peru woollens, mules, European manufactures and the products of China brought in from the Philippines, and took in exchange wine and silver.

To carry these trades routes were pioneered across the Pacific, from Europe to the Americas and through and round the continent on a scale of, and to an extent eclipsing, Norse and Portuguese achievement. Fleets assembled in Havana to carry to Seville, in a trade channelled like that of the rest of the overseas empire through ports specified by the crown, the produce and silver of Mexico (shipped in from Vera Cruz) and the treasure of Potosí brought from Nombre de Dios (see pp. 342ff.). To cater for the tastes of Peruvian magnates, whose silver allowed them to spend 'without heed or argument', cargoes came from Seville to either Nombre de Dios or Puerto Bello in the Isthmus. From there they went by lighter and mule train to Panama, and so, together with slaves imported through Cartagena and various local products, by sea down the long Pacific coast to Callao, the outport of Lima. Ladings were there disembarked and taxed. Some continued to the capital; the remainder were shipped to Arica for forwarding either by land to Potosí or by sea to Chile. It was also at Callao that the silver of Potosí, brought down by llama convoy to Arica and thence north by sea, was assembled. Part was destined for the Philippines, and part for Panama, Nombre de Dios and eventually Seville. With the prevailing south-easterly winds and north-setting currents of the west Pacific coast, the outward voyage from Mexico to Peru was so lengthy – seven or eight months – that there were attempts to find a better way through the Straits of Magellan. Meanwhile men of enterprise pioneered their own – and illegal – route over the Andes to the Río de la Plata, and were by the early 1600s exporting about 25 per cent of Potosí's silver output in exchange for goods and slaves for Chile and Peru (see pp. 249f.). Only the length and risks of the sea passage from Europe to the south Atlantic and the determined opposition of the allied monopolists of Lima and Seville curbed the traffic's further growth.

But however voracious Europe's appetite for silver it was modest compared with that of China (see pp. 241, 270). To feed and profit from this, the produce of the mines of Peru was carried from Callao to Acapulco in Mexico. From there the Manila galleons – two to four vessels of 300t apiece from the late 1500s – took it to the Philippines in a voyage almost as arduous as that of the Portuguese Indiamen, with the homeward leg along the route opened by Urdaneta lasting six months 'without the ships calling in any port or touching any land' (see pp. 271ff.). The volume of the trade, as indeed that of most of Spain's imperial commerce, is any one's guess. At the beginning of the seventeenth century it was estimated that exports were ten times the legal maximum, with anything from 94t to 350t of silver leaving America annually by an infinity of clandestine ways. From Manila coin and bullion spread to China, Cochin-China, Cambodia, Siam and Macassar, making the city the focus of a rich and extensive commerce, and an entrepôt where Malabar, Armenian and Chinese merchants could be seen haggling together. Junks – fifty at a time by the 1630s – brought from China silks and such other luxuries as musk and pearls. These, along with Filipino wax, cottons and gold, the Spaniards sent to the Americas. Some, most notably silk, went on to Europe, and the rest were for local, and especially Peruvian, consumption. From Japan native merchants and the many Iberians resident there[16] imported into Manila foodstuffs, weapons and silks – some also destined for the Americas – and took away Chinese textiles, together with Spanish and American goods. Prohibitions notwithstanding, the Portuguese of Malacca and Macao exchanged spices, textiles and a host of luxuries for bullion, precious stones and Spanish produce, and it was the Manila trade that largely sustained Macao's commerce after the Portuguese loss of Malacca and expulsion from Japan (see pp. 241, 287). Conducted in the leisurely style of Goa, the trade between the Philippines and America required no more than three months' attention in a year, and returning profits of 300 per cent and above relieved its Spanish participants from the need to engage in any other business. Not surprisingly, a major part of the imperial economy was for a time pulled irresistibly towards Asia. Oriental goods sold so cheaply in America, and Peruvian silver was in such demand in China, that Mexico became the entrepôt for Peru's Asiatic commerce. There were plans to divert the flow of spices to Europe through the Philippines and Mexico, whilst in the easy opulence of Manila wild schemes were concocted for the indefinite expansion of Spanish power (see p. 320).

III   *Masters and slaves*

In the New World the fortunate of Hispanic colonial society, living in climates so agreeable, surrounded by willing menials and among such natural riches, appeared to many to have inherited paradise. Nor was it a simple rustic paradise. Spain, from its Roman and Arab past, was intensely urban, a land in which the countryside was dominated by city-based power. Hence Spanish colonization, like that of the Germans earlier, was characterized by the founding of new towns and cities on a scale equalled only in modern times. Their basic plan was that chessboard pattern, centring on a main square, already used by the Germans, as also by the Spaniards themselves in the resettlements of the *reconquista*. Though built wherever possible without defensive walls, the American towns resembled those of Hanseatic eastern Europe in that they contained, living in their own suburbs, unprivileged indigenous inhabitants, and that they were focal points of authority in colonial territories (cf. pp. 43, 69ff.). Some, like Mexico City and Lima, were viceregal capitals, rich, populous and handsome. Many, however, were no more than villages, whilst commercial entrepôts ranged from wealthy Panama to Acapulco, still with only twenty rudimentary buildings in the late 1500s. And besides these were fortresses as powerful as Havana or as desolate as those posts resisting the Araucanians, and 'continuously assaulted by the Chilesians'.

The rapid and prolific establishment of such communities reflects Spain's acquisition of empire by conquests swifter and more complete than those achieved by any precursor. As a result, by 1650 a growing European minority (some 700,000), reinforced by about 850,000 enslaved and free Africans, held in subjection an Indian population roughly twelve times its size. Much of the continent the Spaniards never ruled, settled or even saw, and for long whole areas of their empire consisted of little more than a series of Spanish townships engulfed amongst alien subjects of uncertain loyalty if not downright hostility. Indians were accordingly denied European weapons, and evacuated, as at Lima in 1615, from areas attacked by Spain's European enemies. Spaniards worsted by the English in the late 1500s preferred to surrender to Protestant marauders rather than risk themselves amongst the natives of the Isthmus.[17]

Nevertheless nowhere was the pattern of European society more rapidly and completely reproduced, down to its basis of chronic poverty, than in the Spanish Americas. Not even in the years of conquest did most Spaniards secure lands or riches for themselves. And as the European population grew, and as more emigrants arrived, there was created a substantial class of poor whites. Some eked out an inglorious existence with their Indian woman on some patch of Indian land. Others lived by robbing and plundering Europeans and Indians alike in a way to which neither the Portuguese, constrained by the primitive Amerindian economy of Brazil and the powerful civilizations of Asia, nor any other European expatriates, could aspire. By the late 1500s such were the numbers of what, in familiar European style, were described as this 'idle and undisciplined rabble' that it was proposed to despatch them to conquer Cambodia and Siam.

Yet in the same continent and at the same time universities had been established in Hispaniola, Mexico and Peru. The proliferation of courts and tribunals with the extension of royal authority, and the growth of urban and provincial administrations, supported large numbers of lawyers. Trade, regional and oceanic, was handled by a powerful body of merchants. They may not have enjoyed the political influence of the business communities of the great Dutch and Italian cities, nor did their activities demand or produce any comparable financial or commercial virtuosity. Nevertheless expansion from the first footholds on the continent was often backed by American merchants whose presence also did much to ensure the survival and tenacity of Spanish rule. Money from Panama was invested in the conquest of Peru, just as in the 1540s the Lima business community helped finance the reassertion of royal authority in the colony (cf. pp. 314, 316). A century later, trade with Spain was controlled by a small, but imposingly wealthy, group. Almost all were immigrants from the mother country, replaced, when they withdrew to the pleasures and prestige of landowning, by the young associates they had brought in from the peninsula.

The demands of opulent colonists, and royal insistence, as early as 1501, on the emigration of skilled men, had meanwhile produced a class of artisans and craftsmen, ranging from confectioners to silversmiths, who already in the mid-1500s accounted for about 10 per cent of Peru's European population. Industrious, conservative, and often men of substance and property, employing Negro and Indian labour, they constituted a further major stabilizing influence. And of none was this truer than of the European women in the Americas. Conquest and colonization were everywhere in their initial stages essentially male, and in empires of trade, or those whose possessions were in the disease-ridden tropics, continued so (cf. pp. 185ff., 251, 415ff.). But emigration from Spain was to benign and healthy climates, and was encouraged by statesmen conscious of the virtues of Roman-style settlement. Married colonists guaranteed permanence and stability, besides providing in their domestic bliss an example for emulation by indigenous peoples (cf. p. 312). Women accompanied Columbus in 1498. The crown insisted (1501) that emigrants should be married, and, in course, that those who were should have their wives with them, whilst European wives should be provided for the bachelors. Often enough the unwillingness of wives to emigrate was equalled only by the reluctance of spouses to receive them. Nor were all Spanish women necessarily models of domestic virtue. Potosí had its high class European and creole[18] prostitutes; widows of *encomenderos*, richer with every husband they buried, could end as formidable as any termagant in Europe. But that emigrants were women of spirit is perhaps no more than should be expected, and of their numbers and influence there is no doubt. By the 1570s roughly one-third of the passengers registered for the Americas were women. In fact many more left than are recorded – the fleet of 1604 alone taking 600 instead of a supposed 50. In the admirable climate and easy environment of upland Mexico and Peru they flourished, with their death rate below that of their male compatriots. Hence the apparent predominance of men and the imbalance of the sexes in the colonies was less marked than would at first appear, with, for example, the European population of Lima comprising in 1610 5527 males and 4359 females.

The presence of women from the mother country on a scale equalled only in Norse and German colonization previously, and in the English North American settlements later, meant that Spanish custom and usage were much less affected by those influences native women exercised on the Portuguese in Brazil and Africa or the Italians in the Black Sea (cf. pp. 185ff., 290). Not that males from a society which, like Portugal, considered fornication with unmarried women no sin, were impervious to the charms of Indian girls, who commonly clung tenaciously to tough and masterful aliens. Heroes of the conquest took indigenous mistresses – Cortés his 'princess' Marina; Francisco Pizarro the sister of Atahualpa. In the early years, before the arrival of European wives or marriage to European women, humbler Spaniards lived in virtually monogamous relationships with their Indian mistresses. So, as in the empire of Portugal, there was engendered a large and generally depressed *mestizo* caste. But only among the frontiersmen of Paraguay – that 'paradise of Mahomet' – was there any Spanish equivalent to the voluptuous harem society of Portuguese Asia and Brazil. European women were relatively plentiful, the indigenous civilizations were in decay, Spanish royal policy opposed any such regime and Spanish settlers were rarely as isolated as their Portuguese equivalents.

Thus there developed in the Americas a closely knit, white, ruling minority, descended in part from those humbly born Spaniards (and others) who had established, settled, and briefly controlled the empire. Elsewhere, whether with the Norse or the Portuguese, the founding and rule of colonies was largely the prerogative of those of noble blood. But Spanish patricians were forbidden to engage in private imperial ventures. Generally affluent in the early 1500s they had, as far as is known, no economic reason to do so,[19] and there were in any case more fitting opportunities for them in war and service in Europe in the great days of Habsburg power. Their conversion to empire came with the realization of its increasing riches, and with the assertion of royal authority. Magnates became viceroys, their relatives the ornaments of viceregal courts and determined suitors for pensions, rewards and the hands of colonial heiresses. A society once plebeian and egalitarian, which had seen Pizarro – known to all simply as 'the Marquis' – engage in horseplay with his troops, was soon as rigidly hierarchical as that of the mother country. *Encomenderos* struggled to secure hereditary succession to their fees – as that formidable warrior, the duke of Alva, thought they should have, and as the crown momentarily contemplated conceding (1554). But if some of the new colonial aristocracy were, like the Cortés dynasty, descendants of conquerors of modest or obscure origins, many *encomenderos* left no heirs, and such was the royal tenacity in limiting tenure that by 1642 all but 140 *encomiendas* in Mexico had reverted to the king. The new nobility were in general owners of land acquired either with wealth accumulated in commerce or through political influence.[20] In Mexico in the mid-1600s there was a tiny handful of titled lords (relatives of Spanish aristocrats or descendants of the conquerors), and beneath them a larger group of untitled creole nobles. Rarely reinforced from Europe, tightly interrelated, obsessed with pedigree and embarrassingly unmartial, they seemed, like the magnates of Norse Iceland, a parody of the culture from which they stemmed. Sustained by native labour, and surrounded by relatives and retainers, they lived either as the virtual sovereign lords of vast and more or less self-sufficient estates, or, in equally grand style, in their town palaces, supplied from the surplus produce of their lands. They willingly paraded their wealth in Europe, but made no attempt to enter Spanish politics, and though originating in a distinguished civilization they remained, like the planters of Brazil, addicts of vulgar ostentation. Nor surprisingly. The Spanish aristocrats despatched to administer the empire served only limited terms, so offering no inducement to artists and writers to abandon vital associations in Europe to seek their patronage in the New World. There, unlike the Venetians in Crete and Greece, the Spaniards encountered no culture already held in high esteem. Nor, by royal policy, were the Indies a haven where, as in English North America, dissidents might practice their beliefs. And with their easy living, and (from 1570) the Inquisition to 'root out error', they had, unlike Norse Iceland, no incentive to intellectual curiosity and creative vigour (cf. pp. 33ff., 213ff. 488ff.).

The economy and society of Spanish America rested, to a degree unparalleled elsewhere, on what in law or effect was the forced labour of non-Europeans. Even Portugal had colonies where Europeans tilled the soil, but in the Indies there were no white peasants, and all arduous and menial tasks were discharged by others to such an extent that Creoles visiting Spain were amazed to discover Europeans working. Colonists thirsting for riches, and from a country long familiar with slavery, had no difficulty in persuading the crown that the natives of the Caribbean should be compelled to labour (1503), and had no scruples about reducing whole peoples to servitude. In Mexico Cortés had rebels and prisoners of war branded and auctioned. For primitive and intractable populations, such as the nomads of northern Mexico and the Araucanians, slavery was widely accepted to be the only proper fate, particularly since without the profits of slave-raiding – the so-called 'chases' in Chile, for example, with Indians rounded up like animals – soldiers were reluctant to serve in such territories.

Elsewhere the enslavement of the Amerindians was, after much hesitation, finally prohibited by the crown (1542). But Indian slaves could still be got from Portuguese

Brazil, whilst the Spanish adaptation of the traditional Aztec and Inca systems of forced labour enabled them successfully to set the Indians to work – in a way the Portuguese, dealing with far less advanced peoples, were unable to do – in conditions tantamount to slavery (see pp. 248–9). Initially they were obliged to render tribute, widely taken to mean labour, to the masters to whom they were commended, so that by the mid-1500s 80 per cent of Peru's male population was employed by the Spaniards in anything from mining to the carriage of artillery on their backs. The strenuous denunciation of such behaviour by an influential Spanish minority, and the disastrous fall in the number of Indians, brought a change of policy (see pp. 349, 354). Royal officers were appointed to supervise and protect the native peoples, who from 1549 were compulsorily allocated on a rotational basis by state officials to Spaniards requiring hands. In 1632 this, too, was abolished, except for mining and royal and ecclesiastical works, and the Indians thereafter supposedly received wages. Meanwhile in Peru those of the highlands were compelled to mine silver and mercury, though their use in the cities and plantations of the coast was restricted. But there were countless abuses. Tribute labour continued in Chile and elsewhere into the 1700s. Wages were often derisory and debt-slavery common – the verb 'to owe' significantly entering the Nahuatl language of Mexico c. 1600 – whilst the fall in the indigenous population meant the exaction of the same work from fewer people. Of the callous indifference, even by the standards of the day, of the Spaniards to the sufferings of their new subjects, there is no shortage of testimony, and in the early 1600s Carletti, an enthusiast for the splendours of the Americas, remarked that this paradise was not for the Indians, abused and treated 'like beasts'.[21]

In the later sixteenth century the changing nature of the American economy and the pressure of royal policy did something to ease their lot. They were paid wages from 1549, and they were exempted (1601) from industries such as the production of sugar. Furthermore, as Indians became fewer, and as reformers excited concern for their plight, the colonists turned, as did the planters of Brazil, to the Negro slave. Black slavery Spain, like Portugal, knew from its long Moorish past, and the first Africans – introduced in 1502 to replace the rapidly disappearing and unsatisfactory Tainos – came from those born or held in Iberia. But soon the Spaniards were clients of Portuguese slavers in a trade quickly established as the most important to America.[22] About 75 per cent of the Africans supplied were, like those shipped to Brazil, males. They were, and remained, expensive, with a 'prime piece' selling in Mexico and Peru in the early 1600s at up to twenty times the price of an Indian. And their numbers rapidly increased. The *asiento* of 1615 set annual imports at 3500. But many others were smuggled in, and with Africans in the Americas encouraged (from 1527) to marry African women, there was by 1650 a black population variously put at between 300,000 and the best part of 1,000,000.

Even before the conquest of Mexico was completed, Negro slaves were so numerous in the Indies that there was alarm at the likelihood of mass revolt, and by the end of the century they were owned by anyone from *hacendados* with several hundred to Spanish artisans and hispanized Indians with a handful each. The men served as soldiers in the Peruvian civil wars, as ranch hands in Mexico and Paraguay, as labourers on sugar, cotton and tobacco plantations, as seamen and shipwrights in the Pacific and as skilled artisans almost everywhere. Women became domestic servants, and were commonly taken, and often cherished, as mistresses on whom silks, pearls and jewelry were lavished. Rarely able to tolerate the climate of the high plateaux, Africans flourished in the Caribbean and the tropical lowlands of Ecuador, Colombia, Venezuela and Peru – on whose coast they outnumbered Spaniards before the end of the sixteenth century. As in Brazil, many escaped into wild country to live in independence under their own rulers – in Venezuela in the sixteenth century, and in Mexico in the seventeenth. Continuing rivalries amongst peoples from differing tribes precluded their concerted action, but of the dangers from such communities the Spaniards had no doubts, those of the Isthmus being 'our mortal enemies' in the late 1500s.[23] Sometimes bands of escaped slaves joined the more bellicose Indians – royal attempts to segregate the two peoples notwithstanding – in attacks on Europeans. But they were more likely to be plundering Indian settlements and making off with Indian women. Outbreaks of drunken violence were widespread. There were revolts in Hispaniola (1522), Mexico (1537) and elsewhere later, and until well into the 1600s large-scale risings were apprehensively expected. Slaves were forbidden to travel without permission, to drink wine or to carry weapons. Offenders were castrated and mutilated, captured rebels roasted alive.

Even so, Africans in the Indies were better off than their compatriots in Brazil and North America because of the survival under Spanish rule of a large and employable indigenous population (cf. pp. 249 and 487). Irrevocably torn from their own cultures, Negroes were readily hispanized, accepted Christianity to the extent of knowing their prayers and the commandments, and joined their masters in a common contempt for the docile Indian. Hence, though slaves, expensive Africans were widely used as skilled specialists, and as overseers, and brutal ones at that, of Indian labour. Furthermore, they inserted themselves by enterprise or force as intermediaries between Spanish consumers and Indian producers, whilst in a colonial society more urban than those of Protestant America or Portuguese Brazil many were employed not as field hands, but, like the slaves of the Italian maritime republics, in less arduous domestic servitude (cf. pp. 107–8 and 174–5). They frequently undertook duties which elsewhere might be entrusted to friends or relatives, acting as armed guards or the custodians of a merchant's money and papers. As craftsmen – whether metalsmiths or confectioners – they could achieve the substance, if not the status of freedom. And many, indeed, became legally free, particularly in the towns, more so than in the Protestant empires. Some were rich enough to buy their liberty, others were redeemed by relatives and many, particularly the old and useless, together with favourite mistresses and their offspring, were emancipated by owners. Hence the Indies had a substantial class of free

Africans and mulattos – about 20,000 in Mexico alone by 1650. The more fortunate were, like the Negro captain of a troop of 'free Negro' soldiers, trusted associates of Europeans. Others prospered as artisans, sub-contracting work from Spanish colleagues, living in Spanish style, forming their own mutual aid associations in the Spanish fashion, and constituting a coherent, socially and economically interrelated group. Nevertheless they remained both inferior and dangerous in European eyes. They were excluded from the professions, and the character of their womenfolk's dress was humiliatingly regulated. The less fortunate sank, as did many poor whites, into that impoverished mass common to America and Europe alike. Apprehensively (but spasmodically) the government attempted to restrain their robberies, violence and riots by taxing them, checking their migrations, and bringing them into Spanish employment, or at least under Spanish surveillance.

IV   *The roots of empire*

Of no empire were the origins less obscure than that of Spain. In the late fifteenth century the country had no reason or desire to search for distant lands. Energies were not directed abroad by the royal will, as was so largely the case in Portugal. The Spanish sovereigns had overriding ambitions in Europe, and where, in imperial matters, royal power was most decisively exercised was in ensuring the crown's share of the profits and in curbing the aspirations and excesses of its subjects, not in identifying and appraising new opportunities. Nor, in the early 1500s, had Spain a surplus population – though propagandists claimed it had – obliged to seek a livelihood elsewhere. However, with some 7,500,000 inhabitants in 1550, their numbers increasing almost to the end of the century, the country was better able than Portugal to people new territories, and had no cause to use convicts and paupers. For the majority indeed there seems little enough reason to have remained at home. Agriculture was primitive and inefficient, unable adequately to sustain life. Aristocrats (about 1.5 per cent of the population) owned in effect 97 per cent of the land. Much of it was barren, 'utterly deserted', infertile, or (as in the centre and south) devoted to grazing. Even so, no more than in Portugal was there any marked urge to emigrate. All was changed with Columbus' revelation of the possibility of access to the wealth of Asia, and his opening of a way to that of the Indies. In pursuit of gold and silver – riches in the most acceptable form known to man – Amerindian states were overthrown, the Andes scaled, and the Amazonian jungle invaded. In the end territories with silver became the heart of the empire, those without, its borders. Doubtless few realms have been conquered, and few peoples subjugated, without some expectation of gain. But Spain was unique in that its overseas expansion began with, and was largely shaped by, the pursuit of those precious metals for which, as an Aztec chronicler bitterly commented, Spaniards 'lusted like pigs'. Even so, the rate of emigration was in relative, and often in absolute terms, modest compared with that from Portugal or early Scandinavia. Throughout the sixteenth century the annual average, according to official (and unreliable) statistics, was about 550, and probably in fact at most no more than 5000 in peak years (cf. pp. 2, 282, 292). Lords did their best to prevent the departure of their peasants. There were nearer outlets in Granada, newly conquered from the Moors, or in service in Spain's almost incessant wars in Europe until the mid-seventeenth century. But not all emigrants were so bellicose. The rich and growing settlements in the New Worlds soon needed alike merchants, officials, artisans and domestic servants. Nor were all emigrants crude materialists. Soaked in the fantasy of contemporary romances, some pioneers searched Florida for the delights of the Fountain of Eternal Youth, whilst others sought the realms of the Amazons, those martial ladies of daunting charms, inhabiting the kingdom of California, 'near the earthly paradise'. And with the same energy and determination Spanish missions endeavoured to protect the crown's new Amerindian subjects, and to convert them – as indeed many others – in one of the greatest efforts ever made to spread the Catholic faith.

To accomplish such feats the bellicose and (relatively) wealthy and populous Spain of Ferdinand and Isabella was better endowed than any previous imperial power. The nature of its strength must not, however, be misunderstood. No more than that of Portugal was Spanish expansion the outcome of precocious nautical skills. Carvels were certainly used by Columbus, but in the southern and more kindly waters of an ocean already crossed by Norse vessels, and where they were, as in the east, shortly either modified or replaced. Before long ships of every sort and condition, from German hulks to (occasionally) Mediterranean galleys, were sailing to the Americas, showing that oceanic passages were not the peculiar preserve of some specially designed craft. And whilst in time Spain drew on Portuguese navigational advances, in the Indies fleets the fixing of longitude was never attempted and that of latitude rarely achieved, and the way to America was opened by Columbus navigating, like his Spanish colleagues on the first voyage, by the age-old techniques of dead-reckoning and the sharp observation of natural phenomena (cf. pp. 263ff., 303, 306).

But of Spain's real advantages there is no doubt. Geography obliged its southern province of Andalusia to seek, like Portugal, outlet by sea, and it lay as near as Portugal to the favourable wind systems of the Atlantic, and nearer still to Africa (see p. 261). Both the kingdoms of Castile and Aragon had a long and vigorous history of war, trade and maritime achievement. By *c.* 1300 Catalan subjects of the crown of Aragon had, like their Venetian and Genoese rivals, developed a seaborne commerce which embraced Atlantic Morocco, England, Flanders, the Levant and the Black Sea. In the early fourteenth century Catalan adventurers established in Greece and the Balkans regimes foreshadowing those of Spanish America. Compatriots were notorious slavers in the Mediterranean, whilst Catalan seamen searched the west coast of Africa for the source of Saharan gold and took part in expeditions to conquer and convert the Canary Islands (see pp. 164, 227). From such experience, and from a rich heritage of Jewish and Arab science, the Catalans developed an impressive cosmography, evidenced in the magnificent Atlas of 1375. By the late Middle Ages this economy and civilization were in decline, but their traditions, and the dynastic ambitions of the house of Aragon, turned Spanish interests to the Mediterranean in the fifteenth and sixteenth centuries, culminating in the domination of Italy and the decisive contribution to the defeat of the Turks at Lepanto (see pp. 132–4).

Equally lengthy was the maritime history, and far more vigorous the maritime economy and Renaissance culture of Castile. Backed by rich resources in timber, iron and manpower, Biscayan shipbuilding had long been widely renowned. In the late medieval centuries Biscayan and Basque vessels were to be found working anywhere from the Levant to Flanders, those of Andalusia from the Canaries to the English Channel and (by the 1450s) West Africa, to whose coast as far south as Bojador the duke of Medina Sidonia laid claim in 1449 (see pp. 301–2). And even if by 1500 the Spanish kingdoms were not amongst the most highly developed regions of Europe's economy, they nevertheless contained important pockets of mercantile wealth and skill. Andalusian magnates owned and operated ships. In the Basque provinces landed aristocrats and a large middle class – exempt from taxation by its pretensions to nobility – were widely active in business. At Burgos, rich on the export of wool, and where can still be seen the remains of their splendid town houses, were families like the Haro – future associates of Magellan – and Pardo, wealthy enough to handle the distribution of Portuguese spices in northern Europe (see p. 264). And throughout the peninsula, and in the south in particular, were powerful communities of Italian, and especially Genoese, merchants and bankers (see pp. 178ff.). Seapower in itself would not, as Dutch and English experience was to show, establish an empire. Nor did international high finance initiate expansion, and both Cortés and Pizarro were backed locally in America, not from the money markets of Europe. But such resources were vitally to sustain the new empire.

To some it has seemed that the speed and totality of the Spanish conquests reflected, as did Portuguese success in Asia, the triumph of European technology. The Aztecs and Incas were indeed without writing, the wheel and firearms. But though Spaniards might occasionally attribute their victories to an opponent's lack of artillery, and though gunfire did at times quell those unaccustomed to it, this was not necessarily so. The Maya, on their first encounter with firearms, fought on undeterred (1517), whilst neither guns nor the celebrated Spanish sword made much impression on the Chichimeca and Araucanians. Nor were firearms widely employed in the conquests. They were expensive, crude, unreliable and commonly useless through lack of powder and shot, or because rain had extinguished the slow match needed to fire them. What ensured Spanish success against numerically overwhelming odds was their use of cavalry in a continent with no indigenous equivalent to the horse, giving them enormous advantages of mobility and surprise over those moving only by foot. Horses were ridden Moorish style, i.e. bitted at the neck, singly reined, guided by pressure of the knees, and with the rider kneeling jockey-like on his mount. Standing in his stirrups, he towered over infantrymen, hacking at densely packed masses with his sword, and when in open country they broke and ran, charging them and spearing them by the score with his lance. Time and again small groups of armoured, and seemingly invulnerable horsemen, scattered, demoralized and decimated vast bodies of Amerindian foot soldiers. Like Portuguese reformers in Asia commanders wrote, as did Cortés from Tenochtitlán, of their indispensability, and when in Peru iron was not available horses were shoed with silver to keep them in the field.

Besides cavalry the Spaniards used dogs 'so fierce', it was reported, 'that in two bites they laid open their victims to the entrails'. These tactics, pathetically portrayed in native art, had already proved so successful in the Canaries and the Caribbean that before long 'to hunt' and 'to dog' Indians were synonymous in Spanish. Against such onslaughts the peoples of the Americas fought hard, and often with impressive weapons and skills. Inca slings, the Spaniards admitted, were 'not much less effective than an arquebus', their quilted cotton armour excellent. 'The wild Indians' of Mexico had arrows, it was discovered, 'that will pierce any coat of mail', and archers who could hit running hares, or oranges tossed into the air.[24] Some Amerindians soon acquired European weapons and even European mounts. They found that stake-lined pits would dispose of cavalry charges, that horses could be brought down with *bolas*, and that in passes or defiles horsemen were as vulnerable as any to ambush (cf. pp. 317 and 340).

Yet in the end the majority were conquered. Attacking by sea, the Spaniards were able to choose their points of access and to mobilize relief and reinforcement with comparative ease. The indigenous land empires, on the other hand, could offer no maritime resistance, and living in isolation gave each other no assistance against the invaders. They were, moreover, as disastrously weakened by Spanish-borne disease[25] spreading in advance of Spanish armies as were Europeans by endemic fevers in Asia and Africa. Whilst Spaniards flourished in highland America, the Maya, at their first encounter with Europeans, were afflicted with some unspecified epidemic, and the Inca Huayna Capac and much of his army were destroyed *c.* 1525 by malaria or smallpox. Indigenous resistance was further crippled by the Spaniards' disruption of the agrarian economy which had ensured the cultivation of the quick-growing maize, whose rapid succession of harvests alone allowed Mexico and Peru to support populations of a size so disproportionate to their resources. And even such numbers were a liability. Without cavalry Aztec and Inca armies had nothing of the Spaniards' mobility. Their operations were difficult to co-ordinate, and with their exorbitant needs for food they could rarely hold the field more than briefly. Nor were these their only shortcomings. Aztec warriors fought less to annihilate the enemy than to secure prisoners for sacrifice, and like those of the Incas they usually dispersed if their leaders fell.

Against them were troops from Europe's most formidable military power, where martial achievement rated above all else and illiteracy was no shame in a gentleman.[26] The blazing heat of Spain's summers and the biting cold of its winters, the rigours of its great mountains and endless plains produced men equal to most things, and of a physique and appearance the Indians found awesome. Nor were the *conquistadores* professional soldiers, bound like so many English leaders in North America by the conventions of their calling. They had risen to command from modest and obscure origins by ability and force of character. They were experienced in Indian fighting in the Caribbean and Isthmus, and as fertile in military and political expedients as were the Portuguese of equally humble birth in adapting to the business opportunities of the east (cf. pp. 274f. and 482–4). From a country renowned for its infantry they proved themselves bold and original cavalrymen. Troops were drilled especially to impress the Indians; horses went into battle festooned with rattles to unnerve opponents. Though certainly not without their moments of terror and despair, the Spaniards fought with a determination unsapped by any such pessimism as the Aztec religion inculcated, and sharpened by the prospect of riches to come, and the realization that in Mexico and Peru there was no alternative to victory.

Such qualities might, however, have been deployed in vain had not the invaders encountered societies fatally flawed, whose weaknesses, it was widely remarked, they adeptly exploited.[27] In Mexico they won the support of tribes opposed to, or imperfectly subdued by, the Aztecs – the Cempoalans, Guacingo, Otomi and Tlaxcalans amongst others. Hence when Cortés entered Montezuma's lands he had with him at least 4000 native auxiliaries, soon allegedly swelled to 150 000. Many were simply porters, labourers or scouts, but many, like the Tlaxcalans who served in the final capture of Tenochtitlán, were fighting men. In Peru the Spaniards were aided by the Incas' Colla, Huanca and Canari opponents. Their execution of Atahualpa brought them the goodwill of his adversaries, and with the installation of a puppet emperor they were able to enjoy invaluable Inca assistance. Almagro invaded Chile accompanied by Inca troops and an Inca prince who smoothed his passage through onetime imperial lands. In the absence of any spontaneous affection, native rulers and princelings were forced or tempted into Spanish service, with the Indian council of Huejotzingo recalling in 1560 how Tlaxcalan nobles had been hanged 'for making war poorly'.[28] The dangers of such policies, as the Portuguese already understood, were considerable, but the advantages enormous. Europeans obtained troops who knew the terrain. They acquired essential specialists, like those native engineers whose rapid repair of the roads and bridges damaged by retreating Inca armies permitted the swift Spanish advance into Peru. Their numerical inferiority was redressed, and their strength and resources conserved.

Thus, like the Portuguese, the Spaniards came to rely heavily on indigenous allies, auxiliaries and mercenaries, including those primitive peoples to whom military service was a more acceptable form of tribute than labour. French raiders were repelled from Cubagua in 1528 by Indian archers under Spanish command. In northern Mexico 'friendly natives' were sent to fight the Chichimeca, who, like the bloodthirsty Araucanians, were incorporated into Spanish units once 'pacified'. Hence frontier garrisons might consist of no more than a few dozen Europeans together with 2000 or

3000 Indians, and in the seventeenth century Dutch and English incursions were resisted by handfuls of Spaniards reinforced by large bodies of 'loyal Indians'. More ambitiously, in 1586 the mooted conquest of China was to have been mounted from the Philippines with 10,000 or so Europeans and the same number of Japanese and Visayan warriors. Japanese mercenaries fought in Cambodia (1595), and the force to expel the Dutch from Ternate (1601) included 400 Filipino pioneers serving, like so many of Portugal's indigenous auxiliaries, at their own cost and with their own equipment (cf. pp. 267–8).

Allies, prisoners and native mistresses also provided advice and intelligence. The Spaniards debating the fate of Atahualpa were warned by 'two Indians in their service' of approaching Inca relief. Information from his Indian mistress and interpreter, Doña Marina, helped to shape the course of Cortés' Mexican campaign. And once the native empires were overthrown, it was from amongst their former subjects that the conquerors recruited aid in their exploitation and administration, as did, on a smaller scale, the Portuguese in their eastern possessions (cf. p. 267). Nevertheless it was not the whole of the Americas that fell to the Spaniards. They succeeded spectacularly where they encountered peoples living under central, and vulnerable, authorities which they replaced with their own, leaving the basic indigenous state intact. Where there was no sedentary population accustomed to obey such authority, where there were no social or political divisions to be exploited, where there was no prospect of bullion to inspire them and outside the benign climate of the temperate highlands, they advanced slowly and spasmodically. As with other imperial powers the going against primitive nomads was hard (in northern Mexico) or impossible (in Florida and Georgia). In southern Chile – 'the Flanders of the Indies' – the Araucanians soon had their measure. They destroyed pastures that might support Spanish horses; halted cavalry with the pike; frustrated the aim of Spanish gunners by alternately leaping in the air or lying on the ground; exhausted their attackers by deploying reserves to sustain resistance. Before long they were using captured Spanish weapons, firearms included, and once they had horses, raiding Spanish settlements at will. When challenged they melted away to bases which if destroyed were easily replaced, and whose loss hardly affected the ability of nomadic clans to live and fight (cf. pp. 313, 317). To many observers it seemed, and not without justification, that the extent of Spanish success was determined by the degree of co-operation offered by, or exacted from, native peoples.

v *The practice of empire*

The Spanish monarchs were at first indifferent to the grand oceanic schemes of Columbus. But once the potential of the discoveries was apparent they rapidly asserted their authority. Rarely has any imperial power so consistently sought to regulate every aspect of imperial life, or to understand its native subjects. Such attitudes reflect, like Venetian rule in the Levant, the subjugation of organized societies whose effective control demanded a knowledge of their structure, and are not to be found in empires lacking substantial territorial conquests. But purposeful government also depended on the attitudes of imperial administrators – on the humanist and self-consciously Roman servants of the Venetian republic; on the lawyers and Erasmian bureaucrats of early-Habsburg Spain. And in Spain, as in Portugal, it depended on the character of a succession of remarkable sovereigns, from the pious Isabella to the office-bound Philip II, conscious in varying degrees of royal responsibilities to non-European subjects, acutely aware of the financial prospects of empire and of the dangers inherent in the ambitions of its founders (cf. pp. 120ff., 210, 261, 349).

It was quickly established that the discoveries were made in the royal name, and they were indeed regarded, in the tradition of the *reconquista*, as personal royal possessions until after the death of Ferdinand. The patrimonial and feudal concessions made to Columbus were swiftly undermined, the alarmingly successful (like Cortés), were supplanted and the disposal of lands, rights and offices brought, with difficulty, under the crown's control (cf. pp. 305, 312). It nominated (from 1508) to all ecclesiastical preferments overseas. It admitted to the empire (after 1538) only such papal decrees as it saw fit, and it held the missionary Orders in strict subjection. Emigration was by royal licence. African slaves, who had to be Christians, could only be imported into the Indies by royal permission. Undesirable persons and classes – the poor, the unemployed, foreigners, Jews, Moors, pagans, heretics – were all to be excluded from the colonies, and though some convicts were sent to the Canaries, settlement was to be, in the Roman style so beloved of the Renaissance, by farmers, artisans and respectable married men, whose passage overseas was subsidized. To ensure the permanence and stability of Spanish rule the founding of towns was encouraged, with comprehensive instructions provided for their construction and government. Starting with the shipment of aboriginal slaves from the islands of the West Indies to Europe (1495), an Indian policy was painfully evolved. The powers and privileges of *encomenderos* were, after a struggle, reduced. Europeans, except those collecting tribute, were to be excluded from Indian territories. Provision was made in Mexico for landless whites (1531), and eventually, in a way unthinkable to the Portuguese, the segregation of the races was attempted (cf. pp. 266–7, 351–3).

Equally clear was that the conquests were to be exploited for the royal benefit. Precious metals and other natural riches could only be taken with the approval of the crown, which initially received one-fifth of all gold and silver mined. It took tribute from the Indians together with whatever surplus colonial treasuries might accumulate. It drew revenues from ecclesiastical tithes, the sale of indulgences, and the proceeds of a variety of monopolies it instituted. Goods were taxed on its behalf leaving Spain, arriving in the Americas, and on sale there. To these exactions the demands of impecunious kings shortly added an array of desperate expedients. Private bullion shipments were confiscated in the early 1600s. Licences to breach regulations, notably those prohibiting the emigration of Jews and foreigners, were sold, as were governmental posts.

To reap this rich harvest, and to keep the Americas in economic (and hence political) dependence on the mother country, the colonial trade was supposedly conducted under the strictest control, in the style of Portugal and the Italian maritime republics. The Spanish monarchs were not, however, like the rulers of Portugal, in business themselves. Their view of kingship was more lofty, their commitments and interests more diverse, and imperial revenues in any case of less significance than in Portugal. Instead they defined, as did the Venetian state, the scope and nature of an ambitious monopoly (cf. pp. 114–25). The colonies were to trade only with Spain, and commerce, after a brief liberal interlude in the 1520s, was restricted to members of the Seville *consulado* (guild). It was in this fashion that other groups of merchants were elsewhere in Spain monopolists of particular trades, and in the Americas the Seville guild dealt with similar select bodies in Mexico and Lima. In the same way, after another short-lived liberal episode, Seville and (from 1519) Cadiz, became the only ports to and from which traffic with the Indies was allowed. Unlike those of the Portuguese and Venetian monopolies, none of the ships working to the Indies were state-owned – too many were needed – and in the early years sailed independently (cf. pp. 125, 271). But as the volume of traffic, and the attacks of privateers, increased the trade was, from the mid-1500s, carried by convoys moving, like those of the Venetians and Portuguese, under armed escort.[29] In this way there was some prospect of mutual support in case of trouble, and some hope, in an age of notoriously insecure navigation, that a fleet's position might be discovered by the combined skills of its pilots. Merchants were assured that no competitor's goods would arrive before theirs and the crown could (optimistically) assume that precious metals would be kept from the wrong hands.

From 1564 two fleets, each of some fifty vessels, were supposed to leave Spain every year. One departed (if ready) in the spring, passing from the Atlantic islands to the Lesser Antilles, from where the main body made for Vera Cruz (an overall passage of about 7500km), and the remainder for either Honduras or the Greater Antilles. A second fleet sailed (if ready) by much the same route in the summer, again dividing in the Lesser Antilles, from where most of the ships went to Nombre de Dios (Puerto Bello later) in a total run of about 6900km. There they loaded the bullion which even in the eighteenth century accounted for 80 per cent of the value of (known) incoming cargoes, and then took shelter in Cartagena. The following spring they rendezvoused with the other returning flotillas in Havana, passed together through the dangerous Florida Strait in early summer, and sailed northward along the Florida coast to pick up a favourable wind for the Azores (cf. p. 261). There the fleet halted, awaited stragglers, refreshed and topped up cargoes for the final leg homewards.

To this remarkable organization war and economic disaster brought radical modification. Defences became for a time more elaborate, administration more complex, and expenses consistently more onerous. By the late 1500s regular protective squadrons were stationed in the Caribbean and eastern Atlantic. Convoys were guarded by escorts – as numerous as their wards during the Dutch attacks of the 1620s – which also carried the royal silver and whatever else the influential could persuade them

Fig. 13 Heavily-armed Spanish *gallizabra* or treasure frigate used in the transport of bullion to Europe; late sixteenth century, from a contemporary draught by an English spy. A note at the bottom reads '104 foote by the keele'.

to take. In the hope of improving safety and efficiency the stops in the Lesser Antilles outwards and the Azores inwards were abandoned in the 1600s. As the nature of trade settled convoys became, by a familiar process, smaller, and the vessels in them larger – 70t on average in 1504; 400t in 1650 – as from the mid-1500s the carvel was replaced by the galleon. Of this the origins are uncertain, but in Iberia it developed in the sixteenth century as a heavily armed fighting ship of up to about 500t, distinguished by its fine lines, low bow and high stern. Rigged, like the bigger carvels, with an admixture of square and lateen sails, it was faster, handier and smaller than a Portuguese Indiaman (cf. pp. 263, 279). Such peninsula-built craft became rarer as Spanish commitments increased and Spanish resources dwindled, and by 1650 over two-thirds of those in the Indies fleets were from English, Dutch and South American yards.

The weaknesses of the *carreira*, even in its prime, were legion. Supplying, unlike the Portuguese Asian monopoly, the needs of a sizable colonial society, it demanded a large, but generally underemployed, volume of tonnage. With the onset of Protestant attack its defence costs became exorbitant, with the levy on cargoes for this purpose soaring from 2 per cent in 1585 to 35 per cent in the early 1600s. However rigidly defined, with no other contact between the colonies and Europe allowed, except (from 1597) two ships annually to the Río de la Plata and (from 1618) two biennially to Buenos Aires, the monopoly was never watertight. Treasure ships, the English learned in 1586, commonly carried twice the amount of their declared cargoes.[30] Bullion was freely unloaded in the Portuguese Atlantic islands. Foreigners, supposedly excluded from the commerce of the Indies, traded in one way or another – smuggling, using native agents, becoming naturalized, or simply paying for the privilege. Provided they were not too obtrusive Dutch, French and (after the peace of 1604) even English merchants were tolerated. The Portuguese, often crypto-Jews, were seemingly everywhere. They settled in Mexico City, Lima and Cartagena; openly traded to Vera Cruz even during Portugal's struggle for independence from Spain; and were the main agents in a clandestine commerce linking Pacific America to Europe and Africa through Brazil and the Río de la Plata (cf. pp. 246, 249–50, 365).

Nevertheless the system was effective enough to induce the usual difficulties of a capricious monopoly. Convoys caused congestion and delay in the ports of arrival and departure. Their movements, through the hazards of war and nature, were unpredictable – the return from the Americas taking anything from eight to forty-four weeks – trade consequently erratic, and ships commonly either half-empty or overloaded. The late arrival of the Indies fleet in Spain deprived merchants of the capital needed to assemble cargoes for the outgoing convoy, so diminishing the already inadequate flow of goods to the colonies, and driving settlers, who in any case required little encouragement, into dealings with smugglers. Yet all this was no monument to Iberian folly. The annual volume of Atlantic traffic *c.*1600 might not have amounted to more than 1 per cent of that of the Dutch to the Baltic, and the distances sailed were not those of Portuguese Indiamen (cf. pp. 271–2 and 378). The round trip none the less took at least fourteen months, and involved a larger amount of tonnage than did the *carreira* – about 70 000t a year at its peak. It also entailed the inevitable high rate of loss and wastage, averaging something like 30 per cent of the ships engaged annually. Yet the essential task of carrying the riches of the Americas to Europe was in general successfully accomplished. The English captured occasional vessels in the late sixteenth century, but not until 1628 did the Dutch take the Mexico ships, and only in 1656–7 did almost the whole Indies fleet fall into English hands.[31] The story was much the same in the Pacific. Entrepôts were established, routes ordained, but contraband – the very word is Spanish – flourished. Protestant raids in the late sixteenth and early seventeenth centuries led to some fortification of the Isthmus and elsewhere, and to the basing of a squadron of galleons at Callao for the carriage of silver and the defence of local shipping. Even so, the Dutch found the town as ill-defended in 1615 as had Drake in 1579, and smuggling continued unabated. Yet though English and Dutch seamen might enter the Pacific from the South Atlantic, causing momentary alarm, they did little serious damage, and secured no permanent footholds on the western coast of the Americas.

To control, exploit and defend its overseas possessions, Spain created an imposing imperial administration. Many of its features recalled earlier Aragonese colonial experience, and many were reminiscent of, and like as not derived from, institutions and practices already employed in the government of the empires of Venice, Genoa and

7   Mexico and the West Indies *c.*1600

Portugal (cf. pp. 120, 209, 269). Yet in sheer scale, and for a time in the remarkable dedication of its officials, it was of an order and nature unparalleled since imperial Rome. Colonial trade and maritime affairs were entrusted, as in Genoa and Portugal, to a special department, the *Casa de la Contratacíon*, set up in 1503, probably under Genoese inspiration. Here every cargo and ship to or from the Indies was supposedly registered. In addition the *Casa* came to exercise civil and criminal jurisdiction in maritime and commercial matters, besides developing a widely admired navigational school which trained and licensed pilots, recorded the progress of geographical discovery, and like its Portuguese counterpart produced and corrected a master map (cf. pp. 276, 279). Imperial questions themselves were, except in moments of crisis, handled by what eventually (1524) emerged as the Council of the Indies (*Consejo Real y Supremo de las Indias*), one of the many such bodies which, subordinate to the king, governed the ever-growing Habsburg domains in the 1500s. Its members, professional jurists, often with overseas experience, corporately held, under the crown, supreme authority in the colonies, debating, drafting and issuing legislation, nominating to offices within the royal patronage, investigating the behaviour of incumbents. Later, as the volume of business increased, many of these functions were delegated to other specially created bodies.

Overseas, after the short-lived episode of the hereditary and feudal concessions to Columbus, and some experiment with royal governors, viceroyalties were established (1535, 1543) in Mexico (New Spain) and Peru (New Castile). The office, long familiar in the Spanish kingdoms, and already used by the Portuguese in Asia, met the obvious need for some overall authority besides providing a suitably imposing focus for Indian loyalty, and a definitive stop to *conquistador* ambition (cf. pp. 321–2). Viceroys were usually aristocrats, appointed always at the royal will, and holding office for six years as a rule. Inevitably some were incompetent, but many were of outstanding ability, devoting the best part of their lives to imperial service. With palace, court and guard their style was impressive, and their powers extensive. They distributed posts and favours to friends and relatives, and ruling months, not to say years, removed from royal surveillance, they could adapt instructions and legislation as they saw fit. But no more than any Venetian proconsul could they aspire, even had they wished, to independence. They could raise no army to speak of, since unmartial creoles were unwilling to serve, yet resisted the introduction of peninsula troops. Nor could they dispense money on their own initiative. In civil matters the authority of subordinate provincial governors had to be respected, and in all difficulties viceroys had to consult, not to say contend with, the local *audiencia*. Appeal courts in Castile, these tribunals were introduced early into the Americas to restrain the excesses of conquerors and to adjudicate between inchoate jurisdictions. In so congenial an atmosphere they quickly grew in numbers and power. Those of the viceregal capitals shared, or usurped, viceregal authority. Corporate bodies, with long-serving and influential members (some destined for the Council of the Indies), grandees were no more than equals in their eyes. The remaining *audiencias* were in some degree subject to one or other of the viceroyalties, but all were supreme courts of appeal within their territories, all exercised extensive powers of inquiry and all, with admittedly varying enthusiasm, ensured the royal dues were collected and watched over the well-being of the Indians. Thus the crown devolved authority but not power. Viceroys were restrained by *audiencias*, *audiencias* by viceroys, and both by the separation of the colonial treasuries – which collected royal revenues in each province, and paid all official salaries – from the rest of the administration. And alongside, and frequently in conflict with the secular government, was that massive instrument of the king's will, the imperial church.

At the basis of this ingeniously balanced hierarchy was a network of local officers, larger and more complex than in any other empire, ranging from magistrates with judicial, administrative and even legislative responsibilities, to those *corregidores* who in 1565 were set over Indian communities. Everywhere were towns and cities governed by assemblies (*cabildos*) of justices (*alcaldes*) and councillors (*regidores*). But here again power lay elsewhere. Royal officers presided over town councils, which by viceregal pressure, co-option and the sale of office were converted to quiescent hereditary oligarchies. Civic representatives could only meet with express royal consent, and their attempts to develop municipal assemblies were effectively quashed by kings embittered

8 The Iberian empires in South America c. 1600

by experience of the ambitions of the cities of Castile and the Netherlands. Amerindians were required to live in similar fashion. Where, as in Mexico and Peru, they were accustomed to urban life, Indian *cabildos* appeared, with elected Indian officers. They issued orders, discharged judicial functions, and recorded their business in the vernacular. But as the indigenous population declined, and since Indian officials were responsible to the Spaniards for the tribute and labour of their compatriots, and were thus particularly exposed to European pressure, willingness to serve soon dwindled. Elsewhere, as amongst the Pueblo (i.e. village-dwelling) Indians of the Río Grande, and in the Philippines, there were attempts to modify native institutions to some approximation to Spanish forms, whilst in many places scattered families and communities were forcibly congregated into townships. This was the fate of about one-and-a-half million Peruvians in the sixteenth century, and of some 250,000 Mexicans between 1602 and 1605 alone.

Yet often as not the royal will was ignored or imperfectly implemented. The Spanish kingdoms, with their immense secular and ecclesiastical commitments, could not long provide or pay an administration of the size, quality and dedication required for the effective government of so vast an empire. Slow and uncertain communications meant its close supervision was impossible, besides aggravating all the inherent defects of a legalistic bureaucracy – the leisurely accumulation and annotation of evidence; procedural nicety; the evasion of decision and responsibility. Furthermore, to raise money, to placate postulants for favour, and to ensure the discharge of functions beyond the capability of the state, offices were farmed, sold or granted to private persons. One consequence of this generally accepted expedient was further to acerbate friction between Spaniards and the creoles who were largely excluded from such posts in the Americas. Another was that appointees, eager to reimburse themselves, were irresponsible and corrupt, whilst many officials who began honest came to see the error of their ways. Antonio de Morga, once a zealous servant of the Habsburgs in Manila, arrived to become president of the *audiencia* of Quito (1615) with a cargo of smuggled goods, set himself up with a young mistress, and opened a casino in his office. Left to their own devices, those in charge of Indians – humble and uncomplaining – were able to perpetrate massive frauds. In the Americas trade the appraisal of goods for taxation at Seville became purely nominal, and though emigration to the Indies was supposedly restricted to inhabitants of the Spanish kingdoms and those licensed by the crown, people of every sort nevertheless settled there, from humble Jewish shopkeepers to representatives of major European commercial houses.

Even so, Spanish imperial government worked. In its early years it was flexible and adaptable, retaining wherever possible – as did the Portuguese – indigenous political and social practices (cf. pp. oo–o). The succession of faithful (and converted) tribal chiefs was recognized, and their authority ostentatiously confirmed. They were given coats of arms and grandiose names, declared to rule 'by just and legitimate right and title' and allowed to ride horses and carry European weapons. In exchange they raised troops, fought 'unpacified' natives, collected tribute and ensured the loyalty of their peoples. But the real strength of Spain's imperial bureaucracy in its heyday in the sixteenth century lay in its very nature. It attracted, like the missions, many outstanding men. The majority were lawyers, ranging from colonial rural magistrates to the magnates of the Council of the Indies. Hence the general obsession with formalities and written opinions. But hence, too, from a country engulfed in the Renaissance resurgence of Roman law, a desire for just and ethical rule, and an intense professional spirit and corporate loyalty.

But no lawyer, and no ruler with the experience of a Habsburg, would expect virtue to flourish unaided, and as in the empire of Venice there were sustained attempts to stimulate the honesty and efficiency of officials (cf. p. 120). Viceroys and members of *audiencias* were forbidden (1575) – as were the lower ranks later – to marry within their jurisdictions, or to become in any other way vulnerable to local pressures. But royal officers made especially desirable husbands for creole ladies, lifting them to the top of the social hierarchy, and the legislation, as its reiteration shows, was ineffective. Besides law and exhortation there was – also as in Venice – inspection and investigation. In inquests ever more extensive – 200 heads in 1567, 355 in 1605 – the crown inquired into every aspect of colonial life. Reports of official neglect or inefficiency were investigated in the *visita*, and all, viceroys included, retiring or suspended from duty, accounted for the discharge of their office.

This remarkable administration closely resembled that which later enforced the last half century of British rule in India. Both restricted high office to Europeans, employed an élite of university graduates, and were inspired by a sense of imperial mission. With the colonial regime of Aviz Portugal there was a more immediate affinity. The two countries alike created special central offices to handle imperial affairs, set up ambitious commercial monopolies, and like Genoa were obliged to alienate power and influence to private persons or bodies. With Venice the parallel is closer still. Both states shared a common Roman and medieval heritage, and applied to colonial government high classical ideals enforced by techniques of inspection and inquiry long known in the government of the medieval church (cf. pp. 120ff., 210). Spain's administrative short-comings are self-evident. Nevertheless royal policies were in some measure enforced, much of the wealth of the Indies was at the disposal of Spain's rulers, and their major European rivals were effectively excluded from the Spanish Americas.

VI *Spaniard and Indian*

All this, however, brought no comfort to native Amerindians, exposed, like no other non-European peoples, to the full force of invaders unimpeded by climate, disease or powerful states and cultures. The gentle and inoffensive Arawaks of the Greater Antilles had been wiped out by the 1540s. In Mexico, whose thronged towns and villages had amazed the conquerors, a population of about 27,000,000 in 1519 had fallen to little over 1,000,000 by *c.* 1600, and that of Peru from some 7,000,000 to about 1,750,000 in roughly the same time. In short, in an unequalled record of genocide, the Spaniards had destroyed about 90 per cent of their new subjects in the course of a century. This they had in part accomplished, as a wide body of testimony confirms, by what a royal official described as 'unheard of cruelties and tortures'. Yet Spaniards were rarely psychopaths. That Indians should give tribute and service to their masters seemed only proper, just as most Europeans accepted that primitive peoples had to be 'civilized', and prepared for Christianity by accustoming them to the drudgery demanded of peasants in the homeland. So, with devastating effect, the pattern of life of whole societies was destroyed (cf. pp. 325, 348). In the West Indies colonists dressed, fed, and freed their Taino women from work, only to find that unable to adapt to new circumstances they declined and died. Amerindians, male and female, unused to such labour, were set to pan for alluvial gold in the islands. As a result their reproductive cycle was disrupted, for in lands without domestic animals to provide milk, children were weaned late and died if separated from their mothers. At the same time agriculture was deprived of essential labour, and crops damaged or consumed by European livestock, wild or herded, wandering at will (see pp. 323–4). Nutriment accordingly deteriorated, resistance to disease weakened and people starved.

Much the same happened in the more advanced mainland states, where the Spaniards created a society resting on Negro and Indian backs. Populations were arbitrarily moved from one climatic zone to another, and scattered communities forcibly congregated. The rendering of tribute and labour were well-established features of the Aztec and Inca empires, but Spanish demands were more extensive, more ruthlessly exacted, and exacted for the benefit of a growing European community from a rapidly dwindling native populace. Indians were expected to provide commodities – even beds and linen in Mexico – unknown or unobtainable. They had to obey with alacrity orders which on occasions reduced them to demolishing their own houses to supply the necessary materials and they had to undertake brutally arduous and unaccustomed toil in anything from plantation agriculture to mining (see pp. 325, 333). To these tribulations were added the demands of tribal chiefs, no longer restrained by Aztec or Inca authority, and Spanish destruction or disruption of an agriculture which only by assiduous care could support the existing population.

Yet not only the ill-treated died, but cherished native mistresses, and inhabitants of regions, such as the coastal lowlands of Mexico, barely touched by Europeans. Here, as elsewhere, societies which had evolved in isolation had no resistance to those endemic diseases of the white man to which Europeans had developed some immunity (cf. pp. 248 and 451). What Spaniards baldly described as 'plague' – in fact smallpox, typhus, measles, influenza – killed Amerindians by the million. 'They ail', Carletti recorded in Mexico, 'bleed from the nose and fall dead.' Simultaneously indigenous civilizations disintegrated, as did with awful inevitability all less-advanced cultures, under European pressure (cf. pp. 248 and 451). Without the restraints of the old imperial governments, and encouraged by Spanish willingness to profit from such cravings, there was an upsurge in drug-taking (as with *coca* in Peru) and drinking, which now included Spanish wines, for which, as was said, 'Indians will sell their wives and children'.[32] To escape the consequences of defeat, people fled – some Filipinos as far as the Coromandel coast of India – or killed themselves. In Mexico men 'sought to prevent the conception, or to cause the miscarriage, of their women', ceased to procreate, and sank into idleness. These views of a sympathetic Spanish official may be overdramatic, but they catch clearly enough the abject despair of defeat and failure.

Some peoples were irretrievably destroyed. Those of the Andes were saved by their inaccessibility, whilst in Mexico royal policy allowed the survival under Indian rule of Indian-speaking villages, the basis of eventual demographic recovery. But there was no recovery of the once vigorous indigenous civilizations, deprived of their natural patrons by the destruction of the imperial families and the decline or hispanization of the surviving aristocracies. Without their support, and oppressed by superior European cultural techniques and the hostility of the Spanish church and state, the most distinctive indigenous arts died. Great vernacular buildings remained, but were not renewed or repaired. Skills such as manuscript painting and feather design had disappeared from Mexico by the early 1600s, and only at the base of society, tenacious here as everywhere, did simpler cultural traditions survive. Yet as in any conquest not all the vanquished were losers. The chaos following the fall of the Aztecs allowed the emergence of a new Indian ruling class in Mexico, composed of erstwhile tribal chiefs and upstart commoners. Aping Spanish ways, collaborating with the victors, its members became entrepreneurs or men of property, and the agents of Spanish control of their compatriots. As the nature of the American economy changed, other Amerindians worked for Spanish wages. Employed as estate hands, mining technicians, urban clerks and craftsmen, they too dressed and behaved in Spanish fashion, taking to crime when nothing else suitable offered, and wearing their hair long to signify independence (cf. pp. 322, 325). Indians other than the most primitive usually welcomed, and presumably benefited from, new styles of clothing – shirts, trousers, hats, blankets. Their houses came to be better roofed, Iberian fashion, with tiles, and the more efficient ox-drawn plough from Spain in some measure replaced the hoe. The diet of the fortunate was enriched and variegated by the flesh of European animals – also providers of milk for infants – and by that mass of cereals, fruits and vegetables introduced by the Spaniards, with which, it was complacently observed, 'the Indies have been better repaid than in anything else' (cf. pp. 323–4).

But there were more fundamental interactions of peoples and economies. Spaniards, like most other European expatriates, were unwilling to forgo the consolations of native women. Indeed there were for a time lofty royal hopes – very different from the racial views of the Portuguese crown – that Spanish subjects and Arawak islanders would marry 'freely and without co-ercion' (1501) (cf. p. 266). Once, however, the full impact of European presence was appreciated, royal policy was to keep Spaniards and

Amerindians apart. In Mexico towns designated as Indian were enveloped in protective institutions, and Indian communities, from which Europeans were prohibited, were encouraged to practice, after suitable missionary modification, their traditional ways. But the fusion of races, begun with the conquest, continued all the same. Indian women might be too malodorous and Asiatic-looking for some tastes, but that they were often pretty was widely agreed. They were, moreover, there for the taking, and like their Brazilian sisters 'neither resisted nor contradicted immodesty should those with any power over them demand it'. Hence there was engendered a sizeable *mestizo* population, every degree of racial mix defined in a vocabulary of prejudice as rich as that of the Portuguese (cf. p. 251). But it is a population not easily counted, since its members were known as 'Spaniard' or 'Indian' according to how and where they lived. From the union of *conquistadores* with aristocratic Inca and Aztec ladies there sprang a generation of *mestizos* as spirited as any Brazilian Paulista (see pp. 249, 331). The legitimate were often, in the early years, absorbed into Creole society to strengthen Spanish presence, as were *mestiza* girls, protected by Spanish chivalry and needed to fill the shortage of white women. Such, however, were the restrictions soon imposed on *mestizos* in a culture increasingly obsessed with purity of blood, as to reduce those of Peru to plotting revolt (1567). Furthermore, since Spaniards, like Portuguese, and for the same reasons, were unwilling to marry their Indian mistresses, *mestizo* meant illegitimacy and inferiority (cf. p. 251). Those of mixed Spanish and Indian parentage were, it was allowed, rational, unlike mulattos and *zambos* (see p. 353), but were not good enough for public office. Some became craftsmen, secular clergy or officials in Indian villages. But many, obliged to marry Indian or *mestiza* girls, sank down the social scale, Natural selection reinforced human prejudice. In temperate zones, where European settlement was densest, *mestizos* of dominant European traits were most numerous. In harder climates, where Spaniards were fewer, those of predominantly indigenous characteristics were common. With European hegemony so clearly established, and with the European population so rapidly increasing, *mestizos* could become at best an intermarrying middle class of farmers, traders and clerks, whilst large numbers had no alternative but to live off the Indians.

There were other radical demographic changes. Within the Americas whole peoples were bodily transplanted. From Europe there arrived, royal edicts notwithstanding, Jews and crypto-Jews. The Manila galleons brought in Filipinos, Indonesians, Japanese and Chinese, and from Africa there were massive imports of slaves (cf. pp. 328, 333). Despite the crown's efforts to reduce Negroes to a separate caste, African and mulatta girls – titillating in jewels and Iberian finery – were as irresistable to Spanish as to Portuguese expatriates. From them colonists sired such progenies that by 1650 mulattos accounted for over 2 per cent of the population of the Indies (see pp. 334–5). Many remained, like their mothers, slaves. Some succeeded as artisans, becoming free and employing Negro, Indian and even Spanish apprentices. The most ambitious, in a society ever more convinced that black was inferior – seventeenth-century Spaniards debating the likelihood of creoles turning dark-skinned and degenerate – sought to 'whiten' themselves by ardently supporting the *status quo* and zealously serving Europeans (cf. p. 255). Similarly, though crown and church endeavoured to keep Indians and Africans apart, Negroes mated with appreciative indigenous women to produce those singularly unfortunate *zambos*. As the offspring of free Indian females they were in law themselves free. But if they claimed to be Indians they became subject to demands for tribute and labour, whilst if they claimed to be Africans they were forced into the racial group most despised by Europeans.

The culture of the self-contained and victorious white society of Spanish America was far less susceptible to indigenous influences than was that of the polyglot ruling class of Portuguese Brazil. Amerindian craftsmen might, like their oriental counterparts, embellish colonial architecture with exotic ornament, but to most creoles 'Indian' was the contemptuous generic for all things and persons non-Spanish in appearance or behaviour (cf. p. 290). On native cultures the impact of a triumphant Spain was inevitably more extensive. Co-operative tribal chiefs and some favoured survivors of the Indian imperial dynasties became, like Don Pedro Enrique Moctezuma, completely hispanized. In the post-conquest years descendants of the Inca and Aztec royal houses were successfully encouraged to write the histories of their peoples, and in Mexico the missions educated young aristocrats as European gentlemen. Hence there was produced the celebrated *Badianus Herbal* (1552), a systematic catalogue of Mexican plants classified in a European tradition, but depicted in Indian style, and with the vernacular glosses of one learned native translated into Latin by another. Other cultural fusions were curious rather than significant, with, for instance, Indian notaries in Mexico writing a Spanish which employed Aztec syntax and stylisms. More commonly indigenous peoples were taught, or acquired, some European skill. Many learned, as in other empires, to use and manufacture European weapons. To meet the demands of the expanding American market of the sixteenth century Indians were apprenticed to Spanish masters, and native craftsmen encouraged to produce European-style goods. Towns and cities soon had groups of Spanish-speaking Indian artisans, able to undertake 'any trade or craft', and who, by working alongside Negro, *mestizo* and Spanish colleagues, were integrated into a genuinely multi-racial Mexican society. At a lower level primitive nomads in northern Mexico, having acquired a taste for European beef, became under missionary guidance pastoral farmers, whilst on the remotest imperial frontiers tribesmen of the Argentinian pampas eventually took to the horse for hunting.

Even so, the cultural impact of Spain in America was modest. Manifestly European cities, schools, churches and universities adorned the continent, but only a relatively small part of it, and for the benefit of Spaniards living in a new Spain. The Spanish tongue, which scholars hoped would exercise that same civilizing and unifying role in the Americas as Latin in the Roman empire, made little headway in the countryside since no formal education was provided for the Indians. Like any other imperial language it penetrated along trade routes, and by 1600 Atjeh had Spanish-speaking Chinese merchants.[33] It was used, too, by Amerindians in close and regular contact with Spaniards – loyal chiefs, estate labourers, native mistresses, urban artisans. Yet few of these gave up their own languages, just as few others cultivated European crops, raised European livestock, or ceased to practise traditional arts and crafts, whatever Spanish fashions and usages they might adopt. Many Indians were, through climate or geography, beyond Spanish reach, and the rest, as far as most colonists were concerned were there to work, not to be improved.

Nevertheless the Spanish church brought the best part of the continent within the bounds of Christendom in a missionary effort comparable to the conversion of barbarian Europe or indeed the empire of Rome. More remarkably still, Spain, to an even lesser degree than Portugal, had no tradition of such endeavour, with the insignificant exception of the Christianization of the Canaries. In the *reconquista* Moors who accepted Spanish rule and paid Spanish dues were left to practice their own religion and to occupy their own privileged quarters in towns.[34] The reputation of the Spanish secular church was of the worst. Its dignitaries, according to Cortés, if allowed into Mexico, would merely devote themselves to high living and the accumulation of wealth for the benefit of their relatives and illegitimate offspring. And if Christian enthusiasm was aroused by the fall of Granada, it made little mark on the early voyages. There was no expectation, as with the Portuguese, of meeting fellow Christians, and few attempts by commanders to convert the peoples they encountered.

The spiritual conquest of the Americas was, like that of Asia, the work of the regular Orders, though with the Jesuits initially less prominent than the Franciscans and Dominicans (cf. pp. 285ff.). Unlike the cosmopolitan Portuguese missions, those of Spain, able to tap far greater resources in manpower, were almost exclusively Spanish, their Christian fervour reinforced by national ardour. The recently reformed Orders of friars were inspired by an admixture of millenarianism – greatly strengthened by Italian influences in the late fifteenth century – Renaissance classicism, and Erasmian humanism (cf. pp. 215, 281). Classical views on 'noble savages' combined with deep Christian compassion led the friars to attempt to preserve the Indians from contamination by European decadence, so that they might be purified and reformed to achieve their potential for greatness. Already in 1509 the Dominicans were in Hispaniola, outraging the settlers with their denunciations of the 'cruel and horrible servitude' they had imposed on the native population. The Franciscans began their labours in Mexico in 1524, and by the end of the century 2200 of their Order, together with 1670 Dominicans, 470 Austins, 300 Mercedarians and 350 Jesuits had left Spain for the Americas.

With the same fortitude and determination as the *conquistadores* the friars, barefoot and unarmed, entered Indian lands conquered and unconquered alike. Many endured formidable hardships, struggling against the machinations of witchdoctors and the blandishments of 'the fairest and most seductive women', and many were martyred. In the late 1530s the aging Apostle of the Indies, Bartolomé de las Casas, and some fellow Dominicans successfully – though briefly – introduced Christianity by peaceful means into parts of Guatemala which had resisted military conquest. Such patience was by no means universal, and where opposition was stubborn force was used. Even so, the conversion was in general undertaken with exuberant idealism and remarkable ingenuity until the mid-1500s. Spaniards and Indians were to live and pray together, and even the wants of Negro slaves would be ministered to. In Mexico – more intensively worked than the remoter Peru – European education was to produce a class of well-born and well-bred Christian Indians. Also in Mexico, the learned Vasco de Quiroga, fortified by his reading of Lucian on the Age of Gold, attempted to segregate those he identified as living in pristine innocence from pernicious influences by housing them in communities modelled on the precepts of More's *Utopia*. Franciscans and Jesuits congregated the nomadic inhabitants of the frontiers, where there was little to attract Spanish colonists, into settlements like those of the missions in Brazil. In California and Texas some of these became elaborate economic complexes, worked by Christian natives under the supervision of the fathers, where Indians were taught European skills and accustomed to the habit of regular toil. The most extensive were those of the Jesuits, who in Paraguay established in 1604 what was soon virtually an independent state comprising 100 000 Indians, and by 1641 powerful enough to defeat the attacks of Brazilian slavers.

All this was accomplished in the face of formidable difficulties. The conversions effected by *conquistador* brutality – torture, burnings, hangings – created a hostility intensified by subsequent *encomendero* behaviour. Many Amerindians were hostile primitive nomads, some inhabiting regions as climatically intolerable to white men as tropical Africa. The continent possessed a bewildering variety of tongues, which, to be fully understood by Europeans, had to be converted from oral to written languages. But in America, as nowhere else on any scale, Europeans were conquerors, enjoying the prestige of victory, and with the state so manifestly supporting the church little could stand in the way of the missions. They were not confronted, as in India and China, by mature civilizations and complex and subtle theologies (cf. pp. 285–9). Instead they met the meek and submissive subjects of the Incas, accustomed to convents, temples and a paternalistic priesthood, and the equally docile inhabitants of the Aztec lands, to whom penance, fasting and even – to the amazement of the Spaniards – the cross and the idea of a second coming were familiar. Nor were converts only attracted by what Christianity offered them in the next world, for as some astute Mexican tribal chiefs realized, it could provide a new justification for their authority after the fall of the old gods. But the success of the missions stemmed primarily from the energy, idealism and determination they absorbed from the vigorous and ebullient civilization of the Spain of Charles V. Such qualities can, however, by their very nature rarely endure long. Already in 1562 it was thought that only one-third of the indigenous Christians of Mexico City were any longer receiving the sacraments. Even on the frontiers, whose dangers continued to attract some of the ablest missionaries, disciples rebelled or fled, whilst elsewhere the noble ideals of the friars slid into bizarre fantasy and millenarian heresy. Challenge and euphoria gave way to routine and disillusion; dazzling new prospects opened in Asia; the quality and reputation of the Orders declined. 'It is', a distinguished royal servant sourly remarked in the late 1500s, 'as safe to loose a stallion among a herd of mares as to let a friar out among the Indian women.' As in the east, the Orders quarrelled amongst themselves, and turned their talents – the Jesuits especially – to business (cf. pp. 286–8). They operated ships, used Indian labour to produce textiles, and by 1600 owned about one-third of the real estate in Mexico. Their message became less persuasive in Indian ears as they accepted *encomiendas*, and employed forced labour, very often to build those magnificent convents in which they lived in the grandest style. Indian enthusiasm for Christianity, once kindled by ambitious and co-operative chiefs, cooled as their power declined, and as it became clear that the new religion offered no help against the ravages of disease, and that non-whites, scorned, humiliated and excluded from the priesthood, were not considered full Christians. And whatever the missions might preach, and for a time practise, was, as always, flagrantly contradicted by the behaviour of the majority of European colonists (cf. pp. 251, 288, 352).

Equally depressing was the general record of the secular church, whose clergy, according to a sixteenth-century viceroy of Peru, devoted such energies as they could spare from women to gambling and trade. Sustained by a rapidly acquired and massive endowment, the church raised sumptuous buildings, supported its hierarchy in luxury, and staged ceremonies and spectacles of an opulence and splendour soon proverbial. Priests owned property, bred horses, and were active in every branch of trade and speculation, whilst in seventeenth-century Mexico an enterprising archbishop set up a meat store next door to his palace. Most parochial clergy exacted illegal fees for baptism and confession from their flocks. Others favoured more direct methods. The vicar of Popayán (Mexico) ransacked native tombs in his parish for buried treasure – whereas other priests buried men, it was said, he resurrected them – and the archbishop of Cuzco complained (1636) of Indian reluctance to reveal the whereabouts of gold and silver 'even if put to death'. And no more than at any other time did church, state and Christian society long present neophytes with the edifying spectacle of united endeavour (cf. pp. 285ff.). The Orders denounced the colonists, and sought to segregate the Indians from them; the colonists denounced the greed, idleness and ostentation of the Orders, and sought to have the Indians where they could best be used. Within the Orders peninsular and American-born Spaniards quarrelled over preferment. The imperial administration suspected, and not without reason, that the missions aspired to independence, theocracy or worse; zealous friars saw royal bureaucrats as unimaginative procrastinators deluded by 'two pennyworth of the law of Salamanca'. The age-old antipathies between seculars and regulars remained as strong as ever. In the post-conquest decades the Orders had been highly favoured by the crown, providing 108 out of 171 bishops appointed to the Indies before 1600. Initially they had been freed, in the areas of their mission, from episcopal authority, and allowed to discharge parochial functions normally the prerogative of secular priests. But from the mid-1500s they saw themselves hindered and oppressed, since the secular church endeavoured to take over their parishes, to oblige Indians to attend parish church and not mission chapel, and to subject all clergy to episcopal control, as the decrees of the reforming councils of the church required. Such questions were the subject of acrimonious erudite exchanges between bishop Palafox and the Jesuits in mid-seventeenth century Mexico, whilst in an equally venerable, but less edifying tradition of the church militant, mobs of rival clergy and their supporters did battle.

By the very nature of the evidence such clashes probably now loom larger than they did in life, and whatever its troubles the achievement of the Spanish church was impressive and largely enduring. The Philippines were converted, and from there the missions penetrated to China, Cambodia and Japan (cf. p. 287). An area of the Americas about twenty times the size of Spain became Catholic, with rival Christian creeds excluded. Undesirable native practices – incest, polygamy, bare legs and bosoms, cannibalism, human sacrifice – were checked, if not eradicated. Pagan priesthoods, shrines and temples were destroyed, marriage was instituted and much of the continent was brought within the organizational framework of the Catholic church. Amerindians accepted with an admixture of fatalism and enthusiasm such spectacular manifestations of Christianity as images, processions and the burning of heretics. Indeed the friars urged that a colourful, not to say theatrical, religion was needed 'to redeem them and infuse in them a deeper love for the faith'. Hence there developed a distinctive Latin American Catholicism, with its own music, dances and rich accretion of Indo-European magic and witchcraft. To what extent its adherents, like many of the missions' converts in other continents, were Christian is a moot point. Churches were built, as in the conversion of medieval Europe, on the sites of pagan shrines; peoples were allowed to observe, it was reported from the Philippines, 'such of their old heathen customs as were not contrary to natural law', which meant that pagan worship continued. Native tenacity and incomprehension combined with shortcomings in guidance and instruction to create, in America as elsewhere, a curious syncretic Catholicism, in which Christianity was amalgamated with, or became complementary to, the old faiths, or even turned to downright blasphemous nonsense. God, the villagers of Oxtchuc (Mexico) explained to a visitor some years ago, had many sons, of whom Thomas was the best and Christ the worst. In his malevolence Christ sought to destroy the world, only to be thwarted by the vigilant Thomas, who removed his magic coat as he lay in a drunken stupor.

And such was the true impact of Spain. A white society was established in the Americas. Some primitive peoples were wiped out, the native populations almost everywhere drastically reduced. But in many parts of the continent Spanish influence was modest or negligible. In the heartlands of the empire indigenous states were overthrown, the ruling classes and the most notable expressions of native culture eradicated. But for the survivors life though modified by Spanish custom and belief, and lived in societies more fragmented, remained essentially Indian.

VII   *From Cortés to Quixote*

Conquests of a scale unknown since Antiquity produced in Spain all the usual features of imperial success. Castilian pride became Castilian arrogance. By and large – though there were some views and deeds to the contrary – Africans were assumed to be predestined slaves, and the defeated and passive Amerindians, the least Spanish of any people, dismissed as 'weak and imbecile'. The redoubtable Japanese indeed elicited respect, and from the intermarriage of Spanish men with Chinese women there would spring, thought a learned Jesuit in the late sixteenth century, a race of superior mortals. Even so, some of Philip II's soldiers and clergy in Manila regarded the conquest of China as no great matter for Spanish arms. Like the Portuguese the Spaniards came to believe themselves God's chosen instrument to subjugate and convert the world. Conflict with the pagans, infidels and heretics who everywhere threatened Spanish safety or obstructed Spanish ambitions bred that bigotry and intolerance which characterized Iberia from the mid-1500s, and intensified the xenophobia produced by the survival in the peninsula of a large and unassimilated Moorish minority.

Spain was not lifted, like Portugal, from obscurity and insignificance by empire. Already before the triumphs of the *conquistadores* she was western Europe's major power, and the home, according to German Protestants, of 'beastly tyranny'. By the end of the century Spain had apparently limitless treasure to command, and not only most of Europe but most of the known world in her grasp. To her enemies she was an object of terror, hatred and revulsion, from whom, the Dutch informed Venice (1635) only slavery 'even more wretched than that of the Indians' could be expected. Attempts to forestall the manifestations of such hostility, and to protect such interests as the flow of silver from the Americas, brought new emphases in Spanish policy, turning the country to the west and to the Atlantic. Interest in North Africa, lively in the early 1500s, flagged, allowing the emergence of Moslem pirate states, soon the allies of Spain's Protestant enemies. Yet even if by 1585 the Atlantic was of such importance to Spain that there was talk of making Lisbon the imperial capital, there was no weakening in the pursuit of traditional Habsburg ambitions. Philip II sought to make France a Spanish satellite. Spanish rule was defended in Italy, and in the sixteenth century Spain's greatest effort by land was to retain the Habsburg patrimony in the Low Countries, and by sea to defeat the Turks in the Mediterranean and to destroy the Dutch rebels and their English allies in the north (cf. pp. 132–4, 373, 468ff.).

The acquisition and exploitation of overseas possessions enhanced, as in Portugal, royal prestige, and for a time royal power. Jurists demonstrated that in the Indies royal authority was untrammelled. Royal control of the imperial church – in whose affairs, ruled Philip II in 1574, 'none should dare to intrude' – was absolute. New trades were under royal surveillance; new royal commercial monopolies were created; the requirements of oceanic empire stimulated the idea, and occasionally produced the reality, of a state navy. A vast imperial administration extended the scope of royal patronage, and colonial revenues the resources of royal munificence. The empire absorbed ambitions and potentially dangerous subjects, and significantly enough it was those provinces – Valencia, Catalonia and Aragon – whose access to the colonies was most restricted that had the highest crime rates in the sixteenth century.[35] But above all empire meant wealth. Trade to, from and within the Indies was taxed (cf. p. 341). Tribute was imposed on *zambos* (1572) and mulattos (1574) and a sales tax introduced into Mexico and Peru in the late 1500s. The slave trade provided the lump sums paid by *asiento* holders, and the taxes exacted from slavers and levied on the sale and ownership of Africans. Much of this revenue was consumed in the Americas, but from the residue and the one-fifth on precious metals, the crown had an income over which its authority was complete. Its relative importance was not so great as in Portugal – at best it amounted to no more than 20 per cent of annual disposable revenue – and with the Castilian Cortes already in decline it merely confirmed royal freedom from the uncertain generosity of representative assemblies (cf. p. 277). Nor did it dictate Habsburg policy. Spain was at her most bellicose and expansionist in the early 1500s, before there was any appreciable wealth from the Americas; and willing to make terms with England (1604) and Holland (1609) when imports were at their peak, but the country in effect bankrupt (see pp. 325, 369). Even so, the very possession of an income in ready cash, often augmented by impounded private treasure – not to mention Protestant imagination – was a considerable asset, increasing Spain's already formidable reputation and providing security for massive loans. Indeed by the end of the reign of Philip II, with Castile's taxable potential exhausted, it was only American silver that staved off financial disaster.

Whatever else it did for Spain is less certain. Its influx was once thought to have driven up Castilian prices and eventually ruined the country. But Spanish prices and wages had more or less doubled by the mid-1500s, when silver imports were negligible. By the late sixteenth century prices and wages were rising more slowly, and after 1600 actually falling, whereas bullion receipts at Seville reached a peak between 1580 and 1620. Nor is there any paradox here. Rarely, if ever, and then only in Seville, was there a sufficient concentration of American silver in Spain to inflate prices. Much never reached the country at all, and much that did was quickly smuggled out or migrated to foreign bankers to secure or service loans (cf. p. 179). Large sums were transmitted abroad to buy goods demanded in the peninsula and the Indies, so that by the 1560s it was worth pirates lying in wait for English ships returning with 'coin' after delivering cargoes of cloth and grain in Spain. Still more was poured into the Low Countries to pay for Habsburg wars and vain attempts to suppress the revolt of the northern provinces. More again flowed through Iberia to Asia for use in the west's oriental trade, or to be profitably sold in a world where silver was at a premium as the current monetary standard. It was for long the principal means of exchange in Portugal and much of its empire, and by the seventeenth century, initially through war and ultimately through commerce, American silver was increasingly coming into Dutch and English hands (cf. pp. 270, 406, 465ff., 494ff.).

Yet clearly enough empire affected Spain's economy. Conquerors and administrators were enriched, with the Cortés family rising from obscurity to be amongst the wealthiest of Iberian aristocrats, and Hernando Pizarro building the sumptuous Palace of the Conquests at Trujillo, besides leaving a staggering collection of precious objects, money and property in his will (1578). The rich could enjoy the delights of tobacco and chocolate introduced from the Americas, whilst the robes of magnates were adorned with those Cubaguan pearls which still glisten on the dress of Eleanor of Portugal in Titian's portrait. The diet of the less opulent was reinforced by Indian maize – already cultivated in Spain in the mid-1500s – and fish taken off the coasts of West Africa and Newfoundland. Colonial demand stimulated the production of Castilian woollens, Granada silks and Andalusian wines. The need for ships kept the yards of northern Spain and their ancilliary industries busy. But with Seville the monopoly port for the Indies it was the south that prospered whilst the north, further weakened by Protestant attacks on its Low Countries' trade in the second half of the sixteenth century, declined. Thus the Indies sealed Castile's supremacy within Spain, completing that shift of balance from north to south which had begun with the *reconquista*. Andalusia provided the empire with a high proportion of its colonists, with many of the merchants and seamen who controlled the arteries of its commerce, and with its most widely spoken dialect. In the course of the sixteenth century merchants and sailors from northern Spain migrated to Seville and its adjacent ports; the economy of Burgos foundered; and Madrid replaced Valladolid as the capital. Seville, meanwhile, handling the bulk of the registered Indies trade was, like Lisbon, transformed into one of Europe's wealthiest and greatest ports, with its population rising from 49,000 to over 100,000 between 1530 and 1594 (cf. p. 278). The very nature of its commerce – the erratic arrival of silver in a voracious European market; the inadequate provision of goods for an equally voracious American market – combined with its role of entrepôt for cargoes to and from the Indies, made it a centre of speculation and vast profits. Such wealth, together with the large, shifting and cosmopolitan population of a seaport in touch with lands as different as those of the Baltic and the South China Sea brought accusations that Seville was the New Babylon. And perhaps it was. But if money was squandered in vice and high living, it was also spent on beautifying the city with such buildings as its magnificent Hall (1545) and the elegant *Casa de Pilatos*.

But not more than in Portugal was the culture of the mother country fundamentally influenced by the experience of founding, exploiting and governing an overseas empire. Triumphs were celebrated and follies satirized by men of letters. The nature of imperial responsibility was debated, and masses of geographical information were accumulated and plotted. Spanish soldiers, seamen and missionaries wrote, as did their Portuguese contemporaries, of their achievements (cf. p. 280). Many examined and recorded new phenomena with rational curiosity – Cortés himself despatching a party up the volcano Popocatepetl 'to discover the secret of the smoke'. University chairs were established for the study of native languages, and dictionaries of such tongues as the Quechua of Peru compiled. The history and traditions of non-European high cultures were examined, often sympathetically, by learned missionaries and officials, like Alonso de Zorita, the chronicler of Aztec disaster.[36] Enlightenment of this order was, however, both short-lived and far from widespread, and no more than elsewhere was it evidence of a sudden and fundamental change in outlook. Spaniards in Asia might bathe, or sail in junks and sampans. But in the Americas, a self-contained society ruling defeated peoples, they were resolutely unaffected by all things native. If they read at all it was books from, or in the style of, the mother country. In Iberia there was little enthusiasm for the literature produced by the discoveries and conquests. For men of learning there were the classics, law and theology, and for the less demanding the improbabilities of popular romance. With the passage of time Counter-Reformation Spain became, like Portugal, increasingly intolerant and unreceptive, and was moreover enmeshed in urgent domestic and European problems in the century after 1550 – financial crisis; the advance of the Turks in the Mediterranean; the revolt of the Dutch in the north. And as in Portugal where there was rational speculation and impartial factual description, its inspiration was an admixture of classical and Erasmian precept and practical need. Officials surveyed and investigated native societies to establish their potential for labour and tribute, or to determine how they might best be brought to the Christian faith; Francisco de Toledo examined the origins of Inca rule in Peru in the sixteenth century to reach the satisfactory conclusion that Quechua authority was invalid because usurped (cf. pp. 280–2).

It is against this background that the fierce and far-ranging debate that flared up in Castile in the early 1500s on the question of Spain's title to her colonial empire and the rights of its indigenous peoples has to be placed. Famous names – most notably Bartolomé de las Casas – were involved, and some remarkably humane and liberal views expressed. Yet the whole controversy stemmed from a long Iberian tradition of public debate among the religious, and of doubts as to the validity of forced conversions of infidels and pagans, most recently expressed in relation to the fate of the Canarian Guanches in the late 1400s (cf. pp. 279, 301). Indeed the arguments adduced were of venerable ancestry. As in Portugal it was widely accepted that papal grant and confirmation bestowed title, implicit even in the view of Spanish Dominicans that popes could give kings no more than the right to spread Christianity. Some argued, like the Portuguese, that title came from prior possession and the costs entailed, and went on to prove that the Visigoths of medieval Spain had not only ruled North Africa but also conveniently found their way to the Indies (cf. pp. 269, 279). Others derived Spanish authority from the universal lordship exercised by the Holy Roman Emperor, to which office Charles Habsburg was elected in 1519. In the same way, Amerindian rights stood or fell on the word of the church and the tenets of Aristotle and medieval political theory. Papal grant justified the demand (*requerimiento*) initially made of the peoples of the New World that they either accept the authority of church and state or be enslaved. Natural law, medieval thinkers argued, since it was universal, justified the rule of heathen princes and prohibited its overthrow. But this same unity of mankind could likewise vindicate alien intervention in supposed defence of human rights. Similarly if, as las Casas and others maintained, Amerindians were rational, then by Aristotelian reasoning their states were justified. But if, as Sepúlveda believed, they were irrational, 'though not like bears or monkeys completely lacking in reason', the same logic destined them to such restraint as would prevent their reversion to 'primitive and evil ways'.[37] And for those resisting the Christian message the only fate, according to a powerful tradition of the medieval church, was enslavement and the destruction of their societies (cf. p. 288).

Nor should the scope and impact of the debate be overestimated. Condemnations of slavery were nothing new. The Castilian Laws of 1265 branded it as 'evil and despicable', whilst to an Italian humanist of the 1520s it was contrary to the brotherhood of man in Christ. Moreover, in Spain controversy was not about slavery as such, but about the lot of certain South American peoples. Enslavement of Africans had incurred some half-hearted papal disapproval since the mid-1400s. It was denounced by Albornoz in 1573, eventually accepted to be wrong by las Casas, and subsequently condemned by a handful of clergy. But these were voices crying in the wilderness. The traffic in Africans was economically indispensable and accordingly flourished (cf. pp. 255–7). And whatever speculation this and other problems of empire may have stimulated was destroyed by the intolerant Spain of the later Philips, itself very largely the product of imperial experience.

Much the same happened in other fields. The range of knowledge was enormously expanded; new lands, peoples and phenomena were found and recorded. But neither in Spain nor elsewhere was information, however accurate, that clashed with existing preconceptions, assimilated. The main concerns, assumptions and stimuli remained European, and the response of a country to the demands of empire was conditioned by the character of its own society and civilization. Spanish techniques of colonial government were the adaptation and extension of familiar peninsular and European practice. Empire enormously increased Spanish maritime commitments and strength – which in 1580 with that of Portugal added was, at about 250,000t, probably the greatest in Europe. Yet in comparison with the economically more advanced Italians earlier, or equally advanced Dutch later, Spaniards made few significant innovations in the design and operation of ships (see pp. 206 and 425). Their celestial navigation, like much of their cartographical method, they took from Portugal. Carvels and galleons, though modified at their hands, were the creation of others. Then, as difficulties at sea grew, there were thoughts in the mid-1500s of using English craft in the Indies trade, and by

Fig. 14   Spanish carrack, 1592, from an unspecified contemporary
source. The mainyard is lowered to the deck, as was common
practice in storms.

the end of the reign of Philip II warships were being built in the English style.[38]

Ultimately empire was, as always, a crippling burden. To all Spain's problems in
Europe – further exacerbated in the first half of the seventeenth century by economic
disaster, resurgent French power and risings in Catalonia, Portugal and elsewhere –
were added those of protecting her overseas possessions. To France, England and
Holland the Spanish Americas were a magnificent prey for plunder, a splendid market
from which they were wrongly excluded, and the source of Castile's sinister strength.
Spasmodic attacks on Spanish shipping in the eastern Atlantic gave way in the 1530s to
French and English projects to seize the treasure fleet. In 1553 the English had plans to
attack Peru. Two years later the French took Havana, and the following decade were in
Florida (see pp. 438–9). By the 1570s and 1580s, with the seas from the Channel to the
Atlantic swarming with Protestant privateers, Spanish intelligence reported to a
government already believing the Netherlands lost, one impending catastrophe after
another. Aided by the Araucanians the English would take Chile. With the help of

escaped Negro slaves they could 'accomplish any evil deed they may wish', including colonizing the vital Panama Isthmus. Nor, once Drake had appeared in the Pacific (1579), did any of this seem entirely improbable, and worse was to come. English expeditions attacked the Iberian coast (1595–6), and English privateers, who by now had taken the lead from the French, sacked the major Spanish centres in the Caribbean (see pp. 467ff.). By blows too strong to be parried locally, and too swiftly delivered to allow aid to be summoned from Europe, they destroyed the region's commerce and attempted to subvert the colonists, demoralizing many and trading with the rest. And whilst North African corsairs harried Spanish shipping in the Mediterranean and North Atlantic, the French, English and Dutch began, in the early seventeenth century, to settle West Indian islands unoccupied or abandoned by Spain. In this they were soon aided by the weakening, not to say destruction, of Spanish control of the area by the onslaughts of the fleets of the Dutch West India Company, established (1621) specifically to attack the Spanish-Portuguese empire in the Americas and West Africa. Meanwhile the even more formidable Dutch East India Company was destroying Iberian commerce and rule in Asia (see pp. 385ff., 396ff.).

Thus Spain lapsed into that inescapable cycle of empire in which the defence of what had been cheaply and relatively easily acquired became an exorbitantly expensive duty, and one which through dynastic or national pride, and the fear of direr consequences, it was impossible to renounce. In the 1550s Spain had no naval forces to speak of, the emperor confessing his lack of ships 'to scour the seas and protect our subjects and vassals'. Twenty years later, at enormous cost, galleys were simultaneously provided for service in the Caribbean and against the Turk in the Mediterranean. In the 1580s fast and well-armed frigates were introduced for the carriage of American silver, a squadron of powerful royal fighting ships created for the Atlantic, and an oceanic fleet assembled, very largely from private owners. This force was abortively launched against England and Holland in 1588, costing Spain about half her Atlantic tonnage and most of her deepwater seamen (see pp. 468–9). The loss of ships at least was soon made good, and intermittently into the seventeenth century Spain sent both fleets into the Atlantic and smaller forces to the Caribbean. By an admixture of self-help and metropolitan aid imperial defence was organized. Fortification of vital areas of the Indies was begun. Locally built warships appeared in the Pacific; in the Caribbean commercial interloping was held in check in the early 1600s by locally recruited flotillas. Militias were later established in Cuba and Mexico, and a standing army in Chile.

All this demanded men and money which Spain no longer possessed. The Dutch revolt deprived her of the wealth of the northern Netherlands. The Americas supplied less treasure, and of this the royal share declined, dropping from over 10,000,000 *pesos* in 1596–1600 to little more than 600,000 in 1656–60. Privateering and war disrupted the traffic, discouraging merchants who in any case found it increasingly unattractive because of royal seizures of private bullion (cf. p. 341). Nor was there so much silver to be shipped. The deeper and poorer veins which had to be worked once the most easily accessible had been stripped required greater technical skills than the Spaniards possessed, and by the 1630s European merchants in Asia were complaining of the poor silver content of Peruvian coins, and the Habsburg administration of the incompetence and dishonesty of its officials. There was good ore in northern Mexico, but mining amongst wild aboriginals was a risky and expensive business (see p. 313). Royal monopoly ensured that the mercury needed for refining was everywhere costly or unobtainable, whilst food, equipment and labour were universally scarce and dear. Indians were now few, and made fewer by Spanish policies (see pp. 322, 327). The *mita* force for Potosí, decimated by ill-usage, disease and desertion, fell from 81 000 in 1574 to about 10 000 a century later. The survivors, moreover, could buy exemption from service. This encouraged some lessees to live on the resultant income rather than work their mines, and at the same time deprived others of labour. Nor was there any alternative except to pay wages. African slaves were unsuited to mining at such altitudes, besides being prohibitively expensive since monopolist suppliers kept imports down to guarantee themselves high prices (cf. pp. 175–6, 253, 333).

Nevertheless the American economy was far from being in ruins. Peruvian shipyards and ancillary industries prospered in the seventeenth century from the demand for men-of-war for use against the Dutch. Mexican fiscal yields were still rising in the 1630s. More adeptly than the less bureaucratic Portugal, Spain turned colonial affluence to her advantage, obliging the two unwilling viceroyalties to meet the costs of defending the Indies in the early 1600s. But this left less treasure for export and the purchase of goods provided by Spain. And since, through the mother country's economic and maritime difficulties, these were now in short and unpredictable supply, colonial wealth was diverted elsewhere. The entire Atlantic economy thus contracted, and annual sailings between Spain and the Americas which had once stood at 300 or so, were down to a mere 50 in the mid-1600s. Instead, the colonies traded with each other and outside the Seville monopoly (cf. pp. 327–9). Agents of rich Peruvians bought what their masters desired in Europe, leaving Spanish imports unwanted in the Americas. Less opulent Caribbean creoles were meanwhile supplied by a succession of enterprising interlopers – Canary Islanders and Portuguese in the first half of the sixteenth century; French, English and Dutch later.[39] Yet by the mid-1600s the whole American economy was in decline. Privateering and war had already ruined the West Indian colonies, where the sugar industry had failed to survive the sixteenth century. The natural concentration of merchants on the quick and guaranteed profits of the mainland bullion trade starved it of capital and shipping. The destruction of the indigenous peoples deprived it of labour – African slaves being too expensive – and Brazilian competition finally overwhelmed it. In these same years the Mexican silk industry failed in face of cheap Chinese imports, and because of that Iberian hostility to products threatening those of Spain itself and lack of Indian workers which likewise hampered the manufacture of woollens. By mid-seventeenth century Mexican and Peruvian silver production was – for the time – disastrously reduced, provoking in turn contraction in the agrarian economy dependent on mining needs.

All these difficulties government policies aggravated. Colonial industries were discouraged in case economic self-sufficiency should bring political independence. Tobacco production in Venezuela and adjacent lands was prohibited (1606) to prevent sales to interlopers. Bullion smuggling to the Philippines, and the flow of Peruvian wine and silver to Mexico for the purchase of Chinese goods brought in 1634 a ban on trade between the viceroyalties. As a result the Mexican economy was further depressed, whilst in Manila, starved of treasure, attempts to increase taxation led to political crisis and the Spanish massacre of the Chinese community (1639–40). In the Americas, fewer Indians for exploitation combined with a growing mulatto and immigrant population brought widespread vagrancy and disorder. Colonial government in Mexico degenerated into that corruption and inefficiency the Caribbean had long known. Jewish plots were rumoured; creoles were at loggerheads with peninsular Spaniards; friars and viceroys with bishops and creoles. In the first half of the seventeenth century several viceroys more or less lost control of the colony, and efforts to step up taxation drove one from office (1624) and another to predict (1640) popular revolt.

Nevertheless the decline of Spain was neither precipitate nor, like that of Venice and Portugal, marked by substantial losses of colonial territory.[40] The truce of 1609 with the Dutch indeed conceded in effect that they could trade where they wanted.[41] Ternate and Tidore were abandoned in the seventeenth century, there were fears for the Philippines, and islands in the Caribbean were lost (see pp. 386, 440). But nothing more. By and large Spain's colonies were too difficult of access, and too well populated and hispanized to become such easy victims as the isolated coastal and island possessions of Venice and Portugal (cf. pp. 143, 240). Despite enormous burdens, the mother country showed surprising resilience in the course of what, like that of modern Britain, was a lengthy recessional. Inquests in 1575–80 revealed growing population and widespread prosperity. Spaniards of these years wrote with authority on naval architecture, and Spanish yards could still furnish redoubtable naval forces in the early 1600s and vessels which foreign seamen unhesitatingly identified as 'Biskay builte'.[42] Even in 1625 one Spanish port alone had 41 ships and over 1400 men in the Newfoundland fishery, and the Biscayan iron and Basque whaling industries continued to flourish almost till mid-century. None the less decline there was. The northern Netherlands, Portugal and her empire were all lost. Naval control of the Atlantic and even the Caribbean collapsed, and throughout most of the seventeenth century Spain had no force of any consequence in the West Indies, and no more than 20 fighting ships in the Atlantic by the mid-1600s. As with Portugal the material benefits of empire all too clearly went to others, whilst Spaniards, 'like Indians', merely carried, at their own expense, New World treasure to Europe. The Sevillan monopoly was ignored by some foreigners (and Spaniards) and manipulated by others, whilst through privateering and interloping bullion flowed to alien and usually enemy hands. In the early 1500s the combined demands of a growing metropolitan population and new colonial markets had stimulated Spanish industries – woollens, wine, silk, shipping. But not for long. Private vessels were taken for (and commonly lost in) royal service. Naval wars from the

Mediterranean to the Moluccas, involving disasters such as that of 1588, were inordinately costly in ships and men. Huge demands for new and replacement tonnage – with fifty craft under construction for the crown alone in Biscay in 1583–6 – exhausted Spain's resources in shipbuilding materials and led to dependence on those, increasingly costly, of the Baltic. The inflated wages paid in the trans-Atlantic trade denuded other routes of seamen. Royal policy dictated the construction of large, heavy ships, unpopular with merchants who preferred the more numerous, more suitable and less expensive vessels of the Dutch or the English, who in the 1630s could offer freight rates only one-sixth of those of Spanish owners.[43] Castilian arable farming, crippled by taxation, shortage of labour and the traditional bias in favour of stock-raising, contracted, increasing the country's reliance on foreign food, and in its poverty denying a market to such domestic industry as there was. The manufacture of woollen textiles, enmeshed like that of Venice in a rigid guild system, failed to expand with sufficient speed and flexibility. Its prices rose as the quality of its products declined. The Americas produced some cloth themselves, whilst increasingly the domestic and colonial markets were served by the industries of France, England and Holland, using very often raw materials provided by Spain. With the added burden of the cost of more or less incessant wars the country was particularly vulnerable to the general inflation of the sixteenth century – Castilian prices more than quadrupling – and became dependent on, and indeed the prey of, economies less extended and more efficient than its own. High finance was dominated by a succession of German, Italian and Portuguese-Jewish bankers. Grain came from the Hanse and the Dutch. Seaborne commerce passed into the hands of the Hollanders and (in the 1630s) the English (see pp. 63, 179, 203, 381). And whilst Venice in decline drifted into primary production, Spain was to end with virtually nothing of any value to sell, and obliged to pay for everything with decreasingly abundant treasure (see pp. 364–5). Furthermore, to economic ruin war and empire added the destruction of the state they had been so influential in creating. Moribund provincial representative assemblies were revived in the seventeenth century by privileges they bought from the crown. To save or raise money, kings sold office and alienated state powers, with military administration becoming, from the 1580s, a matter for contractors and local authorities. Society was re-feudalized, and whilst Genoese *condottieri* provided galley squadrons, oceanic fleets were supplied by entrepreneurs such as Alvaro de Bazán and the Menéndez clan, equally accustomed to raising and commanding ships or running colonies.

All this reflected an admixture of inherent economic weakness with problems beyond the administrative resources of any early state and downright political ineptitude. After the death in 1598 of Philip II, Spain came into the hands of kings and ministers of unrelieved mediocrity – Philip IV's favourite, Olivares, apart – and a frivolous and irresponsible ruling class converted even more willingly than that of contemporary Venice from public duty to private pleasure. Wealth and manpower far more abundant than that of Portugal was consumed in imperial policies and commitments of impossible grandeur. To sustain these Spain's economy, essentially one of pastoral farming, was too primitive. The country had too few people, and too many – 10 per cent of Castile's population as opposed to 2 per cent of that of France – who, claiming noble birth, would neither work in trade or industry nor submit to being taxed. Even worse, since Spain was no more than a dynastic amalgam of disparate kingdoms and not a union of peoples, it was Castile alone that financed royal ambitions. The discovery of the seemingly limitless treasure of America bred in such a society the not implausible belief that money was wealth. Combined with the long supremacy of Spanish arms, the triumphs of Spanish missions, and the subjection to Spanish whim of thousands of Africans and millions of Indians, it vindicated and intensified the whole martial and aristocratic ethos of Spanish society. To labour was demeaning: gentlemen lived with style, ate without working, devoted themselves to *armas y letras* – to war and to writing. The less bellicose entered the equally unproductive – in the economic sense at least – callings of the church or the bureaucracy.

Such attitudes might found empires, but for colonies to benefit the mother country required it to possess business and technical skills. These, however, were qualities which flourished in tolerant mercantile communities like Holland and Venice, not in beleaguered and increasingly bigoted Iberia. A bad situation was accordingly aggravated by political and economic folly. Jews – important as financiers, artisans and merchants – and those that ever more sensitive noses sniffed out as such, were persecuted,[44] as were the equally valuable descendants of the Moors. In the mid-1500s the import of foreign manufactures was encouraged, and the export of those produced in Spain prohibited, with predictably disastrous results. An enormous burden of taxation, trebling in the first two decades of the reign of Philip II, was laid on Castile alone – the remaining Spanish lands being considered too impoverished and politically inflammable to be troubled – and there only on the poorest section of the country's population. Royal confiscations of private bullion deprived commerce of capital, destroyed business confidence and stimulated wholesale illicit, and therefore untaxed, imports of silver. From the consequences of these and many other ill-considered acts, Spain could, given the chance, recover. But not from a shortage of manpower, and especially skilled manpower. At the end of the reign of Philip II war alone was probably costing the country 8000 men a year. By 1600 some 300,000, equalling about 8 per cent of Spain's male population, had left for the Americas. Fifty years later emigration from a now radically enfeebled society may have reached an annual rate of 5000, mostly from the once economically important south, where in the sixteenth century Andalusia alone accounted for about one-third to one-half of all emigrants. To these losses were added those inflicted by disease on an undernourished populace – the vagabonds of picaresque literature and the gaunt figures of El Greco's art – with plague killing about 500,000 between 1599 and 1603. This haemorrhage was in some measure staunched by foreign immigration (about 150,000 by 1650) and the influx of some 100,000 African slaves into the south in the sixteenth century. But this was of little help, and Castile's population fell from 7,000,000 in the 1590s to 5,000,000 by the mid-1600s. And no more than in Portugal can the real loss be measured statistically, for emigrants, like the many young skilled and professional men who left for the Americas, included those with the ambition and enterprise to seek a better life.

By the end of the sixteenth century the armies of Spain were only in part recruited in the peninsula, and her ships were increasingly built and manned by foreigners – Germans, Greeks, Ragusans, Italians. The power of her English, French and Dutch enemies increased, whilst royal debts of 20,000,000 ducats in the mid-1500s had quintupled by 1600, and the Spanish crown repeatedly declared itself bankrupt. Such credit as it could muster was largely dependent on the decreasing and uncertain flow of American silver, carried in foreign vessels along a route open to ever more effective attack, to a country living on foreign imports of everything from naval stores to food. Spain's still considerable naval and military resources and skills were dissipated in fighting, more or less single-handed, too many opponents. So Spanish fleets were destroyed by the Dutch at Matanzas (1628) and the Downs (1639), a Spanish army routed by the French at Rocroi (1643), and a civilization once characterized by the ebullience and confidence of Cortés and Francis Xavier succumbed to that disillusion and sense of futility expressed in *Don Quixote*.

Bibliographical note

Here, as in the preceding bibliographical notes, there is no attempt to present an exhaustive survey, but merely to indicate where information on archives may be found, to notice the most important modern works on Spain and her colonies, and to list some of the books and articles I have found particularly useful.

With Spain a world power under the Habsburgs, there are few archives which do not throw some light on the country's history in the sixteenth and seventeenth centuries, as may be seen from the discussion of sources in Fernand Braudel's *The Mediterranean and the Mediterranean World in the Age of Philip II*, trs. by S. Reynolds (2 vols, 1972–3). There are good brief introductions to the archives of Spain's former American possessions, and the guides to them, in R.R. Hill, *The National Archives of Latin America* (Cambridge, Mass., 1945) and J.H. Parry, *The Spanish Seaborne Empire* (1966). Iberian archival (and other) resources for the period with which this book is concerned are discussed in vol. VIII, I of H. and P. Chaunu's *Séville et L'Atlantique 1504–1650* (8 vols, Paris 1955–9), but the essential introduction to the rich, extensive and still largely unworked archives of Spain and her onetime colonies is the *Guia de Fuentes para la Historia de Ibero-América conservadas en España* (2 vols, Madrid, 1966–9). There is a general survey of archival material relating to Latin America in *Itinerario*, I (Leyden, 1977). Some idea of the nature and potential of Mexican vernacular (Nahuatl) sources is provided by A.J.O. Anderson, Frances Berdan and James Lockhart in *Beyond the Codices* (Berkeley, 1976).

A convenient but inevitably dated summary of the bibliographies, journals, guides and catalogues relating to Spanish colonial history is given by B.W. Diffie, *Latin-American*

Civilization (rev. edn, New York, 1967). Indispensable is B. Sánchez Alonso, *Fuentes de la Historia Española e Hispano Americana* (3 vols, 3rd edn, Madrid, 1952). Since 1953 the huge flow of publications on Spain and Spanish America has been listed in the *Indice Histórico Español*, produced by the University of Barcelona. Of the reviews dealing with the colonial period the most important are the *Revista de Indias* (Madrid, 1940–), the *Revista de Historia de América* (Mexico, 1938–) and the *Hispanic American Historical Review* (Baltimore, 1918–22, Durham, North Carolina, 1926–).

The best general survey of the history of Spain and her colonies in the sixteenth and seventeenth centuries, equally authoritative on the peninsula and the Americas, is that of John Lynch, *Spain under the Habsburgs* (2 vols, Oxford, 1964–9). Briefer, and more concerned with Europe, is the attractively written *Imperial Spain, 1469–1716* (1963) of J.H. Elliott. Much the same ground is less excitingly covered by Antonio Domínguez Ortiz, *The Golden Age of Spain* (1971). Peter Pierson's *Philip II of Spain* (1975) is an exemplary biography. Fundamental to any understanding of Spanish policy in these years are Braudel, *The Mediterranean*; I.A.A. Thompson, *War and Government in Habsburg Spain, 1560–1620* (1976); and Geoffrey Parker, *The Dutch Revolt* (1977). The founding of Spain's colonial empire is grippingly narrated by F.A. Kirkpatrick, *The Spanish Conquistadores* (1934), and equally readable accounts are provided by J.H. Parry, *The Age of Reconnaissance* (1963) and *The Spanish Seaborne Empire*. Characteristically vigorous and individual opinions are expressed by P. Chaunu in *L'Amérique et les Amériques* (Paris, 1964) and his *Séville* is a rich mine of ideas, perceptions and (whatever their imperfections) statistics. Charles Gibson, *Spain in America* (New York, 1966) and R. Konetzke, *Die Indianerkulturen Altmerikas und die Spanisch-Portugiesische Kolonialherrschaft* (Frankfurt a/Main, 1965) both provide good descriptions and analyses of the American empire.

The origins of Spanish overseas expansion are discussed in Chaunu, *Séville* and V. Magalhães-Godinho, *L'Économie de l'Empire Portugais aux XVᵉ et XVIᵉ siècles* (Paris, 1969), which contains on this, as on many other subjects, more facts and ideas than its title would suggest. J.W. Blake, *European Beginnings in West Africa, 1454–1578* (1937) examines Castilian policies in West Africa and the conflict with Portugal. The discovery and exploration of America are admirably handled in the writings of the late Professor/Admiral S.E. Morison. A final synthesis appeared in *The European Discovery of America*, of which the second volume, *The Southern Voyages, 1492–1616* (Oxford, 1974) – shrewdly, trenchantly and magnificently written – summarizes a lifetime's work and reflection on Columbus, and contains an excellent appreciation of Magellan. Important material relating to the Columban voyages is given in three essays of D.B. Quinn – 'The Conquest of the Atlantic', 'The Atlantic Perspective' and 'England and the Atlantic' – now available in his *England and the Discovery of America* (1974). Spanish exploration and settlement of what is now the USA is examined in both the first volume of Morison and in W.P. Cumming, R.A. Skelton and D.B. Quinn (eds), *The Discovery of North America* (1971).

There is a fine study of pre-conquest Aztec society by Jacques Soustelle, *La Vie Quotidienne des Aztèques à la Veille de la Conquête Espagnole* (Paris, 1959). An important, though over-sympathetic early Spanish account which depicts the impact of Spanish behaviour, is Alonso de

Zorita's *Breve y Sumaria Relacíon de los Señores de la Nueva España* (written *c.* 1570), of which there is an English edition and translation by Benjamin Keen, *The Lords of New Spain* (1965). The classic account of the conquest of Mexico is that contained in the artfully composed letters written by Hernán Cortés, translated and edited by A.R. Pagden, *Hernán Cortés, Letters from Mexico* (New York, 1971). They, and the equally famous account by Bernal Díaz del Castillo (*Historia Verdadera de la Conquista de la Nueva España*, trans. by J.M. Cohen in *The Conquest of New Spain* (1963)), are subjected to an idiosyncratic but stimulating analysis by Eberhard Straub, *Das Bellum Justum des Hernán Cortés in Mexico* (Cologne, 1976). Spanish relations with the peoples of northern Mexico are described by P.W. Powell, *Soldiers, Indians and Silver* (Berkeley, 1952).

J. Alden Mason describes pre-conquest Inca society in *The Ancient Civilizations of Peru* (rev. edn, 1964), and *Power and Property in Inca Peru* are examined by Sally Falk Moore (New York, 1958). The economic background to the Spanish invasion, and trade and politics in the Isthmus of Panama, are the subject of an illuminating study by Guillermo Lohmann Villena, *Les Espinosa: Une Famille d'Hommes d'Affaires en Espagne et aux Indes a l'Époque de la Colonisation* (Paris, 1968). The best account of the overthrow of the Incas in English is that of John Hemming, *The Conquest of the Incas* (1970). A number of contemporary Spanish narratives of the subjugation of Peru and subsequent events are available in translation. Selections from Pedro Cieza de León's *Crónica del Peru* (1550) appear in Sir Clements Markham's *The War of Chupas* (Cambridge, Hakluyt Society, 1918). They are also edited and translated, together with illustrative material and extracts from Agustín Zárate's *Historia del Descubrimiento y Conquista del Peru* (1555) by J.M. Cohen as *The History of Discovery and Conquest of the Province of Peru* (1968). A. Jara describes Spanish policy and behaviour in Chile and the struggle with the Araucanians in *Guerre et Société au Chili* (Paris, 1961).

Spanish settlement and exploitation of the Americas is detailed and evaluated in studies such as that of the Valley of Mexico, 1519–1810, by Charles Gibson, *The Aztecs under Spanish Rule* (Stanford UP, 1964); by James Lockhart's *Spanish Peru, 1532–1560* (Wisconsin UP, 1968); and by P.J. Bakewell's *Silver Mining and Society in Colonial Mexico: Zacatecas, 1546–1700* (Cambridge, 1971). Marie Helmer, 'Cubagua, l'Isle des Perles', *Annales*, 17 (1962), 751ff., discusses a particularly unsavoury area and episode of Spanish rule in the early 1500s. For the Spanish seaborne economy in the Pacific I have used Godinho, *L'Economie*; Marie Helmer, 'Le Callao (1615–18)', in *Jahrbuch für Geschichte von Staat, Wirtschaft und Gesellschaft Lateinamerikas*, 2 (1965), 145ff.; C.R. Boxer, 'Plata es sangre', in *Philippine Studies*, 18 (1970), 457ff.; and the observations of Antonio de Morga, *Sucesos de la Islas Filipinas*, ed. and trs. by J.S. Cummins (Cambridge, Hakluyt Society, 1971). Francesco Carletti (*My Voyage Around the World*, trs. by H. Weinstock (1965)) has much to say on the Spanish Americas of his time. The opinions and impressions of English prisoners, travellers and propagandists in the sixteenth century can be found in E.G.R. Taylor's edition of the *Original Writings and Correspondence of the two Richard Hakluyts* (2 vols, Cambridge, Hakluyt Society, 1935). There is much valuable information on the condition of the Spanish Caribbean in the late 1500s in K.R. Andrews' edition (Cambridge, Hakluyt Society, 1972) of documents concerning *The Last Voyage of Drake and Hawkins*. Colin

A. Palmer, *Slaves of the White God* (Harvard, 1976) is a more scholarly survey of African slavery in Mexico than its title would suggest. For Peru there is the standard work of Frederick P. Bowser, *The African Slave in Colonial Peru, 1524–1650* (Stanford UP, 1974).

The history of Spain prior to the main wave of expansion in the Americas is narrated by J.N. Hillgarth, *The Spanish Kingdoms, 1250–1516*, of which the first volume (Oxford, 1976) covers the years 1250–1410. For the Spanish economy on the eve of the discoveries I have used J. Heers, 'Le role des capitaux internationaux dans les voyages de découvertes aux XVe et XVIe siècles', in *CIHM*, 5 (1966); Cl. Carrère, 'Barcelone et le commerce de l'Orient a la fin du moyen age', in *CIHM*, 8, and R.H. Bautier, 'Points de vue sur les relations économiques des occidentaux avec les pays de l'Orient au moyen age', in *CIHM*, 8 (1970); and the admirable study by Wendy R. Childs of *Anglo-Castilian Trade in the later Middle Ages* (Manchester UP, 1978). For the literature on the Genoese in Spain, see above, pp. 222–3.

The most convenient summaries of Spanish techniques of imperial rule, control and exploitation are in Lynch, op. cit, and Konetzke, op. cit. For the Spanish missions and colonial church I have used Konetzke, op. cit, and M. Bataillon, *Etudes sur Bartolomé de las Casas* (Paris, 1965), especially 'La Herejia de Fray Francisco de la Cruz' and 'Le Clerigo Casas'.

The most useful and comprehensive surveys of Spanish navigation and cosmography are provided by D.W. Waters, *The Art of Navigation in England in Elizabethan and Early Stuart Times* (1958), and E.G.R. Taylor, *The Haven-Finding Art* (1956). The impact of the discovery and conquest of America in Spain is outlined by G.V. Scammell in *HJ*, XII (1969), and discussed by J.H. Elliott, *The Old World and the New, 1492–1650* (Cambridge, 1970). The nature of Spanish political thought, and the opinions of leading publicists on imperial obligations and indigenous rights are summarized in J.A. Fernández-Santamaria, *The State, War and Peace: Spanish Political Thought in the Renaissance, 1516–1559* (Cambridge, 1977).

For the various projects to attack Spain's overseas possessions, and the attempts to realize them, see Lynch, *Spain*; Elliott, *Imperial Spain*; and G.V. Scammell in *HJ*, XII (1969) and in D.B. Quinn (ed.), *The Hakluyt Handbook* (2 vols Cambridge, Hakluyt Society, 1974), 'Hakluyt and the Economic Thought of his Time'. Of outstanding value is Kenneth R. Andrews, *The Spanish Caribbean: Trade and Plunder, 1530–1630* (New Haven, 1978).

For Spain and her empire in decline the evidence of Lynch and Elliott is usefully supplemented by J.I. Israel, 'Mexico and the general crisis of the seventeenth century', *P&P*, 63 (1974), 33ff., expanded in his *Race, Class and Politics in Colonial Mexico, 1610–1670* (Oxford, 1975). For the volume and nature of Spanish emigration to the Americas, see P. Boyd-Bowman, 'Patterns of Spanish emigration to the Indies until 1600', *HAHR*, 56,4 (1976), 580ff.

7

Holland

I *Dominion of the seas*

By the early seventeenth century it was clear to many, and not only Iberians, that what Spain and Portugal lost, Holland gained, just as it was soon apparent to English patriots that the Dutch were the main threat to their country's economic survival. Such was Holland's commercial and maritime success that emulation of Dutch methods was advocated by publicists as the surest recipe for prosperity with the same enthusiasm that the adoption of Venetian institutions was urged as the panacea for political ills. Nor without reason, for in little more than fifty years the Dutch republic had not only gained its independence but, in the process, risen from insignificance to become a major world power. In origin it was a part of that Netherlands principality assembled by the dukes of Burgundy in the late Middle Ages, and subsequently inherited, like the crown of Spain, by the Habsburgs. This ill-assorted collection of states and towns, restive under the emperor Charles V, broke into rebellion under Philip II, a rebellion sustained from 1579 by the northern and predominantly Protestant lands. After prolonged fighting the independence of these was tacitly recognized by Spain in the truce of 1609, but not formally admitted till 1648. By then the republic, or more strictly speaking its seafaring provinces of Holland and Zeeland, had established the most extensive and exclusively maritime seaborne empire so far seen, consciously extending into the waters of the world a dominance of carrying trades initially exercised in those of the Baltic and northern Europe. In the mid-1600s Holland[1] controlled perhaps 500,000t of shipping, constituting a maritime strength of an order never previously approached and inspiring in Germanic imagination the spectre of the Flying Dutchman roaming the oceans forever. Dutch admirals destroyed Iberian fleets in distant seas and flouted English pretensions in the Channel. Dutch boats drifted for herring off the British coasts. Dutch ships pursued whales in the Arctic, seals off South Africa, carried coal from England to Europe, grain from the Baltic to Iberia, slaves from West Africa to Brazil, silver from Europe to Asia, and spices from Asia to Europe, convincing many that before long the trade of the whole world would be monopolized by these 'oracles of commerce'.

As indeed seemed all too likely. The republic rapidly came to exercise, directly and indirectly, an economic influence similar to, but more potent and far-ranging than that once exerted from a scarcely more promising base by Genoa. Like the equally mercantile Genoese and Hansards, the Dutch were little concerned with the acquisition and control of territory. They made few such colonial settlements as did the Iberians or the English, implanting only in South Africa a society and culture recognizably Dutch (cf. pp. 53ff., 183ff., 390). Their power was instead that conferred by superiority in commerce, finance, industry and shipping. Capital accumulated in business was in the seventeenth century fruitfully and influentially invested anywhere from Protestant Scandinavia and England to Catholic France and Iberia. The dependence, for as long as they could still manage to fight, of the Portuguese and Spanish monarchies on Holland for munitions (including those used against the republic itself), naval stores and food gave the Dutch an economic hold on the peninsula as tight as that of any Genoese financier or entrepreneur. By the mid-1600s they dominated much of Europe's seaborne commerce to a degree that the Hanse and the Italian maritime republics had only attempted and achieved more restrictedly (cf. pp. 47, 90). In Asia, Africa and the Americas Dutch trading posts appeared, whilst many of the cargoes carried along the routes linking Europe to the wider world were shipped, from ports Dutch and non-Dutch alike, in the republic's vessels. Rarely did this reflect the outcome of deliberate voyages of exploration (of which the Dutch made few) or discovery (of which they achieved relatively little). Instead, with business skills and resources in shipping far superior to those of any previous nascent imperial power, Holland turned to its advantage, as it had already done in the Baltic, existing maritime economies.

In the Atlantic and the east this was largely done at the expense of the Iberians, making the Dutch overseas empire the first to be established by Europeans at the cost of fellow white men. Together with the strivings of the English, Holland's success marked the emergence of Protestant imperial ambition and the first enduring breach of the Spanish and Portuguese monopoly of the New Worlds, just as it marked the shift of maritime and oceanic supremacy from Iberia and the Mediterranean to northern Europe. All this the Dutch accomplished in ways that rendered them as unpopular in many eyes as the Italian maritime cities had once been for similar reasons. Holland traded with Spain throughout the very years of its revolt against Spanish rule. Dutch energies were so unashamedly concentrated on the pursuit of wealth as to make the country the epitome of distasteful business ethics to high-minded Orientals and impecunious European squires. 'The nature of the Dutchman', Sir Walter Raleigh warned the English House of Commons in 1593, 'is to fly to no man but for his profit.'[2] Some years later the Chinese found the same nation 'covetous and cunning . . . clever in seeking profits . . . and sparing not even their lives in looking for gain.' Much the same could doubtlessly have been said with equal justice about the majority of Europeans abroad. But like the Genoese earlier, the Dutch as a rule sought gain more systematically, ruthlessly, unscrupulously and successfully. An English commander in Asia, worsted by the stratagems of his Dutch opponent, and outraged by Dutch behaviour, expressed the widespread opinion of those of aristocratic and patrician assumptions when he complained that the ways of Hollanders were not those of gentlemen (1609)[3]. Significantly enough, whilst some of the most distinguished writing in imperial Spain was on the question of title to empire and the rights of subject peoples, in seventeenth-century Holland it was on freedom of navigation and legality of prize (cf. pp. 361–2).

The basis of Dutch wealth and seapower was their control of Europe's ancient and vital commerce with the Baltic (see pp. 47ff.). This they secured by destroying, in the late Middle Ages, the leaking Hanse monopoly, and so effectively that from the early 1500s the trade employed the bulk of their tonnage. Though it might not at first appear so, there was much to help them. The future republic lay in an area so geographically obscure and, to begin with, so politically and economically insignificant, that its activities for long provoked no such apprehensions in the Hanse as did those of the English, subjects of a succession of militarily aggressive and dynastically acquisitive kings (see p. 458). Indeed the very presence of the English in the Baltic in the fourteenth century conveniently diverted the League's attention from the more serious encroachments of the Dutch. True enough, the economy of the northern Netherlands *c.* 1300 gave little promise of things to come. A few modest towns were set amongst generally poor or flooded lands which sustained some pastoral agriculture and produced a little grain and flax. But this poverty was in itself an incentive to the Dutch to seek, like the Vikings, sustenance and livelihood abroad. Nor did it have to be in distant parts. From the Zuider Zee a relatively protected sea route led, in the shelter of the Frisian Islands, to the Danish peninsula and the Baltic. To the south and east a network of waterways connected the northern Netherlands both to the flourishing commercial centres of the Rhine and to most of the rest of the Low Countries. More important still, what was to become the Dutch republic was an integral, though initially a minor part of the great medieval entrepôt of Flanders, centred first on Bruges and then on Antwerp, where routes, merchants and goods from most of the continent converged (cf. pp. 44, 58, 420). Holland's history of commerce and seafaring was accordingly a lengthy one. In pre-Viking days the Frisians had traded from the northern Netherlands to France, Denmark and beyond (cf. p. 28). In the 1200s emigrants from the flooded Low Countries settled on the Baltic littoral, where a century later many Hanse skippers were of Dutch origin. Vessels from the Zuider Zee towns penetrated the Baltic through the Kattegat, avoiding the League's stranglehold on trade across the foot of the Danish peninsula, whilst some of the commerce of the Hanse itself flowed through Holland. Goods from the eastlands completed their journey to Flanders along Dutch waterways to escape the hazards of the passage round Jutland; those from the Rhine towns travelled down similar routes towards England.[4] Hence the northern Netherlands became for a time an essential part of the commercial empire of the League, benefiting enormously from the association, even though Dutch towns were excluded from formal membership by the Hanse's rabid conservatism.

From such beginnings the Dutch, by skills and methods shortly to become universally familiar, were able to undermine the monopoly of the already ailing League. This they did not by force, but, as the Germans had formerly done with the Vikings, by

Fig. 15   Dutch herring buss of the 1560s.

superior commercial organization and the use of more and better ships (cf. pp. 24, 77ff.).
To keep alive the inhabitants of lands singularly unblessed by nature, and never more
so than in the early Middle Ages, they developed what was to become Europe's largest
sea-fishery, and one which initially provided them not only with food but with vessels
which when unemployed could be used in the carriage of cargo. Driven from the great
but increasingly barren herring grounds off the Baltic coast of Denmark by the
Germans in the fourteenth century, the Dutch turned to the resources of the North Sea,
long known to them. Their development, *c.* 1400, of new techniques of barrelling and
pickling (the word itself is of Dutch origin) meant the better preservation of catches,
which in turn enabled boats to work further from home and herring to be marketed
further afield. Such expansion demanded more and larger busses[5] (as the fishing vessels
were called), and by the late fifteenth century the Dutch had a fleet of about 300 of these
craft, ranging from 40t to 160t.

   Profits from the fisheries and other enterprises were invested, with a flexibility not
shared by the Hanse, in industry. Formerly importers of German beer, the Dutch
began to produce, particularly in Gouda, Delft and Haarlem, brews which soon sold
well and widely in the onetime Hanseatic preserves of the ever-thirsty German east.
Dutch North Sea herring, inferior to those of the Baltic, but more plentiful and less
expensive, were sufficiently popular by the mid-1400s to be on sale as far away as

Novgorod and Cracow. In the fourteenth and fifteenth centuries, encouraged by the counts of Holland, and aided by the influx of workers from Flanders, there grew up in towns such as Leyden, Amsterdam and Rotterdam – not to mention many still smaller centres – an important woollen textile industry, with Leyden alone producing nearly 30,000 cloths a year by about 1500. Heavy, cheap and in every way better suited to the market and climate of the Baltic, these textiles soon cut into the sales of the lighter and costlier Flemish varieties in the eastlands, accounting for roughly one-half of Danzig's cloth imports in 1500.[6] Thus outward-bound Dutch ships, often carrying some locally produced cargo, could offer lower freight charges for a round voyage to the Baltic than could less happily placed competitors. Dutch merchants could also obtain for themselves (and others) Baltic goods in exchange for Dutch manufactures – and manufactures which, together with other cargoes, they could sell cheaply because of their low carriage costs. Hollanders, who in the thirteenth century had appeared only spasmodically in the Baltic and Scandinavia, were well-established there a hundred years later, trading along routes their ships had first penetrated as carriers for others. Neither here, nor elsewhere, did they share the aspirations of aristocratic societies to exact tribute from an existing commerce (cf. pp. 266, 269). Their aim, as the Hanse eventually appreciated, was to take into their own hands all that they found. Wherever possible they avoided headlong collision with the League – though should occasion demand, their privateers attacked its shipping everywhere from Brittany to Norway – and instead they pushed in through the chinks in its armour as they were later to do with the Spaniards in the Caribbean (cf. pp. 384ff.). The competitive rates their ships offered for the movement of salt and textiles soon allowed them to expand into the carriage of other goods. In the 1440s they advanced from shipping salt from the French Atlantic coast for use in their own fisheries to importing it into the Baltic, whilst in Latvia and Estonia their merchants sought to reach hinterland markets. The Dutch formed partnerships with local traders, and cultivated relations with restive clients of the League (Denmark, Norway, Sweden) and with those cities, most notably Danzig, resentful of Lübeck's pre-eminence (cf. p. 55). As a rule their vessels kept clear of the major German entrepôts, and in Livonia and Prussia the Dutch dealt, in suitably obscure havens, with large-scale local grain producers, only too glad to dispense with the services of Hanseatic middlemen and to receive, at lower prices, urgently needed western goods.

Intermittently in the fourteenth century, and for most of the fifteenth, there was friction or open war as the League strove to stem the Dutch advance. But in vain. Economic recession in the west made the Hollanders even more determined to market their textiles in the eastlands. To do this, as to trade in general, they had a better and more flexible commercial organization than that of the Hanse. Selling their own produce, they had no need of middlemen at home and sought to avoid them abroad. They nowhere limited trade to specified towns, as did the League, nor did they impose restrictions on non-Dutch merchants.[7] Their freight charges were lower than those of the Hanse, which in any case lacked the tonnage to bring in all the salt required in the north or to take out all those Baltic products in such demand in the west. And as in the establishment of any hegemony, there were always those willing, whatever their masters, rulers or allies might say, to do business with, or join the intruders. In the fifteenth century Danzig shipwrights eagerly seized the opportunity to build for Dutch owners, just as the Teutonic Order, struggling for survival, welcomed merchants wanting grain and able to supply textiles and munitions. Hence whatever policies the League might proclaim – war, the boycott of Dutch goods, the enforcement of the Bruges staple, the prohibition of the teaching of Russian to Hollanders – they were rarely supported, let alone enforced by all members (cf. pp. 55ff.). In 1411, a general embargo on Dutch trade notwithstanding, the grand master of the Teutonic Order allowed the Dutch to export grain from Danzig, and when in 1438 the Wendish cities attempted to make the ban effective, he ordered the sequestration of the property of Lübeck merchants in Prussia. And whilst its opponents were in this disarray, Holland enjoyed, even if only briefly, something of that powerful state support which underlay most successful expansion, coming first from the dukes of Burgundy and then from their Habsburg successors, most notably the emperor Charles V, who in 1544 secured the exemption of his Dutch subjects from the Danish Sound tolls (cf. p. 61).

Hence Dutch control of the trade of the Baltic inexorably tightened. By 1498 their ships carried one-half (by value) of Danzig's imports.[8] In the century after 1550 they accounted for between one-half and two-thirds of all passages recorded through the Danish Sound. Towards 1600 some 1200 Dutch vessels were annually engaged in the Baltic, outnumbering in all its ports, with the possible exception of Lübeck, those of the Germans or any other nationality – many of which were, of course, in reality Dutch-owned (see pp. 65 and 383). Cologne and the rest of the inland members of the Hanse were denied access by water to the Netherlands' coast, whilst in many Baltic ports, major and minor alike, Dutch factors appeared, dealing all year round in commodities with seasonal peaks of production, holding stocks, advancing credit and generally easing and speeding the flow of trade. Like that of the League earlier, it was a trade predominantly in bulk goods, consequently demanding for their carriage a volume of tonnage dwarfing that employed by Holland, or any one else, on the new oceanic routes (cf. p. 44). For their own use, but increasingly for the use of others, the Dutch took from the Baltic such familiar cargoes as timber and timber products. But outstripping all else was grain, with exports of rye and wheat running at about 110,000 a year by the mid-1600s. In its heyday this traffic enriched producers and stimulated the growth of new settlements in Poland. To Dutch merchants it brought profits of reputedly 100 per cent at times, and was agreed by both Low countries' statesmen and Spanish strategists planning its destruction in the 1580s to be the republic's very lifeblood.[9] In exchange the Dutch shipped into the Baltic salt, herring, wine, textiles and, as the range of their commerce widened, products of the Mediterranean and of the Iberian colonial empires – like silver, spices and tobacco (cf. pp. 48ff. and 380ff.).

Such growth was not unimpeded. Clashes with their Burgundian overlords and internal upheavals disrupted some north-Dutch towns in the fifteenth century. By and large, Holland's struggle for independence from Spain aided rather than retarded its economic advance. All the same, renewed fighting with the Habsburgs after the expiry of the 1609 truce in 1621 drove up Dutch freight rates by about a half, exposed the ever-vulnerable fisheries to the depredations of Spanish men-of-war and privateers from Spanish-held Dunkirk, and meant that Holland had to contend with substantial competition from the shipping of the English, neutral in the general European war which broke out in 1618.[10] But with Spain engulfed in global conflict, the English distracted by political strife, and the Hanse in irrevocable decline, the Dutch were not to be stopped. English explorers seeking the north-eastern passage to Cathay in the mid-1500s found them already in Moscow and entrenched in the Russian fur trade (cf. p. 472). Before long they had, it was complained, engrossed the best part of the commerce of the Czar's dominions with the west. Their fishermen worked the White Sea grounds, and in the early 1600s their freighters were carrying grain from Archangel and Lapland to Amsterdam as cheaply as they did from Danzig, driving out English competitors by their ability and willingness to pay in silver, as Russian merchants and officials demanded. More impressively and more significantly, the great fishery in northern waters continued to grow, employing, it was thought in 1662, 1000 busses and nearly 500,000 persons directly or indirectly. Such was its importance that in 1601 the Spaniards, desperate to subjugate their rebellious provinces, discussed improbable schemes for the conquest of the Orkneys and the stationing there of a fleet to destroy 'this Indies whence [the Dutch] draw their resources to keep up the war in Flanders'.[11] but the republic was not to be handled in such ways, and was indeed itself, like any other imperial power, increasingly willing to use or threaten force to protect its interests, annexing bases in Asia and despatching in 1645 a squadron into the Baltic to ensure the safety of its trade.

Pragmatically governed, economically advanced, and controlling impressive resources in shipping, foodstuffs and munitions, the Dutch were able to extend their influence in the sixteenth and seventeenth centuries into those countries of western Europe whose economies were weaker or less developed than their own. As a result Amsterdam, Holland's leading city, became both the continent's greatest entrepôt, where goods of every description, usually brought in by Dutch ships, were to be found, and its greatest grain market, re-exporting in the early 1600s about half its stocks and purchases. For a time Italy was amongst its clients, when in the late sixteenth century, unable to feed its growing population, it was obliged to import northern grain. So Holland's maritime connection with the Mediterranean, where Dutch vessels had once sailed in the twelfth and thirteenth centuries, was vigorously renewed.[12] In 1592 the English met near Gibraltar '100 sail of Flemings from Genoa', and the city's own records show 58 vessels from Amsterdam alone there in the first half of the same year.[13] This trade, opened by the Hanse, the Dutch rapidly appropriated (cf. p. 64). They possessed an abundance of cheaply run freighters essential for the profitable handling of a traffic in which carriage costs were the prime charge. From its reserves and suppliers Amsterdam could usually provide all the grain needed, and by reason of its sophisticated money market, on attractive terms. The passage from the Netherlands to the Mediterranean was shorter than that from the Baltic, and Dutch waters less likely to be frozen in winter than those of the eastlands. By the end of the century Dutch grain carriers were working to Livorno, Genoa, Venice and Rome, and Dutch firms had opened branches in the peninsula, where Jan Coen himself, that austere Calvinist and future governor-general of the Dutch East Indies, served a spell with the house of Pescatore (alias Visser) in the papal city.

These footholds were quickly expanded when after the truce of 1609 the Dutch could give the Mediterranean their fuller attention. Fluctuations and shifts of emphasis in their trade there indeed were. But if the south's need for northern grain dwindled, its need for northern shipping did not. Nor did the zeal of Dutch merchants to exploit the opportunities now revealed. As earlier in the Baltic, the Hollanders were eager and able to market their own textiles, now using, however, cheap and light cloths better suited to Levantine tastes than the heavier and dearer products of Venice. Should occasion demand, as it frequently did in the early 1600s, they could pay for their purchases in the eastern Mediterranean with bullion obtained from the Iberians (cf. pp. 142 and 382). Carefully avoiding political entanglements, undercutting competitors, combining hard-living and hard-fighting in a way which identified them in southern eyes with violence of a new order, the Dutch rapidly spread throughout the Mediterranean, where soon after 1600 their trade was second in value only to that with the Baltic. Hanse competition was eradicated, partly because of the League's preference for Iberia, but largely through superior Dutch business practice (a legacy from Flanders), and the advantages enjoyed by economically run Dutch ships exporting, as in the Baltic, Dutch manufactures. Rightly enough, English merchants predicted (1595) the overthrow of their commerce with the Ottoman territories if exposed to Dutch challenge since 'they can maintain [the trade] with flyboats, and would do it so cheaply'.[14] The ancient Venetian commerce with the Levant they had penetrated by 1597, profiting from the skills of Portuguese Jewish refugees in Holland, long experienced in the trade. They sold their widely admired ships to southern owners (cf. p. 144). Together with the English they came to monopolize Venice's seaborne commerce with the north in the same way that they soon dominated many local trades, with their craft accounting for about 40 per cent of the arrivals in Valencia from Naples and Sicily in the early 1600s.[15] Dutch vessels brought to Italy Spanish salt and wool, Greek and Turkish grain, and the products of the Iberian colonial empires. They shipped fish (much of it English) and textiles down the Mediterranean, and on their way back picked up cargoes for northern Europe in the south of Spain. Nor were Hollanders engaged only in peaceful commerce. Renegades took service, as did the English, in the ships of North African corsairs, who thus reinforced were able, it was alleged, to commit even worse excesses and undertake still bolder designs (cf. pp. 137 and 471). Dutch traders sold arms to

Barbary pirates, whilst, so it was said in the 1620s, refugee Portuguese Jews in Morocco, amongst them Eleazor Ribeiro, the 'Captain Jew', not only provided the corsairs with weapons, but even disposed of their loot in Holland.[16] What private initiative began, the Dutch state, as was so often the case, prudently continued, supplying arms and manufactures (1621) to those North African sultanates then, like itself, fighting Spain.

If at one extreme of Europe the Baltic was the foundation of Dutch prosperity, at the other it was Iberia. From Portugal the Dutch had obtained since the fifteenth century increasing amounts of the salt needed in their fishery. The diversion of so much Portuguese shipping and manpower into the exploitation and defence of overseas possessions, and Portugal's growing need for food and manufactures quickly strengthened the link (cf. p. 293). By the 1540s Dutch vessels were handling much of Lisbon's trade with Antwerp, bringing in oriental wares and taking out textiles, metals and metal goods in a commerce which, re-routed to Holland itself, continued to expand in volume and variety. Much the same, and for similar reasons, was Dutch trade with Spain, little impeded by the republic's struggle for independence which began in earnest when the Sea Beggars – a formidable body of pirates, privateers and Calvinist zealots – seized in 1572 a base near Rotterdam. In the ensuing war the Dutch talked of attacking the Spanish treasure fleets (1578), co-operated with their English allies against the Armada ten years later, and mounted (as in 1599 and 1606) some generally undistinguished campaigns in Spanish waters. More effective was their privateering, especially from Flushing, the depredations of whose ships had already provoked complaints from England in the 1540s, and which by the middle of Elizabeth's reign had reached such a pitch as to oblige her to send out a squadron 'to scour the Narrow Seas' and arrest all craft belonging to the port.[17] But to little avail. Controlling the approaches to the great entrepôt of Antwerp (in Spanish hands from 1585), its ships continued to attack everything, English included, suspected of trading to Spain or the Spanish Netherlands.

Nevertheless Dutch privateering involved no such diversion of maritime resources as did the contemporary oceanic operations of the English. Even less than Venice could Holland allow conventional morality to interfere with business (cf. pp. 114, 134, 420). Accordingly whilst for the best part of a century Dutch and Spanish armies were locked in a war of siege and counter-siege, and whilst the overseas commerce of Antwerp – and indeed the whole economy of the southern and Spanish Low Countries – was largely ruined, Holland's trade with Iberia flourished. By virtue of its own industries and the ramifications of its commerce the republic dominated the supply of those naval stores, foodstuffs and manufactures that Spain and Portugal desperately lacked, and – the Hanse apart – it alone could provide in sufficient volume the tonnage to carry them, and to replace that so lavishly consumed by the Iberians. As Walter Raleigh bitterly observed in 1593, it was the Dutch, England's supposed allies, who maintained 'the king of Spain in his greatness . . . were it not for them he were never able to make out such armies and navies by sea'.[18] Nor was he wrong. Dutch seamen regularly served in Iberian ships, and some, in 1613, would have taken Biscay whalers to Spitsbergen had the Amsterdam admiralty not objected.[19] Even in the years of the bitterest fighting in the Low Countries Dutch vessels sailed, often forty at a time, for every major port in Iberia from Bilbao to Malaga, and in the peninsula many were purchased or impressed for Spanish service.[20] From the north they carried textiles (German, English, Dutch), Scandinavian and German timber, Baltic grain and other foodstuffs, naval stores, copper, guns and armour. Ironically enough it was from Holland that the Portuguese had to buy the weapons to defend their empire against the Dutch and, after 1640, their own independence against the similarly equipped Spaniards.[21] All such opportunities the Netherlanders improved with characteristic enterprise, manufacturing in Amsterdam cheap devotional objects and paintings specially designed for the mass market of Iberian piety.[22] In exchange they took from the peninsula local products (wine, olive oil, wool, salt), together with those of the Portuguese and Spanish colonial empires, ranging from cochineal to silver. On this trade with the enemy the Navy Boards of the independent provinces levied taxes which more or less financed the fleets used to defend Dutch commerce, and to attack Iberian coasts and shipping, ensuring that war, like everything else, was conducted according to the best business practice.

By the end of the sixteenth century Dutch vessels were working a nexus of routes which linked, whatever their supposed religious or political affiliations, the ports of the northern seas, the Atlantic littoral and the Mediterranean. In North Africa they provisioned indiscriminately the strongholds of the Iberians and the armies of their Moslem opponents.[23] They carried the goods of Antwerp merchants to Spain, and at the very height of the Anglo-Spanish war brought cargoes, sometimes even insured in London, from the peninsula to England.[24] In the early 1600s they sailed from Amsterdam to Portugal to load wine (much in demand in Poland) and salt. After discharging in the Baltic, they took on grain either for home or for Iberia and the Mediterranean, from where they eventually returned to Holland with southern and colonial produce. Only towards the end of the Hispano-Dutch wars did this traffic decay. One of its initial attractions to the Hollanders had been the opportunity to obtain in Iberia Asian and American goods, particularly, and relatively cheaply, the silver they could sell so profitably in the eastlands where it was at a premium. But by the mid-1600s the flow of American bullion to Spain had been drastically reduced, leaving the country, moreover, without the means to balance the deficit on its Baltic trade. At the same time the centres of grain production were shifting, whilst punitive Spanish taxation drove up the price of colonial imports, which the Dutch were now in any case fetching directly themselves (cf. pp. 364ff., 384ff.).

But whilst this trade flourished, its conduct meant that in most major Iberian ports there were, as in the Baltic, groups of Dutch merchants and factors, sometimes living, like those in Cadiz in the 1590s, together 'all in one row'.[25] Indistinguishable to Iberians in speech and appearance from Germans or Flemings from the Spanish

Netherlands, these subjects of a Protestant state in open rebellion against the Habsburgs overtly conducted their business in intensely Catholic Spain and Portugal. Blank bills of lading printed in Dutch were despatched to the peninsula;[26] young men came out from Holland to learn the languages, which many obviously did well, for travellers noticed how widely Spanish was spoken in the republic.[27] Naturally enough such a commerce had its problems. The Portuguese Inquisition was empowered in 1561 to search alien vessels – which it did with increasing rigour – for 'indecent pictures' and heretical writings. There was always competition, at times serious, from the Hanse. Protestant England, openly or in effect at war with Catholic Spain for much of the late sixteenth and early seventeenth centuries, sent out privateers which regularly and gleefully seized Dutch ships as lawful prize, whilst English merchantmen, benefiting from their country's neutrality in the Thirty Years War, pushed into the Iberian trades (cf. pp. 471, 496). In the peninsula itself Dutch ships were always liable to arrest, and in 1621 Dutch merchants were expelled from Spanish ports. Furthermore there were from time to time grandiose Habsburg projects 'to put the Netherlanders from our commerce', such as the attempted alliance with the vestigial remains of the Hanseatic League.[28] Nor were they without effect, and in the 1620s the Dutch were driven to the expense of defending their shipping in northern waters against the damaging attacks of Spain's newly organized armada of Flanders.

Nevertheless the needs of both Iberia and Holland were too great, and the weaknesses of Spanish naval and administrative resources too many, for such disruptions to be more than temporary. And in any case they rarely deterred men of purpose. In 1595, after local officials had been bribed with what were contemptuously dismissed as 'half a dozen *reals*', a Dutch flotilla left Cadiz loaded with contraband silver ostensibly bound for Hamburg.[29] The more circumspect carried on their trade in vessels wholly or partly owned by Hollanders in Spain, or in neutral ports anywhere from Biscayan France to the Baltic and Scotland, whose arms, indeed, it was alleged in 1601, some prudent Dutchmen were having emblazoned on their newly built ships.[30] Meanwhile Dutch factors in Spain passed themselves off as Germans and Dutch merchants acquired *de facto* Spanish nationality by marriage, or claimed to be honest citizens of some conveniently neutral state. And in times of especial difficulty cargoes were moved through entrepôts, as when in the 1630s grain was shipped to Bordeaux for forwarding to Spain. Such arrangements demanded and revealed entrepreneurial boldness and ingenuity of a high, not to say brazen, order. In the late sixteenth century the great Amsterdam commercial house of le Maire (Calvinist and once of Antwerp) had representatives in Seville, London and the Low Countries. Factors in Spain handled business for Dutch and English merchants alike, a London agent secured, amongst other things, the release of any of the firm's goods taken by English privateers and a network of intelligence and influence allowed cargoes shipped from Iberia by the family to be sent, as circumstances dictated, to Hamburg, Holland or England.[31]

War and trade with Spain had other and more dramatic effects on the nature and spread of Dutch power and influence. The Habsburg reconquest of the southern Netherlands in the late sixteenth century and recapture (1585) of Antwerp, drove into exile intransigent Flemish Calvinists, many of them merchants. Some took refuge anywhere from Portugal to the Baltic, and some, including many leading business families like the le Maire, Moucheron and Usselincx, in Holland itself. As a result the tolerant northern Netherlands became the focus of an international network of wealth and commercial experience as the emigrés, like the Portuguese Jewish refugees in Holland, traded with their widely scattered relatives and co-religionaries (cf. pp. 64, 344, 428). Hence with Antwerp's commerce effectively strangled by Dutch blockade after 1585, the commercial and maritime ascendency of Holland, and more particularly of Amsterdam, was assured. Finally, too, Spanish policies provoked Dutch penetration of the entire Iberian seaborne economy when periodic arrests of alien shipping in Spanish ports in the late 1500s, and the closing of Lisbon in 1595–6, drove the Hollanders to seek for themselves colonial products they had formerly obtained in the peninsula. This way they could ensure the vital salt for their fisheries, safeguard their sales of exotic goods in Europe, avoid the expense of clandestine trade in Iberia, and with any luck reduce the risk to their shipping from Anglo-Spanish hostilities. But their motives were not exclusively those of the counting-house. Amongst the most insistent advocates of Dutch oceanic ventures were refugees from Flanders, where distinguished cosmographers had already discussed the desirability of a search for the north-west passage to Asia (cf. p. 473). Many of these exiles had previously traded to the Spanish Canaries, and some – as also some Dutchmen – to the Spanish Americas. Now, so it seemed to them, could old dreams be revived, great gains be had, and a godly and mortal blow delivered at the author of all their misfortunes.

The last decade of the sixteenth century saw Dutch ships in the Atlantic islands – which some had once visited in the early 1500s – and off the coast of West Africa. Schemes to colonize the Americas were aired, the Moucherons opened a direct trade to the Caribbean (*c.* 1596) and companies sprang up to exploit the opportunities of the entire wider world. Nor did it seem there was much to impede them. The Dutch could turn existing routes and economies to their own use, as other fortunate maritime powers had earlier done, and all the easier since many of their seamen had been in Iberian service (cf. pp. 293, 382). None knew better than the Hollanders, suppliers of ships and goods to Iberia, that Spain and Portugal were weakened at sea by English attacks, and that their economies were incapable of meeting the needs of their colonial subjects (cf. pp. 293, 365). Hence the initial Dutch imperial impulse was of the simplest: to damage the arch-enemy; to obtain familiar products; to trade with local peoples. These ambitions, prosaic compared with those of the Portuguese or Spaniards in their years of expansion, were swiftly implemented. Salt to replace that of Portugal was found first in the Cape Verdes and then more abundantly in Venezuela. In the wake of the French and the English the Dutch appeared in increasing numbers, and increasingly openly, in the Caribbean (cf. pp. 439ff., 471). By 1600 sporadic visits had given way to the annual arrival of fleets of 100 or so large craft, leading amongst other things to a massive increase in the long-established contraband trade of the region and on the coast between the deltas of the Orinoco and the Amazon (cf. p. 365).

Working, as they had once done in the Baltic, away from the main points of commerce and population, the Dutch loaded salt near Cumaná (Venezuela), hides in Cuba, tobacco in Venezuela, dyewoods in Guiana. Much they paid for with textiles and other manufactures; occasionally, as in Trinidad in 1605, they offered African slaves; and the rest, pearls particularly, they simply took. Such was the volume of their trade, and such their methods of business, that already in 1600 Spanish merchants alleged that what little remained of their own commerce had to be conducted nocturnally by canoe. Initially Spain was ill-prepared to meet these incursions. Nor, whatever the government might propose, were many of its subjects and officers willing to forgo the offers of intruders who could meet their needs whilst the official channels of supply were so inadequate that in 1608 the governor of Venezuela reported that his chronicle of disaster was only curtailed by a lack of paper on which to write it (cf. p. 344).

But the original pace and direction of Holland's advance was not sustained. In the years of their truce with Spain (1609–21) the Dutch found it cheaper, not to say safer, to buy salt in Portugal, especially since a series of Habsburg naval sweeps had destroyed many of their Caribbean footholds and obliged them to turn to the Leeward Islands. At the same time Spanish prohibition of tobacco-growing in coastal Venezuela and elsewhere, although only partially successful, drove the Dutch, like the English and the French, into areas remoter from a still (spasmodically) formidable Habsburg authority, where they could attempt to produce for themselves what they had formerly obtained by trade (cf. pp. 365ff., 440, 492–3). One such region was the so-called 'Wild Coast' of South America, between the Orinoco and Amazon deltas. Here they faced only the most primitive Amerindians, and though far-removed from the major Iberian bases were yet well-placed to trade with Spanish Trinidad. In Guiana they bartered knives and textiles to the aboriginals for slaves and tobacco, sought for gold, and hoped to produce, in Iberian style, cotton, sugar and tobacco. But with little success. Their settlements on the Amazon were destroyed by the Portuguese in the 1620s, and those on the Essequibo ended more Indian than Dutch, with the few colonists, according to the Spaniards (1637), intermarrying 'with the Carib women as well as those of other tribes' (cf. pp. 247ff.). Nowhere was a commerce of any significance established, but in 1648 Spain accepted, with only a loss of prestige, the right of the Dutch to trade in Guiana, and the legality of their possessions on the Berbice and Essequibo rivers.

Very different were events in the Caribbean with the renewal of the Hispano-Dutch war in 1621, and Holland proposing the boldest schemes yet envisaged for the destruction of Iberian power. One of the objectives of the newly founded West India Company was 'to take away from the Spaniard the American treasures . . . with which he has so long battered the whole of Christianity'. Not that such sentiments or schemes were anything new in Protestant thought (see pp. 438–9, 465ff.). Now, however, powerful Dutch squadrons undertook full-scale naval operations against the bullion fleets. No more than Portugal was Spain as easy a victim as had been anticipated, but in 1628, off Cuba, the Mexico ships surrendered to Piet Heyn, a onetime Spanish galley slave, without a fight. This coup neither Heyn nor his fellow admirals could repeat, but their raids along the western shores of the Gulf of Mexico and the Caribbean, and amongst the Greater Antilles, had by 1635 brought all local Spanish trade and communication to a stop. Furthermore, as bases in which to refit and from which to keep the enemy under surveillance, the Dutch seized a number of islands on the fringes of Spanish power. The most important were those off the Venezuelan coast, many providing vital salt, and the majority suitable, like the onetime insular outposts of the Venetians and Genoese in the Levant, as entrepôts for trade with an ostensibly hostile neighbouring landmass (cf. pp. 103, 173). From Tortuga cloth was sold throughout the Gulf of Mexico. Maize was grown on Bonaire, horses raised on Aruba, and African slaves redistributed from Curaçao (taken in 1634) to Spanish and other colonists. Territorially insignificant, these miniscule possessions were collectively of the highest strategic and economic importance. By the peace of 1648 the Dutch accepted total exclusion from the Spanish Indies. In no time they were in fact the biggest interlopers there, trading everywhere in the Caribbean from their islands (and elsewhere). Moreover, after the arrival of Hollanders driven from Brazil, these bases became the centres from which there were transmitted – as to the English in Barbados – techniques of producing sugar, molasses and rum learned from the Portuguese (cf. pp. 248ff. and 492–3). And often enough it was the Dutch who supplied the capital to establish this new industry in the Lesser Antilles – those 'useless islands' to the Spaniards – the slaves to run it, the ships to market its produce, and the European goods the colonies needed.

No such success attended other even more ambitious schemes in the west. The economic attractions of Portuguese Brazil – its valuable sugar, dyewoods and cotton, its demand for textiles, its lack of shipping – the Dutch had early appreciated. In 1587 English privateers found a Flushing hulk at Bahia, and a few years later (1595) met 'great Holland ships' in Pernambuco.[32] No more than in Europe was so profitable an enterprise to be overthrown by the enmity of the Hispano-Portuguese monarchy, and their supposed exclusion from the colony the Dutch either simply ignored or transparently circumvented. They coloured their trade by partnerships with Portuguese merchants, usually New Christian converts from Judaism, or worked in association with refugee Portuguese Jews in Holland who were in vigorous contact with their co-religionaries in Brazil and Portugal. Thus with the Portuguese increasingly short of ships whilst Holland's tonnage was growing spectacularly, and with their onetime English competitors directing their energies to privateering, the Dutch had something like two-thirds of the carrying trade between Brazil and Europe in their hands by the 1620s (cf. pp. 249, 291, 465).

This profitable and effective hegemony was then sacrificed, with a folly worthy of Spain, to a grandiose, ill-executed and ultimately abortive attempt to conquer the colony. The enthusiasm of hotheads for a direct assault on Spain's overseas possessions had cooled after reverses in the Caribbean and the Philippines in the early 1600s, and the acceptance, following a reconnaissance, that the Pacific coasts of Spanish America were well defended. Brazil, on the other hand, seemed a much more likely victim after the expiry of the truce with the Hispano-Portuguese monarchy in 1621. Not only was it rich, but its coast could provide admirable privateering bases, whilst the country itself gave access to the source of Spanish silver at Potosí (cf. pp. 328). Its few cities lay on the Atlantic littoral, vulnerable to seaborne attack, and their inhabitants were thought – by some at least – to be less formidable opponents than Spaniards. It was also optimistically assumed that in a land containing so many refugees from Iberian oppression, disaffection to Spanish rule would be widespread. Nor, considering the frictions within the Hispano-Portuguese empire, and the equanimity with which Spain had accepted the loss of Portugal's base at Hormuz, did it appear probable that an attack on Brazil would provoke as vigorous a reaction as an assault on a Spanish colony (cf. pp. 247, 250). Such confident prognosis turned out to be, as is not unusual, ludicrously wrong. Moreover the West India Company, within whose generous monopoly Brazil fell, added to its difficulties by attacking, under government pressure, not only the colony (and the Spaniards in the Caribbean as well), but also Portugal's possessions in West Africa which provided its slaves. It was the most ambitious operation so far planned against the Iberian overseas empires, demanding for its success control of Bahia and Pernambuco (to prevent the establishment of any bridgeheads for counter-attack), the co-operation or at least the acquiescence of the Brazilian planters, and Holland's ability to supply sufficient African slaves for Brazil's needs. With its assumption of the disruption and subsequent control of an entire economy it was strategically, and in every other way, an enormous advance on the usual obsession with Spanish silver, and its realization well within the republic's maritime resources.

Yet Dutch rule in Brazil, established (as in Africa) only after a series of humiliating setbacks, lasted less than twenty-five years. Bahia was easily taken (1624), then lost the following year when its unsupported, unsupplied and mutinous garrison succumbed to a vigorous counter-attack inspired by fears that the whole of Habsburg America was in danger. Nor did the Dutch do any better until Heyn's capture of the treasure ships restored their morale and finances, and stimulated their ambitions. They took Pernambuco in 1630, and within thirteen years controlled about half the colony, including its best sugar-growing regions. For a time it seemed that there might emerge in Brazil a Dutch colonial regime of the Iberian pattern. A governor of high birth, Johan Maurits of Nassau, was appointed in 1637. Success in West Africa allowed the import of 23,000 negro slaves into Pernambuco alone in the decade after 1636, whilst Portugal, now struggling for independence from Spain was reconciled (1641) to accepting the loss of some part of the colony (cf. p. 249). But not so Brazil's creole inhabitants. Catholic and abstemious, they found their bibulous Protestant conquerors little to their liking. They resented dependence on the capital of the Dutch and their Jewish protégés to restore plantations damaged in the wars, just as they resented Holland's control of the Angolan slave trade, and their consequent indebtedness to Dutch merchants for their Africans (see p. 390). Nor did Luso-Brazilian society hold many charms for the Hollanders. Some, in the absence of Protestant females, did indeed marry Portuguese women, and like other isolated males in similar circumstances, accepted the religion and customs of their wives (cf. p. 290). The majority, however, found such women, used as they were to seclusion, dull and unattractive. Thus there was neither any substantial Dutch settlement in Brazil, nor miscegenation on a sufficient scale to root there an essentially Dutch society. Hence when the Portuguese settlers rose in revolt to save their homeland, West India Company rule disintegrated. Massive losses the Dutch might inflict on the Portuguese at sea, but by 1654 the Brazilians, with some belated help from the mother country, had not only driven the Hollanders out, but also defeated them at sea (see pp. 249, 297).

This last and dramatic collapse reflected less Luso-Brazilian skills and strength than Dutch ineptitude. Mercantile and non-aristocratic Holland was never able (or cared) to recruit for overseas service a cohesive and Dutch army of the quality of its naval forces, or indeed of the quality of the troops that Spain and even (occasionally) Portugal could muster from their less advanced societies (cf. pp. 338, 368). Then the Dutch reduction of their military strength in Brazil (1643–4), with the dismissal of the able Johan Maurits, whose tolerance of Catholics offended zealots at home, was but one manifestation of the inevitable hazards of the corporate direction of any enterprise. The West India Company, like the republic itself, was an amalgam of many and often conflicting interests (see pp. 417, 422). The province of Zeeland had no concern for colonization. It advocated privateering, looked to the Wild Coast and the Caribbean, and demanded that the trade of Dutch Brazil (slaves apart) should be a company monopoly. This discouraged immigration and further alienated the Portuguese. Worse still, it alienated the rich and powerful city of Amsterdam which, living by trade and confident of its ability to triumph anywhere by economic superiority, condemned monopoly as 'the most odious thing in the world'. So Amsterdam merchants, and Amsterdam directors and erstwhile directors of the company, openly violated, and eventually secured the abrogation of the monopoly (1637). The antipathy was heightened by the city's distaste for what it saw as the dangerous political ambitions of the house of Orange, reflected in the doings of Johan Maurits, and its disapproval of the diversion of resources from the far more lucrative opportunities of Asia (see pp. 393ff.). Thus by the 1640s the company's chronic financial difficulties had become desperate. Already after Heyn's victory, prudent investors had taken their 50 per cent dividends and gone elsewhere, leaving it to shoulder the cost of grandiose strategies. And as these failed, the government itself lost interest, making little effort to exact from the largely autonomous states of the republic the aid the company needed and the sums they were supposed to provide (see p. 422).

Whilst the provinces squabbled, and their respective admiralties failed to supply fleets on time, or indeed at all, the company faced in Brazil and Africa an opposition far more tenacious and effective than anticipated. It faced, too, if it was to implement its grand schemes, the need for sustained and co-ordinated naval operations such as those that had once ensured the flow of Venice's 'rich trades', and still ensured that of American silver to Spain. But no more than the English in the preceding century could the Dutch devise or enforce any such policies. Their energies and resources were dissipated in a variety of often mutually incompatible projects, reflecting the interests of particular provinces. Furthermore, with abundant ships, and with command divided amongst several autonomous admiralties, they often attempted, in a way impossible to achieve before the development of more rapid communications, the re-routing or re-deployment of fleets already at sea. And to all the republic's many difficulties there was added, at the very time its Brazilian empire was disintegrating, the re-emergence of vigorous and substantial English maritime hostility, culminating in the Navigation Act of 1651, discriminating against Dutch shipping, and the outbreak in the following year of the first Anglo-Dutch war (see pp. 466ff., 497).

These failures reflect even more fundamental weaknesses in Holland as a putative imperial power. Unlike Iberia or England, it was unable to produce that flow of emigrants essential, as classical precedent and contemporary experience showed, to settle and hold a colony. With its mass of efficiently run shipping it could, with comparative ease, penetrate, extend and exploit an existing economy. But, tolerant and prosperous, it was a country to which, not from which, people fled (see pp. 384 and 428). Its mercantile oligarchs were of that class only parted from the fountains of business and profit in the direst circumstances. Hard though life was for the masses, it was not so hard as in Iberia or medieval Scandinavia, those great exporters of men, nor was Dutch society so oppressively ossified as to debar, as in Spain and Portugal, the able but uninfluential from opportunity. The republic was equally free of those of noble, or allegedly noble birth, demanding lands and offices to enable them to live in proper affluence, whilst for such few martial aristocrats, squires and peasants as it possessed, there was steady employment in the almost incessant wars against Spain in the Low Countries before 1648. Meanwhile the enterprising could secure satisfactory returns from trade or from a shipping industry which itself absorbed a mass of manpower. Then, like other Protestant countries, Holland was imbued with no such missionary urges as Catholic France and Iberia, and no such aspirations as Renaissance Venice to rule colonial subjects with Roman justice (cf. pp. 121, 415, 423). In short, there were no pressing economic, political or religious reasons why its inhabitants should wish to dwell in distant lands, nor, as the most inchoate of states, had the republic any machinery to oblige them to do so.

In West Africa the story was much the same, with the Dutch so rapidly penetrating, from the late 1500s, those trades established by the Portuguese, that by 1613 it seemed to the Spaniards that it was the profits of the Guinea traffic that paid for Holland's onslaught in Asia and the Americas. Though palpably untrue the extent of Dutch success was none the less impressive. By the early 1600s they had quashed most English competition (slaving apart) on the north coast of the Gulf of Guinea, and gained so effective a hold on the gold markets around Mina that after *c.* 1620 their gold coinage was minted from Guinea ore. Their commerce was conducted with the usual skill, a Portuguese writer remarking in the 1620s that in the Congo they took ivory and other goods neglected by his compatriots; and the English had found them sealing near the Cape of Good Hope a decade earlier.[33] But Dutch attempts to dispossess the Portuguese and to establish a formal authority in West Africa were barely more successful than their similar efforts in Brazil. Only in 1612 was a post founded near Mina, following a sequence of earlier failures in and around the Gulf of Guinea. Nor did the subsequent grand schemes of the West India Company come to anything more until in 1638 Mina itself was taken, followed by the capture of Luanda three years later, and the occupation of São Tomé and the Angolan and Benguelan coasts (cf. pp. 254–5).

The boldest dreams of Dutch strategists were now apparently realized, with Holland holding both the prime sugar regions of Brazil and the main slave markets of West Africa. The Portuguese Atlantic economy was in ruins, and instead Dutch vessels brought to Africa the goods – the copper, sugar, Indian cloth and beads – with which slaves were purchased; shipped Africans to Brazil and the Caribbean at what was reckoned would soon be the rate of 15,000 a year; and carried tobacco, sugar and other colonial products to Europe. But this maritime supremacy notwithstanding, Dutch conquests were quickly and easily reversed. In 1648 whilst the Hollanders were engaged in clearing up the last remains of Portuguese resistance in the interior of Angola, assisted by the Catholic ruler of the Congo and assorted Jaga subjects of that 'cunning and prudent virago', Queen N'Zinga – who dressed, in as far as the words are applicable, in male attire – they were surprised, isolated and forced to surrender to an expedition from Brazil. To the accompaniment of defeats in South America they were, for the same reasons, driven from the rest of West Africa, retaining, however, some coastal footholds and, for a time, their commercial supremacy.

They likewise failed (1607–8) against Portuguese Mozambique in East Africa, but in the south of the continent, at the Cape of Good Hope, they achieved their sole colonial success outside Asia. Ignoring English claims, the Dutch East India Company established in 1652 a post for the benefit of its fleets in a virtually empty land whose climate, unlike those of the Brazilian and West African coasts, was superbly suited to Europeans (see pp. 407–8). With no Iberian or indigenous opposition there was no call for large-scale settlement, and the few Africans (Hottentots) encountered succumbed to either European violence or disease, or were reduced to servitude. Even so, failure was well within the Dutch capability. The company, apprehensive at the likelihood of smuggling and desertion from its ships calling at the Cape, imposed impossible restrictions. Colonists were few and labour scarce – provoking talk of the desirability of bringing in slaves or Chinese workers – and only with the later arrival of European settlers did the colony eventually begin to grow.

Equally indifferent was the Dutch achievement in North America. Here, too, there was the familiar demonstration of economic primacy, with Holland's shipping penetrating trades established by others. The first half of the seventeenth century witnessed, after some precarious years, the growth of English settlements on the north-eastern American seaboard, and the tenuous survival of those of the French in Canada (see pp. 447, 484). But already in 1606 it was the Dutch who were handling the bulk of the furs exported from the St Lawrence, whilst in the following decades their vessels and merchants were increasingly active in the trade of England's American colonies, to the alarm of shipowners at home (see pp. 496–7). Yet characteristically the Hollanders took little part in the long and arduous exploration of North America. Only in 1609 did Henry Hudson, an Englishman in Dutch service, searching for the north-west passage to Asia, investigate the river that now bears his name. In so doing he brought the Hollanders into contact, as the French and English had long been, with a land and peoples far different from any they knew elsewhere (cf. pp. 443, 481). Whatever its obvious riches in fish, fur and timber, North America offered nothing of the wealth of Africa, South America or Asia. It contained no tempting Iberian settlements, its winter climate was of the worst, and its Atlantic coast as uninviting, for the most part, as any. Unlike Asia or South America, it supported, though vast, no more than a handful of people – perhaps 500,000 in 1500 – who were of the same distant Asian origin as the aboriginal inhabitants of South America, had developed in similar isolation, and likewise spoke an enormous diversity of languages. Their cultures ranged from more or less static agrarian economies, such as were found east of the Mississippi, to the hunting communities roaming the Great Plains. Their political organization was not as imposing in European eyes as that of the Aztecs or Incas, but the confederacies which ruled them, such as that of the Iroquois,[34] could be of formidable military strength. Despite internecine wars, as between the Huron and Iroquois, European penetration of the homelands of these peoples was slow (see pp. 447, 490). Hence, unlike the majority of their distant relatives in the south, they were able to acquire and become expert in the use of white men's weapons, making them both redoubtable foes (or allies) and invaluable customers for arms.

Despite the fact that the Hudson river lay well clear of those centres of Spanish power which tempered most non-Iberian ambitions in America, and notwithstanding the rapid emergence of a considerable fur trade, the republic's interest was tepid. Not till 1614 did it grant a monopoly of the commerce of what was now described as the New Netherlands to a group of merchants whose agents, housed in a few scattered posts, obtained furs from the neighbouring Indians. Then, as in Africa and Brazil, came bolder schemes. The territory was transferred to the West India Company (1621), which was not only to export furs, but so to develop its holding that it would be able to support traders with cheaply grown American produce, and even become a supplier of timber and grain to the mother country. Unlike the Iberians, or as it was itself to try in Brazil, the company attempted no conquest, but prudently bought land from the

Indians – Manhattan Island, where there slowly emerged the town of New Amsterdam (later New York), and the site of the future Hartford.[35] Nor was there any Iberian-style intervention in Indian affairs. Instead, indigenous traders were encouraged to come to the Dutch posts, with the company counting on its better and cheaper goods to woo them from the French in Canada (see pp. 450ff.).

Such policies needed the support of colonization, and in 1624 thirty Protestant families from Flanders were brought out. But though the company gave them land and abundant good advice, and though the settlement was to be one based on the restraints and responsibilities of family life, and thus most likely to succeed, little came of the venture. The oppressed of many parts of the world, including some fleeing the godly excesses of Puritan New England, were magnanimously received with subsidies and free lands (see p. 491). But no more than the Dutch themselves did they come in sufficient numbers, and many that came found little to please them. They aspired to the riches to be had from the fur trade (with the company doing its best to curtail or prohibit their activities), not to the tribulations of agricultural toil. So, in that familiar cycle of the attempted settlement of lands without easily accessible loot and freely oppressible natives, the colonists failed to produce enough food to feed themselves. In 1629, therefore, the company, retaining in its own hands the profitable fur trade, resorted to the equally familiar strategem of devolving responsibility for colonization on others. In a way roughly resembling Genoese and Portuguese practice, lands were granted to 'patroons', who then had to settle and exploit them. Though in theory vassals of the company, they obtained in effect, like Brazilian *donatorios*, outright possession of their holdings (see p. 248). They enjoyed a similar monopoly of justice over their tenants, whose tenural rights were, however, ensured by contract. But here again there was little success, obliging the company once more to resume (1635) the task of colonization itself, urged on, like as not, by the government's improbable ambition of making the New Netherlands an integral part of a recently devised American economy. The colony could supply food to the Dutch in Brazil and Curaçao, and in return receive slaves and horses from the latter. But these were the least of its problems. Underpopulated, it failed to withstand the pressure of the English settlements to the north, which by the mid-1630s had taken much of its former Indian trade, whilst the French were likewise drawing away furs to the St Lawrence (see pp. 450, 488). Against the indigenous peoples of North America the Dutch perpetrated no such excesses as the Iberians in the south, or their own compatriots in Asia, if for no better reason that they were in no position to do so. The amity of the Iroquois they secured by treaty and the supply of arms. Nevertheless this proud, independent and formidable people kept them east of the Hudson, and discouraged any lengthy wanderings through their territories.

Thus compared with the growth of the neighbouring English colonies, that of the New Netherlands was insignificant, leaving them by the mid-1600s little more than a few settlements concentrated in the upper Hudson Valley and along the Jersey shore. From forts at Orange (Albany) and Nassau[36] the Dutch, in pursuit of the company's main aim, traded for furs – chiefly otter and beaver – with the Iroquois, who supplied them first from their own lands, and then by sending hunting parties further afield. By 1633 exports were running at over 15,000 beaver skins a year, with Holland supplying a vigorous demand in Poland and Germany, the main centres of much of its Baltic commerce. Characteristically the Dutch converted furs from being a prerogative of the rich to a commodity of almost mass consumption. The beaver hat, made from the animal's felted wool, became a popular article of headgear, and Amsterdam naturally the headquarters of the felt industry. All the same, the Dutch hold on North America was tenuous. Much of the land they proposed to cultivate was of mediocre quality. They were overshadowed by the neighbouring English settlements, inspired by forceful ideologies, whilst their own territories had no more than about 5000 colonists in 1664, and these of the most diverse origins (cf. pp. 488ff.). Many refused to endure the scant rewards of a precarious agricultural existence, voicing their discontent in language which would have done credit to any Iberian or English squire. 'They had not', it was explained in 1628, 'come here to work, for that to work they might as well have staid at home.'[37] Nor did the West India Company improve things, devoted – in as far as it had any time for America – simply to the profits of the fur trade. To protect these it endeavoured to ensure that its possessions would remain simple agrarian settlements, whose inhabitants would neither develop manufactures or the mining of precious stones and metals nor practise or teach 'handicrafts upon which trade is dependent'. To policies more Iberian than those of the Iberians it added the refusal to provide adequate machinery of government, and a consequent failure to inspire, let alone retain, the loyalties of its heterogeneous subjects. Its rule was predominantly military, with a measure of consultation only eventually forced on its reluctant officers by circumstances. The resultant bodies were, however, an embarrassment with their demands for reform, so ensuring that no formal representative institutions developed – a fatal weakness in a colony surrounded by the English, to whom the New Netherlands easily succumbed in 1664.

Yet whilst enduring these ignominies in the west, in Asia the Dutch destroyed most of Portugal's empire, drove the English out of the spice trade, and set up their own extensive authority. As earlier in the Baltic, they found a situation which was to reveal little of their political shortcomings, whilst allowing the fullest deployment of their economic strength. They encountered a large and complex series of regional economies, linked in varying degrees to one another, and precariously to Europe, by sea. These they could control or exploit, like the Portuguese before them, not by colonization, but by maritime strength. No more than Portugal could they, or did they need to, challenge any powerful indigenous state. Unlike the Portuguese, moreover, who had been introduced to the east along the routes of Arab commerce, and had so been drawn to India, the Dutch first established themselves in Indonesia, far-removed from the sources of Iberian strength in the Pacific and the Arabian Sea. In part this was by design, in part by accident since, always worse by land than sea, they were long unable to subdue any major Portuguese base. Here, fortunately, the spices they sought were produced by countless islands, none of any naval or military consequence, and many willing to welcome opponents of the Iberians. From such a foothold, and backed by the government of the republic and (as the West India Company only briefly was) by the business skills and wealth of Amsterdam, the Dutch were able successfully to contend with both the largely unconcerted and failing opposition of the Portuguese and Spaniards, and the faltering hostility of the English.

Like that of the Americas, their penetration of Asia was provoked by Philip II's closure of the Iberian entrepôts to them, threatening their profits from the redistribution of exotic goods in northern Europe. But the Dutch reached a distant world about which they were far from ignorant, since many Netherlanders had been in Iberian service in the east, or were, or had been resident in Portuguese and Spanish ports (cf. pp. 382–3). One such, Jan Huyghen van Linschoten of Enkhuizen, despatched in 1580 to relatives in Seville, became clerk to the archbishop of Goa there and spent five years in the capital of the *Estado da India*. He returned home (1592) to compile, in collaboration with an erudite compatriot, his now celebrated *Itinerary*. Based on Portuguese information and sailing directions, it revealed more immediately and comprehensively to the Dutch than had any confidences of Arab pilots to da Gama, the whole nature of the Asian maritime economy, and rightly urged the opportunities of the Indonesian archipelago. Soon after (1594), following inquiries in Lisbon as to the requirements for such an undertaking, and the acquisition there of charts, a company was formed in Amsterdam to back an Asian voyage. Using Portuguese experience, and inspired by relatively prosaic ambitions, this first Dutch venture had, like Holland's other pioneering expeditions, little of the epic quality of the earlier Spanish and Portuguese investigations of the unknown. But the hazards of the sea were the same, and to them was to be added, as Jan Coen calculated, the fact that the Dutch, attempting to breach the monopoly of the Iberians in Asia, mustered only about one-fifteenth of the capital that their opponents had there.

In 1595 a flotilla under Cornelius Houtman – a singularly unfortunate choice as it transpired – sailed for the east after preparations as meticulous as those for da Gama's voyage. Having touched at the Cape of Good Hope the fleet, ineptly led, made a disorderly and mutinous passage to Java where, though not without much trouble, commercial privileges similar to those of the Portuguese and Chinese were obtained from the Moslem sultan of Bantam (1596).[38] Then, following further disagreements and failure to reach the Moluccas, the remaining vessels returned home after an absence of two years and with only one-third of their complements still alive. Nevertheless the expedition had shown that Asia was as accessible from northern as from southern Europe, and in Bantam the Dutch had a base from which they could work the whole year round, unhindered by the seasonal restrictions of the monsoons, and unimpeded by any European or indigenous power. Inspired by such prospects, thirteen fleets, financed by almost as many companies, were sent to the east between 1598 and 1603, with the fortunate making as much as 200 per cent profit. Their declared objectives were commercial, and backers, apprehensive of any threat to their investments, instructed commanders to keep clear of Portuguese vessels. But some, unwilling or unable to find cargoes, could no more resist a tempting prize than could their compatriots in the Caribbean, and their loot on one occasion was, according to Hugo Grotius, the learned advocate of the freedom of the seas, 'the most beautiful and worthiest fruit of voyaging to the Indies'.[39]

Ensuing Dutch expansion was, however, determined less by such predatory urges than by an appreciation of the opportunities of Indonesia. Here the Portuguese had no more than a few fortresses, and were usually at war with the local sultans who, since they dealt in spices themselves, welcomed the Hollanders both as allies and customers. Spice, moreover, was grown in coastal regions conveniently vulnerable to Dutch seapower, as was the seaborne import of rice, textiles and other goods to the Moluccas from Java, Malaya and India. Better still, there was no paramount indigenous authority in the archipelago, but instead a collection of Moslem sultanates usually fighting each other and the Portuguese as well. Each – Atjeh, Bantam, Macassar, Tidore, Ternate – aspired to control the traffic in the adjoining waters, but only one, Mataram (Java), was of any strength. Its ruler's ambitions were, however, exclusively military, and as it transpired he was to destroy those very principalities in the island whose shipping might have been some obstacle to the Dutch.

Yet if Holland's objectives were thus early defined, there was no agreement – reflecting the rivalries, conflicting ambitions and financial independence of the republic's many seaports – as to how they might best be achieved. Fleets were accordingly sent out, often simultaneously, by all the known routes to the east. One, sailing by the Cape of Good Hope (1598), was again commanded by Houtman and had John Davis, an English spy, as its chief pilot.[40] Its members soon showed that whatever high ideals might be aired in the Low Countries, Protestants conceded nothing to Catholics in their brutal contempt for indigenous peoples, inflicting 'rude wrong' on the inhabitants of southern Africa, 'shameful disorders' on those of Madagascar, and dismissing the sultan of Atjeh as 'the great Bacchus'.[41] Other squadrons entered the Pacific (1598) through the Straits of Magellan. The remnants of one ended in Japan, whilst those of another, under Oliver van Noort, reached the Philippines, having thrown their Spanish pilot overboard en route. There the admiral attacked Chinese and Japanese shipping, and fired on survivors in the sea in the course of an action against the Spaniards before returning to Europe *via* Borneo, Java and the Cape of Good Hope (1601) to complete the first Dutch circumnavigation.[42] Meanwhile there were attempts, emulating those of the English earlier, to open a short and easy north-eastern passage to Asia – which indeed there is, but not for wooden sailing ships – through those north-Russian waters known to Dutch seamen since the mid-1500s (see pp. 379 and 472). Efforts in the early 1590s, inspired by Balthasar Moucheron, to push into the icy and fearsome Kara Sea culminated in 1596 in the voyage, as desperate as any, of Willem

Barentsz. Spitsbergen was discovered, and the expedition reached as high as 81°n. Then, blocked by ice, Barentsz and his companions turned for Novaya Zemlya, on which, with their ship crushed in the frozen sea, they wintered in 'a house built in the Norwegian style'. With the following year's thaw the survivors – the first Europeans since the Vikings to have endured the rigours of an Arctic winter – reached Russia by open boat.

Thus by 1600 Holland, considering its resources, had achieved remarkably little in the east, and certainly nothing comparable to what the Portuguese had accomplished in their first few years there. Dutch ports, all capable of raising fleets, all unwilling to concede any advantage to another, squabbled amongst themselves, producing as little concerted oceanic endeavour as contemporary England. And whilst Amsterdam claimed the monopoly of the new trade on the old familiar grounds of the expenses already incurred, the competition of rival Dutch companies drove up the price of spices in Asia and promised to lower it in Europe. To avert these and other difficulties – not least the threat from the English – there was created in 1602, by the intervention of the effective head of the Dutch state, the Grand Pensionary Johan van Oldenbarnevelt, the United East India Company (Vereenigde Oost-Indische Compagnie = VOC, see pp. 403ff.). Formed from the fusion of existing interests, it was given a complete monopoly of the Asian trade, and endowed with enormous powers and privileges. Commerce indeed remained the principal Dutch objective, but in the eyes of Oldenbarnevelt the company was much more than an instrument of private gain. It was, as the commander of the 1603 fleet was ordered, 'to attack the Spaniards and Portuguese wherever they are found', and so divert Habsburg energies and forces from the war against Holland in the Low Countries.

Such things, as the Dutch were to discover elsewhere, are easier said than done, and these very ambitions led a number of major investors in the original companies, who had no taste for such doings, to withdraw their money. Nevertheless, after about a decade, and Iberian resistance notwithstanding, the VOC was trading throughout Indonesia and had established itself at the very heart of nutmeg and cloves production in the Bandas and Moluccas, 'the principal targets', as the company proclaimed in 1608 in a significantly martial metaphor, 'at which we shoot'. Amboina was taken in 1605, Banda Neira occupied four years later, and, after a struggle with the Spaniards, half of Ternate. Such was the weight of Dutch assaults on the Portuguese interport trade, and such their harrying of Goa, Malacca and Macao as to have opened, it was said in 1607, 'a wound almost incurable', and by the 1609 truce with Spain they were in effect admitted to Portuguese Asia. In many places indigenous peoples, seeking, as was alleged – at least by Protestants – relief from the 'intolerable pride' of the Iberians,[43] welcomed the Dutch, allowing them to negotiate or extort treaties like that whereby the sultan of Ternate promised them a monopoly of the spices produced in his dominions in exchange for protection against Portugal and Spain. Nor, as in the Caribbean, was there any shortage of Europeans – inevitably lumped together as Portuguese Jews by the

Spaniards – ready to trade with the intruders. None the less the company failed to achieve the expected success, and was notably unable to take either Goa or Malacca. Portuguese resistance was often remarkably tenacious, and the Portuguese could tap resources other than those deriving from seaborne commerce. They raised loans from local peoples, their territorial possessions brought them money from rents and tributes, which in the 1630s accounted for about one-third of the royal revenues in southern Asia[44] and, however impoverished the empire itself, many of its inhabitants remained impressively wealthy. Furthermore, some eastern communities which had at first welcomed the Dutch, grew tired of them, as did the inhabitants of the Moluccas, disillusioned, so it was reported, by their inability (or unwillingness) to distribute silver with the same lavishness as the Spaniards.[45] Even worse, the company imported so much pepper to Europe as to glut the market, bringing a fall in its return on capital from 75 per cent in 1606 to 20 per cent two years later, and causing the outbreak of acrimonious disputes amongst shareholders and directors.

The disgruntled established, or invested in, rival organizations abroad, and the search for routes to Asia outside the area of the company's supposed jurisdiction brought the discovery of the Le Maire Straits and Cape Horn at the southernmost tip of Latin America. The VOC itself, quickly learning from Iberian experience, appointed a governor-general to reside in the east, and repeatedly and stridently insisted on the absoluteness of its monopoly of the spice trade against all, including the English who had reached Indonesia before the Dutch (see p 467). Notwithstanding the doubts of many Hollanders, their fellow Protestants were to be excluded from those benefits of the freedom of the seas so recently described by Grotius (*Mare Liberum*, 1609) on the grounds of the existing commitments of local peoples to the Dutch, and the expenses incurred by the latter in establishing the trade. Nor, in any case, could economically minded Hollanders accept that whilst they were bearing the heat and burden of war with Iberia, the English should be allowed freely to pursue their business.

Such policies found a vigorous exponent in Jan Coen, twice governor-general (1619–23; 1627–9), a man of the sternest Protestant beliefs and holding the lowest opinion of the natives of Asia. With his commercial experience acquired in Italy and the east, his sharp eye, remorseless energy and strong and simple faith, he played in the early stages of Dutch expansion a role much like that Albuquerque had once occupied in the founding of the *Estado da India*, down to his splenetic correspondence with his superiors (cf. p. 238). He recognized that in Java the Dutch would be better off in Djakarta, the future centre of their rule, provided, as he wrote in true Albuquerquian style, 'we build a stronghold . . . to guard our merchandise' and establish colonies so '[we are] no longer at the mercy of these perfidious moors'. The town was accordingly conquered (1619), a new city – for which dressed stone was shipped in from Europe – laid out, a powerful fortress erected, and the whole named Batavia, the classical designation of the Low Countries. At the same time the company's claims were ruthlessly enforced, not least against the English. An agreement reached in 1619 between the high-minded James I of England and some of the more accommodating Dutch, concerning joint operations against the Iberians in Asia and the rights of their respective East India companies, was ignored by Coen. The English were deprived of their agreed share of the Moluccas trade, excluded from Bantam, tolerated in Djakarta only by Dutch licence, and offered no co-operation by VOC officials on the Coromandel coast of India. This bickering culminated (1623) in the Dutch 'massacre' of ten Englishmen in Amboina, executed it was alleged for plotting to seize the company's fort there with the aid of Japanese mercenaries. Be that as it may, the process was set in train which ended with the withdrawal of the English from both Japan and the spice trade, and their reduction to being clients of Holland for their Indonesian luxuries (see p. 477).

Meanwhile Iberian commerce between Manila and China, in the Straits of Malacca and on the Malabar coast was to be stopped. And besides overthrowing European rivals, the Dutch would turn the maritime economy of Asia to their own benefit. No time should be wasted on exploration or the conversion of the natives, but Holland was to exploit the country trades in which profits eclipsing those made in the traffic with Europe were to be had. A post was to be set up off the Chinese coast. Gujarati textiles were to be obtained at source to be exchanged for spices. Indigenous merchants were to be replaced in the trade in rice and textiles to the Moluccas by time-expired VOC employees and Dutch settlers. The inhabitants of Amboina were to be obliged, 'with a little poverty and pressure', to accept the company's monopoly, and the whole rich interport commerce of Asia was to be carried on by select Dutch nationals. For all this, and for dealings with Europe, Batavia was to become the central entrepôt.

Not all in Holland were willing to accept that Portuguese practice should be so closely emulated, and colonization on the scale advocated by Coen was rejected, though already in 1610 the English had remarked the arrival at Bantam of Dutch ships bringing 'great store of women to inhabit those places which they had conquered'.[46] Nor was there much enthusiasm among company shareholders for the opening of the country trades to their compatriots, likely, it was thought, to squander investors' funds in private ventures. Nevertheless there was no fundamental disagreement between Coen and his masters, however irreverently, not to say contemptuously, he addressed them, or however little they liked his brutality, and he no more revolutionized VOC policy than did Albuquerque that of the Portuguese crown. Like any other commercial power the Dutch needed factories, or more substantial bases, from which to conduct their business and defend routes and sources of supply considered vital. The VOC's acquisition of territories and privileges had commenced before Coen's arrival, and continued after his death. In some cases the company was content with concessions obtained or exacted from local rulers, whom it could then, like the Hanse in the Baltic in its heyday, hold as clients (cf. pp. 54ff., 67). When, however, indigenous power was weaker, or the Portuguese in prior possession, the Dutch resorted to conquest. This was notoriously the case in the Spice Islands, where, pursuing a course begun in 1605, the

Bandas were subjugated with Japanese aid in 1621. Eight hundred of their population – 'indolent people of whom little good can be expected', according to Coen – were shipped to Batavia, over 2000 left to perish in the mountains, and their lands given to Dutch planters. Economic pressure was equally formidable. Cloves were bought by advance payments to local growers, and when these failed to deliver – usually since they had sold the same crop to another buyer – Coen had the company foreclose on the debt, fell the trees on the offending plots, and establish Dutch authority. By 1634, according to the Portuguese, the trade in cloves, nutmeg and mace was all in the hands of the Hollanders. And with the passage of time their control became more formal and extensive, eventually embracing in some degree or other – from local acceptance of the VOC monopoly and a VOC fort, to outright subjection – most of Indonesia.

At the same time, in the course of wars with Spain and Portugal, through rivalry and skirmishes with the English, and through sheer commercial necessity, the Dutch penetrated much of the rest of the maritime economy of the Far East. After a run of earlier failures they were established in Japan (1609), greatly aided by the influence of the Englishman, Will Adams, formerly pilot of a Dutch ship which had arrived there nine years before. Though not allowed to leave the country, Adams had risen to high favour, teaching the *shogun* (see p. 286) geometry, talking to him of other wonders – doubtless a relief from the earnest discourse of missionaries – and receiving in exchange for such intellectual stimulus the comforts of an estate and a Japanese wife. Through his good offices the Dutch were permitted to trade, and granted a factory, first at Hirado and then on Deshima island in Nagasaki harbour. Like most Europeans they recognized and prudently respected the virtues of their hosts, 'good of nature, courteous above measure, valiant in war . . . governed in great civility'.[47] Yet though they were well received, the position of the Dutch was, to start with, far from strong. They had to contend with Portuguese hostility, and lacking as they did a base in China, they were short of the silks vital to European commerce in Japan. Some of these problems they solved for themselves, buying silk in Bantam, Cambodia and elsewhere, or simply removing it from Chinese and Iberian ships. The rest the Japanese solved for them, expelling the Portuguese in 1639 to leave Holland the sole European country allowed to trade in Japan until the nineteenth century (see p. 287).

In China the Dutch had no such success. Here, in Macao, the Portuguese, whose clear lack of martial aspirations the Chinese recognized, had a substantial foothold. It was, moreover, one whose prosperous inhabitants had the means and will to resist, and though the Hollanders might damage the trade of the City of the Name of God, neither by assault nor by blockade could they take it (cf. pp. 275, 295). Their military performance was, as so often, well below the standards of their naval operations, and they lacked in any case a forward base from which to work. Nor were their attempts (1604, 1607) to negotiate admission to China itself any more successful. They had no Adams to counter Iberian influence in imperial high places, whilst their assaults on Chinese shipping served only to make them more unacceptable still. Undeterred, they developed a vigorous clandestine trade from islands off the Chinese coast, in some of which they endeavoured to establish bases – first in the Pescadores, from which the Chinese soon ejected them, and then in Taiwan, where they found Chinese merchants trading with the aboriginal inhabitants, and groups of Chinese engaged in the production of sugar. Forts were built, the spreading of the Calvinist faith begun, and most of the island brought under Dutch control by 1642. But Taiwan was to be no oriental Curaçao, and twenty years later was reconquered by a Ming war-lord.

Where, however, they had to contend with no powerful state, no entrenched Iberian influence, and only such resources as the Portuguese could muster against them, the Dutch could succeed. On the south-eastern (Coromandel) littoral of India political authority was divided between the king of Golconda in the north, and the remnants of the empire of Vijayanagar in the south (cf. p. 237). From the northern coast grain, and more important, cotton piece goods (calicoes, muslins) and ready-made clothing were exported to markets ranging from the Red Sea to the Spice Islands. In exchange Coromandel received commodities such as Indonesian pepper and Burmese gold in a trade basically in indigenous hands, apart from what the virtually independent Portuguese communities in São Tomé and Negapatam had been able to secure for themselves. Control of Coromandel textiles, the Dutch quickly appreciated, could be the basis of a vast and self-sustaining interport commerce. By 1610 they had posts in and around Pulicat, and a foothold in Golconda six years later. From then, until the intervention of the English and the resurgence of indigenous power in the late 1600s, their hegemony was strengthened and extended. More factories were acquired, Negapatam and São Tomé taken (1658, 1662), and attempts made to limit the eastern trade of local merchants. Similarly in Ceylon – under a fragile Portuguese authority – the Dutch had a fort by 1612, and soon developed a vigorous commerce. Amongst other things they imported rice and opium and exported elephants and cinnamon, finally converting economic dominance to political supremacy with their conquest, by 1658, of the entire island except for the mountain kingdom of Kandy. Progress elsewhere in the Bay of Bengal and southeast Asia was more difficult. The Portuguese, briefly ejected from Bengal, were soon back (1632). For a time, but only in face of vigorous Indian and Portuguese competition, the Dutch traded to Burma. By the mid-1600s they were active in Arakan, Siam, and to a lesser extent in Cambodia, and some eventually reached Laos. Further south, Portugal's base at Malacca, its economy already in advanced decline, was taken after prolonged blockade (1641), and Holland's control of the region's commerce tightened (cf. pp. 241–2).

So, too, in the Arabian Sea the empire of the Portuguese was undermined, despite their efforts, by influence at the court of the Mogul emperor and by an admixture of threats and concessions to local peoples, to maintain their lucrative position on the north-west coast of India (cf. p. 242). But a decisive Dutch naval victory (1625) lessened Mogul respect for Portugal's maritime strength, and led to the admission of the VOC to Sind. From here its ships were soon carrying both Dutch- and Asian-owned cargoes to the company's base at the mouth of the Persian Gulf. Here, indeed, inspired by English success, Holland momentarily succumbed to those large and improbable ambitions so readily generated in a region of such commercial and strategic importance (cf. pp. 234 and 478). The export of Persian silk was to become a Dutch monopoly, and its shipment to Europe – from which England would naturally be excluded – re-routed round the Cape of Good Hope. When this was found impossible, the company developed instead an important trade through the factories it acquired in the lands of the shah, selling Bengal sugar and Coromandel cottons, and obtaining some of the silver it needed in Asia. And though in western India prudent regard for Mogul authority limited the scope of Dutch attacks on Portuguese seaborne commerce – much of it carried in local vessels – and though the VOC was unable to suppress a vigorous Portuguese inshore traffic handled by assorted small craft, the wealth and extent of the *Estado da India* were dramatically reduced. Goa's commerce was seriously damaged by blockade from 1636 to 1644, Craganore was taken in 1662, and Cochin was taken the year after.

ii *Private profit and public good*

With these triumphs, and with its economic supremacy in Europe, Holland reached the zenith of its power. In the later seventeenth century the country itself was threatened by the military might of France, and its commerce endangered by English hostility. The republic fought a series of costly and destructive naval wars against the resurgent seapower of its Protestant neighbour, whose Navigation Acts marked the first effective attempt to exclude Dutch shipping from valuable trades. Even so, as the English statistician Gregory King wrote in 1695, and the Scottish savant Adam Smith agreed eighty years later, Holland was Europe's richest state. Its wealth, like that of the Italian maritime republics and the Hanseatic towns, came essentially from trade by sea and rested, as did theirs, on the slenderest of territorial foundations. Like that of Genoa it was accumulated by a ruthless and efficient dedication to business, reflected in the republic's reputation, its domination, to a degree hitherto unapproached, of much of Europe's economy, and its acquisition by war of a maritime empire for the benefit of Dutch commerce (cf. pp. 155ff.). Holland's initial imperial ambitions stemmed largely from the desire to continue a trade formerly conducted through Iberian entrepôts, and threatened in the late 1500s by Habsburg enmity. But such mundane pragmatism swiftly burgeoned into a grandiose global strategy. William Usselincx envisaged (1592), in a tradition already well-established in England, the founding of colonies in the west to provide the mother country with a market for its manufactures and to supply it with raw materials (see p. 482). The precepts of sound business were less in evidence in a project (1600) to convert the Amerindians of the Wild Coast to the blessings of Calvinism and agriculture, to teach them – significantly enough – to fight on horseback, and then to loose this godly horde against the very heart of Habsburg America.[48] By the

1620s there were dreams of overthrowing Spanish rule in Chile with the aid of the fierce and unsubdued Araucanians, of occupying the Straits of Magellan, and even of an overland assault on Spanish Peru.

Of these, and the grander schemes of the West India Company, the ultimate outcome was modest. Nevertheless where, outside Europe, the republic enjoyed territorial sovereignty, and where its maritime hegemony was enormously expanded, was largely at the expense of the Iberians, and more especially the Portuguese (cf. pp. 297–8). As a result Holland saw little reason, and showed little inclination, to expend energies and resources on voyages of exploration and discovery. Some indeed there were, but few of the significance of those of the Spaniards and Portuguese earlier, or of the French and English later. A small area of the north-east seabord of America was explored by Henry Hudson, Spitsbergen discovered by Barentsz, the tip of southern American examined, and the Kuril Islands and Sakhalin reconnoitred during searches (1639, 1643) for lands rich in gold and silver rumoured to lie near Japan. Characteristically Dutch seamen opened an easier and more direct route to south-east Asia than that used by the Portuguese when, in 1611, Hendrick Brouwer found that below the Cape of Good Hope, in latitudes approximately 40° to 50° south, there blow strong and constant westerlies giving a ship a run eastwards through temperate climates until she picks up the south-east trades, fair for the Sunda Straits. Such winds, combined with the imperfections of pilots, navigation and craft brought, as with other maritime peoples, accidental finds (cf. pp. 14, 240). A commander persisting too long in the 'roaring forties' – as many were to do – sighted and explored part of the western coast of Australia (1616), the north of which continent had already been seen and misidentified by a compatriot (1605), if not by the Portuguese earlier. Over the next half century spasmodic exploration of the region continued, culminating in Tasman's demonstration of Australia's insular nature and his discovery (1642) of Tasmania, Fiji, Tonga and the mountainous and inappropriately named New Zeeland (Zealand). But there was nothing here to whet businessmen's appetites or to excite the interest of a commercial society notably lacking in colonial zeal and resources, and after Tasman's examination of the Gulf of Carpentaria in northern Australia (1644) his discoveries were ignored.

Equally characteristic was that Holland's overseas empire was very largely established and exploited by the East India Company and the West India Company, both powerful public joint-stock organizations. In itself the use of similarly financed corporations in such a role was nothing new. They were needed where, unlike in Iberia or Venice, there was no royal or state monopoly of some valuable trade, operated in some degree by royal or state money, and providing, if not always ships, then at least fleets for their protection together with the essential colonial bases and forts. But where these were dependent on private initiative, and where, unlike in the Spanish conquests, there was no prospect of great and immediate gains from the occupation of rich territories, then the costs and risks, as of lengthy voyages themselves, were greater than any individual or small group of individuals were prepared to accept. Hence at one stage companies controlled some of Genoa's colonial possessions, were set up in the mid-1500s by the English to open new trades, and had been employed by the Dutch themselves in their earliest eastern ventures (cf. pp. 191, 472, 477). But the two great monopoly companies which finally emerged were of a size and power hitherto unequalled. Nevertheless their use did not mark, as in Genoa, the surrender by an impoverished state of public responsibility to private hands. Nor were they, like the Russia Company in England, merely business concerns. They were founded to reconcile existing interests, and to mobilize them, together with the widely disseminated wealth of the Low Countries, for private profit and public good – that of the ruling merchant oligarchy in fact – by combining the establishment of a Dutch colonial trade with a global war against the overseas empires of Spain and Portugal.

The United East India Company, formed by the amalgamation of existing companies, eventually achieved such wealth and authority that until Japan's destruction of Netherlands' imperial rule in the 1940s, *Compagnie* and Holland were one and the same thing to the indigenous peoples of Indonesia.[49] The VOC was initially granted a twenty-one-year monopoly of the Asian trade by the republic, in whose name it could make treaties with local rulers. Besides this it could occupy lands, declare war, own ships, raise armies, erect fortresses and appoint officers to their command. Its constitution and organization reflected all the strengths and weaknesses of the Dutch state – its economic precocity, its dominant mercantile oligarchy, the uneven distribution of wealth within its borders, its precarious political unity. The company comprised six so-called 'chambers' (Amsterdam, Middelburg, Delft, Hoorn, Rotterdam, Enkhuizen), deriving from the earlier companies. Each had its own directors, and each retained considerable independence in the operation of its ships and commerce. But between them Amsterdam and Zeeland provided over half the directors, just as Amsterdam and Middelburg provided twelve of the VOC's seventeen-man governing body (*Heeren*-17), recruited from amongst the directors. All the same, anyone, irrespective of race, religion or sex could invest, and on the most attractive terms. Only for directors was a minimum holding stipulated, the liability of subscribers was limited to the purchase price of their shares and they were not burdened by subsequent calls for further cash, since additional capital was raised by short-term loans. Hence whilst the directors themselves put up no more than 7 per cent of the company's capital, money flowed in from the whole range of society. Amongst the vast number of modest subscribers were such humble or prudent figures as starch-makers and university professors; amongst the magnates merchants from Nürnburg joined those of Hamburg and the two greatest holdings belonged to men originally from the southern Netherlands. Thus in Iberia members of nearly every social class were drawn into the implementation of imperial enterprises, but in Holland they could less arduously forward them as investors.

The shortcomings of the VOC were many and obvious. It was, as was soon evident, short of capital. No more than the Iberian monarchies could it restrain the illicit entrepreneurial urges of its servants who, regardless of restrictions, built up a substantial private trade – both in Asia and to Europe – in competition with its monopoly. And for the offspring of a successful commercial state its accounting system was of such complexity as to persuade many that it was a cunning stratagem to conceal from prying eyes the scale of profits being reaped in the east. There, in Batavia, details of receipts and expenditure at all the company's posts from Mocha to Nagasaki were held. From these information was extracted and sent home, but since the VOC had no central accounting office in Europe, and since separate accounts were kept by individual 'chambers', an overall view of business was difficult to obtain. Nor were suspicions as to the company's proceedings allayed by its constitution. Unlike the West India Company, or the English East India Company, the VOC was under a powerful central management which gave purpose to its policies and ensured resources for their implementation (cf. pp. 417, 480). This management was provided by the *Heeren*-17 and the major shareholders, especially those of the Amsterdam and Zeeland 'chambers'. The position of these magnates was, to say the least, enviable. Directors held office for life and had the decisive voice in the selection of their successors. As a body they received various commissions on business, and since they alone knew the true financial position of the company they were particularly well-placed to speculate on loans and shares. Nor was there anything to inhibit such enterprise. They were in fact virtually independent of the will of the shareholders, to whom they were required to account only once every ten years. And since there was no body of company shareholders as such, but only those in the individual 'chambers', the directors were rarely embarrassed by any concerted opposition, and the smaller investors effectively deprived of any say in company affairs. So the doings of an oligarchy as tight and secretive as that of Venice, and of an administration as labyrinthine as that ruling the Spanish colonies, aroused suspicions – and not ill-founded – that the VOC and its plutocrats were doing much better than was indicated in the dividends they were prepared to pay to investors.

Nevertheless the company soon showed itself to be one of the most efficient instruments of colonial exploitation as yet devised. Its form of government, however cumbersome and archaic, was superior to that of its English rival (cf. pp. 480–1). And unlike the latter it enjoyed that state support conducive to imperial success, developing a highly organized secretariat in the capital, the better to protect and advance its interests in ruling circles. True, in 1644 the *Heeren*-17, ostentatiously affirming mercantile faith in the supremacy of profit, declared that 'the places and strongholds which have been captured in the East Indies ought not to be regarded as national conquests, but as the property of private merchants who are entitled to sell these places to whoever they wish, even if it were to the king of Spain or some other enemy of the United Provinces.'[50] Yet it was to the state as well as to the company that VOC personnel took their oaths – as was indeed required by the founding charter. When the office of governor-general was introduced the republic spoke of 'these lands, fortresses and settlements which we and ours possess in India', and it was for state approval that the first incumbent's instructions were submitted. That such practices soon ceased merely reflects the fact that the power of the governing oligarchs of the republic was so strong in the VOC as to make them superfluous. Admittedly, directors might on occasion overrule the decisions of their officers in the east, but in general they accepted them, and by and large company and state policies were identical to the point that when, on the renewal of the VOC charter, shareholders demanded some say in the running of the organization, the republic declared the more radical proposals treasonable.

Moreover, developed and directed by successful merchants in a successful commercial state, the policies of the East India Company were economically more rational, and their implementation more effective, than those of its rivals. Often enough they were in fact those of its precursors, with the VOC borrowing from Asian merchants in the same way and at the same high rates of interest (30 per cent p.a. and above) as did the Portuguese in Goa or Japan (cf. p. 267). But unlike the Portuguese crown the company normally paid its servants (albeit inadequately), and whereas the English sent only fourteen ships all told to the east before 1609, the VOC regularly sent out as many every other year. The company aimed, as the Portuguese did not, to secure control of as much as possible of the centres of spice production (like the doings of the similarly mercantile Genoese earlier with Levantine alum and the resources of Iberia), and whilst the Portuguese crown was content with rents and tribute, and with a monopoly of the shipment to and from Asia of certain commodities, the aspirations of the VOC were far more ambitious (cf. pp. 181, 269). Not only would it monopolize the long-distance traffic between east and west, but it also attempted – after some hesitation, and however imperfectly – to keep in its own hands the enormously valuable interport commerce it developed, just as it kept in its own hands the marketing of its imports in Europe. The company's monopoly was thus both more extensive than those of the medieval maritime states and the Iberians, and more intensive in that its operation was assessed, as was not the case in Spain and Portugal, in terms of profit and loss. Though the VOC had no machinery of annual audit the management received a yearly balance sheet from Batavia, covering the year's trading results and outlining plans for the coming twelve months. It reported profits and losses not only in individual posts, but in the east as a whole, and in addition, like the reports of Venetian ambassadors and consuls, summarized from the mass of information that flowed into Batavia from every factory, the political situation and commercial prospects of all the areas in which the company traded. The VOC's true overall financial position was, and is, difficult to ascertain, not least since the directors merely compared the costs of setting out ships for Asia in a given year with the value of sales in Europe in the same period, making no allowance for other commitments, let alone depreciation. But in Asia the management could and did watch the profitability of every commodity and every factory in the general context of the company's business. Furthermore, circulating capital ('the Indian fund') was built up, retained and employed in the east in ways which again demonstrate the skill and sophistication of the VOC's trading. Its accumulation was possible because the company, unlike its English rival in its early years, did not wind up and distribute its capital at the end of each venture (cf. p. 481). Instead it remained invested and thus continued to grow, whilst money to cover current ventures and to pay the dividends necessary to placate investors was raised by loans secured on incoming cargoes and existing stocks of spice. Moreover the company neither comprised, nor was responsible to, aristocrats and squires who expected from empire those lavish rewards tantamount to plunder. It accordingly paid its shareholders, as indeed they complained, relatively modest dividends[51] – none till 1611; an average of 7 per cent annually for the first fourteen years of its life and 18.7 per cent for the first century – and these often including spices the management had failed to sell. Hence unlike the English company, whose backers expected large and immediate returns on their money, the VOC was able to build up its Asian capital, holding in the east roughly 60 per cent of the profits earned there before the mid-1600s. Resources of this order allowed the widespread diversification and co-ordination of trade in a way that individual Portuguese merchants and officials had appreciated was possible, but on a scale beyond their reach and beyond the means and indeed comprehension of the Portuguese state.

In essence, however, the VOC's commerce was identical with that of Portugal. The company shipped home spices – which in 1648–50 accounted for nearly 70 per cent of the value of its Asian purchases – and by the mid-1600s was supplying about two-thirds of Europe's pepper. In exchange the Dutch exported silver, which they acquired from Spain in the war years by piracy and illicit trade and then directly from Cadiz after the peace of 1648. By then they were taking something like half the American bullion reaching Europe, and with such voracity and efficiency that a VOC ship lost off western Australia in 1656 was carrying coin minted in Spanish America only two years before.[52] These basic exchanges gradually turned, as with the Portuguese, to a widely variegated commerce. The textiles of Bengal, Gujarat and Coromandel, it was soon found, sold well not only in Europe and Asia Minor but also, as 'black Guinea cloths', in Brazil and Angola, and by 1700 made up the bulk of the company's west-bound cargoes. To textiles were added metals, precious stones, indigo, coffee, saltpetre for the manufacture of gunpowder, and porcelain by the shipload, whilst at the same time a growing range of European products was sent to Asia where, for example, the martial Japanese were connoisseurs of plans and paintings of battles. And like the Portuguese the Dutch developed an extensive eastern interport trade, the profits from which, together with locally raised loans and the earnings of their shipping eventually provided them with most of the capital needed for the purchase of goods for Europe. Indeed, inspired by the spectacle of Portuguese activities, Jan Coen envisaged (1619) a commerce in which select Dutch colonists would exchange the products of every part of Asia for spices which could then be sent to Holland. All that was needed was a central entrepôt, Dutch ships and 'a little water [money] to prime the pump'.

The reality was less ambitious, but impressive all the same. By the mid-1600s the Dutch were shipping Sinhalese and Malaysian elephants to Bengal, employing Chinese gold obtained in Taiwan to buy cloth in Coromandel, exchanging Indian textiles for Indonesian spices, selling Japanese copper throughout the east, and using local rather than imported silver where necessary. In short they had developed a trade in which goods from factories anywhere from Persia to Japan were drawn to Batavia which, redistributing them to Europe and Asia, exercised in the east a role similar to that of Amsterdam in the west. This great country traffic, with spices and metals flowing westwards and textiles eastwards, had a vigorous life of its own to which trade with Europe was ancillary, except for the stimulus provided by silver imports. Even so, it was the VOC's control of Japanese bullion, freeing it from close dependence on that coming from Europe and the Americas, that gave the Dutch the edge over their less happily placed English rivals.

But if this was a commerce deriving from a Portuguese and indeed an indigenous pattern, the pristine model was, as in every other field, improved, and business conducted more rationally and ruthlessly (cf. pp. 234–43). The intensive cultivation of the widely salable sugar was encouraged in Java. In Coromandel, where the Portuguese had been happy to buy more or less any sort of local cloth and make small profits on a high volume of sales, the Dutch confined themselves to a limited range guaranteeing high returns. And to ensure adequate supplies of the right quality they issued samples for producers to copy and in Pulicat prohibited (1627) the manufacture of any other. Elsewhere competitors were embarrassed or ruined (see p. 294). In Banda English prices were undercut by up to a third (1609).[53] Later, when there was a danger that rivals excluded from the Moluccas might purchase cloves in Malaysia and Macassar in exchange for Coromandel textiles, the VOC bought up all the cottons it could (1637), raising the necessary capital by loans – some at nearly 40 per cent interest – from Asian merchants.

Similarly in the organization of their oceanic commerce the Dutch accepted but improved current practice. Monopoly it was generally agreed was justified since costs were high, risks and distances great, and indigenous assumptions as to the conduct of business not those of Europeans (cf. pp. 269ff.). Hence the creation of privileged companies, and Holland's extension by law into the wider world of monopolies elsewhere created and sustained by economic superiority. The West India Company was soon in trouble, but the monopoly of the VOC was strengthened and extended. The company's cargoes were carried, in a fashion roughly analogous to that of the Portuguese and Venetians, in its own vessels (see pp. 23, 270). Those working to and from Asia were the powerful 'return ships' resembling in general, with their high-built sterns, three masts and admixture of square and lateen sails, the big craft of other European states (see pp. 147, 194). They were, however, only about half the burthen of the largest Portuguese carracks. Also they had a lower galleon-style bow and beak, finer lines and were rigged in the more complex fashion favoured in the early 1600s, setting an additional square sail on all masts and a spritsail topsail on the end of the bowsprit. With the passage of time their lines became bluffer, their hulls more squat, their masts relatively shorter and the weight of their artillery greater, so that with up to 250 men on board they were frequently bigger than the republic's largest men-of-war. For their country trade the Dutch, like the Portuguese, used in part smaller western craft and in part local vessels such as junks.

The VOC's Indiamen worked, in the same way as those of the Portuguese, to a pattern determined by the oceanic wind systems. Three fleets left Europe annually and usually arrived in Batavia after seven or eight months, though longer passages were by no means uncommon.[54] There was some improvement on Portuguese practice in that if the vessels that sailed in the autumn arrived on time, their ladings for the major oriental markets could be re-shipped without waiting for the onset of the south-westerly monsoon. So also the departure of the second of the two return fleets for Europe was delayed until goods coming to Batavia from China, Japan and the Bay of Bengal were available for loading. For the rest things ran much as they did with the Portuguese, and at the usual high cost in ships and men. The average rate of loss of crew in VOC Indiamen was perhaps about 15 per cent in 1625–31, but conditions could easily be much worse. The English reported meeting near the Cape in the early 1600s 'a Dutch ship which . . . had but eight or nine men standing, the rest sick and forty-six dead'. In mid-century the company itself described one of its vessels as 'like a plague house . . . scurvy, the bloody runs, dropsy, burning fever, insanity, delirium'.[55] Yet to those accustomed to Portuguese ways, the manning structure of Dutch Indiamen seemed businesslike and uncomplicated. Equally characteristically discipline was maintained, in the pursuit of efficiency and profit, with a ferocity notorious even in its own day, but bonuses paid to pilots who got their ships home in good time.

Then again, in Asia the Portuguese crown had been content to abandon the country trade to private merchants. The VOC, on the other hand, after a brief liberal interlude, and notwithstanding some grudging concessions, was adamant that this was its business, even if its employees were equally resolute in disregarding its claims (cf. pp. 274–5, 413–14). Furthermore, though the company's monopoly was initially envisaged as excluding from Asian commerce only other groups and individuals within the republic, the VOC soon assumed it was empowered to prohibit both Europeans and Asians from its preserves. Already in 1608 there was talk of 'how much greater would be the profits' if the company had Moluccan cloves to itself. Seven years later, to improve its position in the Bandas, the directors believed 'the inhabitants must be subjugated, their leaders killed or driven out, and if need be the country turned into a desert'.[56] Nor were these idle words. The Chinese were excluded from the Indonesian ports in which Holland claimed a monopoly. Macassar, since it persisted in trading with the company's rivals, was bombarded (1660) and later occupied. Bantam's trade was diverted by blockade to Batavia, and the Sumatran pepper towns obliged by similar means to make deliveries to the Dutch. Everywhere the VOC pressed for monopoly, and indeed for a time entertained still more remarkable ambitions. At one stage Jan Coen, clearly impressed by Portuguese pretensions and practice, was urging that Indians should be taxed for the right to use the sea, and later (1623) that all indigenous maritime competition should be eliminated. Even for Dutch naval power this was patently impossible, though the *Heeren*-17 found the idea a sound one. As it was they resigned themselves to tolerating Asian competitors as 'a constant plague' to be checked by regulation when too vigorous.[57]

Europeans were treated in similar style. Spanish Manila was blockaded; Spain attacked in the Spice Islands; Portugal's Asian trade and empire vastly reduced; French and English ventures crippled (cf. pp. 400–1, 442, 477ff.). Thus in the mid-1600s, with the capture of Malacca and the occupation of Macassar (1669) – the prime smuggling base – the Dutch spice monopoly was more or less complete, and certainly more complete than that of any predecessor. It was least satisfactory in pepper, which was too widely grown to be controlled by any single power. Even so, the VOC, with its hold on the Malabar coast and its exclusive contracts with Sumatran producers, eventually dominated the best part of the market. With the cloves, nutmeg, mace and cinnamon of countless islands there were difficulties since smuggling, and therefore competition and prices, could never be adequately regulated. Nevertheless with the Bandas and Ceylon in its hands the company had a tight control over nutmeg and cinnamon. The problem of cloves, available in most of the Moluccas, it attempted to solve in characteristic fashion. Their cultivation was to be restricted to Dutch Amboina, alone capable of meeting the combined demands of Europe and Asia. Only those indigenous peoples co-operating in this grand design would be allowed the cloth and rice they needed, and whose import the Dutch controlled. VOC garrisons would ensure that crops were handed over, and VOC naval sweeps would destroy trees found elsewhere. The acquiescence of the local ruler was secured by a suitable reward – 'extirpation money' as it was ominously known. So effective were these proceedings that by 1656 supply was below demand and the majority of the local inhabitants reduced to abject poverty. This triumph of business logic was guaranteed by Dutch seapower and the absence of any significant Indonesian states. Ubiquitous company vessels harried or destroyed indigenous commerce and drove out European competitors, whilst the VOC's concentration was, unlike that of the West India Company in its proposed preserves, undisturbed by over-ambitious commitments and internal dissensions.

In Europe the company displayed similar skills and attitudes. Its aim – far different from that of the Portuguese crown which simply hoped for the highest possible payment for its spices in any year – was to ensure a wide, regular and steady market. This it attempted to accomplish by selling at stable and predictable prices, set, however, sufficiently low to discourage any potential rival from entering the field. Falling prices, as of pepper in 1619–22, were stabilized by a refusal to sell; rising prices restrained by the release of stocks – also used to flood the market, and so depress prices that would-be competitors were destroyed. No more than in Asia was the company's monopoly watertight, nor – man being fallible and nature perverse – could it ever fully implement its economic grand strategy. Crops failed; ships sank; agents ignored or disobeyed instructions. Even so, at the very time costs were rising in Asia the VOC was able to more than halve the price of pepper in Europe (1600–30) and thereafter keep it well below sixteenth-century levels, as well as holding the price of other spices roughly constant.

What profit the company drew from such operations, or indeed what profit the republic drew from its empire, are less certain. Holland's American and eastern ventures were an expression and extension of that dominance of Europe's seaborne carrying trade on which the country lived so well. In comparison with this they remained insignificant – dealings with Asia producing no more than 10 per cent of the total value of the republic's commerce before the eighteenth century. After some brief years of glory the West India Company and its enterprises were anything but rewarding (cf. pp. 386–90, 417ff.). The fortunes of the VOC, before it fell into debt in the late 1600s, are more enigmatic. Cloves might well sell at 300 per cent clear gain in Europe, but throughout the 1620s and 1630s the Moluccas, Amboina and even the Bandas demanded more – chiefly for defence – than they yielded and company dividends were paid with borrowed money. Once Portuguese and English competition had been scotched impressive profits were made in some country trades. Even so, only about 10 per cent of the gross gains were transmitted to Europe and the rest consumed locally in operating and maintaining the monopoly. Hence whilst as in every empire individual entrepreneurs flourished exceedingly – VOC directors working the share market; VOC employees enriched by smuggling – new burdens were laid on the parent state, though not, in prudent Holland, so onerously as in Iberia (cf. pp. 290, 364). It was the company and not the republic that in the first half of the seventeenth century conducted the war in the east against Spain and Portugal, and sustained the expense of running the resultant acquisitions. Whatever commerce the VOC had in Asia was denied to other Europeans – notoriously not the case with the oceanic economies created by the Iberians – and the republic's re-export of eastern goods became yet another element in its commercial and maritime primacy. Manpower the colonies indeed demanded, but of necessity the Dutch employed the resources of others. Nor, as was well understood, were the blessings of empire to be evaluated in simple accounting terms. The Asian possessions were largely acquired at the expense of the Iberians, conveniently contributing, together with similar campaigns in the Atlantic, to Spain's inability to deal with the Dutch revolt in Europe.

III   *The business of empire in Asia*

Like those of the Hanse and the Italian maritime cities Holland's empire was primarily one of commerce. In Asia this meant the attempt to create a monopoly, which in turn demanded the control of sources of supply, the acquisition of bases dominating the routes used by Dutch shipping, and the establishment of trading posts. These factories, similar to those of the medieval seaborne empires or the Portuguese, enjoyed varying degrees of autonomy according to the nature of the societies amongst which they were set. In Coromandel they soon developed an organization of some sophistication. Each had a chief factor, a staff of assorted assistants and clerks, various local officials and servants and a garrison of either European or native troops and their followers. At first these factories were under the general jurisdiction of Pulicat, created in 1615 a 'government', or in other words enjoying in the company's eyes sovereign status. Six years later those in the north were put under Masulipatnam, and a central administration with a governor and a court of justice exercising powers of life and death over company employees set up. But not all eastern peoples, and certainly not the Japanese – who as the Dutch themselves recognized 'care not the least about us, and fear no harm we can do them' – were prepared to concede such liberties. At Deshima they imposed on the company restrictions so stringent as to make Dutch acceptance of them a matter for scorn in the west. VOC vessels were disarmed and immobilized on arrival. Hollanders were forbidden to contaminate Japanese soil by burying their dead ashore, and prohibited, since Christianity was outlawed, from observing Sunday aboard their ships.

Holland's empire was not, however, to remain as did that of the equally mercantile Hanse, simply one of routes, factories and economic hegemony. Like Venice the republic was territorially large enough to be able to advance from trade to dominion, and like Venice it was involved in areas where this was possible. It enjoyed, as the Hanse did not, sufficient political unity – though only just – to undertake such ventures, for which Calvinist hatred of Spain and Catholicism provided the necessary will, occasionally sharpened by the ambitions of the house of Orange and its satellites (cf. pp. 420ff.). In the west Brazil was attacked and even grander visions were entertained, whilst in Batavia there was talk (1643) of so organizing affairs in the Persian Gulf 'that we no longer need to reside under Moorish rule, but can enjoy our own and demand taxes'. And there were thoughts too of the joys of a less strenuous imperialism. The Dutch could trade, like the Portuguese did, with others, money (i.e., on commission), or live, as the Spaniards did in the Philippines, on the fruits of native labour.

So by force and fraud – by foreclosure for debt; by conquests as ruthless as any – the republic's territorial empire was founded in the east. No more than any other did it result from unaided European effort (cf. pp. 367ff. and 339ff.). Its creation, like its survival, was assisted by the adept utilization of conflicts and divisions in indigenous societies. Pagan tribesmen from the interior were used against the coast-dwelling Moslems in Ceram and Amboina, and a variety of local allies employed in the conquest of Java. Indonesia was the heart of the empire, and Batavia its capital. From here Holland's possessions were governed, and through its entrepôt the Dutch operated their commercial monopoly, organized much like Venice's trade with the Levant had once been. By the 1620s the newly founded city, 'Queen of the Eastern Seas', was a flourishing fortified settlement. No more than Holland's colonies in the west was it allowed any such quasi-representative institutions as those of Portuguese Goa and Macao, let alone the liberties of English fellow-Protestants in America. Nor, in comparison with the two Portuguese cities, or those of Spanish America, was it of more than modest size, its population amounting to only about 2000 – and half of these Chinese, the inescapable intermediaries, as the Dutch came to recognize, between themselves and the peoples of Indonesia.

Yet merchant-made and merchant-owned, the eastern empire had little of the propensity of those produced by less advanced aristocratic-peasant societies to almost indefinite expansion in the pursuit of gain or glory. Some territories, like Cape Colony on the vital sea route to and from Asia, were acquired for strategic reasons. The rest, mostly small islands, were occupied to destroy their competition or to guarantee Dutch control of their produce. Thus in the Bandas the indigenous population was driven out and the land divided amongst Dutch planters, each working a holding of fifty nutmeg trees with slave labour. Even so, the economy was not in Iberian or Mediterranean style. The VOC supplied the slaves, bought the crop at its own price and taxed the planters.

How, or indeed whether, such possessions were to be colonized – questions unthinkable in Iberia – were for a time matters of contention. Coen as usual had definitive answers. Orphans, male and female, Dutch and foreign, could be shipped to the east. Dutch colonists would populate Holland's new territories, supplying by the labour of their slaves the spices the VOC required. Dutch 'free-burghers', married like Portuguese *casados* to Asian women, and hence indestructibly rooted in their adopted homeland, would conduct the interport trade (cf. pp. 274–5). And to avert the dangers of ever-present oriental temptations the settlers' morals would receive the undivided attention of Calvinist pastors, who would waste no time on the native peoples. Hardly surprisingly such plans met with little response, and even though the company itself, conscious of the pressing problems of defence, acknowledged the virtues of coloniz-ation, its officials in the east, sensitive to any threat to their own profitable dealings, did not. Thus though by the late 1600s the VOC might have as many as 18,000 men in the east, the majority were soldiers, seamen, artisans and officials, not colonists. Admirable schemes to send out respectable married couples or 'honest but impoverished families' were all largely abortive, and of such settlers as there were the reports – admittedly no novelty – were generally disobliging. The company animadverted against the drunkards and libertines with which it was saddled in Coromandel, whilst an English merchant sourly noted a Dutchman living wild on an island in the Molucca Sea 'with as many women as he pleaseth . . . he will sing and dance all day long, near hand-naked . . . and will be drunk two days together'.[58] No more than other contemporary strictures on colonists as the dregs of humanity are such criticisms to be accepted at their face value. Yet clearly when men to whom Europe had offered very little escaped from the shackles of its conventions and joined indigenous women who had been rejected by or (as slaves) torn from their own cultures, there flourished that immorality which so fascinated European observers. And equally clearly the Dutch, in east and west alike, were short of settlers. There was little reason why any one should wish to leave the republic, least of all on the VOC's terms. 'Free-burghers', largely recruited from time-expired company employees, were only permitted to settle – and under the most stringent conditions – in Batavia, Amboina and the Bandas, where their doings could be watched. Private trade was forbidden – in theory at least – to VOC servants, and before long only permitted to burghers in a few places outside the Indonesian archipelago where the company was unable or unwilling to operate. In short, Dutch settlers, who also faced intense Asian and European competition, had little chance of those lucrative ventures that had once attracted men to Portugal's *Estado da India*. Nor were other prospects any better as the company jealously guarded the interests of shareholders. Far from there being any Mexico or Peru to plunder, the lands for lease around Batavia went only to high-ranking ex-VOC officials who had the influence to secure them and the capital to work them. Small-scale farming, for which in any case European expatriates had no taste, could hardly challenge indigenous agriculture, leaving little for rank-and-file colonists apart from the modest rewards of petty usury, tavern-keeping and, in Batavia – could they survive Chinese competition – a rudimentary building industry.

The Dutch accordingly had to recruit who they could where they could, inevitably including many aliens, and many fleeing the consequences of crimes and misdemeanours. In so doing they produced a colonial society almost as polyglot in origin as that of Portuguese Brazil, but also one that allowed – as indeed empire did everywhere – opportunities to men who might otherwise have been denied them. Antony van Diemen, an erstwhile undischarged bankrupt, became one of the VOC's most distinguished servants, and François Caron, a former ship's cook, the director-general in Batavia (1647). In other ways, however, the colonial society of Dutch Asia was unique. It had none of the aristocrats and squires found in empires as different as those of Portugal and Venice. Nor did it have anything of that middle class common to most overseas possessions and particularly characteristic of the republic itself. More remarkable still, given the origins and aims of the VOC, was the pre-eminence not of merchants, as in the Hanseatic world, but of what amounted to a managerial class, the rough equivalent of the Iberian imperial bureaucracies. Like these it proliferated luxuriantly since, according to van Diemen (1631), it was recruited not on the criteria of merit and aptitude, but by influence and connection, with all the 'chambers' despatching to Asia whoever they wished. The sum result in many eyes was to burden the VOC with men of the lowest calibre – 'clownish boors' – who lauded it over the mass of underpaid and ill-treated clerks needed in a regime dependent on comprehensive book-keeping and minute-taking. That many of the company's servants, like their similarly recruited Portuguese counterparts, devoted their energies chiefly to their own financial interests is clear enough. The accounts of remote factories were fraudulently kept and company assets used in private dealings. Even so, the VOC's very record in the first century of its existence would suggest that other influences were paramount in its operation.

Equally remarkable was the manner in which Holland's eastern (as indeed western) empire was governed. No more than England, where representative institutions tempered royal authority, had a republic born of revolt the means or will to attempt the Iberian-style control of its overseas possessions. Instead these, together with strongholds, fleets and trade came under the jurisdiction of officers of commercial companies. In Asia an elaborate administration soon emerged. Its head was the governor-general, assisted by a council, and with the directors and governors of other possessions – largely independent in fact – regarded as his local representatives. A central judiciary was set up in Batavia and attempts made, though hardly of Spanish or Venetian zeal and efficacy, to oversee the condition and running of posts and territories. In fact the empire was considered one vast business enterprise. Dependency accounts were checked on receipt in Batavia and occasionally locally by inspecting officers from the capital. The company was exercised to know every detail of the doings, and especially the expenditure of its servants, whilst they in turn reported on commodities, prices and likely profits. No sooner had the Dutch arrived in Taiwan and evaluated its economy than they taxed the Chinese there and would have done the same to the Japanese had they permitted.

Other matters were of little consequence, and since few VOC directors had that experience of the colonial world common amongst high-ranking officials of the Iberian crowns they were usually guided by the almost invariably bloodthirsty views of their local officers. Thus there was no desire, as with the Venetians, to bestow the blessings of orderly government on alien subjects. And no more than in the medieval commercial empires or amongst fellow Protestants was any significant provision made for the conversion of indigenous peoples. Some there admittedly was, with the VOC – which assumed the same powers over the reformed clergy as did the Iberian monarchs over the Catholic missions – despatching *predikants* to Asia. Indeed in Taiwan there were hopes of creating a native and happily inexpensive clergy.[59] Here and there Asians were converted to the reformed faith – in Amboina, in some tiny islands of the Banda Sea, in Coromandel and in Ceylon. Amongst the 'wild aborigines' of Taiwan, untainted by Islam, Hinduism and Buddhism, there were allegedly 1800 neophytes by 1639 and a rosy future seemed likely for the island. Idols were burned, schools founded and promising youngsters sent to Holland 'where if they do not behave properly they must be scourged'.[60] But in the end little remained. Taiwan was lost. Elsewhere the reformed faith was repulsed by entrenched Catholicism or overthrown, so it was said of the Spice Islands, 'by the cunning of the Moors'. Perhaps so, but the doctrine of John Calvin was not at best particularly attractive to non-Europeans. Its requirements for baptism were especially exacting, and austere and introspective it was alien to oriental conventions. It lacked, unlike Catholicism, ritual, images and ceremony just as it lacked

Catholicism's respect for the sacramental attributes of the priesthood, akin to that veneration accorded to Hindu and Buddhist equivalents.

Nor was Dutch effort of the scale and quality of that of the Iberians, as the company admitted. The Protestant churches had nothing of the organization, resources and traditions of the Catholic missionary Orders, nor in prosperous, tolerant and commercial Holland did the religious vocation attract as many men of talent as in impoverished, embattled and imperial Spain and Portugal (cf. pp. 285ff. and 354ff.). And for such as it did there were congenial outlets to hand in the violent theological controversies that raged in the republic in the early 1600s. Clergy the company admittedly despatched to the east. But there, in Calvinist eyes, their prime responsibility was to attend to the faith and morals of existing believers. And in any case the VOC, conscious that spreading the word of God was yet another drain on its resources, sent on average no more than five *predikants* a year during the whole of its life. 'Jesus Christ was good', the English pithily observed, 'but trade was better.' Dutch clergy in Asia were therefore both few in number and commonly of the poorest quality, often bibulous and chosen by the company chiefly for their willingness to accept its authority. Worst still, they were assisted by lay-readers and schoolmasters, frequently former soldiers or seamen, who not surprisingly, like a trio in Taiwan, interspersed their godly labours with 'drunkenness, fornication and the ill-treatment of the natives'.[61]

The ideal of Calvinist zealots was admittedly far different. In Batavia theirs should be the only religion. Catholicism was to be eradicated in the onetime Portuguese territories and a proper morality inculcated by, amongst other things, rounding up prostitutes into Houses of Correction where they would be brought to better ways 'under sharp supervision . . . and severe punishment'.[62] But the company had neither the machinery nor the will to enforce such measures effectively. And whatever the enthusiasm of the Dutch for education and literacy at home, abroad they were no more anxious than Spanish *encomenderos* to have the minds of their servants and slaves inflamed by the Christian message. Despite, therefore, what was said, the empire, like the republic itself, became and remained in general remarkably tolerant. Moslems, Confucians and Buddhists practised their faiths at the very gates of Batavia, and the Chinese, particularly valued as artisans and traders, were exempted alike from military service and Dutch law.

But for the rest Dutch colonial society was of a familiar pattern. It was predominantly male, though some European women were in the east from an early date, usually the wives of senior company officers or of missionaries. A certain Mrs Lindeborn, accompanying her husband to Taiwan, occasioned great amazement by arriving in Japan (1636) 'where no foreign lady had been before', with a broken leg.[63] But these were even rarer exceptions than amongst the Iberians. Hence the usual and inexorable European pursuit of indigenous girls, the consequent engendering by the late 1600s of a sizable Eurasian population, and the incessant complaints about the superabundance of 'light women'. Hence, too, since it seemed impossible to produce in any other way the population needed to inhabit and defend the empire, the emulation of the Portuguese practice of marriage with Christianized Asian females (cf. pp. 266–7). In Amboina this was a failure. In Coromandel it worked in some measure, with men, so the English reported, 'bound and tied to everlasting service' there, and living in ways 'more heathenlike than the people of the country itself'. A similar process, it might be less pejoratively put, occurred in Batavia where Dutch burghers generally married, for lack of any one else, Indo-Portuguese women – *mestiças*, many of them former slaves, and many of them of striking beauty – from what used to be Portugal's possessions in the subcontinent (cf. pp. 267–8). Usually, and as happened elsewhere in like circumstances, their culture engulfed that of their husbands, so producing a Eurasian lower class predominantly oriental in language, dress and habit (cf. p. 290). That this was not as they had hoped, the Dutch were well aware. But almost universally Asian females refused to marry Hollanders. In many places the hostility engendered by earlier European presence was the stumbling-block, but more fundamental was the humble standing of 'free-burghers' and what the English gleefully described as the 'base pay' of company employees, making them unacceptable spouses for daughters of high-caste and upper-class families in societies well convinced of the merit attaching to wealth and rank.

Then again, though in Holland the evils of slavery were denounced, and though the great chartered companies prohibited the enslavement of Amerindians, Hottentots and Javanese, slaves were widely employed in the republic's colonies and slaving an important element in its commerce. Since, as Coen observed of Amboina, for the Dutch to engage in manual toil would be to make themselves objects of ridicule, slaves were needed to work the spice plantations, just as they were needed, as in the Iberian empires, for all demeaning tasks and to signify the opulence and importance of their owners. By the late 1600s married women in Batavia were escorted everywhere in public by retinues of slaves, and VOC officials accompanied by their 'little black boys'.[64] Young Indians (aged between 8 and 20) were therefore to be imported into Indonesia for Dutch use by the thousand, with 30,000 demanded in 1622 alone. Other prospective slave markets were Arakan and Madagascar, whilst for a time in the 1620s prisoners taken in raids on the Chinese mainland were employed in the Pescadores. Eventually islands such as Timor and Bali became the regular suppliers of Netherlands' Indonesia, though slaves were also sent, and at the usual high cost in lives, from Malabar, Bengal and Coromandel, which in 1646 provided Batavia with over 2000 'essential for the maintenance of forts and settlements'.

Meanwhile the VOC's major officers, servants though they were of a prudent state and a commercial company, lived in something of that grand style inseparable from empire. 'Most noble, wise, equitable, respected, pious and discreet', or similar grandiloquent terms, were used to address the governor-general in Batavia. The company acquired a pleasure house with grounds of its own on the outskirts of Masulipatnam, and in Golconda its officials were carried in palanquins by native bearers and accompanied and announced by native musicians.

IV *The rise and fall of the West India Company*

In the very different setting of the west Holland's empire was again to be founded and exploited by a public company pursuing what were believed to be the complementary aims of commercial gain and the destruction of Iberian power. But that imperial success was not the necessary corollary of business acumen, and that merchants could be as ardent in the pursuit of chimera as squires and peasants was shown by the history of the Dutch West India Company (WIC= *West Indische Compagnie*). This, unlike the VOC, sprang from no existing trading organizations, but was created in 1621 'to do all that the service of this country and the profit and increase of trade shall require'. In other words it was to attack Iberian possessions, commerce and shipping in the Atlantic and in so doing both benefit the republic's merchant oligarchs whilst diverting, at little cost to the state, Spanish strength and resources away from the Low Countries. The better to accomplish these objectives the company was given a twenty-five-year monopoly of Holland's trade and navigation with the Americas and West Africa, and granted the same semi-sovereign powers as the VOC. It was of a similar federal structure, comprising five 'chambers', each entitled to conduct a more or less autonomous commerce with some particular area. Like the VOC, the company was dominated by a self-recruiting oligarchy of directors who, however, held office for only six years and accounted to the shareholders at a similar interval. The WIC was financed, as was the East India Company, by the sale of shares on the open market. It attracted money from the same wide range of investors – with serving girls and merchant plutocrats alike contributing to its capital – and was again dominated by Amsterdam and Zeeland. Between them their 'chambers' were entitled to two-thirds of the company's trade, and together they provided twelve out of the WIC's nineteen-man central management (*Heeren*-19). But because of the company's strategic purpose state direction was closer than with the VOC (cf. pp. 403ff.). The nineteenth member of the *Heeren*-19, who also had the deciding vote, was the nominee of the republic, which further required that all decisions on military matters should be referred to it. So, also, any profits the company might make by war were to be re-invested in war, and to encourage its martial purpose the WIC was for a time exempted from taxation, strengthened with a subsidy, furnished with troops and munitions at cost price, and promised – provided it could raise an equal number – a fleet of twenty state ships.

Yet despite pressure from the republic, money was slow to come in, and was only made up by a timely influx of French and Venetian capital. A major deterrent to many investors was the domination of the company's management by Calvinist emigrants from the Spanish-occupied southern Netherlands, and particularly from Antwerp. These, more patriotic, like most refugees, than their new compatriots, demanded that there should be no compromise with the perfidious Spaniard and were fertile in bold schemes for the overthrow of Anti-Christ. But policies so overtly bellicose and inordinately expensive were not to the liking of such plutocrats as the oligarchs of Amsterdam, reluctant to see commercial opportunities wasted or, as in the plans for

Brazil and Angola, the powers and standing of the house of Orange enhanced (cf. pp. 386–8). Hence the ultimate backers of the WIC – seamen, Orangists, Calvinist clergy – formed a far less cohesive and influential group than did the wealthy merchants who controlled the VOC. Nor were they helped by the company's constitution, for since directors were only briefly in office they never attained the authority of their VOC counterparts and were unable to restrain the particular ambitions of the various 'chambers'. And all these problems were further aggravated by the fact that in the west the Dutch faced Spain and were obliged, as was not the case in Asia, to balance the strategic advantages that colonial war might confer against the commercial setbacks it could entail in both Europe and the New World (cf. pp. 381ff.). Thus when in 1646–7 the WIC's position in Brazil was desperate, Holland would only come to the rescue if Zeeland agreed to peace with Spain – the merchants of Amsterdam, that is, saw more sense in a trade with Iberia which would provide them with salt, silver and an outlet for Dutch goods, than in continuing Spanish hostility and the pursuit of prizes and military victories dear to the privateer-owners and Calvinist zealots of the neighbouring province.

But for a time the company was able to conduct an extensive and devastating war against the Iberian Atlantic empires, bringing to oceanic privateering a consistency of strategy and a wealth of resources hitherto unapproached. In the first sixteen years of its existence the WIC sent out over 800 ships manned by some 67000 men. They destroyed Spanish commerce in the Caribbean and forced the Habsburgs into expensive counter-measures. In a massive blow to Spain's prestige and finances they took the bullion fleet in 1628 and by 1636 nearly 600 other Spanish vessels as well. At the same time they were capturing Portuguese craft working from Brazil at such a rate that sugar planters dejectedly referred to themselves as 'Dutch farmers'. Yet though these operations, together with similar successes in European waters, established the primacy of Holland's naval power, and damaging as they were to the Iberians, they brought – Heyn's victory apart – no suitable rewards to investors (cf. pp. 297, 386). Their very scale meant they were costly to mount, and their very efficacy meant that they were strangling, if not killing, the goose that laid the golden egg. Worse still, the company became enmeshed in Brazil, failed to exclude the English and the French from the Caribbean and was disastrously weakened by internal dissensions over such matters as the proper commercial policy to pursue. Thus whilst in Asia the VOC, enjoying the full support of Amsterdam's wealth, and engaging only in limited military operations, was able to create by seapower an extensive trading monopoly, in the west the WIC foundered. It met from Spain and Brazil a resistance more effective than that of the Portuguese in the east. Its shrinking resources were distributed amongst a variety of ambitious projects. And it became committed to schemes of colonization for which the republic had neither the means nor the inclination to pursue and to the success of which, as the English had already found, privateering was inimical (cf. pp. 484, 494). For such expensive debacles Amsterdam, eager and able to trade to Asia and West Africa, had no time, whilst the peace of 1648, which re-opened Spain's markets to Holland and recognized the republic's possessions on the Wild Coast, removed the company's whole purpose. Thereafter its sole surviving asset was its hold on the Atlantic slave trade, and this was soon challenged by the English. Hence with Brazil and the New Netherlands lost, it continued only as an increasingly decrepit slaving and smuggling corporation until its bankruptcy and suppression in 1674.

Economic failure was accompanied by colonial failure. The WIC's grand strategy entailed the capture or the creation of overseas settlements. At its most ambitious this involved the attempted seizure of Brazil. Elsewhere aspirations were more modest, as with the founding on the Wild Coast of a few fortified posts whose occupants traded with local peoples. For the good of its traffic in furs the company attempted to colonize the New Netherlands. But in vain. There was little reason for men to leave Holland, and less for them to go to North America. The Dutch had found no precious metals and subdued no highly organized and easily exploitable indigenous societies. And in any case colonists, like their fellows in Asia, were to be excluded from the major and most profitable trades in the interests of investors. The failure of such policies led to equally (as a rule) unsuccessful attempts to delegate the settlement of difficult and unrewarding lands in both the New Netherlands and Guiana to Mediterranean and Portuguese-style 'patroons' (cf. p. 392).

This heterogeneous collection of possessions was governed in roughly the same way as were the eastern factories and colonies. The company asserted, like the VOC, its supremacy, conceded little to its subjects, and experimented with the ways in which they might be supervised (cf. pp. 411–14). At best this meant the liberal rule of Johan Maurits in Brazil. At worst it meant the semi-military regime of North America or the scheme of Venetian complexity devised for Curaçao at one stage. By this the island – eventually united with the New Netherlands for administrative purposes – was to have its own governor. He, assisted by various councils, was to be subordinate to yet another council sitting in Brazil, which was in turn to be responsible to the WIC.

Similarly the evolution and character of the colonial societies under the company's jurisdiction were of the same general pattern of those in the east. They were, with the partial exception of the New Netherlands, predominantly male. Hence, though here and there high company officials might be found, or accompanied by European wives of sound Protestant beliefs, the rank and file, as in the east, commonly had to make do with such indigenous women (as in Essequibo) or such Catholic *mestiças* (in Angola and Brazil most notably) as would have them. So, too, in the west as in the east intolerance was preached (by the Calvinist clergy) but tolerance practised. In the New Netherlands there was supposedly no public worship not consonant with the reformed religion as established in the republic. In Curaçao the entire population – Iberian, Negro and Amerindian alike – was to be converted to the True Faith (1638). But even less was accomplished than in Asia by a missionary effort almost everywhere feeble and ineffective. True, Calvinism had some limited success amongst those Brazilian cannibals untouched by Catholicism. But it was not to last, and of their chances with the Indians of North America the *predikants* were rightly pessimistic. Thus, as in the East, what was said was not what was done. Catholic priests continued to work in Curaçao, Jews were invited to settle in Guiana and freedom of conscience was conceded in the New Netherlands. Dealings with the North American Indians were marked by a similar (and prudent) liberalism, as when in 1626 Manhattan was bought, and not seized Spanish-style, from the local peoples. But no more than in Asia were such pragmatic tolerance and high ideals any obstacle to Dutch involvement in slaving. As practised by the Iberians this the Hollanders indeed denounced, and in 1596 100 Africans brought to Middelburg were set free – 'put', it was said, 'into their natural liberty'. Admittedly not all in the republic disapproved of slavery on such exalted grounds, and William Usselincx found it undesirable for no better reason than that more work could be got out of Europeans than Negroes. All the same, slavers the Dutch became. In 1605 they were dealing with the Spaniards in Trinidad, and soon after they had virtually complete control of the main West African centres of the trade to the Americas. Driven from Angola and Brazil, they made Curaçao the base for their operations, supplying both the Iberian mainland possessions and such new sugar-producing colonies as the English Barbados (cf. pp. 386–8 and 492–3). Nor, whatever the official policy of the WIC, did they overlook any useful victims, enslaving Amerindians in Guiana and the Lesser Antilles and even some of their Portuguese prisoners taken during the fighting in Brazil.

v 'Oracles of commerce'

The emergence of the Dutch republic in the seventeenth century as Europe's, and like as not the world's, leading maritime, commercial and industrial state was, as an English publicist wrote, 'the envy of the present, and may well be the wonder of future generations'. But already in 1548 Holland knew the roots of its strength, explaining to its then lord, the emperor Charles V, that the inhabitants of a small and impoverished land 'in order to make a living must maintain themselves by handicrafts and trades in such wise that they fetch raw materials from foreign parts and re-export the finished products'. The truth was in fact more complex. Throughout the Middle Ages the future republic was part of a region of vital economic consequence, lying at the confluence of commercial routes linking the Baltic to western Europe and the north to the Mediterranean. In the southern Netherlands there developed an outstanding civilization, an advanced economy and the great entrepôt and financial centre of Antwerp to which in the early 1500s there came everything from the textiles of England to the products of the Baltic and the Iberian colonial empires. In the late sixteenth century the roles of Flanders and Antwerp were usurped by Holland and Amsterdam. In part this was the outcome of economic accident. The declining Hanseatic League succumbed to the Dutch push into the Baltic; Antwerp was weakened as piracy in the

English Channel disrupted its sea-link with Iberia and as the resurgent Venetian spice trade drew South German merchants and financiers back to Italy (cf. pp. 139, 269). From these opportunities, and from the political blunders and difficulties of their opponents Dutch statesmen and entrepreneurs extracted the maximum advantage. Distance, shortage of money and the weight of their global commitments prevented the Spaniards from bringing to bear a force sufficient to subdue the Dutch revolt. But in their very attempts to do so they effectively removed one of Holland's major competitors by their sack and occupation of Antwerp, drove into the northern Netherlands men whose wealth and talents enormously benefited the Dutch and provoked and permitted the republic's penetration of much of the Iberian economy (see pp. 381–4). Furthermore, their lengthy campaigns against Holland produced those crises (as in 1572) which brought to office Calvinist extremists whose fanaticism, reinforced by that of emigrants from the southern provinces, ensured a continuing strand of intransigence in Dutch policy. And by pure good fortune the republic was free of any other strong and dangerous neighbours until about 1650. English energies were devoted first to privateering and then to civil strife; those of the French to dynastic ventures in Italy and subsequently to internecine religious and political feuds (see pp. 452–3, 494).

Yet Genoa apart, no putative imperial power seemed worse endowed than Holland. Its total geographical area was no more than 26,000 sq.km, supporting a population of at best only 1,500,000 in the mid-1600s. Its heart was a strip of low-lying land adjoining the North Sea. All that protected it from inundation were sand dunes, already breached in the north by the sea to leave a chain of islands and a number of large and shallow *zees* and *meers* ever threatening to expand. Cut by rivers great and small, the whole region had an amphibious appearance, impressing visitors with the constant dyking, pumping and draining needed to hold back the waters. As travellers often remarked, the country had some regions of rich pasture and intensively worked arable land, but it also had much unused and unusable acreage. In comparison with England, Holland had a shorter spring, a hotter summer and a colder winter, and like many other damp and low-lying areas it was subject to malaria and typhoid, with its inhabitants 'not generally so long-lived as in better airs'. As a maritime power it laboured under several major disadvantages. It had little or no timber (just as it had little or no stone). Many of its ports had to be reached through treacherous shoal and shallow waters. Its harbours, unlike those of England and the Iberian peninsula, could freeze up in winter – though not to the same extent as the Baltic ports – and its shipping westward bound down the English Channel had to face prevalent headwinds.

To the difficulties bequeathed by nature were added those made by man. Before the seventeenth century there was no recognizable Dutch state, but instead a loose confederation of provinces of widely differing wealth and social organization ranging from the prosperous, urban and populous Holland to the impoverished and agrarian Gelderland. Until the mid-1500s these territories had some focus for their loyalties and discontents in the representatives of the Habsburgs sent to rule them. But after the revolt of 1568 the republic became, as a perceptive observer remarked, a collection of states each of which 'so professes liberty that it cannot recognize any superior'.[65] All the provinces that subscribed to the Union of Utrecht (1579)[66] – the juridical beginnings of the Dutch state in effect – had their own governments and considered themselves sovereign. Referring to one another as 'the Allies', they formed at best a military alliance, and one beset with the usual weaknesses of any such association. Of central government there was little, and the States-General, which in foreign eyes embodied the power of the republic, was in reality only a gathering of ambassadors and as impotent as a Hanseatic assembly to impose its decisions on constituent members. Each province contributed to the federal budget – through levying its own taxes. But once again there was no way of compelling dissidents to pay for policies of which they disapproved. So, too, the great trading companies were amalgams of regional 'chambers', and the naval forces of the republic directed by five independent admiralties. And worst still, in the early 1600s the country was torn by violent internecine disputes. These arose from the rivalries between the house of Orange and the urban oligarchs, and were exacerbated by, and inextricably entangled with, squabbles in the Reformed church between the Remonstrants (supported by Oldenbarnevelt) and the orthodox (supported by prince Maurits).[67]

Moreover, Holland's wealth depended, as did that of Venice, on the profits of a vulnerable seaborne trade, and, as did that of no other maritime power, on the rewards of even more vulnerable fisheries. Yet no more than in medieval Scandinavia or Genoa were such obstacles insuperable. Unlike Venice, whose vital commerce was at the mercy of all her enemies, Holland could benefit even in war from the needs of opponents (see pp. 132, 381). Nor, before the mid-seventeenth century, was the republic obliged to meet, as the Venetians repeatedly were, the full weight of any hostile seapower, since in the crucial years of the late 1500s the bulk of Spanish naval strength was usually deployed in waters well clear of Dutch interests in the Baltic (cf. pp. 134, 364). And paradoxically enough, the disparities of wealth within the country, and its curious political structure gave it something of a *de facto* unity by allowing the predominance of the province of Holland. This was the wealthiest and most highly developed part of the northern Netherlands, providing over half their federal revenues and doing so with an ease and promptitude that further enhanced its authority. By 1622 it had 670,000 – including the majority of the richest and ablest – of the republic's total population of some 1,500,000, and in Amsterdam it had the republic's most populous, affluent and influential city. This economic preponderance was converted to political supremacy by Johan van Oldenbarnevelt, who whilst chief minister of the province – from 1586 until his overthrow by Maurits in 1618 – brought the general direction of Dutch affairs into his own hands. Indeed the structure of effective power was relatively simple. Paramount in the state was Amsterdam, occupying in relation to the rest of the northern Netherlands a position something similar to that of Venice in relation to its mainland possessions (cf. p. 88). And in association with Amsterdam were the urban oligarchs (regents). Rulers of the towns of this most intensively urban area of northern Europe, they belonged to the closed corporations controlling those – eighteen in number – represented in the Estates of Holland which they dominated in the same way that they dominated the machinery of federal government. Like Venetian patricians they came from a tightly knit class, though one more flexible and receptive than its older Italian counterpart, since it was regularly reinforced by the admission of new families of appropriate wealth, and preserved from ossification by repeated political crises and the ever-present threat of Orangist ambitions. And such were the resources and influence of the regents that undertakings of which they approved, or in which they were involved, received a state backing as purposeful as that provided by any monarchy (cf. pp. 403ff.).

This burgher and mercantile predominance reflected the economic precocity of the northern Netherlands. It reflected, too, the fact that in the early Middle Ages the country – remote, unappealing, insignificant – had neither developed nor attracted an aristocracy of any importance. Some provinces had, it is true, nobles (e.g., Groningen) and in backward Gelderland they were the dominant class. But in Holland itself there were by the mid-1500s only twelve identifiably aristocratic families owning less than 10 per cent of the province's cultivated land between them. The one considerable exception was the house of Orange, influential in Holland and more so in Zeeland. All the same, the Dutch aristocracy was in no position to dominate the countryside, let alone the government of the region. Nor was their lot to improve. Their powers were trimmed by the Habsburgs before the revolt, and their influence further weakened after its outbreak as many families withdrew to possessions elsewhere. This gave pre-eminence to the Orange dynasty, but at a price. The generally unfortunate career of William the Silent left him impecunious and increasingly dependent on the towns. His successors, seeking support, found themselves allied to Calvinist zealots who generally saw little to their liking in aristocratic ways.

And if, to the benefit of its urban oligarchs, the republic was largely free from the burden of an ostentatious and bellicose nobility and its satellites, it was equally free from the burden of an oppressed peasantry – and equally short of would-be adventurers and colonists. Not indeed that the Netherlands were any paradise for the poor and humble, with merchants and manufacturers expressing their distaste for 'the sottish and ill-natured rabble'. Nevertheless in Holland itself peasants owned nearly 50 per cent of the land they worked in the early 1500s, and were nowhere in such subjection to lords as were their Iberian counterparts. For some the growth of the country's trade and shipping brought new opportunities. Areas of specialized agriculture developed; profits could be invested, as by that group of small farmers from one village who in 1638 held shares in ships and boats. Nor did Dutch colonial and commercial expansion entail those tribulations that empire inflicted on Castile. Manpower was not drained away by war and emigration, nor were the survivors crippled by taxation. Labour the country indeed lacked, notwithstanding that its population, like that of the rest of Europe, increased in the sixteenth century. But resources were husbanded, with the republic, like the equally provident Venice, recruiting most of its troops abroad. Immigrants were attracted and retained, as was the existing workforce, by pragmatic tolerance and relatively high wages which withstood better than those elsewhere the erosion of purchasing power by the general inflation of the 1500s and early 1600s.

All this was the outcome of the rule of a mercantile oligarchy. Its deficiencies were clear enough. 'Unqualified and mean persons' were excluded from politics, and their lot attracted less concern than in Venice. Influence and connection sank inevitably into corruption and nepotism. Nor, like Venetian magnates – or modern businessmen for that matter – did Dutch oligarchs live merely on the rewards of a tireless dedication to commerce and industry, and already in the early 1600s many existed quietly and comfortably on rents from real estate. None the less they formed a governing class which overall conducted business and politics efficiently, single-mindedly and with outstanding common sense. They were, by the standards of the time, remarkably liberal, and this despite the presence in the state of an intransigent Calvinist party. Their talents and resources were not diverted into land – scarce in any case – on the scale of those of their English equivalents. Aristocratic ideals were not deferentially accepted, nor was public office and its attendant status for sale. And a merchant's property was divided after his death equally amongst his children, giving heirs that initial capital otherwise so hard to accumulate and depriving eldest sons of the prospect of subsidized indolence.

Hence in a region whose very nature impelled its inhabitants to live, as they repeatedly acknowledged, 'by navigation and maritime trade', there emerged a state in which the tenets of good business and not the illusions of dynastic ambition or imperial destiny prevailed. In this Holland resembled the Hanse, Genoa, and to a lesser extent Venice (cf. pp. 53, 155). But to a degree unequalled elsewhere the Dutch turned their country's limitations to advantage. Water, it was remarked, became Holland's land. Towns were linked to one another, and to the countryside, by a network of canals and rivers, allowing the cheap movement of goods, the comfortable carriage of passengers and the unimpeded flow of business, since a merchant could 'write, eat or sleep as he goes'. By the mid-seventeenth century the Dutch had built up the greatest volume of shipping so far known in western Europe, and owned not in a handful of large ports but in a host of relatively obscure towns and havens. The seamen manning these vessels enjoyed in the 1500s and 1600s the highest reputation. Carletti, experienced in Iberian ways, wrote in 1602 that 'voyaging with this nation is so safe that I hold shipwreck to be impossible'.[68] The same year, whilst the Spaniards were engaged in constructing warships in the English style, the English themselves were seeking in Holland books 'concerning shipping or navigation' and attempting to discover all they could of the Dutch 'mode of building and victualling ships'.[69] Not that the republic was without problems. As everywhere else, seamen were scarce, and though to its great advantage Holland could tap the reserves of manpower of north Germany and the Baltic lands, complements of VOC Indiamen often had to be brought up to strength with drafts of whatever unfortunates crimps could ensnare. Nor was Dutch navigation free from the usual hazards of the times, with the fleet in which Jan Coen returned to Asia (1627) reckoned by its pilots to be well offshore when it was in fact on the point of being wrecked in Australia.

Even so, the reputation of the Dutch was well deserved. They opened the most satisfactory sea route to Asia, and the vessels they used to establish their eastern empire and to handle their eastern commerce were in all ways – quality, condition, performance – superior to those of the Iberians. In general their lightly built merchantmen had a lower life expectation than the ships of other European maritime powers, but they also had a much lower delivery price – about 40 per cent below English levels in the mid-1600s. They were, moreover, sparingly (and hence economically) manned, with crews about half the size of those on equivalent craft elsewhere by the late sixteenth century. Thus in many trades Holland gained the decisive advantage by using inexpensively constructed, easily worked and cheaply run freighters. The first of these which can be identified with any confidence was the *boyer*, widely employed in the mid-1500s, and whose carvel build, low hull, bluff bow and high stern suggest a mixed northern and Iberian ancestry. It was rigged with a bowsprit (setting a spritsail below) and two masts. The forward carried a sprit-mainsail (like that of the modern Thames sailing barge, and demanding few men to handle it) and two square sails, and the after a lateen mizzen. Its successor, which appeared in the late sixteenth century, was the *fluit* – possibly developed from the *boyer*, possibly descended from the so-called Vlieboot (flyboat) of the Zuider Zee, or perhaps adapted from one of the bulk carriers long used by the Hanse, since to Elizabethan seamen flyboat and hulk were one and the same thing.[70] The *fluit's* basic features were a shallow draught – to cope with the shoal-ridden waters of the Dutch coast – light build and good lifting capacity (*c.* 200t). To give a reasonable performance it was comparatively long in relation to its beam and was rigged with unusually tall masts and short yards, whilst its sail area was more subdivided than was customary to permit easy handling by a small crew. Moreover, though above the waterline its breadth was modest, it swelled out below to allow the maximum lading and to defeat the letter of the Danish Sound regulations in which (1577) tolls were calculated on hold-depth and deck-level dimensions. But the *fluit* no more conferred control of Europe's seaborne commerce on the Dutch than the carvel opened the oceans of the world to the Portuguese. It appeared when Holland's hegemony was already established, and it was not employed in all the republic's trades. Nor is it certain that when contemporaries spoke of the *fluit* or flyboat they were talking of some single distinctive type of vessel. To many it was the quintessential merchantman, cheap to build and run, and the very opposite of those heavily armed, toughly constructed and expensive craft that the English, with their tradition of privateering, favoured. But to other experienced seamen flyboats could be powerful men-of-war – like that 600t 'new double flyboat' which was one of the opponents of the

Fig. 16A   Dutch *fluit*: mid seventeenth century, reconstructed by Gregory Robinson.

Fig. 16B   Dutch *fluit*: late seventeenth century, from the *grisaille* by the
contemporary A. van Salm.

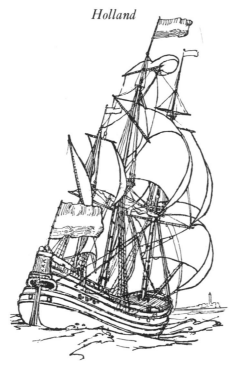

Fig. 17 Dutch East Indiaman off Batavia, 1649, from
the contemporary painting by A.D. Willaerts.

Revenge in her last fight – small and nimble privateers, or cumbersome bulk carriers.[71]

Yet clearly Holland's strength was to have developed ships – whether the herring buss (see pp. 516, n5) or the *fluit* – closely adapted to the particular demands of its major trades. Such enterprise was no novelty, but what was new was the scale and the degree of economic rationality of the adaptations. To save on scarce manpower, and to handle bulk goods on routes where overt naval hostility was rarely encountered, the Dutch produced vessels to carry an optimum lading with the minimum of hands and defences and so at the minimum cost. With no patrician or royal idiosyncrasies to be indulged, they were of a design and construction primarily determined by the nature of the cargoes to be moved and the harbours to be used in a given traffic, with, for example, those working to Königsberg in the early 1600s more or less standardized craft of 200t.[72] Nor, to keep freights low and competitive advantage high, was anything wasted on the creature comforts of crews who, it was complacently observed in the early seventeenth century, are 'so economical in their feeding that they save our shipowners at least a third of the expenses in men and rations which other nations demand in greater quantity and better quality.'

Such was the voice of a society uninhibitedly devoted to the pursuit of profit. Not only were its peasants, but even its ruling classes accustomed to austerity, with the frugality imposed by the nature of their homeland reinforced for many by the tenets of

Calvinism. Ships were not christened with Iberian religiosity or English ebullience, but bore instead much workaday names as *Whalefish*, *Posthorse* or even *Bread and Beer Pot*.[73] The state itself was run efficiently and profitably. Taxes, from which none were exempt, were in general light, public credit good, and talk of bankruptcy – a commonplace with monarchies – unknown after the early years of the revolt. In every sphere of business the Dutch revealed an enviable flexibility, enterprise and ruthless concentration on essentials. In the medieval centuries Flemish skills in the manufacture of textiles and those of North Germans in brewing were emulated and improved, and the products of those regions undercut. The inflation of the sixteenth century, disastrous for Iberia, benefited the Dutch who, paring their own costs to the bone, resold goods which appreciated as prices rose. From the late 1500s new industries were developed as a corollary of Holland's commercial and maritime supremacy, using imported raw materials (sugar, beaver skins) or half-finished manufactures (English woollens) the greater part of which were re-exported after being worked up. Money, as with the capital of the VOC and WIC, was raised wherever it could be found; foreigners were encouraged to trade in the republic. Since Chinese and Japanese porcelain sold well in the west, Delft potters were set on producing imitations. To speed up the repair and building of ships, timbers were cut to standard sizes by mechanical (wind-driven) saws and stored to be available on demand.

To all the advantages conferred by such business acumen were added those bestowed by a remarkable tolerance and enlightenment. It was not, of course, of unlimited scope, particularly when, as in the 1570s and again in the early 1600s, Calvinist zealots were in power. Yet the republic required no more than that its inhabitants should adhere to the 'true Christian Reformed Religion', and attendance at Calvinist services was not – whatever *predikants* might demand – compulsory. Maybe this was the only possible policy for a state in which by the mid-seventeenth century one-half to two-thirds of the population were Catholic or non-Calvinist Protestant. And that such tolerance sprang from little more than the inability of one party to suppress the other and from a pragmatism which, as in Venice, appreciated the material benefits it would bring, detracts nothing from its importance. It drew to Holland a galaxy of daring and original thinkers. It allowed and encouraged the literacy imperative to an advanced economy and an education whose quality was widely remarked. It stimulated a printing industry whose output in the 1600s – including works in Syriac, Arabic and Chaldean – probably outstripped that of all other European presses together. And it attracted an imposing range of commercial, industrial and financial talent. Sephardic Jews, influential in sugar and slaving, came in from Iberia together with Calvinists – some 80,000 before 1600 – from the Spanish-reconquered southern Netherlands. Many of the latter were textile workers whose skills in the manufacture of lighter cloths were transmitted to the Dutch industry, so enabling it to open up new markets. Many were also from the great entrepôt of Antwerp, and expert in sophisticated techniques of accounting, banking and insurance learned by long association with south European merchants. A large number settled, to its immense benefit, in Amsterdam, one-third of whose inhabitants were in 1622 immigrants, or first-generation descendants of immigrants from the south. Such families provided nearly half the city's major VOC investors, some of the most strenuous exponents of colonial expansion, and extended Holland's connections with an international network of commerce and finance.

As a territorial colonial power the republic was unsuccessful and insignificant. But where capital, business skill and maritime strength could be brought to bear the Dutch carried all before them. In Europe they largely destroyed the commerce of the Hanse and hastened the collapse of German economic primacy in the Baltic. By the mid-seventeenth century most of the overseas trade of England and Iberia was in their hands, and the Iberians their economic dependents. Their arrival in Asia killed to all intents the ancient commerce in spices through the Levant which, as a Venetian complained from Cairo in 1623, 'have chosen another route after the Dutch found the new way'. And as a result the Hollanders were able further to extend their power in the Mediterranean by importing not only grain and textiles but oriental spices as well, including to those very Levantine ports which had once sent them to Europe. Such indeed was their ubiquity as to convince a harassed Englishman that 'the Devil shits Dutchmen'. They owned sugar refineries in France, exploited mines in Sweden, sold ships everywhere, invested in land reclamation throughout Europe, supplied both Catholics and Protestants with munitions, manned Japanese craft in Asia and Iberian vessels in the west. Not surprisingly it was generally agreed that Dutch practice was the only remedy for ailing economies, with the Spaniards establishing an equivalent to the WIC (1624), the Portuguese setting up a Brazil company and the French a series of replica VOCs (cf. pp. 265, 442).

In the wider world the republic's influence, if less pervasive, was nevertheless considerable. The Dutch (together with the French and English) destroyed Spain's hold on the Caribbean, and unaided turned the Iberian Atlantic economies to their advantage. They transformed the whole nature of the English West Indian islands by introducing sugar as a staple crop and African slaves to produce it. Even their brief stay in North America left its mark. With disastrous consequences they distributed disease and alcohol, whilst with their encouragement (and that of the English) the Iroquois became the predominant Indian people in the north-east colonial lands. In Asia they annexed much of the onetime Portuguese empire and most of Portugal's former long-distance and interport commerce. In so doing, and in the course of establishing their own monopoly, they destroyed or disrupted indigenous economies. Particularly devastating was their impact in Indonesia. By the mid-1600s the once flourishing trade of Atjeh to the Red Sea was virtually defunct. With clove production limited to Amboina, other former suppliers (such as Ternate and Tidore), their trees extirpated and their local commerce destroyed, sank down into subsistence agriculture. The trade of Batavia grew at the expense of that of Bantam, and the major Sumatran pepper ports, forced to make deliveries to the VOC, were by the end of the seventeenth century so impoverished that their inhabitants could no longer afford the Coromandel textiles imported by the Dutch (cf. pp. 392, 408–9).

Yet as ever some were to benefit from the imposition of alien political or economic hegemony. Methods of cloth production were improved, and the whole industry stimulated in Coromandel by Dutch demand. The influx of bullion into the Orient, to which the VOC notably contributed, had an impact whose nature has already been noticed (cf. p. 283). Dutch insistence that the inter-Asian trade should pay for itself and, as far as possible, for cargoes to Europe as well, intensified commercial relations between the various parts of the east, just as Dutch energy and enterprise brought into direct association regions previously only in indirect contact. From this came opportunities for indigenous merchants, encouraged by the spectacle of European success, enriched by the profits from dealings with westerners, and favoured by the VOC's inability – lacking as it did a network of imperial possessions – to restrain a growth its own presence had occasioned. Hence by the later seventeenth century a Surat-based syndicate had interests stretching from northern India to Indonesia, and Coromandel merchants were trading as far afield as the Philippines.

But on the whole the influence of the Dutch in Asia, unsupported as they were by any significant missionary endeavour, was even slighter than that of the Portuguese. On the general political balance they had a minimal effect, though naturally enough there were localized repercussions. Their containment of Atjeh allowed the growth of Johore, and their very presence in Indonesia encouraged, as had the activities of the Iberians before them, Asian appeals for Ottoman and Arab aid, so further assisting the spread of Islam there. To a handful of rich and influential Asians their arrival was acceptable and rewarding. Rulers, aristocrats and officials had a new source of bribes and could obtain western luxuries and novelties; usurers gained new clients. But for the huge majority of the peoples of the east life was unaltered.

Nor was the pattern any different in other ways. The Dutch were not conquerors, colonizers or proselytizers in the Iberian mould, and consequently made little impression on indigenous civilizations. Notwithstanding the creation in 1623 of a *Collegium Indicum* at Leyden to give *predikants* a knowledge of Malay and of oriental religions, the Calvinist church achieved little in the way of conversions. For Taiwan there was, for instance, brave talk of suppressing nudity, polygamy, abortion, 'lewdness and fornication', but even in 1645 such neophytes as there were were said to be Christian only in name 'and like magpies merely utter such sounds as have been repeated to them'.[74] So Dutch cultural influence was a matter of curiosity rather than significance. European motifs appeared in Japanese and Javanese carving; Japanese artists painted world maps based on European cartographical knowledge (1644–8); a Dutch creole tongue emerged in Guiana. In ways familiar in the rest of the colonial world some oriental peoples took from the Hollanders the trappings of western civilization. European watches, clocks, toys and even musical boxes appeared in Java. Local houses in the immediate vicinity of Dutch settlements in Indonesia were often constructed in the general style of the domestic architecture of the Netherlands, and towards the mid-1600s some Japanese ships assumed a roughly Dutch appearance.

Equally unimportant was the influence of the non-European world on the Dutch republic. There were, it is true, some remarkable experiments in the use of joint-stock companies in overseas expansion. But this was the adaptation of an already well-established financial technique, and one which, though on a smaller scale, the English had already attempted (cf. pp. 472, 477). There were also the usual consequences of imperial and economic triumphs. Poets sang, with varying degrees of felicity, of the achievements of their compatriots, and how

> Wherever profit leads us, to every sea and shore
> For love of gain the wide world's harbours we explore.

Exotic themes were treated by Dutch artists – most notably in Frans Post's Brazilian paintings – and oriental artefacts and curiosities collected by Dutch scholars. Occasionally, though on nothing like the Iberian scale, non-European languages and religions were studied, with one of the Houtmans publishing (1603) a Dutch-Malay vocabulary, and some learned *predikants* in India writing on Hinduism and Tamil. Merchants, seamen, missionaries and officials left careful descriptions of travels in distant parts, ranging from the survey of Taiwan by the Rev. George Candidius in the 1620s to the investigation of the flora, fauna and society of northern Brazil by the protégés of Johan Maurits during the Dutch occupation. These, and much else besides – often in languages other than Dutch, and often, unlike their Iberian counterparts, richly illustrated – were printed by the republic's presses. In this way geographical knowledge was increased and refined, helped particularly by the VOC's requirement that its pilots should submit their charts, as corrected by their own observations, to the company cartographer. And by experience direct or indirect the errors of Antiquity were exposed, with a visitor to the Ladrones bitterly remarking 'there men may plainly . . . behold that golden world whereof the poets write'.[75] There was some acceptance of exotic usages and products. Chinese porcelain was widely employed in Holland, and tea and arak drunk by expatriates in Asia. Indeed some men of learning and some honest pragmatists could admit the rationality of native behaviour, with Dr Jacobus Bontius castigating the folly of these who called the peoples of Indonesia barbarians 'whilst they excel us not only in the knowledge of plants and herbs but in economic management as well'. But as in other empires these were the views of a minority, and most Hollanders, like most Europeans, were soon disillusioned with the inhabitants of the outside world – not that their expectations had in any case ever been very high – and no more than fellow merchants or Protestants did they waste much time or money on missionary endeavour. Admittedly, the attitude of the Dutch to the Indians of North America was sensibly liberal. Prior indigenous title to land was recognized, and consequently the legal necessity – as well as the practical expediency – of paying for what was needed before appropriating it. And some servants of the republic were to wonder by what right their compatriots could propose (1618) to exterminate native trade in the Moluccas. But where profit called such scruples quickly faded. Indigenous peoples were dismissed as idle, immoral and innately vicious, and those of mixed blood vilified as 'crows' and 'cockroaches'.

Such reactions reflected, however, the already established character of Dutch civilization, which was even less influenced by experience of non-European societies than the cultures of other imperial powers. Naturally enough there were in this supremely maritime empire some advances in navigational science and cartography, though none of the importance of those of the Italians and Iberians earlier, or of the English later. Lucas Janszoon Wagenaer published (1584–5) a *Mariner's Mirror* (*Spieghel der Zeevaerdt*) – a volume of sailing directions far superior to any predecessor. It contained not only the usual nautical tables but also all current charts and harbour plans for the coasts of western Europe, printed in a uniform and manageable size. Assorted commercial information was provided, and for the first time such aids to navigation as the buoys and beacons of the Dutch coast and the Thames estuary were shown. Navigators were further assisted in identifying their whereabouts by profiles of coastlines and sketches of the types of vessels most commonly encountered in particular areas. It was also from the republic, with its celebrated skills in engraving and printing that there came, especially in the early 1600s, a distinguished sequence of globes, atlases and wall maps. Yet much of Holland's early nautical science derived from that of the Iberians, with many of the first manuals of navigation no more than translations of standard works, just as later the Dutch made extensive use of the findings of English specialists. Equally important, as in everything else, was the legacy of Flanders. There Abraham Ortelius had already produced (1570) a critically edited selection of maps, and it was Gerhard Mercator, once of the university of Louvain, who accomplished (1569) the adequate projection of the earth's sphericity on to a plane surface, and who planned the great *Atlas* – the first time the word was used of a collection of maps – later amplified and re-edited in Holland.

Nor was much of this of extra-European inspiration. The republic's colonial possessions never involved more than a fraction of its resources, produced more than a fraction of its wealth, or occasioned sufficient emigration to weaken the parent state. Such colonies as Holland acquired were established in the course, and largely as the consequence of, the revolt against Spain. The justification of this war in political and religious terms monopolized whatever intellectual energies were not absorbed in business, theological disputes or the pursuit of themes bequeathed by the republic's rich Burgundian and Renaissance heritage. With no imperial conquests of any substance there was no incentive to speculate on imperial rights and duties, least of all in a state whose own governmental machinery was rudimentary and whose colonies were run by commercial companies. Holland's wealth came from its domination of much of Europe's seaborne commerce. It was the demands of the great European trades that most profoundly influenced the development of its ships, just as their problems inspired Grotius' famous assertion of the Dutch right to the freedom of the seas. The rewards of these trades ensured that until the mid-1600s the republic was controlled by its towns, and in every way dominated by the province of Holland. They further ensured that the civilization of the northern Netherlands in the great years of the seventeenth century was in large measure the expression of the tastes of a generally Protestant and almost exclusively mercantile ruling class. Dutch art was accordingly little concerned with saints, monarchs or military heroics. Nor was it concerned with the grandiose or the exotic. Instead it realistically depicted towns, civic dignitaries, buildings and ships. And significantly and appropriately enough it portrayed the sea – a disciplined background in Venetian marine art – in all its moods, and with a power and intensity only equalled in the painting and music of the last century and a half.[76]

Bibliographical note

The historical records of Holland consist of a central archive in the Hague, provincial archives housed in each provincial capital, municipal records and a number of special collections. There is a good general introduction to these materials in Jan de Vries, *The Dutch Rural Economy in the Golden Age, 1500–1700* (New Haven, 1974). For those – still insufficiently explored – relating to the eastern colonial possessions, and for some indication of the records now held in the former colonies in the east, see Tapan Raychaudhuri, *Jan Company in Coromandel, 1605–1690* (The Hague, 1962) which appears as vol. 38 of the *Verhandelingen van het Koninklijk Instituut voor Taal-Land-en Volkenkunde*. Archival accessions – and much other useful information as well – are reported in *Itinerario*, which is published by the Leyden Centre for the History of European Expansion.

There is an excellent bibliographical guide to the literature on Dutch domestic and colonial history in C.R. Boxer, *The Dutch Seaborne Empire, 1600–1800* (1965), whilst a 'Bulletin critique de l'historiographie Néerlandaise' has appeared annually since 1954 in the *Revue du Nord* (Lille). *Itinerario*, nos 3–4 (1978) carries an annotated bibliography of recent Dutch expansion studies. Amongst the Dutch historical journals which cover the themes and centuries with which this book is concerned are the following: *Bijdragen en Mededelingen van het Historisch Genootschap* (Utrecht, 1877–1968), continued as *Bijdragen en Mededelingen betreffende de Geschiedenis der Nederlanden*; *Bijdragen voor Vaderlandsche Geschiedenis en Oudheidkunde* (The Hague and Arnhem, 1837–1944), continued as *Bijdragen voor de Geschiedenis der Nederlanden*; *Economisch-Historisch Jaarboek* (The Hague, 1916–1968), continued as *Economisch-en Sociaal-Historisch Jaarboek*; *Tijdschrift voor Economisch en Sociale Geografie* (Rotterdam, 1949–   ), formerly *Tijdschrift voor Economische Geographie*; *Tijdschrift voor Geschiedenis* (Groningen, 1919–   ).

George Masselman, *The Cradle of Colonialism* (New Haven, 1963) is a leisurely but good introduction to Dutch history *c*. 1500–1650. Boxer's *Dutch Seaborne Empire* is a work of characteristic verve, distinction and fascinating erudition. Also valuable are J.L. Price, *Culture and Society in the Dutch Republic during the Seventeenth Century* (1974); the already mentioned volume of de Vries on the *Dutch Rural Economy*, and Geoffrey Parker, *The Dutch Revolt* (1977).

The beginnings of Dutch maritime power are best summarized in P. Dollinger, *The German Hansa* (1970) – an English translation by D.S. Ault and S.H. Steinberg from the French – and Klaus Spading, *Holland und die Hanse im 15.Jahrhundert* (Weimar, 1973). The admirable outline in Boxer's *Dutch Seaborne Empire* of Holland's rise to maritime and commercial supremacy in the Baltic and northern Europe is now supplemented by M. Bogucka, 'Nowe Badania na temat handlu Amsterdam-Archangielsk w XVIIw', in *Komunikatij Instytutu Balltyckiego*, 16 (1972), 57ff; by the same author's important 'Amsterdam and the Baltic in the First Half of the Seventeenth Century', *Ec. Hist. Rev*, XXVI (1973), 433ff.; and by Simon Hart, 'Amsterdam Shipping and Trade to Northern Russia in the Seventeenth Century', in *Mededelingen van de Nederlandse Vereeniging voor Zeegeschiedenis*, 26 (1973), 5–30, 105–16. Virginia Rau's *Subsídios para o Estudo do Movimento dos Portos de Faro e Lisboa durante o Século XVII* (Lisbon, 1954) contains invaluable information on Holland's penetration of the maritime economy of Portugal, and her *A Embaixada de Tristão de Mendonça Furtado e os Arquivos Notariais Holandeses* (Lisbon, 1958) throws light on both Portuguese commercial dealings with Holland in general and the purchase of arms in particular. The whole subject of the Dutch economic hold on Iberia is admirably discussed in vol. II of John Lynch's *Spain under the Habsburgs* (2 vols, Oxford 1964–9). For the Dutch in the Mediterranean, see the bibliographical notes of chapters 2 and 3 on the Hanse and Venice. M. Aymard, *Venise, Raguse et le Commerce du blé pendant la second moitié du XVIe Siècle* remains fundamental, as does Fernand Braudel's *The Mediterranean and the Mediterranean World in the Age of Philip II*, trs. by S. Reynolds (2 vols, 1972–3).

There is an important, if diffuse and badly written study of *The Dutch in the Caribbean and on the Wild Coast, 1580–1680* (Assen, 1971) by Cornelius Ch. Goslinga. The subject is briefly and authoritatively re-examined by Kenneth R. Andrews, *The Spanish Caribbean: Trade and Plunder, 1530–1630* (New Haven, 1978). Of the many writings of C.R. Boxer on the Dutch in Brazil I have found his *Salvador de Sá and the Struggle for Brazil and Angola, 1602–1686* (1952) particularly illuminating, whilst there is a good survey of Dutch-Portuguese relations in West Africa in A.F.C. Ryder, *Benin and the Europeans, 1485–1897* (1969). New light is thrown on Dutch beginnings in North America by Simon Hart, *The Prehistory of the New Netherlands Company* (Amsterdam, 1959), and the economic policies of the WIC there are briefly – if rather portentously – discussed by Van Cleaf Bachman, *Peltries or Plantations* (Baltimore, 1969). The history of Dutch North America is outlined in the lavishly illustrated volumes, *The Discovery of North America*, by W.P. Cumming, R.A. Skelton and D.B. Quinn (1971) and *The Exploration of North America, 1630–1776*, by W.P. Cumming, S. Hillier, D.B. Quinn and G. Williams (1974). Henri and Barbara van der Zee detail the early history of New York in *A Sweet and Alien Land* (1978).

The establishment of Dutch maritime and commercial power in Asia, and the assumptions and behaviour of the VOC are discussed in M.A.P. Meilink-Roelofsz, *Asian Trade and European Influence in the Indonesian Archipelago between 1500 and about 1630* (The Hague, 1962) and in the same author's 'Aspects of Dutch Colonial Development in Asia', in *Britain and the Netherlands in Europe and Asia*, ed. J.S. Bromley and E.H. Kossmann (1968). Niels Steensgaard, *Carracks, Caravans and Companies: The Structural Crisis in the European-Asian Trade in the Early Seventeenth Century* (Copenhagen, 1973) is as fundamental – and as difficult – here as for Portugal. There is an excellent concise history of the VOC by C.R. Boxer, *Jan Compagnie in Oorlog en Vrede* (Bussum, 1977). For the shipping employed in the VOC's Indies trade, and for conditions on board, I have also used the same author's richly documented study, 'The Dutch East-Indiamen: Their Sailors, their Navigators, and Life on Board, 1602–1795' in *MM*, 49 (1962), 81ff. There are several first-class studies of Dutch commerce in particular areas of the east, most notably Raychaudhuri's *Jan Company in Coromandel*, and C.R. Boxer's *Francisco Vieira de Figueiredo* (The Hague, 1967) – reprinted from vol. 52 of the *Verhandelingen van het Koninklijk Instituut voor Taal-Land-en Volkenkunde* – which illuminates Dutch activity in southeast Asia and rivalry with the Portuguese in the 1600s. M.A.P. Meilink-Roelofsz edits a volume by many hands on *De VOC in Azie* (Bussum, 1976). For Dutch behaviour and policies in Taiwan (Formosa) I have used the materials collected, edited and translated by William Campbell – who served as a Presbyterian missionary on the island – in *Formosa under the Dutch described from Contemporary Records* (1903).

In addition to the works of J.L. Price and Jan de Vries already mentioned, the basis of Dutch economic and maritime power is also briefly, but perceptively, analysed by C.R. Boxer in *The Anglo-Dutch Wars of the Seventeenth Century, 1652–1674* (1974). Dutch navigational techniques and competence are assessed by D.W. Waters, 'The Navigational Instruments of the *Batavia*, Dutch East-Indiaman, 1629', *CIHM*, 8 (1970). For Dutch ships, shipbuilding and the Dutch shipping industry reference should be made to the section covering the years 1585–1680 of the *Maritieme Geschiedenis der Nederlanden*, ed. P.M. Bosscher, J.R. Bruijn and W.J. van Hoboken (Bussum, 1977) and the excellent study of R.W. Unger, *Dutch Shipbuilding before 1800, Ships and Guilds* (Assen/Amsterdam, 1978). Much is still unknown of the characteristics of important types of early Dutch vessels. The *boyer* is briefly discussed by R.W. Unger in *MM*, 61 (1975), 109ff. For the *fluit* contemporary views can be found in W.G. Perrin (ed.), *Boteler's Dialogues* (Navy Rec. Soc., 1929), p.249, and cf. K-F. Olechnowitz, *Der Schiffbau der Hansischen Spätzeit* (Weimar, 1960), p.13. In 1634 the rig of a Dutch flyboat (*c.* 200t) – also, alas, known as a *boyer* to confuse confusion worse – was recorded as follows: a spritsail (i.e. set under the bowsprit); a foresail and foretopsail on the foremast; a mainsail, maintopsail and topgallant on the mainmast; a mizzen; a spritsail topsail (i.e. set on a mast perched at the end of the bowsprit). Bonnets (additional areas of canvas to be attached to sails) were carried for the main and foresails (PRO HCA 13/51, fo.69v).

Dutch influence on indigenous Japanese culture is examined with a wealth of fascinating detail by C.R. Boxer, *Jan Compagnie in Japan, 1600–1817* (Oxford, 1968). M.H.J. de Graaf draws on a wide knowledge of the east in an essay on 'L'influence involontaire de la Civilization Néederlandaise sur les Indonésiens des XVIIᵉ et XVIIIᵉ Siècles' in *CIHM*, 8 (1970). There is a good short discussion of Flemish and Dutch cartography in G.R. Crone, *Maps and their Makers* (1962).

8

France

○○

1 *Promise unfulfilled*

In striking contrast to the achievements of Catholic Iberia and Protestant Holland was the failure of the early colonial ventures of Catholic France and Protestant England. Yet both were countries with lengthy traditions of conquest and crusade, and both were amongst the pioneers of Europe's overseas expansion. In the early Middle Ages the French had taken a leading role in the establishment of a Latin state in the Holy Land, just as in the thirteenth century they had fought the infidel in North Africa. In 1494, after the ignominy of the defeats of the Hundred Years War had been obliterated by the expulsion of the English from most of France's soil, French armies had triumphantly invaded Italy. True, the first half of the next century was to see France engaged in a sequence of generally undistinguished campaigns against Spain, and the second half saw it sunk in civil war. Nevertheless this prolonged strife produced a body of fighting men, in particular minor and often Protestant gentry, whose energies could – and indeed it was argued by some must – be diverted into colonial enterprise in the interests of domestic peace. Nor did such ambitions seem improbable. In 1500 France was the largest single political unit in western Europe. By the end of the century its population was twice the size of that of Spain and ought, some patriots believed, to be reduced and improved by the despatch abroad of its less desirable elements. The country, moreover, was closely linked to Iberia by economic and cultural ties. Its civilization, like theirs, was profoundly influenced by that of Renaissance Italy, and its economy, like theirs, familiar with Italian merchants and bankers (cf. pp. 441 and 454ff.).

More important still, France in the early sixteenth century was a considerable maritime power. Its regular naval forces were admittedly of little consequence before the late 1600s, but its real strength lay, as did that of Spain, in the resources of a number of widely dispersed ports. In the south was the ancient city of Marseilles. Since the late 1300s its competition had troubled Venice in the Levant, to where, as to North Africa, it had with royal encouragement a thriving commerce in the late sixteenth century. It served (*c.* 1500) in the west Provence, the Genoese Riviera and, through the Rhône Valley, a massive hinterland. It was also in vigorous contact with Atlantic Iberia, supplying manufactures and receiving such native and colonial produce as sugar, spices, wool and bullion (cf. p. 172). On the Atlantic itself France had a seaboard reaching from the Basque lands of the Gulf of Gascony to the waters of the English Channel. Roughly the length of that of Spain, its climate and hazards were far worse,

Fig. 18   Galleon-style ship, perhaps French, mid seventeenth century.

producing seamen who, whether from Bayonne or Dieppe, Brest or Rouen, were second to none. Using ships very like those of their English contemporaries (see pp. 459–60), they were by the early 1500s engaged in trades extending from Portugal's Atlantic possessions to northern Europe, and from Castile to the coasts of north-eastern America. They could, as events were to prove, tap alike the skills of Portuguese navigators, Florentine exiles and Dutch entrepreneurs. Nor were their strengths merely material. The already intense local patriotism of the French western ports, and their virulent rivalries, were further sharpened when, in the course of the sixteenth century many became strongholds of the Calvinist faith – Rouen, Dieppe and Caen in Normandy; St Malo and Vitré in Brittany. And of none was this truer than La Rochelle, rich on the export of the salt and wine of western France, and controlling by *c.* 1600 some 150 ocean-going vessels. With its liberties enshrined in an abundance of royal charters it was to all intents an autonomous maritime republic, conducting its own anti-Catholic policy in alliance with its Dutch and English co-religionaries.[1]

There were thus apparently present in France the majority of the necessary ingredients for imperial success. And to these there was added, as a result of the wars between aristocratic factions and between Catholics and Protestants that filled most of the later sixteenth century, the desire of the oppressed to find refuge abroad. Indeed the country's oceanic beginnings were impressive. The French participated in such early Atlantic voyages as the proposed conquest of the Canaries in 1344. At the beginning of the following century a Norman adventurer took three of the islands, and in the course of their colonization and conversion raided the Saharan coast (1405) in search of slaves, Christians and gold. Within a few years Bretons were trading to Madeira, and by the late 1400s the French were established as the most formidable opponents of Portugal and Spain in the Atlantic. They were known and feared in the sugar islands in Columbus' day. They were in Brazil in 1504 and at the same time selling weapons in Morocco. In 1537 the Spaniards complained that their privateers lay in wait for vessels returning from the Americas.[2] And with reason. A squadron belonging to the Dieppe shipowner, Jean Ango, took a cargo of Aztec treasure despatched from Mexico in 1523, whilst some 300 Portuguese craft were captured by his compatriots between 1500 and 1531; and such was their reputation that inward-bound Indiamen assumed any strange sail sighted in the Atlantic islands would be French.[3] Next, in the course of the almost incessant Franco-Spanish wars of the first half of the sixteenth century, the French – in general Norman Huguenots – invaded the Spanish Caribbean. Their raids, in which royal warships were soon participating, culminated in an attack on Havana itself (1555), and plans to seize the bullion lying at Nombre de Dios and to march across the Isthmus to take the treasure fleet in Panama. Such an operation, later in part accomplished by Francis Drake, was well within French capabilities. As it was, the scheme was abandoned when a Franco-Spanish peace was agreed in 1559, one of the corollaries of which was the French crown's acceptance of Spanish hegemony in South America and the Spaniards' admission that the north was open to France.

But this was far from the end of the story. The ensuing civil war certainly diverted France from any coherent imperial policy. To the Huguenots, however, it demonstrated the strategic value of colonies and their merits as havens for the True Faith. At the same time the wars brought an intensification of French privateering and piracy. Catholic and Protestant ports sought to destroy their opponents' trade, and to ensure their own ability to receive aid, such as that provided for their fellow-Protestants by the English. In the late 1500s shipping bound for Huguenot Rochelle was plundered by the Catholic Bretons, whose captains also took any passing English vessels they encountered. Crews, it was alleged, were reviled as 'Huguenot dogs' and in the heyday of Elizabethan seapower set adrift 'all naked and miserable'.[4] Meanwhile Normandy, whose Protestantism England intervened to save, had become 'a den of thieves' – or so London merchants complained – whose men-of-war seized their ally's ships and put the complements of those returning from Spain to torture to discover what bullion they had on board.[5] Which is to say that the war, like any such, had deteriorated into a general *mêlée* with French privateers and pirates of uncertain provenance and persuasion attacking anything they chose anywhere from the Channel approaches to the East Anglian coast. Nevertheless the Protestant campaign had its grand strategy. Spain was to be weakened, and its energies turned away from France, by the taking of the American treasure fleets – proposed by the English as early as 1533 – and by the setting up of bases within Iberian preserves.

Hence in 1562 Jacques Ribault attempted to establish a Protestant foothold in Florida, backed by the Huguenot leader Coligny who saw the value of colonies both in the global struggle against Spain and Catholicism and as outlets for the dangerous ambitions of fighting men unemployed between campaigns. A settlement was eventually made at Port Royal (Battery Creek, South Carolina) within easy reach of the route by which the Spanish silver fleets left the Gulf of Mexico and – so it was fondly believed – the riches of the supposed Seven Cities of Gold. The scheme collapsed, however, when Ribault, seeking reinforcements in France, was obliged by the mishaps of war to flee to England. There a plan was concocted for a joint Anglo-French attempt on Florida, but with its betrayal to Spain Ribault ended in prison. His compatriots in America had in the meanwhile fallen out and abandoned the settlement. The project was resurrected in 1564 when 300 soldiers and colonists under Laudonnière established Fort Caroline, near the modern Jacksonville (Florida). But there were soon disagreements as to how the local Amerindians were to be handled. Then some of the force, taking to the sea to look for prizes, fell into Spanish hands. Amongst the remainder the usual European reluctance to engage in agriculture led inexorably to starvation and mutiny. The situation was momentarily eased by supplies provided by an English expedition, and by the re-appearance of Ribault with reinforcements, including many women and children. But this was intolerable to Spain, and in 1565 the French posts were destroyed, and the majority of such colonists as had not been lost by incompetent leaderships massacred. In revenge another Protestant force surprised and overthrew three Spanish forts in Florida, to the embarrassment of France's Catholic rulers.

After this the French made no more attempts to penetrate to the heartlands of the Spanish empire. All the same their steady erosion of Iberian power and pretensions continued. Over the next half century their privateers were signalled everywhere from Cape Bojador to the Gulf of Mexico, threatening Panama in 1571 and sailing 'for Peru' in 1595.[6] And like the Vikings before them or the English and Dutch after, the French soon progressed from war to business or a combination of the two, 'plundering with one hand and trading with the other' (cf. pp. 384ff. and 471). In the 1560s they were operating on the Venezuelan coast, in the Panama Isthmus and among the islands, supplying the needs of settlers in the remoter Spanish possessions. Spain complained in 1570 of the 'continual trade' to Hispaniola and thereabouts as Normans and Bretons in particular brought in African slaves and those French textiles colonists had once spasmodically received through Seville. In exchange they shipped home tobacco, sugar and hides that France otherwise imported from Spain. By the end of the century the French were probably the major interlopers in the Antilles, engaged in a commerce of increasing complexity, and often working in conjunction with the Dutch and English. Yet within a matter of years they had been eclipsed in the region, as had all others, by the Dutch (see p. 386).

Nor, when like Holland and England, France turned to settlement on the periphery of Spanish power in the hope of producing commodities made scarce by Habsburg policies, were the results impressive (cf. pp. 385 and 492–3). In the Leeward Islands St Christophe (St Kitts), long a pirate base, was seized (1625) and held in uneasy association with the English. By the mid-1600s, under the Company of the American Islands, colonies had been established on Martinique, Guadeloupe and other islets of the Lesser Antilles. But their future was far from certain. There was friction with the English, Spanish reprisals could still be effective, French ambitions were almost exclusively European and on many of the islands France faced the man-eating Caribs. Like the Araucanians or the Iroquois they were yet another of those primitive peoples whose tenacity and adaptability taxed to the full European techniques of conquest and subjugation (see pp. 340 and 444). They were redoubtable and resourceful fighters, too impoverished to become customers and too fierce to be converted or enslaved. Only when they had either been contained or expelled could settlement progress. As in the neighbouring English islands it was initially by small-holdings, soon producing tobacco at such a rate – in Martinique, for instance – that prices were hopelessly depressed. With no suitable indigenous slaves to hand, and before the importation of Africans commenced, most of the labour had to be provided, as it was in French Canada and much of English North America, by white indentured servants (see pp. 449, 486). These, often to all intents slaves, showed themselves before long as restive as elsewhere, rebelling in St Christophe in 1640 and Martinique six years later. Hence when the expected revenues failed to come in the Company of the Islands, which had originally owned the territories, took that familiar imperial course with unprofitable and intractable colonies or undertakings and abandoned them to private venturers. It sold off its interests (1649–51) to the governors it had appointed, and only at the end of the century, with the emergence of large-scale sugar planting, did the islands begin to prosper.

Equally disappointing was the outcome of French efforts elsewhere in the tropical Atlantic. In the 1530s Francis I, hoping for Portugal's support against Spain, had repeatedly forbidden his subjects to trespass in Portuguese West Africa. But for Portugal and its claims they cared even less than for Spain, and by the mid-1500s were conducting a vigorous traffic – mainly Norman and Rochelais – to the shores of the Gulf of Guinea. Though plans to seize a base near Benin (1558) came to nothing, French vessels regularly worked to West Africa, and from there to the Caribbean and Brazil, throughout the later sixteenth century.[7] But once again it was a trade quickly undermined by the Dutch. More promising still were relations with Brazil itself, known to the Normans and Bretons since at least 1504. Before long posts were set up in areas not under Portuguese control for the loading of brazilwood and cotton, and French seamen were soon so familiar with the route to Brazil as to be in demand as pilots for others – such as some Englishmen in 1539 – seeking to trade there.[8] Already at this stage there was some settlement as sailors deserted, took up with Amerindian women and went off to live the usual native-style existence of frontiersmen. But in 1555, at the instigation of a colourful and experienced soldier, the Chevalier de Villegaignon, and with Coligny's support, the systematic colonization of an island in the magnificent bay of Rio de Janeiro was attempted. It was an even bolder move than the subsequent Florida venture, since not only was the site at the very heart of a major Iberian possession but its settlers were also to include, as no other imperial power had as yet permitted, both Catholics and Protestants. Predictably enough its success was short-lived, ruined not by the rigours of the climate or the strength of local or European opposition, but very largely by the inadequacies of the leader himself. Villegaignon turned out to be a vindictive and arbitrary paranoid, who having exacerbated religious dissensions – no difficult task, admittedly – abandoned the squabbling factions. The settlement was taken by the Portuguese in 1560, but the survivors escaped to the mainland where, with Indian aid, they lived for several more years. After this fiasco there were a number of other attempts to settle, mostly on Brazil's north-eastern shoulder, or – in the hope of obtaining tobacco to replace that of Spain – on the coasts of Maranhão and Pará. But with the exception of that of Cayenne (1604) all these putative colonies were dispersed by the Portuguese. French trade, however, was more tenacious, and in the late 1500s the English regularly met, or heard of, French ships in Brazil – including seven that 'had gone to traffic with the wild people' and been destroyed by the Portuguese.[9] With the arrival in strength of the Dutch this commerce, too, declined, but even so Alagôas still had its 'French port' in the 1630s.[10]

Similarly in Asia the pattern was one of unfulfilled initial promise. French vessels were already in the Indian Ocean in 1518, and five years later the Verrazzani brothers of Florence, probably inspired by the outcome of Magellan's voyage, and claiming knowledge of the spice trade, sailed from Dieppe. Their intention was apparently to seek a passage to the Orient through those still unknown regions of America lying between Spanish Florida and Cape Breton. The enterprise was in the Iberian style. France was to have the monopoly of Asian spices; the undertaking had royal patronage; much of its capital came from Italian financiers in Paris, Lyons and Rouen; one of the ships employed belonged to the king, the other to the celebrated Jean Ango. The first attempt (1524) ended as a reconnaissance of part of the eastern coast of North America (see p. 443). Two years later, equipped with Portuguese sailing directions and probably with Portuguese charts, the brothers tried again. This time they aimed to pass through the Straits of Magellan, and in the end one of their ships – none of them bigger than 70t – reached Sumatra, though via the Cape of Good Hope. But on the return it was lost, after which came the final and fatal Verrazzani expedition (1528), reputedly ending in the Lesser Antilles where the Caribs ate its commander.

Other less-publicized voyages were more successful. Under Portuguese pilots two Honfleur craft reached Kilwa in 1527, from where one went on to Diu. Another three were intercepted at the same time making for the Cape of Good Hope, and two years later some vessels of Jean Ango – his ambitions as bold in the east as in the Atlantic – returned safely from Sumatra. Setbacks there were in plenty, but there was clearly no lack of French ships and seamen capable of accomplishing the voyage. Equally clearly there was a considerable knowledge of Asia in the Atlantic ports, whose seamen often served in Iberian ships and whose privateers regularly captured incoming Portuguese Indiamen. Nor was there any difficulty in recruiting Portuguese pilots – and hence in obtaining the latest charts and sailing directions – who indeed so willingly departed for France that in the 1530s Portuguese agents were trying to bribe them back to their proper allegiance. Even so, French interest in Asia was waning well before the outbreak of civil war. It received no such encouragement as that given in Portugal by the royal house. The Normans and Bretons were profitably employed in the west, and with the revival of the Mediterranean spice trade in the later 1500s – to the benefit of Marseilles – there was even less point in undertaking the risks and burden of the oceanic passage (see pp. 140–1, 436, 453).

Not that such activity ceased. The English heard in 1582 of 'six ships of Frenchmen' bound for the Straits of Magellan,[11] and later, prompted by Dutch success, a spate of companies – usually Norman or Breton – was founded. Some were proposed by adventurers, some by exiled Flemish Calvinists and some by Dutch renegades. Richelieu, the effective head of the French state sought (1624) to entrust the whole of the country's colonial commerce to two great corporations, whilst in 1642 there was set up the Eastern Company, which was to colonize and trade with Madagascar and the neighbouring islands. Yet remarkably little was accomplished. Dutch hostility was unremitting, and such few vessels as reached or returned from Asia they usually seized. Of French capital there was no shortage, but France was incapable of opposing the VOC with anything like that purposeful energy the Hollanders directed against the Portuguese. In a country whose history and sheer size allowed regionalism to luxuriate there was no cohesive merchant community. Nor, with the crown devoted to its grand anti-Habsburg ambitions, was there any force to produce one. Individual French ports were, on and off, interested in eastern commerce – though never as much as in that of the Atlantic. But for expensive colonial schemes anywhere, or for anything likely to benefit some rival, they naturally lacked enthusiasm. Their mutual hostilities accordingly flourished unabated, as did those between the land-bound Paris and the maritime provinces, and not until 1664 did France eventually produce an effective East India Company.

II *Frenchmen and Redskins in Canada*

Only marginally more successful were French ambitions in North America. Yet here, for a time, there was no powerful European competition, and in the exploitation of the natural riches of the Newfoundland coast and the Gulf of St Lawrence – cod, whales, walrus, furs – the maritime strength of the ports of Atlantic France could be deployed to the full. The prodigious resources of Newfoundland's Grand Bank were known in Europe by the end of the fifteenth century (see pp. 245, 451, 495–6). From about 1500 French seamen joined those from other Atlantic countries in a fishery which rapidly became a considerable undertaking, supplying cod to the population of western Europe which – largely through the dictates of religion and a chronic shortage of meat – was a great consumer of fish. Before long fishermen had some knowledge of the adjoining landmass, and discovered that its Amerindian inhabitants could provide those beaver, otter and other furs and skins in demand for the comfort and adornment of the opulent of Europe (see pp. 49ff.). The common progression to conquest – or at least hopes of conquest – came, however, not from attempts to secure better or sole control of these resources, but in pursuit of a route to Asia. In 1524 Giovanni Verrazzano seeking, like the English (and probably the Portuguese) before him, a north-west passage to the east, reconnoitred the American coast from Cape Fear (North Carolina) to about 49° 50′n, investigating such promising inlets as Narragansett Bay (see p. 441). But since he returned with only some worthless metals, 'potions and other aromatic liquors', and since his royal patron was now a Spanish prisoner (1525–6), the search lapsed.[12] Nevertheless over the next few years Spanish and English expeditions examined the littoral Verrazzano had traced, and as a result the whole Atlantic seaboard of America was soon charted.

French interest revived in 1532 when the bishop of Lisieux brought to the notice of the restored king the St Malo pilot, Jacques Cartier, who, it was urged, by 'virtue of his voyages to Brazil and the New Land' was especially suited to undertake 'the discovery of new territories in the New World'. Assured by the pope that this would not infringe papal bulls in favour of the Iberian monarchies, and encouraged by the bishop's offer of financial assistance, Francis commissioned Cartier to seek in the New Land 'certain islands and countries wherein there is said to be great quantities of gold and other things', and like as not to search for a way to Asia. Sailing in 1534 he touched in Newfoundland, passed through the Belle Isle Straits – meeting French fishermen – and into the Gulf of St Lawrence. Here he encountered Micmac Indians clearly accustomed to trading with white men, and then in Gaspé Bay some Hurons, two of whom he kidnapped.

So began the sustained and ultimately disastrous association of the white man with the primitive peoples of North America. Here, with profound consequences for the course and nature of European colonization, there were no such advanced societies as those of Mexico or Peru. Indeed, because of tribal migrations and fusions it was (and is) difficult to associate particular peoples with particular territories. Some North

American Indians were neolithic hunters and fishers, like the various Algonkian tribes –
amongst them Wanabakis, Montagnais and Naskapis – who, united only by a common
language, inhabited the area roughly bounded by the Mississippi, the Atlantic and
latitudes 50° to 35°n. Characteristic of their existence was that of the Micmac of Nova
Scotia and the Bay of Fundy, who totalling at best about 2000, spent from spring to
autumn by the rivers and sea before retreating to the forests in winter to escape the fury
of the Canadian climate. From animal hides they produced a leather as soft and supple
as any woollen cloth, which they used to make clothing and footwear (moccasins). Their
dwellings were portable tents (wigwams) of birch-bark covering a timber frame, and on
water they moved swiftly and easily by canoe. Groups of families were under the
authority of elected chiefs, and whilst the women toiled the men conducted themselves
according to a code of valour. But despite a luxuriant polygamy this was no primeval
paradise. War was common, fought with stealth, cunning and brutality; vanquished
males were scalped and their women and children enslaved.

More advanced were the Iroquois tribes – Hurons, Neutrals, Tobaccos, Iroquois –
who inhabited parts of the modern Ohio, New York and Pennsylvania. Though still to a
degree neolithic hunters and fishers, some had become farmers, with the Hurons
growing sufficient maize in the sixteenth century to trade the surplus to other peoples.
They possessed what by European standards were recognizable townships, Huron
Hochelaga (Montreal) being described as well-fortified 'completely round and
pallisaded with timber in three tiers'. Their social and political organization was
complex, strongly matriarchal in many ways, but based on the clan which both
allocated land to families and collectively undertook all work.

Such peoples were not, like those of South America, to succumb almost at a blow to
white power, least of all a power as feeble as that France came to deploy. Vulnerable
they were to unaccustomed disease, and vulnerable also to European exploitation of
their divisions and rivalries. But though few in number – with the Iroquois never
mustering more than about 2500 warriors – they were brave and resourceful fighters. In
war most of the advantages were for long on their side. They could move with ease
through a terrain of forests and rivers, withstand virtually naked the rigours of the
Canadian winter, and hunt and travel unimpeded on their snow shoes. Often nomadic,
and divided into an infinity of tribes and clans – though the Iroquois had a loose
federation from about 1450 – no more than the Araucanians did they present any
central and supreme authority as a hostage which some Cortés could seize and
manipulate. The resources they controlled were (like maize) either of no interest to
Europeans, or (as with furs) acquired in ways which, unlike mining and agriculture,
admitted no European supervision. And they benefited, as the Indians of Iberian
America only briefly did, from the rivalries and squabbles of their European invaders
(cf. pp. 337–40).

For a time, however, the prospects were pleasing for the French. Rumours of a great
river and of distant lands rich in copper brought the speedy despatch from St Malo of a

9 North America *c.*1600, showing main areas of European trade and colonization

second expedition (1535), locally backed and with some modest royal support. Cartier found the entrance to the St Lawrence, sailed and rowed some 1600km up river – the last stretch past fast-flowing shallows and rock-strewn rapids – to Hochelaga. His reception was enthusiastic, and from the Hurons, eager to please their visitor and speed him on his way, he learned of the precious metals of the kingdom of Saguenay to the west. Barely withstanding the fury of the winter he and his surviving men returned to France the following year with a handful of kidnapped Indians, some gold and glowing reports of Canada.[13] Once the current war with Spain had ended (1538), Francis I prepared to enter into his heritage in a fashion which does much to explain his country's early imperial failures. At first any of his subjects were free to go to 'the Newlands'

(1540). Then Cartier was to search for Saguenay and establish a colony, the nucleus of which was to be provided by convicts. Finally, with growing hopes of precious metals, the whole of North America – Canada, Hochelaga, the lands 'beyond and bordering the seas, uninhabited or not possessed and dominated by any Christian prince' – was to become French, with Iberian title, other than effective occupation, ignored. All this was to be accomplished under the aristocratic soldier Roberval, endowed with virtually unlimited authority. He was to build towns, forts and churches, and to distribute lands in feudal tenure in the style of Portuguese proceedings in the Atlantic islands. These he was to populate, likewise in Portuguese style, with convicts – though not those who had committed 'too grievous crimes' – and paradoxically enough for a Huguenot he was to ensure the dissemination of Catholicism. Equally paradoxically he and his associates were to take the bulk of the profits whilst the crown bore, unlike the Iberian monarchs, most of the costs.

Whilst Roberval struggled to raise his share of the capital, Cartier sailed (1541) with a powerful force. He set up a stronghold at Charlesbourg Royal (near Quebec), made a perfunctory search for Saguenay, and in the face of growing Huron hostility departed (1542) with a cargo of what he thought to be gold and diamonds. In Newfoundland he met Roberval, accompanied by another sizeable contingent of troops and settlers. Ignoring orders to return to Canada he slipped away home to sell his diamonds (worthless as it turned out) and to ensure his reward. Roberval, in his absence, re-occupied Charlesbourg and was momentarily on good terms with the local Indians whom he thought white enough to pass for Europeans could they only be persuaded to wear clothes. But this goodwill soon evaporated, and after another half-hearted search for Saguenay the French withdrew (1543). They had been given no intelligent or informed royal direction. Their leaders were not potential *conquistadores*, and once it was plain that Canada's harsh climate and terrain concealed no precious stones or metals imperial zeal waned, its decline no doubt hastened by the comforting knowledge that the greater part of the financial loss on the voyage would be borne by the king.

The outbreak of civil war in mid-century damped for a time further thoughts of conquering and colonizing Canada. But whilst Cartier passed his declining years, the records show, in the agreeable company of 'other good drinkers', his compatriots continued to work to North America, doing business with the Indians of Chesapeake Bay in the 1540s and of South Carolina in the 1560s, and profitably engaged in the Newfoundland fisheries and the Canadian fur trade. Later in the century royal imperial ambitions revived, with territorial empire increasingly seen as a necessary adjunct of restored regal power. But such grand projects made little headway against the hostility of the Atlantic ports who saw only the prospect of their money being wasted and their trades handed over to royal favourites. Kings vainly attempted to placate provincial merchants, appointed viceroys, proposed to subjugate 'lands and countries occupied by barbarians', promised territories and privileges to would-be explorers and colonizers. The outcome was a modest settlement in Acadia (New Brunswick, Maine, Nova

Scotia),[14] soon reduced by the English to a few trading posts. Nova Scotia was invaded by Scottish settlers in the 1620s and more or less the whole lost to the English by mid-century (see p. 492).

Only with the arrival (1603) in Canada of Samuel de Champlain was there some improvement. Of seafaring stock, Protestant by upbringing and Catholic by conviction, he was a man of wider vision and experience than his predecessors in North America. He had fought in the civil wars, travelled – or so he claimed – in Spain and its empire, and had a graphic and persuasive pen. Joining a trading expedition up the St Lawrence he examined the Saguenay, heard of lakes and waterways beyond, and realized that goods acquired from the French by local Indians were sent on by them to more distant tribes. The year after he accompanied the new royal lieutenant-general, de Monts, in his attempt to plant a colony on the Bay of Fundy, and explored part of the adjoining coast. He convinced de Monts, who held the monopoly of the fur trade, that this was not where France's future lay. Effort should be concentrated on the St Lawrence, away from the danger of European rivals, offering furs more readily, and offering the chance of a passage to Asia.

Accordingly in 1608 he commanded a force which established a post at Quebec. The following spring he joined an Algonkian war party, travelling with them along the Richelieu river, across Lake Champlain to Ticonderoga. Here, as he wrote like some Cortés or Albuquerque dividing to rule, '*les nostres*' (the Algonkians and Hurons), aided by the firearms of three Europeans, defeated the Iroquois, thereafter the mortal enemies of the French. For a time, however, France could claim to control the region, as is witnessed by the names bestowed on it, and the young Etienne Brulé was left with the Algonkians to 'observe the rivers, what manner of peoples inhabit them, and to discover what mines and rare things may be found'. So commenced a European expansion accomplished not, as in South America, by bands of conquerors, but by individual white men dependent, as they were in much of Asia, on indigenous co-operation and moving along indigenous routes. In 1615 Brulé, accompanying the Hurons – who eventually ate him – left the Great Lakes on a journey which finally brought him to Chesapeake Bay. Twenty years later Jean Nicollet, guided by the same tribe, and carrying a mandarin robe in anticipation of his arrival in China, reached Lake Michigan or beyond to hear not of Cathay but of the mighty Sioux nation to the west.

Champlain meanwhile urged the opportunities of this New France. Its natural resources would bring a fortune, its own trade and that of Asia flowing through it could be taxed for the benefit of the mother country and the French church could convert 'countless souls'. With 300 soldiers and the same number of settler families, France would have within fifteen years a colony sustained by 'military strength, justice, commerce and tillage of the soil'. But Canada, without 'mines and rare things' was the wrong setting for the repetition of Iberian practice. The maritime towns were uninterested, the necessary population was not forthcoming and French aristocrats, appointed by the crown to grandiosely named offices, were more concerned with

Europe. Hence with English colonies planted from Virginia to Newfoundland, and various French ventures having failed, Richelieu established in 1627 a Dutch-style Company of New France (see pp. 391ff., 417ff., 485ff.). Its authority was to extend from Florida to the Arctic circle, and from Newfoundland to the Great Lakes and beyond, 'to broadcast and make known' the might of the house of Bourbon. The company was to have a 15-year tax-free monopoly of all Canadian trade (apart from the fisheries). In return it was to settle 4000 French Catholic families by 1643, supporting them for their first three years, and providing them with cleared lands. To aid the good work there were promises that the normal economic bonds of society would be relaxed. Aristocrats who engaged in trade were guaranteed their status would be unsullied, select commoners were to be ennobled and artisans who served six years in Canada would, on their return to France, be accepted as master craftsmen.

Yet despite these ingenious and comprehensive provisions the company accomplished even less than its Dutch exemplar. To the enmity of the Iroquois, incurred by Champlain, was added, as a result of Anglo-French disputes in Europe, that of the English who had already pre-empted the whole Atlantic coast of America above Cape Fear. Barely had the company begun operations when they invaded Canada and seized Quebec, and even after its restoration (1632) their traders – particularly those despatched by the 'Adventurers in the River and on the Coast of Canada' – remained active far up the St Lawrence. Thus by the mid-1600s France's colony in North America was one far poorer (and more heavily taxed) than its Dutch and English neighbours. It was confined essentially to the St Lawrence, and comprised no more than a handful of lordships, three miniscule towns, a few spasmodically manned trading posts and a total population of about 2000. No more than in Dutch America was a company designed primarily to pursue commercial ends the instrument to populate a colony – indeed its critics alleged it opposed colonization to safeguard its fur trade against interlopers – least of all one as envisaged by feudal and aristocratic France. Land was to be distributed in lordships to those of suitable wealth and standing. For their holdings, elongated rectangles running back from the St Lawrence, the recipients were to render homage to the king's representative, and on them they were to settle their own tenants. But in a country where wealth came from trapping, fishing and trading the system was irrelevant. Even in 1663 there were only about one hundred lordships, and these with little of their land occupied. As a result, and through strict royal control, the feudal powers of Canadian *seigneurs* were far less than those of lords in the mother country.

Nevertheless whatever its ambitions to emulate the Dutch, aristocratic France produced a colonial society much like those produced by the equally aristocratic Spain and Portugal. Canada had indeed no mines or plantations, nor any towns worth speaking of other than Quebec. But it had its aristocracy, stemming like those of Iberian America or English Virginia from diverse and generally obscure origins (cf. pp. 332 and 487). As tightly knit as any, its twenty-three members controlled in 1663 about 80 per cent of the available land, and impoverished though they were, managed to live in the idleness and ostentation characteristic of their kind. They had, however, no indigenous servile class, no African slaves – one or two apart – and no polyglot body of skilled freemen to support them. Instead, as in other French (and English) colonies, there were the white indentured servants (*engagés*) (cf. pp. 440 and 486). These were for the most part peasants, usually young men for whom anything was better than the poverty of the homeland, and who bound themselves to a master for a number of years in the hope of eventually being able to set up on their own. In the meanwhile they could be reduced to what was tantamount to slavery. For the rest, the social pattern was of a familiar imperial order. The European inhabitants of Canada were predominantly male. Many, willingly responding to the advances of naked indigenous females, took up with Indian women, but few married them. And on the fringe of French society were those archetypal frontiersmen, the *coureurs de bois*, hunting, trading and living native-style like their Portuguese counterparts in Africa and Brazil, and occasionally commanding, as did la Salle later, tribal war parties. To obtain furs they undertook long and dangerous treks through Indian country, often accompanied by squaws who prepared their food, dressed their skins and satisfied their sexual needs. Back from the forests to (comparative) civilization they disposed of their profits in what the missionaries denounced as excesses worse than those of 'the poor miserable savages'.

Like the Iberian powers too, and indeed conscious of the march that these had stolen, France attempted to defend the purity and extend the bounds of the Christian faith. After some hesitation it was accepted that all colonists must be Catholic. Equally after some hesitation the French Catholic missions began work. By Spanish or Portuguese standards their efforts were modest, and the outcome, notwithstanding a record of suffering and endurance the equal of any, disappointing. Canada was admittedly a daunting prospect. Its tribes spoke an assortment of tongues and dialects. Some were nomadic; none had a written literature or a familiarity with abstract ideas. Primarily Christianity meant to them restrictive and vexing laws, such as the prohibition of polygamy. But to impose these the French lacked that prestige and authority which as conquerors the Spaniards enjoyed in the south, whilst peoples admiring male prowess were unimpressed by celibate missionaries who neither fought, traded or fornicated. Moreover, whatever the views of the government in Paris, Canadian fur-traders had no desire to see their monopoly endangered by the introduction of those settlers whose benign influence, so the missions believed, would Europeanize the Indians and prepare them for conversion. In fact, as in most empires, the teachings of the church were blatantly contradicted by the behaviour of many white settlers.

Though other Orders were present to begin with, the conversion of Canada was, from 1636, a Jesuit monopoly. The fathers used those techniques so successfully employed by their colleagues elsewhere, just as in moments of exasperation their thoughts similarly turned to the merits of force and of introducing recalcitrant Indians 'onto the road to heaven' by means of the stake. They worked amongst the Montagnais,

Naskapi, Abenaki and even the Iroquois. For a time they regarded 'those headstrong savages' the Hurons with something of the enthusiasm that the Japanese had inspired in the Order. But though many of the missionaries endured fearful hardship living amongst the tribes, and though many suffered martyrdom, with Jean de Brébeuf burned, scalded, mutilated and eventually eaten by the Iroquois (1649), their success was limited. French authority was weak, lay support inadequate, the missions themselves too small and their resources insufficient. And in the mid-1600s most of what they had achieved was undone by the Iroquois wars.

Such tribulations reflect the fragility of France's hold on Canada. The colony failed to attract emigrants, and of those it did many of the most enterprising were in effect absorbed into the indigenous economy as *coureurs de bois*. Nowhere could the French conquer and enslave the Amerindians in the way the Spaniards had done in much of the south, and indeed with furs the most valuable commodity they were little better than clients of the tribes who controlled, for their own benefit, the flow of these precious goods towards the trading posts of New France. The Montagnais, than whom, thought Champlain, 'we have no greater enemy', denied the French direct access to the resources of the northern littoral of the St Lawrence. The Algonkians dominated the passage westward through the upper Ottawa. Still more happily placed were the Hurons, masters of the commerce of the Great Lakes. They collected furs from tribes to the north and west, supplying in exchange provisions and European goods ranging from waistcoats and blankets to scissors and metal arrow heads, which they obtained from the French at Tadoussac. The Hurons were France's allies. Her enemies were the formidable Iroquois, armed by the New Netherlands' Dutch, and alienated by Champlain and Franco-Huron attempts to exclude them from the St Lawrence traffic. Though few in numbers their warriors moved freely through the feebly held French possessions, raiding to start with, in open war from 1636. They harried France's indigenous allies – whom she dare not supply with firearms – massacred missionaries, disrupted agriculture and the fur trade, and reduced New France to poverty and almost to extinction. Having displaced the Hurons, the Iroquois could offer furs to the Dutch in Albany, the New Englanders, or the French on the St Lawrence, exploiting their rivalries to get the price and the guns they wanted. Against them the French retaliated in kind, burning their women and children, but not until 1667 were the Iroquois defeated, and then only by regular troops from France.

Already, however, the North American Indians were as much the losers in their encounter with Europeans as any other primitive people. From those who they regularly designated as 'the savages' the French learned much – how to canoe, toboggan and use snow shoes. The Indians in turn accepted the white man's clothing, weapons and trinkets, even abandoning their traditional shell-currencies in favour of glass beads. But unlike the peoples of the more advanced cultures of the south, they could make none of these things themselves to the consequent destruction of their morale and independence. With French assistance the Huron for a time extended their dominion, and from the European demand for furs Iroquois power grew. Many Indians, however, soon preferred to live by begging from Europeans rather than by pursuing their customary ways of life. Like those of the Spanish lands in the south they became addicted to the white man's liquor, and they succumbed, if not on the same scale, yet with the same ease to European-borne disease, with the Huron lamenting in 1616 'that since the French are amongst them, and have commerce with them, many of them die and their population is decreasing'. Thus, physically weakened, their religions undermined, and their whole existence increasingly dependent upon people whom they regarded as inferiors, many Canadian Indians, unconquered though they were, lapsed into that same melancholy and despair that European military victory had produced in the south.

But if by the mid-1600s France had gained little glory from North America the New Land had nevertheless brought many Frenchmen profit. The cod which abounded off Newfoundland were taken by ships from ports the length of the Atlantic coast. Rarely more than 80t, they sailed against the gales of the winter and spring for the Grand Bank where they launched small boats whose crews fished, as was to remain the practice for centuries, with hook and line. Since France, like Iberia, had salt of its own, catches could be cleaned and pickled directly, and as soon as they were fully laden ships returned to Europe so as to be able to make another trip in the autumn. The industry developed rapidly in scope and nature, with some Normans and Bretons landing (as did the English, who had no salt) to dry their fish on stagings ashore, and ports like La Rochelle and Nantes selling their catches in Spain and Italy. Soon not only cod, but whales (for oil), walrus (for ivory and oil) and seals were being taken. Ports came to have their own specialities and their seamen waged open war against rival compatriots encountered in distant waters. Hence the French fishery was more extensive than that of the English (concentrated off eastern Newfoundland and on the Grand Bank), and in 1578 it was thought there were as many as 150 of their vessels working around Newfoundland, off Cape Breton and in the Gulf of St Lawrence.

Here, too, early chance encounters with the Indians revealed that North America could provide furs. By the mid-1500s a regular trade, ancillary to the fisheries, had sprung up with the peoples of southern Labrador, and before the end of the century ships were going out solely to load furs. From such associations, and from attempts at colonization, the French learned something of the nature of the Indian economy, now influenced by their demands, and of the routes by which furs were brought to the St Lawrence. Trading posts were pushed up river (Tadoussac, Trois Rivières, Cap de Victoire) as far as the Indians would permit – which was not very far – and individual European *coureurs de bois* penetrated further inland to obtain furs or to persuade the Indians to bring them. Before its disruption by the Iroquois and English wars, there had developed an important trade, with the French annually exporting anything from 12,000 to 15,000 beaver skins alone in the 1630s. These sold in the mother country at about ten times their purchase price, persuading projectors of the vast profits Canada could yield, and opening to the king vistas of taxes which would provide sufficient revenues to run the colony and leave a handsome surplus as well. Not surprisingly merchants, like the Dutch in the neighbouring New Netherlands, showed little inclination to be diverted from such opportunities into schemes of colonization and empire.

III *A non-imperial state*

Thus in 1650, after a century and a half of intermittent endeavour, France was Europe's most insignificant imperial power. True, Castile's demographic and economic difficulties allowed French emigration to the peninsula and also enabled France to provide Spain and its colonies with manufactured goods they were incapable of producing themselves (see pp. 367, 439). Even so, the French hold on the Iberian empires was never anything like that of the Dutch, by whom it was in any case rapidly eroded, and the French possessions in the New World, their natural riches notwithstanding, were but a poor reflection of the bold schemes first envisaged and attempted.

French energies were indeed diverted at a crucial moment by the civil wars which lasted until the reign of Henry IV (1589–1610). Yet France had failed to effect any permanent penetration not only of the Spanish, but of the much weaker Portuguese empire before the mid-1500s, and the showing of the restored monarchy of the first half of the seventeenth century was even worse. France's greatest effort was made in Canada. Here, in a region remote from the main seats of Spanish imperial strength, there were the riches of the St Lawrence and the chance of a maritime route to the Orient. But the country itself offered no prospect of a Spanish-style conquest, and seemingly lacked all those things – precious metals, free land, ready labour – to draw men to distant parts and especially to those with a winter so long and fearsome. Elsewhere France was unable, for most of the sixteenth century, consistently to bring to bear that volume of seapower needed to challenge the Iberian oceanic monopolies. And when eventually French effort was renewed the Dutch were entrenched in the east and, together with the English, in the west.

Yet had France, given her resources, seriously attempted the conquest of the Iberian colonial territories when the rule of Spain and Portugal was still only uncertainly established, she might well have achieved what the Dutch were almost to accomplish in Brazil. But only momentarily did the French act with anything like the purposefulness of the Iberians or the Dutch, and only the Huguenot leader Coligny (murdered in 1572) and the Catholic Richelieu after him, had anything of a considered imperial policy. Under Francis I, when the opportunities were greatest, spasmodic enthusiasms were disrupted by attempts to check Spain in Europe and by the king's own imprisonment. The rest of the century was filled by the chaos occasioned by royal minorities and civil wars, whilst after the accession of Henry IV kings were preoccupied with re-establishing royal authority in France and France's position in Europe. This meant, as in the Middle Ages and after the ending of the Hundred Years War, a concern with those traditional spheres of influence, Italy and the Mediterranean. Here royal ambitions coincided with the interests of the merchants of Lyons and Marseilles, the latter city already envisaged in the mid-1400s as another Venice, monopolizing Levantine trade with northern and central Europe. Thus whilst the Atlantic ports were left more or less to their own devices, commercial privileges were acquired in Mameluke Egypt (1507), and shortly after France became the ally of the Ottoman sultan and the first European state other than Venice and Ragusa to enjoy trading concessions within his realms.

But this long history of uncoordinated colonial endeavour reflects more than the follies of statesmen. France, like Spain, was not a united state but an agglomeration of provinces. Between these, rivalries were acute, as in the sixteenth century between Normandy, the pioneer of French oceanic expansion, and Brittany, newly enriched by trade and war with Spain. In France, however, no one province had such a preponderance as did the kingdom of Castile in Spain. French towns and cities were, moreover, unlike those of Holland and Spain, relatively insignificant. The Atlantic seaboard had indeed its powerful, wealthy, particularist and virtually independent maritime communes, their long-standing commercial rivalries now exacerbated by religious differences. Individually, or in small groups they were willing enough to back fishing voyages, assorted forays into Iberian preserves, or even to advance money to infant settlements. But in colonies and the commercial monopolies associated with them – almost inevitably favouring some opponent – they saw only a threat to their prosperity. Such monopolies they accordingly either resisted or simply flouted, setting up rival companies to handle the same trade or demanding exemptions for existing interests.

In all this, however, France differed very little from Spain, Holland or England, except that she had no single port strong enough to establish its hegemony the way Amsterdam and Seville did, and no authority, before the resurgence of royal power in the seventeenth century, able to reconcile, as Oldenbarnevelt did in Holland, divergent ambitions. There was, furthermore, a fundamental lack of sympathy between the royal government in Paris – a city without the maritime and commercial associations of Lisbon, London or Amsterdam – and the masterful, bourgeois and often heretic Atlantic ports. Hence companies set up in Paris, like that of Richelieu's for New France, were backed not by merchants – of whom it had only twenty-six out of over a hundred investors in 1629 – but by royal officials. To these, as to their like elsewhere, empire was a matter of strategy and prestige, of settlement, of the conversion of the natives, and of trade through carefully regulated monopolies. But to the seaports this meant, as did similar projects to merchants elsewhere, nothing but expense and needless annoyance.

Nor was there much in France's colonies to appeal to other sections of society. Aristocrats and gentlemen could expect no lucrative offices, no opportunity to live by peculation, plunder or on the labours of serfs and slaves. For peasants seeking a better life there was little to be said, however desperate their lot, for continuing in servitude in a worse climate on the banks of the St Lawrence – always assuming their lords would let them go. And as in the Dutch New Netherlands the very success of the fur trade was an obstacle to colonization since merchants and monopolists feared that settlers would poach on their commerce. But in any case the sheer size of France itself meant that few ordinary people living inland ever heard of the chances of the New World, whilst many of those that did in the seaports were Protestants, forbidden to settle in Canada after 1627. Indeed this exclusion of the Huguenots, many of them merchants, seamen and craftsmen, seemingly removed a major potential source of desperately needed emigrants. Since, however, the Edict of Nantes (1598) allowed Protestant subjects freely to practise their religion and to hold public office in certain regions of France and under certain conditions, there was little more reason than in liberal Holland for men to seek religious freedom in distant lands.

IV   *The Noble Savage and Indian rights*

Not surprisingly empire, whether her own or any one else's, made little impact on early modern France. Scholars and connoisseurs collected Iberian maps, translations of Iberian chronicles and various exotic curiosities. North American and Brazilian Indians were brought to Normandy in the early 1500s, where Jean Ango had a brazilwood house. It was also in Normandy that, as a result of oceanic voyaging and Portuguese influences, there developed at this time an important and distictive school of cartography and navigation. The French were the first to use artists to depict new lands (as did the English, Spaniards and Dutch later), when in 1564 Jacques le Moyne de Morgues accompanied Laudonnière to Florida. And from a country where humanist influences were early and strongly established, came impressive accounts of the wider world. Verrazzano, recording his voyage to America, distinguished hypothesis from fact, carefully described what he had seen, and admitted the gaps in his knowledge. The Protestant pastor, Jean de Léry, writing on Brazil (1578), gave one of the most sympathetic accounts of any primitive people, contrasting the virtues of the Tupinambá – their hospitality, bravery, unaffected behaviour – with Christian shortcomings. These same qualities of accuracy, perception, sympathy and prejudice, already familiar in Iberian writings, re-appear in the Jesuit *Relations* concerning Canada. Annually from 1632, partly to stimulate interest in their mission and funds to support it, partly to record their achievements, fathers in the field reported on their work. Suitably edited, these narratives were until 1673 published in Paris. They tell of the attempts of white men to live with and to understand primitive peoples, and they contain the observations of able and highly educated priests on what they encountered. They describe the land, its exploration and, with an honest mixture of revulsion and admiration, the behaviour of tribes whose life defied all European conventions and categories. The Huron, thought Jean de Brébeuf, were 'lazy, liars, thieves and beggars', but he willingly admitted their stoicism in the face of every disaster inflicted by man and nature.

But no more than elsewhere did such matters excite general interest or re-shape contemporary thought. Some writers digested information about non-European lands. Pupils in Jesuit schools were expected to study the history of the missions. Romances were set in exotic surroundings, and literature was adorned with exotic trimmings – François Béroalde (d. 1629) claiming to have learned from a Chinese sage the invaluable art of determining female virginity. Yet Jean Parmentier left no account of a visit to Brazil since, like other Renaissance men of letters, he believed scholars should devote themselves exclusively to the study of the classics. The less discerning, meanwhile, preferred to hear of giants, treasure, pilgrimages and the doings of France's redoubtable ally the Turk, on whom twice as many books were produced than on America in the sixteenth century.

Yet paradoxically it was through the writings of the poet Pierre de Ronsard (1524–85) and the essayist Michel de Montaigne (1533–92) that the discoveries were to make their most significant intellectual impact in Europe. Neither had any first-hand experience of the Americas or of France's modest role in exploration, nor was the revelation of new lands a decisive or even a major influence on their thought, but both used what they had heard and read to give striking point to their views. Convinced that the aboriginals of Brazil were living in pristine bliss, Ronsard urged (in his *Complaint against Fortune*) that they should be left uncontaminated by European civilization, a reproach to modern vice. He drew his information from a work of André Thevet which in turn had been influenced by the reminiscences of Normans who had lived happily amongst the Amerindians. All this confirmed a pleasing classical myth, resurrected with Renaissance adulation for everything ancient, that there had been in the remote past a golden age when life was good and simple. Recognizing, like other humanists, primitive societies as the survivors of this lost glory (cf. p. 355), Ronsard demanded that the peoples of Brazil should be neither destroyed, subverted nor proselytized, and asserted their right to resist any attempted colonization by force.

A similar liberalism and relativism were more profoundly and trenchantly propounded by Montaigne, whose humanist scepticism and tolerance were heightened by revulsion from the follies of half a century of civil war. He knew some of the French and Iberian writings on the Americas, and he knew a Norman who had lived wild for over a decade in Brazil. He condemned the Spaniards as 'mere beasts' for their behaviour in the Indies, demonstrated the diversity of human custom, and in his *Cannibals* extolled the virtues of Amerindians living as man had done at the Creation. Their existence was a model for all to emulate, and one indeed that Gonzalo in *The Tempest* by William Shakespeare – who knew Montaigne in translation – proposed to follow in his intended commonwealth. With Montaigne's demand that Europeans should not denounce customs as wrong simply because they differed from their own, a minute step was taken towards genuine toleration. At the same time the philosophy of

Rousseau and the Romantics was foreshadowed, and the myth of the Noble Savage launched on its long and influential career. Yet such views, most fully and forcibly expressed in a country whose imperial achievement was negligible, stemmed not from Europe's colonial experience, but from the legacy of Antiquity and from a disillusionment bred by the violence, bigotry and futility of religious and civil war.

Bibliographical note

There is an admirable introduction to the archives (and bibliographies) relating to French expansion in this period in Patricia Claxton's translation of Marcel Trudel, *The Beginnings of New France, 1524–1663* (Toronto, 1973). For the sources for the study of the French maritime economy *c.* 1500 Michel Mollat, *Le Commerce Maritime Normand à la Fin du Moyen Age* (Paris, 1952) is of especial value. The most useful journals on early French colonial history (though this is by no means their only concern) are: *The Canadian Historical Review* (Toronto, 1920–), which lists all new publications on Canadian history; *The Jamaican Historical Review* (Kingston, 1945–); and *The Caribbean Historical Review* (Port of Spain, 1950–). In France the *Revue Française d'Histoire d'Outre Mer* (Paris 1959–) continues the work of the former *Revue d'histoire des Colonies* (Paris, 1932–58) and *Revue de l'histoire des Colonies Françaises* (Paris, 1913–31).

The whole subject of the beginnings of French expansion is handled with Gallic éclat in C.-A. Julien, *Les Débuts de l'expansion et de la colonisation Française XVᵉ–XVIᵉ siècles* (Paris, 1947). This covers even more ground than its title indicates, and contains, for example a lucid and balanced survey of the impact of the discoveries on French culture. Mollat, *Le Commerce maritime Normand* deals with the background to Norman oceanic ventures. For the commerce of Marseilles and the French interest in the Mediterranean *c.* 1500 see the richly illustrated essay of Domenico Gioffrè, to which I am already heavily indebted, 'Il Commercio d'importazione Genovese alla luce dei Registri del Dazio, 1495–1537', in A. Guiffrè (ed.), *Studi in Onore di Amintore Fanfani* (6 vols, Milan, 1962), V 168ff. The affairs of Marseilles at the end of the century are discussed by many of the writers on Venetian and Genoese commercial history (see pp. 153–4), with a useful summary in Niels Steensgaard, *Carracks, Caravans and Companies: The Structural Crisis in the European-Asian Trade in the Early Seventeenth Century* (Copenhagen, 1973). The financial background to the first French oceanic voyages is examined by Jacques Heers in *CIHM*, 5 (1966), 273ff.

The first French voyages to West Africa and the Canaries are analysed in Raymond Mauny, *Les Navigations Médiévales sur les Côtes Sahariennes antérieures à la découverte Portugaise* (Lisbon, 1960). Much of relevance is hidden (by lack of an index) in vol. II of V. Magalhães-Godinho, *Os Descobrimentos e a Economia Mundial* (2 vols, Lisbon, 1963–5). New light is thrown on Breton oceanic enterprise by J.A. van Houtte and E. Stols in their contribution to the *Mélanges en honneur de Fernand Braudel* edited by Edouard Privat (Toulouse, 1973), I, 645ff. Recent French work on maritime history and the French contribution to the great discoveries are sympathetically assessed by S.E. Morison, *The European Discovery of America: The Northern*

Voyages (Oxford 1971), which on this, as on everything else, is illuminating and entertaining.

For France in the Caribbean A.P. Newton, *The European Nations in the West Indies, 1493–1688* (1933) is still of value, though now corrected and amplified by Kenneth R. Andrews, *The Spanish Caribbean: Trade and Plunder, 1530–1630* (New Haven, 1978). French activity in Portuguese West Africa was long since noticed by Richard Hakluyt, and is admirably discussed in J.W. Blake, *European Beginnings in West Africa, 1454 1578* (1937). France's early interest in Brazil, and French trade and attempted colonization there are examined in Julien, *Les Débuts*, Mollat, *Le Commerce Maritime Normand*, and F. Mauro, *Le Portugal et l'Atlantique au XVIIe Siècle* (Paris, 1960).

Eric Axelson notices, from Portuguese sources, the first French voyages to the Orient in his *South-East Africa, 1488–1530* (1940). The subject is re-examined in detail by M. Mollat in *CIHM*, 6 (1963), 239ff. and by J. Barassin, ibid., 373ff. In *CIHM*, 8 (1970), 453ff., there is a lively and wide-ranging discussion by L. Dermigny of France's difficulties in producing an East India Company and her shortcomings as a potential colonial power.

French beginnings in North America are colourfully and exhaustively discussed by Morison, *The European Discovery of America*. Useful, and lavishly illustrated, is W.P. Cumming, R.A. Skelton and D.B. Quinn, *The Discovery of North America* (1971), continued in *The Exploration of North America*. Fundamental is Trudel, *The Beginnings of New France, 1524–1663*. C.-A. Julien, *Les Français en Amérique au XVIIe Siècle* (Paris 1976), though essentially a work composed many years earlier, has valuable insights and opinions. There is a good analysis of the economy and society of French Canada in its early years in S. Diamond, 'Le Canada Français du XVIIe siècle, in *Annales*, 16, 2, (1961) 317ff.

For the Grand Bank and St Lawrence fisheries I have used G. Musset, *Les Rochelais à Terre-Neuve, 1500–1789* (La Rochelle, 1899); R.G. Lounsberry, *The British Fishery at Newfoundland, 1634–1763* (New Haven, 1934); D.B. Quinn, 'England and the St Lawrence, 1577–1602', in John Parker (ed.), *Merchants and Scholars* (Minneapolis, 1965). There is a fine description, based on personal reminiscence, of the French Grand Bank fishery at the beginning of this century, in Morison, *The European Discovery of America*, authoritative on the whole subject.

There is much of value on the weaknesses of France as an imperial power in Julien, *Les Débuts*; Dermigny in *CIHM*, 8; and in an excellent article by David Parker, 'The Social Foundation of French Absolutism, 1610–30' in *P&P*, 53 (1971), 67ff., which is particularly illuminating on the power and privileges of La Rochelle.

The impact of the discoveries on French culture is examined by G. Atkinson, *Les Nouveaux Horizons de la Renaissance Française* (Paris, 1935). The most perceptive analysis remains that of Julien in *Les Débuts*. There are some brief essays of relevance in the vast work by various hands edited by Fredi Chiappelli, *First Images of America, The Impact of the New World on the Old* (2 vols, Berkeley, 1976) and an enormous amount of curious information in the even vaster work of D.F. Lach, *Asia in the Making of Europe*, vol. II bks 2 and 3 (Chicago, 1977).

9

England

1 *Armed and aggressive beginnings*

More promising still, but only belatedly brought to fruition, were England's colonial beginnings. Yet the country enjoyed most of those advantages which elsewhere produced imperial success. Like Portugal it was small, and for most of the time more or less under the effective control of rulers who between roughly 1550 and 1650 had no serious political ambitions or commitments in Europe. Its capital was at once a political and commercial centre and a port of some consequence. As a producer of wool and woollen textiles widely in demand, England had for centuries been linked to the great commercial and industrial regions of Italy and the Low Countries. Furthermore, for much of the late 1500s and early 1600s its textile industry was in difficulty, inspiring searches for new markets and, combined with a growing population, convincing statesmen that disorders and worse could only be avoided by the despatch abroad of 'the offals of our people'. And since in the half century after *c.* 1580 there was a striking increase in the size of aristocratic and gentry families, these influential classes were attracted, like their Viking or Genoese counterparts earlier, to colonial and similar schemes.

Nor was there any reason why these should not have succeeded. England's medieval magnates and sovereigns had been amongst Europe's most strenuous crusaders. They had also been amongst its most persistent empire-builders, conquering Wales and failing to conquer Scotland in the thirteenth century, and overrunning much of France in the opening campaigns of the Hundred Years War. With conquest came skills in subjugation. The royal hold on Ireland, it was urged in 1398, would be improved by settling a family from every parish in England on the frontier lands.[1] A few years later Danzig was convinced that if the English got a foothold in Prussia it would end, like Gascony, in their hands. Just as lengthy and vigorous was England's tradition of war and trade by sea. Magnates had long possessed ships and even fleets, commonly employed, like the vessels of the king-making earl of Warwick in the mid-1400s, in grand-scale piracy. Then, from the late fifteenth century, the country had a body of royal ships. They did not constitute the equivalent of Christendom's only other state navy, that of Venice, but these heavily armed royal men-of-war – nineteen of over 200t in 1588 – gave England the decisive edge over the Armada, and when employed, as they commonly were, by private owners, they brought invaluable strength to commercial and privateering ventures. Well before their assault on the Iberian oceanic empires the

Fig. 19 Engraving of the circumnavigator Thomas Cavendish's ship entering the harbour at St Helena.

English were generally regarded as a singularly formidable maritime people, whether by the Hanse in the late Middle Ages, or by the Venetians who in 1551 thought them 'very powerful at sea'.

A major element in this strength was the quality of English ships. The men-of-war enjoyed such a reputation that their design was copied by the French in the 1550s, and by the Spaniards from the 1570s. Spain was similarly advised (1566) that there were no better craft for the Indies trade than those built in England, and by the end of the century English ships, or those of English inspiration, were widely employed in both European and distant waters. The distinctive features of the Elizabethan man-of-war were its low freeboard and its speed and manoeuvrability. A representation (*c.* 1580) of the royal *Tiger* shows a long, low, flush-built hull, far removed from the towering height of the Mediterranean carrack and her descendants. The ship has three masts – the forward pair setting two square sails each, the mizzen carrying a lateen – and a bowsprit with a spritsail.[2] But such lines, in part Mediterranean and Iberian in origin, reflect no revolution. There were indeed big (700t or more) and high-charged merchantmen and warships in England *c.* 1500 – often German or Spanish in origin. But the *Tiger's* profile is foreshadowed in that of the earlier (1546) royal *Greyhound*. And earlier still English merchantmen are depicted in carvings from the beginning of the fifteenth century with squat hulls, sharpish lines, and a two-masted rig comprising a square main and a lateen mizzen. There was, that is, a long-established English style of building. There was also a long-established English style of fighting. The country's larger warships and some of its larger merchant vessels mounted effective artillery from *c.* 1450. According to a Spanish report of 1574 the men-of-war carried their heavy pieces near the waterline, using them in broadsides whose smoke confused an opponent. And thus, it continues, they had fought in the 1540s. Broadside firing was admittedly common enough in the early sixteenth century, but it is clear that with tactics as with ships what was regarded as something identifiably English had been established before the opening of Elizabeth's reign (1558).

Meanwhile the country's vessels had penetrated to distant waters. In the late 1200s it was the English who, together with the Dutch, pioneered a direct passage from the North Sea to the Baltic. Far more significant, and marking – together with Portugal's exploration of the Atlantic coast of Africa – the real beginnings of Europe's overseas expansion, east-coast fishermen, seeking new grounds since fish 'had abandoned their former haunts', re-opened (*c.* 1412) the continent's trade with Iceland. In so doing they demonstrated that the country already possessed the ships, seamen and navigational skills needed for the regular conduct of difficult and dangerous voyages. More promising still were the prospects of the Mediterranean, notwithstanding the strength of Italian opposition. Occasional English vessels appeared there in the late 1300s, and more in the second half of the following century when England, now recovering from the political and economic troubles of the Wars of the Roses, could better afford such luxuries as silks, spices and Aegean wines. From the late 1470s royal ships on charter to merchants, and before long private vessels as well, were carrying cloth to Pisa and Livorno. Once established, the English rapidly expanded their operations. They were at Chios by 1479 – where some settled and married – and at Oran two years later. By the turn of the century they were in Marseilles and Sardinia, Asia Minor and Alexandria, and shipping wine from Crete despite Venetian protests. Their commerce was soon one of some sophistication. Bullion obtained from the sale of textiles in southern Italy was used to purchase silk and wines in the Aegean, and English ships entered such local trades as that between Chios and Genoa. England's success, part of a general Atlantic intrusion into the Mediterranean at this time, stemmed from a number of factors, not least the willingness of the Florentines, embattled with their neighbours, to welcome her merchants. To this was added the security brought by the initial use of royal warships, the commercial concessions obtained in Italy by the first Tudor, and the weakening of the hold of Genoa and Venice on some traditional commercial routes (cf. pp. 142, 177). Nor was England's southward drive confined to the Mediterranean. A

Fig. 20 English man-of-war, *c.* 1580

trade had been opened with Morocco by the early 1500s, whilst in 1481 the Spaniards thought the English would make admirable partners for a venture to Portuguese West Africa, to which, indeed, some Plymouth ships made several voyages in the 1530s.

Meanwhile Bristol, in close touch with Iberia and the Iberian Atlantic colonies, seemed on the point of becoming another Lisbon or Seville. Searching for new fishing grounds and those delectable islands with which medieval imagination had populated the Atlantic (cf. pp. 245–6), its seamen may have reached Newfoundland *c.* 1480. Inspired, perhaps, by reports of such achievements, the Venetian John Cabot appeared in England (*c.* 1495). He proposed, as Columbus had done, to make a westward passage to Asia, but one by those channels which according to late medieval cartographers threaded through the islands of the Arctic. He eventually left Bristol with some modest royal backing to make a landfall (1497) in either Labrador, Newfoundland or Maine, which he optimistically identified as 'the country of the Grand Khan'. Despite his loss on a subsequent voyage there was some further northern exploration in the early 1500s, sometimes in conjunction, and sometimes in competition with, seamen from the Portuguese Azores. Grander ambitions revived when Cabot's son Sebastian, again sailing from Bristol, attempted to get to the east by outflanking what was now coming to be recognized as a vast new continent. What he achieved is uncertain, though perhaps he found the entrance to Hudson Bay and examined the eastern shores of North America (1508–9).

Yet despite the English failure to reach Asia or to reveal, as had Columbus and his successors, any attractive substitute, interest in the North Atlantic persisted. A learned relative of Thomas More of *Utopia* fame led a disputatious and abortive colonizing expedition westwards in 1517. Four years later Henry VIII (1509–47) himself vainly attempted to involve sceptical London merchants in a scheme of Cabot's for 'the New Island'. In 1527, possibly inspired by news of Verrazzano's findings (cf. p. 443), the king commissioned one of his own officers to seek a way to 'the lands of the great khan' between Newfoundland and Labrador. No such strait was discovered, but the expedition coasted down America, attempting to make contact with the aboriginal inhabitants, in the end reaching the Caribbean from where, after a brush with the Spaniards, it returned safely home (1528). Accomplished by an ordinary English vessel,[3] the voyage showed that oceanic passages were not the prerogative of some specially designed craft. Equally clearly they were already at this date well within the capabilities of English mariners. Yet apart from a disastrous expedition (1536) to Labrador and Newfoundland, the undertaking had little sequel. The coastline of northern America was neither benign nor welcoming and notably lacking in precious metals or priceless luxuries. Spanish opposition in the Caribbean was resolute, and in any case Tudor policy still required good relations with the Habsburgs. The project of Robert Thorne for a northern voyage to the Moluccas was accordingly ignored (1530), and the proposal (1540–1) of Roger Barlow, another English merchant resident in Seville, for a similar venture to Cathay, left unprinted. The spendthrift king was naturally enough impressed by reports of the riches accruing from commerce with Asia, to the point that in 1541 he (vainly) sought Portuguese permission to send out a man with the India fleet. At the same time there was some inconclusive talk of finding a way 'between Iceland and Greenland' to regions likely to welcome English cloth. Nothing, however, was done.

But this was not the sum of England's Atlantic enterprise. Fisheries which were to endure and prosper were opened off Iceland and Newfoundland. The country had, moreover, long traded with Spain. This meant that from the early 1500s some members of the English community in Seville were able to own or invest in ships working to the Indies, or to do business there themselves. More remarkably still, Robert Thorne and Roger Barlow both backed Cabot's unhappy Cathay expedition, in which Barlow himself sailed (cf. p. 317). Meanwhile compatriots, and not always Catholics, settled and even married in Mexico and Hispaniola.[4] At the same time there was an English commerce with the Iberian Atlantic islands – with Madeira, known to Bristol merchants by 1480, and with the Canaries where John Hawkins' hopes of the Indies were later aroused. And from south- and west-country ports ships went to Brazil, from where William Hawkins had a local 'king' brought to Henry VIII's court, and where there was a Southampton trading post in 1542.

Yet in these very years, and without the intervention of any such catastrophe as the civil wars that crippled France, the whole range of England's seaborne commerce and endeavour contracted, with voyages to Africa, Brazil and North America abandoned. English merchants were still effectively excluded from the Baltic by Hanseatic privileges which the first two Tudors were in no position to revoke (cf. p. 59). Relations with Spain cooled from the 1530s as Catholic rulers looked with growing suspicion on a now Protestant England whose king had set aside a Spanish wife and whose seamen took Iberian ships. Sailings to the Mediterranean declined in the mid-1500s in face of the uncertainties and perils arising from the Turkish advance. Trade to the Moslem Levant was subject to embargo by Spain, and ships were attacked by Ottoman pirates or commandeered in Spanish ports for Habsburg service.[5] And accompanying, and in part reflecting, these difficulties were changes in the pattern of England's cloth trade.[6] Exports, whose volume grew dramatically, were increasingly channelled through London to the great northern entrepôt of Antwerp. The capital accordingly came to dominate the country's commerce – handling about 90 per cent of its exports in the mid-1500s – to the detriment of the provincial ports. Their ability to engage in oceanic ventures was undermined, whilst London's resources and interests were concentrated on the pleasing prospects close to hand. Nor had the Crown much taste for expensive and speculative forays into distant regions, and neither Henry VII (1485–1509), only recently and precariously established on the throne, nor his son, preoccupied with continental and domestic ambitions, were willing to give more than token assistance to projects both potentially unrewarding and politically embarrassing.

England's association with the wider world was not, indeed, broken. Trade, though much of it now overland, continued to the Mediterranean, whilst in 1555 a cargo shipped from Portuguese India to the west was insured in London.[7] But with the political and economic crises of the mid-sixteenth century came renewed expansion and the generally armed and aggressive beginnings of what was to end as the most extensive of all empires. The fierce and futile reign of the Catholic Mary Tudor (1553–8) left the country irretrievably Protestant, with its radical Puritans the intransigent enemies of Catholicism and the willing allies of Spain's opponents. At the same time the Antwerp market for English textiles collapsed, and after some years of friction with its Habsburg rulers the English merchant community withdrew from the Netherlands (1564). New markets were needed, and bold views as to how and where they might be found were aired with the rise to power under Edward VI (1547–53) of John Dudley, shipowner, onetime naval commander and briefly (until his execution in 1553) duke of Northumberland. The patron of cosmographers, men of learning and men of action (amongst them John Dee, Sebastian Cabot and Jacques Ribault) (see pp. 317, 439, 472), he encouraged attempts to open a trade with China and to renew that with Morocco and the Gold Coast, besides planning an attack on Peru.

Particularly promising, or so French and earlier English experience seemed to suggest, were the opportunities of Portuguese West Africa, to where in 1553–4 William

Wyndham, already something of an old Africa hand, led an expedition. Like his previous ventures it was backed by a strong London syndicate, and under a renegade Portuguese pilot arrived safely at Mina and Benin. Commercially it was a success, though the commander's insistence on entering the Niger delta brought, through fever, his own and many of his company's deaths. After something of a lull under Mary, the voyages recommenced in earnest early in Elizabeth's reign (1558–1603), notwithstanding that the obstacles, as was soon clear, were formidable. The climate was lethal; tenacious Portuguese resistance entailed the use of royal or other powerful craft, always expensive to hire and operate; and without a foothold in Africa the English found it difficult to establish regular contacts with local traders and slavers. All the same a traffic developed, producing pepper, gold, ivory and palm oil in exchange for cloth and iron. Soon ambitions were bolder. A factory could be established on the Mina coast (1561), and by venturing her ships the queen herself became involved in the breach of Portugal's pretended monopoly. Finally there was an attempt to break into the trade in Negro slaves to the Americas. It was made by John Hawkins, of a Plymouth family long versed in such operations, commanding a force of royal and private vessels, and with powerful London, naval and government backing. On his first voyage (1562) Hawkins was able to obtain the Africans he needed by intervention in a tribal war, and to sell them, with a certain amount of forceful persuasion, to colonists in the Caribbean. Subsequent voyages were of a more normal commercial pattern, but the enterprise ended when in 1568 Hawkins was trapped in San Juan de Ulúa (near Vera Cruz) by the incoming bullion fleet, only escaping with difficulty and loss. Yet it is doubtful whether in any case a commerce involving such high costs and risks had much future. The Caribbean market at which Hawkins aimed was one of the least prosperous in the Americas, and the least able to afford his cargoes. He was, moreover, in competition with the French and with the Portuguese who were considerably aided by compatriots settled in the area (cf. p. 365).

Nevertheless an African commerce continued, despite Portuguese protest in the 1570s, and despite the fears of English merchants trading to Iberia that their interests would be damaged. But it was a commerce far less grandiosely conceived and executed, though one whose true scale remains, by its very nature uncertain. The Portuguese themselves alleged that all the gold of Mina was now taken by the Moors, the French and the English. But in fact most English endeavour from the later 1500s was concentrated in Senegambia and Sierra Leone, admittedly often with the encouragement of Portuguese renegades or those who, after 1580, opposed Spanish rule.[8] It was a trade in which west-country ports were particularly active, concerned to start with with gold and ivory, but increasingly with slaves. A treaty (1642) with the newly independent Portugal finally gave England legal access to what remained of Lusitanian Africa, and though unable to compete with the Dutch, the English shipped Negro slaves to their own growing Caribbean colonies, and by mid-century had a fortress on the Gambia.

Much the same happened in Brazil to where trade, abandoned *c.* 1550 – probably in favour of piracy in home-waters – was vigorously renewed under Elizabeth. In 1578 an Englishman, about to marry into a Genoese plantation-owning family in the colony, envisaged a traffic in which English textiles and Canarian wine (obtained with English textiles) could, with other things, be exchanged for Brazilian sugar. Nor was this merely pre-nuptial euphoria. There were English factors in the country in the 1580s, and in 1582 it was said that the whole sugar crop was 'promised to certain London merchants'.[9] But again the English, with their energies deflected into privateering, were no match for the Dutch. They were further hampered, too, by the hostility engendered in Brazil in the late 1500s by their compatriots' attacks on Iberian shipping and by the opposition of their fellow countrymen trading to Portugal, who saw in a direct Anglo-Brazilian commerce a threat to their re-export of Iberian colonial produce. And, as a result of the enmity between Spain and England, the English were (until 1642) excluded from all the former Portuguese colonies following Philip II's annexation of Portugal and her empire. But this was the least of their troubles. By some the prohibition was blatantly ignored, whether by those shipping timber (1615) from a post at Cabo Frio, or the would-be colonizers of the lower Amazon (cf. pp. 247 and 492). Others conducted a successful commerce by the usual subterfuges, and particularly through Portugal with the assistance of local New Christians. By the 1630s they were shipping from Brazil anything from sugar to tortoise shells, and providing in exchange a remarkable variety of commodities – amongst them cloth, butter, cheese and pots for sugar-loaves.[10] But though the trade flourished, especially after the renewal of Holland's war with Spain (1621), it never achieved the volume or importance of that of the Dutch (cf. p. 368).

That the expansion of the range of English maritime endeavour brought no expansion of English commerce comparable to that of the Low Countries reflects, in part, the amount of English energies and resources devoted to privateering. To many the country had long seemed little better than a nest of seaborne thieves, whose aristocrats, like Warwick in the fifteenth century, engaged in massive depredations, and where whole communities lived and grew rich by piracy. These aptitudes were turned against Spain in a war which was to reach its climax under Elizabeth. Already in 1533 there were plans to take the bullion fleet; a decade later, whilst assaults on Iberian vessels in the Channel were said to be 'worse than open war', a Southampton flotilla was awaiting the incoming Indies ships. Early in Elizabeth's reign these haphazard tactics were converted into a considered policy by which England would be enriched and Spain crippled. The volume of American wealth reaching the peninsula was now appreciated, and whereas Spain appeared to prosper, and Castilian arms universally triumphed, the lot of England, and with it the safety of the True Faith, or so it seemed to devout Protestants, was worsening. The remedy, as the French had shown, was to attack Spain in the Atlantic and the Caribbean, a policy welcome, through convenience or conviction, to some in high places, and especially welcome to seamen like Hawkins and to piratically inclined west-country squires. Nor was there any shortage of suitable men and material for its realization. Private owners possessed a number of powerful ships. There were many commanders, often erstwhile pirates, only too willing to exercise in a new oceanic setting skills perfected in home waters. And the ways in which such forays could be mounted – arrangements for formal partnerships between vessels and for the distribution of prizes – had long since evolved.

The key figure in this new strategy was Francis Drake, a west-country seaman of modest origins and little or no formal education. Like many of his kind he held the most fundamental Protestant views, taking round the world with him a copy of Foxe's *Book of Martyrs*, extracts from which, recording the sufferings and deaths of Protestants under Mary, he read to Spanish prisoners, and the pictures in which he passed his leisure time colouring. Weaknesses he had in plenty, and his behaviour was frequently irresponsible, unreliable and lacking in judgement. But of his qualities there is no doubt. He was, as any commander worth his salt must be, personally brave. As a man of plebeian birth he understood his crews, and by his urgent eloquence, rough humour, character and achievements earned and held their respect and admiration. And whatever the disasters of his closing years, he was at his prime, as his successes demonstrated and even his opponents agreed, one of Europe's greatest seamen.

In 1570–1, backed like as not by the Hawkins and Winter families – shipowners, associates of the Huguenots, and old enemies of the Portuguese in Africa – he raided the Indies, established a base on a secluded stretch of the northern coast of the Isthmus of Panama, and penetrated almost to the city itself, to the focal point that is of the bullion route from Peru to Europe (cf. pp. 327–8). Two attempts to seize Spanish treasure either in or on its way to Nombre de Dios failed. But then, with French and *cimarrón*[11] aid, Drake ambushed a mule-train carrying bullion near the town (1573), effecting the first successful armed incursion into mainland Spanish America. His example was quickly, though as a rule unsuccessfully, followed, except that in 1576 John Oxenham crossed the Isthmus and reached the Isle of Pearls, from where, until his capture soon after, he controlled the approaches to Panama.

Yet such happenings did not seriously damage Anglo-Spanish relations. Philip II had other and more pressing problems, Elizabeth was chronically cautious, and trade between England and the peninsula was in any case flourishing. But the imaginations of ardent Protestants, ambitious courtiers and professional seamen influential in the administration of the navy were inflamed. Cuba and Hispaniola could be seized; a settlement could be made in the 'Kingdom of the Magellanes' from where Peru could be attacked; Spain, so Hawkins believed, could be crippled by the disruption of the shipments of American treasure. Hence in 1577 Drake sailed in command of a squadron financed by court and navy money, and ostensibly bound for Alexandria. His instructions are unknown, though very likely he was simply to examine both sides of the southernmost tip of South America, make contact with the Indians known to be resisting the Spaniards, and assess the prospects for an attack on Peru. All this was to be paid for by the capture of Spanish prizes. As it was, necessity and Drake's characteristic independence turned the voyage into a circumnavigation of the world, and one of the greatest of all feats of seamanship.

Under a Portuguese pilot impressed in the Cape Verde Islands the fleet made a slow passage to Brazil. It then moved down the coast of South America where (1578) at Port San Julián Drake had Thomas Doughty, one of the leading gentlemen in his force, executed on the suspicion of mutiny and on account of his role in the dangerous antagonisms that had arisen between the seamen and the gentry of the expedition. The three surviving ships cleared the Straits of Magellan in the remarkable time of 16 days, but then Drake was driven south by storms which scattered his vessels, destroying one and allowing another to turn back. Once recovered, he worked north up the Pacific coast of Spanish America, sacking Valparaiso, attacking Callao (1579) and effortlessly taking an unsuspecting treasure ship on passage to Panama which, when hailed, incredulously replied 'What old tub is that?' By now any thoughts of a return through the Straits had probably evaporated, and loaded with booty Drake continued north, capturing pilots who could guide him to Manila, and in California searching either for a strait leading to the Atlantic, or for some remote base in which he could prepare for the Pacific crossing. Eventually he put in near the modern San Francisco, and when the Indians appeared to crown him king, took possession of what he described as Nova Albion in the queen's name. From here he made the arduous passage across the Pacific, and in Ternate gave a further demonstration of his parts by negotiating – though without any credentials to do so – a commercial agreement with the ruler, and loading a cargo of cloves. Surviving a grounding in the Celebes (January 1580), he called in Java, and from there returned in the autumn to his home port of Plymouth (1580) by the Cape of Good Hope and West Africa.

The achievement was superb. Drake was the first commander to complete a circumnavigation of the world. In its course he had shown himself an excellent seaman, an outstanding officer, and a man bold and ingenious in the interpretation and execution of orders. He returned, moreover, unlike the survivors of the even more momentous Magellan voyage, not in a state of distress, but with most of his ship's company alive, and with an enormous haul of booty that ensured, in the expressive contemporary phrase, the venture was made. As relations with Spain – hardly surprisingly – deteriorated, and with the awesome spectacle after 1580 of Philip II controlling much of the known world, Drake's triumphant return suggested to ardent and acquisitive spirits profitable ways to England's salvation. The riches of the Pacific were now open to her, and the claims of Portugal, a Spanish satellite, could be ignored. The empire of Spain could be universally assailed, footholds could be established in Peru or Panama, slaves and Indians incited to rebel, and the treasure fleets taken.

Yet apart from an ill-organized and unsuccessful foray under Edward Fenton (1582), which ended as a piratical cruise in Brazilian waters, nothing was done. But all was changed when in 1585 Philip seized English shipping in Iberian ports. Holland, in similar difficulties, began a direct trade to Asia and the Americas; England opened against Spain a privateering war now backed by the considerable resources and skills of those merchants and shipowners – from London, the south and the west in particular – whose commerce with the peninsula, if not destroyed was certainly disrupted. Until the accession in 1603 of the pacific James I ended the campaign, over seventy expeditions were sent out. Some – in general the most successful – were financed and run by merchants and seamen; others were organized by courtiers, aristocrats and influential officers of state. Ultimately squadrons might include craft which, like the earl of Cumberland's *Red Dragon*, with her full broadside of heavy artillery, were tantamount to men-of-war. Most expeditions were, however, less powerfully armed and were destined for plunder and trade in the eastern Atlantic[12] and the Caribbean, though towards the end of the century, as more and more of Iberia's commerce was carried in non-Iberian ships, some, and these usually of considerable strength, looked to the Mediterranean for their prey. At the same time vessels belonging to magnates such as Cumberland – who was alone responsible for eleven ventures between 1586 and 1598 – attempted more ambitious operations, sacking Puerto Rico on one occasion. Meanwhile fleets comprising royal and private craft carried out raids whose supposed strategic objectives barely concealed a prime concern with loot.

In 1585 Drake, backed by royal, court and London money, sailed with twenty-two ships and over 2000 men – the strongest force as yet to invade the Spanish maritime empire – to seize the treasure fleet, attack the Indies and establish a base in the Caribbean. Triumphantly demonstrating the vulnerability of Spain and her possessions, he plundered the Iberian coast on the way out, sacked Santiago (Cape Verdes), took Santo Domingo (1586), pillaged Cartagena, attacked Florida and finally made contact with the English at Roanoke (cf. pp. 482–3). The blow to Spanish commerce and – more important – to Spanish prestige and morale was considerable. 'We have all come to extreme poverty, being in want of everything both to eat and to wear', it was reported from Santo Domingo. All the same Drake had achieved none of his strategic aims, and his loot failed to cover the costs of the raid. But appetites were whetted, and he was out again in 1587, this time to disrupt Spanish preparations for an assault on England. Proceedings were in characteristic style. Drake made a dashing (and unsuccessful) descent on Cadiz, failed at Lagos, effected little at Sagres, and then, with no further heed for any larger considerations, set off for the Azores to seek an incoming Portuguese Indiaman. His force disintegrated, but the prize was taken, making the voyage a financial success. And since the Spaniards felt obliged to pursue Drake to the Azores, so delaying the sailing of the expedition against England, the whole undertaking was also, even if accidentally, a strategic success.

Goaded by these and other English forays, and by England's continuing association with the rebellious Low Countries, Spain at long last despatched the Armada which was to subjugate the country (1588). It was the most ambitious and difficult seaborne operation as yet contemplated in the west, and made the more so by the intention of embarking the necessary troops in Flanders, since with the prevailing south-westerlies the Spaniards, once off the Belgian coast, were more likely to end in Denmark or Norway than in England. Even worse, their plan demanded that a large and polyglot concentration of ocean-going shipping – including anything from Ragusan carracks to Hanseatic hulks hired or impressed for the occasion – should be brought into the shallows of the Flemish coast for an operation whose success depended on improbable Dutch quiescence, the unpredictable weather of the Channel, and the unlikely co-operation of two commanders, the prince of Parma on land and the duke of Medina Sidonia, and he no sailor, by sea. Everything indeed favoured England. On the day she mustered more fighting ships (105 as opposed to 71 Spaniards).[13] In general they were better armed than their opponents, and enjoyed a crushing superiority in firepower, both by range and weight of shot.[14] They were also smaller, handier and livelier craft than the Spanish, and amongst them were the queen's men-of-war – 19 of which were big, fast, powerful, manoeuvrable and weatherly vessels – together with many merchantmen of much the same quality, developed in response to the demands of privateering. Neither side had any experience of handling such a mass of shipping (166 operational English craft; 124 Spanish) under sail. Some Spanish officers were used to the precise and concerted movements of oared-galley war, and others to conducting convoys across the Atlantic. The Spaniards had behind them the record of the best part of a century of military invincibility and carried contingents of Europe's most formidable soldiery. The English had a higher percentage of seamen. They also had many commanders, of whom Drake was the most celebrated, veterans of years of piracy and privateering, who were accustomed to fight often and to win frequently.

The Spanish fleet passed safely down Channel, impressively holding formation, and losing only three ships – and two of these in collisions. The English, with their better vessels, got up to windward, and stayed for the most part out of reach of such short-range artillery the Armada had, and well out of the way of the Spanish infantry. In the midst of these tactical manoeuvrings Drake secured himself a rich prize. But when the Spaniards anchored off Calais the English chance had come. Fire ships were drifted down on them, and many, in their haste to get clear, cut their cables or slipped their anchors, which was soon to cost them dear. For a time, until their food and ammunition gave out, the English edged the Spaniards into the North Sea, damaging several and sinking one by gunfire. By now, given the wind and weather, the demoralized Armada's only hope of survival, as the German skippers with it probably advised, was to run north and pass round Scotland into the Atlantic. This it did at the cost of fifty vessels which, damaged and without ground tackle, either foundered in the autumn gales or were driven ashore on the western coasts of Scotland and Ireland. Worse still was the loss of skilled men, drowned or massacred, the crushing blow to morale and prestige, and the fact that at such a price nothing had been accomplished.

But though the English, so the Venetians reported, had established themselves as *grandissimi guerrieri* and Europe's finest sailors,[15] they were uncertain how their advantage might be exploited, and they had in any case by no means ruined Spain. Splendid strategic plans were formulated, reflecting a healthy ebullience and a disastrous lack of overall direction. Some, like John Hawkins, obsessed with bullion, advocated a sustained naval blockade of Spain to cut its supposed life-giving flow. Court bloods, like the reigning royal favourite, the earl of Essex, aspired to display their military talents. The queen herself insisted that the remnants of the Armada, recuperating in Iberia, should be destroyed. The privateering interest demanded some bold and profitable venture, and Drake believed that Portugal could be induced to throw off Spanish rule. The outcome (1589) was an expedition under divided command and with no specifc objective. Drake led a large force (150 ships and about 20,000 men) against Coruña, where he did little more than forewarn the Spaniards of his presence. After moving south, the troops were put ashore at an ill-chosen spot. In the course of a bibulous week they advanced no more than fifty miles, and since they had no siege guns – which the queen had failed to provide – they were unable to take Lisbon. The fleet made no move against the city, the Portuguese showed no signs of rising, and the expedition broke up in disorder. Its leader, whom it was felt had 'framed himself to do what came into his own brain and fancy' and conducted his campaign 'more for profit than for service', received no substantial command for the next six years. Nor did Hawkins' disciples do any better. A flotilla under Cumberland forced the treasure fleet into the Azores, but was of insufficient strength to manage anything more. Intermittent blockade in the same waters only temporarily disrupted the influx of American silver, whilst in 1591 a weakened English squadron was surprised by the Spaniards and forced to withdraw with the loss, in a celebrated action, of the royal *Revenge*. After this the queen was more unwilling than ever to risk her own ships, but successes there still were, with a Spanish foothold in Brittany destroyed in 1594 and Cadiz sacked two years later in the old familiar style.

It was against such a background that the ill-fated last voyage of Drake and Hawkins was finally mounted (1595). Their fleet was an admixture of royal and private ships, largely financed by the queen and the two commanders. The expedition was crippled from the start, like that of 1589, by the division of its leadership, this time between the cautious and methodical Hawkins and the imperious and impulsive Drake, both now past their prime. It was similarly crippled by the absence of any agreed objective. The queen wanted preparations for another Armada destroyed; the commanders hoped for loot in the Panama Isthmus. And it was for Panama that they eventually headed, with, however, the intention of first seizing a crippled treasure ship reported to be in Puerto Rico. But in an operation demanding above all speed and secrecy the preparations were prodigiously lengthy and progress acrimonious and dilatory. By the time the English reached Puerto Rico the Spaniards were ready for them and the attack was repulsed. No worthwhile loot was taken in the Isthmus and the assault on Panama failed. Hawkins died off Puerto Rico, and Drake off Puerto Bello, where he was buried at sea as the trumpets sounded 'and all the canon in the fleet were discharged'. The remnants of the expedition then ignominiously retired to England (1596).

But this was far from the end of the maritime war against Spain. Privateering continued, and even more boldly, combined with an extensive trade, like that of the French and Dutch, with Spanish colonists in and around the Caribbean. At the same time, as Spanish defences improved and prizes became more elusive, the range of English operations was extended. True, the treasure fleet was never taken, but in the eighteen years of war lasting until James I's peace of 1604, the English captured over 1000 Spanish and Portuguese vessels, plundered many more of other nationalities, and obtained prize goods worth about 15 per cent of the country's then imports. And when the war officially ended many seamen continued their depredations from bases anywhere from North Africa to the Channel (cf. p. 137).

Tactically and strategically the English had worsted Spain. In the Caribbean they had penetrated, and were in some measure to remain in, an area of vital concern to the Habsburgs. Their raids, together with those of the French and Dutch, forced the Spanish government into costly defensive measures. Admittedly England had not defeated the Armada in some overwhelming engagement, nor had she damaged Spain's naval forces as opposed to her merchant fleet (cf. p. 364). Nevertheless the Spaniards were unable to invade England – apart from a foray in 1596 – and to fulfil those plans which were to have solved all their difficulties in the north. As it was, Philip II was drawn into an expensive and futile operation, whilst the English continued to attack, with varying degrees of success, both the Indies and the coasts of Iberia. The fruits of these endeavours, combined with an intransigent Protestant hatred of Catholicism, fostered in England the widespread belief that the country's only proper foreign policy was one that would permit a gentleman 'to get a ship and judiciously manage her'. Just what this meant was shown in the course of renewed war with Spain and France in 1625–9. French, Dutch, German and Iberian craft were attacked. Privateers fell with gusto on anything they alleged was bound for Spain – including, on occasion, fellow privateers from Flushing. Three hundred English vessels were lost, some 600 prizes taken, and the colonial empire of Spain further penetrated. After peace had supposedly been made, the associates of the Puritan earl of Warwick – whose maritime interests embraced piracy, slaving and privateering – used an island off Nicaragua as a base to attack Spanish trade, and when expelled briefly held Jamaica (1642–3).

II *Routes to the east and the rise of the East India Company*

If one major objective of English ambition was the produce and bullion of the Americas, another, and intimately related one, was access to the wealth of Asia. This had been the aim of John Cabot's voyages and of other early Tudor ventures. With the passage of time the call of the east became more insistent. What it could provide was known from English merchants trading to Portugal, from the occasional involvement of Londoners in the insurance of cargoes coming from Asia, and through the presence in the capital of Portuguese Jews who, like the elusive Dr Hector under Elizabeth, were carrying on a commerce with the *Estado da India*. But what brought home most forcefully to the English the staggering riches at stake were the captures by privateers – as by Drake in 1587 – of Portuguese Indiamen, whilst with Portugal under Spanish rule after 1580 the few remaining restraints to attacks on its possessions were removed (cf. pp. 296, 475).

Serious interest in the east revived with the re-appearance in England, during the political and economic crises of the mid-1500s, of Sebastian Cabot who, since his departure in 1512, had spent thirty-five years in Spanish service and risen to become Pilot-major (cf. pp. 317, 461). Aged and authoritative, he was now disillusioned with the possibilities of a northwestern or southern passage to the Orient and advocated instead a route via the northeast, in which he was backed by the erudition of Dr Dee, another of Northumberland's protégés (cf. p. 463). They argued, following medieval precedent, that the coast of Asia ran in a northwesterly direction from Cathay, and must therefore run southeast from Muscovy. Hence an expedition sailing for China northeast past the North Cape of Norway would for much of the time be in waters already partially known, and near lands enjoying a temperate climate and inhabited by civilized peoples who could well be potential purchasers of English textiles. Obstacles it was admitted there were, though none that could not be overcome, 'as Pliny and others write'. Assured by these truths, not indeed entirely divorced from reality, there recommenced an English search for a northern way to the east which was to continue for the best part of a century in a sequence of voyages of astonishing endurance. But they were doomed to failure, and England was to receive no such reward for her tenacity as did the Portuguese from their equally arduous struggle to by-pass Africa. What can now be accomplished by atomic icebreakers and submarines was not to be achieved in minute wooden sailing ships.

In 1553 a joint-stock company, some 200 strong, embracing court, government and London interests, was established under Cabot's governorship. Guided by his comprehensive instructions, of the familiar Iberian style, Hugh Willoughby and Richard Chancellor departed northwards for Cathay. Off Norway their fleet was scattered in a storm. Willoughby sailed east to reach Novaya Zemlya and die in the Arctic cold; Chancellor arrived in the Russian White Sea port of Archangel, from where before long a trade with the realms of the Czar was opened, to the detriment of the Hanse (cf. pp. 60–1). But of China there was no sign, though renewed attempts brought Stephen Borough, in a small boat with a crew of only eight, into the Kara Sea (1556). After this, and the revelation of the fearsome obstacles of distance, climate and ice, there were only intermittent voyages in the late sixteenth and early seventeenth centuries, with Henry Hudson, in the service of the Russia Company (see p. 474), reaching Spitsbergen (1607) and exploring part of Novaya Zemlya (1608).

Meanwhile the north-western passage, sought by John Cabot and others, had been resurrected. Influential cosmographers of the mid-1500s came to believe in a strait, that of Anian or The Three Brothers, leading from the Atlantic to the Pacific. It lay somewhere above the modern Labrador, separating the island of America from the polar land-bridge which linked north-east Asia to north-west Europe. It was recorded, if not invented, by the distinguished Louvain scholar Gemma Frisius, and accepted by the equally distinguished Mercator and Ortelius (1564). From them it was taken up by the ever-persuasive Dr Dee and the Oxford-educated squire, Humphrey Gilbert, active in assorted colonial and maritime projects. The first search for the passage, which like that by the north-east exists, though hardly in the form envisaged, was mainly backed by the Loks, a London merchant family long experienced in similar ventures to Russia and West Africa. It was commanded by the equally versatile Martin Frobisher – tough, quarrelsome, unscrupulous – an erstwhile pirate and slaver. In 1576 one of his ships reached as far to the north-west as the modern Baffin Island where in a blind inlet (now Frobisher Bay) the long-sought strait was optimistically identified. By then the expedition, weakened by skirmishes with the Eskimos, who were as little intimidated by the English as they had been by the Vikings (see pp. 6ff.), was unable to do more and returned with a kidnapped native fisherman and his kayak, and samples of what was thought to be gold ore. The Cathay Company was promptly established to pursue these discoveries, though its subsequent operations were directed less to finding China than shipping home alleged gold. However in 1578 Frobisher examined part of the modern Hudson Strait, reporting it an even better way to the orient. But when the supposed gold ore turned out to be worthless, and with the ensuing bankruptcy of the Cathay Company, interest in the northwest once more languished.

It revived at the end of the century, this time in association with the radical anti-Catholic party's advocacy of a base in North America – equally useful for attacking Spain and her empire and for finding a way to China – and with the search for a less arduous sea route to Asia than that of the Portuguese (cf. pp. 481ff.). In 1585 John Davis, a seaman and navigator of outstanding parts, sailed in a venture supported by London money and by such members of the war party as Walter Raleigh and Humphrey Gilbert. He worked up the west coast of Greenland to the site of the modern Godthaab, carefully observing the Eskimo inhabitants of this onetime Norse colony (see pp. 481ff.). There he turned to explore the south-east of Baffin Island, and in Cumberland Sound thought himself in the approaches to the strait. On a later voyage (1587) he pushed as high as 72° 12′n into the ice of Davis Strait (between Greenland and Baffin Island) and seeing clear water to the north-west triumphantly reported 'the passage is most probable, the execution easy'. But war with Spain and the diversion of Davis' skills elsewhere meant that it was left to others to test his opinions, some in the service of great chartered trading corporations like the Russia and East India companies (see pp. 474, 477), others employed by specially created associations. In 1610 Henry Hudson penetrated the Bay which now bears his name, barely survived the fearsome winter of 'that desolate place', and the following year was set adrift together with his son by his mutinous crew. That he had found only another blind opening was shown by Thomas Button (1612). But four years later Robert Bylot, with William Baffin as his pilot, reached 78°n in the waters between Greenland and Canada. They searched Baffin Bay, and in its north-western extremity discovered and named Jones Sound and Lancaster Sound which lead, though they failed to appreciate that this was so, into the Arctic Ocean. Further projects and expeditions followed, like that of Thomas James (1631–2) to Hudson Bay, the account of whose frightful experiences was to inspire Coleridge's description of seas where 'ice mast high came floating by'. But with the Cape route now in use by the English any further exploration of the north was abandoned until the eighteenth century (see pp. 477ff.). That Englishmen, with an endurance as dogged as that of Spanish *conquistadores* in pursuit of American treasure, should have persisted so long in ventures so unrewarding is testimony to the respect accorded to the views of contemporary cosmographical experts. It is also testimony to the volume of resources that from the mid-1500s could be attracted to almost any undertaking offering the remotest possibility of gain. And it is testimony to the quality of ships – such as Hudson's *Discovery*, six times in the Arctic – and seamen who, like John Davis, could repeatedly endure voyages to seas and climates so cruel.

There were in the same years other abortive attempts to reach the East. One possibility, already proposed by a Genoese in the 1520s, was across Russia to where, as a result of the Willoughby-Chancellor voyage, a commerce had been opened under a monopoly company (1555). Anthony Jenkinson, one of its agents, reached Bokhara from Moscow in 1558, only to find that the presence of the Portuguese in Asia had destroyed the flow of spices and other luxuries, and that the way which Marco Polo had once travelled was unusable (cf. p. 269). On a subsequent journey to Persia (1562), though rebuffed by the shah, he struck up a friendship with a local khan, and a trade began in which English textiles were exchanged for Asian products. But the link was tenuous and vulnerable, involving a passage of roughly 1500km through Russia alone to reach Archangel, and dependent on the precarious stability of the empires of Persia and Russia. And when in 1579 the Ottomans invaded Persia it was summarily severed. Even so there were plans (1582) to establish an entrepôt near the present-day Volgograd through which eastern spices could be funnelled northwards across Russia and English goods distributed throughout the Levant.[16] Nor had hopes of a trade with the east through Russia entirely faded at the beginning of the next century.

More promising were the ancient routes from the eastern Mediterranean – where the English were in business in some strength by the late 1500s – to the orient (cf. pp. 102ff. and 143). It was by this way, which he had reconnoitred the previous year, that in 1583 John Newberry and seven other employees of the Turkey Company proposed to reach Asia. Leaving two of their number to open a trade in Baghdad, and two more in Basra, the remainder, after an odyssey as colourful as any – including escape from imprisonment in Portuguese Goa – arrived at the court of the Mogul emperor in northern India (1584). Newberry disappeared attempting to return by the north-west frontier, but Ralph Fitch went on further, travelling through Bengal, Burma, Siam and Malaysia before eventually finding his way back home in 1591. That trade was possible along such routes the experience of Venice amply demonstrated (see pp. 140–1). But they were long and arduous, besides which the English repeatedly found themselves worsted, as in the Mogul empire in the early 1600s, by the intrigues of Italian merchants conducting a commerce through the Middle East, and by those same Portuguese missionary influences of which the Dutch complained. But in any case after 1580 the influential war party in England saw no reason why their compatriots should not use either the route of the Portuguese *carreira* or that, with its additional attractions of pillage, followed by Drake in his circumnavigation.

In 1581 it was proposed that the newly knighted hero should himself lead an expedition to Calicut. The following year Edward Fenton, backed by Drake and Leicester and accompanied amongst others by half-a-dozen compatriots familiar with the Portuguese east, sailed for Good Hope and Asia, whilst Frobisher was said to be preparing a similar venture. In 1586 the youthful Suffolk squire Thomas Cavendish, with influential court and privateering support, set out for the Straits of Magellan and whatever lay beyond. After being repulsed on the Chilean and Peruvian coasts, now better defended, he took a Manila galleon with a lading of enormous value off southern California. He also obtained, by ways which remain obscure, a map of China and details of its commerce. Now down to a single ship he passed (1588) through the Philippines to Java, and from there home across the Indian Ocean and via the Cape, running in for Plymouth with one of those westerly gales which was elsewhere destroying the remnants of the Armada.

Cavendish was no Drake. He had prisoners tortured and his stormy relations with his officers and men were the first signs of the mental instability soon to overtake him. But he had shown that Drake's way to the east remained open, that there were riches there for the taking and that others than Drake himself could accomplish this most exacting and arduous of all voyages. But not many. John Davis, an old associate of Raleigh and the Gilberts, failed on his own in 1590 and again in 1591 in company with Cavendish in an expedition intended both for the 'South Seas and China' and the discovery of the Pacific end of the north-west passage. Even by the standards of the time preparations were casual and inadequate. Cavendish, now mad, failed to clear the Magellan Straits (1592) and died at sea. Davis sailed and re-sailed the same waters in an unseaworthy ship in a tenacious search for his commander before returning home (1593) with only sixteen survivors from a crew of sixty-seven. More disastrous still was the attempt (1591) by the Cape route under George Raymond and James Lancaster. Backed by London privateering money it was supposedly a reconnaissance of the prospects of trade with the east. In fact it was a thinly disguised armed raid. The one surviving vessel finally reached south-east Asia, and there achieved very little other than demonstrating the lack of any organized Portuguese opposition. Incipient mutiny led to a mishandled return, involving six weeks in the Doldrums, and with the ship eventually lost in the West Indies after trying to reach Newfoundland. Lancaster himself, however, at last got back (1594) and lived to accomplish much else by land and sea.

Nothing deterred, yet another faction tried its hand, this time the Hawkins dynasty which had long combined an interest in Asia with commercial, naval and privateering operations in the west. Commanded by Richard Hawkins, the only son of Sir John, a fleet comprising the family's powerful *Dainty* and two smaller craft left Plymouth (1593) 'for the islands of Japan, of the Philippinas and Moluceas, the kingdoms of China and the East Indies' in a voyage whose costs were inevitably to be met by privateering. But Hawkins, though a brave and honourable man, was an indifferent commander. With the *Dainty* alone he passed safely through the Straits into the Pacific, where the demands of his crew for loot led to an attack on Valparaiso which brought only modest returns and alerted the Spaniards as to his presence. By sheer good luck he escaped from a Callao squadron sent out after him – finding to his amazement it could outsail him – but instead of getting clear he returned, at his company's insistence, to look for prizes. As a result he was trapped shortly after on the Peruvian coast and taken, though only following a hard fight and with his surrender dictated by consideration 'for them which should be partakers of life' (1594). Undismayed, optimists proposed yet further projects, and two years later Benjamin Wood, fortified with a royal letter addressed to the emperor of China, sailed with a small flotilla. Behind the venture was Robert Dudley – illegitimate son of the earl of Leicester and grandson of Northumberland, both protagonists of bold oceanic schemes – whilst Wood himself was an experienced privateer and an old servant of the family (cf. pp. 463 and 475). His original intention was to go via the Straits of Magellan, but instead he eventually went by Good Hope. Once in the Strait of Malacca he set about plundering Portuguese shipping with his two remaining vessels. But the loss of men from disease obliged him to abandon one, and sailing north with the other he was wrecked in Burma.

Compared with that of the Portuguese and the Dutch this was a sorry record (cf. pp. 235, 398). With nobody to exercise such an overall control as had been provided by the house of Aviz or as Oldenbarnevelt was to do, expeditions had no specific objective and often barely any specific destination. They were despatched by many and conflicting interests, and were all too often haphazardly prepared and organized. For the majority of captains, crews and investors loot and not trade was the primary objective. Fleets were accordingly drawn to the Straits of Magellan and to those Pacific waters where, as Drake and Cavendish had shown, magnificent prizes were to be had. But, as the Spaniards had long since realized, this was a route of impossible length and insupportable rigours for a regular commerce. It was also one on which, before long, the English came up against effective Spanish opposition. Furthermore it entailed an intolerable loss of life, since the large crews demanded by privateering had to be crammed for long periods of time into inadequate and insanitary accommodation where they were the easy victims of disease. Such a sequence of consistent and expensive failure convinced prudent investors that their money was better employed elsewhere.

But interest revived with the appearance of the Dutch in Asia, threatening the lucrative commerce of English merchants who shipped home oriental goods from the

Levant – where they arrived by those ancient land and sea routes now likely to be cut or rendered superfluous by the Hollanders (cf. pp. 141–3). Moreover, with an Anglo-Spanish peace in the offing it was all too probable that England would be excluded from Habsburg preserves. Hence in 1599 a group of London merchants petitioned the queen that they might be incorporated to trade to Asia. They were refused on the grounds that such a move would prejudice negotiations with Spain, but when these collapsed permission was granted, and in 1600 the East India Company (EIC) was founded. At its heart was a group of city magnates long dominant in both the Levant trade and in privateering. They provided much (about 25 per cent) of the initial capital together with large and powerful ships developed in privateering and men experienced and successful in their command. The company received a fifteen-year monopoly of commerce 'beyond the Cape of Good Hope and the Strait of Magellan', and was to operate on a joint-stock 'the Indias being so farre and remote from hence'. Such a form of financing was common in risky and expensive undertakings – shipowning, privateering, new trades – demanding a greater capital than individuals or limited groups were willing or able to venture. And the company was widely used in colonial commerce and rule in states which did not provide, unlike the Venetian and Iberian empires, naval protection and overseas trading posts and fortresses (cf. pp. 402–3).

In pursuit first of all of spices the English, sailing by the Cape route – better-known since John Davis had followed it in Dutch service – reached Indonesia (see p. 395). But before long the hostility of the Hollanders and an appreciation of opportunities elsewhere brought their widespread penetration of the network of Asian trade. A factory was established at Bantam (1602), and shortly after the company had posts in eastern and western India, Siam (1612), Macassar (1613), Sumatra (1615), the Bandas and at Jask in Persia (1616). But few were to survive. In Japan, where they arrived in 1613, the English made nothing of the influence enjoyed there by their compatriot Will Adams (see p. 399). Their attempts to sell their inescapable woollen textiles – which, as the Japanese pointed out, they refrained from wearing themselves – were abortive. And unable or unwilling to employ the forceful methods of the Dutch, they failed to acquire sufficient quantities of the silk vital to any commerce with Japan. A trade so fragile was not to endure, and in 1623 the VOC drove the English out, as it did from most of Coromandel, from the Spice Islands and from elsewhere east of India in due course. Yet even after its expulsion (1623) from Amboina the EIC could still get all the pepper it could sell through factories such as Bantam, together with whatever cloves could be smuggled to Macassar – 'one of the especialest flowers in our garden' – from Amboina, until all these fell to the Dutch too (see pp. 398, 408ff.).

As a result of these reverses the company turned its attention to western Asia, a traditional field of interest for Levant merchants. Here the Dutch were not as yet particularly strong, and the Portuguese weak. Nor, unlike the VOC in the Spice Islands, could the servants of the *Estado da India* openly attempt to exclude the English from lands not under Portuguese sovereignty – though they could do their best to persuade local rulers to do so. Thus England prospered at the expense of the Portuguese, who were defeated at sea off Surat in full view of Mogul troops and officials (1612, 1615), and again off Jask (1620). Two years later English ships helped a Persian army to take Portuguese Hormuz (cf. p. 296). The EIC had already been trading to the realms of the shah for some years, first trying to dispose of woollens unsalable in India, then hoping to obtain silk from the imperial monopolist on especially favourable terms. Now, however, it seemed to some bold (or drunken) spirits that the English might tax trade from Hormuz as the Portuguese had once done, and keep a fleet in the Persian Gulf. But the aspirations of (some at least) Protestant merchants to lead a parasitical Portuguese-style life did not accord with the views of the fierce and idiosyncratic shah. In the end all the company effected was a modest commerce to the west and a more vigorous one with India.

Meanwhile the assault on the *Estado da India* continued. EIC ships joined those of the Dutch in the blockade of Goa (1621–3) and in an attack on Bombay (1626), and for a time there were thoughts, revived again in mid-century, of acquiring the town, had not the cost been considered prohibitive. Following the Anglo-Portuguese truce of 1635 the English were allowed some trade in Cochin and Calicut. Their vessels were used by Portuguese merchants to safeguard cargoes from the Dutch, and a rival English concern, having failed to gain access to China, was after some bluster allowed by the Portuguese to trade to Macao, where English ships appear in the 1630s and 1640s.[17]

But it was in India that the company achieved its greatest success. In the north-west, producer of the textiles vital for the purchase of spices, relations were established with the Mogul emperor, increasingly impressed by English naval power, and at whose court an ambassador was resident (1615–19) 'to prevent any plots that may be wrought by the Jesuits to circumvent our trade'. From its factory at Surat the EIC opened a commerce to Indonesia and Persia, whilst the reputation of its vessels for strength and safety allowed them to ship native passengers and cargoes to and from the realms of the shah. In the 1630s trade was extended to Sind and Rajapur, and in the following decade into the Red Sea and the Persian Gulf. On India's eastern seaboard the first factory was established at Masulipatnam in 1611, and within a few years there was a string of English footholds running from Madras (1639) in the south to Bengal (1651) in the north. But this expansion was not the outcome of any such considered strategies as those of the Portuguese or the Dutch. It reflected in part frustrations elsewhere; in part the company's rapid absorption into the complex economy of Asia; and in part its discovery, like its European precursors, that there was a western market for other oriental products than spices.

England's Asian trade was thus of the same general nature and pattern as that of Portugal and Holland, though without – except briefly – their access to China and Japan. The major import was pepper, paid for with metals, cloth and bullion. In addition the company developed a country traffic, exchanging Indian textiles for Indonesian spices, and financing some of its eastern purchases with the freights obtained from the carriage of local cargoes and with loans from local merchants. With the passage of time its homeward shipments became, like those of the Portuguese and Dutch, more variegated, and included large amounts of Indian calicoes – used in Europe for dresses, hangings or domestic linen – together with some silk, sugar and saltpetre (cf. pp. 273, 406).

Like the VOC the English company was a joint-stock monopoly corporation. It was managed by a small group of directors (twenty-four) elected annually by an assembly of investors, which also ratified (or modified) their decisions. Factories like those of the Portuguese and Dutch were established in the East, and by the 1630s brought under some general control, the earlier absence of which had put the company at a disadvantage compared with the VOC. The EIC's chief officer (President) at Surat was in charge of Indian and Persian affairs, and of the posts in western Asia. His colleague in Bantam – from where there were soon familiar reports of the company's servants 'dangerously disordering themselves with drink and whores'[18] – was responsible for the diminishing group in eastern India, Indonesia and Indo-China.

But the EIC was not an instrument of state like the Portuguese royal spice monopoly or the VOC (cf. pp. 269, 396). It was an independent commercial association conducting its business as best it could to its own liking. Thus whilst the early Stuart rulers of England sought in general good relations with Iberia and Holland, the company was at war with the Portuguese in Asia until 1635, and with the Dutch on and off. As a body of merchants its prime concern was with profits, and an organization which in later life was to develop an insatiable appetite for territory was in its infancy far more modest in its ambitions than the Portuguese or the Dutch. It made no more than a half-hearted attempt to regulate indigenous commerce, and was even more indifferent than was the VOC initially to conquest, colonization and the conversion of local peoples (cf. pp. 410–15). Not that it was entirely innocent of such aspirations, but it lacked the strength to realize them in the regions where it was established, and elsewhere (as in the Spice Islands) where this might have been possible, it was up against overwhelming Dutch power. Nor indeed was there any urgent reason for it to pursue such policies. Entering an established economy it could in general – the VOC permitting – participate in existing trades and use existing entrepôts, and there was little reason (or opportunity) to set up fortified posts in regions of established and comparatively stable government.

Hence England nowhere ruled the east, though with local assistance and connivance, and without the company's intervention, a fortress was eventually acquired in Madras (1639). But not even when it became the seat of the eastern presidency did the EIC's writ run there. For the rest the English had achieved only a partial and precarious penetration of the network of Asian commerce. Some of their posts, such as Agra and Ajmer in northern India, were, unlike those of the Portuguese and the Dutch, hundreds of kilometres from the sea and totally at the mercy of local indigenous officials. And everywhere the company was dependent on the goodwill of rulers who, like the shah of Persia or the Mogul emperor could suddenly and arbitrarily reorganize or re-route some particular trade. All the EIC could do to seek redress was to withdraw its agents; attempt (but only against lesser potentates) naval blockade; or buy its way back into favour, even to the extent of paying compensation for damage for which it was not responsible.

Such behaviour is a measure of its weakness. It lacked on the one hand the skills, resources and devotion to profit of the VOC. And on the other hand, though the product of a state and society as predatory as any, it lacked that aristocratic dedication to loot and tribute which had been so powerful an incentive to Portuguese expansion in Asia, just as it lacked any equivalent to the missionary zeal of the Iberians. The English indeed arrived in the east with the reputation, assiduously fostered by the Portuguese, of a nation of pirates, and to find that the Japanese had a representation in song and dance of their misdeeds.[19] Nor surprisingly, since in 1604 Sir Edward Michelbourne had led a successful plundering raid on Java and Malaya. That he was not a servant of the EIC reflects the fragility of its authority. The company enjoyed no such state direction as had benefited the Portuguese, and no such state backing as aided the VOC (cf. pp. 261, 405). The very opposite in fact. Its interests soon clashed with, and were opposed by, merchants trading to the Levant, whilst the ever-impecunious Stuarts, to hold the affections of favourites, or simply to raise cash, sold or granted licences to contravene its monopoly. James I himself approved Michelbourne's raid, and his recognition of a Scottish company (1618) the EIC only averted with a loan.

To contend with such problems, and with Portuguese and Dutch hostility, the company was ill-suited and ill-prepared. It lacked even the fragile cohesiveness of the VOC, for though initially an association of merchants it was before long invaded by a powerful, vociferous and disruptive group of gentry and courtiers demanding quick and generous returns on their investments. Furthermore its constitution was such that its committee of management had neither the continuity nor independence of that of the VOC. It was elected annually and obliged to submit its decisions to the assembled freemen of the company. Moreover, since every voyage was a separate venture the committee was merely a connecting link between various groups of investors and it was powerless to co-ordinate company business (cf. pp. 404–6). In Asia the EIC had no real equivalent to the Portuguese viceroy or the Dutch governor-general to give some direction to its affairs and to control the private commerce of employees, from whose competition the company's trade suffered to a far greater extent than did that of the VOC from the enterprises of its servants. More crippling still, the EIC lacked the resources of the Dutch. Without their hold on the commerce of Spain it was short of the bullion essential in eastern trade, and had besides to withstand fierce domestic criticism of its export of what little it could muster (cf. p. 406). And whatever England's post-Armada naval reputation, the country owned nothing like Holland's amount of shipping. Between 1613 and 1622 the EIC sent only 82 vessels to Asia as against the 201 of the VOC, to whose maritime ubiquity it attributed Dutch success. Nor did England have the business skills of the economically more advanced Netherlands. The EIC did not attempt, as did the Dutch, to regulate the price of oriental goods in Europe. In Asia it developed no more than a modest country trade, which meant that to a greater degree than the VOC its purchase of homeward cargoes was dependent on the sale of those from Europe – a considerable problem for merchants from a country which could offer little in addition to bullion except woollen textiles. And whilst (Brazil apart) Dutch energies and resources were concentrated on commerce, those of the English were consumed in privateering and the attempted colonization of Ireland, North America and the West Indies (cf. pp. 405ff., 482ff.).

But nowhere was the EIC's weakness more apparent than in its financial organization. Unlike the VOC it had, to start with, no capital of its own. Instead, until the mid-1600s, trade was conducted in a series of separate ventures.[20] The accounts of all these were kept separately, each was wound up separately, and the profits of each distributed separately. Every such undertaking was financed by a group of investors who bore all its costs and shared in its profits. Hence a company member could be involved in all, some or none of these ventures, but only in this way (in theory) could anybody trade to the east, and only under EIC supervision. Proceedings of this order meant that in various parts of Asia there could be rival English factors representing what were in reality rival concerns. They also meant, since partnerships and stocks were terminated at the end of a venture, that the EIC was unable to accumulate and deploy in the east a circulating capital such as contributed to Dutch commercial flexibility and success (cf. pp. 405–6). Hence whilst the VOC grew – though not without crises – the EIC, its commitments ever increasing, struggled to satisfy the demands of investors for quick profits, borrowing wherever it could even as its share capital remained unpaid. Throughout most of the first half-century of its existence it was in more or less continuous trouble, obliged to employ large, powerful and expensive ships whilst trying to sell its imports in an inelastic and already overstocked market dominated by the Dutch. And by the mid-1600s, hopelessly overshadowed by the VOC, its operations denounced at home and its monopoly disregarded abroad, it was on the point of collapse.

III *Pioneer and planter in America and the West Indies*

In the course of the search for a way to Asia English attention was drawn to the possibilities – for long equally disappointing – of North America. But apart from some abortive schemes in the early 1500s nothing was proposed or attempted until the second half of the century (cf. pp. oo–o). Then there were plans first (1560–70) for a colony somewhere in the southeast – in regions up to about the latitude of the modern North Carolina – handy for assaults on Spanish treasure fleets (cf. p. 439). Following, however, the misfortunes of the French in Florida, interest thereafter fluctuated between the north-east (Newfoundland, New England) and the littoral further south

(Virginia, North Carolina). To some extent this reflected the experiences of the English themselves and their reactions to the policies of other European states. It reflected, too, the supposed requirements of current grand strategies, to which colonies were often seen as necessary adjuncts, and most simply the balance of power at Elizabeth's court where there were those who favoured projects unlikely to offend Spain and others who advocated the open bridling of Spanish might. A further factor was the argument, most notably propounded by the younger Richard Hakluyt, that an American colony in a temperate climate could supplement England's products, provide a home for the country's surplus population, stimulate its economy by offering new markets, and indeed generally act as a panacea for all current ills.

Hence there was an attempt *c.* 1580 to colonize the suitably uncontroversial Gulf of St Lawrence where, so it was believed, the English could engage in large-scale ranching like the Spaniards in the Caribbean, and where settlement would reinforce the sea-fisheries. Barely disillusioned by the failure of this venture, the equally unpromising Newfoundland was next tried. In 1578 Humphrey Gilbert, a ferocious would-be colonizer of Ireland prominent in many bold maritime projects, was licensed by the queen to occupy lands in America not already belonging to any European power. Funds were raised by the allocation of holdings to sub-patentees who ranged from the most implacable members of the anti-Spanish party to a Catholic squire seeking a sanctuary for his oppressed co-religionaries. The enterprise also had the support of much erudition, with Richard Hakluyt printing a mass of evidence demonstrating what others had achieved,[21] and Dee concocting a royal title to the new lands. After some inept reconnaissances – one of which did no more than fall to the congenial pursuit of piracy – Gilbert himself sailed in 1583. His precise intentions are uncertain. The presence in his large force (260 men) of artisans to construct buildings suggests that settlement was envisaged. But though he also hoped to find the supposed Indian city of Norumbega with its rich silver mines – sited by French imagination on the Penobscot – no more than his successors did he contemplate a Spanish-style conquest. Following a tumultuous crossing of the Atlantic he eventually reached St John's in Newfoundland, of which he took possession in the queen's name, to the disgust of the fishermen he found there, unwilling to be subjected to any jurisdiction. He then sailed to Cape Breton, and having accomplished nothing of any consequence set out for England, only to be lost when his tiny ship was overwhelmed in a storm, his last imperishable words recorded by a fellow captain: 'we are as near to heaven by sea as by land'.

Gilbert's plans were taken up by his kinsman and former associate, the disastrously abrasive soldier and courtier Walter Raleigh, a man better fitted to expound than to accomplish his wishes. He proposed a settlement further south, where the climate was expected to be better and where the Spanish treasure fleets would be within easy reach. A reconnaissance of 1584 returned with glowing accounts of the North Carolina coast and of the particular suitability of the island of Roanoke. Raleigh, ever felicitous in phrase, named the area Virginia in honour of the queen. In 1585 he sent out an expedition containing an astonishing galaxy of talent, including in its number the painter John White and the future circumnavigator, Thomas Cavendish (see p. 475). But once again virtually nothing was achieved. An essentially military force attempted no conquest but instead proposed to set up at Roanoke an agrarian settlement of the sort advocated by Hakluyt. But the only virtue of the site was that it was hard for an enemy to find, and before long the leaders, narrowly confined, had fallen out. Moreover, no more than the majority of colonists did the settlers, and least of all the soldiers, intend to demean themselves in agricultural labour. They lived for a while on what they could get from the local Algonkian Indians, but these had neither the resources nor the desire to supply the intruders, whilst the English, unlike the *conquistadores* in the south, were in no position to exact what they needed by force. With the Indians increasingly threatening, and indeed attempting to starve them out, the colonists gladly took passage home with Drake's fleet which passed along the coast in 1586 on its way back from the West Indies. The following year Raleigh sent out another party – including about thirty women and children – to settle this time on Chesapeake Bay. His pilot took them, however, to the ill-fated Roanoke, where they were left whilst their commander departed to England for supplies and reinforcements. Because of the Armada campaign and its aftermath it was not until 1590 that he returned to find the post abandoned and its inhabitants gone – either massacred or refugees with some friendly tribe.

After this there were only some spasmodic, un-coordinated and commonly abortive ventures before the early 1600s. Inspired by reports of the value of the French fishery and fur trade in the Gulf of St Lawrence, there were plans (1597) to settle the Magdalen Islands with those of Puritan inclinations distressed by the recent enforcement of uniformity of doctrine and observance in the Anglican Church. But the scheme was killed by Basque and French opposition, whilst another proposal to ship out 'rogues, vagabonds and paupers' was stillborn. Nevertheless Englishmen continued to visit America. Vessels fishing off Newfoundland put ashore parties to hunt for furs. Others touched and traded in New England – seeking sassafras, that 'sovereign remedy for the French pox' – and Maine, and in 1607 a colony briefly appeared on the Kennebec river.

Thus the English had very little to show for something like a century of endeavour in North America except the Newfoundland and Greenland fisheries, and even these not their exclusive preserves. Yet the country was not one of insuperable natural obstacles. It was rich in game and fish and its climate was tolerable to western Europeans, even if in the north the winters were colder and the summers hotter than they were accustomed to. True, for strategic and political reasons much English effort was directed to the northeast. Here winters were bitter, and a rocky coast backed by marshes and virgin forests reaching to the water's edge was swept by fierce storms. Nor were things easier once ashore. Access to better terrain inland was limited to the Hudson-Mowhawk gap, since the other rivers of what was to become English America were navigable only to a line of falls and rapids relatively near the coast, whilst from New York to Pennsylvania the way to the interior was obstructed by the Appalachians. There were, furthermore, no indigenous empires to be subverted for the benefit of Europeans. Instead along the north-eastern littoral were various Algonkian tribes, all quite capable of defending themselves, and beyond them the redoubtable Iroquois (cf. p. 444).

Yet the Iberians had overcome similar and far greater difficulties, and before long they were to be surmounted by the English. But not as yet. America was seemingly without precious metals. It offered no easy access to Asia, proved a disappointing base against Spain, and was – as the translations of Spanish materials published by Hakluyt and his successor Samuel Purchas showed – part of a continent inhabited by brutal and savage heathens (see pp. 498–9). Something more was needed to attract men to such lands – abundant riches, escape from persecution – than earnest schemes to provide the mother country with raw materials and a market for unwanted woollen cloth. The worst repression of religious dissent in England was, however, still to come. Meanwhile for those seeking wealth, land and glory there were ample opportunities to hand. Much money and energy went into the attempted colonization of Ireland begun by the crown itself in the 1560s and 1570s, and then handed over to private venturers. And in the last two decades of the century the privateering war against Spain was at its height. But equally important in explaining English failure were the inadequacies of the proposed plans and the commanders who were to implement them. No English Cortés marched inland, but instead expeditions of the same strength of those of the *conquistadores* disintegrated on the coast, their members unwilling to work and unable to find any other acceptable occupation. Many of the captains were professional soldiers trained in the wars of the Low Countries. There campaigning was predominantly a matter of fortification and of siege and counter-siege, so that their natural inclination in America was to establish a beach-head, dig in, and keep open communications with home. And unlike the Spanish conquerors of the south, many of the leaders were not men of humble origins with nothing to lose and everything to gain. They were courtiers and gentlemen, such as Gilbert and Raleigh, reluctant to accept hardship, and with their many interests to watch, projectors of schemes rather than commanders of great enterprises.

Efforts were renewed with the changing circumstances of the early seventeenth century. The privateering war ended, and James I's interpretation of the Anglo-Spanish peace of 1604 was that whilst his subjects might colonize lands not settled by the peoples of other Christian princes, they traded to the Spanish Indies at their peril. Nor was the trade any longer so attractive. Force was now debarred, Dutch competition was increasing, Spanish reaction could still be effective, and Habsburg prohibition of tobacco-growing in areas most easily accessible to interlopers rendered profitable cargoes scarcer. English energies were thus deflected on the one hand, like those of the French and Dutch, to the 'Wild Coast' of South America and to the Lesser Antilles, and on the other, with the founding of the Virginia Company (1606), to North America (cf. pp. 385, 440). This association, empowered to colonize lands between 34° and 45°n was an amalgam of two barely compatible interests. One, based in the west country, hoped to exploit the region's natural resources. The other, backed by London merchant wealth and with support in government circles, though sharing some of these aspirations, hankered after gold, Asia and strategic checks on Spain. Like the EIC the company could draw on resources accumulated in privateering and on the skills of commanders the war had produced, whilst mercantile involvement gave some realism to its plans. The colonists sent out would be its employees, producing goods which could then be sold for its benefit.

Even so the probability of failure was long present. The regions chosen for settlement were those of previous disasters, and within months a post on the Kennebec had collapsed. Further south the former privateering captain Christopher Newport landed 144 assorted aristocrats, gentlemen, artisans and labourers in Chesapeake Bay (1607). Jamestown was founded on a scarcely defensible site surrounded by malarial swamps, and by the end of the year half the pioneers were dead. Undismayed the survivors commenced a search for gold, casting the local Algonkian Indians in the role of providers of food and labour. But there was no gold and the confederated tribes were guided by Powhatan, a chief more astute than any Montezuma or Atahualpa, who soon appreciated that the intruders could be starved out. In 1608 the colony was down to 38, in a state of siege, and with the military and those claiming gentle blood refusing to work. It was saved by the arrival of the able soldier Captain John Smith, who with an experience acquired in adventures from Russia to Morocco enforced St Paul's simple precept that 'he that will not work shall not eat'.

Nevertheless the future was far from assured. Military-style government provoked, as in Dutch America, discontent. There was little to attract immigrants, particularly since there was the alternative of Ireland for those seeking land. Of such as arrived many were soon killed by disease or the climate, whilst others fled, as they did elsewhere, to live amongst the indigenous peoples in the hope of better things, and notwithstanding the fearful punishments inflicted on any recaptured. Nor were the Algonkians reconciled to European presence, though relations improved when John Rolfe married Powhatan's daughter Pocahontas, their love overcoming the biblically inspired doubts of many pioneer Virginians as to the propriety of an alliance with one who as a girl was to be seen cart-wheeling naked around Jamestown. But English pressure on Indian lands and Indian acquisition of European weapons brought risings such as that of 1622 when 300 settlers were massacred. And since Virginia produced no returns, merchants lost interest, reducing the company, before its dissolution (1624) to merely an authority for licensing the ventures of others.

But the colony was made when John Rolfe introduced the cultivation of tobacco. Smoking was already an established habit amongst the affluent of Europe, with what was denounced as 'this chopping herb of hell' provided from the Spanish Americas partly through Seville, but largely by interlopers in the Indies. When, in the early 1600s, their commerce was disrupted there came an opportunity rapidly and profitably seized by Virginia, whose exports rose from a puny 24t in 1619 to over 600t by 1639.

Unlike that of Spanish America, its tobacco faced only a relatively short sea passage to Europe. Its producers were unhampered by any such restrictions as those the Habsburgs placed on what was a relatively insignificant element in the wealth of their possessions, and the colony soon took measures to ensure prices were held at a satisfactory level. Thus whilst Spanish tobacco remained a high-cost luxury, that of Virginia became an object of mass consumption. Its impact on the colony's society and economy was as profound as that of sugar in Brazil. Demanding neither the skills, capital or labour the latter required, it could be grown on small-holdings. And needing access to water for its transport, and the clearing of new land to increase output, it produced a pattern of settlement dispersed and riparian like that of Brazil.

The Virginia Company's original intention had been to establish a colony comprising landlords, tenants and labourers. And, in exchange for their subscriptions, a few ex-soldiers and members of the gentry did indeed receive modest grants (usually 200 acres or less). But with the response so poor and the potential rewards from tobacco so great, responsibility was handed over (1618) to syndicates which, like entrepreneurs elsewhere, undertook to colonize given areas. Even so there remained the problem of the provision of a suitable work-force. The unsubdued local Indians, few and nomadic in any case, could hardly be used. African slaves, the usual answer, were impossibly expensive, especially as England lacked substantial access to the sources of supply. Hence, after some Portuguese-style experiment with the shipment of vagabonds and convicts, the English turned, like the French, to the use of indentured servants who, after working anything from three to seven years in bonded servitude to a master, were entitled to freedom and either a lump sum or a holding of their own. Their supply, like that of slaves, became a substantial industry. Some were acquired by the agents of potential employers, and some by specialist contractors not averse to the use of kidnapping. But the majority came from enterprising shipmasters who in a business bringing profits of 300 per cent clear signed up whatever they thought the market would bear.

Most of those indentured were country lads who entered into an existence resembling apprenticeship in some ways, but serfdom and slavery in more. They were denied any sexual life, were regularly bought and sold, and could find themselves at the mercy of a man who could, unpunished, flog his servants, male and female alike, to death. But their passage to America was paid, and there they lived at their master's charge, sustained by hopes of land – which in fact only about 10 per cent obtained – or the high wages of a freeman. In England they had little prospect other than starving in the overpopulated countryside or in some crowded and disease-ridden town. Propaganda may have ensnared some, the wiles of recruiters others, but the rest were drawn to easily accessible ports by that same innocent optimism which supplied Portuguese and Dutch East Indiamen with crews.

With some 1000 bondsmen arriving annually in Virginia between 1625 and 1640 they accounted by mid-century for about half its population, and made it, with so high a percentage of the unfree, the closest English approximation to a Spanish-style colony. And it was a parallel intensified by the 'headright' system, under which those responsible for the importation of a servant received fifty acres. This naturally favoured the rich, who alone could afford such expense, and so to those that had was it given, fostering the rise of the big estate and accentuating inequality. Nor were these the only similarities with the Iberian south. Virginia was founded at the expense of an indigenous people, for though the Algonkians might avoid English counter-measures against their raids by melting away into the forests, in the end, weakened by disease and pushed off their lands, they had to recognize white suzerainty (1646). As in Spanish America Europeans turned to agriculture following the failure of other prospects, becoming, like the Brazilians, producers of a major cash crop, though one basically grown on small-holdings. The profits from this, and the labour policies it entailed, eventually led to the emergence, from the usual obscure and uncertain origins, of a colonial aristocracy in which the descendants of gentry families were soon eclipsed by those whose forbears had been shipmasters, merchants and artisans. It was a class as intellectually undistinguished as its equivalents in Iberian America – plans for a university were shelved, the provision of schools meagre – but one enjoying considerably more political power, even if ruling over no such latifundia as existed in Brazil and Mexico. Virginia had no indigenous servile class, like that of Spanish America – though some Indians were employed in the strictest servitude – nor as yet many African slaves. But their place was filled by indentured whites whose conditions were such that masters regarded them with the same apprehension as did Spanish authorities the Negro slave, particularly once weapons began to circulate widely as a result of the requirement that all freemen should own guns. And from the ranks of this servant class there came the freed but unsuccessful poor white, the associate often enough, like his Spanish counterpart, of the Indian, despite attempts to segregate the races. Similarly Virginia's white population was predominantly male – about 80 per cent so in 1660 – with the normal colonial bias accentuated by the large-scale importation of servants (cf. pp. 320ff., 329ff.).

Following the collapse of the Virginia Company the colony became, like those of the Iberian crowns, a royal possession. It was also one where, though by local and not metropolitan requirement, there was to be uniformity of faith and no toleration of heresy (cf. p. 341). Virginia's religion was that of those who, whilst demanding further radical reform of the Anglican church in a Protestant direction, were willing to remain within its ranks. Hence whilst there flourished some measure of that ostentatious immorality inseparable from colonial life, settlers were required by law to attend church and eschew idleness, and were much given (or at least urged) to Bible-reading and psalm-singing.

Virginia, however, was far from being another Mexico or Peru. Its Amerindian populace had nothing of the economic importance of those of Spanish America (or French Canada). Nor was there any serious attempt to convert it. Some of the usual pragmatic associations of races there were, but despite learned clerical advocacy of the duty and benefits of Christianization there were few, as amongst the Calvinist Netherlanders – and for similar reasons – willing to undertake the task. But the most fundamental difference from any Iberian (or Dutch) settlement was the growth of representative institutions, fostered indeed from home, here as elsewhere, to shore up the local government, confer some cohesion on the colony, and firmly saddle it with financial responsibility for its affairs. These were policies diametrically opposed to those of the strong and bureaucratic Spanish monarchy, apprehensive lest the flow of wealth from its rich and populous possessions be disrupted, or they came to hanker after independence. They were policies equally unacceptable to the Dutch WIC, a commercial organization exercised primarily to further its fur trade (cf. pp. 346, 393). But in Virginia, alongside the governor and council initially exercising authority, there appeared in 1619 an assembly representing the interests of freemen. Before long, with the vote safely restricted to freeholders and power in the hands of plantation owners, it saw itself as another House of Commons, enjoying fiscal and legislative authority and claiming, during the English civil wars, to appoint both governor and council.

Neighbouring Maryland, which together with Virginia had a white population of some 30,000 in the mid-1600s, was of much the same social and economic pattern, though a proprietary colony, of the type once favoured by the Portuguese, and belonging to the Catholic Calvert (Baltimore) family, who intended it as a refuge for their co-religionaries (1632). But of a radically different order were the settlements established in that New England mapped and named by John Smith in 1614 in the service of the Council of New England. This was a reorganized association of what was once the west-country interest in the Virginia Company, and which in 1620 was incorporated and empowered to colonize lands bounded by the Atlantic, the Pacific and latitudes 40°n to 48°n. It soon, however, became by a familiar progression yet one more authority for leasing concessions to others. The first of these were the Plymouth Pilgrims, a body of settlers whose hopes were of a nature quite unparalleled in any previous European overseas colonization, since they sought only the freedom to practise their own religious beliefs. They too were Puritans, but separatists convinced of the need to leave the Anglican church in order to maintain their corporate life according to their interpretation of the Bible. Harried by the late-Elizabethan drive for conformity, a small group took refuge in Holland. Then, disappointed, some of the most resolute entered into an agreement with a body of backers, promising, in exchange for supplies and a free passage to America, to send back cargoes to England. Emigrating, unlike all but the Norse before them, as an organized social group, they sailed – 102 men, women and children – to make a landfall at Cape Cod and establish themselves (1620) at Plymouth Harbour.

The land, one of their leaders wrote, was a 'hideous and desolate wilderness full of wild beasts and wild men'. Half their number perished in the first 'sharp and violent' winter, but reinforced, the tiny community survived. The local Indians, weakened like other coastal tribes by diseases probably contracted in chance encounters with earlier European visitors, had little inclination to resist. The pilgrims, unlike the Roanoke and Jamestown adventurers, expected nothing from mortal life but hardship. Many were countrymen, all were willing to work, and all were sustained by an unflinching faith. Furthermore, to their leaders, who were capable and determined men, they accorded the fullest authority, drawing up a solemn agreement before they landed – a covenant of the sort they were accustomed to enter into with God – which bound them to accept whatever laws their elected governor and his associates should make.

So this unique society, still only 300 strong in 1630, took root, its birth and struggles recorded in the moving biblical prose of Bradford and Winslow. After some initial friction (and a show of force) the Pilgrims lived in generally amicable terms with the neighbouring Indians, whom they had no wish to exploit, and from whom indeed they desired to remain aloof. They developed a simple agrarian economy, farming holdings allocated annually to all families by lot. They traded with the nearby Dutch, and with the Indians for beaver, and so successfully that they were shortly able to dissolve their association with their backers and afford to bring in more settlers. Troubles they had. Interlopers pushed into the fur trade, sold guns and liquor to the Indians, and drank and danced with them. Such affronts to the Lord were suppressed, just as those who killed Indians were executed. Thus stern, earnest and purposeful the Pilgrims lived, as they wished, in independence. Their community was predominantly one of small-farmers, without any such clerical-graduate caste of leaders as that of neighbouring Massachusetts, and politically a republic, though not a democracy, since only church members could vote.

Similar pressures soon brought others to New England. A group of west-country Puritans settled on the site of the future Salem in the 1620s. Shortly after (1629) there was founded, with the backing of aristocrats, gentry, lawyers and merchants, the powerful and largely Puritan Massachusetts Bay Company. Its undertakings, declared one of its most influential members, would result in no such fiasco as Virginia, where 'the main end was carnal' and settlement by 'the very scum of the land'. This righteous eloquence doubtless brought in recruits. Not, however, that they were lacking. Puritans were dismayed by the disasters everywhere overwhelming Protestantism in the decade after 1620, and by the Catholic and absolutist tendencies of the rule of Charles I. They were equally alarmed by the persecution of radical Protestantism – developing in England since the mid-1500s – which reached a climax under the king's servant William Laud.[22]

A colony was planted in Boston (1630), only to endure all the now familiar hardships. Like Plymouth it was saved by the unbending faith of the emigrants and their total commitment to the founding of a godly sanctuary. But unlike the Pilgrims the Massachusetts pioneers had money. The company was able to send out a further 8000 colonists by 1635. Many paid their own passage, whilst others, in return for their subscriptions, received 200 acres together with the same 'headright' bonuses as in

Virginia. They found a climate less arduous than that of the more southerly settlement, and once again a weakened Indian population little inclined to trouble them, and against whom in any case they had the strength to use force, wiping out the Connecticut Pequots in 1637. As with the Pilgrims, their theological assumptions led to their complete acceptance of the authority of their leaders, amongst whom were such outstandingly able men as the first governor, John Winthrop. He quickly appreciated that the colony might divert the Dutch fur trade into its own hands. With an equally shrewd eye he made Boston, on the defensible Shawmut peninsula, his base and hired experts to build fortifications and teach his charges the arts of war. The population soon began to grow, as to the flow of immigrants was added the natural demographic increase of a society in which women married young, the birth-rate was high, and – in the absence of disease-infested towns – the death-rate low. With 15,000 white inhabitants in 1642 the colony was the most important Protestant settlement in America, or indeed anywhere.

Its economy, though far more prosperous, was like that of the Pilgrims, one of fishing, fur-trading and farming. But with the resources and enterprise available there quickly emerged something more than an unspecialized subsistence agriculture. Cattle were exported to the West Indies, food to the partial monocultures of Virginia and Maryland, and cod, grain and timber to Europe. As elsewhere in English America few of the colonists moved far from the coast. In part they were prevented by natural obstacles, but in Massachusetts chiefly by their own beliefs. They were not seeking gold, and what contemporary language described as 'wandering abroad' was condemned as undermining that mutual edification and supervision essential to the maintenance of purity of faith and morals. Frontiers and forests were not, as in Canada and the Iberian empires, gateways to riches and opportunity, but only to realms of evil and temptation. Nor did Massachusetts aspire to exploit or convert the local Indians, who were regarded in much the same light as by the Pilgrims. They were yet another manifestation of the evil and hostility of the environment, perhaps, it was first thought, to be Christianized by godly example, but in general best left alone. Only in mid-century – and then largely to eradicate pockets of heathenism from lands colonized or about to be colonized – was there any serious evangelization. The Bible was translated into Algonkin, and some Iberian-style communities of 'praying Indians' were established. But the effort, like that of the Dutch, was modest, and Protestant theology in any case too complex and exacting for easy transmission.[23]

Massachusetts sprang, as did Plymouth, from the emigration of entire families and congregations, so that there came to America, as there never did in Iberian colonization, ready-formed, highly organized and closely integrated communities, embracing young and old, males and females. Their numbers included, like those of the Spaniards, no aristocratic settlers. Neither did Massachusetts intend to attract or entertain the poor, though it had its indentured servants and a miscellaneous lower order comprising by the mid-1600s 'Scotsmen, Negers and Indians'. Its society was essentially one of gentry and yeomanry, of family-worked freeholdings, of artisans and merchants. It was remarkable for its domination of the clergy, particularly once Laudian persecution drove so many Puritan ministers to the New World, and it was equally remarkable for its high level of literacy and education. Puritanism, by its very nature and with its high moral purpose, inculcated the need to read in order to study the word of God. Many of its adherents who arrived in Massachusetts were products of the educational renaissance of sixteenth-century England, and often prosperous Oxford or Cambridge graduates. And in a world in which individualism could easily lead to anarchy the affluent soon felt an urgent need to produce a clergy who could confute the socially dangerous teachings of 'mechanic tailors and cobblers . . . and lewd fellows of the lower sort'. So schools and colleges proliferated on a scale unapproached elsewhere in America, and with the founding of Harvard, Massachusetts became the only colony other than those of Spain to establish a university.

The settlement's political organization was theocratic, with power rigorously confined to church members. This select body elected a governor who, together with a legislature, behaved as though sovereign. Adult male church members similarly chose their clergy and, from the 1630s, deputies who formed a general assembly. The view as to what constituted a proper ordering of life was a severe one, and not only were wages regulated by legislation, but the death penalty was imposed for adultery. Born of uncompromising independence, the settlement led a turbulent existence, its troubles exacerbated by the intense introspection of the Puritan mind, the free play of individual inspiration over the highly charged language of Old Testament texts, and the pressures of prosperity. Ministers became disenchanted with the powers of congregations. Gentlemen were alarmed when the militia proposed to elect its officers. And with the influx of merchants, servants and seamen – few of them actual or potential church members – political rights became vested, to the great discontent of the disenfranchised, in the hands of about 20 per cent of the population. Nor was this minority prepared to tolerate heresy. Dissidents were punished – which included hanging some Quakers, both men and women – or ejected, so that as in the Norse and Iberian empires disputes within the initial settlements were potent incentives to further expansion. Providence came into existence with the expulsion of Roger Williams (1635); Connecticut was established to practise primitive austerity and improve the fur trade (1635); Rhode Island grew from a fusion of the disciples of Williams with those of the refugee Anne Hutchinson (1636); New Haven was founded by a disillusioned congregation (1637).

Thus successful Protestant settlements had at last been planted in America. Those of New England, whose population had reached about 30 000 by 1660, were the outcome of the adamant will of a number of people, many of them endowed with considerable skills in mundane matters, to find a sanctuary for the unhindered practice of their beliefs. The only contribution of the English monarchy, despite the urgings of propagandists, was to eject some particularly vigorous (and fractious) subjects, and to accept, like the Norse or Genoese earlier, but as no contemporary state did, that colonies should be receptacles for those whose opinions could not be tolerated in the mother country. Colonization was accordingly a function of entrepreneurs, producing not an empire but a number of virtually autonomous settlements. In New England the environment, the social backgrounds of the emigrants and their religious beliefs gave rise to an agrarian society without the cities of Spanish America or its vast estates and their vestigial feudalism. The arrival of the Puritans brought the usual disasters to the primitive indigenous population, depriving them of lands, afflicting them (unwittingly) with diseases. But in the absence of precious metals, and with the Puritan dedication to work, the colonies were not parasitic on what remained of the native economy. Nor did they result in any appreciable miscegenation. Indians were grudgingly accepted to have rights, and by some groups treated in general honourably. They were, however, far from being equals, and their women were unacceptable as spouses. The Old Testament enjoined the faithful 'to live separate from the people of the land and from strange wives'. But in any case European females were present in the colony from the very beginning, and a farming community had no use for those unaccustomed to English practice, and no desire, unlike Canadian frontiersmen, to learn native skills. As they intended, the Puritans maintained their way of life virtually intact.

The English claimed or settled other lands in the west, acquiring Bermuda (1609), colonizing Newfoundland the following year, and reconnoitring the future South Carolina in the 1630s, whilst the Scots pushed into Nova Scotia (cf. p. 447). Inspired by Spanish belief in the bullion-laden realms of El Dorado, the golden-painted ruler of Manoa, Walter Raleigh had the Orinoco delta and the Guiana coast examined (1595–6) (cf. p. 318). Here for a time there was much powerfully backed activity, sustained by hopes of gold, tobacco and some strategic advantage against Spain. Eventually Raleigh himself, now a broken man, was released from imprisonment by James I to undertake the ascent of the Orinoco (1617), a fiasco whose main outcome was the disruption of the clandestine tobacco trade with the region (Trinidad in particular) and his own execution.

In the Caribbean, long the scene of English privateering, piracy continued after the peace of 1604, accompanied before long by bolder strokes as England, like France and Holland, attempted to seize unoccupied islands, or those weakly held by the Spaniards, especially with the renewal of war against the Habsburgs under Charles I (cf. p. 471). After rebuffs and failures in the face of Carib resistance and Spanish reprisals, St Kitts, Barbados and other of the Lesser Antilles were occupied from the 1620s, and in 1655 Jamaica was taken. The first acquisitions were largely settled by young men hoping to make a quick fortune in tobacco growing and then return home. Of none was this truer than Barbados, occupied at such a rate that within two decades all its land was taken, and by the mid-1600s its population (among them royalist refugees from now republican England) alleged to have reached 50 000. Whatever the truth, this minute territory, with its virtually exclusively male society dreaming of rapid enrichment, its unfree and restive (though white) labour force, epitomizes the hopes and methods of

European colonization. Yet it was the only Caribbean island – perhaps the only European overseas settlement – to be brought to anything like full productive capacity solely by the toil of whites. Its economy, and that of the neighbouring islands, was one of small plantations growing, with the labour of young indentured servants, cotton and a tobacco described by one disgruntled purchaser as 'foul and full of stalks'. But all was changed, as it was in the other islands later, with the difficulties of the Dutch in Brazil and their ultimate expulsion. Sugar production soared from the 1640s, stimulated by the capital and skills of refugee Hollanders, to meet European demand (cf. p. 386). With such growth came the development of big plantations on which African slaves – their numbers already put at 20 000 by mid-century – had to be employed. This was so partly because of the nature of the crop, but also since the absorption of land into larger units diminished the chances, formerly good, of an indentured worker being able to obtain a holding, and so weakened the incentive to immigrate.

English expansion thus reached its greatest momentum only as Iberian resistance faltered. Its period of gestation, from the first Bristol voyages of the fifteenth century, had been one of prodigious length. This cannot be explained by the alleged inadequacies of English maritime technology and nautical science, or by the supposed insufficiencies of the country's economy. That England had ships capable of crossing and recrossing the Atlantic was shown by the early Tudor voyages, and in any case English owners had in their possession from the mid-1400s, either by purchase or piracy, many of the same types of craft as were used by the Iberians. Renegade pilots, Portuguese in particular, were not hard to recruit, and that financial resources were available is suggested by the funds directed, from the mid-1500s, into a vast variety of maritime projects, by the existence of relatively advanced joint-stock methods of mobilizing capital, and by the volume of money poured into privateering. Furthermore, England could draw on the wealth (or credit) of an aristocracy willing, not to say eager, to engage in speculative undertakings, about one-third of whose members were, for example, investors in the Virginia Company at any one time in the early 1600s. Indeed that projects of expansion excited the interest of so wide a range of society, in turn producing so rich a variety of ventures – from aristocratically owned proprietary colonies such as Barbados to the independent Puritan theocracy of Plymouth – was one of the country's main weaknesses in comparison with Holland or Iberia. Martial gentry like Gilbert and Raleigh, or Puritan grandees like the Caroline earl of Warwick, favoured the founding of a territorial empire and a vigorous war, particularly by sea, against Spain, so defending Protestantism and bringing the rewards of loot and honour. But no more than elsewhere were merchants attracted by schemes promising little but expense. North America produced no bullion or cash crops, Ireland only failure and the arrival of settlers in Newfoundland was thought likely to disrupt the profitable fishery. Merchants were willing to seek new trades should the old founder, or to engage if need be in businesslike privateering. But rarely were such ambitions compatible, nor were there the resources available to indulge them all. One of the reasons for the failure of the attempted colonization of North America in the late sixteenth century was the deflection of men, money and interest to Ireland and oceanic privateering. Friction between merchants and other backers helped ensure the failure of Drake's 1589 expedition, whilst in 1600 the London merchants of the infant EIC were apprehensive lest court and aristocratic involvement should drive away investors, and wished to deal only with those 'of their own quality'.

Such problems were not diminished by the behaviour of the Tudor and Stuart sovereigns who, unlike their Iberian counterparts, generally regarded colonial and oceanic projects as dangerous and expensive, and rarely directed the forces available to any specific objective. The delicate balance of power at Elizabeth's court meant that several policies were entertained simultaneously but none pursued wholeheartedly, whilst in the reigns of James I and Charles I intrigue and ever-pressing royal financial difficulties resulted in conflicting privileges being conferred on, or sold to, competing bidders and favourites. In Asia the English made slow going against entrenched Portuguese opposition, and there as everywhere suffered from their economic inferiority to the Dutch and their lack of a comparable volume of efficiently operated shipping. In America little was initially effected since, in face of Spanish power, the English, like the French, devoted their energies to regions which in their very nature – lacking bullion and indigenous societies that could be geared to European wants – could never live up to the expectations of immigrants. Only with the persecution of the Puritans, and with new opportunities in the west for the production of tobacco and sugar did English settlement belatedly take root.

IV   *New commercial horizons; old intellectual boundaries*

The major impact of oceanic enterprise in England was economic. From the mid-1500s the geographical area of the country's commerce was rapidly enlarged. New trades to Europe came into being, some accidently, like that with Russia through the White Sea, the outcome of a search for a northern passage to China. At the same time old routes were penetrated by, or re-opened to, English vessels. The weakening of the Hanse and English troubles in the Netherlands brought increased sailings to Scandinavia and the re-appearance in some strength of English ships in the Baltic in an expansion checked only by Dutch competition and the economic recession of the 1620s. Similarly Mediterranean demands for food, England's search for allies against Spain and for new outlets for her textiles, and the changing economy and maritime balance in the southern sea produced an important commerce through the Straits of Gibraltar. By *c.* 1600 the English had a network of trading posts reaching from Morocco to the eastern Levant. Their powerful ships, able to fight off corsairs, were gladly freighted by Christians and Moslems alike, allowing them to conduct trades ranging from such local traffics as that

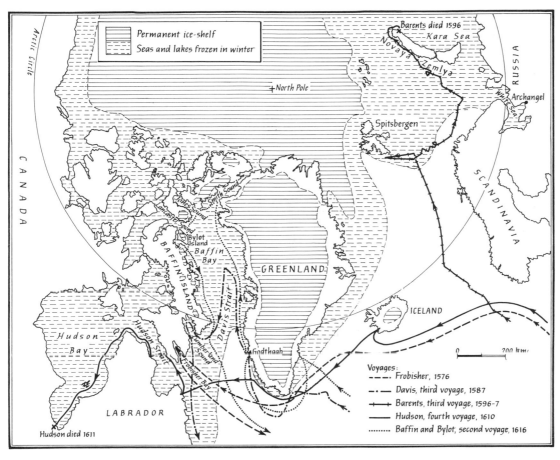

Permanent ice-shelf
Seas and lakes frozen in winter

Voyages:
- – – Frobisher, 1576
- · – Davis, third voyage, 1587
+ + Barents, third voyage, 1596-7
——— Hudson, fourth voyage, 1610
········· Baffin and Bylot, second voyage, 1616

10   The Arctic Waters *c.*1600

between Ragusa and the Aegean Islands to the provision of oriental spices to Venice or textiles and munitions to the Ottomans (cf. p. 143).

To these trades were added those with the newly found (or re-found) overseas territories. From the mid-1400s, and throughout the sixteenth and early seventeenth centuries the English dealt, legally or illegally, in the Portuguese and Spanish Atlantic islands. They became poachers in Iberian West Africa, in the Spanish Caribbean and Portuguese America. Their enterprise re-opened contact with Iceland, and they discovered, and were amongst the first to exploit, the enormously rich Newfoundland fishery. By about 1600 they probably dominated the grounds where, in the following decades, there were as many as 300 craft from the west country alone present. The products of these lands and waters English ships carried to European markets old and new. Newfoundland cod joined Yarmouth herring and Plymouth pilchards in cargoes to the Mediterranean; American tobacco went to southern Europe. In some cases important multilateral trades developed. From the late 1500s Atlantic fish was exchanged in the Mediterranean for ladings of southern goods for England, whilst by the early 1600s ships which had taken emigrants to America returned with Newfoundland cod to be sold in the Canaries or Spain for wine destined for England.

The range of English seaborne commerce was further enlarged in the first half of the seventeenth century as a result of the country's neutrality in the majority of the great European conflicts of the time, which brought its ships into wide demand as safe carriers. Hence they were able to penetrate most of the maritime economy of Iberia – with which, in any case, a trade had continued throughout the Anglo-Spanish wars – and by the 1630s they were transporting the products of the Portuguese and Spanish colonial empires to Europe, sailing from Portugal to Asia, Brazil and Africa, working between Goa and Macao, and carrying American bullion to Spanish Flanders (cf. pp. 367, 478).

Such activities, momentary gains elsewhere at the expense of the Dutch, and the stimulus of the privateering wars, led to an increase in English tonnage from about 70,000t in 1582 to something like 115,000t in 1629. But it was not unimpeded. English ships suffered from the depredations of the increasingly powerful North African corsairs. Trading to Iberia they were, for much of the time, legitimate prey for Dutch privateers, whilst during the years of England's war with Spain after 1625 they were also harried by the craft of the still redoubtable Basques and by Dunkirkers from the Spanish Netherlands. Against such opponents England deployed naval forces whose effectiveness declined disastrously under James I, and whose reputation reached its nadir when, in 1639, in the presence of the royal ships, the Dutch destroyed a Spanish fleet sheltering in the English waters of the Downs. A still greater weakness was the inability of English vessels to compete in terms of freights, costs and efficiency with those of Holland (cf. pp. 425–6). Some Dutch *fluits* the English bought or took as prizes, and some Dutch-style craft were produced by English builders. But not as yet in sufficient numbers to give England a merchant fleet in any way comparable to that of Holland. Consequently whenever the Dutch were unhampered by war with Spain England's share of the carrying trade declined.

Nevertheless the nature of the country's overseas commerce remained fundamentally unchanged. By the end of Elizabeth's reign English ships were bringing back some of the oriental goods formerly acquired through intermediaries, or taking whales off Greenland whilst English textiles appeared anywhere from Spanish America to Portuguese East Africa. But exports were still chiefly of woollen cloths going largely to Europe. New opportunities had, however, some local influence. London became, though to a lesser degree than Amsterdam and Lisbon, an entrepôt for dyes, spices and Asiatic textiles, just as it became, on privateering hauls of Iberian sugar, a major centre of refining. Similarly areas of the country's economy were in some degree affected. Continuing trade with Spain – which bought many of its imports with specie –

combined with the captures by privateers, brought into England sufficient bullion for enemies to attempt to intercept it, and probably enough to aggravate around the ports of entry (such as London) an inflation basically due to population growth. Again, in the late 1500s the rewards and requirements of privateering persuaded some English owners to build large (200t and above[24]), strongly constructed and heavily armed vessels of a size not favoured in the country since the late Middle Ages. These, requiring big crews, and thus expensive to run, were unable to compete with Dutch craft except in trades where safety was the prime concern. But ironically enough it was descendants of ships of this type which in the later seventeenth century helped England to regain by force from Holland what had previously been lost by economic innocence.

Colonial and maritime ventures also influenced economic organization. They encouraged the use of joint-stock financing, and they stimulated the growth of chartered companies, from whose incorporation the crown drew a fee whilst the members were granted the monopoly of some particular undertaking, be it trade with Russia or the colonization of New England. They likewise had important social repercussions. Between 1620 (when emigration began in earnest) and 1640 some 60,000 people left England for the New World and another 20,000 or so for Ireland. That so many should depart at a rate much like that of the Iberians (i.e., about 4000 per annum) for lands apparently offering so little is a measure of their determination, just as the economic flowering of the Puritan colonies is an indication of their quality (cf. pp. 489-90). For others opportunity came nearer to home. Elizabethan privateering and the (often associated) rich trades to the Orient and the Mediterranean handsomely rewarded the enterprise of a group of London plutocrats increasingly influential in city and national life by the early 1600s, and from whose ranks there emerged such crown financiers as the Bayning and Myddelton families. Privateering and associated ventures similarly made the fortunes of a number of professional seamen, increasing the opportunities for advancement – always considerable in a calling in which the incompetent rarely survived to make the same mistake twice – for those who had nothing but their natural talents to recommend them. The biography of Drake was the maritime equivalent of those of a Cortés or a Francisco de Figueiredo (cf. pp. 275, 310). And so, too, once there developed a commerce with the new North American settlements it passed, being unattractive to magnates dealing with Asia or the Mediterranean, into the hands of provincial merchants, squires, yeomen and shipmasters trading under no corporate privileges. By the mid-1600s they formed a class some of whose members were powerful enough to demand the abrogation of the rights of the chartered monopoly companies, and to urge and eventually secure the defence and expansion of English commerce by force.

But whoever else might have gained from oceanic trade and the nascent colonies, it was not the English crown, which received no such enhancement of its reputation or strengthening of its powers as empire brought to the Iberian monarchies. England inflicted damaging blows on Spain at sea, on Spanish Atlantic and Caribbean commerce, and on Portugal in Asia. But most were delivered by privately organized forces, whilst in overseas settlements largely created by companies or proprietors English rulers had no real authority. Again, privateering expeditions were organized like the great Spanish military undertakings (*entradas*) of the years of conquest. That is they were licensed by the crown, which in one way or another took some part of their haul, but they were privately financed. Since, however, Elizabeth herself was often an investor she ultimately became, not the visible director of some great enterprise, but a partner in policies conceived and executed by an influential faction. And at the same time the state navy which had loomed so large under Henry VIII was eclipsed by privately owned flotillas.

Yet if the triumphs of Drake, the defeat of the Armada and the success of the privateering war intensified in England a sense of nationality and Protestantism, and inspired a euphoria only dissipated by Stuart incompetence, in general the country was as little influenced intellectually by its experience of the outside world as was Holland. Many new phenomena were indeed encountered. There appeared, for example, in England, occasionally as guests, but more usually as slaves or prisoners, handfuls of Amerindians (the first *c.* 1500), Eskimos, Icelanders and Africans. As elsewhere, and for similar reasons, much new information was mapped by cartographers and recorded, and often sympathetically evaluated by seamen, scholars and travellers (cf. pp. 280, 361). Giles Fletcher produced in 1591 the first systematic account of the structure of Russian government and society, Thomas Hariot an excellent description of the Indians of Virginia, and Henry Lord the first serious English study of Hinduism (1630). Men of learning obtained maps, narratives and treatises from abroad, and from the mid-1500s onwards there became available, chiefly through the labours of Richard Hakluyt[25] and his successor Samuel Purchas,[26] a mass of material ranging from the eyewitness accounts of English sailors to translations of European geographical writings.

The literature of England, like that of many parts of Europe, was adorned with exotic themes and references. John Donne addressed his mistress as 'my new-found-land' and John Milton enthroned Satan amidst riches eclipsing those of 'Ormus'. But of any profounder influence there is little evidence. The great importance accorded to colonies in Thomas More's *Utopia* (1516) probably stemmed from classical inspiration rather than from that of the as yet insignificant Iberian conquests and settlements. And whilst the New World appears in Shakespeare's *Tempest* it is seen in a light deriving from the views of Montaigne. In general there was little speculation about, or concern for, such indigenous peoples as were encountered. True, the circumnavigator Thomas Cavendish admired the skills of the Chinese craftsmen in Manila, whilst the Amerindian Algonkians – to whom indeed some Europeans in Virginia fled to live – were favourably portrayed by that aimiable toper Thomas Morton.[27] And in the early seventeenth century occasional doubts were expressed, as was earlier the case in Europe, about the morality of colonization.

There was also some discussion of England's responsibility to Christianize the North

American Indians. But despite plans in Virginia and Massachusetts, English, like Dutch, Protestantism, lacked Catholicism's organization and will for such work. Its demands on putative converts were exacting, the energies of many of its exponents were devoted to intense internecine disputes, and its more radical adherents were concerned to keep themselves separate from the rest of mankind. Yet the views expressed were of a familiar ancestry, demonstrating once again how new experience was accommodated within the existing mental framework of European civilization. The English accepted, as had the medieval church, that force could be used on heathens who resisted the word of God to save them, for their own good, from their 'barbarous kind of life and brutish manners'. They similarly accepted that in servitude such peoples would find a beneficial prelude to conversion, the use of Indian 'servants' in Virginia being the equivalent of the enslavement employed by the Iberians elsewhere. The English likewise defended their title to the New World on the venerable grounds of prior possession, whether stemming from an alleged Welsh conquest in the twelfth century or the supposed later achievements of John Cabot (cf. pp. 288, 361). The existence and condition of its inhabitants they explained by reference to the Old Testament, and their portrayal was coloured by European preconceptions and by political convenience. They were initially shown in a generally unfavourable light because of the nature of the Iberian material circulating in translation, from which the sympathetic opinions of las Casas were largely absent.[28] When, however, there were hopes of recruiting emigrants the picture became more roseate, only to revert to its former hues as a result of such events as the Virginia rising of 1622.

Indian title to land was handled in much the same way. That the indigenous peoples of America had rights was pragmatically conceded by the private purchases of holdings from them in New England, or in the Virginian treaty of 1646, defining Algonkian territories. But such agreements, like the equally politic behaviour of the Dutch, owed as much to convenience as to conviction, and it was still widely assumed that in law America was 'empty' and so available for colonization. For the rest, English debate centred not on large ethical questions, but on those economic and strategic problems to which Tudor and Stuart experience was mostly confined. The threat of Spanish world hegemony in the sixteenth century produced the first tentative English oceanic strategy (cf. pp. 467ff.). In the same years Habsburg strength was identified (as by Richard Hakluyt)[29] with Castile's control of American bullion – the classical equation of money with power put in a new setting – whilst the inflationary impact of New World silver in England was suggested by the reviser of the *Discourse of the Common Weal* (1581). The irresistible advance of Dutch commerce in the early 1600s, the contemporary misfortunes of that of England, and argument on the dangers arising from the export of 'treasure' (the silver needed to trade to Asia, the Baltic and the Mediterranean), led Thomas Mun to speculate (*c.* 1625) that there could be a larger commercial world in which his compatriots could win assets with which to solve problems nearer home. His assumptions were an advance on those of predecessors who maintained that the volume of trade was limited, or that a nation's share in it was more or less predetermined by its natural resources.

But in nothing was the influence of the oceanic world more notable than in establishing England from the late sixteenth century as the major centre in the development of those navigational techniques pioneered by the Italians and Iberians. Interest in such matters was first aroused when, in the mid-1500s, as part of the general penetration of English culture by continental Renaissance influences, something of the mathematical and cosmographical learning of Flanders was introduced into the country by John Dee. It was strengthened by Northumberland's patronage, amongst others, of Sebastian Cabot, and by the visit to the *Casa de la Contratación* in Seville of Stephen Borough during the reign of Mary Tudor, the wife of Philip II of Spain (cf. pp. 345, 463). But from the acceptance of Spanish methods and the emulation of Spanish practice there had evolved by *c.* 1600 a distinctive English science whose practitioners wrote on such matters as the behaviour of the compass or the trigonometric relationship between course and distance sailed. Many were academics, or, like Thomas Hood and Edward Wright, men of academic education whose achievements were part of a wider scientific resurgence in the north. Nor did their work reflect a re-orientation of modes of thought occasioned by the new experiences of the extra-European world, but the fact that English seamen could, as had those of Portugal earlier, call on the skills of compatriots for the solution of some practical problem (cf. pp. 263-4). Not all, however, were inclined to do so. Despite sustained attempts to ensure a wider diffusion of the knowledge of mathematics and celestial navigation demanded by oceanic voyages, some, like Frobisher, claimed they lacked the wit to understand such things, and others, like the pilot of the Elizabethan *Galleon Leicester*, professed to give 'not a fart for cosmography'.

In England, as in Europe, the opening of the oceans and the discovery of new lands brought an accumulation of new information and some interest in newly revealed objects. But in a country in which, in the first half of the seventeenth century, there was conflict between putative royal absolutism and the Commons, and between an increasingly Catholic Anglicanism and various radical Puritan sects, the discoveries were matters of little moment. Nor could what clashed with existing preconceptions, whether those deriving from the classics or from the authority of the Bible – increasingly influential with the growth of more extreme Protestantism – be accepted or assimilated. Walter Raleigh, who had some, and claimed more, competence as a navigator and explorer, used the nonsense of Mandeville's *Travels* – which indeed he considered vindicated by recent findings – to support his curious belief in the existence of a race of headless mortals. Samuel Purchas, indefatigable in the collection of assorted geographical information, emerged from his perusal of this vast accumulation convinced that Europe was the sole home of 'Arts and Inventions'.

Bibliographical note

The main body of archival material relating to early English maritime and colonial history is in the national archives in London. To these there is an exemplary introduction in HM Stationery Office, *Guide to the Contents of the Public Record Office* (1963). Sources for colonial history are outlined in C.S.S. Higham, *The Colonial Entry Books. A Brief Guide to the Colonial Records in the Public Record Office before 1696* (1921). Also useful is A.R. Hewitt, *Guide to the Resources for Commonwealth Studies in London, Oxford and Cambridge* (1957), though naturally largely concerned with a later period than this book. The nature of the sources available in the Library of the India Office in London is indicated in K.N. Chaudhuri, *The English East India Company* (1965). Maritime history cannot, of course, be studied from the records of one particular country, and for England reference needs to be made to those of the Hanse, Holland, Iberia and the Mediterranean (as set out in the bibliographical notes to chapters 2, 3, 4, 5, 6 and 7).

A mass of documents, correspondence, etc. is summarized in J.S. Brewer, J. Gairdner and R.H. Brodie, *Calendar of Letters and Papers, Foreign and Domestic, Henry VIII*. This series is continued (chronologically) by the Stationery Office publication of *Calendars of State Papers: Domestic* (1547–); *Foreign* (1547–); *Colonial* (1513–); *Spanish* (*Relating to Negotiations between England and Spain*, 1485–); *Venetian* (*Relating to English Affairs in the Archives . . . of Venice*, 1202–). W.L. Grant and J. Munro, *The Acts of the Privy Council, Colonial Series* (6 vols, 1908–12), extracts from the privy-council registers entries relating to the colonies. Private collections of archives are described, and extracts from them published, in the *Reports and Calendars issued by the Royal Commission on Historical Manuscripts* (1870–). Material of great value is printed in the volumes of the Navy Records Society (1894–) and those of the Hakluyt Society which since 1847 has made available a vast array of geographical records and narratives both English and (in translation) European. The rich store of information contained in the collections of Richard Hakluyt and Samuel Purchas has already been noticed.

An excellent and trenchant bibliographical survey (to the date of publication) of English maritime beginnings and the American voyages is provided by S.E. Morison in the relevant section of his *The European Discovery of America*, 2 vols (Oxford, 1971–4). The *Annual Bulletin of Historical Literature* produced by the Historical Association briefly indicates, though somewhat in arrears, new books and articles. Current publications in journals are noted each year in *The English Historical Review*.

The major periodical publications in England dealing with the country's early maritime and colonial history are *The English Historical Review* (1886–); *The Mariner's Mirror* (1911–); *History* (1912–); *The Economic History Review* (1927–); *The Historical Journal* (Cambridge, 1958–), continuing the former *Cambridge Historical Journal* (Cambridge, 1923–57); and *Past and Present* (Oxford, 1952–). *The William and Mary Quarterly* (Williamsburg, Virginia, 1921–) is particularly concerned with North America and the English Caribbean. For the West Indies there are *The Caribbean Historical Review* and *The Jamaican Historical Review* (see p. 456).

Such older works as A.P. Newton (ed.), *The Great Age of Discovery* (1932) and J.A.

Williamson, *The Age of Drake* (5th edn, 1965) still make useful introductions to the beginnings of England's overseas expansion. They are now supplemented by vol. I of Morison's *The European Discovery of America*, the opening chapters of D.B. Quinn's *England and the Discovery of America* (1974), and by the present writer in *Ec. Hist. Rev*, XIII (1961), 327ff.; *Trans. Royal Hist. Soc.*, 12 (1962), 105ff.; and *HJ*, XV (1972), 385ff. For the early history of the Iceland trade see G.J. Marcus, 'The First English Voyages to Iceland', *MM*, 42 (1956), 313ff. There is a wealth of information on English beginnings in the Mediterranean in P. Argenti, *The Occupation of Chios by the Genoese and their Administration of the Island, 1346–1566* (Cambridge, 1958), in the paper of Domenico Gioffrè, cited many times already, in A. Guiffrè (ed.), *Studi in Onore di Amintore Fanfani* (6 vols, Milan, 1962), V, and in M.E. Mallet, 'Anglo-Florentine Commercial Relations, 1465–91', in *Ec. Hist. Rev*, XV (1962), 250ff. I have also made extensive use of HCA Examinations (PRO HCA 13/vols 1–5). G.D. Ramsay, *The City of London in International Politics at the Accession of Elizabeth Tudor* (Manchester, 1975), has a valuable discussion of English commerce and its problems in the mid-1500s.

English intervention in West Africa is described in J.W. Blake, *European Beginnings in West Africa 1454–1578* (1937), and English commerce there in A.F.C. Ryder, *Benin and the Europeans, 1485–1897* (1969). The early slaving activities of John Hawkins are convincingly re-appraised by Kenneth R. Andrews in his *The Spanish Caribbean: Trade and Plunder, 1530–1630* New Haven, 1978). There is a valuable study of the English in Brazil in the same author's *Elizabethan Privateering* (Cambridge, 1964) and some additional material in F. Mauro, *Le Portugal et l'Atlantique an XVIIᵉ Siècle, 1570–1670* (Paris, 1960).

K.R. Andrews also re-examines the career and influence of Francis Drake in his stimulating *Drake's Voyages* (1967), which supplements his study of *Elizabethan Privateering*, of which I have made extensive use. English piracy after 1604 is the subject of C.M. Senior's lively *A Nation of Pirates* (1976). For the privateering war of 1625 I have chiefly used HCA 13/vols 44–7.

The opening of an English trade to Russia is analysed with a wealth of detail in T.S. Willan, *The Muscovy Merchants of 1555* (Manchester, 1953). The search for a northern passage to Asia is described in Morison's *European Discovery of America*, vol. I, and in W.P. Cumming, R. Skeleton and D.B. Quinn, *The Discovery of North America* (1971) and G.W.P. Cumming, S. Hillier, D.B. Quinn and G. Williams *The Exploration of North America* (1974). English activity in the Levant in the late sixteenth century is placed in its European context in Fernand Braudel's *The Mediterranean and the Mediterranean World in the Age of Philip II*, trs. by S. Reynolds, (2 vols, 1972–3). His account is modified by Niels Steensgaard, *Carracks, Caravans and Companies: The Structural Crisis in the European-Asian Trade in the Early Seventeenth Century* (Copenhagen, 1973) and by Susan Skilliter's important study, drawing on Ottoman archives, of *William Harborne and the Trade with Turkey, 1578–1582* (Oxford, 1977).

The disastrous voyage of Edward Fenton is discussed, and an important source for its history published, in Elizabeth Story Donno's edition for the Hakluyt Society (1976) of Richard Madox's diary, under the title of *An Elizabethan in 1582*. Thomas Cavendish's even more disastrous expedition is illuminated by David Quinn's edition of *The Last Voyage of Thomas Cavendish, 1591–2* (Chicago, 1975). The origins of the East India Company are analysed in Andrews, *Elizabethan Privateering*, and its early history discussed by Chaudhuri, *The English*

East India Company. The development of its trade is the subject of D.K. Bassett's important contribution, 'Early English Trade and Settlement in Asia, 1602–1690', to *Britain and the Netherlands in Europe and Asia* (1968), ed. J.S. Bromley and E.H. Kossmann. The company's structure, weaknesses and operation are discussed by Chaudhuri, by M.A.P. Meilink-Roelofsz in her *Asian Trade and European influence in the Indonesian Archipelago* (The Hague, 1962), by Steensgaard in *Carracks, Caravans and Companies*, and by L. Dermigny in *CIHM*, 8 (1970).

The definitive account of the first English attempts to colonize North America is that of David Quinn, whose various papers on the subject are now available in *England and the Discovery of America* (1974). Iberian materials available in translation, and their influence on English views of the Americas are investigated in systematic detail by Colin Steele, *English Interpreters of the Iberian New World from Purchas to Stevens, 1603–1726* (1975). The first settlements are briefly described in Cumming, Skeleton and Quinn, *The Discovery of North America* and in *The Exploration of North America*. A mass of information, especially valuable on emigration, is brought together by Carl Bridenbaugh in *Vexed and Troubled Englishmen, 1590–1642* (Oxford, 1968). The evolution of the English colonies is brilliantly treated by K.G. Davies, *The North Atlantic World in the Seventeenth Century* (Minneapolis, 1974), equally stimulating on their politics, economies or theology. An interesting light is thrown on government and society in Massachusetts by T.H. Breen, 'English Origins and New World Development: The Case of the Covenanted Militia in Seventeenth-Century Massachusetts', in *P&P*, 57 (1972), 74ff. Two recent large-scale studies make further reference to a secondary literature of overwhelming proportions superfluous. One is the collection of essays in honour of David Quinn, edited by K.R. Andrews, N.P. Canny and P.E.H. Hair as *The Westward Enterprise, English Activities in Ireland, the Atlantic and America, 1480–1650* (Liverpool, 1978). The other is that of H.C. Porter, *The Inconstant Savage: England and the North American Indian, 1500–1660* (1979), a work of enormous if diffuse erudition, ranging far beyond the ostensible subject of its title. Andrews re-assesses the motives, and examines the course, of English penetration of the Caribbean in his *Spanish Caribbean*. The economies and societies of the first English settlements in the West Indies are analysed in Davies, *The North Atlantic*, and some colourful detail supplied by Bridenbaugh, *Vexed and Troubled Englishmen*.

The general pattern of English overseas trade in this period, and the changes it underwent, are most concisely described and lucidly explained in D.C. Coleman, *The Economy of England, 1450–1750* (Oxford, 1977). Ralph Davis discusses England's penetration of the Mediterranean from the late sixteenth century in 'Influences de l'Angleterre sur le déclin de Venise au XVIIᵉ siècle', in *Aspetti e Cause della Decadenza Economica Veneziana nel Secolo XVII* (Venice/Rome, 1961). The fortunes of English shipping in the first half of the seventeenth century are examined by Harland Taylor, 'Trade, Neutrality and the 'English Road', 1630–48', in *Ec. Hist. Rev*, XXV (1972), 236ff., and by J.S. Kepler, 'Fiscal Aspects of the English Carrying Trade during the Thirty Years War', ibid., 261ff. I have also used HCA Examinations, vols 23ff. The influence of oceanic ventures, colonization and the new trades on English society is discussed by Andrews, *Elizabethan Privateering*, and by Robert Brenner, 'The Civil War Politics of London's Merchant Community', *P&P*, 58 (1973), 53ff.

For the intellectual impact of the New Worlds in England, see the remarks of the present writer in *HJ*, XII (1969), 389ff., and of Porter, *The Inconstant Savage*. England's contribution to navigational science is definitively treated, in its European setting, by David W. Waters, *The Art of Navigation in England in Elizabethan and Early Stuart Times* (1958).

Conclusion

The world envisaged by scholars and known to travellers in Catholic Europe in the early Middle Ages was a tiny one. It was conceived in terms deriving from vestiges of classical geography modified by Christian piety, and had Jerusalem as its focal point. By 1650, and indeed in many cases much earlier, cartographers were depicting an earth easily recognizable to modern eyes. The size and general outline of the huge African continent were understood, a sea route to India had been opened, China and Japan had been identified with the Cathay and Cipangu of Marco Polo, the Americas discovered, and European ships were sailing the waters of the globe from the Pacific to the Arctic Ocean.

All this had been accomplished in voyages which, whether by land or sea, were of a duration and rigour now hard to grasp, and generally at an appalling cost in human life and suffering. Outward-bound Portuguese Indiamen commonly reached the southern tip of Africa with half their crews dead through disease. Commanders couped up for weeks on end in tiny and overmanned ships, contending with the hostility of the elements and the frustrations and antagonisms that inevitably developed amongst their complements, suffered nervous breakdown, as did Columbus, or, like Thomas Cavendish, went mad. But of the outcome of their achievements there can be no doubt. There were important technical and technological advances, most notably in cartography, even if outside Europe it was coastlines rather than the interiors of continents (still largely unknown) that were recorded. There was a considerable improvement in navigational techniques. Nevertheless the establishment of longitude at sea remained impossible, and that of latitude fairly haphazard with all but the ablest seamen. The carrying capacity, fighting strength and comfort of ships were all substantially bettered. Yet if the vessels of the mid-1600s are compared with those of the Norse, improvements in seaworthiness and performance were little more than marginal.

The widening of horizons, the discovery of new lands, new continents and new peoples meant an enormous increase in factual knowledge in Europe, with savants recording – to their pleasure and surprise – matters on which Antiquity was now proved to be ignorant or ill-informed. It meant, too, the opportunity for an enterprising, bold, unscrupulous or simply lucky minority to become rich, just as it meant the enhancement of the wealth of prudent mercantile states, the momentary prosperity of the Iberian monarchies, and the eventual hastening of the shift in economic preponderance in Europe from the Mediterranean to the north. For some, whether Vikings in Normandy, Genoese expatriates in the Black Sea, Portuguese *casados* in Asia or Spanish *conquistadores* in South America, there came opportunities they could never have enjoyed in their homelands. But such gains meant in general indigenous loss. Whole peoples were in one way or another destroyed in the Americas. The presence of the Italians in the medieval Levant enlarged the net of slavery, whilst its dimensions were still further extended by the European shipment of Africans to the New World to work in anything from plantations to silver mining. Nevertheless on the vast majority of the populations of Africa, Asia and even North America European presence had as yet little or no influence. Limited areas of non-European economies were stimulated or disrupted, some elements of European technology here and there absorbed. Some indigenous merchants similarly found new chances of profit, and those chiefs or rulers who co-operated with the intruders might benefit from the association. And to many peoples – though even so an insignificant proportion of the world's inhabitants – there was brought, sometimes by persuasion and argument, sometimes by less delicate means, the Christianity of Catholic Europe in a missionary endeavour reaching from the islands of the Pacific to the forests of Canada.

Equally remarkably there came into being first a larger European economy and then, as never before, one of a tentative global nature. Through the trade of the Hanse the rich resources of the Baltic littoral were known from Norway to Italy. European products sold alike in imperial China and Norse Greenland in the high Middle Ages. By the sixteenth century American silver had both penetrated old trading routes – such as that from western Europe to the Baltic – and come into use in Asia, whilst Chinese silk was selling in Peru and Mexico, or reaching Spain from her colonies. But though maize introduced into Africa from the Indies might now help to keep its population alive, and though American tobacco was imported for the contentment of some Europeans, these were again changes which left the mass of mankind untouched. Amongst states, however, the acquisition of new territories brought, as in medieval Venice and Habsburg Spain, impressive experiments with the forms of colonial government. And what one power possessed, whether in the Black Sea or the Caribbean, became the object of the ambitions of others, widening the area of conflict, encouraging the growth of navies, and stimulating strategic debate.

Increases in knowledge and technological or political developments were one thing. The willingness to accept as fellow humans those millions of people whose conventions were not of a familiar order, whose skins were not of a familiar whiteness, and whose beliefs were not Christian, was a very different matter. Acceptance – let alone admiration – of other cultures was confined to a tiny minority of Europeans. Nor was it an attitude of mind evolving by linear progress. There were acute and often sympathetic accounts of alien civilizations written by merchants and missionaries in the Middle Ages. The first European encounters with Amerindians produced some euphoric schemes for their improvement (and admittedly others for their enslavement). But to know one's neighbour was not to love him, and on the whole non-European peoples were viewed with growing disillusionment, not to say contempt. Where toleration and intellectual curiosity flourished it had little to do with a realization that the world was a bigger place and its inhabitants more diverse than had previously been known. The (comparatively) open and tolerant nature of Dutch and Venetian civilization in its heyday needs no extra-European explanation, and significantly enough the countries which in the sixteenth and seventeenth centuries made the most distinguished contributions to science were those least directly involved in the New Worlds – Germany, Holland, England and Italy.

The most striking result of European penetration of the wider world, and indeed of the creation of maritime empires within the waters of the Continent, was to produce what, according to temperament, can be regarded as proper national pride or crude complacent arrogance. The Genoese set up a testimony to their own merits in the Holy Sepulchre in Jerusalem. The Portuguese referred to their overseas possessions, however acquired, as 'the conquests'. The Spaniards, like the Venetians, scattered throughout their colonies mottoes extolling the might and excellence of their rule. Some of the empires engendering these attitudes enjoyed only a brief existence; some survived into our own age. But they had brought together for the first time in enduring association, and with enduring consequences, many of the peoples inhabiting the earth. So at last, as a contemporary wrote of Francis Drake's great voyage, was 'The World Encompass'd'.

Notes

Chapter 1   The Norse

1   Vikings were pirates – literally men who lurked in bays. In race they were a mixture of Norwegians, Swedes, Danes and others. 'Viking' or 'Norseman' were terms used indiscriminately by contemporaries as generics to describe the raiders irrespective of their origins.

2   Such birch woods as they found the original settlers soon destroyed.

3   These were probably Eskimo remains, but just possibly Irish.

4   For the nature of the Sagas, see pp. 35–6.

5   These were Eskimo of the so-called Thule culture. When the Norse first arrived the traces they found were probably of the earlier (Dorset) Eskimo. *Skraeling* is used in the Sagas to describe both Indians and Eskimo.

6   On the Vinland Map there are exhaustive discussions in the relevant pages of S.E. Morison, *The European Discovery of America: The Northern Voyages* (Oxford, 1971) and D.B. Quinn, *England and the Discovery of America* (London, 1974).

7   This is the story as told in *The Greenlanders' Saga*. It does not appear in *The Saga of Eirik the Red*. There are good but complicated reasons for accepting the version of *The Greenlanders' Saga*. For some of the literature on this, and for the sources, see pp. 35–6.

8   The exact location of Vinland is much disputed, and some would place it in New England. The difficulties of accepting northern Newfoundland as a land of vines and wheat have called forth much subtle exegesis. The Saga descriptions, however, may well include conventional pictures of some earthly paradise. And in any case the vines may have been nothing more than red currants, gooseberries or cranberries, and the wheat Lyme Grass, a wild grass with a wheat-like head, all of which could be found in Newfoundland.

9   For the difficulties of the Saga evidence see pp. 35–6 and above, n. 8.

10   The earliest compass was a magnetized needle either suspended on a pivot, or pushed through a straw and floating in a bowl of water, cf. pp. 206–7.

11   Nor were these the only merits of the early Norse rudder. That of the Gokstad ship is so arranged that the turning axis divides the blade area into two parts, one forward and one behind the turning axis. Correctly balanced, the rudder, and thus the ship, could be turned with no more effort on the part of the helmsman than was required to overcome the friction of the mounting. Other rudders have been found which appear to have been of deliberately unsymmetrical construction to counterbalance the effect of being hung on one side.

12   The famous and hard-driven Black-Ball liners of the early nineteenth century averaged 3.2 knots on the crossing.

13   A strake is a continuous line of planking in the hull of a ship.

14   The change was perhaps also encouraged by the use of sawn planks which meant it was no longer easy, as when the adze had been used, to leave on the planks those cleats through which they were lashed to the ribs.

15 Ceded by Charles the Simple to Rollo in 911.

16 There had been trading contracts between the Black Sea and the Baltic in Antiquity.

17 A dynasty which had established itself in Khorasan and Transoxania by the end of the ninth century.

18 Norway was recorded as a peninsula in 1285.

19 For similar reactions elsewhere in Europe at a later date, cf. pp. 280ff.

20 The *Heimskringla* is the thirteenth-century history of the kings of Norway.

Chapter 2   The Hanse

1 Hanse, like Viking, is a word of uncertain etymology and has inspired an equally extensive exegetical literature. It is an ancient Germanic work which by the twelfth and thirteenth centuries meant, amongst other things, a group of merchants being or living abroad. Not until 1343 was it used of the whole community of north-German merchants, and soon after, the towns having become an association, were described as 'of the German Hanse' (*van der dudeschen Hense*).

2 Wismar, Rostock and Hamburg founded in the one-time lands of a Slav tribe.

3 Until the late thirteenth century their trade was not a direct maritime one, and initially goods and merchants having reached Lübeck continued from there by land to Hamburg, and thence to England or the Netherlands.

4 For the *kontor*, see pp. 67–8.

5 Fifty per cent of Narva's exports were still going to Lübeck in the seventeenth century.

6 Its medieval level is unknown.

7 This relates to the eastern towns. Those of the western wing of the Hanse from Cologne to Magdeburg (i.e. in Westphalia and Saxony) are of stone, as, in the east, was Reval.

8 Modified and enriched, as occasion demanded, with elements of Latin, Estonian (at Reval), Polish (at Lublin), Italian, Czech and Ukranian; see Henryk Samsonowicz in *Studia Maritime*, I (Warsaw, 1978).

9 The remains of a cog of 130t were found at Bremen in 1962. Its length was 23.5m and its beam 7.4m.

10 The height of the deck above water.

11 Lübeck *fluits* are noticed in 1590 in PRO HCA, 13/28, 56. For this type of vessel, see below, pp. 425–7.

12 Depositions in, for example PRO HCA, 13/32 give ratios of men/tons served as 1:11 or 1:13. These compare favourably with many ratios to be found elsewhere. See G.V. Scammell in *MM*, 56 (1970), 131ff.

Chapter 3   The Venetian Republic

1 It was in the Levant that goods brought from further east by non-European merchants were acquired for redistribution in the west (cf. pp. 90, 102ff.).

2 In north-eastern Italy, some 130km south of the modern Venice.

3 Then surrounded by more extensive lagoons than those now surviving.

4 A doge (duke), who was the military representative of the Byzantine emperor, first appears *c.* 700. Orso, elected in 726, is now regarded as the forerunner of the independent doges.

5 Between Constantinople or the markets of the Levant, that is, and the west.

6 They penetrated to the fairs of Champagne in east-central France, and at the intersection of ancient land routes leading from the Mediterranean to the north German frontiers, and from Flanders to central and eastern France.

7 Zara is on the Adriatic coast of modern Yugoslavia, roughly opposite to Ancona.

8 So, in the north, there was no invasion of Hanseatic preserves.

9 Lajazzo is a port in (Christian) Armenia, just north of Syria.

10 Like Epirus and Nicaea, Trebizond had not been taken in 1204.

11 The khanate of the Golden Horde (the Kipchak empire) covered, very roughly, the lands of the great rivers of southern Russia. In what are now Iran and Iraq was the khanate of Persia (the Ilkhan empire).

12 Soldaia was, however, never more than a factory at the mercy of the Tartars and overshadowed by Genoese Caffa. It was lost to Genoa in 1365 (see pp. 185–6).

13 See p. 103. In 1328 Venice acquired commercial privileges in Cyprus roughly equivalent to those she had previously enjoyed in the Holy Land.

14 The shah proved to be as big a disappointment as did his successors and the emperor of Ethiopia to the Portuguese in similar schemes (cf. pp. 237, 252).

15 Joints, that is, that required considerable time, skill and accordingly money to make.

16 These were rewards of services in the crusades (cf. pp. 92, 116).

17 One guess is that *c.* 1400 Europe imported 700t of spice a year, of which Venice accounted for 500t.

18 Cyprus did not come under formal Venetian rule until 1489. Before this, however, the Venetian family of Corner were engaged in the large-scale production of sugar on their plantations in the Episcopi district.

19 They were usually Orthodox. The late Middle Ages witnessed some revulsion in the west against the enslavement of Greeks.

20 This was both because purchasing power was limited and because there was little that Asia could not itself provide.

21 Another was the carriage of slaves (see also pp. 2, 106ff., 282, 368).

22 Jaffa is now Tel Aviv.

23 For some contemporary estimates and recent calculations, see *P&P*, 79 (1978), 10–11.

24 This coin and bullion were, of course, supplied to eastern merchants to enable them to make their purchases in the Orient. Silver was also needed in the Black Sea trade where, in dealings with primitive Tartars, or the nomads of Turkestan, the market for manufactures was limited.

25 There was, however, a strenuous but brief reaction, in the mid-1500s, when there were a number of executions for proven Protestantism.

26 The *fondaco* was either a warehouse together with some accommodation, or a complex of shops, houses and other buildings (cf. also pp. 54, 67–8, 73).

27 The city carefully ensured that convoys suffered no competition from vessels sailing independently.

28 The fleets, to the obvious benefit of merchants, in general returned by the way they had come out, though the Barbary galleys sailed more directly from Valencia to Tunis and thence home.

29 By the late fifteenth century the fleets to Flanders, Aigues-Mortes and Barbary were running at a loss, but subsidized to ensure that Venice's position as an entrepôt was maintained.

30 There was, that is, little of the galley above the water to offer resistance to the elements (see also pp. 130, 149–50).

31 The rowing arrangements in galleys are described on pp. 129.

32 A lateen sail was triangular, its leading edge attached to a long curved spar by which it was hoisted, and set so that the same point or corner was always kept to windward.

33 A sail set at the stern will turn a vessel's bow into the wind, one set at the bow will turn it away.

34 This was what the state enjoined. The practice of commanders might well differ.

35 But the city had a handful of its own warships even in earlier centuries.

36 Four oars to a bench were tried in the fourteenth century; five in 1529, but by the 1530s single oars were instead being pulled by several men. Such experiments were not confined to Venice.

37 Ships were also sent out from Crete and other Venetian possessions.
38 The Ottomans also had an arsenal, bigger than that of Venice.
39 Covered slipways have only recently reappeared in shipyards.
40 See pp. 154, 242–3. Relations between Venice and Iberia were not uniformly bad. Information about events in the east reached Spain and Portugal through Constantinople and Venice, and in the late sixteenth century Venetian ships were used in the Atlantic by Spaniards to avoid arrest by English privateers.
41 Yet not until the late seventeenth century did the arsenal build sailing men-of-war on the now well-tried lines of those to the north.
42 According to the wind they could be set to push or pull the ship's bow round.
43 Its colourful history is recounted in PRO HCA 13/32, 41.
44 I.e. associations regulating the commercial or professional activities of their members.
45 Since rarely provisioned for more than ten days.

Chapter 4   The Genoese Republic

1 For the medieval population of Venice see p. 88.
2 For the nature of the west's commercial relations with the Levant, and for its economic importance, see pp. 90, 101ff.
3 North Africa, likewise, had been Moslem since the Arab conquests.
4 Siwas was in the northeast of modern Turkey.
5 These were probably, but not certainly, native craft in Genoese ownership or chartered to Genoese merchants.
6 That it was possible to reach India from Abyssinia and East Africa appears to have been understood by missionaries by the early fourteenth century.
7 The office of the doge was introduced by 'the people' in the early fourteenth century, but was soon converted by its incumbents to a means of acquiring land and rank.
8 Genoa's overseas possessions were run at a loss. Those of Venice – and even for a time of Spain – made useful contributions to the mother country's revenues, cf. pp. 106, 359.
9 For western knowledge of the coasts and interior of Africa in the late Middle Ages see pp. 164, 208, 227.
10 Flemish textiles also reached Genoa after re-shipment from Cadiz.
11 See pp. 177ff. The Habsburgs were rulers of both Spain and southern Italy.
12 The trade was of such an extent that, combined with that in European textiles, it meant that Genoa's commerce with Egypt, unlike that with Syria, balanced.
13 Cf. pp. 107–8 and 257. Even in the twelfth century the Genoese had distinguished between black and white among their Moslem slaves.
14 The enslavement of Balkan Christians was condemned by Popes Urban V and Clement VII in the fourteenth century, and by St Antonino of Florence in the fifteenth.
15 The di Negri were a family regularly engaged from the late 1500s in the provision of African slaves to the Iberian Americas, see p. 256.
16 For the import of American bullion to Spain, see pp. 324ff.
17 The Algarve is the most southern region of Portugal.
18 The *Cortes* was the representative assembly of Portugal.
19 Lisbon, Arquivo Nacional da Torre do Tombo, *Inquisição de Lisboa-Processo* 5451, f.34.
20 Jewish and Portuguese to the Habsburg officials in the Netherlands.
21 Troubles with the disintegrating Mongol power were such that the Genoese boycotted Tabriz in 1342 and never officially re-used it thereafter.

22 In particular with Greeks – witness the ubiquity of those *gasmoules* of the Franco-Greek parentage – who conformed most nearly in behaviour, appearance and colour to Christians of the central and western Mediterranean. For consciousness of differences of colour see p. 174.

23 Hence such craft were known as *uscieri*.

24 For the *bucius* see p. 146. Those of the Genoese had in the thirteenth century two masts of equal size, each setting a lateen sail, although other suits were carried according to the weather.

25 *Dromon* was once the name of a large-oared Byzantine fighting ship. It may have come to mean a great galley. For the cog see pp. 77–80.

26 The mizzen would, for example, bring the ship's head into the wind, so helping her, amongst other things, to change tack.

27 For the meanings of these terms see pp. 125ff., 129ff.

28 Archivio di Stato di Genova, *Notaro Agostino Cibo Peirana*, f.6–10.

29 For other rates of manning see pp. 126ff., 509 (n 12).

30 For Venetian naval policies and organization see pp. 128ff.

31 The Armada probably had 130 ships carrying about 22,000 men. In 1295 Genoa set out 200 galleys and 40,000 men (see above, p. 161). All such figures are of course highly suspect. For Lepanto see p. 134 and for the early Genoese fleets see p. 158.

32 For the *mahona* see p. 191. Northern joint-stock finance could, however, have had a more purely local inspiration in the old-established practice of shareholding in ships.

33 BM. Additional MS 7968, f.48v; *CSPD, 1598–1601*, pp. 172, 304, 311.

34 For the nature of sailing directions see p. 18.

35 *Portolans* also describes collections of sailing directions.

36 To the Black Sea at the beginning of the thirteenth century and to northern Europe at the end (see pp. 95, 165).

37 Known only from a revised version still preserved in Venice.

38 Not all such borrowings are of course simply to be credited to the Italians, let alone to the Venetians and Genoese.

39 Yet already in the twelfth and thirteenth centuries Venice was one of the major channels through which the west came to know Aristotle's work more fully.

40 For similar developments in the north see p. 73.

41 Florence, Archivio di Stato, *Balia Familiarum* 317, no. 245.

Chapter 5　Portugal

1 There was already some realization in the early 1300s that Prester John was in fact the emperor of Ethiopia.

2 For Henry's geographical knowledge see p. 260. There was a Portuguese translation of a Latin version of Polo in the library of Dom Duarte (1433–8). This was possibly one of the works which, with other geographical information, Dom Pedro was alleged to have obtained in Venice (see p. 207).

3 So it was reported by Pacheco Pereira who sailed with Dias.

4 Amongst those consulted was the Spanish scholar, Diego Ortiz, in the library of whose college at Salamanca is a Spanish geography of Arab origin (now University of Salamanca MS 2086) containing much information on India.

5 For this technique of navigation see pp. 17, 263.

6 See pp. 139ff. The Portuguese allowed, for political and economic reasons, the continuance of Asian commerce through the Persian Gulf, see p. 272.

7 Swiss infantry was the most renowned in early sixteenth-century Europe.

8 Macao is at the southern extremity of the Pearl River estuary (see p. 241).

9 The Ming emperors had forbidden all direct Chinese trade with Japan (see p. 240).

10 Cf. pp. 328–9. During the union of Spain and Portugal (1580–1640) trade between Macao and Manila was (ineffectively) banned by the Spanish crown. It continued indirectly during the Portuguese struggle for independence, 1640–68.

11 The Province of the North.

12 Where it was difficult to breed horses.

13 Once the cane was cut the first stages of sugar production had to be completed, if possible, in a matter of hours.

14 PRO HCA 13/28, f.156v; 13/45, f.570v.

15 Used as a dye in cloth making (cf. p. 176).

16 See pp. 250, 343. It was also from the Azores that ships caught a favourable wind for Europe.

17 'New Christians' were converted Jews.

18 PRO HCA 13/45, 521v. ff.

19 HCA 13/28, f.30.

20 Of mixed European and negroid parentage.

21 A chart of the Venetian Andrea Bianco shows (1448) what some have identified as the eastern bulge of Brazil, and perhaps records an earlier discovery.

22 It was originally 'The Land of the True Cross'.

23 For the missions, see pp. 285ff.

24 I.e. pioneers or explorers.

25 See BM. Add. MS 36 321, f.251ff., for a Portuguese account (1623) of foreign settlement on the Amazon.

26 PRO HCA 13/45, 522.

27 See Carl Laga, *Estudios Historicos*, (Sao Paulo, 1963) vol. I.

28 *Mestiços* were of mixed European and Amerindian parentage.

29 A coarse pepper-like spice, the so-called 'grains of paradise'.

30 The Congo was bounded on the north by the river Congo, on the south by the Dande, on the east by the Kwango, and on the west by the sea.

31 Lisbon, Arquivo Naçional da Torre do Tombo, *Gaveta* XV/14/28.

32 These are, again, approximate figures. Buenos Aires was officially opened to the slave trade in 1595.

33 Francesco Carletti, *My Voyage Around the World*, trs. by H. Weinstock (London, 1965), p. 9; cf. M. Bataillon, *Etudes sur Bartolome de las Casas* (Paris, 1965), p. 93.

34 Specimens were carried to be shown to peoples encountered (see also p. 164).

35 See Eliahu Ashtor in Edouard Privat (ed.) *Mélanges en l'honneur de Fernand Braudel* (Toulouse, 1973), vol. I, 31ff., (p. 104). The lowest was reached at the time da Gama sailed for India.

36 *APO*, 4 (i.i.), 558.

37 *APO*, 4 (i.i.), 256.

38 *APO*, 4 (i.i.), 201, 202.

39 Gomes Eanes de Zurara, *Crónica dos Feitos de Guiné* (Edição da Agência-Geral do Ultramar, Lisbon, 1949), 11,54.

40 The astrolabe had long been used by astrologers and astronomers. In essence it was a brass disc engraved with a projection of the celestial sphere, covered by a plan of the heavens graduated in degrees around the perimeter. A rotable sight-bar fitted at the centre allowed the altitude and motion of heavenly bodies to be observed and plotted. A simplified version for use at sea was known by *c.* 1540. The quadrant, employed in the fifteenth century, was a quadrant of a circle, marked in degrees from 0° to 90°, and fitted with sighting vanes along one edge. The altitude of a heavenly body as seen through

the vanes was indicated on an arcuate scale by a plumb suspended from the apex. Such instruments could be used on a heaving and rolling ship only with great difficulty.

41 See p. 208; G.V. Scammell in *HJ*, XII, 3 (1969), 403–4.
42 *APO*, 4 (i.i.), 45.
43 *APO*, 4 (i.i.), 43; *Hakluyt*, V,500.
44 *Hakluyt*, VII, 99.
45 *APO*, 4 (i.i.), 252.
46 *APO*, 4 (i.i.), 549ff.
47 APO, 4 (i.i.), 316.
48 Cf. pp. 339–40; *APO*, 4 (i.i.), 105, 126.
49 *APO*, 4 (i.i.), 865.
50 *Hakluyt*, XI, 224.
51 *APO*, 4 (i.i.), 304.
52 *APO*, 4 (i.i.), p. 539; c.f. pp. 241–3.
53 *APO*, 4 (i.i.), p. 657.
54 *Hakluyt*, II, 472; but cf. p. 139.
55 *Casa da India*.
56 *APO*, 4 (i.i.), p. 615; see pp. 274–5.
57 For galleons and carracks see pp. 147ff., 194, 279, 343.
58 A comparable voyage was that of Spain's Manila galleons (cf. p. 328).
59 Identified by soundings, see the description in *Hakluyt*, VI, 382.
60 Cochin was used before 1510, and other ports by occasional vessels thereafter.
61 The *carreira* was the round voyage between Lisbon and Goa.
62 APO, 4 (i.i.), 301; cf. pp.139f. Cambayan ships similarly returned westward from Malacca, Burma and Indonesia *via* the Maldives.
63 The Portuguese carrack of the late sixteenth century was a broad-beamed vessel of three or four flush decks and high poop and forecastle. She had a bowsprit and three masts, the forward pair each setting two square sails, the aft a single lateen.
64 *Com mouros e gente da terra*, APO, 4 (i.i.), 542; cf. ibid., 819.
65 Lisbon, Torre do Tombo, *Livro das Monções* 13 (1620), 79.
66 The Portuguese slave trade was, in fact, worth about 10 per cent of all royal monopolies and taxes in Portugal *c.* 1500.
67 Used from the early 1500s, this was a four-square staff, graduated on one side in degrees and minutes, along which a wooden cross-piece slid. One end was held to the eye, and the cross-piece moved so that by simultaneously sighting the horizon and the observed celestial body, the altitude of the latter above the horizon was given.
68 *Pello direito da propriedade*, *APO*, 4 (i.i.), 71. Other arguments advanced were the expense involved and the duty to occupy empty lands (cf. p. 269).
69 See D.F. Lach, *Asia in the Making of Europe* (Chicago, 1977), vol. 2, bks 2 and 3, 545ff.
70 *De Inst. Oratoria*, II, 5, 15.
71 Antonio de Morga, *Sucesos de las Islas Filipinas*, trs. and ed. by J.S. Cummins (Cambridge, Hakluyt Society, 1971), 323, n.2.
72 PRO HCA 13/29, f.28v: cf. pp. 325, 350.
73 *APO*, 4 (i.i.), 257.
74 Vietnam was evangelized from the late 1500s.
75 I.e. from western India.
76 *APO*, 4 (i.i.), 156.

77 Lisbon, Torre do Tombo, *Livro das Monções* 38, 405.

78 *APO*, 4 (i.i.), 874.

79 *APO*, 4 (i.i.), 214.

80 PROHCA 13/45, f.454. For attacks on Jews in the colonies, Torre do Tombo, *Livro das Monções* 31, f.133

81 *Studia*, 8 (1961), 173.

82 PRO HCA 13/29, 4ff. (cf. p. 264).

83 *Purchas*, III, 354; IV, 158.

84 Torre do Tombo, *Livro das Monções* 51, f.19 (cf. p. 242).

85 PRO HCA 13/28, f.19v, 109v, 156v; 13/32, 311, 318v, 329v; 13/45, 331v. The evidence comes largely from arrests made by English privateers.

86 *APO*, 4 (i.i.), pp. 292, 306, and cf. p. 265.

87 *Purchas*, IV, 153.

Chapter 6   Spain

1 The marriage of Ferdinand and Isabella had united the kingdoms of Aragon and Castile; that of Maximilian of Habsburg and Mary brought together Austria and Burgundy. Between 1516 and 1519 succession of all four houses devolved on Charles Habsburg, who in 1519 was also elected Holy Roman Emperor.

2 Columbus was therefore perhaps influenced by knowledge gained in Iceland about the west (cf. pp. 5ff.).

3 With the fall of Granada in 1492.

4 Elsewhere in these waters, however, the Spaniards were to meet the fiercely bellicose and cannibal Caribs.

5 The indigenous population was so named by Columbus as early as February 1493.

6 The Golden Chersonese of Antiquity.

7 Council, see p. 346.

8 The romance, *Amadis of Gaul*.

9 *Bolas* were balls connected by thongs and thrown so as to entangle the limbs of whatever was being hunted.

10 The Taino were known also as Arawaks (cf. pp. 304, 349–50).

11 From which came ivory tusks.

12 *Purchas*, II, 195.

13 *Purchas*, II, 197.

14 In the defeat of Richard Hawkins in the *Dainty* by Beltran de Castro (1594), cf. p. 476.

15 *Hakluyt*, IX, 390.

16 Before their expulsion in the 1630s.

17 K. R. Andrews (ed.), *The Last Voyage of Drake and Hawkins* (Cambridge, Hakluyt Society, 1972), 189.

18 Creoles were American-born Spaniards.

19 See Helen Nader in *Ec. Hist. Rev.*, XXX, (1977), 411ff.

20 For *hacendados*, see pp. 322–3.

21 Francesco Carletti, *My Voyage Around the World*, trs. by H. Weinstock (London, 1965), 49, 60.

22 Before the introduction of the *asiento*, Portuguese slavers bought permits to supply the American market from the Spanish licensees of the trade (cf. pp. 175–6, 256).

23 Andrews, op. cit. 196; cf. p. 249.

24 Augustín de Zárate, *The History of Discovery and Conquest of the Province of Peru*, ed. and tras. J.M. Cohen (London, 1968), p. 164; *Hakluyt*, IX, 388.

25 To which, living in isolation, they had developed no natural resistance (cf. pp. 248, 350).
26 Zarate, op. cit., 199.
27 *Hakluyt*, IX, 56.
28 A.J.O. Anderson, Frances Berdan and James Lockhart (eds), *Beyond the Codices* (Berkeley, 1976), 183; cf. pp. 310–16.
29 Their armed escort was financed by a levy on cargoes.
30 *Hakluyt*, XI, 264.
31 See below, pp. 386, 471. Wastage figures are inflated by the retention of tonnage in the Americas, often to be cannibalized.
32 *Hakluyt*, IX, 372, and cf. p. 323.
33 *Purchas*, II, 315.
34 Such agreements, like those made with some Canarian peoples, had been abrogated by the time of the American conquests.
35 See I.A.A. Thompson in *Ec. Hist. Rev*, XXI, (1968), 261.
36 In his *Breve y Sumaria Relacíon de los Señores de la Nueva España*, written *c*. 1570.
37 Juan Ginés de Sepúlveda, *Democrates Alter*, ed. A. Losada (Madrid, 1951), 35ff.
38 See G. V. Scammell in *HJ*, XV (1972), 387.
39 The trade of the Canaries to the Indies was the only substantial exception to Seville's monopoly. It was regulated by the Casa from an early date, and shipments were recorded from 1548. Much, and probably most, of the traffic escaped control (cf. pp. 344, 384ff., 439ff.).
40 Cf. pp. 133, 297. This refers to colonies initially settled by Spaniards.
41 The agreement appeared to open unoccupied parts of the New World to the Dutch, but they made no promise to curb those who, at their own risk, continued to trade to the Indies.
42 PRO HCA 13/45, f.405v.
43 Working routes to the Americas.
44 Jews were expelled from Spain in 1492, but many converts, real and nominal to Christianity, remained in the country.

Chapter 7   Holland

1 Holland was a term used to denote both the provice of that name, or, as in this instance, the united provinces of the Dutch Republic.
2 Quoted in A.L. Rowse, *Raleigh and Throckmortons* (London, 1962), 172.
3 *Purchas*, II, 532.
4 Klaus Spading, *Holland und die Hanse* (Weimar, 1973), 13, 95.
5 The buss is known as little more than a name before the late sixteenth century. It then appears as a box-like craft, about 25m long, 5m in beam and drawing roughly 3m. It was on average 100t, with a bluff bow, rounded stern and more or less perpendicular sides. It was rigged with three masts, each setting at least one square sail. When fishing both the fore and mainmasts were lowered and only a mizzen sail set. This allowed the vessel to ride to her nets, strung out from her bow, with which she drifted.
6 Spading, op. cit., 158; cf. pp. 50ff., 58.
7 Spading, op. cit. 165.
8 Spading, op. cit., 50.
9 Archivo General de Simancas (Spain), *Estado, legajo*, 592.
10 J.I. Israel, 'A Conflict of Empires: Spain and the Netherlands 1618–1648', *P&P*, 76 (1977), 34ff.
11 *CSP Spanish, 1587–1603*, 692.

12 Cf. p. 136; R. Doehaerd, *Les Relations Commerciales entre Gênes, La Belgique et L'Outrement* (3 vols, Rome-Brussels, 1941) vol. I, 84–5, 92–3.

13 *CSPD, 1591–4*, 224; E. Grendi, 'I Nordici e il Trafico del Porto di Genova: 1590–1666' in *Rivista Storica Italiana*, 83 (1971), 23ff.

14 *CSPD, 1595–7*, p. 102. For the flyboat see pp. 425–7.

15 Calculated from figures in Castillo Pintado, *Trafico Maritimo y Comercio de Importacion en Vanencia a Comienzos del Siglo XVII* (Madrid, 1967); cf. above, pp. 142–3.

16 PRO HCA 13/45, f.624v.

17 *CSP Spanish, 1547–9*, 133–4; *CSPD, 1547–80 (Elizabeth)*, vol. CVIII, 67; vol. CIX, 18.

18 Quoted in A.L. Rowse, *Raleigh and Throckmortons* (London, 1962), 172.

19 Simon Hart, *The Prehistory of the New Netherlands Company* (Amsterdam, 1959), 63ff.

20 Abundant evidence from arrests by English privateers in PRO HCA 13/25, 13/32.

21 Virginia Rau, *A Embaixada de Tristão de Mendonça*. (Lisbon, 1958), 99.

22 Virginia Rau, *Subsídios para . . . Faro e Lisboa* (Lisbon, 1954), 214.

23 PRO HCA 13/32, f.13v.

24 PRO HCA 13/25, f.298vff; 13/32, f.25v, 36v, 322.

25 PRO HCA 13/32, f.176.

26 PRO HCA 13/32, f.361v.

27 PRO HCA 13/32, 175; Francesco Carletti, *My Voyage Around the World*, trs. by H. Weinstock (London, 1965), 236.

28 *CSP Spanish, 1587–1603*, 692; cf. p. 63.

29 PRO HCA 13/32, f.174v, 202v.

30 *CSP Spanish, 1587–1603*, 686; cf. pp. 65, 367.

31 PRO HCA 13/32, f.233ff, 243ff, 258 Hamburg was particularly favoured by the Dutch to colour trade and the ownership of vessels, (cf. p. 65).

32 PRO HCA 13/24, f.200; *Hakluyt*, XI, 216; for the hulk see p. 80.

33 *Studia*, 27–8 (1969), 453; *Purchas*, III, 116.

34 The Iroquois inhabited the modern New York, Pennsylvania and Ohio.

35 Hartford is on the Connecticut.

36 Near what is now Philadelphia.

37 Quoted in Van Cleaf Bachman, *Peltries or Plantations* (Baltimore, 1969), 90.

38 In the north-west of the island.

39 Quoted in George Masselman, *The Cradle of Colonialism* (New Haven, 1963), 131.

40 *Purchas*, II, 305. For this distinguished seaman, see pp. 473, 475.

41 *Purchas*, II, 305, 308, 320.

42 *Purchas*, II, 199–201.

43 *Purchas*, III, 555.

44 Calculated by Dr A.R. Disney, cf. pp. 266, 267.

45 *Purchas*, loc. cit.

46 *Purchas*, III, 113.

47 *Purchas*, II, 338ff.

48 C.C. Goslinga, *The Dutch in the Caribbean and on the Wild Coast* (Assen, 1971), 36 (cf. above, p. 337).

49 See H.J. de Graaf in *CIHM*, 6 (1963), 420.

50 Quoted in Niels Steensgaard, *Carracks, Caravans and Companies: The Structural Crisis in the European-Asian Trade in the Early Seventeenth Century* (Copenhagen, 1973), 131.

51 The dividends were modest, that is, compared with the gross profits obtained, or reported to be obtainable in such a commerce, cf. pp. 101, 158, 272, 410.

52 C.R. Boxer, '*Plata es Sangre*', in *Philippine Studies*, 18 (1970), 470. The silver not needed in the Far East was used for the purchase of primary products in the Baltic, silks in the Middle East and Indian textiles in the Red Sea.

53 *Purchas*, II, 534.

54 After 1652 all fleets inward and outward bound called at the Cape of Good Hope.

55 *Purchas*, II, 548–9; Masselman, op. cit., 252.

56 Quoted in Albert Hyma, *The Dutch in the Far East* (Michigan, 1942), 111.

57 Such pretensions were abandoned in the later seventeenth century.

58 *Purchas*, III, 93.

59 William Campbell, *Formosa under the Dutch described from Contemporary Records* (1903), 143, 146.

60 Ibid., 140, 145.

61 Campbell, op. cit., 191.

62 Campbell, op. cit., 209.

63 Ibid., 79.

64 Campbell, op. cit., 326.

65 Carletti, op. cit., 256.

66 Holland, Zeeland, Utrecht, Friesland, Groningen, Overijsel, Gelderland.

67 The Remonstrants, so called from their petition (remonstrance) to the States of the province of Holland, accepted the supremacy of the civil power whose protection they sought against their intransigent (Counter-Remonstrant) co-religionaries. These, amongst other things, advocated discrimination against Catholics and dissenters and the untrammelled freedom of the Calvinist church from the civil power.

68 Carletti, op. cit., 243.

69 *CSPD*, 1601–3, 171.

70 *Hakluyt*, XI, 215.

71 *Hakluyt*, VII, 81; PRO HCA 13/32, f.301v.

72 *CIHM*, 3 (1960), 45ff.

73 PRO HCA 13/32, f.301; 13/45, f.28.

74 Campbell, op. cit., 211.

75 *Purchas*, II, 269.

76 Even a cursory glance at such a work as van der Velde the Younger's 'The Resolution in a Gale' (National Maritime Museum, Greenwich) shows the fatuity of Ruskin's often-quoted opinion that Dutch artists presented the sea as 'small waves *en papillote* and peruke-like puffs of farinaceous foam'.

Chapter 8   France

1 Until reduced to obedience in 1627.

2 *CSP Spanish, 1536–8*, 334.

3 C.F. Beckingham and G.W.B. Huntingford (eds), *The Prester John of the Indies* (Cambridge, Hakluyt Society, 1961), 486.

4 PRO HCA 13/24, f.205v.

5 HCA 13/23, f.238; 13/25, f.220, 223.

6 HCA 13/32, f.8v.

7 Abundant references in *Hakluyt*, VI, 224, 238, 241; VII, 91.

8 Michel Mollat, *Le Commerce maritime Normand à la fin du moyen âge* (Paris, 1952), 257.

9 PRO HCA 13/28, f.35v.

10 HCA 13/51, f.187.

11 E.G.R. Taylor (ed.), *The Troublesome Voyage of Captain Edward Fenton* (Cambridge, Hakluyt Society, 1959), 203.

12 Francis I, who reigned from 1515 to 1547, was captured by the Spaniards in their crushing victory at Pavia (1525).

13 From Cartier's understanding of *caignetdaze*, the Iroquois word for metals other than gold.

14 I.e. Arcadia, Virgil's idyllic rural world, initially sited by Verrazzano in the future North Carolina.

Chapter 9   England

1 J.T. Gilbert, *Foreign and Domestic History of the Viceroys of Ireland* (Dublin, 1865), 561.

2 *MM*, 51 (1965), 194.

3 Belonging to the king, and designed apparently for the Bordeaux wine trade.

4 *Hakluyt*, IX, 347.

5 J.S. Brewer, J. Gairdner and R.H. Brodie (eds), *Calendar of Letters and Papers, Henry VIII* (23 vols, 1862–1932), X, 148; *Hakluyt*, V, 76, 153ff., and cf. pp. 132ff.

6 Woollen cloth, the country's only substantial export, accounted for about 80 per cent of the value of English exports in the mid-1500s.

7 R.G. Marsden (ed.), *Select Pleas in the Court of Admiralty* (2 vols, Selden Society, 1894–7), II, 49–50.

8 *Hakluyt*, VI, 443; VII, 95, 102.

9 E.G.R. Taylor, *The Troublesome Voyage of Captain Edward Fenton* (Cambridge, 1959), 195.

10 PRO HCA 13/25, f.300; 13/45, 331v.

11 Escaped African slaves, cf. p. 334.

12 That is the waters between the western Channel and the Canaries, and in particular those of the Iberian coast between Lisbon and Gibraltar.

13 See R.J. Lander and C.J. Martin in *MM*, 63 (1977), 359ff.; 365ff.

14 See I.A.A. Thompson in *MM*, 61 (1975), 355ff.

15 *CSP Venice, 1581–91*, 349.

16 *CSP Spanish, 1580–86*, 265.

17 Lisbon Arquivo Naçional da Torre do Tombo, *Livro das Monções* 40, f.205; 57, f.99.

18 *Purchas*, III, 406.

19 *Purchas*, III, 448.

20 'Voyages' at first, then longer-term 'joint-stocks'.

21 *Divers Voyages touching the Discovery of America* (1582).

22 Bishop of London, 1628–33, archbishop of Canterbury, 1633–45.

23 Demanding, for instance, the ability of its converts to read the Bible (cf. pp. 414–15, 491).

24 Of which England had 150 in 1629, with a large merchantman then three-masted, carrying topmasts and topgallants, having a topmast on the sprit and setting a mizzen topsail.

25 In his *Principal Navigations* (1589) and *Principal Navigations* (1598–1600).

26 In *Purchas, his Pilgrimage* (1613) and *Purchas, his Pilgrimes* (1625).

27 In his *New English Canaan* (1637).

28 His *Brevissima Ralacíon*, condemning the behaviour of his compatriots, only appeared in English translations in 1583 and 1625.

29 In his *Discourse of Western Planting* (1584).

Index